RUBY

Part One

Workbook Answer Guide

ISBN # 0-9801670-2-7 Teacher's Edition

ISBN–13: 978-0-9801670-2-3

EDITOR-IN-CHIEF
Judith Factor

CREATIVE/ART DIRECTOR
Carla Martin

DESIGN/COMPOSITION
Libby Spero

SENIOR EDITOR
Abigail Rozen

COPY EDITOR
Laya Dewick

CURRICULUM WRITER
Rifky Amsel

JILL'S JOURNALS/POETRY UNIT
Jill Brotman

LESSONS IN LITERATURE
Jim Garrett

TEXT AND CURRICULUM ADVISOR
Rabbi Ahron Dovid Goldberg

Mosdos Press Literature

Anthology Series

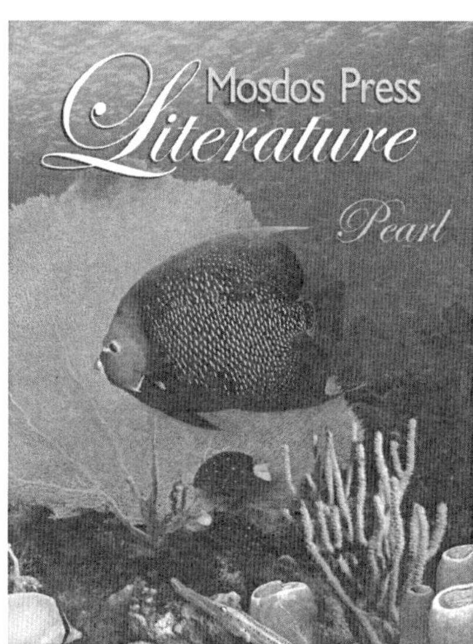

RUBY

CORAL

PEARL

JADE

GOLD

THE THINGS THAT MATTER

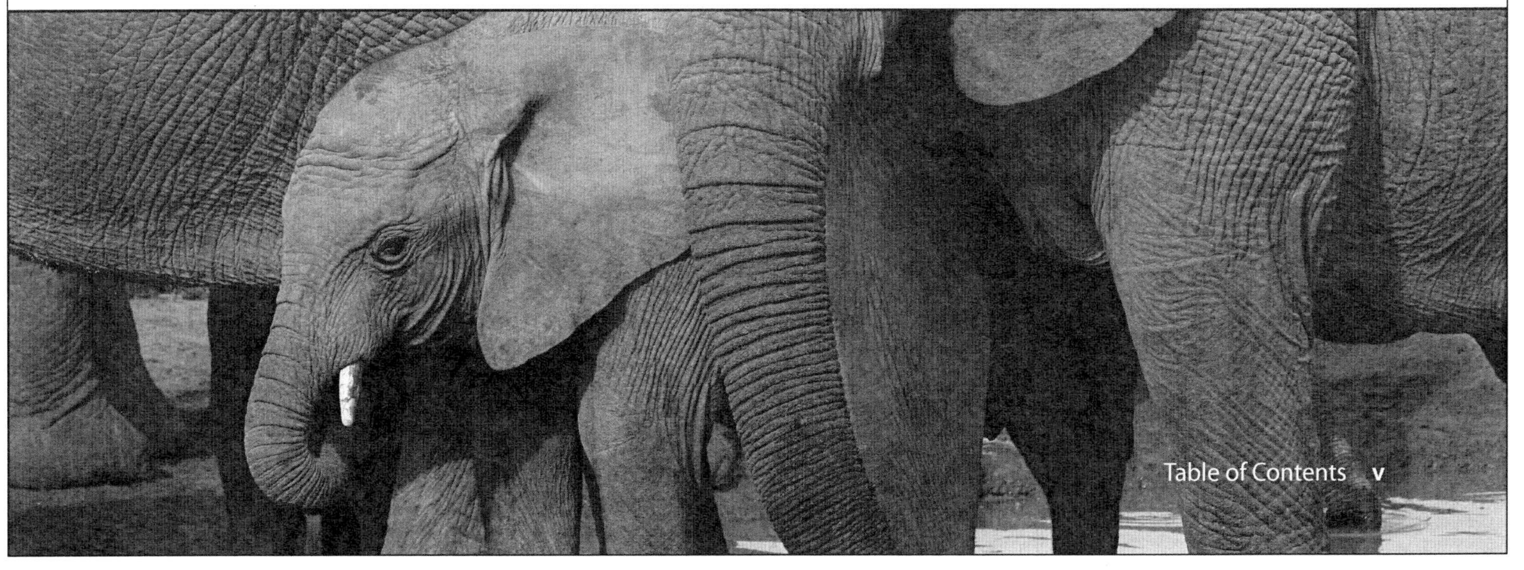

unit 2

CLARITY

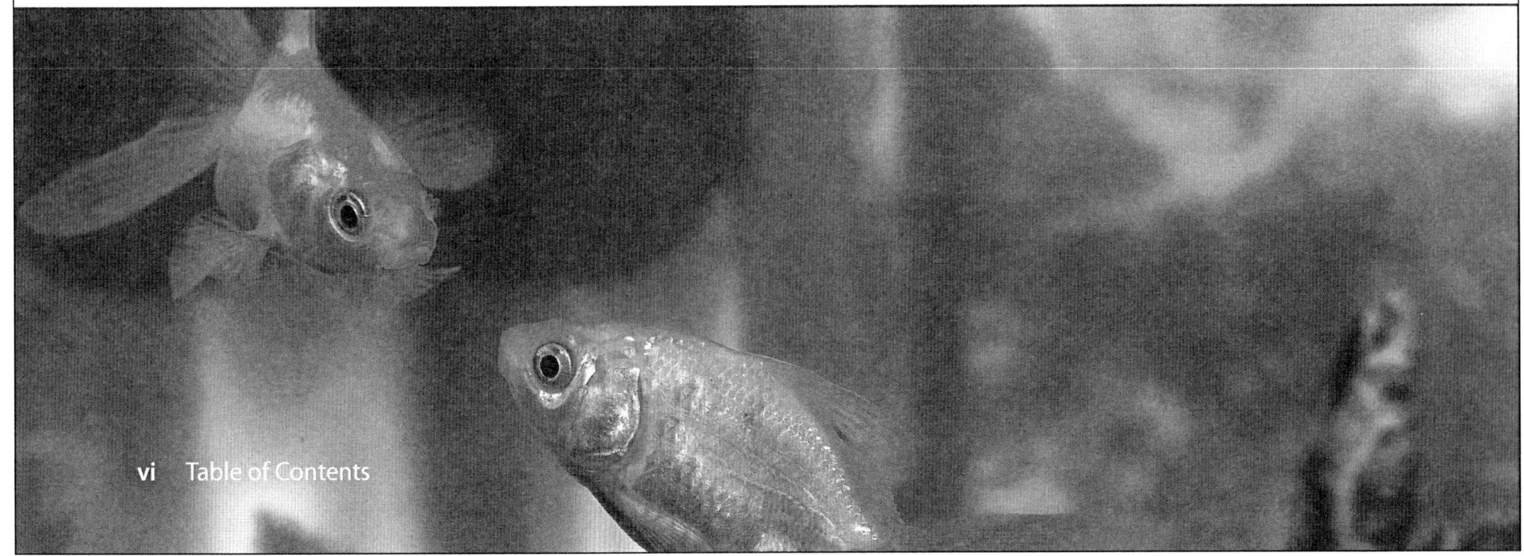

unit 3

HEAD, HANDS, HEART

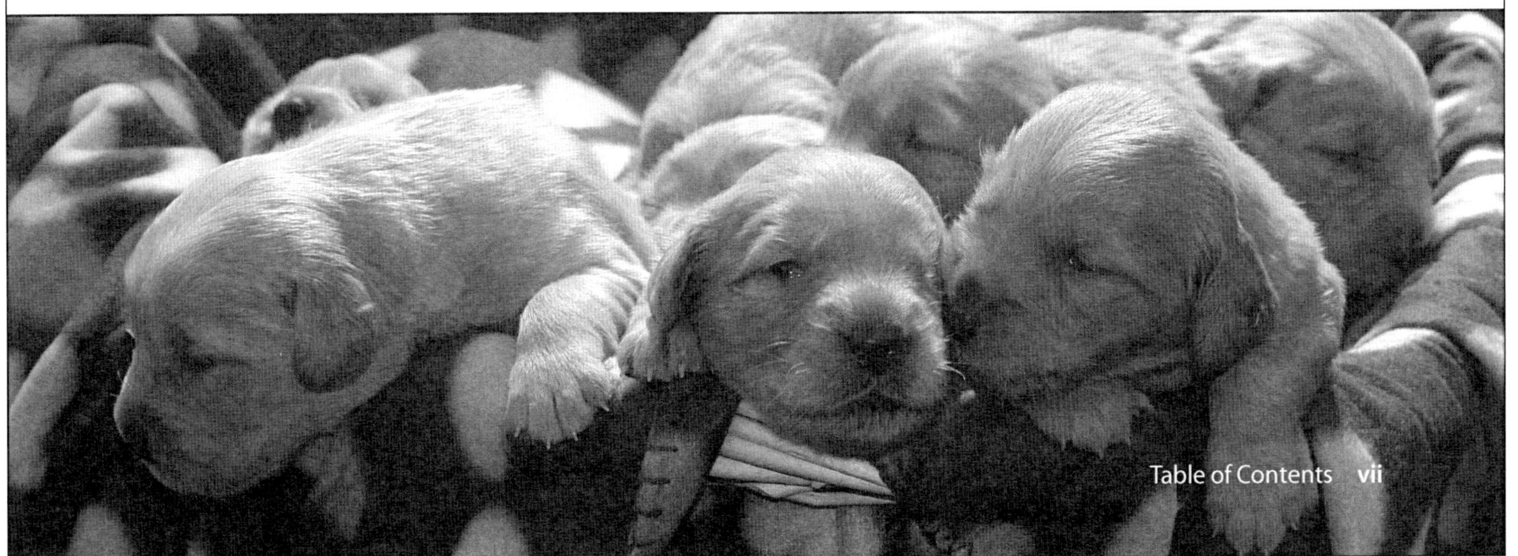

poetry

unit 4

CARING

unit 5

DETERMINATION

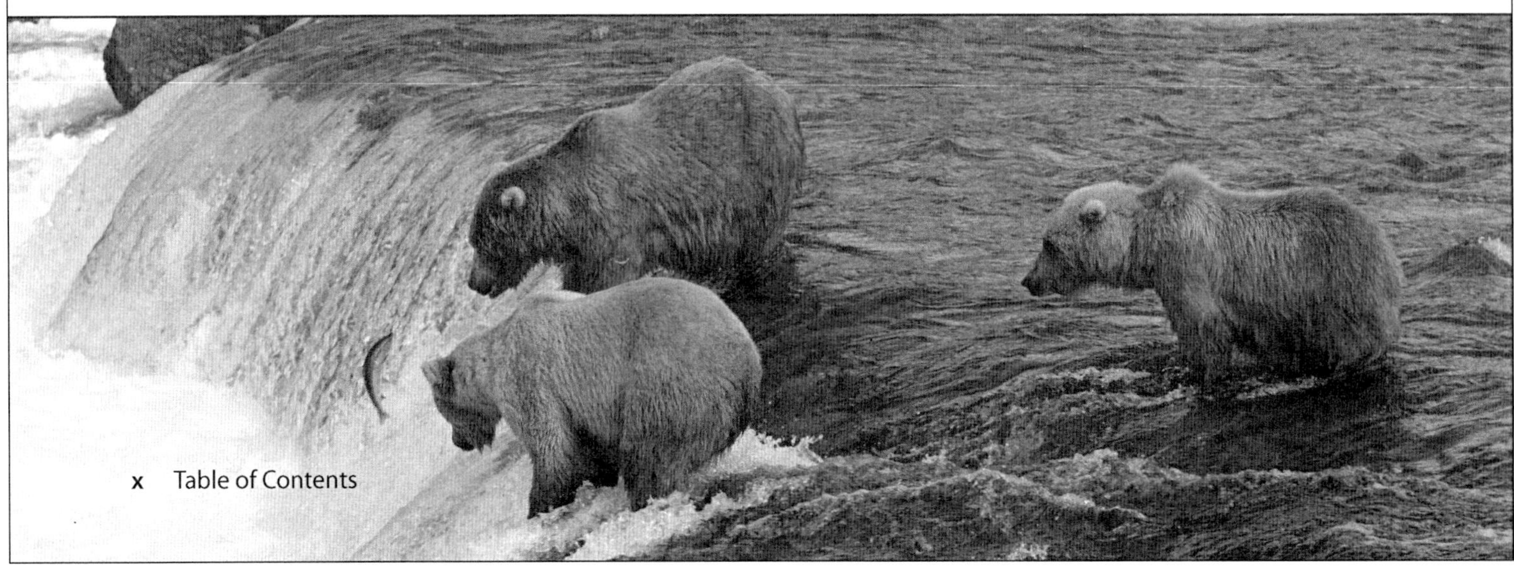

unit 6

THE GRAND FINALÉ

For the Teacher

The information below has been provided so that you can fully appreciate the student textbook, the accompanying workbook, and—most particularly—your Teacher's Edition.

The curriculum for each grade level has been developed in such a way that both new and experienced classroom and home school teachers are able to teach effectively and enjoyably. When a teacher is at ease with the material, and well-informed about what is being taught, the teaching that results is vastly superior to what it would be otherwise.

Please read each of the sections below so that you will be familiar with every part of the curriculum. It will be easier to follow the descriptions if you consult your books as you read.

1. **Scope and Sequence:** *Scope and Sequence* is an overview of the curriculum. *Scope and Sequence* lists the teaching concept of each of the *Lessons in Literature*, as well as the selection theme and the target skill, unit by unit. *Scope and Sequence* also shows the components of the selection: the tie-in poem, *Jill's Journal* and its related power skill, and the student workbook activities for that selection. *Scope and Sequence* will enable you to see where you are going—and where you have been—regarding the sequence of skills. You will also find the target skill listings very helpful for lesson plan notations.
2. **Lessons in Literature:** The *Ruby* pre-curriculum begins with *Lessons in Literature. Lessons in Literature* introduce the literary component, or the language arts skill, that will be taught with the literary work that follows. These lessons are good teaching tools. Use *Lessons in Literature's* original short selections to give your students extra practice with the targeted literary component or skill.
3. **Teacher Resources Section:** Teacher Resources is located at the back of each of the two parts of your Teacher's Edition. There, you will find additional background information for many of the selections. This data will better ground you in the cross-curricular context of the piece—historical, scientific, environmental, or social. Wherever additional resource material is provided in the Teacher Resources Section for a particular selection, it is noted in the body of the Teacher's Edition.
4. **Reviewing Vocabulary:** Teachers should review all vocabulary given in the *Word Banks* of the textbook *before* students read the associated piece. In the Teacher's Edition, the *Word Bank* vocabulary is listed on the *Lessons in Literature* pages that precede each selection. Students should also complete the Workbook Vocabulary Activity I *prior* to reading the selection. In the Teacher's Edition at the bottom of the *Lessons in Literature* pages, there is also a replicated image of Vocabulary Activity I and II. If no vocabulary activities are shown, no new vocabulary is associated with the piece.
5. **Getting Started:** *Getting Started* will make it easier for you to begin a dialogue with your students regarding the selection they are about to read. As such, *Getting Started* is a springboard to the selection. It may be an activity, a question, or information that will intrigue students and generate broader interest. Often, *Getting Started* is an aural exercise that will help students to hone their listening skills.
6. **Teacher's Answer Guide for the Workbook Activities:** The Workbook Answer Guide is located at the back of each of the two volumes of your Teacher's Edition. Notes to the Teacher has been included with suggestions regarding how best to use the student workbook. Please acquaint yourself with the workbook at the beginning of the semester, *before* you begin using the textbook with your students.
7. **Selection Summary:** For each selection, the Teacher's Edition gives a summary of the story—a synopsis that will be a good memory aid when you return to the selection each year.
8. **Blueprint for Reading:**

   Into... Here, the Teacher's Edition parallels the textbook material and both clarifies and elaborates upon the discussion of theme. Theme may be very difficult for many young readers. This fuller explanation enables you to point to specific thematic elements in the selection. *Into...* is an invaluable teaching aid.

   Eyes On... This section of the Teacher's Edition focuses on the featured literary component. *Eyes On...* also enables you to enlarge upon writing style, tone, and language. Here, you will also find insightful teaching hints and thoughtful questions to pose. *Eyes On...* helps your students understand the target skill being taught.
9. **Guiding the Reading:** You can guide your students' understanding of the selection with both literal and analytical questions. These questions appear in the Teacher's Edition below the textbook page from which they are drawn. The literal questions are based on the facts of the piece. The answer requires recall only, and can be derived from the page the class has just reviewed. Analytical questions are inferential. Again, the answer can be drawn from the page just read, but the answer is not stated explicitly, as it is with the literal questions. *Guiding the Reading* lists the literal and the analytical questions separately. However, since the questions build on one another, it makes sense to ask the questions in sequential order. Analytical questions build on literal questions, and often, each literal question builds on the one before it.

10. **Literary Components:** *Literary Components* provides a superior lesson tool. They may even be an education for the teacher. Here, numbers in the margins of the selection provide a legend to a list of descriptions of literary components. The numbered, underlined text provides examples of imagery, style, point of view, plot, characterization, setting, foreshadowing, suspense, rising and falling action, climax, resolution, irony, dialogue, figures of speech, and historical or scientific relevance (where appropriate).

    The details of each literary component are not necessarily meant to be shared in their entirety with your class. Their most important function is to ground the educator in the material. Use your judgment, regarding how advanced your learners are, and how many of these insights you think your class will benefit from or appreciate. Often, the *Literary Components* serve as a way to explain a sophisticated point to the educator, so that he or she can, in turn, explain it coherently to the students.

11. **About the Poem—Tie-In Poems:** A majority of the selections have a tie-in poem that follows the selection in the textbook. In the Teacher's Edition, the poem is analyzed and significant literary components are elucidated for the educator. In the Teacher's Edition, the analysis appears on the page just below the replicated image of the poem. These tie-in poems have been provided in the textbook simply to be enjoyed, and often share a thematic or topical link with the prose selection they follow. There is no student curriculum associated with these poems.

12. **First Impressions:** The Teacher's Edition *First Impressions* parallels the textbook post-curricular questions, and suggests possible student responses.

13. **Studying the Selection in the Teacher's Edition:**

    Quick Review and **Focus** provide detailed answers to the questions posed in the parallel sections of the textbook. Additional material has been included for productive classroom discussion.

    Creating and Writing is the final review element in the textbook. The activities in this section are challenging: one requires creative writing; one is grounded in the theme of the selection and its literary form; and the final activity is non-literate (a work of art, a charitable activity, a fieldwork project, for example). Precise teacher instructions for these projects and activities are provided in the textbook.

    NOTE: The Workbook Comprehension Questions continue the post-curricular *Studying the Selection*. These workbook pages should be assigned after the textbook exercises are completed.

14. **Jill's Journal:** *Jill's Journal* is a unique literary device that is being introduced in *Ruby*. *Jill's Journal* follows twelve of the prose selections.

    This is a four-page spread: 2 to 3 pages are devoted to *Jill's Journal*; the remaining 1 to 2 pages describe a power skill for the young reader or writer. Exercises are given for practice.

    Jill's Journal is an "autobiographical," first-person narrative. Jill imagines herself a reporter on assignment. Her journal entries are connected topically with the selection, and place Jill the Journalist back in time or someplace in the world. These pieces are guaranteed to bring students right into the world of the story. Extensive background material is provided in the Teacher's Edition.

15. **Poetry Unit:** The Poetry Unit in the student textbook follows Unit Three. The Poetry Unit is comprised of seven lessons, meant to be taught lesson by lesson, *sequentially*, throughout the school year, interspersed with the teaching of the primarily prose units. Each of the poetry lessons builds on the other. Please let your students enjoy the poetry as it is presented.

    There is extensive material in the Teacher's Edition to help the educator enjoy the poetry as well, and teach the poetry effectively. The Poetry Unit is the last unit in Part One of your Teacher's Edition. This material is intended for your edification, as it is generally much too sophisticated for elementary school students. The information is meant to make you feel completely comfortable with the poetry so that you will be grounded in its teaching. There are many suggested activities in the teacher notes for each poetry lesson. These activities will enhance both your and your students' experience. Enjoying poetry from an early age will bring your students a lifetime of rewards.

RUBY TEACHER'S EDITION

- Scope and Sequence
- Annotated Teacher's Edition
- Teacher Resources Section
- Workbook Answer Guide

UNIT ONE: *The Things That Matter • Story Elements Overview*

The elements of a story are introduced in this unit—plot, character, setting, and theme—as well as the basic structure of a story. In each of Unit One's five selections, one of these elements is explored.

SELECTION	INTO . . .	EYES ON . . .	POEMS JILL'S JOURNALS	WORKBOOK
Leah's Pony *by* **Elizabeth Friedrich** p. 4 *Genre:* Realistic Fiction *Lesson in Literature* What Is a Story? **Sarah's Room**	• Saving the farm and her family are *The Things That Matter* to Leah in this story of the Dust Bowl era. People react in different ways when faced with a challenge. Leah inspires others to behave with kindness and generosity.	• *Eyes On* Narrative Elements • What is a story? • Introducing the word **elements** • *Target Skill:* Discussing plot, character, setting, and theme	• *Poem:* **The Way** Poetry Shows Us the Way • *On Assignment from the Dirty Thirties* Jill visits Kansas in 1935 and experiences the Dust Bowl firsthand. • *Power Skill:* Learning to read a map	• pp. 2-7 Vocab. Activity I p. 2 Vocab. Activity II p. 3 Comp. Questions pp. 4-5 Graphic Organizer pp. 6-7
Supergrandpa *by* **David M. Schwartz** p. 24 *Genre:* Fiction *Lesson in Literature* What Is Plot? **Jigsaw**	• Competing in the Tour of Sweden bicycle race and being judged for his ability, not his outward appearance, are *The Things That Matter* to Gustaf. Quick judgments vs. thoughtfully drawing conclusions is explored.	• *Eyes On* Plot • What is plot? • *Target Skill:* Students learn that a **plot** is what happens in a story and that an author must have a story plan for the plot	• *Poem:* **If You Think You Are Beaten** Poetry Encourages Us	• pp. 8-13 Vocab. Activity I p. 8 Vocab. Activity II p. 9 Comp. Questions pp. 10-11 Graphic Organizer pp. 12-13
Two Big Bears *by* **Laura Ingalls Wilder** p. 40 *Genre:* Semi-autobiographical fiction *Lesson in Literature* Characters **Starfish**	• The safety of the children and the security of the homestead are *The Things That Matter* to Laura and her parents in this excerpt from *Little House in the Big Woods.*	• *Eyes On* Character • *Target Skill:* Learning how to recognize the **main** character in a story	• *Poem:* **March Bear** Poetry Speaks in Different Voices • *On Assignment in China* Jill visits the moon bears in the rescue center in China. • *Power Skill:* Speaking slowly, clearly, loudly, and with expression	• pp. 14-19 Vocab. Activity I p. 14 Vocab. Activity II p. 15 Comp. Questions pp. 16-17 Graphic Organizer pp. 18-19
Mom's Best Friend *by* **Sally Hobart Alexander** p. 58 *Genre:* Nonfiction/ Autobiography *Lesson in Literature* What Is Setting? **The Pond**	• Gaining her independence through perseverance is one of *The Things That Matter* to Mom. A blind mother handles difficulties calmly and patiently as she trains with a new dog guide.	• *Eyes On* Setting • What is setting? • *Target Skill:* Students learn that **setting** describes the background of a story and that a story may have more than one setting.		• pp. 20-23 Comp. Questions pp. 20-21 Graphic Organizer pp. 22-23
The Tiger, the Persimmon and the Rabbit's Tail *by* **Suzanne Crowder Han** p. 72 *Genre:* Fable *Lesson in Literature* What Is Theme? **For the Birds**	• Overcoming fear is one of *The Things That Matter* in this humorous fable.	• *Eyes On* Theme • What is theme? • *Target Skill:* Students learn that **theme** is the main idea of a story.	• *Poem:* **Here She Is** Poetry Praises	• pp. 24-27 Comp. Questions pp. 24-25 Graphic Organizer pp. 26-27

UNIT TWO: *Clarity • Exploring Elements of Plot*

Elements of plot—internal conflict, external conflict, sequence, predicting outcome, and finding the main idea—are taught in this unit. Students will be taught how the elements of plot are the foundations for understanding literature.

SELECTION	INTO...	EYES ON...	POEMS JILL'S JOURNALS	WORKBOOK
Sato and the Elephants *by* **Juanita Havill** p. 94 Genre: Fiction *Lesson in Literature* What Is Internal Conflict? **The Flower Garden**	• Sato understands his mistake with *Clarity*. Having the strength and courage to change when his mistake is realized is a classic internal conflict for the main character in this story.	• *Eyes On* Internal Conflict • *Target Skill:* Defining **conflict** and understanding and recognizing **internal conflict**	• *Poem:* **Purple Snake** Poetry Opens Our Eyes	• pp. 28-35 Vocab. Activity I p. 28 Vocab. Activity II p. 29 Comp. Questions pp. 30-31 Graphic Organizer pp. 32-35
Amelia's Road *by* **Linda Jacobs Altman** p. 112 *Genre:* Realistic Fiction *Lesson in Literature* What Is External Conflict? **Neighbors**	• Amelia's moment of *Clarity* is when she understands where she belongs. In this story about migrant workers, a young girl's feelings about belonging change as her understanding grows.	• *Eyes On* External Conflict • *Target Skill:* Understanding the difference between internal and **external conflict** and recognizing external conflict in a piece of literature	• *Poem:* **Since Hanna Moved Away** Poetry Is About Feelings • *On Assignment in the Supermarket and the Field* • *Power Skill:* What is fiction? What is nonfiction?	• pp. 36-39 Comp. Questions pp. 36-37 Graphic Organizer pp. 38-39
The Hatmaker's Sign *Retold by* **Candace Fleming** p. 130 *Genre:* Parable *Lesson in Literature* What Is Sequence? **The Tree House**	• *Clarity* is a well-executed sign in this interesting parable.	• *Eyes On* Sequence • *Target Skill:* Students learn to recognize the elements of **sequence** in a well-organized story.		• pp. 40-45 Vocab. Activity I p. 40 Vocab. Activity II p. 41 Comp. Questions pp. 42-43 Graphic Organizer pp. 44-45
Dad, Jackie, and Me *by* **Myron Uhlberg** p. 146 *Genre:* Autobiographical Fiction *Lesson in Literature* What Is Foreshadowing? **Baseball Card**	• *Clarity* is understanding how to overcome prejudice in *Dad, Jackie, and Me.* Through his father's example, a young boy gains a deep understanding of how one overcomes intolerance and prejudice.	• *Eyes On* Predicting Outcome • *Target Skill:* **Foreshadowing** is defined and students are asked to recognize hints and clues in a story to predict outcome.	• *Poem:* **Analysis of Baseball** Poetry is About the Things We Cheer	• pp. 46-49 Comp. Questions pp. 46-47 Graphic Organizer pp. 48-49
And Now the Good News *by* **Margery Facklam** p. 162 *Genre:* Nonfiction Essay *Lesson in Literature* What Is a Main Idea? **Turtle, Tortoise, or Terrapin**	• Realizing what we must do to protect endangered animals with *Clarity* is the good news in this nonfiction piece. Students learn that preservation is the process of keeping something safe.	• *Eyes On* Main Ideas and Details • *Target Skill:* Recognizing the **main idea** that holds a piece together and understanding how new ideas are connected to the main idea	• *Poem:* **Hurt No Living Thing** Poetry Makes Us Care • *"They Loaded Up Their Trunks and They Moved to Tennessee"* • *Power Skill:* Making a table	• pp. 50-55 Vocab. Activity I p. 50 Vocab. Activity II p. 51 Comp. Questions pp. 52-53 Graphic Organizer pp. 54-55

UNIT THREE: *Head, Hands, Heart • Exploring Elements of Character*

Recognizing a character's attributes, understanding the difference between a major and minor character, dialogue, internal dialogue, and point of view are elements of character explored in this unit.

SELECTION	INTO . . .	EYES ON . . .	POEMS JILL'S JOURNALS	WORKBOOK
Eddie, Incorporated *by* **Phyllis Reynolds Naylor** p. 188 *Genre:* Realistic Fiction *Lesson in Literature* Simple and Complex Characters **Hutchman's Heroes**	• The *Eddie, Incorporated* team put their *Heads, Hands, and Hearts* together for an important recycling project. This story explores the importance of teamwork when working with others.	• *Eyes On* Character • *Target Skill:* Recognizing a character's attributes • Learning about **characters** from their language, actions, thoughts, and feelings	• *On Assignment at the Town Dump* • *Power Skill:* Conduct an experiment; keep a log of the results	• pp. 56-61 Vocab. Activity I p. 56 Vocab. Activity II p. 57 Comp. Questions pp. 58-59 Graphic Organizer pp. 60-61
Heatwave! *by* **Helen Ketteman** p. 214 *Genre:* Fantasy *Lesson in Literature* Major and Minor Characters **Snowstorm!**	• In this humorous fantasy selection, the main character uses ingenious problem solving skills and her *Head, Hands, and Heart* to help her family.	• *Eyes On* Major and Minor Characters • *Target Skill:* Recognizing the difference between **major characters** and **minor characters** in a selection	• *Poem:* **Be Glad Your Nose Is On Your Face** Poetry Is Silly	• pp. 62-67 Vocab. Activity I p. 62 Vocab. Activity II p. 63 Comp. Questions pp. 64-65 Graphic Organizer pp. 66-67
The Wright Brothers *by* **Quentin Reynolds** p. 232 *Genre:* Fictionalized Biography *Lesson in Literature* What Is Dialogue? **Horses**	• Using their *Heads, Hands, and Hearts,* and the self-confidence instilled by their mother, the Wright brothers will accomplish great things.	• *Eyes On* Dialogue • *Target Skill:* **Dialogue** helps us understand characters and make them more believable • Learning about a character's attributes through what they say	• *Poem:* **The Inventor Thinks Up Helicopters** Poetry Teaches Us to Ask Questions • *On Assignment in Dayton, Ohio* • *Power Skill:* Creating another time and place	• pp. 68-71 Comp. Questions pp. 68-69 Graphic Organizer pp. 70-71
The Imperfect/ Perfect Book Report *by* **Johanna Hurwitz** p. 252 *Genre:* Realistic Fiction *Lesson in Literature* What Is Internal Dialogue? **Bicycle**	• In *The Imperfect/Perfect Book Report* the main character has to use her *Head, Hands, and Heart* to really understand that friendship is more important then competition.	• *Eyes On* Internal Dialogue • *Target Skill:* **Internal dialogue** tells us about the character's inner thoughts. When we overhear internal dialogue, it is as if we're hearing the characters talking to themselves.	• *Poem:* **You and I** Poetry Is About You and Me	• pp. 72-77 Comp. Questions pp. 72-73 Graphic Organizer pp. 74-77
Justin Lebo *by* **Phillip Hoose** p. 268 *Genre:* Nonfiction Article *Lesson in Literature* Point of View **Nicaragua**	• Justin Lebo selflessly gives of himself with his *Head, Hands, and Heart.* When one is selfless, one puts someone or something first. In this story, the reader sees what Justin gains from being selfless and giving.	• *Eyes On* Point of View • *Target Skill:* Recognizing point of view • Identifying the **point of view** from which a story is told	• *Poem:* **Holding Up the Sky** Poetry Shares Big Ideas	• pp. 78-83 Vocab. Activity I p. 78 Vocab. Activity II p. 79 Comp. Questions pp. 80-81 Graphic Organizer pp. 82-83

UNIT FOUR: *Caring • Exploring Elements of Setting*

How an author establishes a setting, understanding imagery, comparing settings, understanding mood and how an author creates it, and the use of setting in a biography are explored in this unit.

SELECTION	INTO…	EYES ON…	POEMS JILL'S JOURNALS	WORKBOOK
Earthquake Terror *by* **Peg Kehret** p. 326 *Genre:* Adventure/ Realistic Fiction *Lesson in Literature* Establishing a Setting **Cross Country**	• A *Caring* brother protects his disabled sister with quick thinking and skill in *Earthquake Terror*. The reader learns that it is not how we feel that makes us courageous, it is what we do.	• *Eyes On* Creating a Setting • *Target Skill:* Learning to recognize setting • Understanding why **setting**—the way things look and feel—plays an important part in a story	• *Poem:* **Michael Is Afraid of the Storm** Poetry Is Not Afraid to Be Afraid • *On Assignment in New Madrid, Territory of Missouri* • *Power Skill:* The five W's of reporting	• pp. 84-91 Vocab. Activity I pp. 84-85 Vocab. Activity II pp. 86-87 Comp. Questions pp. 88-89 Graphic Organizer pp. 90-91
The Gift *by* **Helen Coutant** p. 350 *Genre:* Realistic Fiction *Lesson in Literature* What Is Imagery? **Run In the Woods**	• A *Caring* young girl, a rare friendship, and a creative gift contribute to this poignant story. As we read we understand why two such different people become such loving friends.	• *Eyes On* Imagery • *Target Skill:* Understanding **sensory images** and recognizing that they tell us to picture, smell, hear, feel, or taste something in a story	• *Poem:* **For You** Poetry Is Giving	• pp. 92-97 Vocab. Activity I p. 92 Vocab. Activity II p. 93 Comp. Questions pp. 94-95 Graphic Organizer pp. 96-97
Toto *by* **Marietta D. Moskin** p. 368 *Genre:* Fiction *Lesson in Literature* Comparing Settings **The Color of Water**	• Suku's *Caring* nature engages him in a risky adventure as he overcomes his fear in *Toto*. Leaving what is familiar and trying something new encourage the two main characters to gain more than they lose.	• *Eyes On* Comparing Settings • *Target Skill:* **Comparing settings** and recognizing multiple settings in a story	• *Poem:* **In This Jungle** Poetry Is Quiet and Strong	• pp. 98-103 Vocab. Activity I p. 98 Vocab. Activity II p. 99 Comp. Questions pp. 100-101 Graphic Organizer pp. 102-103
Owl Moon *by* **Jane Yolen** p. 386 *Genre:* Story Poem *Lesson in Literature* What Is Mood? **Driftwood**	• The *Caring* and love between a father and daughter, the beauty of the winter woods at night, and a unique activity are all part of this wonderful story poem.	• *Eyes On* Mood • *Target Skill:* Recognizing and identifying the descriptive words that create atmosphere or **mood** in a piece of literature		• pp. 104-107 Comp. Questions pp. 104-105 Graphic Organizer pp. 106-107
from **Homeward the Arrow's Flight** *by* **Marion Marsh Brown** p. 400 *Genre:* Biography *Lesson in Literature* What Is Biography? **Sandra Day O'Connor**	• Dr. Susan La Flesche Picotte personifies *Caring* in this moving biography. We learn that she is an idealist that puts others' needs first.	• *Eyes On* Biography • *Target Skill:* A **biography** is the story of a person's life. • How does an author compile information about the person they are writing about?	• *On Assignment in Britain to Speak with the Lady with the Lamp* • *Power Skill:* Making a pie chart	• pp. 108-115 Vocab. Activity I pp. 108-109 Vocab. Activity II pp. 110-111 Comp. Questions pp. 112-113 Graphic Organizer pp. 114-115

UNIT FIVE: *Determination • Exploring Elements of Theme*

Elements of theme—author's purpose, stated and implied theme, drawing conclusions, and comparing and contrasting—are explored in this unit. When we understand how a work of literature makes us feel, we comprehend theme.

SELECTION	INTO...	EYES ON...	POEMS JILL'S JOURNALS	WORKBOOK
Underwater Rescue *by* **Wayne Grover** p. 428 *Genre:* Nonfiction *Lesson in Literature* Author's Purpose **Country Road**	• *Determination* and communication helps the author save the baby dolphin. Motions, gestures, and signs enable the communication and trust between the diver and these magnificent mammals.	• *Eyes On* Author's Purpose • *Target Skill:* As we understand the reasons authors write nonfiction, we understand **author's purpose.**	• *Poem:* **Today the Dolphins Came to Play** Poetry Is Wonder • *On Assignment Exploring the Mesoamerican Reef* • *Power Skill:* Learning to write setting	• pp. 116-123 Vocab. Activity I p. 116 Vocab. Activity II p. 117 Comp. Questions pp. 118-119 Graphic Organizer pp. 120-123
The Seven Children *by* **Linda and Clay Goss** p. 448 *Genre:* Fable *Lesson in Literature* What Is Stated Theme? **My Dog Is Best**	• Parents use their *Determination* and ingenuity to teach an important lesson to their seven children.	• *Eyes On* Stated Theme • *Target Skill:* Identifying the **stated theme** and understanding that it is often presented near the beginning of a story • When an author tells us what the story's main idea is, it is called a stated theme.		• pp. 124-127 Comp. Questions pp. 124-125 Graphic Organizer pp. 126-127
The Garden of Happiness *by* **Erika Tamar** p. 462 *Genre:* Realistic Fiction *Lesson in Literature* What Is Implied Theme? **Seeds**	• The people of this urban neighborhood use their steadfast *Determination* to carve out a place of beauty in *The Garden of Happiness.* They plant seeds in a little patch of earth and create a place of hope and dreams.	• *Eyes On* Implied Theme • *Target Skill:* When an author does not openly state what the theme is, but only hints at it, the theme is implied. • The student learns that plot, characterization, and setting contribute to the **implied theme.**	• *Poem:* **Johnny Appleseed** Poetry Plants Seeds • *On Assignment in Crista's Garden* • *Power Skill:* Conducting an interview	• pp. 128-131 Comp. Questions pp. 128-129 Graphic Organizer pp. 130-131
One Grain of Rice *by* **Demi** p. 482 *Genre:* Mathematical Fable *Lesson in Literature* Drawing Conclusions **Forestdale Forever**	• Because of her *Determination* to help the starving people of her city, a young girl ingeniously creates a solution with *One Grain of Rice.*	• *Eyes On* Drawing Conclusions • *Target Skill:* When a reader takes all the information that has been given and predicts how things will turn out, they **draw conclusions.**		• pp. 132-135 Comp. Questions pp. 132-133 Graphic Organizer pp. 134-135
Maria's House *by* **Jean Merrill** p. 500 *Genre:* Realistic Fiction *Lesson in Literature* Compare and Contrast **In the Eyes of the Beholder**	• Maria's *Determination* will lead her to the right decision, as she learns to appreciate her 'real' house. Learning this important life lesson helps Maria learn about herself and others.	• *Eyes On* Compare and Contrast • *Target Skill:* Students compare and contrast the characters and setting to one another. This helps them understand a story's theme.	• *Poem:* **City I Love** Poetry Shows Us Our World	• pp. 136-139 Comp. Questions pp. 136-137 Graphic Organizer pp. 138-139

UNIT SIX: *The Grand Finalé • Reviewing the Narrative Elements and Genre*

Students will read poignant fiction, informative nonfiction, interesting drama, and fictionalized biography in this unit. They will recognize how all the literary elements of plot, character, setting, and theme work together in excellent literature.

SELECTION	INTO...	EYES ON...	POEMS JILL'S JOURNALS	WORKBOOK
The Bridge Dancers *by* **Carol Saller** p. 528 *Genre:* Realistic Fiction *Lesson in Literature* Elements of Fiction **Beyond the Ropes**	• On a path to self-discovery, a young girl learns to value her own strengths in *The Bridge Dancers.* As she reconciles who she would like to be with who she is, her goals become clear.	• *Eyes On* Realistic Fiction • *Target Skill:* Students recognize that **realistic fiction** has real-life problems and although the events in the story did not happen, they could have happened.		• pp. 140-145 Vocab. Activity I p. 140 Vocab. Activity II p. 141 Comp. Questions pp. 142-143 Graphic Organizer pp. 144-145
Dancing Bees *by* **Margery Facklam** p. 544 *Genre:* Nonfiction Science Article *Lesson in Literature* Elements of Nonfiction **Is It a Hurricane?**	• In *Dancing Bees* we learn that taking a good look at the world around us is very informative. We understand that part of science is observing and that the reader is amazed at what people can learn when they watch and wait.	• *Eyes On* Nonfiction • *Target Skill:* Students read a lot of **informative nonfiction** and the skill of association is taught as a helpful memory tool.		• pp. 146-149 Comp. Questions pp. 146-147 Graphic Organizer pp. 148-149
Name This American *by* **Hannah Reinmuth** p. 552 *Genre:* Drama *Lesson in Literature* Elements of Drama **A Beautiful Day**	• *Name This American* is about five Americans who made significant contributions.	• *Eyes On* Drama • *Target Skill:* **Dialogue** is critical to developing plot, character, setting, and theme in a play.		• pp. 150-157 Vocab. Activity I p. 150 Vocab. Activity II p. 151 Comp. Questions pp. 152-153 Graphic Organizer pp. 154-157
Boss of the Plains *by* **Laurie Carlson** p. 570 *Genre:* Fictionalized Biography *Lesson in Literature* Fictionalized Biography **The Way Things Work**	• The secret to success is using your particular talent or skill to its utmost. In *Boss of the Plains,* John Stetson discovers that his success lies in using a skill he already had in an innovative way.	• *Eyes On* Fictionalized Biography • *Target Skill:* Understanding which parts of a fictionalized biography are true and which are fiction		• pp. 158-163 Vocab. Activity I p. 158 Vocab. Activity II p. 159 Comp. Questions pp. 160-161 Graphic Organizer pp. 162-163
Stone Fox *by* **John Reynolds Gardiner** p. 586 *Genre:* Adventure Fiction *Lesson in Literature* Pulling It All Together **Monster**	• *Stone Fox* is a story about a struggle between two good, two strong, and two very determined people. It is not until the very end that we understand who is the winner and if there really is a loser.	• *Eyes On* Narrative Elements • *Target Skill:* Exploring all of the elements—plot, character, setting, and theme—of a well-written piece of literature		• pp. 164-169 Vocab. Activity I p. 164 Vocab. Activity II p. 165 Comp. Questions pp. 166-167 Graphic Organizer pp. 168-169

POETRY

Poetry uses the pleasure we take in sound and the repetition of sound. It is about rhythm, beat, and patterns—all the building blocks of poetry. Poetry is not taught: it is shown. This poetry magazine shows children a celebration of sound.

POEMS	LESSONS
Lesson One: *Poetry Is Sound and Rhythm* • **Birds' Square Dance** *by* Beverly McLoughland (p. 288) • **Thistles** *by* Karla Kuskin (p. 289) • **Whirligig Beetles** *by* Paul Fleischman (p. 290) • **This Is the Key** *by* Anonymous (p. 291)	• Students learn that poets repeat sounds, just as composers repeat notes. Through the rhythms and sounds experienced in the four poems in this lesson, students will learn the various forms of **repetition**, as well as **alliteration** and **consonance**. • Lesson One celebrates sounds with a square dance beat (*Birds' Square Dance*), a tongue twister (*Thistles*), a poem in two voices (*Whirligig Beetles*), and an old nursery rhyme (*This Is the Key*).
Lesson Two: *Poetry Is Sound, Rhythm, and Rhyme* • **A Bridge Engineer** *by* Anonymous (p. 294) • **A Bugler Named Dougal MacDougal** *by* Ogden Nash (p. 294) • **A Funny Young Fellow Named Perkins** *by* Anonymous (p. 295) • **A Native of Chalamazug** *by* Graham Lester (p. 295) • **A Gullible Rancher Named Clyde** *by* Graham Lester (p. 295)	• Students learn that **limericks** are five-line poems that are usually funny. Students are taught that these little nonsense poems have a rhyme scheme (an *aabba* pattern). • Often limericks present words and concepts that need explanation in order to fully appreciate the humor. Teachers should note the small guide in the teacher's edition, highlighting each of these words for each of the limericks in this lesson.
Lesson Three: *Poetry Is Saying a Lot in a Few Words* • **Seasons Haiku** *by* Myra Cohn Livingston (p. 298)	• Students learn the rules for writing **haiku**, reviewing the process of **syllabification**. They learn that haiku—an old Japanese form of verse—depends heavily on subtle imagery, observation, and a compression of thought and words.
Lesson Four: *Poetry Is a Picture* • **A Seeing Poem** *by* Robert Froman (p. 302) • **Popsicle** *by* Joan Bransfield (p. 303)	• After generating a list of different shapes poems can take, students practice writing their own **form poems**. • Students learn that poetry usually draws pictures for us, and in a form poem the poet becomes an actual picture. • Both *A Seeing Poem* and *Popsicle* are excellent examples of concrete poems.
Lesson Five: *Poetry Is Rhyme* • **The Shark** *by* John Ciardi (p. 306) • **Dust of Snow** *by* Robert Frost (p. 307)	• Students learn that the pattern in which the lines of a poem rhyme is called a **rhyme scheme**. In this lesson, they compare and contrast the rhyme scheme of *The Shark* and *Dust of Snow*. • *The Shark* is a wonderful performance piece and should be read aloud as an imaginative, dramatic reading. *Dust of Snow* can be taught as a simple, little poem, but also lends itself to a discussion of what is a symbol.
Lesson Six: *Poetry Is Fun to Write* • **Some Opposites** *by* Richard Wilbur (p. 310) • **Tortillas Like Africa** *by* Gary Soto (p. 311)	• Both of the poems in this lesson incorporate lists, so it will be necessary to review these lists with your students. • Students learn about **free verse**, **repetition**, and the odd punctuation and capitalization that many free verse poems have. • *Some Opposites* is a list of opposites, and *Tortillas Like Africa* begins and ends with the same story, and its middle is a list of countries.
Lesson Seven: *Poetry Is Free* • **Good Hotdogs** *by* Sandra Cisneros (p. 314) • **Jackrabbit** *by* Byrd Baylor (p. 316)	• Students learn that writing poetry is a satisfying release for their ideas and images—a way of letting feelings go, setting feelings down, and communicating with another person. • *Good Hotdogs* lends itself to a discussion of the repetition of vowel and consonant sounds. *Jackrabbit* is a dramatic performance piece that should be performed in class by groups of four to six students.

unit 1

the things that matter

What Is a Story?

Sarah's Room

1. Until now, Sarah has had to wait. In the middle of the story her father tells her she does not have to wait—she has first choice.
2. The six characters are Sarah, her mother, her father, her two sisters and her brother.
3. The new house has a downstairs bedroom with a big window and a big closet. There is a field next to the new house. There are several bedrooms upstairs.

Lesson in Literature . . .
SARAH'S ROOM

WHAT IS A STORY?

- A story has a beginning, a middle, and an end. Something in the story must change before the story is over.
- *What happens* in the story is called the **plot**.
- The *people* or animals in the story are called the **characters**.
- The *time* and *place* in which the events happen are called the **setting**.

THINK ABOUT IT!

1. In the middle of the story, something changes in Sarah's life. What is it?
2. Who are the six characters in the story?
3. Describe the setting of the second half of the story.

2 Unit 1

Vocabulary

sow (rhymes with now) *n.*: an adult, female pig

gullies (GULL eez) *n.*: small valleys or ravines made by running water

clutched (KLUCHD) *v.*: held onto tightly

cultivate (KUL tih vayt) *v.*: to help the plants grow by tending to the soil around them

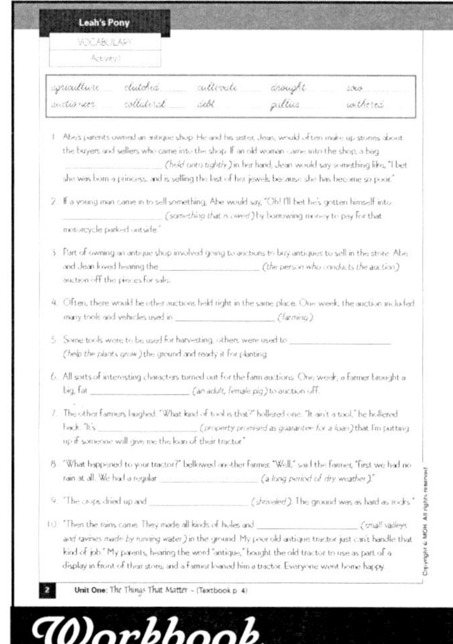

Workbook

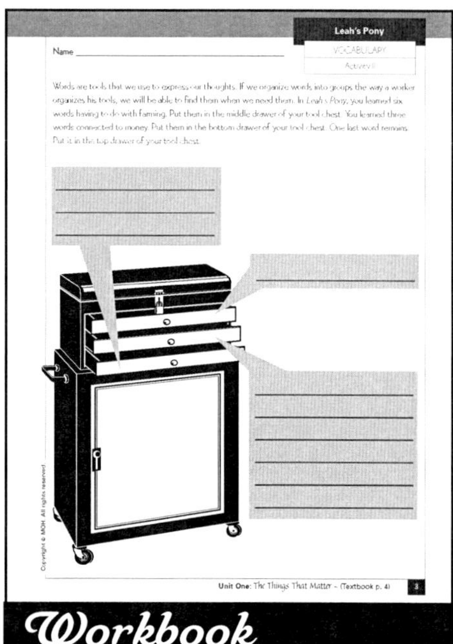

Workbook

Sarah didn't like being the youngest in the family. With an older brother and two older sisters, Sarah always had to wait for them to do things first. On the playground or in the backyard, she had to wait. "Wait your turn!" her sister Emily said when Sarah wanted to go first. When her parents gave her brother permission to ride his bicycle to the park, Sarah asked, "Can I go too?"

"Sarah," her mother said, "you're too young. You have to wait until you're old enough."

"But when will I be old enough?" Sarah asked.

"Soon," her mother said.

Sarah thought about it. When she was younger, she had to wait to go to school. She had to wait to learn to read. She had to wait to ride a bicycle. She had to wait to swim in the pool. Now at twelve she still had to wait. She had to wait to sit at the adults' table for dinner. She had to wait for her older sisters to grow out of their clothes, and she was still waiting for her own room. Sarah didn't want to share a bedroom with her sister Emily anymore. When she asked her father about a room of her own, all he said was, "Sarah, you just have to wait."

So when her family moved into a new house, her father surprised them all when he said, "Sarah has waited long enough. In this house she gets her own room." He smiled at her. "Sarah, you get first choice. What room do you want?"

Her whole face smiled back at her father, but she didn't feel happy. She felt the eyes of her brother and her sisters staring at her. She didn't have to wait anymore, but now they had to wait.

"I like the downstairs room," she said. It was the best room in the house. It had a big window that opened to a field of tall grass behind the house. It had a big closet, too. It was also the only bedroom on the first floor.

Once the movers left, everyone in the family helped with the unpacking, carrying boxes upstairs to the other bedrooms or to the rear of the house to Sarah's bedroom. After a while Sarah noticed that her sister Anne took a long time climbing the stairs with her boxes. Ever since her hip surgery Anne used a cane. She walked slowly and couldn't carry very much, and Sarah's heart jumped when she saw Anne almost fall coming down the stairs.

Sarah liked the downstairs room. She liked the sunlight from the window and the view of the field. She even liked the big closet. But she especially liked first choice. So when her father walked past with a box, she stopped him. "I can't wait to tell you," she said. "I changed my mind. My first choice is to share a bedroom upstairs with Emily. I want Anne to have the downstairs room."

When he heard her new choice, Sarah's father immediately held out his arms to hug his youngest daughter. "You didn't wait to do the right thing," he said. Sarah didn't wait to be hugged, either. She ran into her father's outstretched arms, happy she didn't have to wait for a hug.

Leah's Pony 3

Unit Theme:	***The Things That Matter***
Target Skill:	***Discussing plot, character, setting, and theme***
Genre:	***Realistic Fiction***

The following are some discussion ideas.

- Did your family read to you as a young child? Do you still have stories read to you? Do you/did you enjoy the experience? Why?
- Do you have the opportunity to read or 'make up' stories for younger siblings or other children? Does your audience enjoy your stories? Do you ever have difficulty creating a story? Why do you think so?

If the students do not bring it up on their own, mention that being creative and organizing a story requires a lot of skill. Perhaps they have been in a situation where they started telling a fictional story and, having reached the middle of it, found they had "painted themselves into a corner." Explain that this is why the planning and organizing stage of story writing is so important.

Getting Started

To begin this unit, have an open discussion about stories. Ask your students to think about some stories they have read or heard over the summer. Use the following to guide the discussion.

- What are the different parts of the story? (Acknowledge proper terminology, but do not limit the comments to that.)
- What makes a story interesting or memorable?
- In their eyes, what makes a story a good one or not such a great one?

Convey the idea that one may or may not like a story. Some of this is dependent on the individual's tastes, while some may be a response to the author's talent and style of writing. Throughout the year, if students express an opinion about a story, encourage them to support it with examples from the story and their familiarity with story elements.

Into . . . Leah's Pony

The theme of *Leah's Pony* is life's challenges and how we respond to them. As the story unfolds, many crucial lessons about growing up and what truly matters in life are learned.

What are challenges? A challenge is something that tests one's abilities or resources. Have the students describe situations that, to them, seem challenging. After various responses are given, make it clear to the class that everyone views situations differently—what is challenging to one person may be only slightly inconvenient to another. Here are a few examples of circumstances that will determine how varying challenges will be viewed:

- A wealthy person vs. a poor person
  (How will each react when $100 is stolen?)
- A three-year-old child vs. a ten-year-old
  (A favorite toy is broken beyond repair.)

The next example is of a different nature and can be used as a springboard for the next part of the discussion.

- Becoming seriously injured in an accident

Of the above scenarios, some present greater challenges to certain individuals. No one will argue that point. In some situations, however, the challenge is great for everyone.

There are some challenging situations, though, in which we can control or alter circumstances. Often we cannot change the situation, and a good deal of how we manage stems from our attitude. Point out to students that, despite everything, we can "put on a different pair of glasses" and see things from another perspective.

Students can provide suggestions as to how one might react to any type of challenge. Some examples:

Negative: sulk, complain constantly

Positive: ask others for assistance, share your problem with others, ask for advice

Now, let's examine how the characters dealt with their 'hard times.' Papa did his best to improve things when he took a loan from the bank. When this wasn't enough, he realized he had to auction off his goods to repay the loan. While he was sad, he taught his daughter to be responsible and brave. Mama recycled items and kept everyone's spirits up.

For her part, Leah thought beyond herself. She recognized how the situation affected everyone and she wanted to do something about it. Putting her own feelings aside, she sold her only precious belonging—her pony. Without consulting with an adult, Leah made a mature decision. Her selflessness had an even greater impact when others followed her example.

Every family living in the Dust Bowl was enduring the same brutal weather conditions. Despite the fact that they themselves were struggling, they stepped up to help another farmer in his time of need. The author depicts an atmosphere of caring and warmth. The sense that something special is happening is highlighted by the reaction of the auctioneer, who was not accustomed to seeing this type of generosity.

There are daily opportunities for a fourth grader to perform selfless and kind acts. Explain that some situations require inner strength and selflessness while others call only for a measure of sensitivity and thoughtfulness, without any sacrifice on their part.

Blueprint for Reading

INTO . . . *Leah's Pony*

After many years of comfortable farm life, Leah's family falls upon hard times. People react in different ways when faced with a challenge. One person may react with anger. Another person may react with determination. As you read, think about the way Leah, her family, and her neighbors deal with the difficulties that come their way. Leah has no concern for herself, as she inspires others to behave with kindness and generosity.

Narrative Elements

Why do we tell stories? There are many reasons. A story can have important messages, help us remember something, or create an imaginary world. In order for a story to work properly, a number of **elements**, or parts, must be present. You will learn about these elements, such as plot and setting, in the coming pages. As you read *Leah's Pony*, think about what makes the story interesting. Does anything in the story surprise you?

4 Unit 1

Eyes On Narrative Elements

You can start this *Eyes On* discussion by talking, just briefly, about the elements of a story. A story starts with: a **beginning**, or **exposition**, when we are introduced to the **characters** (the people in the story), the **setting** (the time and the place), and the situation.

Then there is **rising action**, as events unfold, and we see what sort of conflict or problem the main character has. Is the main character having a problem with another person? With a set of circumstances? Within him- or herself, as in a personal struggle over what is the right thing to do?

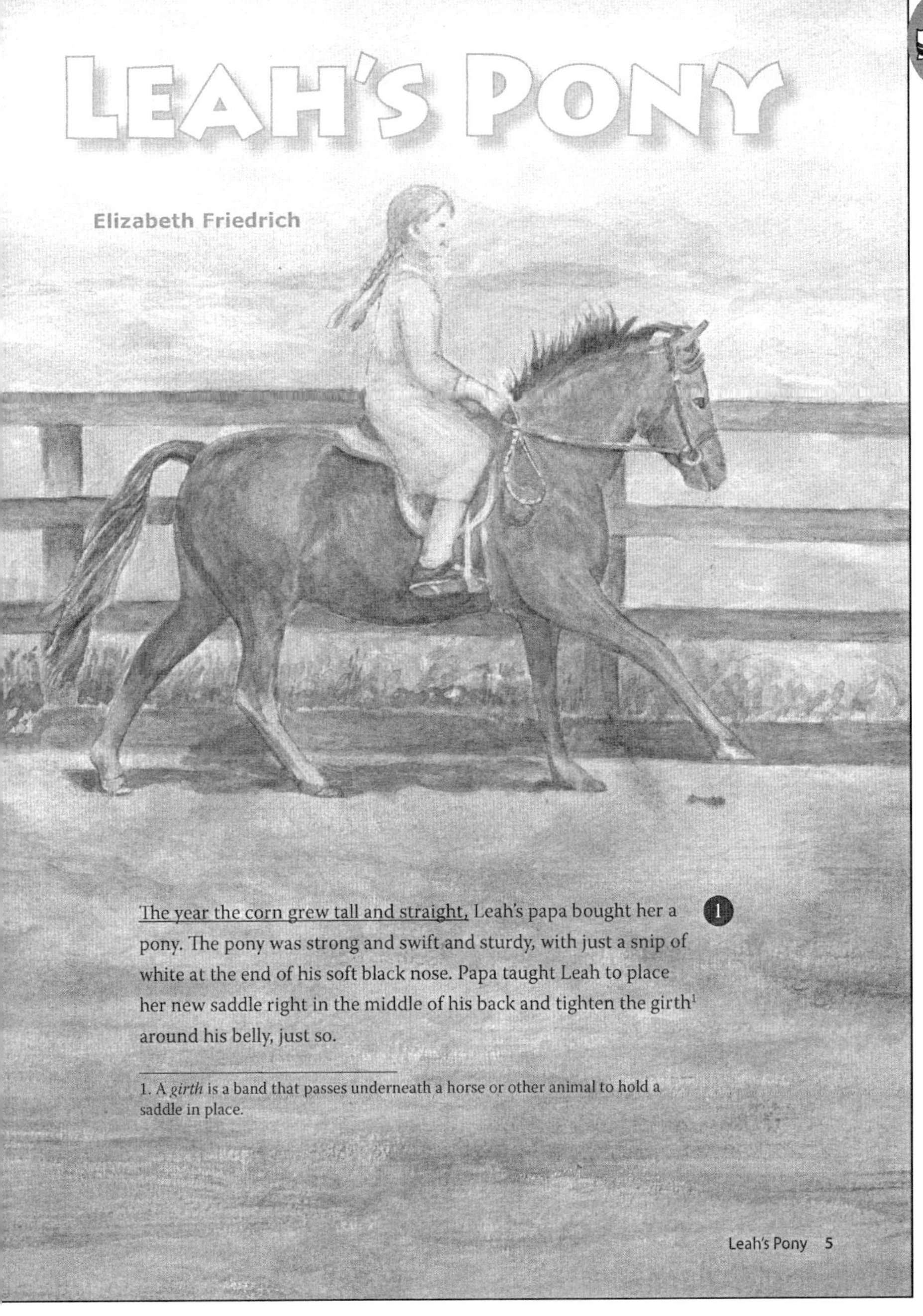

LEAH'S PONY

Elizabeth Friedrich

The year the corn grew tall and straight, Leah's papa bought her a pony. The pony was strong and swift and sturdy, with just a snip of white at the end of his soft black nose. Papa taught Leah to place her new saddle right in the middle of his back and tighten the girth[1] around his belly, just so. 1

1. A *girth* is a band that passes underneath a horse or other animal to hold a saddle in place.

Leah's Pony 5

Selection Summary

It is the early 1930s, somewhere in the south central United States, and Leah's father buys her a pony. Leah loves the pony and rides it all over the family farm and into the nearby town, where it is dubbed "the finest pony in the whole county." When the drought that created the Dust Bowl strikes, the farm begins to fail. Leah's father, almost bankrupted, agrees to auction off his livestock and farm implements. When he does that, he will be finished as a farmer, for even if the drought ends, he will have nothing to start over with.

Leah devises a plan. On the day of the auction, she asks the storekeeper who had admired her pony to buy the pony from her. He does so reluctantly. Clutching the few dollars she now has, Leah runs to the auction, where she witnesses her father's prize livestock being sold. When the auctioneer offers Papa's tractor, Leah raises her hand and bids one dollar. No one in the audience will bid against her. The farmers, inspired by Leah's selflessness, purchase the rest of the tools and livestock for almost nothing, and return them to Leah's father. At the end of the story, the storekeeper returns Leah's pony to her, and the author lets us know that the family recovers and lives to see good times.

Literary Components

1 Exposition; Imagery: The first sentence provides a visual image—a picture that tells us a number of things. We learn that the story will take place in a rural setting. We learn also, that times are good; food and money are plentiful.

At some point, the **main character** has to make a decision, or take action, in order to deal with the conflict. When the main character does this—or decides to do it—this is the **turning point** in the story.

The turning point may or may not be the **climax**, or highest moment, of the story. In the story that follows, the turning point is not the climax. This is because the emotional climax for the main character is not the situational climax of the story.

After the climax of a story there is **falling action**, as the story unwinds, and events come to a **resolution**, or **conclusion**. It is this cycle of opening, rising, peaking, falling, and resolving that makes stories so satisfying.

In the *Literary Components* that are given page for page, the elements of the story are indicated in the appropriate places.

Guiding the Reading

Literal

Q: What did Papa buy for Leah?

A: Papa bought her a new pony.

Q: Describe Leah's pony.

A: Leah's pony was strong, swift, and sturdy. He had just a snip of white at the end of his black nose.

Q: What did Leah need to do before riding the pony?

A: Leah had to place the saddle right in the middle of his back and tighten the girth around his belly. Papa showed her how to do it just right.

Analytical

Q: Why do you think it is important to mention that the pony was purchased during the year the "corn grew tall and straight"? What does that mean?

A: When the corn grew tall and straight, crops were growing well and earning a profit on the market. Papa was able to afford extras like a pony for Leah.

6 Unit 1

That whole summer, Leah and her pony crossed through cloud-capped cornfields and chased cattle through the pasture. 2

Leah scratched that special spot under her pony's mane and brushed him till his coat glistened like satin. 3

Each day Leah loved to ride her pony into town just to hear Mr. B. shout from the door of his grocery store, "That's the finest pony in the whole county." 4

The year the corn grew no taller than a man's thumb, Leah's house became very quiet. 5

Sometimes on those hot, dry nights, Leah heard Papa and Mama's hushed voices whispering in the kitchen. She couldn't understand the words but knew their sad sound. 6

Some days the wind blew so hard it turned the sky black with dust. It was hard for Leah to keep her pony's coat shining. It was hard for Mama to keep the house clean. It was hard for Papa to carry buckets of water for the sow and her piglets. 7

Soon Papa sold the pigs and even some of the cattle. "These are hard times," he told Leah with a puzzled look. "That's what these days are, all right, hard times."

Mama used flour sacks to make underwear for Leah. Mama threw dishwater on her drooping petunias to keep them growing. And, no matter what else happened, Mama always woke Leah on Saturday with the smell of fresh, hot coffee cake baking. 8

One hot, dry, dusty day grasshoppers turned the day to night. They ate the trees bare and left only twigs behind. 9

The next day the neighbors filled their truck with all they owned and stopped to say good-bye. "We're off to Oregon," they said. "It must be better there." Papa, Mama, and Leah waved as their neighbors wobbled down the road in an old truck overflowing with chairs and bedsprings and wire.

WORD BANK

sow (rhymes with now)
n.: an adult, female pig

Leah's Pony 7

Literary Components

2 Alliteration; Visual Image: The musical sound of *cloud-capped cornfields* helps us feel the tranquility and satisfaction that a fruitful field inspires. The reader can visualize the white of the clouds against the blue of the sky and the green and gold of the crop.

3 Simile: The pony's smooth shining coat is compared to satin.

4 Exposition: It is important to the story's plot that the reader be aware how very fine this horse is. (It will help us appreciate, later on, just how great a sacrifice Leah is prepared to make.)

5 Imagery: Contrast this phrase with the opening one. Again, the author uses a visual image to describe the economic/agricultural situation. *The corn* determines prosperity or failure for the farmer.

6 Sensory Images: Instead of telling the reader directly that times are hard and people are frightened and sad, the author uses sensory images (word pictures that appeal to the reader's sense of touch and sound) to portray the atmosphere.

7 Repetition: The repeated phrase illustrates how the drought affected the lives of all the characters, even though each one had a different objective.

8 Characterization: Mama is shown to be kind, thoughtful, loving, and resourceful.

9 Alliteration; Sensory Image: The rhythmic words describing the effects of the drought drive home the sense of monotony and endlessness created by the Dust Bowl.

Guiding the Reading

Literal

Q: What are some ways that Leah spent time with her pony?

A: Leah rode through cornfields, chased cattle in the pasture, and loved to ride her pony into town.

Q: Why did Leah like to ride into town?

A: She loved to hear Mr. B. tell her, "That's the finest pony in the whole county."

Q: Describe how life has changed for Leah's family.

A: In the beginning, they seemed very happy and now they are sad and concerned. The family is not as busy, and the tasks that must be done are very different. Instead of their typical chores, they spend time cleaning and then cleaning again. Everything seems to revolve around the wind and dust.

Q: What problem was there besides the wind?

A: The grasshoppers ate the trees bare.

Q: Why did some neighbors leave for Oregon?

A: They hoped that the situation would be better there.

Analytical

Q: In what ways does Leah show love for her pony?

A: Leah scratched a special spot under her pony's mane and brushed him until his coat glistened like satin.

Q: What were the 'hard times' that befell Leah's family?

A: The family's source of income was almost wiped out as a result of the drought. (They had to sell cattle and other important items, once the drought ended. Leah and her family had to make do with reused items and work hard to keep things clean.)

Q: What is the significance of the fresh coffee cake every Saturday?

A: Even though times were tough, Mama wanted to keep some semblance of routine and normalcy in their lives. This was done especially for Leah who, at this point, did not fully understand the impact these hard times would have on the family. It was a warm and touching gesture on Mama's part.

Q: How do you think Papa, Mama, and Leah felt when they saw so many neighbors leave?

A: Answers will vary. Some answers may include: they were sad that they were going to miss their fellow farmers and neighbors; they considered moving themselves; they were looking forward to hearing good news from them in the near future; they were hoping this wouldn't last long and that they wouldn't have to leave the farm they'd built up.

Literary Components

10 Characterization; Theme: Papa is strong and honest. He wants his family to be the same way. He will try to meet adversity bravely. Courage is one of the story's themes.

11 Characterization: Although Papa is strong, he is also human. He is a character who shows emotion and communicates with his family.

The hot, dry, dusty days kept coming. On a day you could almost taste the earth in the air, Papa said, "I have something
10 to tell you, Leah, and I want you to be brave. I borrowed money from the bank. I bought seeds, but the seeds dried up and blew away. Nothing grew. I don't have any corn to sell. Now I can't pay back the bank," Papa paused. "They're going to have an auction, Leah. They're going to sell the cattle and the chickens and the pickup truck."

11 Leah stared at Papa. His voice grew husky and soft. "Worst of all, they're going to sell my tractor. I'll never be able to

8 Unit 1

Guiding the Reading

Literal

Q: How did Papa try to improve the situation? Why didn't his idea work in the end?

A: Papa borrowed money from the bank in order to buy more seeds, but they dried up and blew away.

Q: What did Papa tell Leah would happen because he was unable to pay back the bank?

A: An auction would be held where many things on the farm would be sold.

Analytical

Q: Why do you think Papa wanted Leah to be so brave?

A: Perhaps he knew that things would only get worse before they got better. He was also keenly aware of the fact that Leah would have to give up certain things because there was no money. (You can also mention the idea that knowing about a hardship in advance can sometimes be helpful.)

Q: How would an auction help Leah's family?

A: The profits from the auction would be used to pay back the money Papa borrowed from the bank. Even though they would be left without any farm equipment, they would still have the farm.

Q: What does the description of Papa's voice tell you?

A: Papa may have lowered his voice because he was not proud to be discussing the auction. Papa was not talking to Leah in a strong, confident manner but in a sad and emotional way; the huskiness in his voice was his manly way of holding back tears.

plant corn when she's gone. Without my tractor, we might even have to leave the farm. I told you, Leah, these are hard times."

Leah knew what an auction meant. She knew eager faces with strange voices would come to their farm. They would stand outside and offer money for Papa's best bull and Mama's prize rooster and Leah's favorite calf.

All week long Leah worried and waited and wondered (12) what to do. One morning she watched as a man in a big hat hammered a sign into the ground in front of her house.

Literary Components

(12) **Alliteration; Rhythmic Repetition:** The phrase helps the reader feel the nagging, repetitive anxious thoughts that Leah had.

Guiding the Reading

Literal

Q: What was the worst part of the auction in Papa's eyes?

A: Selling the tractor was the worst part. This meant that Papa would no longer be able to plant corn and might even have to leave the farm.

Q: What did Leah do until the time of the auction arrived?

A: She worried, waited, and wondered all week long.

Analytical

Q: How do you think Leah knew what an auction was?

A: Auctions were not uncommon at the time. Many farmers were in similarly dire straits.

Literary Components

13 Turning Point: Finally, Leah can do something to help her family. Her position changes from passive to active. There is always a sense of relief when one arrives at a plan of action, no matter how long the odds of success are.

14 Alliteration; Imagery: This is an unusual but very appropriate description.

15 Rhythmic Repetition: The naming of the object, followed by the refrain "sold," evokes the sense of helplessness Papa must have had, as the fruits of his labor slip away from him in a matter of moments.

Leah wanted to run away. She raced her pony past empty fields lined with dry gullies. She galloped past a house with rags stuffed in broken windowpanes. She sped right past Mr. B. sweeping the steps outside his store.

At last Leah knew what she had to do. She turned her pony around and rode back into town. She stopped in front of Mr. B.'s store. 13 "You can buy my pony," she said.

Mr. B. stopped sweeping and stared at her. "Why would you want to sell him?" he asked. "That's the finest pony in the county."

Leah swallowed hard. "I've grown a lot this summer," she said. "I'm getting too big for him."

14 Sunburned soil crunched under Leah's feet as she walked home alone. The auction had begun. Neighbors, friends, strangers—everyone clustered around the man in the big hat. "How much for this wagon?" boomed the man. "Five dollars. Ten dollars. Sold for fifteen dollars to the man in the green shirt."

15 Papa's best bull.
Sold.
Mama's prize rooster.
Sold.
Leah's favorite calf.
Sold.

WORD BANK

gullies (GULL eez) *n.*: small valleys or ravines made by running water

10 Unit 1

Guiding the Reading

Literal

Q: How did Leah feel when she finally saw the auction announcement go up?
A: Leah wanted to run away.

Q: What made Leah turn around and go back into town?
A: A new thought struck her. Leah came up with an idea of how she could help.

Q: What offer did Leah make to Mr. B.?
A: "You can buy my pony."

Q: Did Mr. B. take Leah's offer seriously at first?
A: He couldn't believe that she was willing to sell "the finest horse in the county."

Q: What reason did Leah give to Mr. B. for selling her prized pony?
A: She told Mr. B. that since she'd grown over the summer, she was too big for the pony.

Q: Who was the man in the big hat with all the people around him?
A: He was the man in charge of the auction, known as an auctioneer.

Analytical

Q: Where did you first think Leah was going when she ran away?
A: Answers will vary.

Q: When Leah left on the pony, was it her intention to sell the pony to Mr. B.?
A: No. We know from the words, "At last Leah knew what she had to do. She turned her pony around and rode back into town."

Q: Does the story actually mention that Mr. B. purchased the pony?
A: No, but it does say that Leah walked home alone, so we can infer that Mr. B. purchased the pony.

AUCTION
Leah's Pony 11

Literary Components

16 Rising Suspense: *What* has to be enough? Is there a plan here? A way out?

17 Approaching Climax: As everyone holds their breath, the reader hopes that somehow, Papa's farm can be saved. It is not yet clear how.

18 Climax: This is the high point of the story. Leah's plan has worked, the people are behind Papa, and the farm will be saved.

16 Leah clutched her money in her hand. "It has to be enough," she whispered to herself. "It just has to be."

"Here's one of the best items in this entire auction," yelled the man in the big hat. "Who'll start the bidding at five hundred dollars for this practically new, all-purpose Farmall tractor? It'll plow, plant, fertilize, and even cultivate for you."

It was time. Leah's voice shook. "One dollar."

The man in the big hat laughed. "That's a low starting bid if I ever heard one," he said. "Now let's hear some serious bids."

17 No one moved. No one said a word. No one even seemed to breathe.

"Ladies and gentlemen, this tractor is a beauty! I have a bid of only one dollar for it. One dollar for this practically new Farmall tractor! Do I hear any other bids?"

Again no one moved. No one said a word. No one even seemed to breathe.

"This is ridiculous!" the man's voice boomed out from under his hat into the silence. "Sold to the young lady for one dollar."

18 The crowd cheered. Papa's mouth hung open. Mama cried. Leah proudly walked up and handed one dollar to the auctioneer in the big hat.

WORD BANK

clutched (KLUCHD)
v.: held onto tightly

cultivate (KUL tih vayt)
v.: to help the plants grow by tending to the soil around them

12 Unit 1

Guiding the Reading

Literal

Q: Did the auctioneer acknowledge Leah's "one dollar" as a true bid at first?

A: No. He laughed it off and said, "Now let's hear some serious bids."

Q: Describe the different reactions to Leah's purchase.

A: "The crowd cheered. Papa's mouth hung open. Mama cried." Leah was proud. The auctioneer was upset and frustrated. Everyone else seemed to be proud of Leah and continued what she had started.

Analytical

Q: Where did Leah get the money that she had clutched in her hand?

A: The money Leah had was from the sale of her pony.

Q: When Leah said, "It has to be enough," what did she mean? Enough for what?

A: Answers will vary. They should all indicate that she wanted to buy something at the auction or help pay off the debt in some small way.

Q: How did Leah feel about announcing a bid for the tractor?

A: Leah's voice shook. She was nervous about speaking in front of all the adults and afraid of what they would think of her offer.

Q: Why did the man in the big hat laugh?

A: He could not believe that a young girl really thought she could bid on a tractor with such a low bid. He viewed it as childish and moved on with the auction.

Q: What caused everyone to be silent?

A: Answers will vary. Some answers may include that they were surprised by her offer or that they were contemplating what to do next. Perhaps they were afraid to ruin the moment when this innocent girl was trying to save her family.

Q: What do you think were some of the thoughts of the onlookers and participants?

A:

- They were surprised that a young girl would make a bold and ridiculously low bid.
- Some may have seen it as an opportunity to help Leah's family.
- Others may have thought that this was not the place for Leah to get involved.
- Perhaps some people were confused.

Q: How was Leah's act selfless?

A: Leah really thought beyond herself. She sold the one thing she owned and loved and used the money to try and help her family.

Q: Remember when Papa told Leah to be brave? In what way did she show her bravery at the auction?

A: Without knowing how her parents would react, without asking anyone for advice or approval, Leah spoke up in front of the auctioneer and all of the adults. She was nervous and her voice shook, but she was brave. Leah risked looking foolish or childish because she thought she might be able to help.

"That young lady bought one fine tractor for one very low price," the man continued. "Now how much am I bid for this flock of healthy young chickens?"

"I'll give you ten cents," offered a farmer who lived down the road. 19

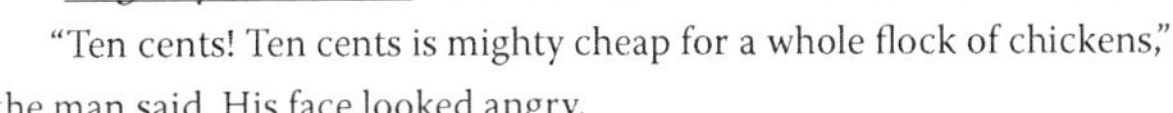

"Ten cents! Ten cents is mighty cheap for a whole flock of chickens," the man said. His face looked angry.

Again no one moved. No one said a word. No one even seemed to breathe.

"Sold for ten cents!"

The farmer picked up the cage filled with chickens and walked over to Mama. "These chickens are yours," he said.

The man pushed his big hat back on his head. "How much for this good Ford pickup truck?" he asked.

"Twenty-five cents," yelled a neighbor from town.

Again no one moved. No one said a word. No one even seemed to breathe.

Leah's Pony 13

Literary Components

19 Conclusion: After the tractor is sold for a dollar, the rest of Papa's possessions are sold at similar low prices. We are not as surprised, and the action slows down as the story comes to a happy resolution.

Guiding the Reading

Analytical

Q: How did Leah save the day?

A: By keeping the tractor in the family, Leah kept hope alive. They would eventually be able to plant again. Additionally, with all of the neighbors in the farming community following Leah's lead, the family didn't lose everything, as they had feared they would.

Q: Why was the experienced auctioneer puzzled about what bid to put up for the other items?

A: After taking a one-dollar bid for an expensive tractor, he couldn't charge the regular price for chickens. He wasn't sure what to do in this unusual situation.

Q: Do you think the auctioneer felt the same way as the rest of the fellow farmers at the auction? Support your answer with quotes from the story.

A: No. It was his job to conduct a proper auction and give the proceeds to the bank.

- "This is ridiculous!"
- "Ten cents! Ten cents is mighty cheap for a whole flock of chickens," the man said. His face looked angry.
- "This isn't supposed to be a penny auction!" he shouted.

Literary Components

20 Conflict: The auctioneer represents those who would wish to benefit from the suffering of others. The neighbors and Papa stand on one side, and the bank and the auctioneer stand on the other.

21 Characterization; Theme: While Papa and Mama can feel happy and secure now, Leah must live with the sacrifice she has made. She does not regret it, but still finds it difficult to behave "bravely" as her father had instructed her to.

22 Sensory Image: Again, the author uses an auditory (sound) image rather than telling us directly what has happened. This draws us into the story and makes us feel as though we are living it, not just reading it.

23 Conclusion; Theme: As the story ends on a happy note, another theme is highlighted. It partners well with the theme of courage, because a belief that better times await us gives us strength and the ability to be brave.

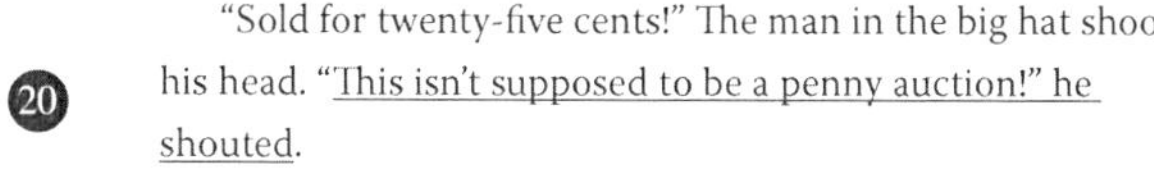

"Sold for twenty-five cents!" The man in the big hat shook
20 his head. "This isn't supposed to be a penny auction!" he shouted.

The neighbor paid his twenty-five cents and took the keys to the pickup truck. "I think these will start your truck," he whispered as he dropped the keys into Papa's shirt pocket.

Leah watched as friends and neighbors bid a penny for a chicken or a nickel for a cow or a quarter for a plow. One by one, they gave everything back to Mama and Papa.

The crowds left. The sign disappeared. Chickens scratched in their coop, and cattle called for their corn. The farm was quiet. Too quiet. No familiar whinny greeted Leah when she
21 entered the barn. Leah swallowed hard and straightened her back.

That night in Leah's hushed house, no sad voices whispered in the kitchen. Only Leah lay awake, listening to the clock chime nine and even ten times. Leah's heart seemed to copy its slow, sad beat.

The next morning Leah forced open the heavy barn doors
22 to start her chores. A loud whinny greeted her. Leah ran and hugged the familiar furry neck and kissed the white snip of a nose. "You're back!" she cried. "How did you get here?"

Then Leah saw the note with her name written in big letters:

Dear Leah,

This is the finest pony in the county. But he's a little bit small for me and a little bit big for my grandson.

He fits you much better.

Your friend,

Mr. B.

23 P.S. I heard how you saved your family's farm. These hard times won't last forever.

And they didn't.

14 Unit 1

Guiding the Reading

Literal

Q: What was the trend that was started?

A: The people began to not only offer low bids, but also to return to the family any purchases they had made.

Q: What was the general attitude of the people about returning the items?

A: They returned the items willingly and in a generous and kind manner.

Q: Why was it "too quiet" on the farm?

A: The familiar whinny of Leah's beloved pony was not heard.

Q: What words show that once again Leah was brave?

A: "Leah swallowed hard and straightened her back."

Q: What surprise did Leah receive in the morning?

A: Leah's pony was back in the barn.

Analytical

Q: Why did the new owner of the chickens return them to Mama?

A: He wanted to be able to assist the family instead of watching them lose everything they owned.

Q: How did Leah inspire her neighbors to behave with kindness?

A: While it's possible that some of the farmers felt bad for Leah's family and what they were going through, it wasn't until Leah took action that they were moved to help as well.

Q: Why couldn't Leah fall asleep?

A: So many 'big' things had taken place during the course of the day. She had been reviewing all of the day's events and her role in them. Often, such thoughts prevent people from falling asleep. Mostly though, she was missing her pony.

Q: Now that you know the true reason that Leah sold her pony, why do you think she invented a reason instead of just telling the truth?

A: Leah was probably embarrassed to discuss her family's financial difficulties. In addition, maybe she didn't want to make a big fuss about selling her pony.

Q: Do you think Mr. B. intended to return the pony originally or was he also influenced by what took place at the auction?

A: Answers will vary.

Q: What do you think would have happened to Leah's family if the outcome of the auction had been different?

A: They would have endured even harder times. They would have had to make do with even less. Without their essential farm equipment, they could not have hoped to work the land once the weather improved. They could have seen no purpose in staying and would have decided to move.

ABOUT THE AUTHOR

As a child, **Elizabeth Friedrich** loved to visit her aunt and uncle's farm. There, she was allowed to ride horses and help care for some of the farm animals. Young Elizabeth thought of the farm as "a magical place." As an adult, Ms. Friedrich was able to fulfill her dream of living on a farm. She, her husband, and their two children live on a New Hampshire farm, where they are raising a small flock of sheep. In addition to writing, Ms. Friedrich enjoys traveling and collecting antiques.

About *The Way*

Poetry Shows Us the Way

The Way is about what it feels like to ride a horse. It asks you to sit in the saddle, feel the sun on your shoulders, sway with the horse's movement, and listen to the sound of the horse's hooves. In short, it asks you to experience, rather than to think. A poem is better equipped to achieve this than is a piece of prose. The short lines of a poem, the evocative language and imagery that a poem employs, even the rhythm, pull the reader away from analyzing and thinking and towards feeling and experiencing. *The Way* is a good companion poem for *Leah's Pony* because it encourages us to feel how wonderful it is to ride on a pony and thus, to value even more highly Leah's sacrifice.

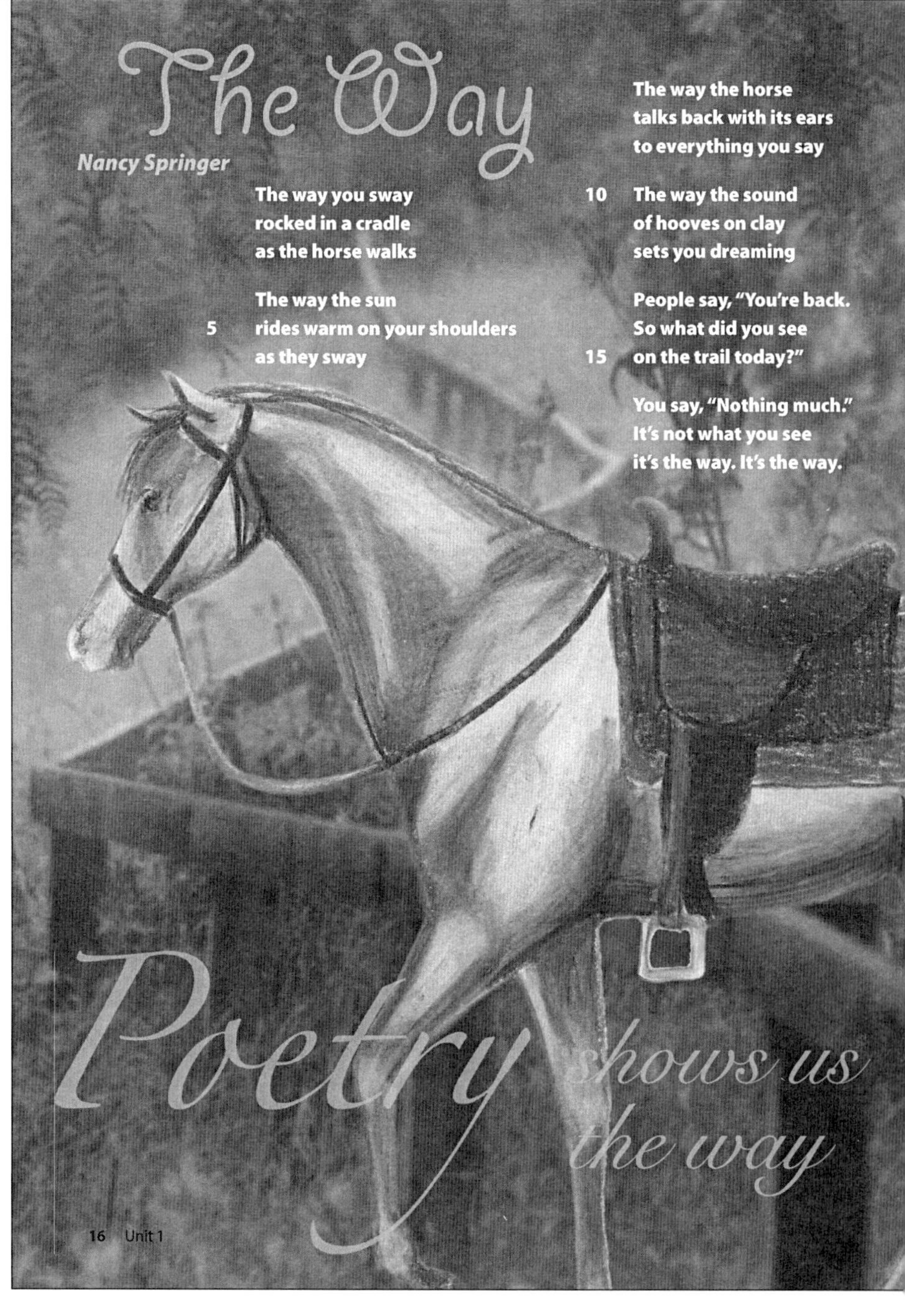

The Way

Nancy Springer

The way you sway
rocked in a cradle
as the horse walks

The way the sun
rides warm on your shoulders
as they sway

The way the horse
talks back with its ears
to everything you say

The way the sound
of hooves on clay
sets you dreaming

People say, "You're back.
So what did you see
on the trail today?"

You say, "Nothing much."
It's not what you see
it's the way. It's the way.

Poetry shows us the way

16 Unit 1

Studying the Selection

FIRST IMPRESSIONS

Do you think you would have the strength to do what Leah did?

QUICK REVIEW

1. Describe Papa's precious gift to Leah.
2. What type of weather conditions brought on the 'hard times' experienced by Leah's family?
3. How did Mama recycle things to save money?
4. Who changed the direction of the auction with a very low bid?

FOCUS

5. Leah's father told her to be brave, and Leah obeyed. What are two examples of Leah's bravery?
6. We know that a good story has a beginning, middle, and an end. Reread the story and write down one important event from the beginning of the story, the middle of the story, and the end of the story.

CREATING AND WRITING

7. Leah acted unselfishly to help her family. Do you think the townspeople would have reacted differently if an adult, rather than a child, had done what Leah did?
8. Leah was selfless during very difficult times. Think of someone you know who gave up something important to help another person. Write a paragraph describing the situation and selfless deed.
9. Create a poster for a "One Kindness a Day" campaign. Encourage people, young and old alike, to do something for others with the understanding that small acts can make a big difference. Be sure that your poster is attractive and explains the purpose of the project.

Leah's Pony 17

First Impressions

Answers will vary.

Discuss the fact that, on the one hand, we often think we are capable of doing great things until we are actually faced with the reality of doing them. On the other hand, when a difficult situation does present itself, we often rise to the challenge and find strength we did not know we possessed.

Encourage the students to relate personal stories of strength and triumph.

Quick Review

1. Papa bought Leah a strong pony with a "snip" of white on its black nose. The pony was swift and sturdy. The pony's coat glistened like satin when Leah brushed him. Mr. B. said, "That's the finest pony in the whole county."
2. The weather was hot, dry, and dusty. This was a period of severe drought with the wind constantly blowing dust and dirt.
3. Mama used flour sacks to make underwear and dishwater to water the flowers.
4. Leah made a bold offer of one dollar for the tractor and no one had the heart to outbid her.

Focus

5. She tried to sell her most precious possession—her pony.

   When she was talking to Mr. B., she bravely pretended that the pony was just too small for her—concealing her despair at having to sell him.

   "Leah's voice shook." Making a ridiculously low bid in front of the entire crowd took courage.
6. Answers will vary.

Creating and Writing

7. Answers will vary. Remind students to include responses to all of the questions.
8. Answers will vary.
9. Provide enough craft materials so that students can do more than just write their message in marker. Tell your students that content is as important as art.

Background Bytes

The material that follows is certainly more extensive than would be normally presented to fourth grade students.

The phrase *The Dust Bowl* refers to (1) a period of time, (2) a region of the country, (3) a condition of the soil and the broader environment, and (4) a catastrophic series of events that had a huge impact on American culture and the American economy.

The Dust Bowl occurred between 1930 and 1940—although the human behavior and the events that caused it existed for many years leading up to this period.

The area that became known as the Dust Bowl included, especially, the driest region of the United States Great Plains, southeastern Colorado, southwest Kansas, and the panhandles of Oklahoma and Texas—100,000,000 acres. But the entire Great Plains region, and eventually the entire country, were affected. The other states most strongly associated with the Dust Bowl phenomena are Nebraska, Wyoming, North Dakota, South Dakota, Montana, New Mexico, Iowa, and Minnesota.

How did the soil become so dry and damaged? What created all that dust? The Dust Bowl was a mostly human-made disaster that came about when the virgin top soil of the Great Plains was deeply and repeatedly plowed, which killed the natural grasses. These grasses had kept the soil in place and moisture trapped for centuries, even in periods of drought and fierce winds.

Moreover, decades of extensive farming without crop rotation had stripped the earth of nutrients it needed to remain healthy and stable.

Finally, where the land was not being plowed (and there was a history of bitter and violent conflict between farmers who wanted the land for raising crops and ranchers who wanted it for beef), overgrazing by millions of head of cattle meant the near obliteration of the grass roots that prevent soil erosion.

Thus, when the drought of the 1930s came, the soil dried out, turned to dust, and blew away eastwards and southwards in large dark clouds. The skies could darken for days. In some places the dust would drift like snow, covering farmsteads. The dust storms were given names such as Black Dark Blizzard and Black Roller because visibility was so reduced. The storms themselves caused further ecological and agricultural damage to the American and Canadian prairies.

During the Dirty Thirties, the clouds that blackened the sky reached all the way to the East Coast. Prairie dust was deposited in New York, Washington, D.C., and the Atlantic Ocean.

The Dust Bowl got its name after Black Sunday, April 14, 1935. More and more dust storms had been blowing up in the years leading up to that day. In 1932, 14 dust storms were recorded on the Plains. In 1933, there were 38 storms. By April 1935, there had been weeks of dust storms, but the cloud that appeared on the horizon that Sunday was the worst. Winds were clocked at 60 mph. Then it hit.

A giant dust storm engulfed Boise City. Cyclic winds rolled up two miles high, stretched out a hundred miles, and moved faster than 50 miles an hour.

The Dust Bowl displaced millions of people and destroyed a way of life for thousands upon thousands of farm families. People who had previously owned their own farms went west looking for work. The only labor available to them was as migrant farm workers. Think about what a change this represented for a family that had lived on and owned its own farm, to now be at the mercy of the crops, their seasons, and more fortunate landowners!

As John Steinbeck wrote in his 1939 novel *The Grapes of Wrath*:

> *And then the dispossessed were drawn west—from Kansas, Oklahoma, Texas, and New Mexico; from Nevada and Arkansas, families, tribes, dusted out, tractored out. Car-loads, caravans, homeless and hungry; twenty thousand and fifty thousand and a hundred thousand and two hundred thousand. They streamed over the mountains, hungry and restless—restless as ants, scurrying to find work to do—to lift, to push, to pull, to pick, to cut—anything, any burden to bear, for food. The kids are hungry. We got no place to live. Like ants scurrying for work, for food, and most of all for land.*

Jill's Journal:

On Assignment from the Dirty Thirties

You will never guess where I am, or what it is like here.

What if it were daytime, but when you looked out your window you couldn't see anything? Wouldn't you think it was scary, if you couldn't see anything but dust so thick you just saw blackness? Well, that is what it is like here.

It is Sunday, April 14, 1935. I am in Dodge City, Kansas. I wanted to go to a town somewhere in the Great Plains. Then I would be able to see for myself what happened on Black Sunday. That's what people called it later on. On Black Sunday, some people thought the world was coming to an end.

I am staying with the Kaufmans, a farm family. They are pretty sure that the black blizzards have come because people have plowed too much. The grass is gone. The roots of the grass used to grip the soil and keep it moist. Also, cattle

Courtesy of Library of Congress Prints and Photographs Collection.

have been grazing the land for years. They've eaten what was left of the grass.

Mr. Kaufman also told me that the farmers on the prairie have been planting the same crop—wheat—year after year after year, on millions of acres of earth. He says that planting just one crop takes all of the good nutrients out of the soil.

18 Unit 1

Then the long and terrible drought started in 1930. There has been almost no rain for five years, so the land has turned to dust.

Mr. and Mrs. Kaufman work so hard. They have been farming this land for eleven years. In fact, five of their six children were born right in this cabin! Each of the children helps (of course, not the baby). Meg is 12, Tim is 10, Robert is 8, Zack is 6, Elizabeth is 4, and little Ruthie is 18 months. I will tell you now that the baby is sick. Her mom is holding a wet cloth over her face so she won't breathe in so much dust. Meg says they are worried that Ruthie has dust pneumonia.

Well, no wonder. The cabin is always filled with grit and dust, no matter how hard everyone works to keep it clean. Tim and Zack are taking wet gunnysacks and waving them through the air. They call that sweeping the air. The gunnysacks turn black with dirt.

Any little holes or cracks in the walls or doors or windows are plugged up with newspapers and rags. But the house is not sealed tight the way our houses are. Dust still gets inside. Meg and Robert are nailing sheets over the windows now and putting blankets over the doors. But it

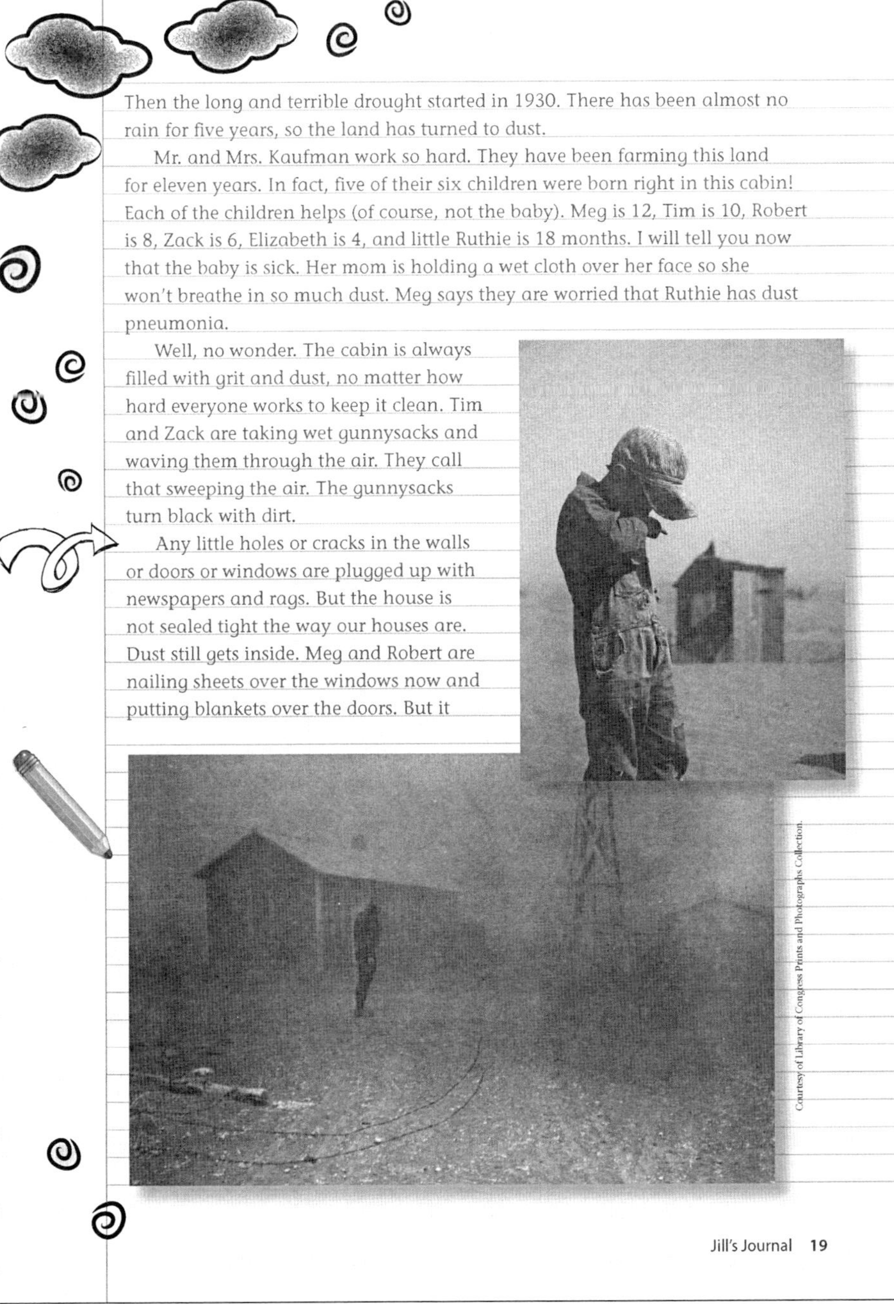

Courtesy of Library of Congress Prints and Photographs Collection.

hardly seems to help. I have only been here a few days, but sometimes it feels like I could choke. The cabin is hot and very stuffy.

You should see the lot of us. Have you ever seen cowboys with kerchiefs tied over their noses and mouths? The cowboy robbers did that so no one could identify them. That's how the Kaufmans and I look. And when we go outside, if we dare, we put on these funny old goggles to protect our eyes. It is dangerous to go out, because you cannot see your hands in front of your eyes. You can get lost only a few feet from the house.

I am helping Mrs. Kaufman do laundry. We wash everything by hand in a large metal tub. Of course, the clothes are gray when we pull them from the soapy

water. Mr. and Mrs. Kaufman carry the heavy tub outdoors together to empty it. Someone has to go to the well to bring in more water. Then it's heated in the big black iron kettle. This takes so long. I can hear grit rattling in the bottom of the kettle as it heats. Even the food we eat has grit in it.

What will happen to the Kaufmans?

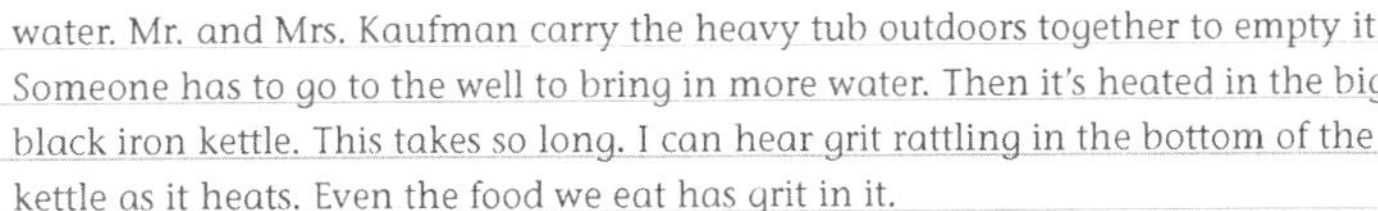

POWER SKILL:

Don't Get Lost! Learn to Read a Map.

It is important to be able to read a map. Maps tell us where we are. They tell us what is around us. A map adds to the information you may have about a place. Maps make it much easier for us to understand events in history.

If you live in the United States, do you know where your state is on the map?

If you live outside the U.S., do you know where your country is on the globe?

Many maps show directions with a compass rose, a circular figure that shows the directions north, south, east, and west. Some maps also have a scale bar to show the true size of the area on the map. These days, we go by airplane to travel long distances. Travel by plane doesn't give us the sense of distance we have when we go by car, train, bus, or on foot. So we *do* need maps.

Exercises

1. Your teacher will give you an outlined, blank map of the United States.
2. Now you are going to put in the Dust Bowl states on your map. Use a large labeled U.S. map to help you. Start at the bottom with Texas. Then add New Mexico and Oklahoma. Now add Kansas and Colorado.
3. Now write in the names of the following states: Nebraska, South Dakota, and North Dakota.
4. Finally, using a U.S. map for reference again, write in the names of other states that were affected by the Dust Bowl: Wyoming, Montana, New Mexico, Iowa, and Minnesota.
5. Now, on your maps, color in the Dust Bowl area. That was the region most badly affected during the Dust Bowl years.

Jill's Journal 21

Power Skill:

Don't Get Lost! Learn to Read a Map.

For the map exercises, you will want to be certain your students have a good, complete larger map of the United States available for reference. You will need to supply them with individual outline maps of the U.S.A. for their use.

What Is Plot?

Jigsaw

1. Katie is afraid of dogs.
2. When Jigsaw jumps on Katie and licks her, he seems so friendly and loving that she forgets her fear of dogs.
3. Katie no longer fears all dogs. Although she is cautious around dogs she doesn't know, she realizes that once she gets to know them, she will like them.

Lesson in Literature . . .

WHAT IS PLOT?

- In the first part of the plot we are introduced to the characters and setting.
- A problem or conflict occurs near the beginning of the story.
- At the middle or near the end of the story, something will change and there will be a turning point.
- As the story reaches its conclusion, the problems presented in the plot are solved.

THINK ABOUT IT!

1. What problem is presented at the beginning of the story?
2. What happens to change the way Katie feels about Jigsaw?
3. How has Katie changed by the end of the story?

Katie was afraid of dogs. Once when she was little, she put out a hand to pet a cute brown-and-white dog, but the dog snarled and bit her hand. Last summer she was playing outside when a large black dog came into her backyard, growling and barking. She ran inside, terrified.

Her mother tried to comfort her. "Katie, some dogs are mean but some dogs are nice. You just have to be cautious around unfamiliar dogs."

Katie didn't think she would ever like any dog. On her way to school, she always walked fast in front of a white house with a big loud dog that barked at her from behind a wire fence. She didn't like it when a neighbor from down the street walked by her house with a little white dog sniffing and pulling on a leash. She was riding her bicycle one day when she and the neighbor with the dog came to the corner of the street at the same time. The little dog jumped at her and almost knocked her off.

So when her father brought home a fluffy brown puppy, Katie was afraid and ran to her bedroom. "Katie," he called up the stairs, "come down and meet Jigsaw."

She refused to budge even when her father came into her room to talk to her. "Katie," he said, "Jigsaw is just a puppy who wants someone to love him."

Katie shook her head and crawled under the bedcovers. "I don't like any dogs. They're scary and mean."

Her mother came in and sat on the edge of the bed. "Not all dogs are mean, Katie. Do you remember what I said about strange dogs and familiar dogs? Once you meet Jigsaw and spend some time with him, you'll see. Once you're familiar with him and he's

22 Unit 1

Additional background information for *Supergrandpa* can be found on p. 2 in the Teacher Resources Section.

Vocabulary

scoffed (SKOFT) *v.*: mocked; ridiculed

sprinted (SPRINT ed) *v.*: raced at full speed for a short distance

craned (KRAYND) *v.*: stretched out their necks (to see)

trembling (TREMB ling) *v.*: shaking slightly from fear, cold, or excitement

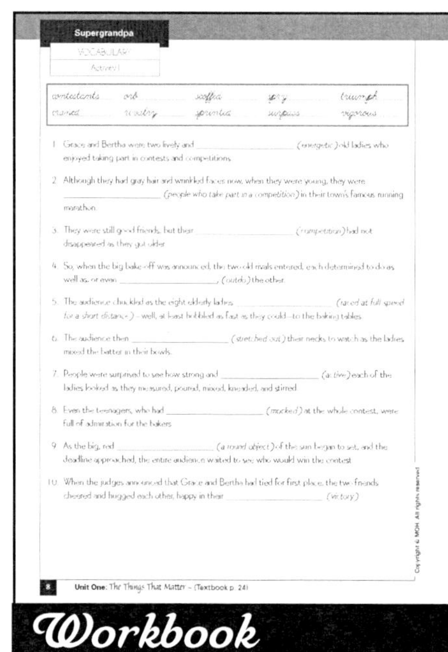

Workbook

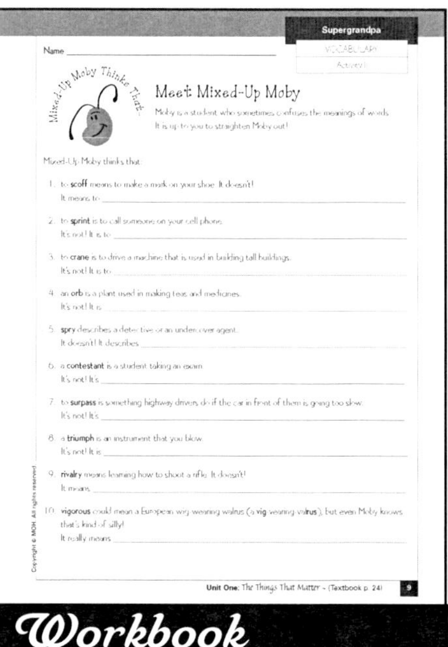

Workbook

JIGSAW

familiar with you, you'll become friends."

After her parents left her alone, Katie wondered why anyone liked dogs. She opened a book to read, thinking she would spend the rest of her life alone in her room.

Just then, the light from outside her door came on. She sat up in bed as a fluffy ball of fur leaped on her. "Oh!" Katie cried as Jigsaw pressed his nose against her hands and licked her face. "Oh!" Katie cried again, but this time she sounded as if she had just jumped into a swimming pool on a hot summer day.

When Katie put out her hand to pet Jigsaw, he just wagged his tail. As her hand stroked his ears and neck, Jigsaw curled up in Katie's arms, and she knew that Jigsaw was not like the mean dogs she knew. He was cute and friendly, and he belonged to her.

Katie's father stood in the doorway. "I'm sorry. He just got away," he said. "But by looking at you two now, I'm glad he did."

The next day when Katie saw the neighbor with the mean dog, she didn't think that all dogs were mean. She thought that she just hadn't met the little white dog yet. On her way to school, she didn't rush past the house with the dog behind the fence. She hoped the dog's owners took him for walks or let him run in the park.

Walking home from school, she couldn't wait to see Jigsaw again. As she opened the kitchen door, Jigsaw ran to her, and the two spent the afternoon getting to know each other better. Soon they became more than familiar; they became friends. Although she always remained cautious around unfamiliar dogs, Katie loved getting to know Jigsaw, a puzzle she loved solving.

Supergrandpa 23

Getting Started

When teaching literature, exercises using several modalities should be implemented. Your students will benefit from the variety, which sharpens both skill and interest. Twenty-five percent of the *Getting Started* activities will be in the form of aural exercises. These will help your students develop the ability to listen carefully and answer questions clearly.

The aural comprehension questions will not be graded or handed in to the teacher. Students can mark down which questions they have answered correctly and see for themselves how they are progressing over the course of the year. Knowing that they are not being graded relieves pressure and allows the students to concentrate on what they are hearing.

Read the story from p. 25 only through p. 27 up to "Go home to your rocking chair." aloud twice. Be sure to enunciate in a clear and loud voice. After reading the story, read each question aloud twice. Allow enough time for your students to record their answers. The correct answers are in bold letters.

1. How old was Gustaf Håkansson?
   a. 82 **c. 66**
   b. 45 d. The story does not give his age.

Unit Theme:	***The Things That Matter***
Target Skill:	***Plot is what happens in a story. Authors must have a story plan for the plot.***
Genre:	***Fiction***

2. The story tells us that Gustaf
   a. felt very old and weak.
   b. looked old, but didn't feel old.
   c. felt old but looked young.
   d. had a lot of young friends.
3. Which of the following was *not* a place that Gustaf passed every day?
   a. the bakery **c. a school**
   b. the butcher shop d. many farms
4. What did Gustaf eat every morning for breakfast?
   a. hot oatmeal with milk
   b. sour milk and lingonberries
   c. freshly squeezed orange juice and toast
   d. cold cereal with skim milk and strawberries
5. What news did Gustaf see in the newspaper?
   a. There was going to be a bicycle race in Sweden.
   b. The Swedish government was going to change the traffic rules.
   c. There was a new mayor in Grantofta, Sweden.
   d. A new bakery specializing in Swedish pastries had opened.
6. The name of the race was
   a. Race of Swedes. **c. Tour of Sweden.**
   b. Tour de France. d. European Annual Race.
7. Which words show that Gustaf's son thought Gustaf would faint from working too hard on the race?
   a. "Go home to your rocking chair."
   b. "You'll keel over."
   c. "His face rippled with wrinkles whenever he smiled."
   d. "This Tour of Sweden is for me."
8. What does "Struntprat" mean?
   a. smart boy c. news
   b. delicious berries **d. silly talk**
9. Which of the following is *not* one of the reasons used by the judges to disqualify Gustaf from the race?
   a. "Men with white beards cannot travel one thousand miles."
   b. "We can only admit racers who are strong and fit."
   c. "You're too old, Gustaf."
   d. "You would never make it to the finish."
10. Gustaf thinks
    a. the judges are right.
    b. about dyeing his beard red.
    c. that perhaps it's time to buy a new rocking chair.
    d. that he is fit enough to win the race.

Into . . . Supergrandpa

Most people thought it was absurd for Gustaf Håkansson to even consider participating in the Tour of Sweden bicycle race. The reaction to his wish to cycle more than one thousand miles is not surprising. A man over sixty would not be encouraged to participate in such a race unless, perhaps, he was exceptionally fit. However, Gustaf *was* able to race and showed people that their assumptions were not correct.

One theme presented here is not to judge others. Explain to students that we should not judge hastily or without knowing the whole story. We should not judge by appearances alone, and ultimately, we should try not to judge people at all.

Inherent in the theme is a valuable lesson. Help students understand that people cannot be labeled like file folders. The fact that a person is young, for example, does not automatically mean that that person is not capable of handling a big job. A child who cannot play ball is not necessarily clumsy or untalented. In addition, even if any of the above were true, it should not prevent us from seeing the whole person.

In this story, Gustaf is measured by his bushy white beard and his age. As the class reads the story, invite the students to put themselves in his shoes. Explain that, while we are talking about an older man in this instance, the lesson learned can apply to their lives as well. They have probably had the experience of being judged unfairly or of judging unfairly. Invite them to share these experiences with their classmates.

There are other themes in the story. The qualities of persistence and determination play an important role in the story. One's inner voice should speak more loudly to an individual than a whole chorus of voices from the outside. A subordinate theme is that small acts of kindness (as we saw earlier, in *Leah's Pony*) can mean a great deal.

Blueprint for Reading

INTO . . . *Supergrandpa*

Gustaf Håkansson does not start out as a Supergrandpa. At first, people judge him by the way he looks. They think that he is too old to do anything interesting or important. Unfortunately, some people make quick judgments based only on what they see. More thoughtful people wait before drawing conclusions. As you read, think about which characters make quick judgments and which characters judge on more than looks alone.

A **plot** is what happens in a story. Before authors write a story, they must have a story plan for the plot. The story plan has many parts. The author will check the plan and ask: Does the story have a beginning, middle, and end? Is there an exciting part or turning point? Can the reader find solutions to the problems presented in the story? Do the events appear in the proper order? Does everything make sense? If the answer to all these questions is "yes," the author is ready to write the story!

24 Unit 1

Eyes On Plot

Although any discussion of plot will be primarily about the story line, we would like to preface our discussion of plot by emphasizing the need for a good *plan* for the story. Students should recognize that a good idea doesn't transform itself into a story on its own. The following is an introduction to the elements of plot. You may introduce the concepts now, while the terms and details will be elaborated upon in later selections.

Beginning: Gustaf wants to join a race, but everyone thinks he is too old to join.

Middle: Gustaf participates in the race despite what everyone else thinks.

End: Gustaf not only races, but wins with the approval of most of Sweden!

Rising Action: After everyone tells him he is too old to race, Gustaf rides for miles and chooses to participate unofficially in the Tour of Sweden.

Climax: The turning point is when Gustaf becomes a famous "Supergrandpa" and gains the support of many Swedish people.

One can argue that the turning point is when the onlookers are cheering for him and are convinced Gustaf is going to win. This is the first time Gustaf even thinks about winning the race.

Falling Action: Although Gustaf is the first to cross the finish line, the judges still decide that he cannot be the winner. No one seems to care and even the king recognizes Gustaf's accomplishment.

Problem: Gustaf wants to ride in the race but family members and the judges feel that he is too old.

Resolution: Gustaf goes on the road to race even though he has not officially been accepted as a contestant. He persists and proves to himself and others that he's capable not only of completing the course, but even of winning the race.

External Conflict: Gustaf vs. Judges

Internal Conflict: Gustaf has to decide whether he will ride or not.

Stiff muscles and the like challenge Gustaf, but the warmth and kindness of the crowd keep him going.

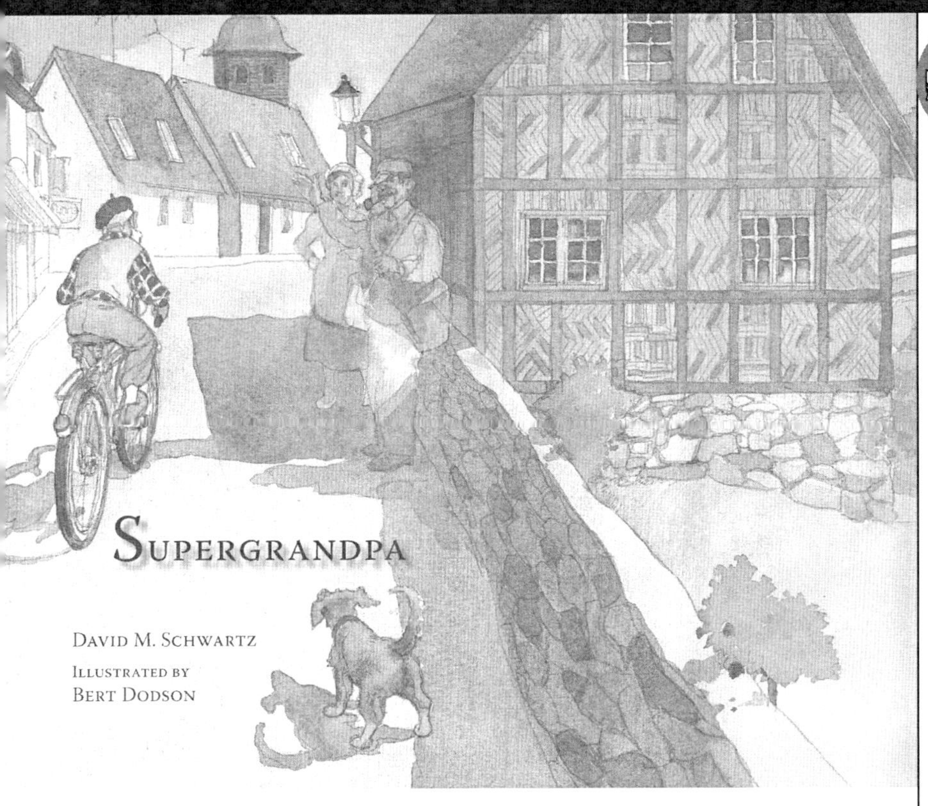

Gustaf Håkansson was sixty-six years old. His hair was snow white. His beard was a white bush. His face rippled with wrinkles whenever he smiled. Gustaf Håkansson looked like an old man, but he didn't feel old, and he certainly didn't act old. 1

Everyone for miles around knew Gustaf. People saw him on his bicycle, rain or shine, riding through the crooked streets of Grantofta—past the baker's and the butcher's and the wooden-toy maker's, over the stone bridge leading out of town, up steep hills scattered with farms, down narrow lanes bordered by stones, then home again to his morning paper and a bowl of sour milk and lingonberries.[1]

One morning Gustaf read something very interesting in the paper. There was going 2 to be a bicycle race called the Tour of Sweden. It would be more than one thousand miles long, and it would last many days.

1. *Lingonberries* are a type of berry that grow in the Scandinavian countries; they are also called mountain cranberries or cowberries.

Supergrandpa 25

Selection Summary

Gustaf Håkansson is a sixty-six year old Swede who lives in the town of Grantofta. He rides his bicycle everywhere, so it is only natural that when he sees a newspaper ad for a thousand-mile bicycle race called the Tour of Sweden, he wants to enter it. It is natural to him, that is. Everyone else, including his wife, son, grandchildren, and the race's judges deem him too old to ride in the race.

Undeterred, Gustaf begins to train for the race, biking more and more miles each day. Because he is not an official racer, he is not permitted to ride on the train to the race's starting point, six hundred miles away. Gustaf bikes the six hundred miles. Still not officially admitted to the race, he starts the race with a makeshift number—Zero! By biking when the contestants are sleeping, and resting only sparingly, Gustaf overtakes the official racers. A little girl spots him and dubs him "Supergrandpa," and he becomes a hero. All of Sweden—or a good part of it—come out to cheer him on and, indeed, he reaches the finish line first. Although the judges refuse to give him the trophy, the king himself hugs Gustaf as the crowds hoist Supergrandpa on their shoulders and celebrate his victory.

Literary Components

1 Characterization; Theme; Exposition: The main character, Gustaf, is an old-looking person who is more youthful and energetic than most of the younger people who surround him. He embodies the story's theme, which is that age should not be a deterrent for activity, accomplishment, or fun.

2 Rising Action: Into the sleepy, idyllic setting of Grantofta, the author injects a bit of excitement.

Guiding the Reading

Literal

Q: How old was Gustaf Håkansson?
A: Gustaf was sixty-six.

Q: Describe Gustaf's physical appearance.
A: Gustaf looked old. His hair was snow white, his beard was a white bush, and his face rippled with wrinkles whenever he smiled.

Q: How well-known was Gustaf?
A: People knew him for miles around.

Q: Where did Gustaf live?
A: Gustaf lived in Grantofta.

Q: What was Gustaf's regular activity, rain or shine?
A: Gustaf always went bicycle riding.

Q: What were some places that he passed on his regular route?
A: He passed the bakery, the butcher shop, the wooden-toy maker, a stone bridge, steep hills, farms, and narrow lanes.

Q: What did Gustaf eat for breakfast every morning?
A: He ate a bowl of sour milk and lingonberries. (Lingonberries are a type of mountain cranberry.)

Q: What was the name of the big bicycle race?
A: It was called the Tour of Sweden.

Q: Where did he find out about it?
A: He read about the race in the newspaper.

Q: What details do you know about the race?
A: It would be more than one thousand miles long and it would last many days.

Analytical

Q: In what ways was Gustaf truly sixty-six and in what ways did he not seem like sixty-six years old?
A: Gustaf looked his age but did not feel or act old.

Literary Components

3 Characterization; Theme: Gustaf is a positive, upbeat person who knows his own strength.

4 Characterization; Conflict: Gustaf's son is just the first of the young naysayers who wish to write off an older person as weak and incapable.

3 "This Tour of Sweden is for me!" exclaimed Gustaf.

"But you're too old for a bicycle race," said Gustaf's wife.

4 "You'll keel over," said his son. "It would be the end of you."

4 Even his grandchildren laughed at the idea. "You can't ride your bike a thousand miles, Grandpa," they scoffed.

"*Struntprat!*" Gustaf answered. "Silly talk!" And he hopped onto his bike and rode off to see the judges of the race. He would tell them that he planned to enter the Tour of Sweden.

Guiding the Reading

Literal

Q: What was Gustaf's reaction to the Tour of Sweden?

A: "This Tour of Sweden is for me!"

Q: How did his family react?

A: His wife thought he was too old and his son thought that he would keel over.

Q: How did Gustaf's grandchildren react?

A: They laughed and said, "You can't ride your bike a thousand miles, Grandpa."

Analytical

Q: Did you expect Gustaf to react to the race the way he did?

A: Answers will vary.

Q: Do you think this is a typical reaction for a sixty-six year old man?

A: Answers will vary. Students will likely lean towards no.

Q: What did Gustaf's son mean when he said, "You'll keel over... It'll be the end of you"?

A: Literally, it means that the race would cause Gustaf to pass out and might even kill him. His son was possibly a bit dramatic and meant that it would be too much for Gustaf at his age. It might adversely affect his health.

Q: Did his grandchildren's comments bother him?

A: No. He felt it was silly talk and went to enter the race anyway.

"But this race is for young people," said the first judge. "You're too old, Gustaf." 4

"You would never make it to the finish," said the second judge.

"We can only admit racers who are strong and fit," said the third judge. "What if you collapsed in the middle of the race?"

"*Struntprat*!" protested Gustaf. "I have no intention of collapsing, because I *am* strong and fit!"

But the judges were not to be moved. "We're sorry, Gustaf," they grumbled. "Go home. Go home to your rocking chair." 4

Gustaf went home, but he did not go to his rocking chair. "They can keep me out of the race," he muttered, "but they can't keep me off the road." 4

The next morning, Gustaf began to prepare for the long ride ahead. He arose with the sun, packed some fruit and rye bread, and cycled far out of town—over rolling hills dotted with ancient castles, across valleys dimpled with lakes, through forests thick with birches and pines. It was midafternoon before he returned. The next day he biked even farther. Each day he added more miles to his ride.

A few days before the race, all the young cyclists boarded a special train to Haparanda, in the far north of Sweden, where the race was to begin. But Gustaf was not an official racer. He had no train ticket.

There was only one way for Gustaf to ride in the Tour of Sweden. He would have to pedal six hundred miles to the starting line! 5

It took him several days to bike there. He arrived just as the Tour of Sweden was about to begin.

Literary Components

5 **Rising Action:** Gustaf now begins to prove that he is more than capable of riding in a marathon.

Guiding the Reading

Literal

Q: How many judges were there?

A: There were three.

Q: What was their opinion of Grandpa Gustaf?

A: They all agreed that he was too old and not in the condition to participate in the race.

Q: What words show Gustaf's determination to ride even though everyone thought he was too old?

A: "They can keep me out of the race," he muttered, "but they can't keep me off the road."

Q: What did Gustaf take with him on his first big practice ride?

A: He took fruit and rye bread.

Q: How did Gustaf prepare for the big race?

A: Gustaf cycled far out of town and back for many days. He rode through all types of areas including valleys and forests. Each day he added more miles to his practice run.

Q: In what location was the race to begin?

A: The race was to begin in Haparanda in the north of Sweden.

Q: Why couldn't Gustaf get on the train with all the other people who planned to bike in the race?

A: He was not entitled to a train ticket because he was not an official racer.

Q: What bold plan did Gustaf come up with in order to get there in time for the race?

A: Amazingly enough, he decided that he would pedal six hundred miles to Haparanda.

Analytical

Q: The judges said, "We're sorry." Did they seem truly sorry?

A: No. They grumbled and said mockingly, "Go home to your rocking chair."

Q: What is meant by the words "Go home to your rocking chair"?

A: The judges are telling Gustaf in a negative and roundabout manner that he should go do what sixty-six year olds usually do and forget about the race.

Q: Do you think Gustaf even owned a rocking chair?

A: Answers may vary. Students should indicate that Gustaf was very active and even if he did own one, it was unlikely that he sat in it for long.

Q: From what you've read so far, do *you* think that Gustaf Håkansson was too old for the Tour of Sweden?

A: Answers will vary.

Literary Components

6 **Humor:** Gustaf's lighthearted response to those who won't let him enter the race makes this story happy and enjoyable rather than heavy and bitter. Perhaps one reason Gustaf enjoys such good health is his positive approach to life!

WORD BANK

sprinted (SPRINT ed) *v.*: raced at full speed for a short distance

All the racers wore numbers, but of course there was no number for Gustaf. So he found a bright red scrap of fabric and made his own.

What number should he be? He had an idea. He wasn't supposed to be in the race at all, so he would be Number Zero! **6**

He chuckled as he cut out a big red zero and pinned it to his shirt. Then he wheeled his bicycle to the starting line.

The starting gun went off and all the young cyclists took off in a spurt. Their legs pumped furiously and their bikes sprinted ahead. They soon left Gustaf far behind.

That night, the racers stopped at an inn. They were treated to dinner and a bed.

Hours later, Gustaf reached the inn too. But there was no bed for him, so he just kept riding. While the others snoozed the night away, Gustaf pedaled into the dawn.

28 Unit 1

Guiding the Reading

Literal

Q: Why didn't Gustaf have a number to wear at first?

A: Only official racers received numbers.

Q: How did he create his own number?

A: He used a bright red scrap of fabric and created his own.

Q: What number did Gustaf choose?

A: Since he wasn't supposed to be in the race at all, Gustaf chose the number zero. (It also shows that Gustaf had a sense of humor!)

Q: Did Gustaf keep up with the pace of the young cyclists?

A: No, they left him far behind.

Q: What did the racers do once night fell?

A: They stopped at an inn to rest for the night.

Q: Did Gustaf stop at the inn with the others?

A: No, Gustaf kept pedaling. Besides, there was no bed or meal prepared for him.

Q: What did he do while everyone was sleeping?

A: Gustaf kept riding until dawn. This gave him a head start and would help him keep pace the following day.

Literary Components

7 Turning Point: Suddenly, Gustaf is in the limelight. From the old man who lagged behind the young racers, slept on park benches, and was looked upon with scornful amusement, emerges a superhero.

WORD BANK

craned (KRAYND) *v.*: stretched out their necks (to see)

Early the next day, the other cyclists passed Gustaf. But he kept up his steady pace, and late that evening he again overtook the young racers as they rested. In the middle of the night, he napped for three hours on a park bench.

On the third morning, Gustaf was the first to arrive in the little town of Lulea. A small crowd of people waited, hoping to catch a glimpse of the racers zooming by. Instead they saw Gustaf. His white beard fluttered in the breeze. His red cheeks were puffed out with breath. "Look!" cried a little girl. "Look! There goes Supergrandpa!"   7

"Supergrandpa?" Everyone craned to see.

"Yes, yes, he does look like a Supergrandpa!"

A few clapped. Others shouted friendly greetings. Some of the children held out their hands and Gustaf brushed their palms as he rode by. "Thank you, Supergrandpa! Good luck to you."

Supergrandpa 29

Guiding the Reading

Literal

Q: Who was ahead of whom on the second day?

A: Gustaf started out ahead, but it didn't take long for the other cyclists to pass him.

Q: Where did Gustaf rest for a short while on the second night?

A: He napped on a park bench.

Q: How was Gustaf able to arrive in Lulea before all of the other cyclists?

A: He overtook the young racers while they slept.

Q: What happened when Gustaf arrived in the town of Lulea?

A: A little girl called Gustaf "Supergrandpa." This drew the attention of many onlookers in the crowd. People shouted friendly greetings, clapped, and touched his hand. Some wished Supergrandpa good luck and one even took his picture.

Q: Which words indicate that Gustaf was working hard to pedal and keep up?

A: "His white beard fluttered in the breeze. His red cheeks were puffed out with breath."

Analytical

Q: Do you think the people of Lulea were disappointed that the excitement was just because of an old man riding by their town?

A: Some may have been disappointed because they had been waiting for a while and were looking forward to catching a glimpse of incredible racers. Others may have been satisfied to see anyone ride by. Perhaps some thought the girl's response was childish but the general response seemed positive.

Q: How do you think Gustaf felt about the reception he got from the crowd?

A: Gustaf may have expected people to be watching along the route of the race, but he did not expect to be the focus of so much attention, himself. At first, he may have been surprised by it all, but later, he seems to have enjoyed it.

Literary Components

8 Characterization; Rhetorical Question: Supergrandpa is not arrogant. He is not vindictive. He does not say "I told you so." He does not wish to lord it over his young competitors. He does not moralize or even use mild sarcasm. Like the air of his native Grantofta, he is pure, sweet, and mild. The question he asks is *rhetorical,* which might be a new term for your students.

9 Foreshadowing: Who will win the race?

A photographer snapped Gustaf's picture. It appeared the next day in the newspaper. The headline read:

SUPERGRANDPA TAKES A RIDE.

Now all of Sweden knew about Supergrandpa Gustaf Håkansson.

When he got hungry or thirsty, people gave him sour milk with lingonberries, tea and cake, fruit juice, rye bread, or any other snack he wanted.

Newspaper reporters rushed up to talk with him. Radio interviewers broadcast every word he spoke. Everyone wanted to know how he felt.

"I have never felt better in my whole life," he told them.

"But aren't you tired?" they asked.

8 "How can I be tired when I am surrounded by so much kindness?" And with a push on the pedal and a wave of his hand, Gustaf was rolling down the road again.

Once again Gustaf rode through the night, passing the other racers while they slept. When his muscles felt stiff, he remembered his cheering fans. He pedaled harder.

And so it went, day after night, night after day. By the light of the moon, Gustaf quietly passed the young racers in their beds, then slept outside, but only for a few hours. Under the long rays of the morning sun, they overtook him and left him
9 struggling to keep up his spirits and his pace. But each day it took them a little longer to catch up with Gustaf.

30 Unit 1

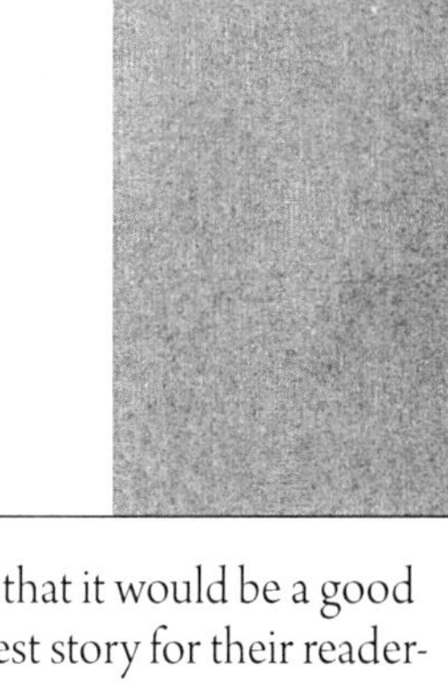

Guiding the Reading

Literal

Q: How did all of Sweden find out about Supergrandpa, Gustaf Håkansson?
A: The paper that carried the article and photograph was read all over Sweden.

Q: What did people offer Gustaf along the way?
A: People gave him sour milk with lingonberries, tea and cake, fruit juice, rye bread, or any other snack he wanted.

Q: What did the newspaper reporters and radio broadcasters want to know?
A: Everyone wanted to know how he was feeling.

Q: What kept Gustaf from being tired?
A: The kindness of all the people he encountered gave him strength when he was tired.

Q: When Gustaf felt his muscles get stiff, what thought helped him to continue?
A: He remembered his cheering fans.

Q: What two things did Gustaf struggle with every day?
A: He struggled to keep up his spirits and his pace.

Q: Each day it took the racers longer to do what?
A: It took them longer to catch up to Gustaf.

Analytical

Q: Why is it important to note what the photographer did with the picture he took of Gustaf?
A: The fact that the photo was printed in a popular newspaper added a new dimension to the story. Now that Gustaf was 'famous,' he had increased support for what he'd set out to do. This helped him prove that even a grandpa—super or not—could finish the race.

Q: Why do you think all of the media people were so interested in Gustaf?
A: It was a unique experience to see someone with a bushy white beard participating in a race intended for young and fit bicyclists. They probably thought that it would be a good human-interest story for their readership.

Q: Do you think Gustaf liked all the attention?
A: The story does not say. However, we can infer that he didn't mind at all, from the words, "I have never felt better in my whole life," and "How can I be tired when I am surrounded by so much kindness?"

Q: Having read up until this point, do you think the judges were correct when they decided that Gustaf was too old to race?
A: Answers will vary. While he certainly seemed fit and was able to race many miles a day, he was not able to keep pace with the other cyclists.

60
Supergrandpa 31

32 Unit 1

On the sixth morning of the race, thousands lined the road. As Gustaf rode by, their joyful cheers traveled with him like a wave through the crowd.

"You're almost there, Supergrandpa!"

"A few more miles!"

"Don't look back."

"You're going to win!" (10)

Win? Gustaf hadn't thought about winning. He had simply wanted to ride in the Tour of Sweden and reach the finish line. But win?

"You're out in front, Supergrandpa."

"A few more miles, Supergrandpa, and you'll be the winner!"

The winner? Gustaf glanced over his shoulder. The pack of racers was catching up. Their heads and shoulders were hunched low over their handlebars. Their backs were raised high above their seats.

Gustaf decided not to think about them. Instead he thought about his many fans. He thought about how they wanted him to win. And suddenly, he wanted to win too!

Gustaf looked ahead. In the distance he could see a bright banner stretched all the way across the road. The finish line!

Gustaf lowered his head. He raised his back. He whipped his legs around with all their might and all their motion.

The next time he looked up he was bursting through the banner and rolling over the finish line—just before another racer thundered past.

Literary Components

(10) Foreshadowing; Secondary Turning Point: Who will win the race? For the first time, Supergrandpa thinks he can win. The reader has come to this conclusion earlier.

Guiding the Reading

Literal

Q: What encouraging comments did people have for Gustaf on the sixth morning?

A: "You're almost there, Supergrandpa!"
"A few more miles!"
"Don't look back."
"You're going to win!"
"You're out in front, Supergrandpa!"
"A few more miles, Supergrandpa, and you'll be the winner!"

Q: Which comment surprised Gustaf?

A: "You're going to win!"

Q: What did Gustaf see when he glanced back over his shoulder?

A: He saw the other racers catching up with their heads and shoulders hunched over and their backs high above their seats.

Q: Whom did Gustaf try not to think about?

A: The racers behind him.

Q: What made Gustaf change his mind about winning?

A: All of his fans were counting on him to win the race.

Q: What could Gustaf see in the distance?

A: He was able to see a bright banner stretched across the finish line.

Q: Describe Gustaf's physical position as he prepared to approach the finish line.

A: He lowered his head and raised his back. He whipped his legs around with all their might and all their motion.

Q: Who (did it seem) won the race?

A: Gustaf rolled over the finish line first.

Q: Was Gustaf far ahead of everyone or was it a close race?

A: It was a close race. Gustaf went over the finish line just before another racer thundered past.

Analytical

Q: Why did it surprise Gustaf that Swedish citizens were rooting for him to win?

A: He'd never thought about winning. It was not the purpose of his riding in the race.

Q: Why did Gustaf want to ride in the Tour of Sweden if he didn't want to win?

A: Answers may vary. Gustaf's original interest in the race was simply to participate and enjoy himself. Once he started, he wanted to prove that his age wouldn't limit him and he would race regardless of what everyone thought.

34 Unit 1

WORD BANK

trembling (TREMB ling)
v.: shaking slightly from fear, cold, or excitement

The crowd roared. People lifted Gustaf onto their shoulders. They showered him with flowers. They sang victory songs. The police band played patriotic marches. 11

The three judges, however, said that Gustaf could not be the winner, because he was never actually in the race. Besides, it was against the rules to ride at night. No, the big gold trophy would go to another racer, not to Gustaf.

But no one seemed to care what the judges said. Even the king stepped up to hug Gustaf and invite him to the palace. And to nearly everyone in Sweden, Gustaf Håkansson—sixty-six years old, his hair as white as snow, his beard a great white bush, his smiling face an orb of wrinkles—to them, Supergrandpa Gustaf Håkansson had won the Tour of Sweden.

ABOUT THE AUTHOR

David Martin Schwartz was born in New York, New York in 1951. After graduating from Cornell University in upstate New York, he took a job as an elementary school teacher. After a short while, he tried a variety of other jobs, such as lumberjack, veterinary assistant, and freelance writer. Mr. Schwartz has written stories and books on many different topics. He has written about restaurant food, animal life, and even about the people of the Amazon. He hopes to always write on new and unusual subjects that interest him.

Literary Components

11 **Climax:** The high point of the story is reached when all the earlier reluctance to validate Gustaf—or just to give him a fair chance—is swept aside and Gustaf is hailed as a hero. His white hair, his bushy beard, and his many wrinkles are now a badge of honor.

Guiding the Reading

Literal

Q: How did the crowd react to Supergrandpa's win?

A: They roared and sang victory songs. People lifted Gustaf into the air and gave him flowers. The police band played patriotic marches.

Q: What was the judges' opinion about Gustaf winning the race? What was their stated reason?

A: The judges said that Gustaf could not be the winner because he was never actually in the race. In addition, it was against the rules to ride at night.

Q: Was the rest of the crowd interested in the judges' decision?

A: No one seemed to care what the judges thought.

Analytical

Q: How do you think the racer behind Gustaf felt?

A: Answers will vary. Some answers may include that he felt it was unfair for Gustaf to get all the attention and win; that Gustaf didn't even follow the rules; that he was proud to ride with such a wonderful man; or that he was impressed that so many people supported Supergrandpa's win.

Q: Why did everyone get so excited and feel Gustaf was the winner even though he didn't follow the rules?

A: They admired his energy and determination and were impressed by this older man's abilities. They felt it proved something. Not everything is determined by rules. It is likely that many of the other racers had similar sentiments.

About *If You Think You Are Beaten*

Poetry Encourages Us

This poem is written in an interesting mix of colloquial language:

"It's almost a cinch that you won't"

and formal, romantic language:

"Full many a race is lost/Ere even a step is run."

Perhaps the author is pointing out that his message is timeless.

If You Think You Are Beaten is linked to *Supergrandpa* thematically. The poem's message is that a defeatist attitude is self-fulfilling. The poem's focus is on the negative, on how thinking that you are beaten, that you can't win, that you'll lose, will actually cause you to fail. The focus in *Supergrandpa* is on the positive: Supergrandpa's upbeat, optimistic, and confident self-esteem is the story's chief attraction. The story and the poem work as two sides of a coin to ... *Encourage Us.*

If You Think You Are Beaten

Anonymous

If you think you are beaten, you are;
If you think that you dare not, you don't;
If you'd like to win, but you think you can't,
It's almost a cinch that you won't.

If you think you'll lose, you've lost;
For out in the world you'll find
Success begins with a person's will,
It's all in the state of mind.

Full many a race is lost
Ere even a step is run,
And many a coward falls
Ere even his work's begun.

Poetry encourages us

36 Unit 1

Studying the Selection

FIRST IMPRESSIONS

Do you think that, at the end of the race, any of the judges felt bad about having misjudged Gustaf?

QUICK REVIEW

1. What was everyone's reaction to Gustaf's announcement that he wanted to participate in the Tour of Sweden?
2. How did all of Sweden find out about Supergrandpa Gustaf Hakånsson?
3. What did Gustaf do each day in order to keep up with the young bicyclists?
4. What kept Gustaf's spirits up when it became tough to continue riding?

FOCUS

5. Explain why the people felt that Gustaf had earned the title "Supergrandpa."
6. In this story, there are people who do not agree. They have different ideas about whether or not Gustaf should ride in the Tour of Sweden. Who is the disagreement between? Is it ever settled? How is it settled?

CREATING AND WRITING

7. Do you agree with the judges' decision? Why or why not? Support your answer.
8. Think of a situation where you were not judged favorably. Perhaps someone jumped to conclusions about you. They may have thought you were at fault when you were not, or thought you were a certain type of person because of the way you dressed. Write a paragraph about what took place and how you felt at the time.
9. Write a cheer for Supergrandpa that people could shout as he bicycled through your town.

First Impressions

Answers will vary. Some points to include in a class discussion are:

- Some of the judges may have felt strongly about following the rules, no exceptions made. These judges would not have been swayed by Supergrandpa's abilities.
- Some of the judges may have felt that they had to stick to what they had said originally, because it is a judge's job to be consistent.
- Some of the judges may have felt differently when they saw how everyone reacted, but uneasy about appearing too malleable.

Quick Review

1. They all thought the idea was ridiculous and discouraged him from participating in the race.
   - "But you're too old for a bicycle race," said Gustaf's wife.
   - "You'll keel over," said his son. "It would be the end of you."
   - Even his grandchildren laughed at the idea. "You can't ride your bike a thousand miles, Grandpa," they scoffed.
2. After a young onlooker shouted, "Look! There goes Supergrandpa!" a photographer snapped a picture. It was printed in the newspaper with an accompanying article the following day.
3. Gustaf rode through the night. He had only a few hours of sleep each night, often in uncomfortable places such as park benches. He didn't stop much for food and relied on the generosity of the people he met along the way.
4. The kindness and encouragement of the people of Sweden kept him going. When it got tough, he thought of his cheering fans and how they wanted him to win.

Focus

5. The word *super* indicates excellence or strength and Gustaf displayed both of these. He certainly showed excellence in his ability to ride a bicycle, especially at his age. Strength of character is evident through his upbeat attitude and confidence in himself. By winning the race he showed both physical and emotional strength.
6. The strong disagreement is between the judges and Gustaf. However, it could be termed as *judges and family vs. Gustaf and citizens of Sweden.* While the disagreement was never officially resolved, Gustaf proved himself capable of riding in the race and proved that those who said he could not were wrong.

Creating and Writing

7. Answers will vary. Students should support their opinions. Answers should include a thematic connection. These may include: judging favorably or not judging one by looks alone; giving people a chance; kindness and generosity; justice or sticking to the rules; and proving oneself.
8. Answers will vary. Suggest that students include both points of view to give the full picture of the situation. Were they embarrassed? Hurt? What were the long-term effects? Did they behave differently towards others after the incident?
9. Answers will vary. This should be encouraging and upbeat without negativism toward the other younger participants.

Lesson in Literature

Characters

Starfish

1. Nana, Jennifer, and Johnny are the three characters.
2. Nana and Jennifer remain the same throughout.
3. Johnny learns the following lessons:
   a. If he wants something done, he should do it himself.
   b. One often has to choose between two things that one wants.
   c. A living thing is more precious than one that is not living.
   d. Helping an animal live in its natural habitat is more rewarding than keeping the animal for oneself.

Lesson in Literature . . .

CHARACTERS

- The characters are all the people in the story.
- The characters who are the most important are called the **main** characters.
- In some stories, the characters remain the same from beginning to end.
- In other stories, the characters change because of something that happens during the story.

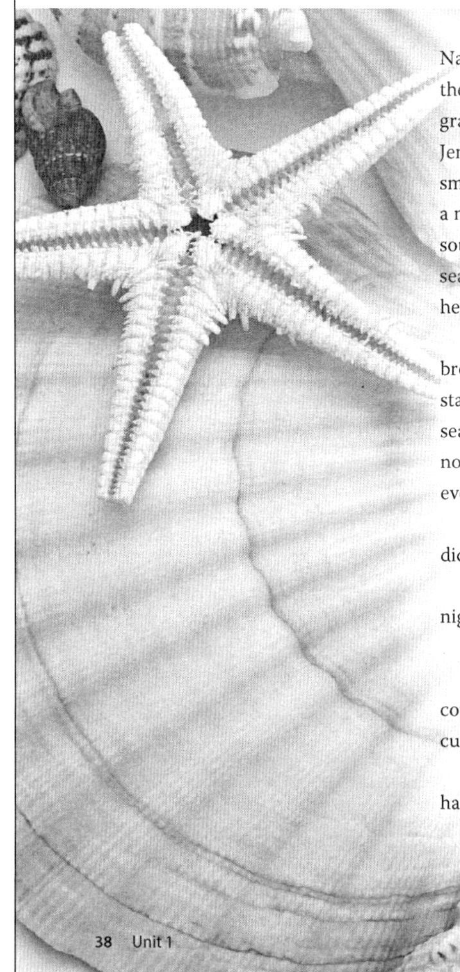

Nana, Jennifer, and little Johnny took long walks on the beach. "North or south today?" Nana asked her grandchildren each time they climbed over the dune. Jennifer liked to go north. That beach was long and smooth with white sand, and they always walked for a mile. Johnny liked to go south. Whenever they went south, they didn't go far. Instead, they hunted for seashells in the sand. Johnny liked to see how many he could hold in his hands.

Today was a beautiful day with a soft, warm breeze. Jennifer said, "I don't care which way." They started south, and Johnny ran ahead, looking for seashells, but he ran only a little ways before he noticed something amazing. There were starfish everywhere in the sand.

"Look!" he cried, holding up a starfish. "Where did they come from?"

"They must have washed up after the rain last night," his grandmother said.

"Throw them back," Jennifer said. "They're dead."

Johnny didn't listen. He gathered as many as he could in his hands, enough that the starfish gave his cupped hands many more fingers.

Hands full, he looked up, but Nana and Jennifer had walked ahead. Down the beach they had stopped,

Vocabulary

thaw *v.*: melt
eaves (EEVZ) *n.*: the overhanging lower edges of a roof
quivered (KWIV erd) *v.*: shook slightly
calico (KAL ih ko) *n.*: a plain cotton fabric printed on one side
chores (TSHORZ) *n.*: the everyday work around a house or farm; a small job that must be done regularly
trembling (TREMB ling) *v.*: shaking slightly from fear, cold, or excitement
pitch *n.*: a black, sticky tar
budge (BUHJ) *v.*: move even slightly
club (KLUB) *n.*: a heavy stick
hearth (HARTH) *n.*: the floor of a fireplace

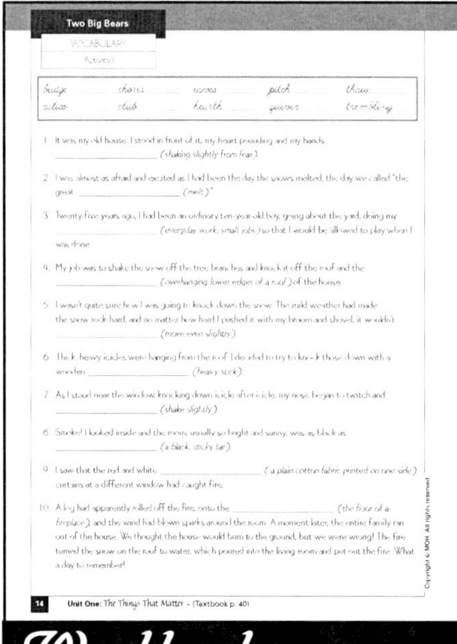
Two Big Bears

Workbook

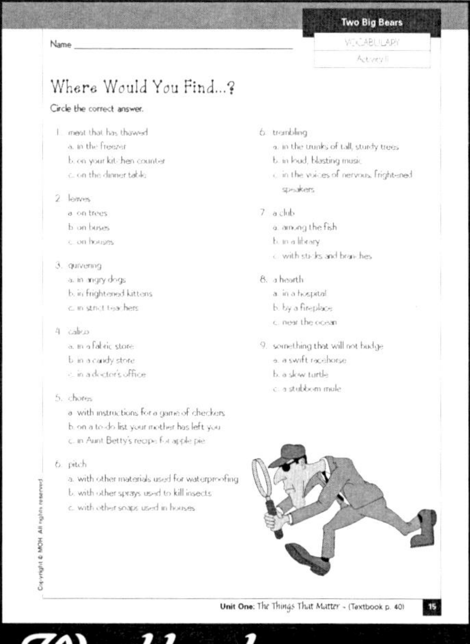
Two Big Bears

Where Would You Find...?

Workbook

Starfish

THINK ABOUT IT!

1. Who are the three characters in *Starfish*?
2. Two of the characters remain the same throughout the story. Which two?
3. The third character learns a few lessons near the end of the story. What is one of those lessons?

and Jennifer knelt in the sand. As he ran up to them, he saw what his sister had found. A live baby turtle squirmed tangled in a clump of seaweed.

"I want it," Johnny said.

"No," Jennifer said, "it's alive." She freed the baby turtle from the seaweed and held it up between her fingers while it swam the air and then gently put it down in the sand. "Okay," she said to the turtle as if it were her favorite pet, "the ocean is straight ahead. Go to the water."

"Nana," Johnny said, "tell her she has to pick up the turtle. I want it."

Nana had been standing nearby watching her grandchildren. "Pick it up yourself, Johnny," she said.

"I can't," he said. He looked at his hands, full of starfish, and looked at the turtle inching toward the water.

"Yes, you can. You have to choose."

Nana and Jennifer stood together and watched as Johnny made up his mind.

Hands full, he squatted and opened his fingers, the starfish falling like shooting stars onto the sand. Then he picked up the baby turtle, letting it swim on the palm of his hand, walked to the ocean, and let it go in the surf.

He didn't go back for the starfish.

Two Big Bears 39

Unit Theme: *The Things That Matter*

Target Skill: *Learning how to recognize the main character in a story*

Genre: *Semi-Autobiographical Fiction*

Getting Started

As a preface to *Two Big Bears*, involve your students in a discussion about animals in general as well as safety around animals.

- How many different types of animals have they encountered?
- In what locations have they seen animals? (household pets; zoos; neighborhood animals such as squirrels, birds, or even deer, etc.)
- Are they afraid of animals? What type? Is the fear due to a specific incident? (Acknowledge that it is okay to feel frightened. The remainder of the discussion should help in conquering some fears.)
- What are some safety rules regarding animals? (Prepare a list in advance.) Would they be the same for a horse, a squirrel, and an elephant? Why or why not?

If it is possible, bring in a member of your local safety squad, animal control, zoo, or veterinarian's office to speak to your students.

Into . . . Two Big Bears

Security and safety are crucial to everyone. Children are familiar with the physical security represented by police, smoke alarms, and double-locked doors. But there is another form of security that is not addressed as often. That is the sense of security people feel when surrounded by those who take care of and love them.

Parents want the best for their children. It is essential that you help your students recognize that love is expressed not only by gifts, but also more truly, by things like wise advice and warm hugs. Reassurance and support help a child get through all types of situations.

It is important for children to acknowledge just how much their parents do for them and to show their appreciation for all they receive. In addition, children should be taught to contribute to the family unit and demonstrate their care and concern.

The following are some examples from the story that illustrate the above theme.

Ma: stood up to the bear, made Laura feel good about helping her with the chores, knew what to do and acted calm, saved Laura from possible harm, hugged Laura when she was crying after meeting up with the bear, reassured her that no harm would come to them or Sukey, complimented her on good listening, locked the door with the special latch, kissed the girls and tucked them in to bed, sewed new clothing for everyone

Pa: worked hard all winter to provide for his family, was strong and brave, brought presents home for everyone, took the girls on his knees, thought of his family and got the courage to fight off the bear, made decisions, hugged Laura, whistled cheerfully

Laura: glad to help with chores, listened to Ma right away when she was told to go back into the house, worried about Pa, glad that Pa got such good prices for the furs, Laura snuggled close to Pa

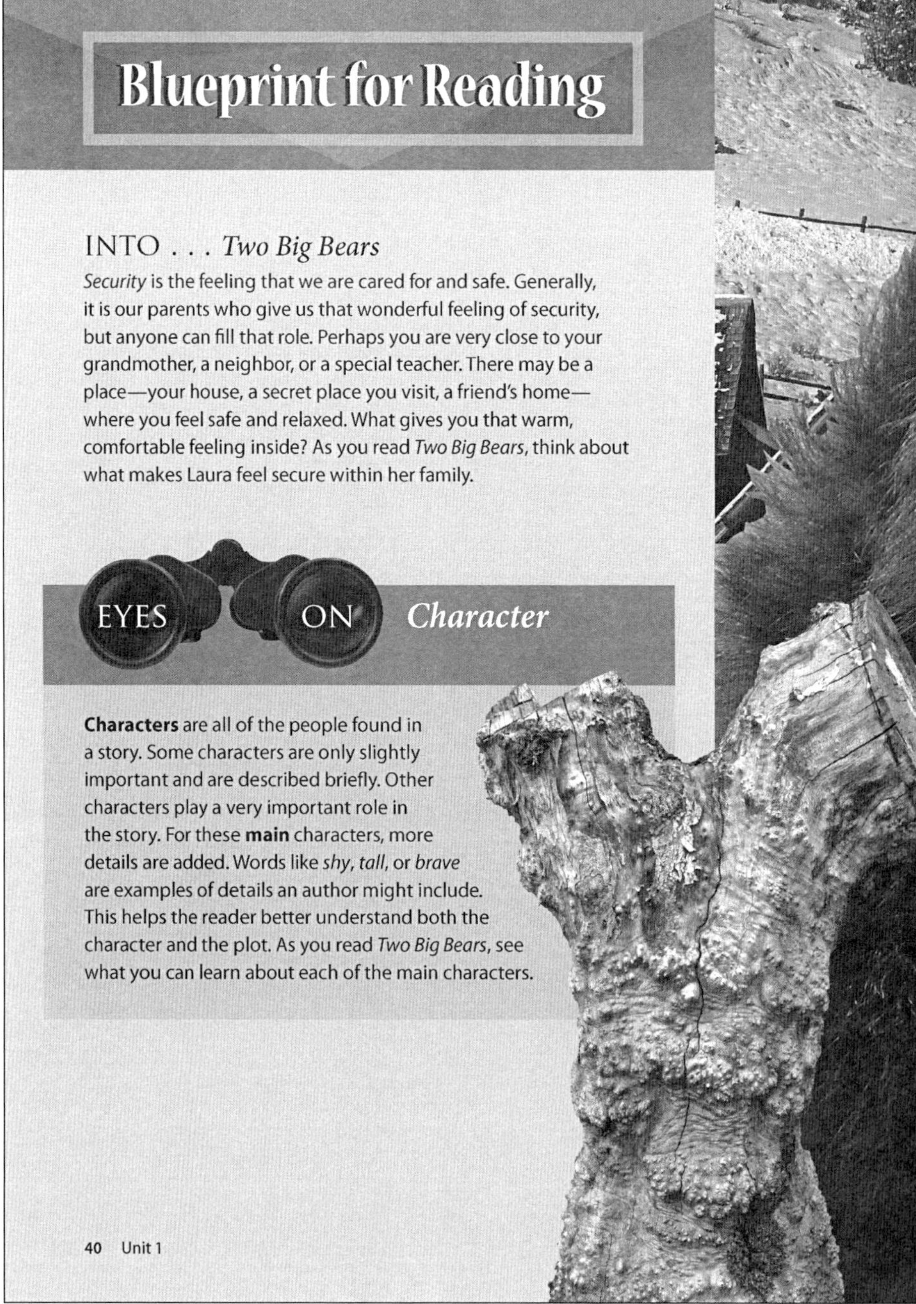

Blueprint for Reading

INTO . . . *Two Big Bears*

Security is the feeling that we are cared for and safe. Generally, it is our parents who give us that wonderful feeling of security, but anyone can fill that role. Perhaps you are very close to your grandmother, a neighbor, or a special teacher. There may be a place—your house, a secret place you visit, a friend's home—where you feel safe and relaxed. What gives you that warm, comfortable feeling inside? As you read *Two Big Bears*, think about what makes Laura feel secure within her family.

EYES ON *Character*

Characters are all of the people found in a story. Some characters are only slightly important and are described briefly. Other characters play a very important role in the story. For these **main** characters, more details are added. Words like *shy, tall,* or *brave* are examples of details an author might include. This helps the reader better understand both the character and the plot. As you read *Two Big Bears*, see what you can learn about each of the main characters.

40 Unit 1

Eyes On *Character*

Characterization, or character development, plays an essential role in most—though not all—stories. Aside from creating a more interesting narrative, characterization works to both explain and propel the action in the story. Characterization may include descriptions of physical features, personality traits, character traits, and tastes.

When there is limited description of a character, the character can be termed **flat**. Once the writer adds more description, the character becomes vibrant and multi-dimensional. Most people prefer to read a narrative with colorful characters whose traits and appearance are well-defined.

Read the following paragraph to your students:

> *Aunt Rachel comes every year to stay with us for a month. She is friendly and dresses nicely. Rachel brings presents and sometimes cooks for us while she's here. I don't use most of the presents she brings. My brother likes Rachel, and I do, too, but by the time she leaves, I'm happy to see her pack up and go.*

First, ask your students to identify the characters in this brief narrative. Then ask them what characteristics were described or hinted at in the paragraph. There are a few that can be identified, but they are vague and limited. We know that Rachel seems friendly and dresses nicely, but we are not sure to what extent and in what way. Rachel also cooks and brings presents. The author likes certain things about her aunt but dislikes others.

Read the following paragraph to your students:

> *Aunt Rachel comes to visit every January and stays with us for a month. While she is kind and generous, it is sometimes uncomfortable for me to have her around for so long. Her generosity often gets in the way of things. Trying to assist me with my homework is great, but not if she goes on and on with a funny story she heard last week. That does not help me remember all the events and dates I need to know for my history test.*

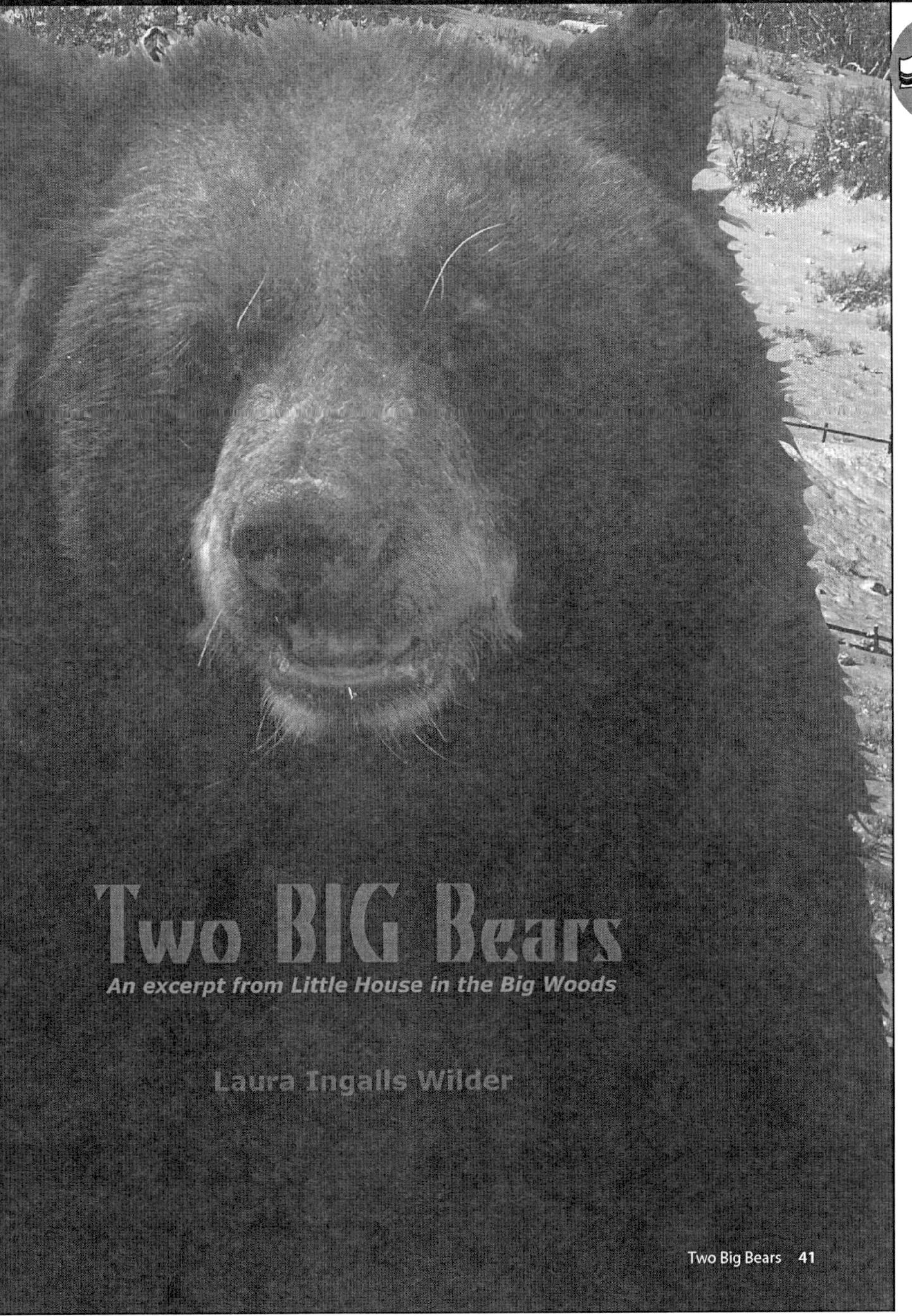

Selection Summary

It is the last quarter of the 19th century and the narrator, Laura (in real life, Laura Ingalls Wilder), is a little girl who lives with her older sister, her baby sister, her Ma, and her Pa near the Big Woods of Wisconsin. The winter is nearing its end, and Pa leaves for town to sell his furs. Ma invites Laura to accompany her to the barn to milk the cow by the light of a lantern. As they approach the barn, they see the figure of what they think is the cow. Ma slaps its shoulder, only to discover that she is standing next to a bear. Horrified, Ma quietly instructs Laura to go back into the house. Miraculously, Ma is able to follow immediately.

Meanwhile, Pa is having his own difficulties. Having successfully sold his furs and loaded himself up with many new purchases, Pa finds himself on the road through the woods as night is falling. Walking along, he encounters what he thinks is a bear. Deciding to stand his ground, he courageously hits the bear with a club, only to discover that the "bear" is a tree stump.

Pa finally reaches home, and the family is happily reunited. They share their stories as the spring air tiptoes through the cracks of their house.

Another example would be the way she helps in the kitchen. I think she wants to feel as if she's doing her part during her stay, but it is not always appreciated. Rachel means well, but often prepares dishes that we don't like, burns the food, or forgets an ingredient. Clothing is very important to my aunt and is another area where she tries to help. Aunt Rachel is always dressed in elegant outfits with matching scarves and hats. She is often displeased with my clothes and offers to buy me new things. But I like what I wear! Aunt Rachel brings a variety of gifts when she comes, and she distributes even more while she's here. As an older, successful businesswoman, she can afford to buy many expensive items. While Rachel is very thoughtful, she does not have children and does not know what to buy for an eleven-year-old girl like myself. She has no idea that I cannot stand shopping, I like word puzzles, or that I enjoy listening to music and playing on my guitar. My little brother Joey is only six, so he doesn't notice all of these things. He loves Aunt Rachel and all of the attention he receives while she's here. I suppose that I, Shelly Kogan, should be more mature and learn from Joey! I should overlook all of the minor issues and appreciate Aunt Rachel's efforts.

Ask your students if they gained more insight into the characters from this paragraph. Certainly, the appropriate response would be that they did, in fact, learn a lot more about the characters. While the author and her brother can now be identified, we can learn the most about Aunt Rachel, the principle character in this narrative.

Different aspects of characterization as they apply to *Two Big Bears*, are listed below.

- **Major Characters:** Pa, Ma, Laura
- **Minor Characters:** Mary, shopkeeper, Sukey, bear
- **Dialogue:** reveals information about character. Some examples: Ma and Laura's conversation outside regarding chores, Ma and Laura's conversation after they reach the house, Pa's story and Laura's comments.
- **Internal Dialogue:** "entering the minds" of characters and hearing their thoughts. An example: Pa's thoughts and rationalizations when he encountered the 'bear.'

Literary Components

1 Exposition: The use of the name, *Pa,* and the mention that spring is coming evokes a rural, old-fashioned setting—which is exactly what this story's setting is.

2 Visual Images: The beautiful visual images that adorn the stories of Laura Ingalls Wilder are legendary. *Quivering icicles, trembling drops of water,* and *holes in softening snowbanks* are drawn with the artist's touch, and our senses are unconsciously engaged. We are drawn into the setting before we even meet the characters. The story's setting is part of what the story is all about.

3 Foreshadowing: When we are told that Pa could not take his gun, we wonder whether he will end up needing it, especially when we are told, in the next sentence, that Ma is worried.

4 Characterization: We are introduced to Laura and Mary, who have never seen a town.

5 Repetition: The repeated phrase reflects the recurring, then growing, anxiety about Pa's failure to return.

1 One day Pa said that spring was coming.

In the Big Woods the snow was beginning to thaw. Bits of it
2 dropped from the branches of the trees and made little holes in the softening snowbanks below. At noon all the big icicles along the eaves of the little house quivered and sparkled in the sunshine, and drops of water hung trembling at their tips.

Pa said he must go to town to trade the furs of the wild animals he had been trapping all winter. So one evening he made a big bundle of them. There were so many furs that when they were packed tightly and tied together they made a bundle almost as big as Pa.

Very early one morning Pa strapped the bundle of furs on his shoulders, and started to walk to town. There were so many furs to
3 carry that he could not take his gun.

Ma was worried, but Pa said that by starting before sun-up and walking very fast all day he could get home again before dark.

4 The nearest town was far away. Laura and Mary had never seen a town. They had never seen a store. They had never seen even two houses standing together. But they knew that in a town there were many houses, and a store full of candy and calico and other wonderful things—powder, and shot, and salt, and store sugar.

They knew that Pa would trade his furs to the storekeeper for beautiful things from town, and all day they were expecting the presents he would bring them. When the sun sank low above the treetops and no more drops fell from the tips of the icicles they began to watch eagerly for Pa.

5 The sun sank out of sight, the woods grew dark, and he did not come. Ma started supper and set the table, but he did not come. It was time to do the chores, and still he had not come.

Ma said that Laura might come with her while she milked the cow. Laura could carry the lantern.

So Laura put on her coat and Ma buttoned it up. And Laura put her hands into her red mittens that hung by a red yarn string around her neck, while Ma lighted the candle in the lantern.

Laura was proud to be helping Ma with the milking, and she

Word Bank

thaw *v.*: melt
eaves (EEVZ) *n.*: the overhanging lower edges of a roof
quivered (KWIV erd) *v.*: shook slightly
calico (KAL ih ko) *n.*: a plain cotton fabric printed on one side
chores (TSHORZ) *n.*: the everyday work around a house or farm; a small job that must be done regularly

42 Unit 1

Guiding the Reading

Literal

Q: What did Pa say was coming?
A: He said that spring was coming.

Q: What were two signs that spring was coming?
A: The snow was beginning to thaw and the icicles were melting.

Q: What was Pa busy doing all winter?
A: He was trapping animals and collecting their fur.

Q: How big was Pa's bundle of furs?
A: It was almost as big as Pa himself.

Q: Why was Pa going to town?
A: He was going to trade all of the furs.

Q: What time of day did Pa leave?
A: He left very early in the morning.

Q: Why did he leave so early?
A: So that he could get home before dark.

Q: What did Pa have to leave at home?
A: Pa left his gun at home.

Q: What had Laura and Mary never seen?
A: They had never seen a store or a town.

Q: What would Pa do with the furs once he reached the store?
A: He would trade them in for things that the family needed as well as presents for everyone.

Q: How did Laura feel about helping Ma?
A: She felt proud and grown-up.

Analytical

Q: Where do you think the family lived if the children had never seen two houses standing together?
A: Answers may vary, however they should all indicate a very open and rural area.

Q: Why does the author repeat, "he did not come" three times?
A: This is for effect. It shows how Papa's not coming was constantly on their minds. Each time it is said it indicates greater worry and even dread about what may have happened.

Q: Why do you think Pa hasn't returned home yet?
A: Answers will vary.

Q: Do you think Laura usually helped her mother this late at night?
A: It seems that Ma gave her special permission to come out with her this time. Laura felt proud in a way that she would not have felt had carrying the lantern at night been an ordinary chore.

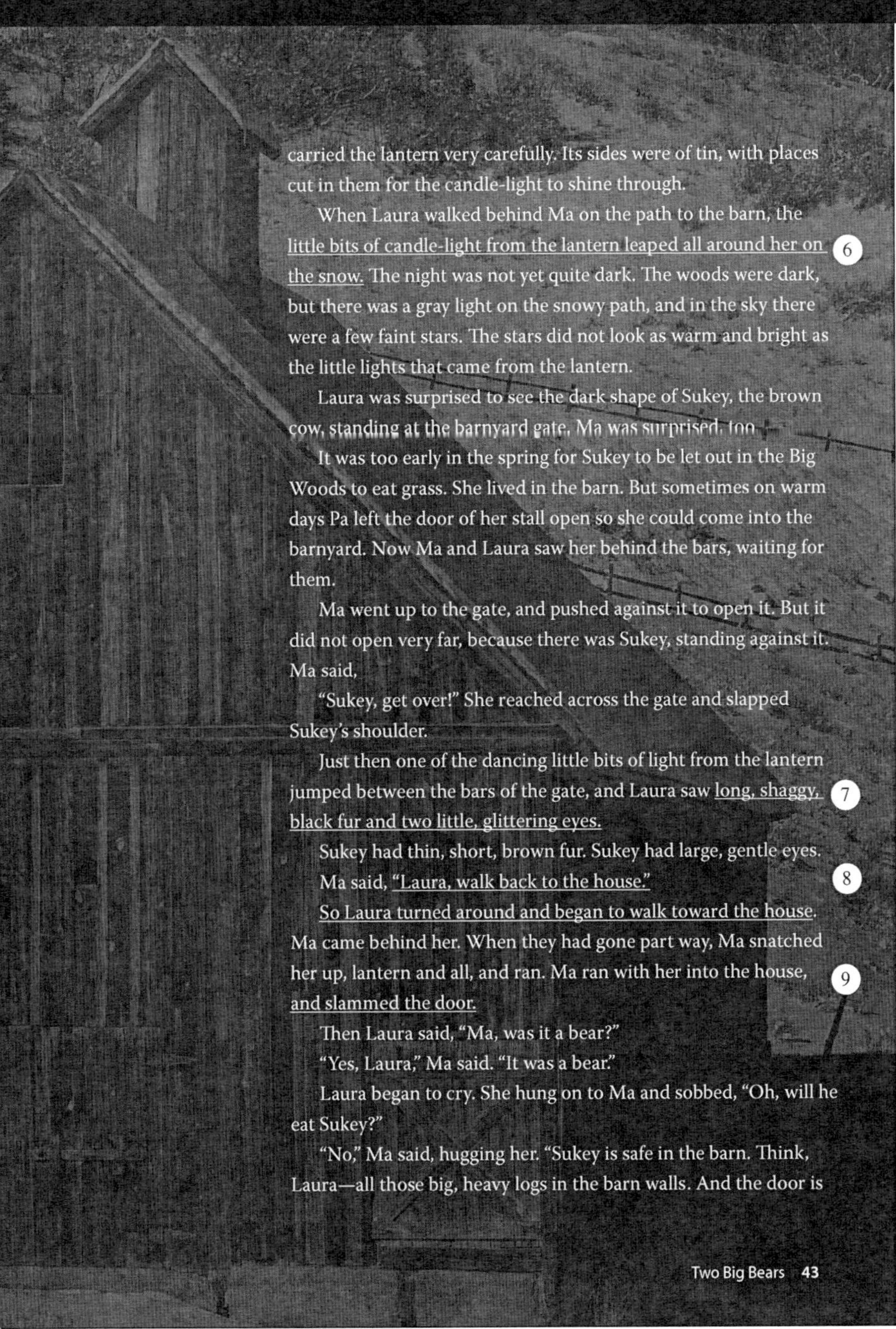

carried the lantern very carefully. Its sides were of tin, with places cut in them for the candle-light to shine through.

When Laura walked behind Ma on the path to the barn, the little bits of candle-light from the lantern leaped all around her on 6
the snow. The night was not yet quite dark. The woods were dark, but there was a gray light on the snowy path, and in the sky there were a few faint stars. The stars did not look as warm and bright as the little lights that came from the lantern.

Laura was surprised to see the dark shape of Sukey, the brown cow, standing at the barnyard gate. Ma was surprised, too.

It was too early in the spring for Sukey to be let out in the Big Woods to eat grass. She lived in the barn. But sometimes on warm days Pa left the door of her stall open so she could come into the barnyard. Now Ma and Laura saw her behind the bars, waiting for them.

Ma went up to the gate, and pushed against it to open it. But it did not open very far, because there was Sukey, standing against it. Ma said,

"Sukey, get over!" She reached across the gate and slapped Sukey's shoulder.

Just then one of the dancing little bits of light from the lantern jumped between the bars of the gate, and Laura saw long, shaggy, 7
black fur and two little, glittering eyes.

Sukey had thin, short, brown fur. Sukey had large, gentle eyes.

Ma said, "Laura, walk back to the house." 8

So Laura turned around and began to walk toward the house. Ma came behind her. When they had gone part way, Ma snatched her up, lantern and all, and ran. Ma ran with her into the house, 9
and slammed the door.

Then Laura said, "Ma, was it a bear?"

"Yes, Laura," Ma said. "It was a bear."

Laura began to cry. She hung on to Ma and sobbed, "Oh, will he eat Sukey?"

"No," Ma said, hugging her. "Sukey is safe in the barn. Think, Laura—all those big, heavy logs in the barn walls. And the door is

Two Big Bears 43

Literary Components

6 Visual Image: Again, a beautiful image with a touch of alliteration: "little bits of candle-*light* from the *lantern leaped all* around ..."

7 Rising Suspense: In the half-dark of the mild evening, danger lurks.

8 Characterization: The characters of mother and daughter are revealed here. The mother is calm and controlled; the daughter is unquestioningly obedient. Surely the mother's own self-discipline plays a role in the daughter's great respect for her.

9 Release of Tension: One can imagine Ma breathing a sigh of relief as she locks and bolts the door against the bear.

Guiding the Reading

Literal

Q: What added to the light aside from the lantern?
A: There were a few faint stars.

Q: Who was Sukey?
A: Sukey was the family's brown cow.

Q: What surprised Ma and Laura?
A: They were surprised that Sukey would be out eating grass this early in the spring.

Q: Why wasn't Ma able to open the gate?
A: It seemed that Sukey was standing against it.

Q: What did Ma do in order to get 'Sukey' to move?
A: She slapped 'Sukey's' shoulder.

Q: What differences were there between Sukey and the animal they saw?
A: Sukey was brown, had short fur and large gentle eyes, and the other animal was black, and had shaggy fur and small glittering eyes.

Q: What did Ma tell Laura to do?
A: "Laura, walk back to the house."

Q: Did Laura question her mother or protest?
A: No, she did not.

Analytical

Q: Whom do you think the glittering eyes belonged to?
A: Answers will vary.

Q: At what point did Ma show a calm demeanor and when did she seem nervous?
A: When Ma told Laura to go back she sounded calm, but she seemed nervous when, immediately afterwards, she snatched Laura and the lantern, ran, and slammed the door.

Q: What type of animal had they encountered?
A: They had met a bear, not Sukey, the cow.

Q: When did you realize that the glittering eyes did not belong to Sukey?
A: Answers will vary.

Q: Why was Laura crying?
A: Laura was afraid that the bear might eat Sukey. In addition, when she realized how narrowly they had escaped, she must have felt overwhelmed. Also, Ma's quick thinking, warm touch, and caring could have brought her to tears.

Literary Components

10 Release of Tension; Humor: It is very common for a person to laugh once the fear or shock has subsided. Part of the laughter is simply relief; the other part is the result of the person's picturing himself or herself in a (now) ridiculous situation.

11 Translating an Emotion into Something Concrete: Laura is actually lonely and worried, but she says the house is cold and still. Were her father safely home, the house would feel just right.

12 Personification; Projection of Emotion: The wind *cries* and *sounds frightened*. Laura not only attributes human emotions to the wind (personification), she attributes *her own* emotions to the wind. This is called projection.

13 Characterization: Ma is calm and confident. When she says Pa will be there in the morning, the reader and Laura know that he will be. Ma is not putting on an act to quiet the girls; she has an innate optimism that characterized the pioneers (for a pioneer, by definition, believes in a better tomorrow).

14 Detail: The detailed account of the fabrics makes the story seem very real; the modern reader feels almost as though a "video" were playing.

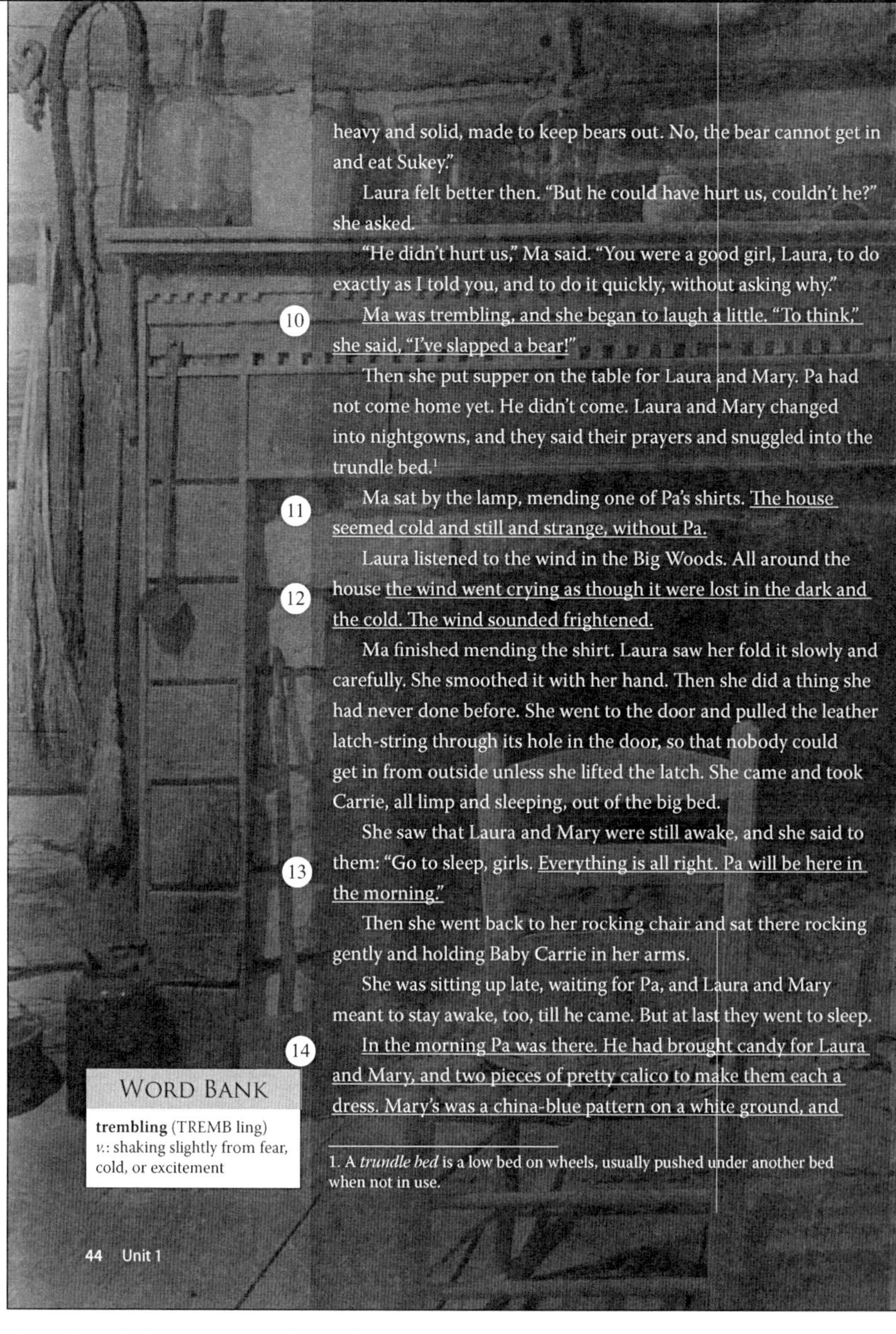

heavy and solid, made to keep bears out. No, the bear cannot get in and eat Sukey."

Laura felt better then. "But he could have hurt us, couldn't he?" she asked.

"He didn't hurt us," Ma said. "You were a good girl, Laura, to do exactly as I told you, and to do it quickly, without asking why."

10 Ma was trembling, and she began to laugh a little. "To think," she said, "I've slapped a bear!"

Then she put supper on the table for Laura and Mary. Pa had not come home yet. He didn't come. Laura and Mary changed into nightgowns, and they said their prayers and snuggled into the trundle bed.[1]

11 Ma sat by the lamp, mending one of Pa's shirts. The house seemed cold and still and strange, without Pa.

Laura listened to the wind in the Big Woods. All around the
12 house the wind went crying as though it were lost in the dark and the cold. The wind sounded frightened.

Ma finished mending the shirt. Laura saw her fold it slowly and carefully. She smoothed it with her hand. Then she did a thing she had never done before. She went to the door and pulled the leather latch-string through its hole in the door, so that nobody could get in from outside unless she lifted the latch. She came and took Carrie, all limp and sleeping, out of the big bed.

She saw that Laura and Mary were still awake, and she said to
13 them: "Go to sleep, girls. Everything is all right. Pa will be here in the morning."

Then she went back to her rocking chair and sat there rocking gently and holding Baby Carrie in her arms.

She was sitting up late, waiting for Pa, and Laura and Mary meant to stay awake, too, till he came. But at last they went to sleep.

14 In the morning Pa was there. He had brought candy for Laura and Mary, and two pieces of pretty calico to make them each a dress. Mary's was a china-blue pattern on a white ground, and

WORD BANK

trembling (TREMB ling) *v.*: shaking slightly from fear, cold, or excitement

1. A *trundle bed* is a low bed on wheels, usually pushed under another bed when not in use.

44 Unit 1

Guiding the Reading

Literal

Q: How did Ma reassure Laura that the bear could not get to Sukey?

A: She reminded Laura that the barn was made of big, heavy logs and the door was heavy and solid.

Q: Why was Ma so proud of her 'good girl' Laura?

A: She did exactly as she was told without asking 'why.'

Q: What humor were they able to find in the situation?

A: Ma couldn't believe that she had slapped a bear!

Q: When Pa still hadn't returned home, what did Laura and Mary do in the meantime?

A: The girls ate supper, changed their clothing, and got ready for bed.

Q: What did Ma do while waiting for Pa?

A: She mended a shirt.

Q: What did Ma do that night that she had never done before?

A: She pulled the leather latch-string through the hole of the door.

Q: What did Ma say to the girls to help them fall asleep?

A: "Go to sleep, girls. Everything is all right. Pa will be here in the morning."

Q: Was Pa actually there when the girls woke up?

A: Yes, he was home.

Analytical

Q: Why did Ma pull the leather latch-string through the door?

A: Ma did it for protection. She may have had a feeling that Pa would wait for morning to come. Even if he was just delayed, she wasn't accustomed to being at home without Pa in the house. She wanted to be sure that the family was safe from bears or other predators.

Q: Why were Laura and Mary having trouble falling asleep?

A: They were worried about Pa and couldn't get him off their minds.

Q: Did Ma really think everything was all right when she said so to the girls?

A: Ma seemed concerned, but probably was not as worried as the girls were. She waited up late for Pa, but knew that he might not come until morning. Whatever fears she did have, she kept to herself so as not to alarm Laura and Mary.

Two Big Bears 45

Literary Components

15 Stark Contrast: The safe, warm feeling the girls have as they delight over the new calico and the candy Pa has brought them, is punctuated by the icy chill of fear they feel when they view the claw marks on the walls.

16 Rising Tension: Pa's mention of being without a gun sets up the tension. Why, we wonder, will he need a gun?

17 Rising Tension: Hearing that the bears are thin and hungry creates even more worry in the listeners.

18 Simile: Pitch is tar; the simile is a common one.

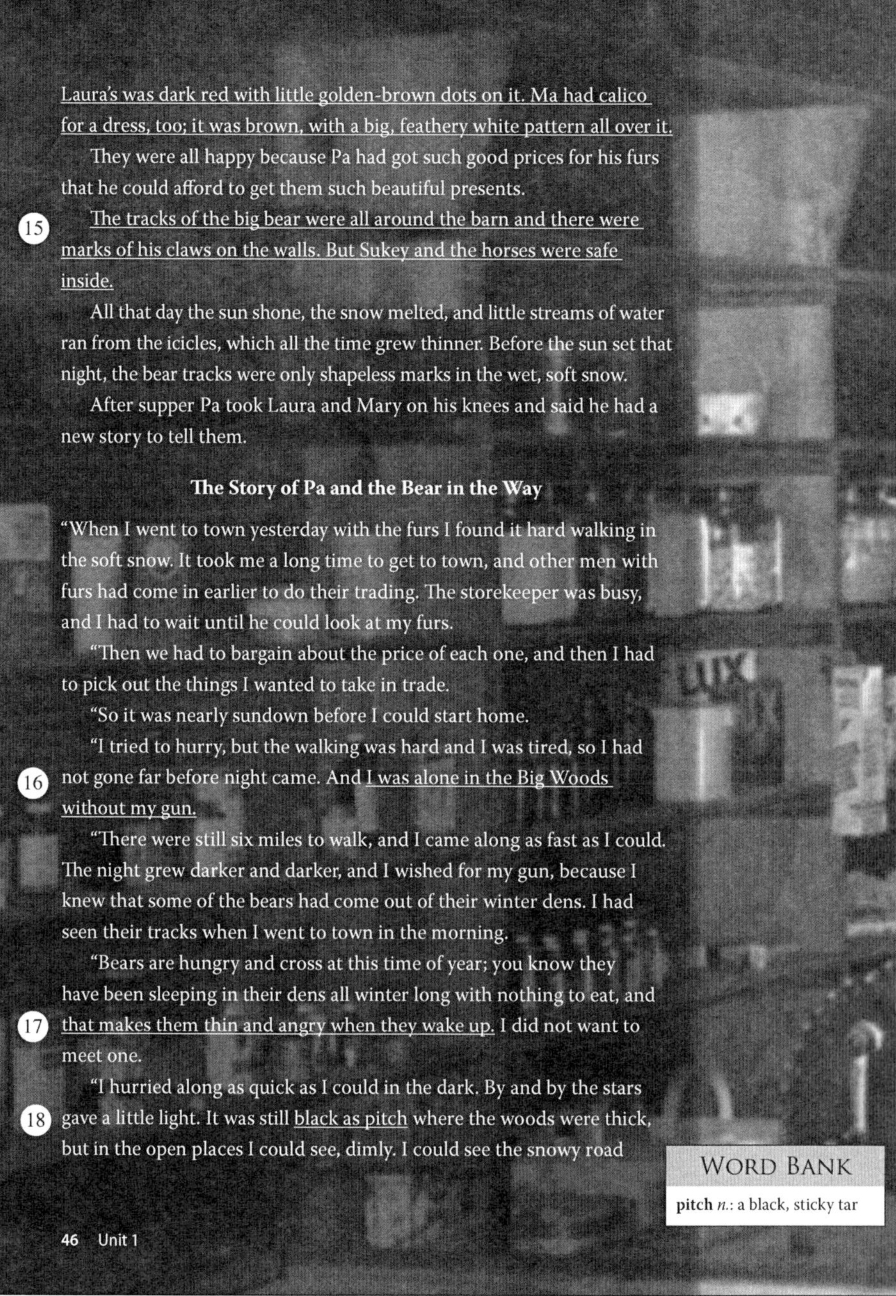

Laura's was dark red with little golden-brown dots on it. Ma had calico for a dress, too; it was brown, with a big, feathery white pattern all over it.

They were all happy because Pa had got such good prices for his furs that he could afford to get them such beautiful presents.

15 The tracks of the big bear were all around the barn and there were marks of his claws on the walls. But Sukey and the horses were safe inside.

All that day the sun shone, the snow melted, and little streams of water ran from the icicles, which all the time grew thinner. Before the sun set that night, the bear tracks were only shapeless marks in the wet, soft snow.

After supper Pa took Laura and Mary on his knees and said he had a new story to tell them.

The Story of Pa and the Bear in the Way

"When I went to town yesterday with the furs I found it hard walking in the soft snow. It took me a long time to get to town, and other men with furs had come in earlier to do their trading. The storekeeper was busy, and I had to wait until he could look at my furs.

"Then we had to bargain about the price of each one, and then I had to pick out the things I wanted to take in trade.

"So it was nearly sundown before I could start home.

"I tried to hurry, but the walking was hard and I was tired, so I had
16 not gone far before night came. And I was alone in the Big Woods without my gun.

"There were still six miles to walk, and I came along as fast as I could. The night grew darker and darker, and I wished for my gun, because I knew that some of the bears had come out of their winter dens. I had seen their tracks when I went to town in the morning.

"Bears are hungry and cross at this time of year; you know they have been sleeping in their dens all winter long with nothing to eat, and
17 that makes them thin and angry when they wake up. I did not want to meet one.

"I hurried along as quick as I could in the dark. By and by the stars
18 gave a little light. It was still black as pitch where the woods were thick, but in the open places I could see, dimly. I could see the snowy road

Word Bank

pitch *n.*: a black, sticky tar

46 Unit 1

Guiding the Reading

Literal

Q: What did Pa bring back for everyone?
A: Pa brought calico material to make new dresses.

Q: Why was he able to buy so much beautiful material?
A: He was able to trade the furs for very good prices.

Q: What were the signs that the bear didn't leave after Ma and Laura went inside?
A: There were tracks all around the barn and claw marks on the wall.

Q: Did the tracks and marks affect Sukey and the horses?
A: No, they were safe.

Q: What caused the bear tracks to fade away?
A: The streams of water from melted icicles affected the tracks.

Q: What did Pa do after supper?
A: He put the girls on his knees and prepared to tell a story.

Q: Why did Pa have a hard time getting to town?
A: It was hard to walk in the soft snow.

Q: Why did it take so long for Pa's trades?
A: It took a long time to get there and the shopkeeper was busy. After he bargained about the price of each fur, he had to pick out the items he wanted for trades.

Q: When did Pa begin his trek home?
A: He began when it was almost sundown.

Q: Why did Pa wish he'd brought his gun?
A: He was alone in the dark and had seen bear tracks.

Q: Why was Pa especially wary of meeting a bear at this time?
A: After sleeping in their dens all winter long with nothing to eat, the bears were hungry and grouchy. He did not want to run into a sensitive bear looking for food.

Two Big Bears 47

Literary Components

19 Suspense: At this point, the story is becoming suspenseful to the listener.

20 Characterization: Pa is not only brave, he is also logical. Conversely, he is not only logical, he is also brave. The two qualities combine to make him the solid, admirable person he is.

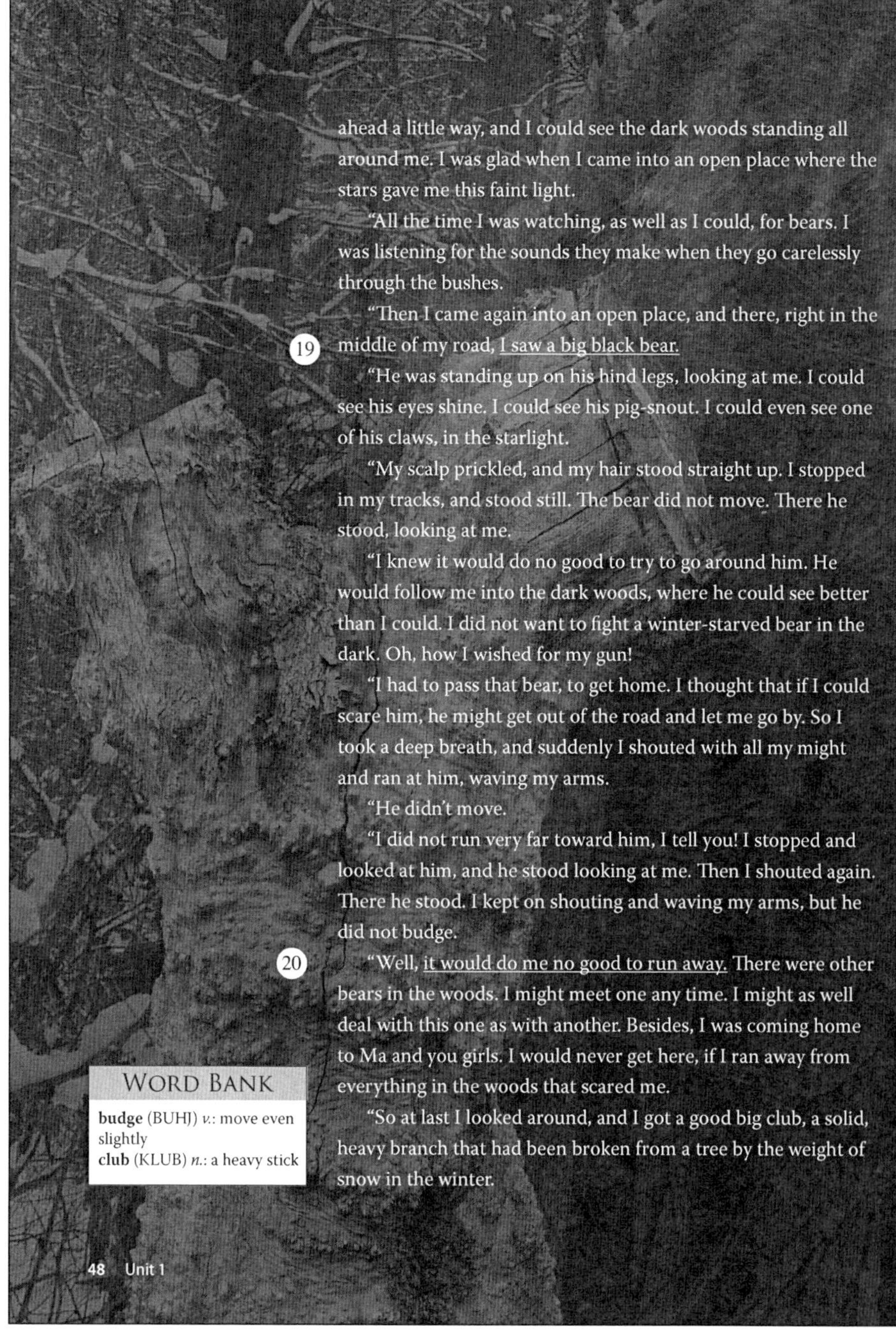

ahead a little way, and I could see the dark woods standing all around me. I was glad when I came into an open place where the stars gave me this faint light.

"All the time I was watching, as well as I could, for bears. I was listening for the sounds they make when they go carelessly through the bushes.

"Then I came again into an open place, and there, right in the
19 middle of my road, I saw a big black bear.

"He was standing up on his hind legs, looking at me. I could see his eyes shine. I could see his pig-snout. I could even see one of his claws, in the starlight.

"My scalp prickled, and my hair stood straight up. I stopped in my tracks, and stood still. The bear did not move. There he stood, looking at me.

"I knew it would do no good to try to go around him. He would follow me into the dark woods, where he could see better than I could. I did not want to fight a winter-starved bear in the dark. Oh, how I wished for my gun!

"I had to pass that bear, to get home. I thought that if I could scare him, he might get out of the road and let me go by. So I took a deep breath, and suddenly I shouted with all my might and ran at him, waving my arms.

"He didn't move.

"I did not run very far toward him, I tell you! I stopped and looked at him, and he stood looking at me. Then I shouted again. There he stood. I kept on shouting and waving my arms, but he did not budge.

20 "Well, it would do me no good to run away. There were other bears in the woods. I might meet one any time. I might as well deal with this one as with another. Besides, I was coming home to Ma and you girls. I would never get here, if I ran away from everything in the woods that scared me.

"So at last I looked around, and I got a good big club, a solid, heavy branch that had been broken from a tree by the weight of snow in the winter.

WORD BANK

budge (BUHJ) *v.*: move even slightly
club (KLUB) *n.*: a heavy stick

48 Unit 1

Guiding the Reading

Literal

Q: Because he did not have his gun with him, what did Pa do to try to avoid bears?
A: He watched and listened carefully.

Q: Where did Pa face a 'bear'?
A: Pa saw the 'bear' when he came to an open place in middle of the road.

Q: What did Pa do to try and scare the 'bear'?
A: Pa shouted, waved his arms, and ran.

Q: How did the 'bear' respond?
A: The 'bear' didn't budge.

Q: Why didn't Pa think it was a good idea to run away?
A: If Pa ran away from one bear, he might very well meet another one along the way.

Q: What did Pa use to beat the 'bear'?
A: He used a solid, heavy branch that was broken from the weight of the snow.

Analytical

Q: Why didn't Pa bring his gun? Do you think he will bring it the next time he goes to town?
A: Pa didn't anticipate that he would be walking at night. Perhaps he didn't like carrying a gun unless it was absolutely necessary. Pa was loaded down with furs and carrying a gun would have added to the load. In all probability, Pa will never again leave on a trip like this without a gun. This is called learning from experience.

Q: How do you know that Pa was frightened even though he didn't say so?
A: "My scalp prickled, and my hair stood straight up. I stopped in my tracks and stood still."

Q: What was Pa's dilemma?
A: He didn't want to fight a bear but he had to try to get home.

Q: What could be a reason that Pa did not want to run away from the bear, aside from the possibility of his meeting another bear?
A: Pa certainly knew that running usually causes wild animals to chase and attack the runner. In addition, he didn't really have anywhere to hide.

Q: How did thinking of his family help Pa decide what to do with the bear?
A: When he thought of Ma and the girls, he knew he had to figure out a way to get back home, instead of running away.

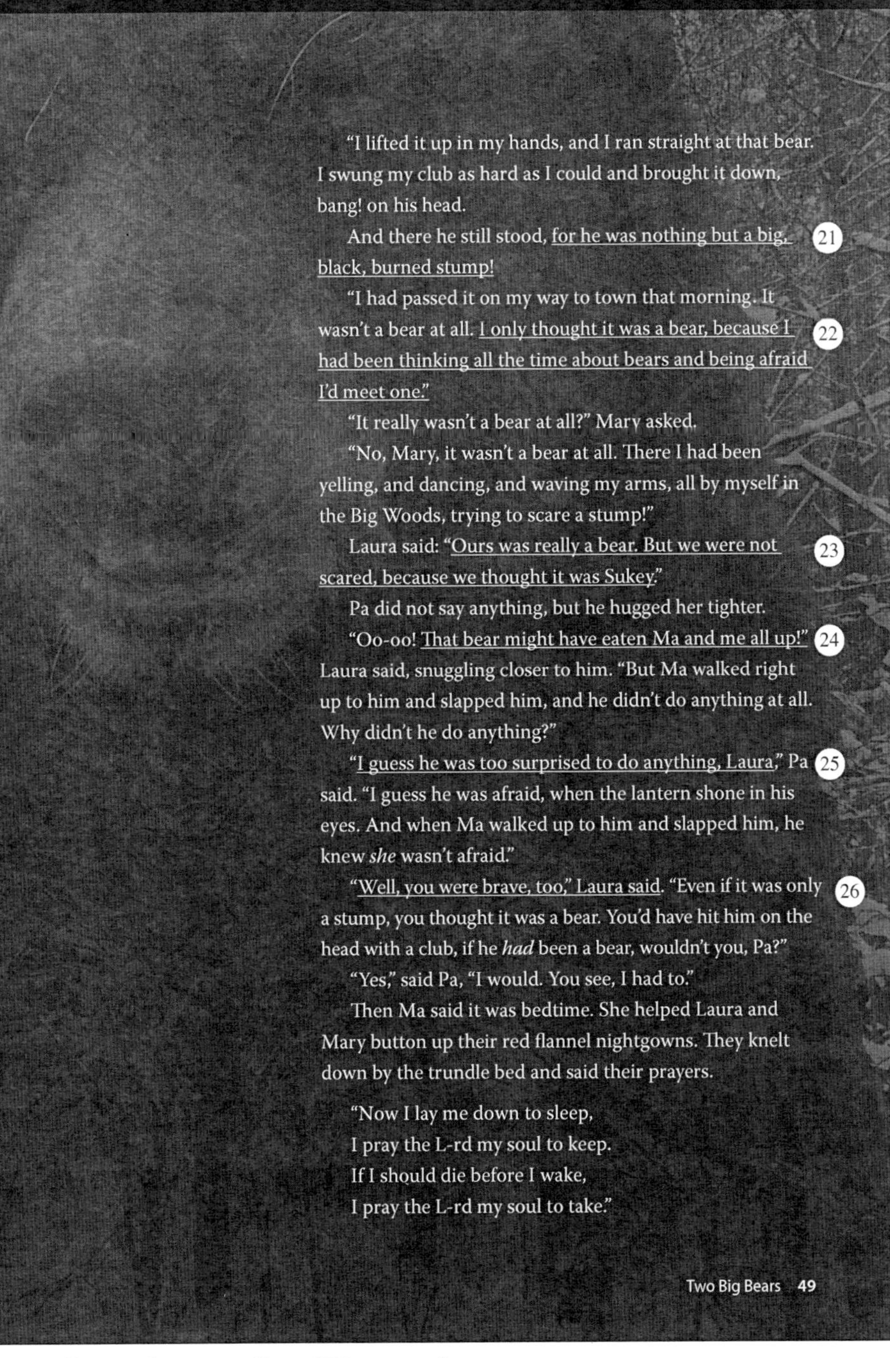

"I lifted it up in my hands, and I ran straight at that bear. I swung my club as hard as I could and brought it down, bang! on his head.

And there he still stood, for he was nothing but a big, black, burned stump! 21

"I had passed it on my way to town that morning. It wasn't a bear at all. I only thought it was a bear, because I had been thinking all the time about bears and being afraid I'd meet one." 22

"It really wasn't a bear at all?" Mary asked.

"No, Mary, it wasn't a bear at all. There I had been yelling, and dancing, and waving my arms, all by myself in the Big Woods, trying to scare a stump!"

Laura said: "Ours was really a bear. But we were not scared, because we thought it was Sukey." 23

Pa did not say anything, but he hugged her tighter.

"Oo-oo! That bear might have eaten Ma and me all up!" 24 Laura said, snuggling closer to him. "But Ma walked right up to him and slapped him, and he didn't do anything at all. Why didn't he do anything?"

"I guess he was too surprised to do anything, Laura," Pa 25 said. "I guess he was afraid, when the lantern shone in his eyes. And when Ma walked up to him and slapped him, he knew *she* wasn't afraid."

"Well, you were brave, too," Laura said. "Even if it was only 26 a stump, you thought it was a bear. You'd have hit him on the head with a club, if he *had* been a bear, wouldn't you, Pa?"

"Yes," said Pa, "I would. You see, I had to."

Then Ma said it was bedtime. She helped Laura and Mary button up their red flannel nightgowns. They knelt down by the trundle bed and said their prayers.

"Now I lay me down to sleep,
I pray the L-rd my soul to keep.
If I should die before I wake,
I pray the L-rd my soul to take."

Two Big Bears 49

Literary Components

21 Release of Tension; Alliteration: One can almost hear the girls' sigh of relief. The use of alliteration reveals a small flair for the dramatic.

22 Projection: Laura is not the only one in the family who "projects." Pa has projected his fear onto a tree stump, making it a scary, wild thing.

23 Point/Counterpoint: Pa mistook a tree stump for a bear and was terrified when he should have been calm; Ma mistook a bear for a cow and was calm when she should have been terrified.

24 Pleasurable Horror: Thinking in hindsight about what could have happened, but didn't, is one of life's little pleasures.

25 Characterization: Pa is able to explain mystifying things in a calm, reasonable way. He and Ma have created a small, secure world for their girls in spite of the dangers that lurk all around them.

26 Characterization: Laura is loving and she is also wise. She is able to understand that whether or not the bear was real, Pa thought it was real and acted with great courage. And she lets him know that she appreciates that fact.

Guiding the Reading

Literal

Q: What caused Pa to believe that the stump was a bear?
A: He had been thinking about meeting bears the entire day.

Q: Did the girls suspect that it wasn't really a bear?
A: No, they did not. Mary asked, "It really wasn't a bear at all?"

Q: What reason did Pa give for the bear not reacting to Ma's slap?
A: The bear was too surprised to do anything.

Q: Why did Laura think that Pa was so brave?
A: Regardless of whether it was a bear or not, Pa had been prepared to face a real bear with a club and fight it off.

Analytical

Q: At what point did you suspect that it wasn't a bear?
A: Answers will vary.

Q: Was there anything humorous about Pa's story?
A: Some students will suggest that it was funny that Pa became so frightened and "attacked" a tree stump. Others will counter that it wasn't funny because it could have been a real bear and Pa was genuinely scared.

Q: What do you think Laura was feeling when she said, "Ours was really a bear"?
A: It could have been a simple statement contrasting the conclusion of Pa's story. Laura may have thought in the beginning that both she and Pa had similar experiences with a bear. After hearing the whole story, she felt proud and brave, stating that they had encountered a real bear and were not scared.

Literary Components

27 Auditory Images; Setting: This time, the author creates a setting with auditory, rather than visual, images.

28 Full Circle: The story that started with the words *One day Pa said that spring was coming* comes to a satisfying conclusion with the words *In just a little while the trees would be putting out their baby leaves...for it would be spring.*

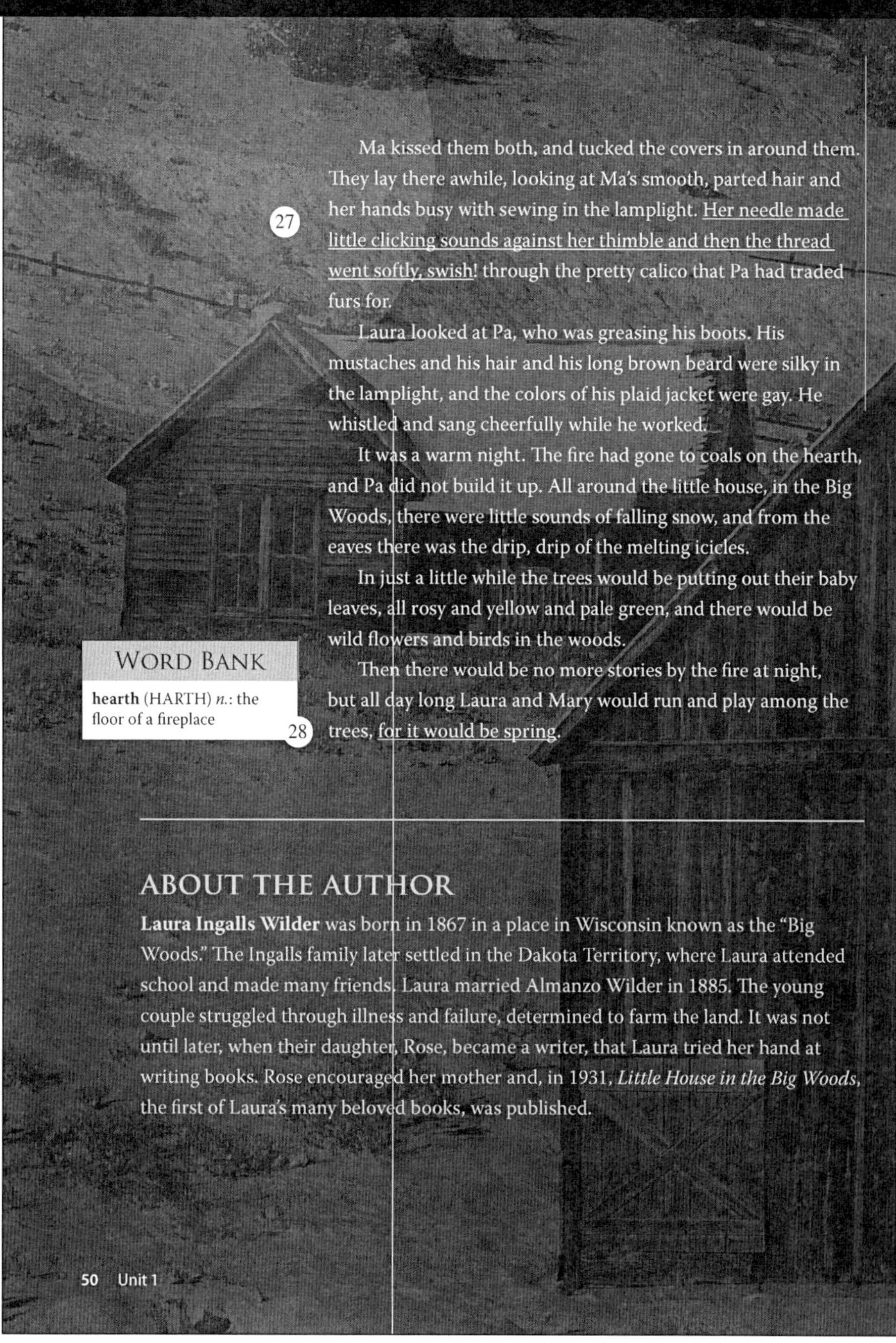

Ma kissed them both, and tucked the covers in around them. They lay there awhile, looking at Ma's smooth, parted hair and her hands busy with sewing in the lamplight. Her needle made little clicking sounds against her thimble and then the thread went softly, swish! through the pretty calico that Pa had traded furs for. 27

Laura looked at Pa, who was greasing his boots. His mustaches and his hair and his long brown beard were silky in the lamplight, and the colors of his plaid jacket were gay. He whistled and sang cheerfully while he worked.

It was a warm night. The fire had gone to coals on the hearth, and Pa did not build it up. All around the little house, in the Big Woods, there were little sounds of falling snow, and from the eaves there was the drip, drip of the melting icicles.

In just a little while the trees would be putting out their baby leaves, all rosy and yellow and pale green, and there would be wild flowers and birds in the woods.

Then there would be no more stories by the fire at night, but all day long Laura and Mary would run and play among the trees, for it would be spring. 28

WORD BANK

hearth (HARTH) *n.*: the floor of a fireplace

ABOUT THE AUTHOR

Laura Ingalls Wilder was born in 1867 in a place in Wisconsin known as the "Big Woods." The Ingalls family later settled in the Dakota Territory, where Laura attended school and made many friends. Laura married Almanzo Wilder in 1885. The young couple struggled through illness and failure, determined to farm the land. It was not until later, when their daughter, Rose, became a writer, that Laura tried her hand at writing books. Rose encouraged her mother and, in 1931, *Little House in the Big Woods*, the first of Laura's many beloved books, was published.

50 Unit 1

Guiding the Reading

Literal

Q: What did Ma do for the girls that made them feel warm, loved, and at ease?

A: Ma kissed them and tucked them into bed. She also stayed with them for a while.

Q: What were Ma and Pa doing as the girls went to sleep?

A: Ma was stitching the calico that Pa had brought home and Pa was whistling while greasing his boots.

Q: Why didn't Pa build up the fire?

A: The weather was warm enough with the coming of spring. This is indicated once again by the melting snow and icicles.

Q: Why wouldn't Laura and Mary hear as many stories during the spring?

A: They would spend much of their time outdoors.

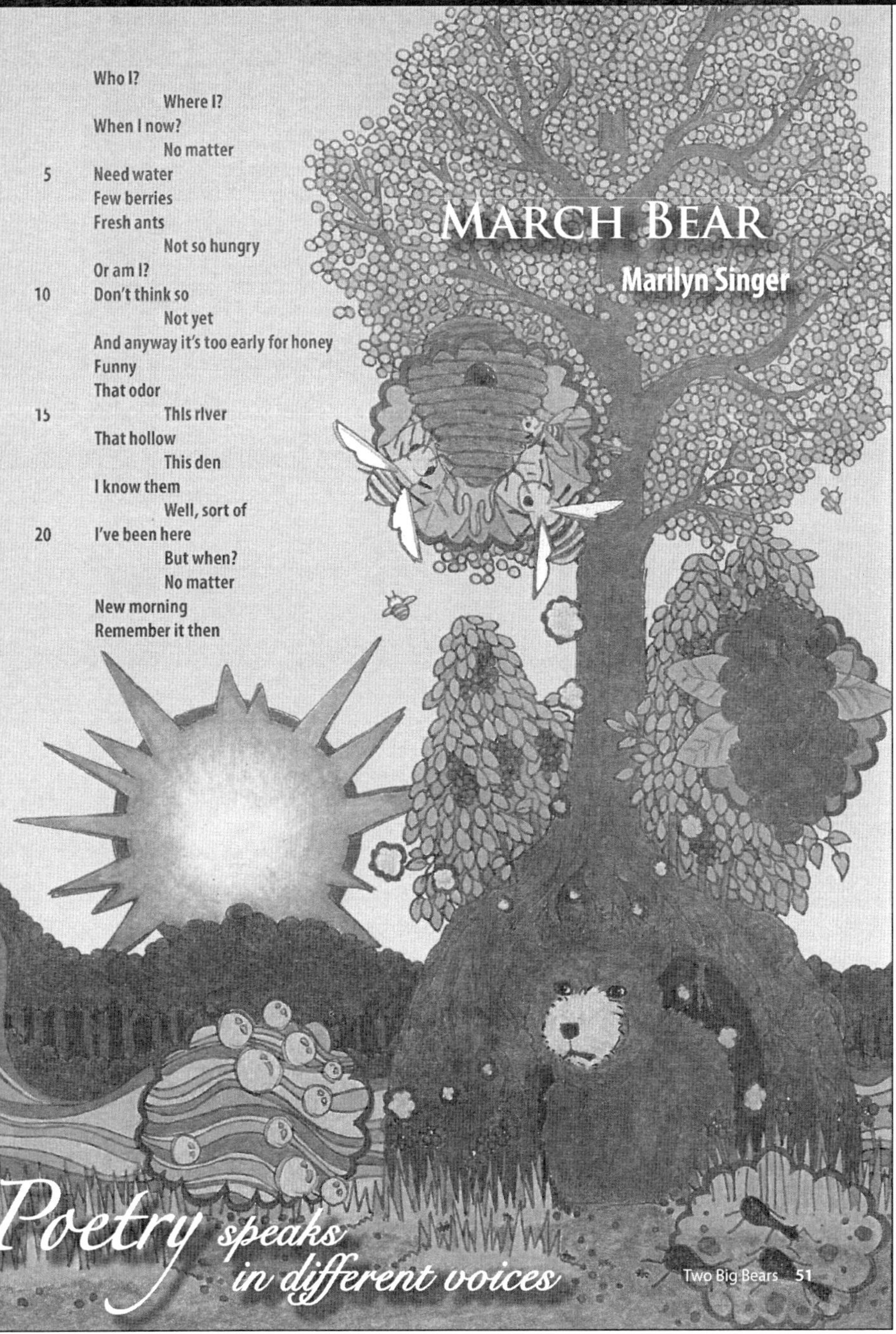

MARCH BEAR

Marilyn Singer

Who I?
Where I?
When I now?
No matter
Need water
Few berries
Fresh ants
Not so hungry
Or am I?
Don't think so
Not yet
And anyway it's too early for honey
Funny
That odor
This river
That hollow
This den
I know them
Well, sort of
I've been here
But when?
No matter
New morning
Remember it then

Poetry speaks in different voices

Two Big Bears 51

About March Bear

Poetry Speaks in Different Voices

Poetry speaks in different voices and this poem's voice belongs to a bear. Like most bears, this one talks in short grunts. It is up to the reader to connect the dots and mentally follow the bear's abbreviated statements. This bear is not nearly as frightening as the one Ma encountered in *Two Big Bears*. It is more like the one Pa "encountered"—essentially harmless!

How does the poem work? First of all, the title tells us that a March Bear is the subject, so we do not have to grope for a meaning when we read the opening lines.

"Who I" tells us that this bear is gruff and unsophisticated—your basic bear.

"When I now?" tells us he has probably just woken up and feels the same way we do when our alarm clock wakes us up from a deep sleep.

"Need water/Few berries/Fresh ants/Not so hungry" spells out the situation in monosyllabic bear grunts. It uses short, sharp words to mirror instinct rather than thought.

"That odor/This river/That hollow/This den" gives the poem a setting and also lets us identify with the bear as he gradually awakens and begins to recognize his surroundings.

The poem concludes with "New morning/Remember it then," the bear's acceptance of his sense of disorientation and his confidence that, by the morrow, he will feel at home in his surroundings.

First Impressions

Laura seemed very aware of her parents' love and concern for her. Some references to Ma and Pa's love are explicit while others can be inferred from the narrative. Ma made sure Laura went straight to the house safely, hugged her after the bear incident, and told her that she was a good girl. She also took care of the house when Pa was not home and reassured Laura and Mary when they worried. Pa bought presents for everyone, took the girls on his knee to tell a story, and hugged Laura tight. Ma kissed her and tucked her into bed.

Quick Review

1. Pa went to town to trade the furs of the animals he had been trapping all winter.
2. On warm days, Pa would sometimes leave the door to Sukey's stall open so she could come into the barnyard. However, it was too early in the spring for Sukey to be let out in the Big Woods to eat grass.
3. The girls were worried about Pa and the fact that he hadn't arrived home before dark. Ma told them, "Go to sleep, girls. Everything is all right. Pa will be here in the morning."
4. Pa left his gun because of the huge bundle of furs he was carrying but later wished for it when he encountered a 'bear.'

Focus

5. Accept all reasonable answers. One key point that must be mentioned is that on the night that Pa was away from home, everyone seemed sad and gloomy and the atmosphere was a little cold. On the evening of the day he returned, everyone seemed upbeat and there was a warm and charged atmosphere. In both situations, though, all family members were caring and supportive of one another.
6. **Ma:** brave, responsible, caring, confident
   Laura: proud, obedient, appreciative

Creating and Writing

7. The most basic answer should include the idea that Laura's life was saved because she did not question her mother's instructions. Ideally, the answer should include two other concepts. One is the fundamental concept of respecting those who are older than you. During the time period in which this story is set, children were very cautious about how they responded to their parents and other adults. The second point is that, because they have life experience, adults tend to see things differently than children. They can see the greater picture, can better predict the outcome of actions taken, and have usually experienced something similar to what the children are now facing.
8. Answers will vary.
9. The children can divide the text as they wish and should create original illustrations. Provide different mediums and materials to enhance the book. This project is a good opportunity to have your students work in pairs.

Studying the Selection

QUICK REVIEW

1. Why was Pa going to town?
2. Why were Ma and Laura surprised to find Sukey out of the barn?
3. Why couldn't the girls fall asleep and what did Ma say to reassure them?
4. What did Pa have to leave at home that he wished for later?

FOCUS

5. Compare the atmosphere in the house on the night Pa was away to the night after he returned.
6. List at least three of Ma's characteristics and three of Laura's.

CREATING AND WRITING

7. Write about why it was important for Laura to follow her mother's instructions without question.
8. When a writer describes something that is not human as though it were a person, the writer is using *personification* (pur SAH nih fih KAY shun). The author uses personification when describing the wind: "All around the house the wind went crying as though it were lost in the dark and the cold. The wind sounded frightened." Imagine that the books and supplies in your desk could think, talk, and move around. Write a paragraph in which you give human traits to something in your desk.
9. Laura will surely want to share stories with her children just as Pa shared stories with her. Make a storybook with illustrations describing Laura and Ma's encounter with the bear.

52 Unit 1

FIRST IMPRESSIONS

Do you think Laura knew how much her parents loved and cared for her? How do you know this?

Jill's Journal:

On Assignment in China

In China and Tibet and Vietnam, there is a bear called the Asiatic Black Bear. This bear has a beautiful yellow crescent on its chest, and so it is called the Moon Bear. For a long time, moon bears have been hunted and trapped. People want to get something called *bile* from their bodies. The bile is used for medicine. But these days, the same medicine can be manufactured from herbs—the bears aren't needed for it.

I had heard about moon bears and about Mrs. Jill Robinson who is helping them. I decided to go see her. So here I am, in Chengdu. In the last twenty-four hours, I have flown on a plane for 17 hours to Hong Kong. Then I took another plane from Hong Kong. It took two more hours to get to Chengdu, which is the capital of Sichuan Province in China. (A province is a bit like a state in the United States.)

Chengdu is a very modern big city with fancy hotels, large businesses, and many cars. There are even some signs in English along the highway. I was very tired when I arrived, but I was also very excited to almost be at my destination. It took another hour to get to the Rescue Center by car.

Mrs. Robinson was waiting. She told me the following story. In 1993, she visited a place where they kept moon bears. It is called a bear farm, and the bears are kept in small cages.

Moon Bear

Jill's Journal 53

Background Bytes

As early as 1933, the National PTA Congress of the United States talked about the power of teaching children to care about animals.

Children trained to extend justice, kindness, and mercy to animals become more just, kind, and considerate in their relations with each other. Character training along these lines will result in men and women of broader sympathies, more humane, more law abiding, in every respect more valuable citizens.

Humane Education is teaching in the schools the principles of justice, goodwill, and humanity toward all life. The cultivation of the spirit of kindness to animals is but the starting point toward that larger humanity of one's fellows.

This *Jill's Journal: On Assignment in China* focuses on the rescue of the moon bears. But this *Background Bytes* opens with a broader discussion of seven bear species in the world over. (Note that this will be a good opportunity for a quick geography lesson, since bears are located in many places with which your students may be unfamiliar. So try to have a world map handy when you share whatever is appropriate for your class from the material that follows.)

Polar Bears

Polar bears are at the top of the food chain—they have no enemies but mankind. Scientists study top predators, because if those at the top are in trouble, it usually means that something has gone awry in the ecosystem as a whole.

Because polar bears live in climates that have been inhospitable to humans, they are the only bears that still live within their original range. However, the area covered by arctic sea is melting now at an unprecedented rate. Polar bears are losing the sea ice they need to get to their food, and to move from hunting grounds to the places where they rest and have families. The ice is crucial to their survival. Without it, they will drown or starve.

Panda Bears

Which animal is more easily identified than the panda bear? Is any large animal more beguiling? But this same creature, the giant panda, is the most endangered bear on the planet. Only 700 pandas are left in the wild. This is a very low number for genetically stable breeding stock. Another 200 live in captivity. But pandas don't like to have babies in zoos and breeding programs have a very low rate of success.

Pandas eat bamboo almost exclusively, and bamboo forests in China are being clear-cut for farms and houses. Clear-cut means that all of the trees in a forest are cut down.

Most of the pandas that live in the wild today remain within a small chain of fourteen reserves set aside by the Chinese government. Like other bears, pandas need corridors between sections so they can safely roam across large territories. (A corridor is a narrow strip of land that provides access to a place.) If there is any chance of saving the panda, a great deal of money will be needed to establish reserves, educate and relocate people who live within the reserves, stop poachers (those who kill when it is illegal to kill), and plant lots of bamboo.

Spectacled Bears

These bears, who look like they are wearing eyeglasses, make their habitat in the South American Andean rain forest, where there is lots of water and vegetation to provide a supplement to their basic diet of roots, leaves, shoots, berries, occasional insects, rodents, and dead animals. Spectacled bears love fruit and spend days eating and sleeping in fruit trees. They are arboreal, which means they live in trees for the most part. When they encounter humans or other spectacled bears, they are submissive and cautious.

There are an estimated 2,000 remaining in the wild. The spectacled bear population is under threat for a number of reasons: (1) they are hunted by local folk who believe they will eat livestock (in spite of their being primarily vegetarian); (2) they are hunted for their gall bladders, which are highly valued in the Asian medicine market; (3) they are losing their habitat to extensive logging and to farming.

Sloth Bears

Most sloth bears live in India and Sri Lanka, others live in southern Nepal, and they have been reported in Bhutan and Bangladesh. Sloth bears are oddly disheveled in appearance, and look like they need a good brushing and combing.

They lead a reclusive life in India's forests, and make noisy grunting sounds as they search for insects and fruit. They are the most nocturnal of all the bears, although mothers with cubs often move about in daylight. They can jump from distances of 10 feet! Like sloths, they can hang upside-down.

Sloth bears are considered vulnerable animals. They lose their habitats to farmers who cut down the trees in which the sloth bears live and from which they derive their food. Then, lacking food, the sloth bears eat the crops the farmer grows. Consequently, the farmer shoots and kills them. Habitat loss also means that sloth bears suddenly find themselves in the vicinity of humans, whom they find threatening. The sloth bears react to feeling threatened by being aggressive. So then they are killed because, under these circumstances, they are dangerous. This is a terrible, destructive cycle that animal preserves and reserves would go a long way toward preventing.

Asiatic Black Bears

Young Asiatic black bears, or Tibetan moon bears, were captured for centuries, and trained to be dancing bears.

Today, this species of bear is listed under the Convention on International Trade in Endangered Species (CITES) in Appendix I, the most critical category of endangerment. In modern times, their numbers have declined dramatically because they are relentlessly hunted and farmed for their bile.

Bears are the only mammals to produce significant amounts of the bile acid, ursodeoxycholic acid (UDCA). UDCA has been used in traditional Asian medicine for 3,000 years. In fact, studies have shown bile acid to be effective in the treatment of some ailments. However, Chinese doctors now agree that it can easily be replaced by herbal and synthetic alternatives that are cheaper, more effective, and more readily available.

Since 1993, the Animals Asia Foundation has endeavored to end bear farming. The Foundation works with the Chinese government and local communities in Asia to reduce the suffering of captive

"I still remember thinking that these bears need to be free. They need to eat berries and nuts. They need to climb in trees to play." Then, she said, she felt a gentle paw touch her shoulder. "I turned around and one little girl bear stared up at me. I knew it could be dangerous, but I reached out and held this little bear's paw. I made a promise to myself and to the little bear that I would help create a safe place for these bears to roam free."

Seven years later, Mrs. Robinson and Animals Asia signed an agreement with the Chinese government. The government said they could rescue 500 farmed bears in Sichuan Province and start a special rescue place for the bears. The first bear, Andrew, came in October 2000. Now there are 235 bears here.

Wait a minute! I'm going to see the bears! Wow! They're so cute. A staff member is telling me who they are. There's Andrew. He is standing on tiptoe, squeezing his eyes shut and eating raisins. The next one is Bottom. She is eating cake that has been stuffed into holes in a big tree branch. Now my guide is pointing out Freedom. The guide tells me that it took a very long time for Freedom to trust humans, but now she is happy—and free. The others who are coming out are Crystal and Banjo. Now Crystal is lying in the grass, gazing into the distance. The guide is talking to me but I can't hear her words. I need a tissue. I feel so happy to be here and meet the bears.

POWER SKILL:
Speaking Slowly, Clearly, Loudly, and with Expression

Have you ever watched a play? You probably have. It can be difficult to watch a play if you can't understand what the actors are saying.

How do you feel about speaking in front of a group? You could be presenting a report, reciting a poem, or performing in a play. Doing these things well is very pleasing. You have shown that you can be grown up, and that you are not feeling embarrassed. You have given clear information to your friends and your teacher. You have entertained your audience.

The same skills are what you need to participate in helping projects. If you want to read to the blind, you have to read clearly and with expression. The same is true for talking with an elderly person whose hearing may be impaired. If you rush through your words, your words won't be understood. This will be hard on you and on the person with whom you are speaking.

Taking your words, and how you speak them, seriously, will make you feel more confident and more sure of yourself. Then you will be able to handle yourself well, when you meet a new person or when you greet guests in your home.

54 Unit 1

bears. They have successfully negotiated with the Chinese government for the release of 500 bears. The "farmers" who relinquish their bears are paid to do so, so that they can retire or find other work.

Brown Bears

Vital Ground is a bear conservation organization located in Montana. They have written the following:

> *The grizzly is a symbol of the American wilderness. It remains one of the most dramatic, imposing life forms anywhere on Earth. Not all that long ago, the great bears shared dominion over the western half of the continent with Native Americans. But as U.S. settlement expanded, grizzly numbers plummeted, first due to unchecked hunting, trapping, and poisoning, then as a result of habitat loss. By 1975, with just one percent of its original population left on barely two percent of its original range, the species was officially listed as threatened with extinction in the lower 48 states.*

Have you ever been in a situation in which you are with people you know but who do not know each other? You have the power to make people feel comfortable, relaxed, and happier, if you can perform the simple task of introducing them to each other.

Exercises

1. Below are five Chinese characters and their meanings. The characters are not simply letters, but stand for words. Your task is to create a picture of a moon bear who has been freed. You are going to draw her. Then you will add the Chinese characters instead of the actual sun, moon, mountains, rain, and trees. Put them where they belong in the picture. Then you can add a river, fallen logs, a bamboo forest, and so forth.
   Chinese Characters:

Sun

Moon

Mountain

Rain

Tree

2. Your teacher will hand out the script of a play and assign parts. Have fun!

Jill's Journal 55

Black Bears

Black bear numbers in much of North America are good. They are listed as a threatened subspecies in Louisiana, eastern Texas, and southern Mississippi under the federal Endangered Species Act. In four additional states, black bears are state-listed as rare, threatened, or endangered (Louisiana, Florida, and within the historic range of black bears in southern Mississippi and eastern Texas). The Florida black bear subspecies is listed as threatened by the state of Florida.

In most of the remaining states, black bears are classified as a game animal. In Canada the bears are classified as a pest species in the agricultural areas of Manitoba, while they are classified as a game animal and/or furbearer in the rest of Canada. In Mexico, the black bear is listed as Endangered by Mexican wildlife authorities.

Black bears are increasingly vulnerable, however, to habitat loss, fragmentation of range, logging, human encroachment, roadkills, and being hunted for sport. According to Defenders of Wildlife, "Highways, homes and other developments built through bear habitat fragment their habitat, sometimes keeping them from large areas they depend on for food, water, and shelter. Habitat fragmentation also makes it difficult for bears to find mates and limits their chances to move into more suitable habitat." Regarding their nature, there is a popular misconception that black bears are vicious. Consequently, as developers build on land located within traditional bear habitat, a growing number of bears are killed when they come into contact with homeowners.

Power Skill:

Speaking Slowly, Clearly, Loudly, and with Expression

For all of the reasons cited in the textbook, becoming comfortable with presentations before groups is a skill that will serve your fourth graders for the rest of their lives. To this end, a play titled *The Drama of the People and the Moon Bears* has been included for your class to perform. The reproducible script can be found in the Teacher Resources Section on p. 8.

If your class has any difficulty with the vocabulary of the play, make changes in the wording.

Parts may be combined or expanded to suit your class size.

Once students become really involved in the play, their embarrassment should be minimized. Make certain that students practice speaking loudly, slowly, and with expression. Encourage them to look at the audience when they are able.

Exercises

1. Please review the Chinese characters with your students by writing them on the board (or by having them write them on the board).
2. Allow sufficient class time for rehearsal.

What Is Setting?

The Pond

1. Details of the setting are: "log"; "a lily pad"; "the shore"; "a nearby tree"; "the grass."
2. "The sky became dark"; "a loud crack of lightning lit the sky"; "a rumble of thunder shook the earth."
3. The story tells us that it is a sunny day, so we know the setting in the pond is daytime.

Additional background information for *Mom's Best Friend* can be found on p. 2 in the Teacher Resources Section.

Lesson in Literature . . .

WHAT IS SETTING?

- Setting includes the **time** and **location** in which the story takes place.
- *Time* refers to the year, season, and time of day in which the story takes place.
- The *location* may be a very specific place, for example, "Macy's Department Store in Manhattan." Or, the location may be typical of a large group of places, for example, "a school building" or "a park."
- In a play, costumes, lighting, and sound effects all help create the setting.

One sunny day a large heron flew over a small pond. Looking down, he wondered, "Is that a good pond?" and swooped down to find out.

At the edge of the pond, he stood on his long, thin legs and looked around. It looked like a perfect pond. Fish swam in cool blue water. A turtle basked on a log. A frog croaked on a lily pad. A duck waddled along the shore. A robin sang in a nearby tree. A rabbit hopped in the grass.

"Is this a good pond?" Heron called out.

Fish swam by, nodding yes.

Turtle stirred. "This log is perfect for me."

Frog croaked, "It's good. It's good."

Rabbit twitched his whiskers. "It's home."

But Duck paddled up to Heron. "There is no place for you here. This pond is ours. No vultures allowed."

"No vultures allowed?" Heron repeated, surprised. He was not a vulture; he was a Great Blue Heron. He flapped his large wings, ready to fly off for another pond where he might be welcomed.

But just then drops of rain began to fall. "That's just rain," Duck said, circling around Heron. "You have to leave this pond. No vultures allowed."

The rain fell softly at first but soon big, fat raindrops fell everywhere. The sky became dark. A loud crack of lightning lit the sky and a rumble of thunder shook the earth.

"What's that?" Duck asked.

"It's a bad storm," Heron said. He spread his two large wings. They looked like two huge umbrellas. "Hide under here."

Duck eyed the outstretched wings. "I will never take help from a vulture," Duck said. He paddled to the other side of the pond as rain fell harder.

Heron called out to the others, "Hide under my big wings!"

Fish swam away.

Turtle shifted on his log. "I can take care of myself, Vulture," he said.

THE POND

THINK ABOUT IT!

1. In the first two paragraphs of the story, the author gives five details to help us picture the setting. The first is "cool blue water." What are two more?
2. One part of setting can be the weather in which the events happen. In the story, "big fat raindrops" fall everywhere. What are two other phrases that tell us about the weather in the pond?
3. What time of day is part of the setting for this story?

Just then the lily pad under Frog sank to the bottom of the pond. Frog swam over to Heron. "Are you a vulture?"

"No, I'm a heron, Frog," Heron said.

"Why didn't you say so?" Frog said and ducked under one of Heron's wings.

Robin flew from her tree and huddled with Frog. "I don't care if you're a vulture or a heron," she said to Heron. "Thank you for sharing your wings."

Rabbit hopped over. "Thanks for the help, Mr. Heron," he said. Before he joined the others under Heron's wing, Rabbit shouted across the pond at Duck. "This is your last chance, Duck!"

But Duck refused to join the others.

After the storm ended, Turtle basked on his log. Frog found a lily pad. Robin flew back to the tree. Rabbit sniffed the wet grass. Fish swam around, and Heron stood in shallow water watching the sun come out.

Duck was last seen waddling away, alone.

Mom's Best Friend 57

Unit Theme:	*The Things That Matter*
Target Skill:	*What is setting?*
Genre:	*Nonfiction/ Autobiography*

Getting Started

Read the story aloud until page 62 up until the words "Would she get along with the new dog? Would they work well together?" Then complete the following aural exercises.

(For more information on aural exercises refer to *Getting Started* for *Supergrandpa*.)

1. Mom needs a dog guide because she
   a. loves pets.
   b. cannot drive.
   c. is blind.
   d. uses dogs to sniff the trails of criminals.
2. What was the name of Mom's first dog guide?
   a. Methuselah
   b. Marit
   c. Joel
   d. Pete
3. What did Joel give his sister to make her feel better about losing the dog?
   a. a stuffed pony
   b. a rabbit
   c. part of his marble collection
   d. some money for candy
4. What did Mom use to guide her after the dog died?
   a. a guide rabbit
   b. a computerized guide
   c. a cane
   d. a braille map
5. What does "go sighted guide" mean to Mom?
   a. Mom would use her dog to guide her.
   b. Mom would use her cane to guide her.
   c. Mom would teach her dog how to guide her.
   d. Mom would hold onto the arm of a seeing person.
6. Which one of Mom's senses is extra special?
   a. hearing
   b. touch
   c. taste
   d. smell
7. The Seeing Eye, the dog guide school that Mom went to,
   a. was located far away in Texas.
   b. was the first dog guide school in the United States.
   c. trained about 100 dogs a month.
   d. changed its name to The Seeing Eye Dog Academy.
8. What type of dogs do they train at The Seeing Eye?
   a. Poodle and Labrador
   b. Great Dane and Cocker Spaniel
   c. German Shepherd and Golden Retriever
   d. Terrier and Bloodhound
9. Mom knew her way around The Seeing Eye building because
   a. she had been there twelve years before and remembered her way around.
   b. she spent three days in the building before the training began.
   c. she had a girl to guide her and describe everything as they walked along.
   d. her friend, who had gone through the training, had told her all about it in advance.
10. Mom became blind because of which of the following reasons?
   a. She was born blind.
   b. She was in a fireworks accident when she was nine.
   c. An illness she had as a young girl caused her to slowly lose her sight.
   d. The story does not say.

Into . . .
Mom's Best Friend

Despite the challenges that Mom has to contend with, she perseveres. Mom's general attitude about her disability is positive. She does not dwell on what she cannot do but rather on what she is able to do. Determination and hard work are part of Mom's regular day. She enjoys being independent and doesn't feel that her blindness should prevent her from performing everyday tasks. It is obvious that she ordinarily does the housekeeping from the fact that, when she is away, the other members of the family have to take over for her. From her conversations with other guests at The Seeing Eye, it is clear that these people are not complainers and are resolute about living as normally as possible. Mom keeps plugging away at Ursula's training even when the dog makes mistakes; she is even able to inject some humor into most situations.

While not everyone has to grapple with a challenge like blindness, every one of us faces our own "bumps in the road." Encourage your students to apply the story's lesson to their own lives. The proverbial "I think I can..." lends itself to this lesson. Explain to the class that we often don't recognize our own potential until we make up our minds to face a challenge head-on and stay the course.

Eyes On Setting

The setting of a story is often, but not always, found within the exposition. Generally, the exposition contains information at the beginning of the story that helps set the scene. The information provided in the exposition helps the reader to understand the background as well as the plot and characters. Details and vivid description help the reader to envision the setting.

Ask your students to come up with details of settings of stories they've read together or of classic fairy tales. Be sure to point out the different elements of setting including: location, date, era, season, weather conditions, mood, and atmosphere.

In *Mom's Best Friend*, there are two crucial settings. One is The Seeing Eye training center and the other is home. Home refers to Mom's hometown and family structure, not just her house. Once the training is completed, Mom and Ursula have to transfer all they've learned to a different setting. Ask your students to identify the details that help them picture the setting better, such as descriptions of the streets Mom has to navigate or the layout of the house.

Despite all the challenges that Leslie and her family face, the tone remains calm. There are traces of anger and sadness coming from Leslie, and Mom does get frustrated at times, but the mood remains light and positive for the most part. Everyone in the family is aware of the fact that blindness is something that they must deal with on a daily basis and that the training will help Mom. There is an upbeat, can-do atmosphere in the house.

Blueprint for Reading

INTO . . . *Mom's Best Friend*

Mom's best friend in this story may not be the kind of friend you were expecting to read about. You will see that Mom is devoted to her new friend no matter what comes her way. Mom displays a lot of *perseverance* (PUR suh VEER uns) throughout the story. To *persevere* is to work steadily at something even when problems come up. One who perseveres handles difficulties calmly. Patience is an important part of perseverance. As you read, you will see some of the challenges that Mom faces and the way she perseveres.

EYES ON *Setting*

Whether it is a snowy mountaintop, an African jungle, or a city street, every story has a **setting.** The setting describes the background of the story. It may include where the story takes place, when it takes place, or even what the weather is like. The mood is part of the setting. Does the author describe a tense and exciting scene, or a calm and lazy one? In *Two Big Bears*, the main setting is a farmhouse on the plains of the United States in the late 1800s. The mood is warm and friendly, but it does get frightening during the bear tales.

Notice what is included in the setting as you read *Mom's Best Friend.* Keep in mind that a story may have more than one setting.

58 Unit 1

The best thing about having a mom who's blind is getting a special dog like Marit, Mom's dog guide. At least that's what my brother, Joel, and I used to think. Then, four months ago, Marit died. And it became the worst thing.

Marit had been with us since before I was born. Her death left a big hole in our family. I kept thinking I heard her whimpering for a game of catch. Any time I left pizza on the counter, I would race back to the rescue. But there was no sneaky dog about to steal it.

For my birthday Joel gave me a rabbit that I named Methuselah.[1] Although it helped to have a soft bunny, I still wanted Marit.

1. *Methuselah* (muh THOO zuh luh)

Mom's Best Friend 59

Selection Summary

Leslie's mother is blind. Mom's beloved dog guide, Marit, has died four months earlier and Leslie and her brother Joel feel lost. Mom tries various techniques to replace Marit's guidance (though nothing could replace Marit's loving nature), but finally decides she must get a new dog guide. Mom leaves home to enroll in The Seeing Eye, a dog guide school where she will get a new dog and learn to work with her. The dog's name is Ursula, and Mom and Ursula slowly learn how to help one another. Leslie is sure she will never be able to love a new dog. She also misses her mother. While the family at home go on with their lives and their daily chores, Mom "vacations" at school, enjoying the company of other blind people and teaching Ursula. Mom writes letters home telling the inspiring stories of her "schoolmates" and of Ursula's progress.

Finally, Mom returns with Ursula. There is still much work to be done with her, but slowly, Ursula becomes part of the family and, though no one could ever replace Marit, she takes her own special place in their hearts and lives.

Literary Components

❶ **Exposition; Theme:** We are introduced to the story's central theme in the first sentence: a child's life that centers on a blind mother and a beloved dog guide.

❷ **Problem that Gives Rise to Internal Conflict:** The narrator's love for Marit is deep and lasting. The loss of Marit makes the narrator feel as though she could never love another dog again. When a new dog guide is brought home, the narrator will resist feeling affection for her, out of loyalty to Marit.

Guiding the Reading

Literal

Q: Who was Marit?
A: Marit was Mom's dog guide.

Q: Why does Mom need a dog guide?
A: Mom needs a dog guide because she is blind.

Q: What benefit did Joel and his sister have from their Mom being blind?
A: They could have a special dog like Marit.

Q: What happened four months ago?
A: Marit died.

Q: How long was Marit with the family?
A: Marit was with the family since before the narrator was born.

Q: How did the family feel about the loss of the dog?
A: "Her death left a big hole in our family."

Q: What were some memories Leslie (the author) had of Marit?
A: She remembered Marit whimpering for a game of catch and stealing pizza that was left on the counter.

Q: What did Joel give his sister to try to make her feel better?
A: He gave her a soft bunny rabbit.

Q: Did the rabbit make her feel better?
A: It was helpful and comforting to receive the gift, but she still wanted Marit.

Analytical

Q: What does the author mean when she says, "Her death left a big hole in the family"?
A: Leaving a hole indicates that something important is missing from their lives.

Literary Components

3 Simile: Mom creeps like a snail, slowly and cautiously.

4 Jargon: We are familiarized with some of the "jargon" of the blind. Having terms or phrases for various obstacles or difficulties makes them easier to handle. A person, confronted with a difficulty, simply "plugs in" the terminology for the problem, and its solution "comes up." This is why armies, hospitals, and all sorts of other problem-solving organizations have their own unique jargon.

5 Characterization: Independence is one of Mom's key character traits.

Mom missed her even more. She didn't lose just a sweet, furry pet. She lost her favorite way of traveling, too. She had to use her
3 cane again, and crept along the sidewalk like a snail. Once, when she crossed the street, she missed the opposite curb and kept walking toward the traffic. I had to holler to get her onto the sidewalk.

After that, I worried about her running errands by herself. I asked
4 her to "go sighted guide," holding Dad's, Joel's, or my arm. Sometimes she did. But mostly she used the cane. She didn't want to depend on
5 us—or on anybody.

A lot of blind people do fine with a cane. It's like a real long arm to help them feel what's around: walkways, hedges, mailboxes.

With a dog guide, blind people use their hearing more than touch. Mom has trained her ears. It's amazing: she can tell when something, like a movie marquee, is above her head, and when she passes a lamppost. She knows from the change in the sound of her footsteps.

Guiding the Reading

Literal

Q: Who missed Marit the most and why?
A: Mom, because she needed Marit to function without constantly asking other people for help.

Q: What did Mom use to help her get around?
A: She used a cane.

Q: Why was the author worried about her Mom running errands by herself?
A: She saw her Mom miss the curb and head toward the traffic by mistake.

Q: What is the meaning of "go sighted guide"?
A: It is a term used to describe a blind person holding onto a seeing person to guide them.

Q: Why did Mom prefer the cane to someone's arm?
A: She didn't want to depend on anyone.

Q: How does a cane help a blind person?
A: It acts as an extra-long arm to detect things like walkways, hedges, or mail-boxes.

Q: Since Mom is blind, which of her senses has she learned to use very well?
A: Mom has trained her ears to help and protect her.

In spite of Mom's special hearing, I worried. I was relieved when she decided to go back to The Seeing Eye for a new dog guide.

Before Mom left, I told her I wouldn't be able to love the new 6 dog as much as Marit. Mom hugged me and said, "The night before you were born, I wondered how I could love a second child as much as your brother. Then you came, and like magic, I 7 was just as crazy about you."

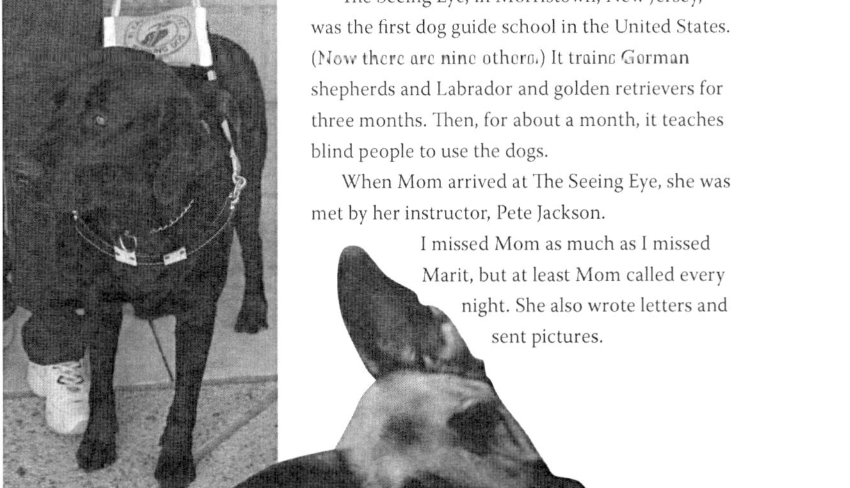

The Seeing Eye, in Morristown, New Jersey, was the first dog guide school in the United States. (Now there are nine others.) It trains German shepherds and Labrador and golden retrievers for three months. Then, for about a month, it teaches blind people to use the dogs.

When Mom arrived at The Seeing Eye, she was met by her instructor, Pete Jackson.

I missed Mom as much as I missed Marit, but at least Mom called every night. She also wrote letters and sent pictures.

6 **Theme; Conflict:** As mentioned above, the narrator's loyalty to Marit causes her to be conflicted about the new dog.

7 **Characterization; Foreshadowing:** Mom is sensible and kind. She is able to identify with the narrator's anxiety, but can also offer a different perspective on the problem. Although the narrator does not accept Mom's words now, she will see later how true they are.

Guiding the Reading

Literal

Q: How was The Seeing Eye school in Morristown, New Jersey different from other dog guide schools?

A: It was the first dog guide school in the United States.

Q: What types of dogs were trained at The Seeing Eye?

A: There were German Shepherds, Labradors, and Golden Retrievers.

Q: How long did it take to train each dog?

A: It took four months total—three for training the dog alone and one with the blind individual.

Q: What helped the author when she missed her Mom?

A: Her mother called every night. She wrote letters and sent pictures.

Analytical

Q: Why was the author both glad and concerned that her Mom was going back to The Seeing Eye?

A: She was glad because she did not believe that a good sense of hearing and the use of a cane were enough to guide her mother safely. She felt that now Mom would be getting the help she needed. She was concerned because she still missed Marit and was sure she wouldn't be able to love the new dog as much.

Q: Why did the author's Mom tell her how she felt just before the author was born?

A: Mom told her the story to comfort her and to compare her own feelings to Leslie's feelings about Marit. While she loved Marit, she could love another dog as well.

Literary Components

8 Characterization: Mom is independent and she is also bright. She compensates for her lack of sight by memorizing her surroundings. She is proactive, not passive; she is positive, not complaining; she chooses to take charge, not to be a victim.

9 Rising Suspense: Although this is not ordinary "suspense," for the person whose well-being depends upon it, the unknown character of the new dog is anxiety-provoking.

10 Important Idea: The author gradually teaches us about how dog guides are trained. The dog is made to correct itself when it does something wrong. It is praised when the correction is made. Does this method work for training people, too?

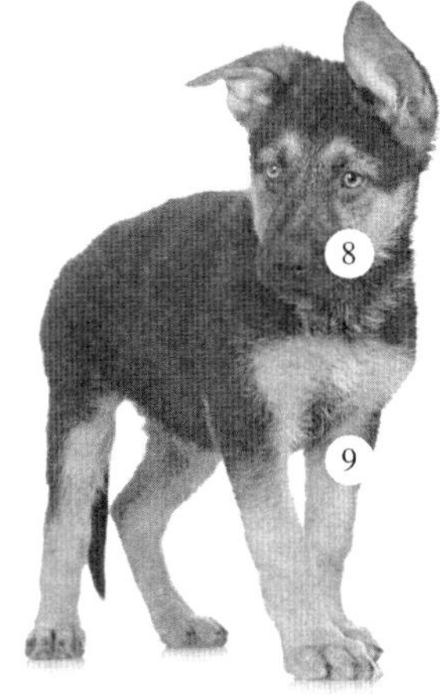

Mom's first day was a cinch. She'd gone to Seeing Eye twelve years before to get Marit, and still remembered her way around. Usually when she's in a new place she has to move from room to room with her cane, memorizing the layout. 8

In the morning Mom walked with Pete Jackson so that he could check her pace. He wanted to choose the dog that would suit her best. Then she was free to play the piano, exercise...and worry. Would she get along with the new dog? Would they work well together? 9

The next day she got Ursula. What a strange name! The staff at Seeing Eye's breeding station had named Ursula when she was born. (Ursula's brothers and sisters were also given names starting with *U.*) Dog guides need a name right away so that Seeing Eye can keep track of the four hundred or so pups born each year. At two months of age, the pups go to Seeing Eye puppy-raising families to learn how to live with people. At fifteen months, they are mature enough to return to Seeing Eye for the three-month training program.

Dad said that Ursula means "bear." But in the pictures Mom sent, Ursula looked too pipsqueaky to be called bear. Mom explained that Seeing Eye is now breeding some smaller dogs. They are easier to handle and fit better on buses and in cars.

My friends thought dog guides were little machines that zoomed blind people around. Until Mom went away, even I didn't understand all the things these dogs were taught.

But on Mom's first lesson in Morristown, Ursula seemed to forget her training. She veered on a street crossing and brushed Mom into a bush. Mom had to make her correct herself by backing up and walking around the bush. Then Mom praised her. 10

After ten practice runs with Pete, Mom and Ursula soloed.[2] Ursula didn't stop at a curb, so Mom had to scold her and snap

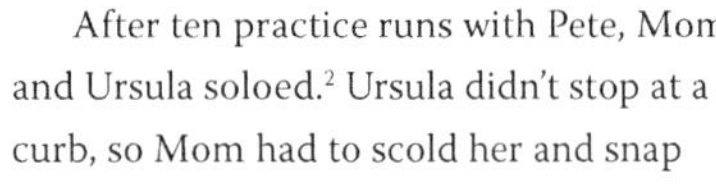

2. *Soloed* means they did it by themselves, without Pete's supervision.

62 Unit 1

Guiding the Reading

Literal

Q: How long ago had Mom gone to The Seeing Eye to get Marit?
A: She went twelve years ago.

Q: Even though it had been twelve years since she was last there, what was Mom able to do?
A: She was able to make her way around since she remembered the layout.

Q: What was the name of the new dog?
A: Her name was Ursula.

Q: Why do pups at The Seeing Eye need names right away?
A: They have to keep track of the four hundred or more pups born each year.

Q: Where do they send the dogs at two months old?
A: The pups go to Seeing Eye puppy-raising families.

Q: At what point are the pups ready for the Seeing Eye training?
A: They are ready at fifteen months.

Q: What does the author find humorous about the fact that "Ursula" means bear?
A: Ursula is a pipsqueak and doesn't look anything like a bear.

Q: Why is The Seeing Eye now breeding smaller dogs?
A: They are easier to handle and fit better on buses and in cars.

Q: How do you know that the author's friends do not know what is involved in training seeing-eye dogs?
A: Her friends think that they are little machines.

Q: What problem did Mom and Ursula have during their very first lesson?
A: Ursula veered into a street crossing and brushed Mom into a bush.

Q: After how many practice runs were Mom and Ursula able to go out on their own?
A: They were able to go out on their own after ten practice runs.

Analytical

Q: Pete Jackson wanted to choose the dog that would suit Mom best. What does that mean?
A: Pete needed to take into account Mom's pace, personality, and specific needs. Just like any other partnership, many things need to be considered before making the connection.

Q: Why do you think it is so important for these pups to go to live with families at a very young age?
A: Dog guides are not just friendly pets or companions; they are life guides to the blind. They must be familiar with the regular activities of a family—household life must become second nature to these special dogs. They must become completely comfortable with human contact.

Q: Why did Mom praise Ursula even though she had made a mistake?
A: Once Ursula corrected herself, Mom praised her. She didn't want to encourage negative behavior, but didn't want to upset Ursula right away, either. By correcting what she did and being praised, Ursula will, hopefully, do the right thing the next time.

her leash, calling, "Pfui." Later Ursula crashed Mom into a low-hanging branch. "Ursula will have to start thinking tall," Mom said that night, "or I'll have to carry hedge clippers in my purse."

Even though Ursula had walked in Morristown a lot with Pete, she was nervous when Mom's hand was on the harness. Mom talked and walked differently. And Mom was nervous, too. Ursula moved so much faster than old Marit had, and Mom didn't trust her. 11

Every day Mom and Ursula made two trips. Every week they mastered new routes. Each route got longer and more complicated, and Mom had less time to learn it. Every night Mom gave Ursula obedience training: "Come. Sit down. Rest. Fetch." I thought she 12
should try obedience training on Joel.

While Mom worked hard, Dad, Joel, and I went on with our normal lives—school, homework, soccer, piano, spending time with friends. We divided Mom's chores: Dad did the cooking, Joel, the vacuuming and laundry, and I did the dishes, dusting, weeding. The first two weeks were easy.

In a phone call Mom said that things were getting easier for her, too. "Remember how tough curb ramps have been for me?" she asked. "They feel like any other slope in the sidewalk, so I can't always tell that I've reached the street. Well, Ursula stopped perfectly at every ramp. And she guided me around, not under, a ladder and right past a huge parking lot without angling into it. But best of all, she actually saved my life. 13
A jackhammer was making so much noise that I couldn't hear whether the light was green or red. When I told Ursula, 'Forward!' she refused to move and kept me from stepping in front of a car. (Of course, Pete would have saved me if Ursula hadn't.)"

Mom barely asked about us. It was all Ursula, Ursula, Ursula! She seemed to be forgetting Marit, 14
too. When a letter came a few days later, I was sure she didn't miss anyone.

Mom's Best Friend 63

Literary Components

11 Conflict: Mom and Ursula are not a perfect match. They will have to work through their difficulties to achieve the interdependence required for a successful dog guide/person relationship.

12 Humor: The narrator finally injects a bit of humor into her narrative. Until now, her sadness at losing Marit and her mother's absence from home have kept the story serious and factual.

13 Turning Point: Ursula has proven herself. Though she may make mistakes in the future, she has shown she will be a good and loyal dog guide.

14 Conflict: The narrator worries that her mother loves Ursula more than her family and more than she loved Marit.

Guiding the Reading

Literal

Q: Did everything go smoothly on their first outing?

A: No, Ursula didn't stop at the curb and caused Mom to go into a low-hanging branch.

Q: Why didn't Mom trust Ursula?

A: She moved so much faster than old Marit.

Q: How did Mom and Ursula progress each week?

A: Each week they mastered new routes that got longer and more complicated.

Q: How did Dad, Joel, and the narrator divide the jobs that Mom usually did?

A: Dad did the cooking, Joel did the vacuuming and laundry, and Leslie (the author) did the dishes, dusting, and weeding.

Q: How did Ursula 'save Mom's life'?

A: While trying to cross the street, Mom couldn't hear all of the regular noises because a jackhammer was making so much noise nearby. When she instructed Ursula to go forward and cross the street, Ursula refused. She didn't actually save Mom's life in this instance, because Pete was there, but Ursula learned how to save Mom's life in such a situation.

Q: Why was the author so sure that Mom didn't miss anyone?

A: It seemed that all she spoke about was Ursula and it felt like she hardly asked about how they were doing at home.

Analytical

Q: Why did Mom say that she would have to carry hedge clippers in her purse?

A: Ursula did not notice branches that were above her height.

Q: Which of Mom's characteristics made Ursula nervous and why?

A: The way Mom walked, talked, and handled Ursula was different from the way Pete did. Every individual has slightly different habits and tendencies.

Q: What was obedience training?

A: To be obedient is to follow instructions or obey commands. Ursula was learning to respond to commands like "Come," "Rest," and "Sit down."

Q: What did the author mean when she said, "I thought we should try obedience training on Joel"?

A: She thought (jokingly) that perhaps they could teach her brother to listen and be more cooperative in the house.

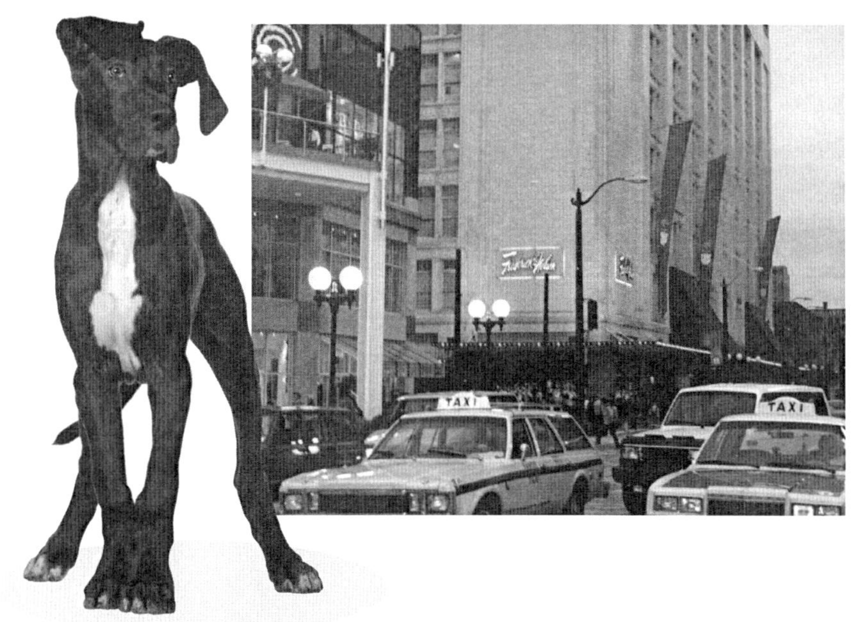

Dear Bob, Joel, and Leslie,

Today Ursula and I faced several disasters! She tried hard to ignore a boxer dog who wanted to play. A few minutes later, a Great Dane lunged out from nowhere, jumped all over her, and loped off. Ursula's instinct is to chase dogs, but she didn't move a paw after that one. As if the dogs weren't enough trouble, fire engine sirens went off. Ursula just strolled down the sidewalk.

Mostly, life is smooth here. Seeing Eye is a vacation—no cooking, no cleaning, lots of time to talk to new friends, like Dr. Holle, the veterinarian. And since I don't have many blind friends, it's a treat to be with my roommate and the twenty other students. We laugh about the same things, like the great enemy of the blind—trash collection day! Every twenty feet there's a garbage can reeking

Guiding the Reading

Literal

Q: What disasters did Mom describe in her letter?

A: Ursula was almost distracted by other dogs a couple times and ignored fire engine sirens.

Q: Why does Mom feel like The Seeing Eye is a vacation?

A: There is no cooking or cleaning and there is a lot of time to talk with friends. She is happy to be surrounded by other blind people, who face the same challenges she does.

Q: What does Mom call the "great enemy of the blind" and why?

A: Trash collection day is the enemy because the dog guides are tantalized by the many smells coming from the garbage cans, and sometimes can't resist stopping to poke their noses in the garbage.

of pizza, hoagies, old cheese. Usually Ursula snakes me around these smelly obstacles. But sometimes the temptation to her nose wins out, and I have to correct her, all the while holding my own nose.

Some trainees really inspire me, like Julie Hensley, who became blind from diabetes at twenty-two. Even though she's been blind for twelve years, she still teaches horses to do stunts. She judges her location from a radio playing music in the center of the pen, and gallops around as fast as she ever did when she could see.

Bob Pacheco used to race motorcycles and hunt. Then, two years ago, when he was twenty-nine, he developed optic atrophy and became blind two months later. He took up fishing, swimming, even trapping. But something was missing. He couldn't get around quickly enough. After the first trip with his dog guide, he was overjoyed. "Sally!" He was so excited. "I don't feel blind any more."

The dogs are wonderful, and the people here are very special. So are you.

Love, Mom

Guiding the Reading

Literal

Q: Who is Julie Hensley and why does she inspire Mom?

A: She is a woman who became blind at twenty-two and has been blind for twenty years. Julie does what she did before she lost her sight—she teaches horses to do stunts. She is tremendously creative in finding solutions to her problem and can actually gallop around as fast as she did when she could see.

Q: Why did Bob Pacheco say that he didn't feel blind anymore?

A: Even though he was still blind, the dog gave him the freedom to get around quickly without depending on other people and to enjoy all of his hobbies thoroughly.

Literary Components

15 Humor; Characterization: Mom, who is the one who has the real challenge, is the most upbeat member of the family. She uses humor to encourage her children and husband.

16 Characterization; Conflict: How interesting it is that each of us views the same event from a different angle. Before Mom meets Ursula, she is afraid Ursula will not be a good dog guide for her. Now that Ursula has been shown to be a good dog guide, the narrator is worried that she will not be able to love her as much as she loved Marit. Does that really matter? Well, it does to the narrator.

17 Resolution: The narrator falls instantly in love with Ursula and her worries evaporate—until she starts to worry about whether Ursula will love *her*.

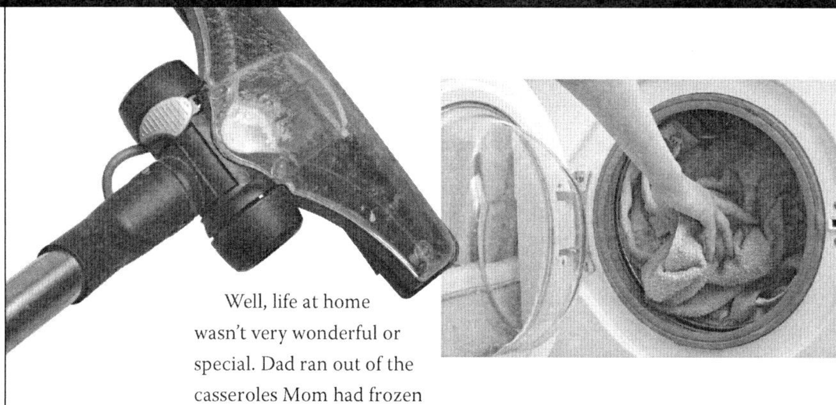

Well, life at home wasn't very wonderful or special. Dad ran out of the casseroles Mom had frozen ahead of time, and although his meals were okay, I missed Mom's cooking. Worse, the dishes kept piling up. I never knew Joel ate so much.

Then things got really bad. While Dad was teaching his American literature night class, Joel and I faced a disaster Mom and Ursula couldn't have dreamed of: the toilet bowl overflowed! We wiped the floor with towels. As Joel took the towels down to the washing machine, he found water dripping through the ceiling—all over the dining room table, all over the carpet. He ran for more towels, and I ran for the furniture polish and rug shampoo. When Dad got home, everything looked perfect. But I wrote a braille letter.

Dear Mom,
Come home soon. The house misses you.
Love,
Exhausted in Pittsburgh

Mom wrote back.

Dear Exhausted,
15 *Hang on. We'll be home to "hound" you Thursday. Be prepared. When you see me, I will have grown four more feet.*
Mom

16 I couldn't laugh. I was too tired and worried. What if I couldn't love Ursula? Marit was the best dog ever.

Soon they arrived. Ursula yanked at her leash and sprang up on me. She pawed my shoulders, stomach, and arms just the way Marit used to, nearly knocking me over. She leaped onto Joel, licking him all over. As she bounded
17 up onto me again, I realized Mom was right. Like magic, I was crazy about this shrimpy new dog.

66 Unit 1

Guiding the Reading

Literal

Q: Why didn't Leslie feel that life at home was wonderful and special?
A: Dad's cooking wasn't the same as Mom's. Leslie realized how many dishes the family used each week. To top it off, the toilet overflowed when Leslie and Joel were at home.

Q: What disaster did Joel and Leslie have to deal with on their own?
A: The toilet overflowed and water leaked through the ceiling. They cleaned up everything before Dad got home.

Q: Why didn't Leslie appreciate the humor in Mom's letter?
A: She was tired and worried and thinking about whether she would be able to love Ursula the way she'd loved Marit.

Q: What happened as soon as Mom and Ursula arrived?
A: She jumped all over Joel and Leslie and licked them.

Q: What was Leslie referring to when she used the word 'magic'?
A: She couldn't believe how quickly she liked the new dog.

Analytical

Q: Why do you think Leslie wrote such a brief letter to her mother?
A: Leslie was exhausted from her chores and her ordeal with the toilet. It was tedious to write in Braille and she simply wanted her mother to come back home.

Q: Mom tried to inject some humor into her letter. What did she mean by "hound" and "grown four more feet"?
A: A hound is a dog but it also means to bother and irritate. The four feet wouldn't actually belong to Mom but would be the feet of the dog accompanying her.

But by the end of the day, I had a new worry. Was *Ursula* going to love *me*? She seemed friendly enough, but keyed up, even lost in our house.

Mom explained that Ursula had already given her heart away three times: first to her mother, then to the Seeing Eye puppy-raising family, and finally to Pete. Mom said we had to be patient. 18

"Remember how Marit loved you, Leslie? When you were little, she let you stand on her back to see out the window. Ursula will be just as nuts about you. Love is the whole reason this dog guide business works." 19

So I tried to be patient and watched Mom work hard. First she showed one route in our neighborhood to Ursula and walked it over and over. Then she taught her a new route, repeated that, and reviewed the old one. Every day she took Ursula on two trips, walking two or three miles. She fed her, groomed her, gave her obedience training. Twice a week Mom cleaned Ursula's ears and brushed her teeth.

"I'm as busy as I was when you and Joel were little!" she said.

Mom and Ursula played for forty-five minutes each day. Joel, Dad, and I were only allowed to watch. Ursula needed to form her biggest attachment to Mom. 20

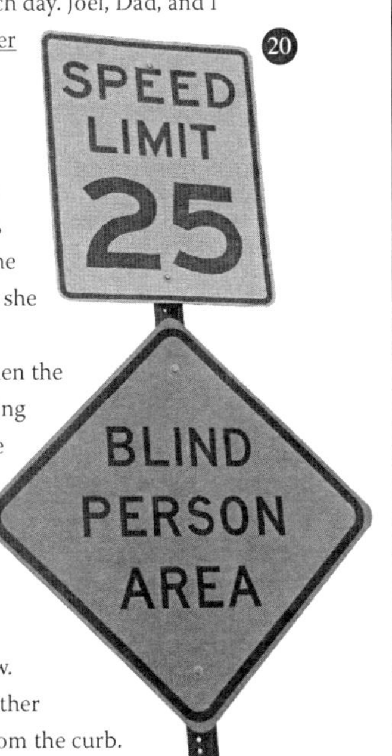

Mom made Ursula her shadow. When she showered or slept, Ursula was right there.

Still, Ursula didn't eat well—only half the amount she'd been eating at Seeing Eye. And she tested Mom, pulling her into branches, stepping off curbs. Once she tried to take a shortcut home. Another time, because she was nervous, she crossed a new street diagonally.

Crossing streets is tricky. Ursula doesn't know when the light is green. Mom knows. If she hears the cars moving beside her in the direction in which she's walking, the light is green. If they're moving right and left in front of her, it's red.

I worried about Ursula's mistakes, but Mom said they were normal. She kept in touch with her classmates and knew that their dog guides were goofing, too. One kept eating grass, grazing like a cow. Another chased squirrels, pigeons, and cats. Still another always stopped in the middle of the street, ten feet from the curb.

Literary Components

18 Characterization; Theme: Mom could not have gotten as far as she has without the quality of patience.

19 Theme: Love and patience work hand in hand to make this family a strong unit.

20 Theme: The strong bond forged between dog guide and person is one of the story's themes.

Guiding the Reading

Literal

Q: What was Leslie's new worry at the end of the day?
A: She wondered if Ursula would love her back.

Q: Who were the three people Ursula had given her heart to?
A: She had given her heart to her mother, to the people at The Seeing Eye, and then to Pete. All of this was before she even met Mom.

Q: Why did Mom tell Leslie to be patient?
A: It would take some time for Ursula to warm up to all of the new people and learn to love them. Then it would be like the good times with Marit.

Q: What is the whole reason that the dog guide business works?
A: It all depends on love.

Q: Describe Mom's work with Ursula.
A: Mom had to teach Ursula all the routes in her new neighborhood. She was constantly teaching and reviewing various routes. Mom continued with the obedience training that they had done at The Seeing Eye. Mom also groomed and fed Ursula, cleaned her ears, and brushed her teeth.

Q: What words show that Mom thinks that training Ursula is like handling toddlers?
A: "I'm as busy as I was when you and Joel were little."

Q: Why were other family members only allowed to watch at first?
A: Ursula had to form an attachment with Mom first. This was because Ursula needed to understand that, regardless of any relationships she might form with family members, she was here to serve Mom.

Q: What were some of the problems that Mom faced with Ursula?
A: Ursula didn't eat well and often tested Mom.

Q: Why was crossing streets tricky?
A: Ursula didn't know when the light would turn green.

Q: How does Mom know when the light is green or red without sight?
A: She judges whether the light is green or red based on the sounds she hears. She can tell which direction the cars are moving in, and uses this information to determine whether or not she can cross.

Q: Why wasn't Mom as worried as Leslie about Ursula's mistakes?
A: Mom said they were normal. (Point out to your students that Leslie mentioned that Mom had Marit even before Leslie was born. Therefore, Leslie is not familiar with the whole training process.)

Analytical

Q: What did Mom mean when she said that Ursula gave her heart away three times?
A: Ursula never actually handed over her heart to anyone, obviously. (You may want to point out that this is figurative as opposed to literal speech.) Ursula grew close to all these people and loved them. Then, when she had grown to love one person, she had to get to know another person. Her heart was broken a few times, meaning she was hurt by the need to sever the relationships.

Q: What is meant by the words, "Mom made Ursula her shadow"?
A: Whatever Mom did, Ursula followed.

Literary Components

21 **Resolution:** The two main problems in the story are now resolved. Mom can get around as easily as before, and the children love Ursula as much as they loved Marit.

Once in a while her friends got lost, just like Mom, and had to ask for help.

Mom said it takes four to six months for the dogs to settle down. But no matter how long she and Ursula are teamed up together, Ursula will need some correcting. For instance, Ursula might act so cute that a passerby will reach out to pet her. Then Mom will have to scold Ursula and ask the person not to pet a dog guide. If people give Ursula attention while she's working, she forgets to do her job.

After a month at home, Ursula emptied her food bowl every time.
21 She knew all the routes, and Mom could zip around as easily as she had with Marit.

"Now it's time to start the loneliness training," Mom said. She left Ursula alone in the house, at first for a short time while she went jogging with Dad. Ursula will never be able to take Mom jogging because she can't guide at high speeds.

Each week Mom increased the amount of time Ursula was alone. I felt sorry for our pooch, but she did well: no barking, no chewing on furniture.

Then Mom said Joel and I could introduce Ursula to our friends, one at a time. They could pet her when she was out of harness.

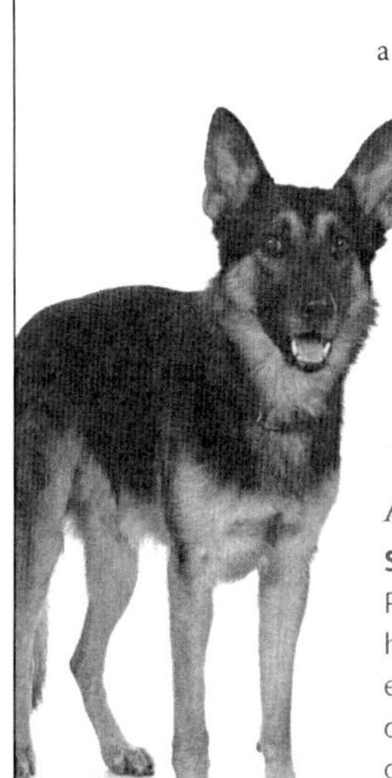

Every morning Ursula woke Joel and me. Every night she sneaked into my bed for a snooze.

Finally Mom allowed Joel and me to play with Ursula, and I knew: shrimpy little Ursula had fallen for us, and we were even crazier about her.

But we haven't forgotten Marit. Joel says that Ursula is the best dog alive. And I always say she's the best dog in this world.

ABOUT THE AUTHOR

Sally Hobart Alexander had a wonderful childhood growing up in the Pennsylvania countryside. As a girl, she liked to write and tell stories. In her twenties, she contracted a rare disease, which caused her to lose her eyesight. She completed a training program for the blind, then earned a degree in social work, and married. Today, she and her husband have two grown children, a son and a daughter. Mrs. Alexander's goal is to live an ordinary life despite her disability. "I write about disabled people trying to do the same thing," she says.

68 Unit 1

Guiding the Reading

Literal

Q: About how long does it take for the dogs to settle down?

A: It takes about six months.

Q: How did Mom know that Ursula was starting to settle in after a month?

A: She was eating better and would zip around the regular routes just as Marit had done.

Q: What is loneliness training?

A: It trains the dogs to be on their own and behave well despite the lack of supervision.

Q: Why won't Ursula accompany Mom while she's jogging?

A: Ursula cannot guide Mom properly at those speeds.

Q: What did Ursula get used to doing every morning and every night?

A: Every morning she woke up Leslie and Joel and every night she crept into Leslie's bed.

Analytical

Q: Why do you think that the children's friends were allowed to meet Ursula one at a time? Why did she have to be out of harness when they petted her?

A: Mom didn't want to overwhelm Ursula. Ursula had to know that she could not just have a good time with a whole group of people and forget her commitment to Mom. The harness was a clear sign to Ursula that she was at work, guiding Mom. When Mom removed the harness from Ursula, she was teaching Ursula the difference between work time and play time.

Studying the Selection

FIRST IMPRESSIONS

Do you know someone who doesn't let a disability get in the way of their success?

QUICK REVIEW

1. Who is Mom's best friend?
2. Why does Leslie's Mom need a dog guide?
3. Why was Leslie so worried about Mom getting a new dog guide?
4. List at least three types of behavior that are included in training a dog at The Seeing Eye.

FOCUS

5. Leslie was very concerned about the new dog at the beginning of the story. How did she feel about Marit and Ursula at the end of the story?
6. Explain why the two main settings in this story are both very important to Mom.

CREATING AND WRITING

7. Write about someone you know who doesn't give up despite a disability or some other challenge.
8. We know what Leslie thought about Ursula. Now, tell us what Ursula thought about Leslie, her Mom, and the whole business of being trained as a dog guide! Write a paragraph—it may be humorous or serious—in which Ursula describes her feelings.
9. Mom's hearing is exceptional. She pays attention to sounds that we take for granted. At home, sit quietly for five minutes with your eyes closed and listen carefully to all the sounds that surround you. You will notice things you may not have noticed before. You may hear the sound of your mother's shoes, the squeak of a floorboard, the grating of the cabinet door that needs to be oiled, or the ticking of a clock. Write a list of six to eight sounds that you hear now, that you ordinarily don't notice at all.

Mom's Best Friend 69

First Impressions

Answers will vary. Some students will be able to come up with numerous examples, while others may not be able to think of any. Explain to your students that many of us have some type of shortcoming, something that limits us that may not be as recognizable a disability as blindness. Some individuals may be clumsy and poor at sports while others may be disorganized or have poor short-term memory. Certainly this is not in the same category as a disability like blindness, but it will help students understand that many of us confront challenges more often than we realize. Encourage students to discuss how one overcomes these obstacles.

Quick Review

1. While Mom loves her family, her dog guide, Ursula, is her best friend.
2. Leslie's Mom is blind and depends on a dog guide to travel around independently.
3. Leslie was still thinking about Marit and was concerned about having to love a new dog.
4. The dog must walk many routes repeatedly, learn to avoid trees and other obstacles, and determine when it is safe to cross the street. It is expected to stay alert and not be distracted by other people, sirens, or other dogs. The dog must also get used to being handled by a new owner.

Focus

5. Leslie still misses Marit and has a warm place in her heart for Mom's first dog guide. She has come to love Ursula but understands that she has not taken the place of Marit. Leslie is happy to have such a wonderful dog in the house as well as a new dog guide for Mom.
6. The Seeing Eye building was crucial for Mom's independence. She needed a new dog to continue leading her life the way she'd led it before Marit died, and needed this institution's setting to train with her new dog. Home is obviously where Mom feels most comfortable and would like to settle back in with Ursula. It is very important that Ursula feel comfortable in this setting as well, if she is to be a competent dog guide for Mom.

Creating and Writing

7. Answers will vary.
8. Answers will vary.
9. Answers will vary. Allow your students to share their 'observations' with the class.

What Is Theme?

For the Birds

1. The student did not care about birds at the opening of the story. By the end of the story, the student would like to help endangered birds.
2. The author would like us to care about saving endangered birds.
3. The author's theme is that all birds, beautiful or ugly, are precious and worthy of being preserved and that people can make the difference in their survival or extinction. The phrase that sums up this idea is, "we too can make a difference."

Lesson in Literature . . .

WHAT IS THEME?

- The theme is the story's main **idea**.
- To discover a story's theme, the reader must think about what happens in the **plot**.
- To discover a story's theme, the reader must think about what the **characters** say and do.
- To discover a story's theme, the reader must think about **when** and **where** the story takes place.

When my teacher invited an ornithologist to talk to our class about birds, I wasn't excited at all. Birds? I thought. I don't care about birds. Why do I need to learn about birds?

The next day I wasn't paying attention when he stood in front of the class, but I looked up when he made a loud noise like a high-pitched bugle call. "That," he said, "is the call of the Puerto Rican parrot."

The ornithologist switched off the classroom lights and said, "Let's look at the first slide." There on the slide was a small, funny-looking green bird with a red forehead and white around its eyes. "The Puerto Rican parrot," the ornithologist said, "is an endangered species. Only thirty-five of these birds are alive in the world today."

That's when I sat up. Only thirty-five of them are alive in the world today? I felt my hand rising. "Why?" I asked.

"Good question," the ornithologist said. "When I started my work, the Puerto Rican parrot was nearly extinct." He explained that he and other ornithologists helped to save these parrots by studying their habitat, raising some of them in captivity, and later releasing them into new habitats in the wild.

I wasn't excited about birds before, but now I was. Finding out about the Puerto Rican parrot interested me.

I was excited about birds until the ornithologist showed the next slide.

"Here's the next slide," he said. I couldn't believe it. On the slide was the ugliest bird I had ever seen. It was very large and very black and had a long, hooked beak and an ugly red bald head. I couldn't stop looking at it.

The ornithologist told us that the California condor was almost extinct. I wondered why anyone wanted to save such an ugly bird. The California condor looked ugly and mean. He switched to a slide of two climbers on the side of a mountain. One of the climbers was the ornithologist!

The next slide was of four big black birds flying high in the sky. "When I took this picture," he said, "those four condors were half of the entire population of California condors."

Vocabulary

stealthily (STELL thih lee) *adv.*: softly and secretly

persimmon (pur SIH mun) *n.*: a large, plumlike orange fruit that is sweet when very ripe

devour (dih VOW ehr) *v.*: to swallow hungrily

FOR THE BIRDS

THINK ABOUT IT!

1. What change takes place in the student's attitude by the time the story has finished?
2. What, in your opinion, would the author like to change in your attitude to birds?
3. In your opinion, what does the ornithologist mean when he says, "we too can make a difference"?

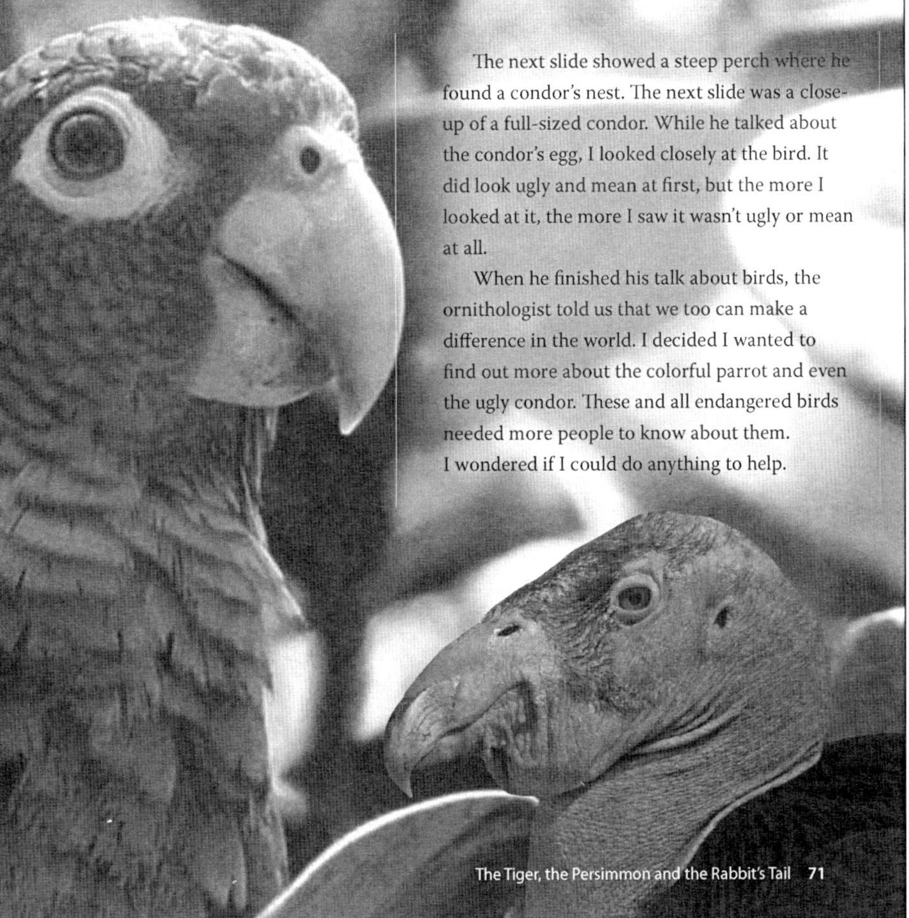

The next slide showed a steep perch where he found a condor's nest. The next slide was a close-up of a full-sized condor. While he talked about the condor's egg, I looked closely at the bird. It did look ugly and mean at first, but the more I looked at it, the more I saw it wasn't ugly or mean at all.

When he finished his talk about birds, the ornithologist told us that we too can make a difference in the world. I decided I wanted to find out more about the colorful parrot and even the ugly condor. These and all endangered birds needed more people to know about them. I wondered if I could do anything to help.

The Tiger, the Persimmon and the Rabbit's Tail 71

Unit Theme:	***The Things That Matter***
Target Skill:	***What is a theme?***
Genre:	***Fable***

Getting Started

Before beginning the next selection, introduce your students to the fable. A **fable** is a short tale that is not true. The characters are usually (though not always) animals who have some particular human flaw. The story has a moral. Often, a proverb is placed at the end to clearly state the moral of the story. Your students are likely to be familiar with classic fables. Read the following fable aloud. Let your students offer their ideas as to what the moral of the story is.

The Boy Who Cried Wolf

There once was a shepherd boy who was bored as he sat on the hillside watching the village sheep. To amuse himself he took a great breath and sang out, "Wolf! Wolf! The wolf is chasing the sheep!"

The villagers came running up the hill to help the boy drive the wolf away. But when they arrived at the top of the hill, they found no wolf. The boy laughed at the sight of their angry faces.

"Don't cry 'wolf,' shepherd boy," said the villagers, "when there's no wolf!" They went grumbling back down the hill.

Later, the boy sang out again, "Wolf! Wolf! The wolf is chasing the sheep!" To his delight, he watched the villagers run up the hill to help him drive the wolf away.

When the villagers saw no wolf they sternly said, "Save your frightened song for when there is really something wrong! Don't cry 'wolf' when there is *no* wolf!"

But the boy just grinned and watched them go grumbling down the hill once more.

Later, he saw a *real* wolf prowling about his flock. Alarmed, he leaped to his feet and sang out as loudly as he could, "Wolf! Wolf!"

But the villagers thought he was trying to fool them again, and so they didn't come.

At sunset, everyone wondered why the boy hadn't returned to the village with their sheep. They went up the hill to find the boy. They found him weeping.

"There really was a wolf here! The flock has scattered! I cried out, 'Wolf!' Why didn't you come?"

An old man tried to comfort the boy as they walked back to the village.

"We'll help you look for the lost sheep in the morning," he said, putting his arm around the youth. "Nobody believes a liar… even when he is telling the truth!"

Into . . . The Tiger, the Persimmon and the Rabbit's Tail

When you discuss fear, make sure that your students understand that fear is a normal emotion. While there are some fears that are irrational, most are real and justified. The problem arises when, instead of identifying the fear and dealing with it, the frightened person runs from the fear and allows their imagination to magnify the danger (precisely as happens in this story).

Probably the most effective preventive measure against fear is building a child's—or an adult's—confidence. A person who is confident in their abilities, strengths, intellect, and courage will be a less fearful person. People who feel that they can cope with life, assume, when they are faced with something new and frightening, that they will learn to cope with that development, too.

The following quotes can be used as a springboard for some very interesting discussions with your students.

- "The only thing we have to fear is fear itself." – Franklin Delano Roosevelt
- "No one can make you feel inferior without your consent." – Eleanor Roosevelt
- "Always do what you are afraid to do." – Ralph Waldo Emerson
- "Courage is not the absence of fear, but the mastery of it."

Eyes On Theme

Young people often have difficulty understanding what is meant by the term "theme." Before you can explain it to them, you must be clear about it yourself! The theme of a story, poem, drama, or novel is the *idea* that underlies and unifies the work. It is to convey this idea that the author has written the work.

For the teacher: Let us take the idea of crime and punishment. One writer had many thoughts about this subject. His name was Fyodor Dostoevsky. He created characters, put them into a setting with which he was familiar, wrote dialogue for them, and invented a plot—all for the purpose of getting across his ideas about crime and punishment. Had he encountered a reader who loved his setting, was hypnotized by his characters, was enthralled by his dialogue, but did not know that the theme was crime and punishment, Dostoevsky would surely have felt that his book was a failure as far as this reader was concerned.

For the student: A concrete way of teaching the idea of theme is to lead the class into a discussion of theme-based parties. Ask them if they've ever been to one. They may have been to a football themed party, a holiday themed party, or a storybook themed party. Let us take a simple example: A Day at the Zoo Party. At this party, everyone was asked to dress up as their favorite zoo animal. A tape of various animal sounds played as background music and each table had a different stuffed animal as a centerpiece. The games were "leapfrog" and other animal themed games, and the treats were jellyfish, chocolate lions, and animal crackers. In short, every aspect of the party contributed to the "zoo" theme. In the same way, every aspect of a story contributes to its theme.

The idea for a theme is usually a broad, general, true (universal) idea. Ask your students for examples of themes. In a short story, the theme could be friendship, sadness, courage, or similar topics. All elements of the story help get the author's idea across. If your students ask you how one identifies a story's theme, ask them how they, had they walked into the zoo party, could have identified its theme. They will say they looked at the decorations, the costumes, and the refreshments, and figured out what they had in common, what *idea* they all conveyed. Tell them that when they have read a story, they must look at the plot, the characters, and the dialogue and try to figure out what idea they all convey.

As the year progresses, your students will grow in their understanding of what a theme is and their ability to identify it in a story.

Blueprint for Reading

INTO . . . *The Tiger, the Persimmon and the Rabbit's Tail*

What are you afraid of? Snakes? Spiders? Being laughed at? Everyone is afraid of something. The question is: How do we handle our fears? The worst thing people can do is to allow their imaginations to run wild. Then their fears grow and grow until, what once frightened them, now terrifies them. The best solution to being afraid is to look directly at the thing you fear, and then face it, find out more about it, and make a plan to deal with it.

In the funny story that follows, the once brave tiger grows more and more frightened. Why? Can you explain why the tiger was so frightened? What could he have done differently?

EYES ON *Theme*

Every story has a theme. The **theme** is the main idea of the story. Sometimes the theme is very clear and obvious. The author might even start the story by telling the reader what the main idea is. Other times, the author hides the theme and makes the reader work at figuring out what the story's message, or theme, is. *The Tiger, the Persimmon and the Rabbit's Tail* is a story whose theme is hidden below the surface. You will have fun reading this humorous tale. When you have read and enjoyed it, ask yourself: Is there a serious message underneath the light words? What is the story's theme?

72 Unit 1

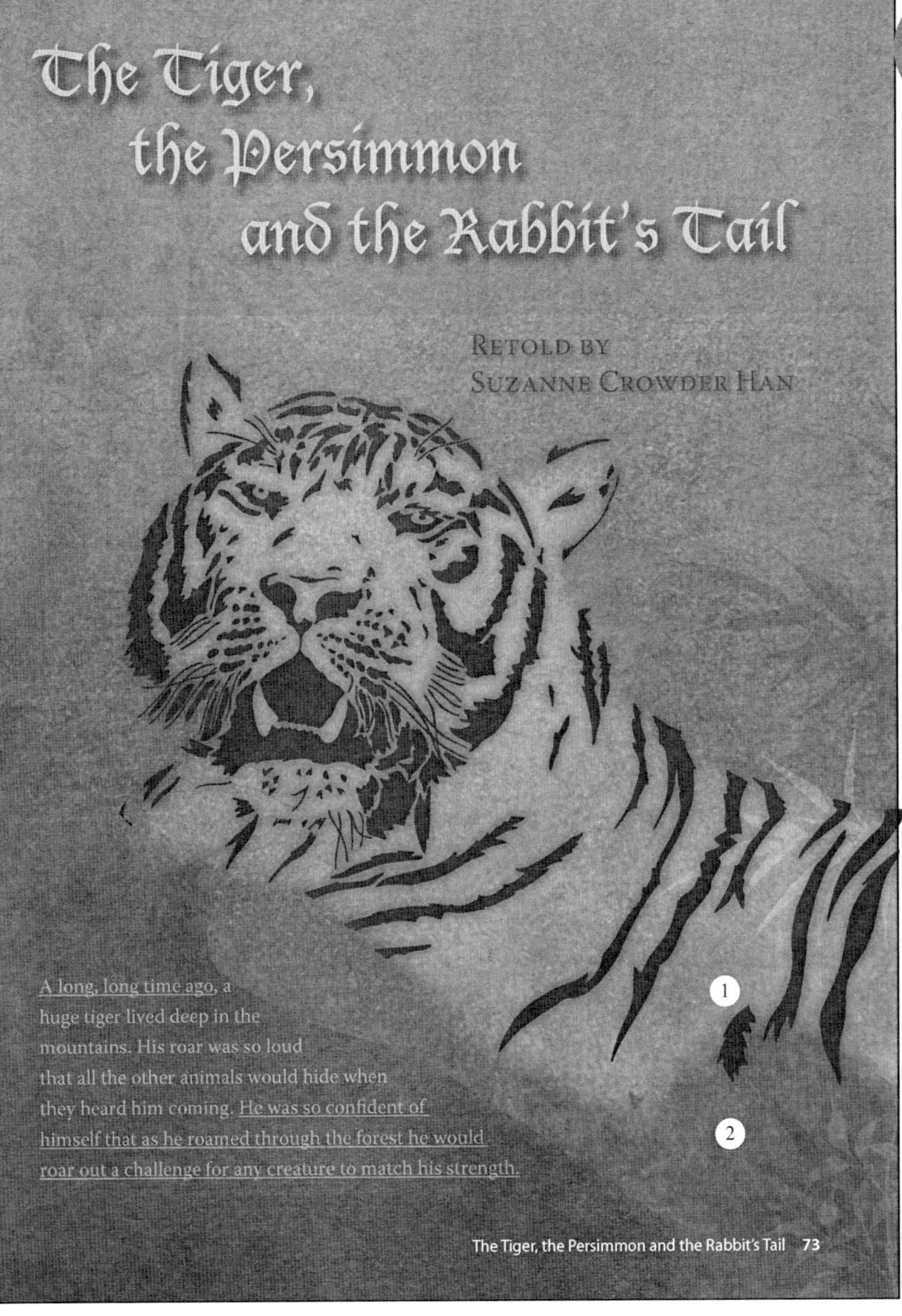

Selection Summary

This is a humorous fable in which a lack of information creates havoc. A tiger overhears a mother trying to quiet her crying baby with the words, "Stop crying! Do you want the tiger to get you?" Much to the chagrin of the tiger, the baby continues to cry. However, when the mother offers the baby a dried persimmon, the baby ceases its crying. The tiger, not knowing what a dried persimmon is, jumps to the conclusion that it is something even more frightening than a tiger.

Persuaded that the dried persimmon will attack him, the frightened tiger goes to the barn to eat the ox. A thief, who is in the barn to steal the ox, mistakes the tiger for a calf and pats his fur. The tiger, convinced that it is the persimmon who is patting him, allows himself to be roped and led out of the barn. The thief, still unaware that he has roped a tiger, gets on the tiger's back, at which point he realizes that he is riding a tiger. The tiger is terrified of the 'persimmon' on his back and the thief is terrified of the tiger he is riding.

After the thief jumps off of the tiger's back and climbs a tree to escape the tiger, the tiger confides to a passing rabbit that he has been miraculously saved from a dried persimmon. The rabbit, doubtful about the identity of the dried persimmon, investigates and finds only a frightened thief hiding in a tree. The rabbit laughingly tells the tiger to come to the tree to see the 'dried persimmon' and stands next to the hole in the tree to prevent the thief from running away. The thief ties a string to the rabbit's tail and pulls. The rabbit howls in pain and the tiger, frightened even further, is validated in his fear of the dried persimmon.

Guiding the Reading

Literal

Q: Where did the huge tiger live?

A: He lived in a forest deep in the mountains.

Q: Why did the other animals hide when they heard his roar?

A: They were frightened of his loud roar as well as of his confidence and strength.

Q: What was the tiger's challenge to all the other creatures in the forest?

A: He challenged them to see if they could match his strength.

Literary Components

1 Opening Line: The opening of the story tells us that we are about to read a fable or fairy tale.

2 Characterization; Theme: The tiger is supremely confident. He looks for a challenge and, presumably, a good fight, in which he will emerge victorious. He is arrogant.

Literary Components

3 Characterization: His arrogance and confidence have a tinge of cowardice and dishonesty.

4 Characterization: Another trait of the tiger is curiosity.

5 Humor; Theme: The overconfident, sly, and curious tiger is funny because he lacks a basic understanding of what is happening. He thinks the mother's invoking of "the tiger" to frighten her baby refers specifically to him. This misunderstanding leads to all the mishaps that befall the tiger in the rest of the story. The story's humor arises from the audience's knowing what the tiger does not know (a common technique employed by writers of comedy).

Then one cold winter day, hunger forced him to leave the snow-covered
3 forest in search of food. Stealthily he crept into the yard of a house at the edge of a village and looked around.

He saw a large fat ox in a stall near the gate. The sleeping animal made his mouth water. He crept closer to the stall. Then, just as he was ready to pounce, he heard a baby crying.

"Human babies certainly have an odd way of crying," said the tiger and,
4 being very curious, he crept closer to the house. "He's really loud. How can his mother stand the noise?" he wondered.

"Stop crying! Do you want the tiger to get you?" shouted the mother.

5 "How did that woman know I was here?" the tiger asked himself and he crept closer to the house.

"Hush! If you don't stop crying, the tiger will get you," said the mother.

But the baby cried even louder, which angered the proud tiger. "That baby isn't afraid of me? I'll show him!" said the tiger, creeping closer to the room.

WORD BANK

stealthily (STELL thih lee) *adv.*: softly and secretly

74 Unit 1

Guiding the Reading

Literal

Q: What caused the tiger to leave his forest home and go to the village?

A: He was hungry on a cold winter day.

Q: What animal made the tiger's mouth water?

A: A large, fat ox made his mouth water.

Q: What caused the tiger to stop before pouncing on the ox?

A: He heard a baby crying.

Q: What made the tiger curious?

A: He thought that human babies cried in an odd way and wondered how the mother could stand the baby carrying on.

Q: What did the mother tell her child?

A: "Stop crying. Do you want the tiger to get you?"

Q: What did the tiger ask himself, as he got closer to the house?

A: "How did that woman know I was here?"

Q: Did telling the baby about the tiger help the crying?

A: No, it did not.

Q: Why did the tiger get upset when the baby continued crying?

A: He was angry that the baby was, apparently, not afraid of him.

Analytical

Q: What does the expression, "make one's mouth water," mean? What was the tiger planning on doing to the ox?

A: When one sees savory food, one begins to salivate in anticipation of eating it. The tiger was going to eat the ox.

Q: Do you think the mother really knew that the tiger was right outside their home?

A: No, otherwise she would have been doing something else to protect herself and her child. It was just a way to get her child to stop crying.

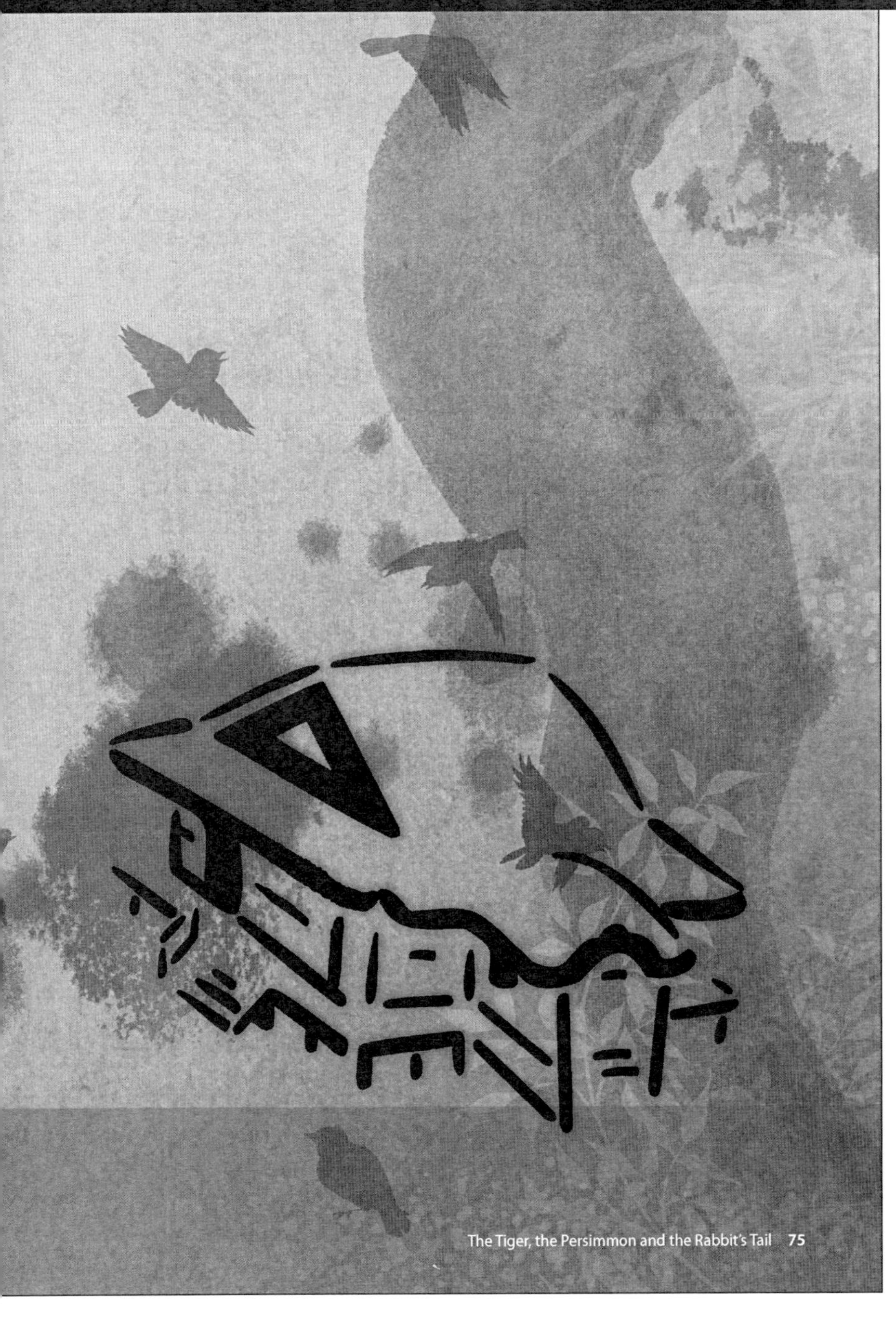
The Tiger, the Persimmon and the Rabbit's Tail 75

Literary Components

6 **Characterization:** The tiger's mixture of ego, ignorance, and cowardliness make him jump to the wrong conclusion.

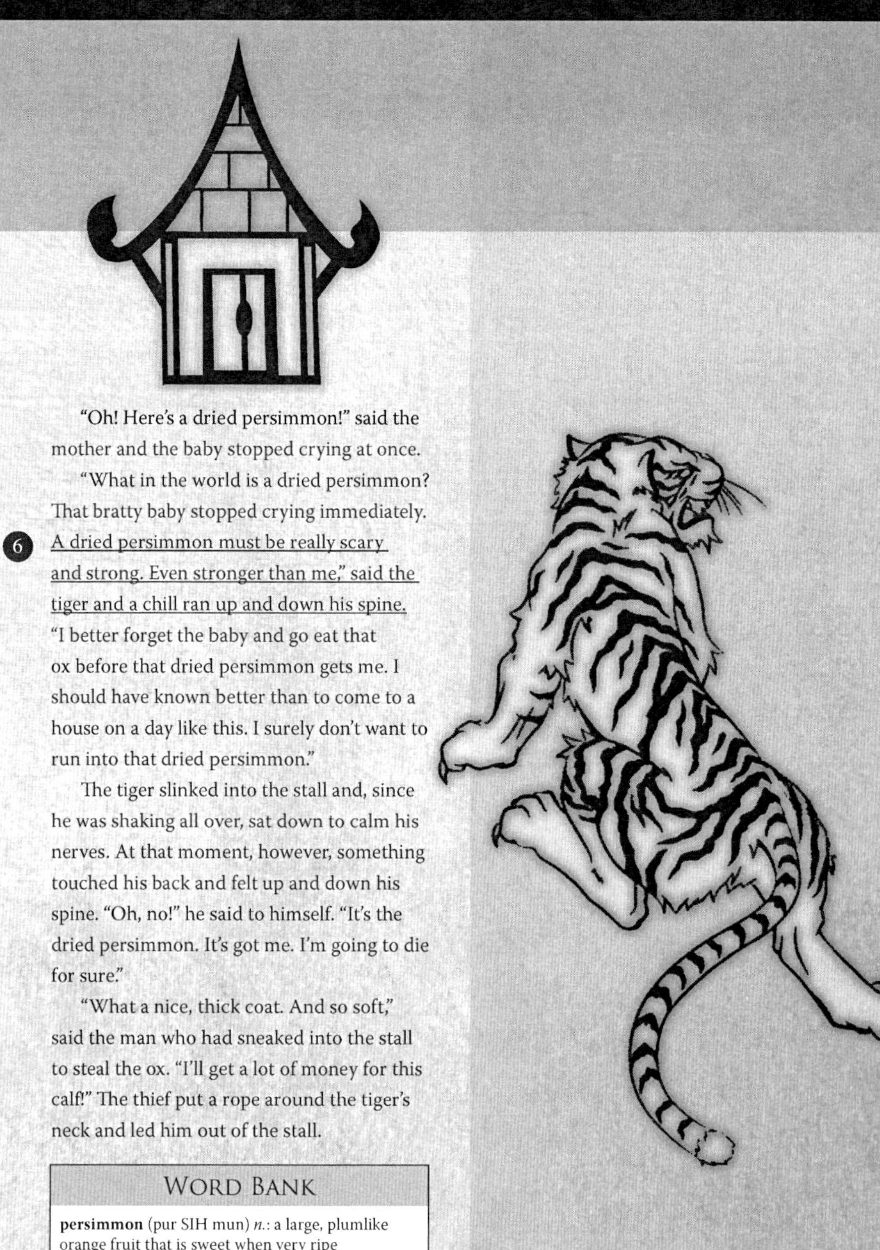

"Oh! Here's a dried persimmon!" said the mother and the baby stopped crying at once.

"What in the world is a dried persimmon? That bratty baby stopped crying immediately.
6 <u>A dried persimmon must be really scary and strong. Even stronger than me," said the tiger and a chill ran up and down his spine.</u> "I better forget the baby and go eat that ox before that dried persimmon gets me. I should have known better than to come to a house on a day like this. I surely don't want to run into that dried persimmon."

The tiger slinked into the stall and, since he was shaking all over, sat down to calm his nerves. At that moment, however, something touched his back and felt up and down his spine. "Oh, no!" he said to himself. "It's the dried persimmon. It's got me. I'm going to die for sure."

"What a nice, thick coat. And so soft," said the man who had sneaked into the stall to steal the ox. "I'll get a lot of money for this calf!" The thief put a rope around the tiger's neck and led him out of the stall.

WORD BANK

persimmon (pur SIH mun) *n.:* a large, plumlike orange fruit that is sweet when very ripe

76 Unit 1

Guiding the Reading

Literal

Q: What did the mother give her baby that stopped the crying?
A: She gave the baby a dried persimmon.

Q: Did the tiger know what a dried persimmon was?
A: No, he did not.

Q: Why did the tiger change his mind about going into the house?
A: He thought that whatever a dried persimmon was, it must certainly be very scary and stronger than him, and he didn't want to meet up with it.

Q: Why did the man go into the stall?
A: He wanted to steal the ox.

Q: Why did the thief think that he would get a lot of money for the animal he caught?
A: It had a nice, thick, and soft coat.

Analytical

Q: Why was the tiger shaking all over?
A: He was afraid of the dried persimmon.

Q: At first, what did you think it was that touched the tiger's back?
A: Answers will vary.

The Tiger, the Persimmon and the Rabbit's Tail 77

Literary Components

7 **Repetition:** The thief sounds like the tiger, exclaiming, "What can I do?" The difference is that the thief really should be afraid of the tiger, while the tiger really has nothing to fear. The thief and the tiger are similarly dishonest and cowardly.

"Oh my. What can I do? This is without a doubt that dried persimmon," moaned the tiger to himself. "Oh what can I do? I can't roar. I can't run. I can only follow it. Oh this is the end of me."

The thief was very happy to have in tow what he thought was a very fine calf that he could sell for a lot of money. Thinking he should get away from the area as fast as possible, he decided to ride the calf and thus jumped onto the tiger's back.

"That's strange," said the thief, "this doesn't feel like any calf I've been on before." He began to feel the tiger's body with his hands. "Oh

7 my. This isn't a calf. It's a huge tiger," he cried. "What can I do? What can I do?"

The thief was so frightened to discover he was riding a tiger, he nearly fell off. "Oh, I have to hold on," he said, grasping the tiger tighter. "If I fall off, that will be the end of me for sure. He'll gobble

Guiding the Reading

Literal

Q: What did the tiger do once it was caught?

A: Nothing, except follow the man. He thought that roaring and running wouldn't help.

Q: Why did the man decide to ride the 'calf'?

A: After stealing it, he wanted to get away as soon as possible.

Q: What made the man think that he wasn't riding a calf?

A: It didn't feel right to him.

me up before I even hit the ground," he said, squeezing the tiger with his legs. "Just calm down," he told himself, "and try to think of how to get away." 8

"I'm going to die. I'm going to die," moaned the tiger as the thief tightened his hold on him. "What rotten luck to die at the hands of a dried persimmon! I must try to get him off my back. That's the only thing I can do," he said and he began to shake his body. Then he tried jumping and bucking. Over and over he shook and jumped and bucked as he ran but the thief held on tight.

After a while they came to a grove of trees. When the tiger ran under a large one, the thief grabbed hold of a branch, letting the tiger run out from under him, and quickly climbed through a hole in the tree trunk and hid inside.

The tiger knew immediately that the dried persimmon was off his back but he didn't even think about trying to eat it. He just kept running as fast as he could deeper into the mountain. Finally he stopped and let out a sigh of relief. "Oh, I can't believe I'm alive. I just knew that dried persimmon was going to kill me." He was so happy to be alive, he rolled over and over on the ground, smiling all the while.

Literary Components

8 Characterization: The thief, unlike the tiger, tries to take hold of himself.

Guiding the Reading

Literal

Q: What were some of the man's thoughts once he realized that he was riding on a tiger?

A: "What can I do? Oh, I have to hold on. If I fall off, that will be the end of me for sure. He'll gobble me up before I even hit the ground. Just calm down and try to think of how to get away."

Q: What was the tiger thinking when the man held him tighter?

A: He thought that the 'dried persimmon' would get him and that he would die.

Q: How did the tiger try to get the man off his back?

A: He shook his body and jumped but the thief held on tight.

Q: What happened when they went under a large tree?

A: The thief grabbed a branch and let the tiger run out from under him.

Q: What happened after they became separated?

A: The man quickly hid in a tree hole while the tiger ran away as fast as he could.

Q: What caused the tiger to roll around on the ground?

A: He was so happy to be alive, having escaped from the 'dried persimmon.'

Literary Components

9 Characterization: The rabbit is one of the only characters that has any sense.

"Oh Mr. Tiger," called a rabbit who had been awakened by the tiger rolling around on the ground, "why are you so happy? How can you be so happy in the middle of the night?"

"I almost died today," replied the tiger, "so I'm happy to be alive."

"What's that?" asked the rabbit, hopping closer to the tiger. "You almost died?"

"That's right," explained the tiger. "A horrible dried persimmon caught me. I've just this moment escaped from it."

9 "What in the world is a dried persimmon?" asked the rabbit.

"You fool! You don't know what a dried persimmon is?" laughed the tiger. "Why it is the scariest, strongest thing in the world. Just thinking about it gives me chills."

"Well what in the world does it look like?" asked the rabbit.

"I don't know," said the tiger, "I was so scared I really didn't get a good look at it."

"Well where is it now?" asked the rabbit.

"I think it must be up in a tree," said the tiger.

9 "Where is the tree?" asked the rabbit. "I think I'll go have a look at that dried persimmon."

"What? Are you crazy? As weak as you are, it will devour you right away," said the tiger.

9 "If it looks like it is going to grab me, I'll run away. After all, there's no one faster than me," laughed the rabbit.

Word Bank

devour (dih VOW ehr) *v.*: to swallow hungrily

Guiding the Reading

Literal

Q: Who was awakened by the tiger?

A: The rabbit was awakened by the tiger.

Q: What did the rabbit ask the tiger?

A: "Why are you so happy? How can you be happy in the middle of the night?"

Q: What did the tiger tell the rabbit the dried persimmon looked like?

A: He couldn't describe it. The tiger told the rabbit that he was so scared that he didn't really get a good look at it.

Q: Why did the tiger think that the rabbit was crazy?

A: He was going to seek out the strong 'dried persimmon' even though he was only a weak rabbit.

Analytical

Q: Why do you think the rabbit felt that it's hard to be happy in the middle of the night?

A: Most people are drowsy and enjoy their sleep in the middle of the night. It is hard to be upbeat and active at that time. Certainly the rabbit didn't seem too pleased to have his sleep disturbed.

Q: Did the rabbit take the tiger seriously when he said that he almost died? How do you know that?

A: No. He laughed and did not take him seriously.

Q: How do you think the rabbit felt when the tiger told him that he didn't know what the dried persimmon looked like?

A: He thought the tiger was a fool for being so frightened of something that he had never seen.

The Tiger, the Persimmon and the Rabbit's Tail 81

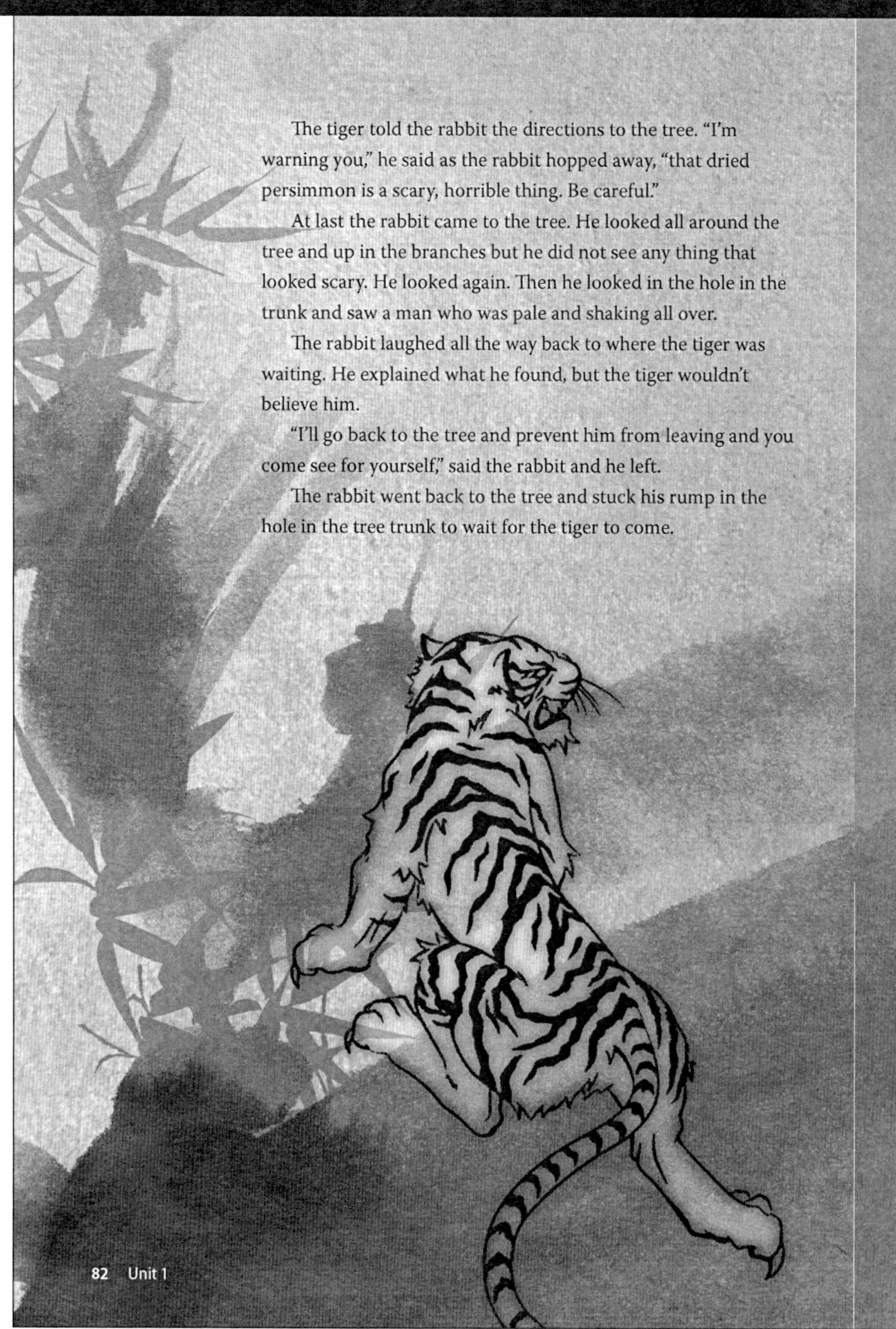

The tiger told the rabbit the directions to the tree. "I'm warning you," he said as the rabbit hopped away, "that dried persimmon is a scary, horrible thing. Be careful."

At last the rabbit came to the tree. He looked all around the tree and up in the branches but he did not see any thing that looked scary. He looked again. Then he looked in the hole in the trunk and saw a man who was pale and shaking all over.

The rabbit laughed all the way back to where the tiger was waiting. He explained what he found, but the tiger wouldn't believe him.

"I'll go back to the tree and prevent him from leaving and you come see for yourself," said the rabbit and he left.

The rabbit went back to the tree and stuck his rump in the hole in the tree trunk to wait for the tiger to come.

82 Unit 1

Guiding the Reading

Literal

Q: What did the tiger tell the rabbit before he left?

A: "I'm warning you, that dried persimmon is a scary, horrible thing. Be careful."

Q: What did the rabbit find in the hole in the tree?

A: A man who was pale and shaking all over.

Q: Was the rabbit scared?

A: No, he laughed all the way back to where the tiger was waiting.

Q: What was the tiger's reaction to the rabbit after the rabbit went to the tree?

A: The tiger didn't believe him.

Q: What did the rabbit do to protect the tiger?

A: He backed up into the hole in the tree so that the man couldn't get out.

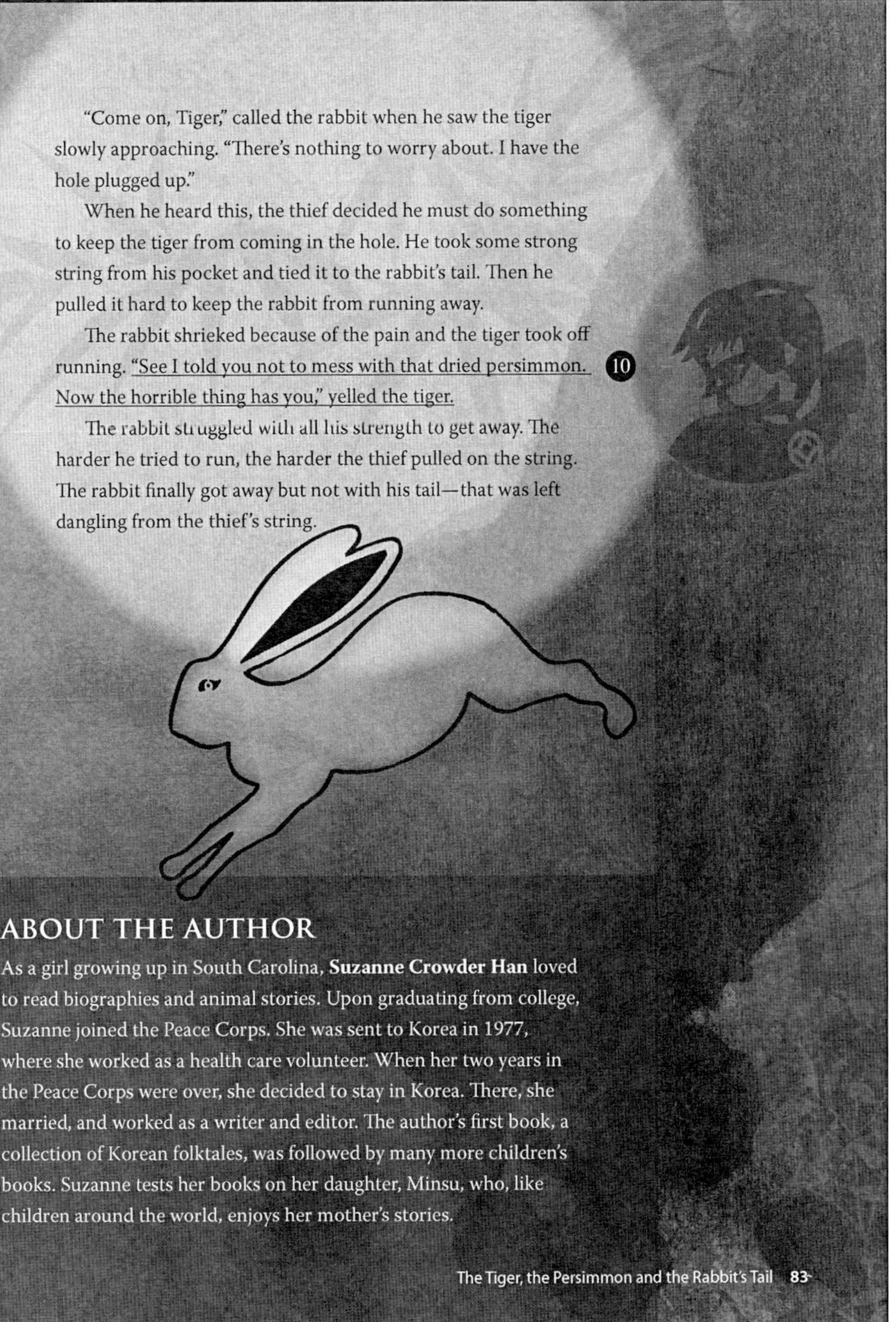

"Come on, Tiger," called the rabbit when he saw the tiger slowly approaching. "There's nothing to worry about. I have the hole plugged up."

When he heard this, the thief decided he must do something to keep the tiger from coming in the hole. He took some strong string from his pocket and tied it to the rabbit's tail. Then he pulled it hard to keep the rabbit from running away.

The rabbit shrieked because of the pain and the tiger took off running. "See I told you not to mess with that dried persimmon. Now the horrible thing has you," yelled the tiger. (10)

The rabbit struggled with all his strength to get away. The harder he tried to run, the harder the thief pulled on the string. The rabbit finally got away but not with his tail—that was left dangling from the thief's string.

ABOUT THE AUTHOR

As a girl growing up in South Carolina, **Suzanne Crowder Han** loved to read biographies and animal stories. Upon graduating from college, Suzanne joined the Peace Corps. She was sent to Korea in 1977, where she worked as a health care volunteer. When her two years in the Peace Corps were over, she decided to stay in Korea. There, she married, and worked as a writer and editor. The author's first book, a collection of Korean folktales, was followed by many more children's books. Suzanne tests her books on her daughter, Minsu, who, like children around the world, enjoys her mother's stories.

The Tiger, the Persimmon and the Rabbit's Tail 83

Literary Components

(10) **Humor; Theme:** The tiger is right for the wrong reason. His toxic mixture of ego and ignorance always leads him to the wrong conclusions.

Guiding the Reading

Literal

Q: What made the man do something to the rabbit?

A: He heard the rabbit calling the tiger. The man wanted to make sure that the tiger didn't come into the hole.

Analytical

Q: Why was the tiger approaching slowly?

A: He was still scared and wasn't sure if he could trust the rabbit.

Q: Why didn't the man want the tiger to come near the hole?

A: Obviously so he wouldn't attack him, but he was extremely worried because he had provoked an attack.

Q: What did the man in the tree do to the rabbit?

A: He pulled on the rabbit's tail with string.

Q: Was the rabbit as calm as before, when he was laughing and reassuring the tiger that there was nothing to be afraid of?

A: He shrieked from pain and ran away.

Q: What did the rabbit lose in the struggle with the man?

A: He lost his tail.

About *Here She Is*

Poetry Praises

The tiger in *The Tiger, the Persimmon and the Rabbit's Tail* is a fairy tale tiger. He is arrogant, foolish, and cowardly. He is the stuff of fables. The tiger in *Here She Is* is a flesh and blood jungle tiger. Although the tiger's markings are described in metaphors—"necklaces," "bracelet"—the tiger itself is realistic. She has strength and grace and her eyes blaze. The one quality attributed to her which is not necessarily an animal quality, is vanity—"she shows off."

Poetry praises in ways that prose can't, because metaphors and similes are so much more evocative than ordinary description. Even the poetic expression "She shows off… her tiger strength" says more to the reader than would the prosaic "She shows off… how strong she is."

The phrases "Her tiger blaze," "her tiger eyes," and "her tiger face" talk directly to us. They do not need to spell anything out because they evoke in us the sensation of awe that we all feel when we look a tiger in the face. Like *The Way*, this poem wants you to experience rather than to think.

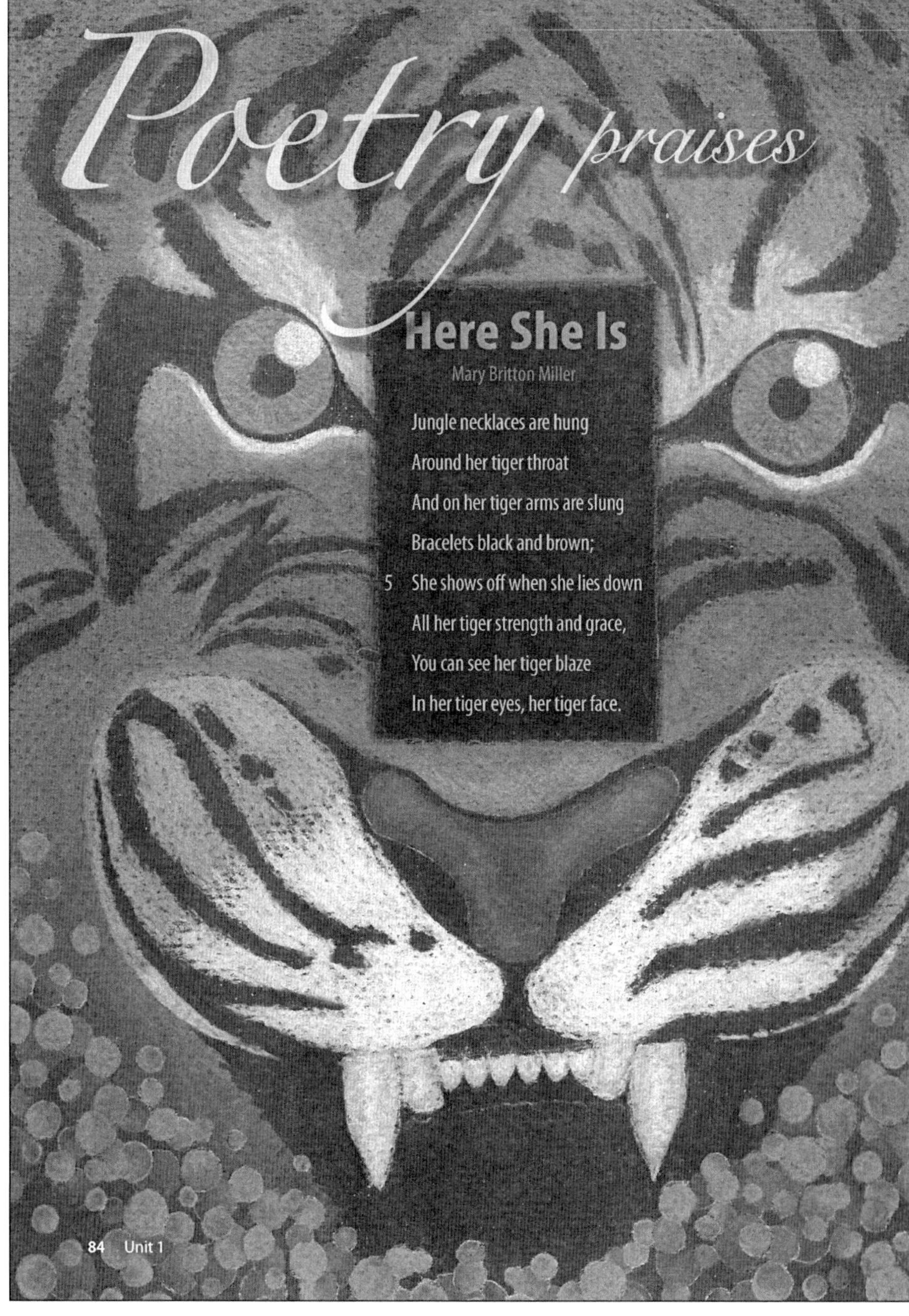

Poetry praises

Here She Is

Mary Britton Miller

Jungle necklaces are hung
Around her tiger throat
And on her tiger arms are slung
Bracelets black and brown;
She shows off when she lies down
All her tiger strength and grace,
You can see her tiger blaze
In her tiger eyes, her tiger face.

Studying the Selection

FIRST IMPRESSIONS

What if the tiger had known what a dried persimmon really is? Would the story be very different?

QUICK REVIEW

1. What caused the tiger to lose confidence and become frightened?
2. Did the tiger know what a dried persimmon looked like?
3. What was the thief thinking after he stole the animal? What was the tiger thinking?
4. What happened to the rabbit at the end of the story?

FOCUS

5. Do you think that the tiger and the rabbit were good friends? What about after the persimmon incident?
6. What, in your opinion, is the story's message?

CREATING AND WRITING

7. Who do you think was more frightened, the tiger or the man? Explain your answer.
8. Choose two animals other than a tiger and a rabbit. Write a story involving these animals and something they are afraid of. You may add a line to give the moral or message of the story.
9. What did the scary dried persimmon look like? Draw a picture of what you think the tiger imagined.

The Tiger, the Persimmon and the Rabbit's Tail 85

First Impressions

Had the tiger looked at the man who had tied a rope around him, he would not have been frightened. Identifying the "enemy" would have changed the whole story; there would have been no fear of the unknown.

Quick Review

1. When the tiger thought that something was greater and stronger than he was, his confidence was destroyed.
2. No, he did not.
3. At first the thief was happy about the money he would make by selling the stolen animal. When he realized that he was riding a tiger, he panicked. He held onto the tiger thinking that if he fell off, the tiger would devour him. "Just calm down," he told himself, "and try to think of how to get away." He finally thought of the idea of grabbing hold of a branch, which he did. Letting the tiger run from under him, he quickly climbed through a hole and into the trunk of the tree.

   The tiger was sure that roaring and running wouldn't do any good and that his life would end. When the thief hung onto him, the tiger thought he was going to die. He figured that if he shook his body wildly he might be able to shake off the 'persimmon.' When he finally felt that the thief was off his back, he was still so terrified that he ran away as fast as he could.
4. The rabbit lost part of its tail when the man tied string around it.

Focus

5. Answers will vary. From the start, the rabbit does not seem apprehensive about the tiger's reputation. Perhaps they had some sort of friendship where they could talk and laugh together. Maybe their behavior was different because it was the middle of the night and they were in an unusual situation. We do see the rabbit mocking the tiger, but then he tries to help. Students will draw their own conclusions.
6. The theme is addressed in the *Into* section at the beginning of this selection. Students' answers should include the ideas that fearing the unknown is a waste of energy, that sometimes scary, arrogant beings (like the tiger) are really cowards underneath, that brains (thief) are more useful than brawn (tiger), and that sometimes injury can come when one least expects it (the rabbit's tail)—when one is being a bit too confident.

Creating and Writing

7. Answers will vary.
8. Guide your students in the writing process. Review the idea of a story having a moral.
9. Pictures will vary. They do not have to be recognizable as people or animals.

wrap-up

the things that matter

ACTIVITY ONE

Don't Forget Your Jacket!

1. Every book has a jacket, or book cover. Your job is to create a jacket for one of the stories you've read in Unit One. Choose one of the following stories to use for your project: *Leah's Pony, Supergrandpa, Mom's Best Friend, Two Big Bears*, or *The Tiger, the Persimmon and the Rabbit's Tail.*
2. Your teacher will distribute paper and explain how to fold it in order to make a book jacket.
3. Draw an interesting front cover for your story. Include a picture that is important to the story. The title and author should be written on this side as well.
4. The *spine* of the book is the thin side that one sees when the book is upright on the shelf. The title and author are printed there.
5. Have you ever stopped to read the back of a book jacket? If you have, you know that two things are usually put there. The first is a paragraph that summarizes the story without revealing the end of the book. The publishers don't want to ruin the excitement for the reader! For the back of your book jacket, write a summary of the story in about five sentences.

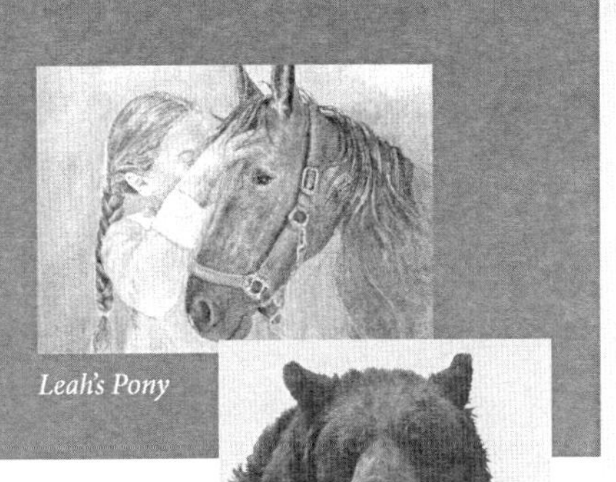

Leah's Pony

Two Big Bears

Supergrandpa

Mom's Best Friend

The Tiger, the Persimmon and the Rabbit's Tail

6. Below the summary found on the back of many books, the publishers often place one or two short *reviews* of the book. A review is comments about the book. Your second job is to write a brief review of the story. Include your opinion of the story along with the reason you have that opinion. You may include an example from the story to support your opinion.
7. Display your projects in a classroom 'library' for all to see.

ACTIVITY TWO

Ladies And Gentlemen.....

1. You have been chosen to present an award to one of the characters in this unit.
2. Think about the different lessons or themes found in each story. Then, think about positive character traits that are described in each story. Making a list or chart may help you organize the information.
3. Choose one character that you believe deserves an award for a positive act and can serve as a role model for others.
4. Write a speech that explains the purpose of the award and why this character deserves to win it. Do not write your explanation in one sentence. Saying that a character is devoted or honest is not enough. Be sure to support your decision with information from the story, and give your award a title!

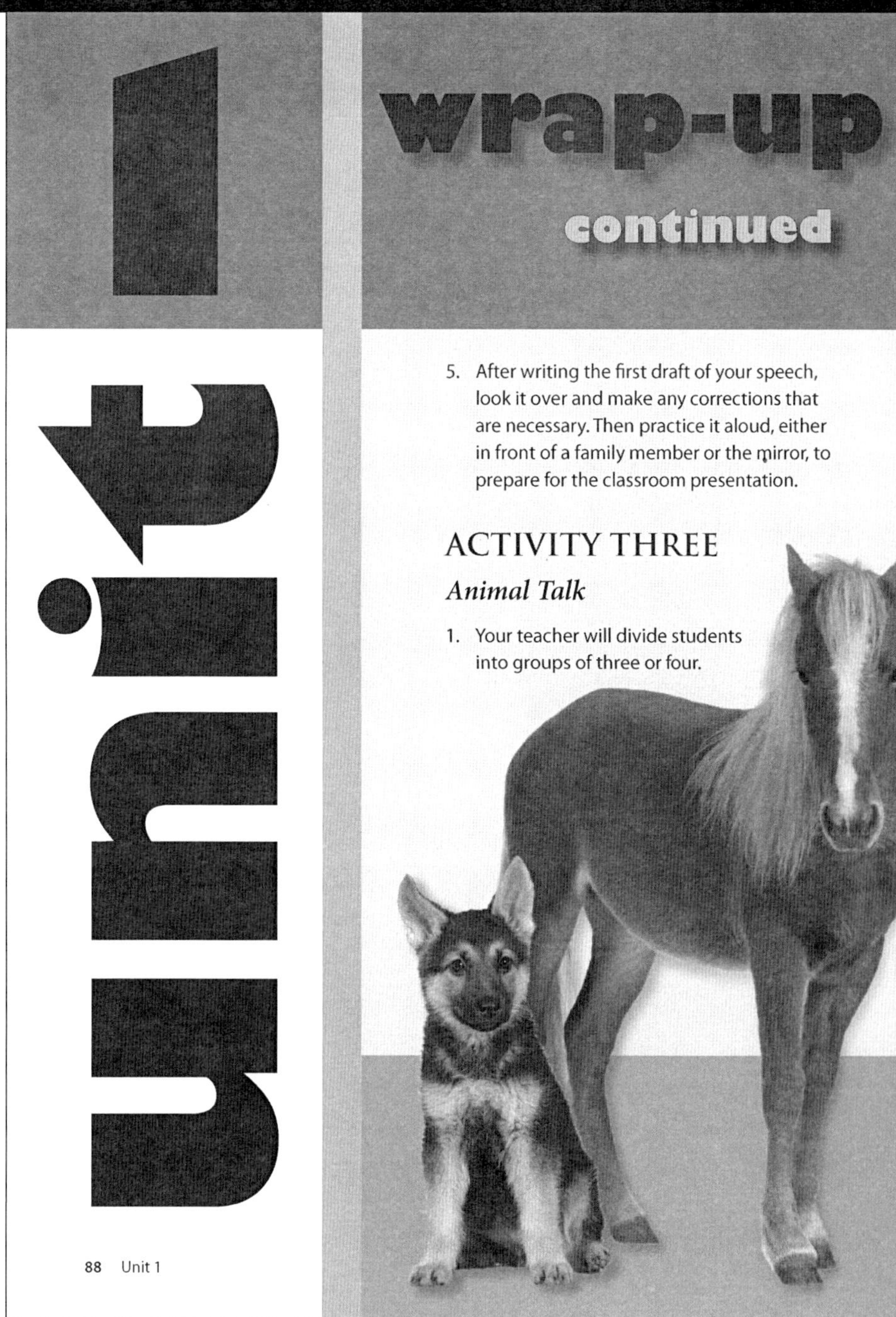

5. After writing the first draft of your speech, look it over and make any corrections that are necessary. Then practice it aloud, either in front of a family member or the mirror, to prepare for the classroom presentation.

ACTIVITY THREE

Animal Talk

1. Your teacher will divide students into groups of three or four.

88 Unit 1

2. Each member of your group should pick an animal character from one of the stories in Unit One. *(Leah's pony, Marit, Ursula, Sukey, Ma's bear, Pa's bear, the tiger, the rabbit)* Each person will act the part of one animal.
3. Imagine that all these animals met. Assume that they are all familiar with all of the stories. What would they say to one another? Would they have some good advice for each other? Would they laugh at or make fun of one another? Would they defend something they had done in the story to the others?
4. Write down the dialogue that would take place and then share it with your class. Be sure to make it interesting and creative.

ACTIVITY FOUR

We All Make Mistakes

1. Many characters in Unit One took risks or made mistakes. To take a risk is to take a chance with the possibility of causing damage to oneself or to others. For example, Leah took a risk by selling her pony and bidding for the tractor. She wasn't sure if her plan would work or if her parents would approve of it. The tiger made several mistakes, while the rabbit took a risk.
2. Think about a time that you took a risk or made a mistake. Write about what happened and what you learned from the experience.

unit 2

clarity

Lesson in Literature

What Is Internal Conflict?

The Flower Garden

1. At the start of the story, Cynthia is not as honest as she should be. [Teacher: please do not say, "She made a mistake." The line, "she stopped, *looked over both shoulders*, and plucked a tulip for herself," tells us that she knew what she was doing was wrong.] What you could say is that she didn't let herself think too clearly about the fact that these flowers belonged to someone. (This parallels, to some degree, Sato, who doesn't let himself think about the fact that the ivory he loves to carve is obtained by killing elephants.)
2. Seeing the owner, Mrs. Hudson, makes Cynthia face the fact that these flowers belong to someone. She is honest enough to see the truth and to feel remorse for what she did. (Similarly, seeing the bullet in the piece of ivory forces Sato to face the facts and then make a choice.)
3. Cynthia goes the extra mile. Not satisfied with just feeling bad, she offers to help grow new flowers.

Additional background information for *Sato and the Elephants* can be found on p. 3 in the Teacher Resources Section.

Lesson in Literature

WHAT IS INTERNAL CONFLICT?

- **Internal** means inside. **Conflict** means struggle, or battle.
- An **internal conflict** is a *struggle* that takes place inside a person's mind.
- A story about internal conflict is about someone who must make a choice.
- The choice will usually be between two moral values, such as right and wrong, truth and falsehood, or kindness and cruelty.

THINK ABOUT IT!

1. In the middle of the story, Cynthia asks herself, "Why had she ever thought it was okay to pluck flowers from Mrs. Hudson's garden?" Can you answer this question?
2. What helped Cynthia see that it was wrong to take flowers from Mrs. Hudson's garden?
3. What extra step did Cynthia take to make up for what she had done wrong?

Vocabulary

precision (prih SIZH un) *n.*: being exact about every detail
dense (DENSS) *adj.*: thick and tightly packed together
pare (PAIR) *v.*: to cut off the outer layer
chiseled (TCHIH zuld) *v.*: carved with a *chisel*, a tool with a cutting edge designed to carve a hard material
beacon (BEE kun) *n.*: a light used as a warning signal
tepid (TEP id) *adj.*: lukewarm
flaw *n.*: a defect; an imperfection
corroded (kuh RODE id) *adj.*: worn away
eerie (IH ree) *adj.*: strange and somewhat frightening
trudged (TRUJD) *v.*: walked slowly and heavily

Sato and the Elephants

Mixed-Up Moby is Back!

Workbook

Workbook

The Flower Garden

Cynthia loved flowers. Whenever she walked to the playground, she admired a neighbor's beautiful flower garden of white tulips and yellow daffodils. She liked to stop and smell the flowers, even touch their delicate petals. One day, though, she stopped, looked over both shoulders, and plucked a tulip for herself.

When she met her friends at the playground, they all said something nice to her about her flower. "It is so beautiful," her friend Katie said.

"I love it!" her friend Rachel said.

The next day Cynthia plucked another flower, a bright daffodil and the next day, another. After a few days she told her friends about the flower garden. "It's not far," she said. "There are flowers for all of us."

It was a warm afternoon in early summer when Cynthia and her friends circled around the garden, choosing flowers for themselves. "This one?" Cynthia asked as she plucked tulips and daffodils for her friends.

All the girls were smiling at their flowers when Cynthia saw a car pull into the driveway of the house beside the garden and an old woman in a kerchief open the car's trunk and remove gardening tools. Cynthia was sure the woman didn't see the three girls with flowers in their hands circled around her garden.

"Let's go," Cynthia said quietly. All that afternoon, at the playground and later up in her room at home, she thought about the woman in the kerchief. Her mother once told her that the woman who owned that house, a Mrs. Hudson, kept to herself and lived all alone because her husband died years ago and her grown children lived far away. That night Cynthia thought to herself, Why had she ever thought it was okay to pluck flowers from Mrs. Hudson's garden?

The next day, on her way to the playground, Cynthia walked around Mrs. Hudson's house, not past her garden, and she didn't have a flower to show off to her friends. She did the same thing the next day and the next day. "We miss your flowers," her friend Rachel said.

Cynthia knew she had been wrong to pluck even one flower from someone else's garden. Even though it was beautiful, it belonged to someone. The flower garden on the way to the playground was hers only to admire. But Cynthia still felt bad, because not plucking any more flowers from Mrs. Hudson's garden just wasn't enough. What else could she do?

It was a sunny morning in July when Cynthia, in a kerchief and garden gloves, knocked on Mrs. Hudson's front door. "I'm Cynthia. Do you need some help in your garden, Mrs. Hudson?" she asked.

"I sure do. That garden's been giving me some trouble," Mrs. Hudson replied, with a twinkle in her eye.

"I think I know what you mean," Cynthia said, a shy smile inching across her face.

Unit Theme: *Clarity*

Target Skill: *Understanding and recognizing internal conflict*

Genre: *Fiction*

You may want to ask your students to write scenarios of situations that they have experienced and read them to the class. And, if you feel comfortable doing so, share a few of your own experiences with your students to demonstrate that adults, too, can have difficulty making important decisions.

Getting Started

Preface the story by having a discussion with your students regarding decision-making. Ask them to think about a time that they made the right choice even though it was very difficult. Perhaps they had to forgo something that was precious or pleasurable. Give them some sample scenarios.

Imagine that you finally made arrangements to spend Sunday afternoon with a new friend in your class and are looking forward to the visit. Your mother asks you to spend the afternoon with your grandmother. She is elderly and enjoys the company as well as needing someone to help her go to the grocery store. You've been waiting for weeks for this special time with your friend; should you cancel the visit to assist your grandmother?

You are asked to watch your little brother while your mother rests to ease her pounding migraine headache. He plays nicely for a while but then gets bored and cranky. After seeing your new art set, he insists that he must play with it now. The art set is a recent birthday gift that means a lot to you. It has a variety of materials and so far you have not shared it with anyone. Should you keep the art set to yourself and let your brother have a tantrum that will wake up your mother? Should you share the art set even though it means that your brother will likely use or break some of the fancy art supplies?

Into . . . Sato and the Elephants

The defining moment in which one recognizes that a mistake has been made can be painful, enlightening, guilt-laden, and disheartening all at the same time. Ask your students how they feel when they realize they've made a mistake. Does the type of reaction they have depend on whether they've made a 'small' or a 'big' mistake? Encourage them to share their experiences—but only if they feel comfortable doing so. Expand on the idea that mistakes can serve as a learning experience. Errors can cause us to feel remorse or anger, but we must move on. Gaining something from the experience is the only way to compensate for the damage caused.

Sato's behavior at the beginning of the story is not so much the product of bad judgment as of a simple lack of awareness. He knows in theory where ivory comes from, but he has never grappled with the reality of the killing of elephants for their tusks. Now, given the facts that Sato's father was an ivory carver and that the culture in which he lives does not view killing elephants as cruel, he can hardly be blamed for not having confronted the issue before it is forced into his consciousness. Sato finds himself having to reexamine what he was led to believe as a child. To his credit, he does not take the easy way out and shrug off his unease with the accepted custom. He—led by his subconscious—faces the truth and immediately changes his behavior, even though it compromises his livelihood.

The two high points of the story are first, when Sato discovers the bullet in the piece of ivory and the connection between the smooth ivory and a living elephant suddenly hits home. The second comes at the end when we are gratified and inspired by Sato's determination to rectify the mistake caused by his lack of awareness. The finality of his decision is represented by the figure of the elephant that he keeps near him.

Eyes On Internal Conflict

We all experience internal conflicts on a daily basis. Some of these are petty and some are vitally important. The petty ones—which outfit to wear, which baseball team to cheer for—are not usually termed internal conflicts. We save that term for questions of moral values, honesty, responsibility, respect for others, sensitivity, patriotism, and the like.

One could, admittedly, experience internal conflict when faced with two perfectly respectable choices. For example, a very artistic person choosing whether to live as a "starving artist" or as a competent accountant would probably qualify as a person with internal conflict. Yet, for the conflict to be interesting enough to write about, there would probably have to be a moral or psychological dimension to it.

Explain to your students that conflict in a story creates excitement and suspense. Most stories revolve around one or more conflicts. Emphasize that conflict means the struggle between two opposing forces, and that generally the character must choose to side with one or the other.

Blueprint for Reading

INTO . . . *Sato and the Elephants*

We all make mistakes. Some, like dialing a wrong number or making errors in addition, are easy to recognize and correct. Others, such as embarrassing someone or blurting out a secret, are more difficult to repair. We do not always realize at first that we have made a mistake. However, when the moment comes, we feel like a light bulb has gone on. We know what we have done wrong and often know what behavior we must change. Will we have the strength and courage to make the change? As you read *Sato and the Elephants,* see if you can find the moment that Sato understood his mistake. Does Sato change his behavior? Is Sato someone you could admire?

Internal Conflict

Have you ever had difficulty deciding whether or not to tell a "little white lie"? Did you ever have trouble deciding whether or not to reveal something that was told to you as a secret? If so, you've had an internal conflict. A **conflict** is a struggle or an argument. An **internal conflict** is a struggle that takes place *internally,* within our own selves, when we are trying to make a decision. As you read the following story, see if you can identify Sato's internal conflict.

94 Unit 2

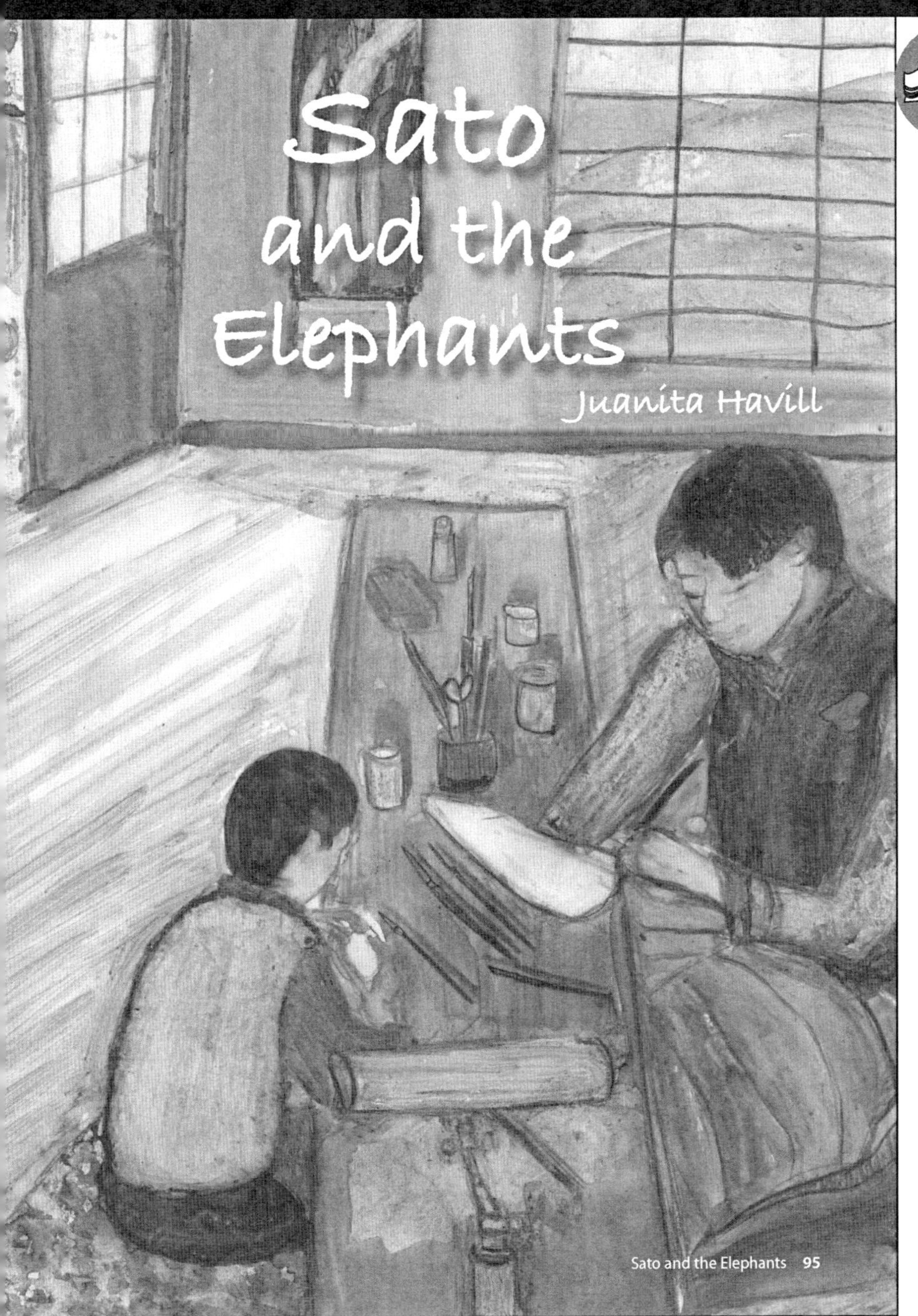

Selection Summary

Sato is a man whose father was an expert ivory carver. As he grew, he learned from his father the trade secrets of choosing the best ivory and carving the most exquisite figures. When his father dies, he continues to work as a carver, seeking continually to perfect his skill. One day, when he asks a dealer for a piece of ivory to carve, the dealer comments that elephants are becoming scarcer. This is the first time that Sato consciously links the beautiful ivory with the death of an elephant.

A short while later, the merchant sells Sato a flawless piece of ivory. Sato sees in it the image of an elephant, just waiting to be carved from it. He works carefully on the carving, day after day, night after night. One night, in the piece of perfect ivory, he finds a flaw. The flaw turns out to be a bullet embedded in the ivory. Sato weeps. He completes the carving and falls into a trancelike sleep. In his dream, or trance, Sato sees the elephant come to life. The elephant takes Sato to the African savannah, where a herd of elephants surround him, swaying back and forth and trumpeting.

Sato awakens, trembling with fear. In his hand is the figure of the elephant. He vows never to carve ivory again. The next day, he buys a piece of stone, determined to learn the craft of stone carving. The ivory elephant remains on his table, the first thing he sees in the morning and the last thing he sees at night.

Literary Components

1 Exposition; Characterization; Setting: The story opens with a simple statement: Sato is a happy man. As the story progresses, we will see that Sato's character will deepen and become more complex. The foreign-sounding name combined with the character's occupation (carver of ivory) indicates to the reader that the setting will be a foreign one, probably Africa or Asia.

1 Sato[1] was a happy man. From morning to night he did what he wanted to do. He carved figures from creamy white pieces of ivory. Rabbits and monkeys. Turtles and fish. Dragons with smooth, delicate scales, and birds that looked as if they would fly right out of his hands.

As a boy, Sato had watched his father work. A master carver of netsuke[2] and okimono,[3] he was famous for the

1. The name *Sato* (SAH toh) means *to come to understand.* As the story progresses, you will see why the author named this character Sato.
2. A *netsuke* (net SOO kee) is a miniature carving attached to the end of a cord hanging from a pouch.
3. An *okimono* (oh kee MOH noh) is an ornament.

Guiding the Reading

Literal

Q: Why was Sato a happy man?
A: From morning to night he did what he wanted to do.

Q: What type of animals did Sato carve?
A: He carved rabbits, monkeys, turtles, fish, dragons, and birds.

Q: Of what material were the figures carved?
A: They were carved from ivory.

beauty and precision of his ivory figures. One day he carved a netsuke and gave the figure to Sato. Sato was so pleased that he hung the figure on a cord and wore it always around his neck. Whenever he touched the smooth, polished figure, he told his father, "Someday I will be a great ivory carver like you." 2

Sato learned much from his father about the secrets of ivory. He learned that the best ivory was hard and dense and fine-grained. He learned how to saw and file the ivory, and to shave and pare it with knives. He learned how to sand, then polish a figure until it shone.

But he was young when his father died. It would take many more years of hard work before Sato could carve with his father's skill. Someday, he promised himself, he *would* be a master ivory carver.

Whenever Sato finished a carving, he took it to Akira, the dealer. Akira admired Sato's work and always sold the figures for a good price. With the money Sato was able to buy more ivory from Akira.

WORD BANK

precision (prih SIZH un) *n.*: being exact about every detail
dense (DENSS) *adj.*: thick and tightly packed together
pare (PAIR) *v.*: to cut off the outer layer

Literary Components

2 Tactile Image: An ivory carver must have an extremely sensitive sense of touch. His hands are his second pair of eyes. The writer makes us feel this by using words that help us "feel" the ivory figures.

Guiding the Reading

Literal

Q: What did Sato learn from his father about ivory?
A: He learned that the best ivory was hard, dense, and fine-grained. He learned how to saw and file the ivory, and to shave and pare it with knives. He also learned how to sand, and then polish a figure until it shone.

Q: What did Sato do with the figure his father gave him?
A: He hung it on a cord and always wore it around his neck.

Q: What did Sato tell his father he would be when he grew up?
A: He said that some day he would be a great ivory carver just like his father.

Q: Was Sato as good a carver as his father?
A: No, it would take many more years of hard work before Sato could carve with his father's skill.

Q: What did Sato promise himself?
A: He promised himself that he would be a master ivory carver.

Q: What did Sato do when he finished a carving?
A: He took it to Akira, the dealer.

Q: What did Sato do with the money he earned from his figures?
A: He used it to buy more ivory from Akira.

Analytical

Q: How were Sato and his father alike?
A: They were both ivory carvers.

Q: Why did Sato stop learning from his father before he was ready?
A: His father died.

98 Unit 2

One Saturday after Akira paid him, Sato asked, "What piece do you have for me to carve?"

Akira shook his head. "I don't have anything today, Sato. Ivory is becoming harder to find. I guess there aren't as many elephants. Maybe next week." 3

Sato walked home slowly, sadly. He would have nothing to carve now. He thought about Akira's words. Then he thought about the elephants. Ivory came from their long tusks, he knew. But whenever he held and carved a piece, he couldn't believe it came from an elephant. Ivory was as hard and heavy as rock. As plentiful as rocks, too, Sato had always thought.

The next Saturday Sato went back to Akira's shop. Again there was no ivory on display. But the dealer, seeing Sato, pulled a parcel from a drawer, unwrapped it, and set it on the table.

"Oh," Sato gasped. It was a beautiful piece, the size of his two fists, and creamy as foam on the sea. His hands shook as he picked it up and felt its strength and firmness. From this ivory he hoped to carve a masterwork. 4

"This is the piece I have been waiting for!" he shouted. 5

The price was high. "It's very rare," said Akira.

"I will take it," Sato said, though he knew it would cost almost all of his savings.

When he got home, Sato sat on his mat before his workbench. He turned the block over and over in his hands, eager to shape and smooth it. What should he carve? This piece was too large to become a netsuke strung on a cord. He didn't want to waste any of it. He studied the ivory. It would speak to him. It would tell him what to carve. 6

Literary Components

3 Rising Action: The innocence of both the character and the reader suddenly develops a crack. Who had thought of elephants until now? One thought only of the ivory, not of the living, breathing elephant from which it is taken.

4 Simile; Visual Image: The color of the ivory is compared to sea-foam.

5 Rising Action; Characterization: Sato's excitement upon seeing the piece of ivory tells us what a true artisan he is. His excitement pushes from his thoughts all shadows of guilt about the elephants.

6 Counterpoint: Whereas the average person looks at a piece of stone, or ivory, or wood, and sees only what meets the eye, an artist sees the potential of each as a piece of art. He sees what he can do with each material, how he can transform each one into a thing of beauty.

Guiding the Reading

Literal

Q: What problem was there when Sato went to Akira on Saturday?
A: Akira told him that he didn't have any ivory to give Sato.

Q: What reason did Akira give for not having ivory?
A: He said that ivory was becoming harder and harder to find. Maybe there weren't as many elephants.

Q: Where does ivory come from?
A: Ivory comes from elephant tusks.

Q: Why couldn't Sato believe that ivory came from an elephant?
A: Ivory was as hard and heavy as rock and he always thought it was just as plentiful.

Q: What did Akira give to Sato even though there was no ivory on display?
A: He gave him a large, beautiful piece of ivory.

Q: How is the piece described?
A: It is described as beautiful, the size of two fists, creamy as foam on the sea, and strong and firm.

Q: How much did this rare piece of ivory cost?
A: The story doesn't say exactly but Akira told Sato that the price was very high and Sato knew it would cost most of his savings.

Q: Why didn't Sato begin carving the ivory as soon as he returned home?
A: He was eager to shape it but didn't want to waste it. He was also waiting for an idea to come to him.

Literary Components

7 Early Turning Point: When Sato "sees" an elephant in the ivory, he is, for the first time, seeing the ivory as part of an elephant. This will set off a chain of new thoughts and feelings in him.

8 Veering Into Mysticism: The story, until now a simple, if poetic, tale begins to take on a mystical quality. Sato sees the image of an elephant in the ivory, and becomes obsessed with it.

For a long time Sato stared. Then suddenly a vision appeared to him, as clear as if magic had already
7 carved the figure: a big head, wide ears, powerful legs.

Sato's heart thumped wildly. He closed his eyes and breathed deeply to control his excitement. He must plan and carve carefully.

First he made a small clay model of the figure he would carve. Then he began to pencil light marks on the ivory to guide his hands. But the image was so distinct that he soon dropped his pencil and picked up a small saw.

He cut away the edges and corners and chiseled a rough shape. With a knife he grated the ivory, making a rhythmic, scritching sound. Then he smoothed the ivory and began to carve again. From time to time, he lay down his knife to flex his hand. But when he turned back, the image still
8 shone in the ivory like a beacon.

Sato forgot about everything but the figure. He ate only handfuls of rice, drank tepid green tea, and slept hardly at all. Week after week he worked, often past midnight, stopping only when he could no longer make his hands obey his mind.

Then late one night, his knife slipped and cut a thin streak across his finger.

"Ai!" Sato cried out.

WORD BANK

chiseled (TCHIH zuld) *v.*: carved with a *chisel*, a tool with a cutting edge designed to carve a hard material
beacon (BEE kun) *n.*: a light used as a warning signal
tepid (TEP id) *adj.*: lukewarm

Guiding the Reading

Literal

Q: What vision came to Sato?
A: He envisioned an already carved figure with a big head, wide ears, and powerful legs.

Q: How did he feel about carving this new figure?
A: "Sato's heart thumped wildly. He closed his eyes and breathed deeply to control his excitement."

Q: What did Sato do to prepare for this new carving?
A: He made a small clay model and made light pencil marks on the ivory.

Q: What were some steps Sato had to take to carve the figure?
A: He had to cut away edges and corners, chisel a rough shape, grade the ivory with a knife, and smooth the ivory.

Analytical

Q: How do you know that Sato worked so hard on the figure that he almost forgot about everything else?
A: The story tells us how he laid down his knife to flex his hand from time to time. He often worked past midnight and hardly slept. He didn't eat well, eating mostly rice and tea.

Only a small cut, he thought. I'm tired. I should rest before I make some horrible mistake.

But as he got up, he noticed something dark within the ivory. What was it? Only a shadow, Sato was certain. But he sat back down to look more closely. The shadow remained. A flaw? In this perfect piece? Sato's body felt weak, his chest so heavy he could hardly breathe. How could he carve a masterwork from a flawed piece of ivory? Hope drained from his heart.

In shock Sato began to cut tiny chips from around the flaw. He had never before seen anything so strange. Why, the flaw wasn't even part of the ivory. It was something else. Hard. Corroded. Metallic.

Suddenly Sato realized what it was: a bullet. A cry filled his mind, eerie and strange, like the trumpeting of elephants mourning their dead. Elephants who had died so that Sato might have ivory to carve. 9

Sato set his tools down. He bent his head before the unfinished figure, covered his face with his hands, and wept.

Word Bank

flaw *n.*: a defect; an imperfection
corroded (kuh RODE id) *adj.*: worn away
eerie (IH ree) *adj.*: strange and somewhat frightening

Literary Components

9 Action Rising to Crescendo; Theme: The theme that has been woven into the action from early on in the story, that art should not be created or acquired at the expense of living things, reaches its climax here. The source of the beautiful piece of ivory is displayed in the most dramatic way.

Guiding the Reading

Literal

Q: How did Sato get hurt one night?
A: His knife slipped and cut him because he was too tired.

Q: What decision did Sato make?
A: He decided it was time to stop and rest before making a horrible mistake on his precious figure.

Q: What did Sato see on the ivory after he cut himself?
A: He saw something dark in the ivory but wasn't sure if it was a flaw or a shadow.

Q: How did he feel about it?
A: "Sato's body felt weak, his chest so heavy he could hardly breathe . . . Hope drained from his heart."

Q: What did Sato discover after cutting the chips around the flaw?
A: The flaw wasn't part of the ivory. It was a bullet.

Analytical

Q: What connection did Sato make between the elephants and his figures?
A: He had always (theoretically) known where the ivory came from but had never really pictured a hunter killing an elephant for the sake of its ivory.

Q: How did Sato feel about finding the bullet?
A: He felt sad and guilty. Seeing the bullet brought to mind elephants mourning their dead. He covered his face with his hands and wept.

Literary Components

10 **Visual Image:** The figure glows because the perfect piece of ivory has been carved and polished by an expert carver.

11 **Fantasy:** The story moves into the realm of fantasy.

12 **Visual Image; Simile:** The elephant's ears spread out like sails—a sight easily imagined.

After a while he began to carve again. As if in a trance, he carved all night. By morning he was covered with a fine, white dust. He wiped the figure with a soft cloth and cleaned and polished the "flaw." Then he set it on the low table beside his futon and lay
10 down to rest. The figure glowed as if sunlight shone within it. It was just as he had imagined, except for one thing. A dark, shiny bullet was buried in its forehead like a jewel.

Exhausted, Sato gazed at the figure.
11 Its white sides seemed to breathe, and with each breath the elephant grew. Its
12 trunk swayed, and its huge ears spread like sails.

Sato rubbed his eyes. He raised himself on his elbow, then rose to his knees. The elephant towered above him. Slowly it bowed, and Sato understood that he was to climb onto its back. As the elephant stood, Sato felt his stomach lurch. He was afraid to look down.

"Where are you taking me?" he cried out.

102 Unit 2

Guiding the Reading

Literal

Q: What did Sato do all night following his discovery?
A: He carved all night.

Q: What did he do when he was finished carving in the morning?
A: He cleaned the fine white dust off the figure with a soft cloth.

Q: What was different about the figure?
A: The shiny bullet in its forehead was different.

Q: What seemed to happen to the elephant as Sato stared at it?
A: It seemed to come alive. It grew and moved and breathed.

Q: What was Sato's reaction?
A: His stomach lurched and he was afraid to look down.

Sato and the Elephants 103

Literary Components

13 **Fantasy:** Note the shift between the fantastic and the real. One part of the fantasy—the elephant—turns back into ivory, but Sato remains in the dream world of the African savannah.

14 **Characterization; Theme:** Compare the Sato of now to the Sato of the beginning of the story. Sato has developed an awareness of where the ivory comes from, and with that awareness comes a sense of shame and sorrow.

The elephant trudged on in silence. Sato felt the wind in his face, first cool, then warm, then hot. The sun drummed down upon him.

Across the African savannah,[4] he saw a herd of elephants. The largest raised its trunk and trumpeted. The white elephant kneeled,
13 and Sato slid off its back. Then it became small and hard, an ivory figure again. Sato picked it up and put it inside his shirt, next to his skin.

Sato walked toward the herd. As he drew near, the elephants parted, forming a clear path to their leader. Sato trembled, but he had no choice. He had to follow the path.
14 How small and helpless he felt, and how ashamed and sorrowful!

When he looked up at last, he was staring at the giant elephant's tusks, as smooth and graceful as stony carvings. He looked into its small eyes. Then he reached inside his shirt for the ivory statue. He held it up for the elephant to see.

The elephant closed its eyes and nodded. Then it raised its front legs. Sato covered his face with his arms, terrified that the elephant would crush him.

4. A *savannah* is a large area of flat land near the tropics that has coarse grass and a few, scattered trees.

WORD BANK
trudged (TRUJD) *v.*: walked slowly and heavily

Guiding the Reading

Literal

Q: How is the temperature described?
A: There was wind in his face. First it was cold, and then it warmed up from the heat of the sun.

Q: Where did Sato see a herd of elephants?
A: He saw them in the African savannah.

Q: What did the elephants do as Sato approached?
A: They parted, forming a clear path to their leader.

Q: How did Sato feel as he walked along the path?
A: He felt small, helpless, ashamed, and sorrowful.

Q: What did Sato show the elephant?
A: He showed him his ivory elephant statue.

Q: What made Sato cover his face and arms?
A: He was terrified that the elephant would crush him.

Analytical

Q: What do you think is going on here? Is this real or fantasy? Why do you think so?
A: Students' answers will vary.

Q: Why do you think Sato showed his carving to the elephant?
A: He wanted the elephant to see that he now understood what the elephants went through before the ivory reached him; that although he was not very thoughtful before, things had changed.

Sato and the Elephants 105

Literary Components

15 Imagery: We see the dust clouds, hear and feel the earth tremble as the elephants' hooves pound it, and see Sato shuddering with fear.

16 Return from Fantasy: Sato wakes up in the real world after a long, fascinating dream.

17 Turning Point: Sato's dream has clarified the truth for him. He has decided to never again carve ivory.

Instead, it backed away to join the others, who now encircled Sato. Their huge bodies swayed from side to side, and their trumpeting echoed as they marched around him, slowly at first, then faster and faster. (15) Dust rose in clouds as their massive feet pounded the earth. Sato felt the ground shake, and he shuddered with fear.

(16) When the dust settled, Sato awoke in his room. He lay on his futon, gripping the ivory elephant in his hands, thinking one thought. (17) He could never become a master ivory carver.

The next day Sato bought new tools. Then he purchased an inexpensive piece of stone. Someday, perhaps, he would carve a masterwork from marble. But for now he had much to learn about the secrets of stone.

Sato never sold the ivory elephant. He kept it on the table by his futon so that he would see it each day when he awoke and each night before he went to sleep.

ABOUT THE AUTHOR

Juanita Havill grew up in Mount Carmel, Illinois. She has lived in France, Illinois, and Minnesota, and now lives in Arizona with her husband and children. As a girl, she would make up poems and recite them to her mother. Fearing she could not earn very much money writing poems, her mother encouraged her to be a teacher. She followed her mother's advice, but also continued to write. To date, she has published fifteen children's books, and teaches at the college level. For Ms. Havill, writing is a way of discovering what you really feel about the important things in life.

106 Unit 2

Guiding the Reading

Literal

Q: What did the elephants do around Sato?
A: They encircled him, swaying and marching, going faster and faster. They trumpeted loudly.

Q: How was Sato feeling at the time?
A: Sato shuddered with fear.

Q: What was one important thought Sato had after he awoke?
A: He could never become a master ivory carver.

Q: What new things did Sato purchase?
A: He bought new tools and an inexpensive piece of stone.

Q: Why wasn't Sato ready to carve marble at this point?
A: He still had a lot to learn about the secrets of stone.

Q: What did Sato do with the ivory elephant after he decided to carve stone instead?
A: He kept it on display on a table where he could see it.

Analytical

Q: What do you think was the meaning of the elephants' swaying and trumpeting?
A: Answers will vary. They have been showing their control and power over Sato, ganging up against him. On a deeper level, this behavior in his dream could indicate their anger at Sato's constant use of ivory.

Q: What can you learn from the words, "When the dust settled, Sato awoke in his room"?
A: One can deduce that the previous scenario was all a dream.

Q: At what point did you think that this might be a dream?
A: Answers will vary.

Q: Why do you think Sato displayed the elephant?
A: He put it in a place where he could see it often. It could remind him of any of the following: that he had made a mistake; that there was a reason he was using stone instead of ivory even though that was not his original plan; that it pays to do the right thing even if it is difficult; and that he would continue to make the right choices in the future.

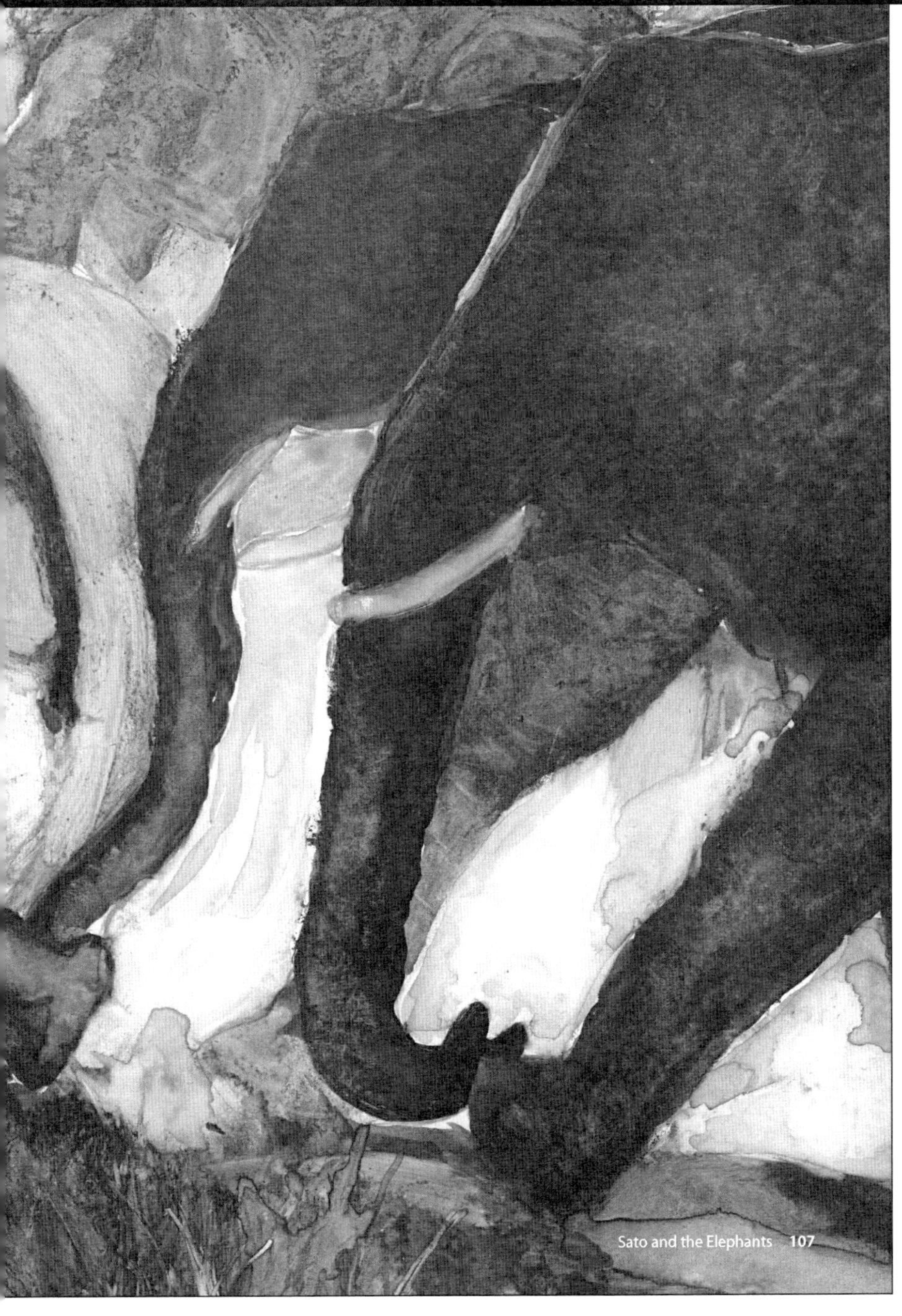
Sato and the Elephants 107

About *Purple Snake*

Poetry Opens Our Eyes

Like Sato, Don Luis is an artist, but where Sato carves ivory, Luis carves wood. The sentiment expressed by Don Luis in the first line, though, could have been spoken by Sato.

" 'It's in there, sleeping' "

The layman sees a material—ivory, wood, stone, or almost anything that can be fashioned into something else—and marvels as the artist makes something out of it. The artist, however, sees what he is going to make within the material before he even begins to work. The narrator is a layman like us:

"He knows I want to feel
the animal asleep in a piece of wood,
like he does"

Though he cannot create, he can admire the sixth sense of the artist who finds life:

"... asleep
in a piece of wood"

The poet is an artist, too, and finds life and meaning in words and images, in rhythms and rhymes, in subtleties and nuances of language. The poet *opens our eyes* in much the same way that a sculptor or a carver can.

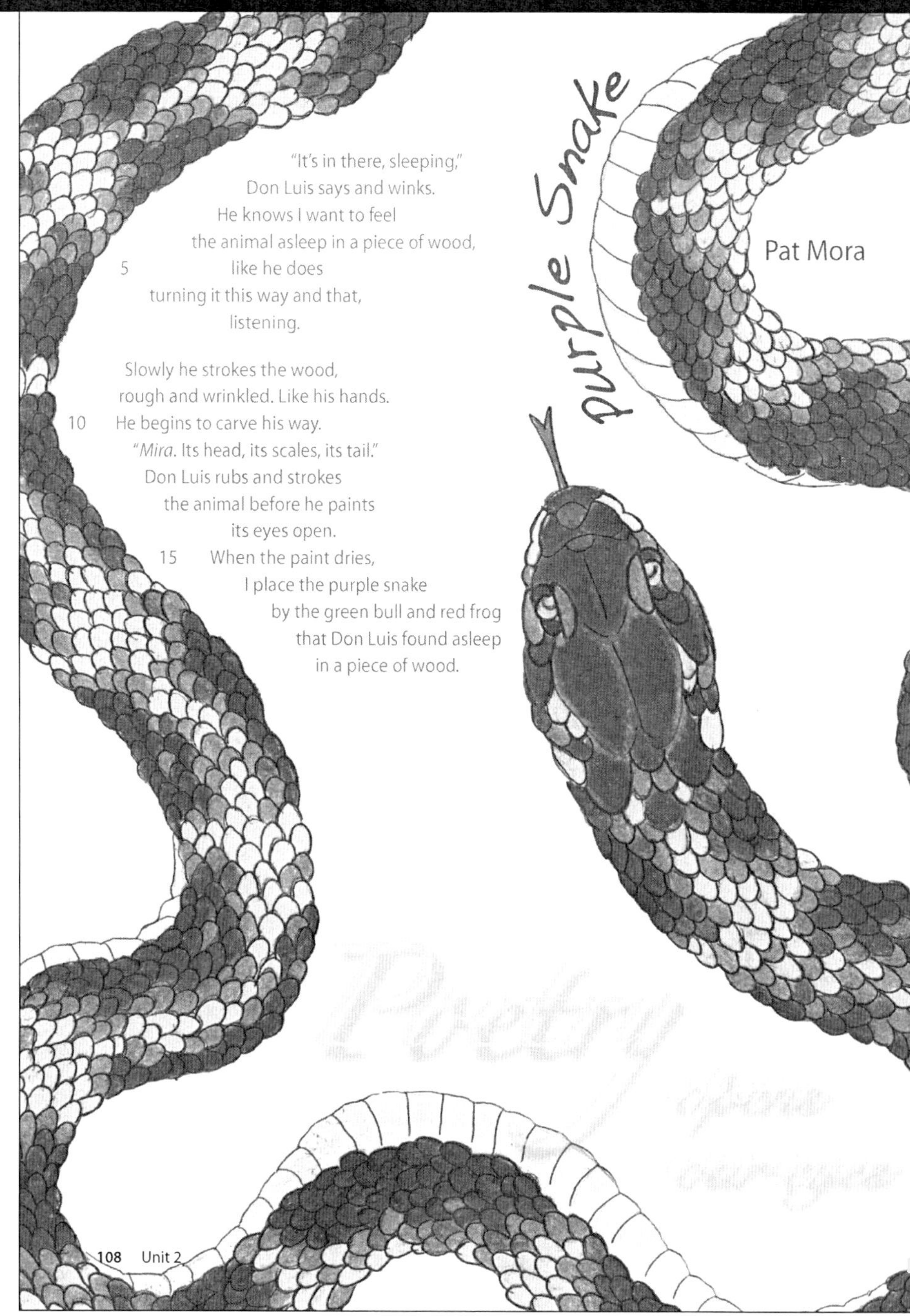

purple Snake

Pat Mora

"It's in there, sleeping,"
Don Luis says and winks.
He knows I want to feel
the animal asleep in a piece of wood,
like he does
turning it this way and that,
listening.

Slowly he strokes the wood,
rough and wrinkled. Like his hands.
He begins to carve his way.
"*Mira.* Its head, its scales, its tail."
Don Luis rubs and strokes
the animal before he paints
its eyes open.
When the paint dries,
I place the purple snake
by the green bull and red frog
that Don Luis found asleep
in a piece of wood.

108 Unit 2

Studying the Selection

FIRST IMPRESSIONS

Do you think most people would have reacted in the same way that Sato did? Why or why not?

QUICK REVIEW

1. What type of work did Sato do? Who did he learn the craft from?
2. What was Sato's dream at the beginning of the story?
3. What was Sato's reaction when Akira brought out a special piece of ivory for him?
4. What "flaw" did Sato find in his new piece of ivory?

FOCUS

5. Do you think Sato should have stopped carving ivory? Why or why not?
6. What was Sato's internal conflict?

CREATING AND WRITING

7. Why did Sato decide to carve stone instead of ivory? Write a paragraph that answers this question.
8. Write about someone who had a dream and then made a change to make the dream come true.
9. Sato carved ivory and then stone. He made a clay figure before he began the actual carving. Use the clay that your teacher gives out to create an animal model.

First Impressions

Answers will vary. The reactions of people would probably run the entire gamut from denying or not caring that elephants are killed for their ivory to being absolutely heartsick about the situation.

Quick Review

1. Sato was an ivory carver and he learned the craft from his father.
2. Sato dreamed of becoming a *master* ivory carver like his father.
3. He was thrilled! He gasped and said, "This is the piece that I have been waiting for!" He hoped to carve a masterwork from this piece of ivory.
4. He found something hard, corroded, and metallic. Sato realized that it was a bullet.

Focus

5. Once the students understand why Sato made his decision, most will think it was the right thing to do. Some may suggest that he could still use ivory so long as it came from elephants that died of natural causes.
6. Until he found the bullet in the ivory, Sato hadn't realized what the elephants suffered before the ivory reached his hands. The bullet made it all real. He felt guilty and couldn't justify working with ivory again. On the other hand, part of him wanted to do what he loved and was highly trained to do. Abandoning his lifelong dream of becoming a master ivory carver like his father was immensely difficult. He had worked so hard to reach this point in his career; it was surely difficult to forfeit all he had achieved.

Creating and Writing

7. Sato realized that he had made a mistake and had to find a substitute for ivory. After finding the bullet and having the disturbing dream, Sato decided that he could no longer use ivory. He felt sad and guilty about contributing to the killing of elephants.
8. Answers will vary.
9. Allow students to be creative and choose whatever animal they wish. You may extend the lesson by asking students to explain why they chose the animal they did.

Lesson in Literature

What Is External Conflict?

Neighbors

1. Marcy felt so bad that she avoided the old neighborhood.
2. Mrs. Watson's illness forced Marcy to return to her old neighborhood.
3. A neighbor is someone who lives near another person. A good neighbor is one who cares about and looks out for those who live near him or her.

Lesson in Literature . . .

WHAT IS EXTERNAL CONFLICT?

- **External** means outside. **Conflict** means struggle, or battle.
- An **external conflict** is a *struggle* with something *outside* of oneself.
- A story about external conflict tells of the struggle of a person or a group against something or someone.
- An external conflict is not always between right and wrong. It can be a struggle between two people or a person and a force of nature, like a blizzard or hurricane.

Marcy loved her house and her neighborhood. She loved her cozy bedroom and the big fireplace in the living room. She loved the backyard and the swing beneath the oak tree. She loved her friends, and she loved Mrs. Watson, the kind old lady who lived next door. So when her father told her they had to move to an apartment, Marcy was upset. She went upstairs and peered out her bedroom window at the lonely swing swaying in the wind. She went outside and sat quietly in the grass under the big oak tree. She even went over to Mrs. Watson's house.

"We have to move!" she complained.

"I know," Mrs. Watson said softly. "But you'll come and visit, won't you?"

"Of course, I will," Marcy said.

But after she moved away, Marcy missed her old house and neighborhood so much she didn't want to go back to visit. When she walked to the park, she took a different street. When she rode her bicycle, she went the other way. When she rode in the car with her parents, she asked, "Can't we go another way?"

"You can't just avoid the old house and the old neighborhood forever, Marcy," her father told her.

She didn't visit Mrs. Watson, either.

But a few weeks later, Marcy's mother brought her bad news. "Mrs. Watson's in the hospital," she explained. "She needs surgery, and she needs someone to collect her mail

Vocabulary

grim *adj.*: serious and unpleasant

shanties (SHAN teez) *n.*: cabins or houses that are roughly built and in a state of disrepair

NEIGHBORS

THINK ABOUT IT!

1. How did Marcy react to the move her family was forced to make?
2. What event caused Marcy to change her behavior?
3. What would you say is the difference between "a neighbor" and "a good neighbor"?

- **Unit Theme:** *Clarity*
- **Target Skill:** *Recognizing external conflict*
- **Genre:** *Realistic Fiction*

and water her plants while she's gone. I promised her you'd go over there tomorrow."

"I don't want to go," Marcy said.

Her mother's eyes softened. "I know you miss the old house," she said, "but Mrs. Watson needs your help."

The next morning a thick blanket of snow covered the ground. School was closed. Snowplows moved slowly up and down the streets. It took Marcy's father two hours to shovel out the driveway. Marcy's mother told her, "The snow's too deep. Mrs. Watson will understand if you don't go today."

"No," Marcy said. "I'll go."

"Here's the key," Marcy's mother said, smiling gently.

Bundled up, Marcy walked all the way from the apartment to her old street, her footprints the only trail in the deep snow. She almost turned back because of the cold, but when she made it to her old street, the houses looked so beautiful under the covering of fresh snow that she was suddenly glad she decided to help Mrs. Watson.

After unlocking the front door, she emptied the mailbox and watered the flowers and plants that seemed to be everywhere. She even shoveled the walkway up to Mrs. Watson's front door. Before she left, she discovered a handwritten note pinned to the back door. "Thank you, Marcy. You're such a good neighbor."

After that, Marcy went back every day while Mrs. Watson was in the hospital, because she finally realized what it means to be someone's neighbor.

Getting Started

Use the following questions as a springboard for a discussion regarding road trips.

- Have you ever gone on a road trip with family or friends? Where have you been?
- What was the trip like? Was it a difficult or long ride? Were you full of excitement and anticipation?
- Did you use maps to guide you?
- What is your reaction when you see one of your parents taking out a map to plan a trip? Are you excited? Are you concerned? Are you bored? Why do you have the reaction you have?
- Have you traveled on a certain road a number of times?
- What are some of the different type of roads?
- Does the fact that a road is small mean that it does not lead to anywhere important?

Into . . . Amelia's Road

Ask your students if some of them remember moving to a new town and whether they felt uncomfortable in their new surroundings. You can easily find other life situations that your students can relate to, such as being new to a summer camp, or attending a relative's wedding where one does not know any of the guests. Other more common scenarios that are socially awkward can be discussed.

- A group of students decides to play a new game and you don't know the rules.
- You were absent for three days and classmates are talking about something that happened while you were gone.
- Cliques of students are talking amongst themselves about an experience that does not relate to you.
- You do something, like wear a particular type of clothing, to be noticed and accepted.

Routine and passage of time foster acceptance and belonging. Amelia is never in any one place long enough to lay down roots or to be accepted as part of the group. Whenever her family travels, she finds herself in a struggle against time, in a struggle to overcome her role as an outsider, in a struggle to break into the group.

Make the point clear that one is entitled to be an individual, but human nature dictates that a person be an accepted member of society. Most people yearn for a sense of belonging and if it is lacking, they will go to great lengths to achieve it.

Eyes On External Conflict

Review the concept of conflict with your students and once again make the distinction between internal and external conflicts. Clarify that an external conflict is not necessarily a physical fight but can be a clash of ideas or forces.

Ask students for suggestions of external conflicts. If your students are up to the task, share with them ways of categorizing these conflicts, as follows:

man vs. man: a conflict between two people—physical, philosophical, and more

man vs. nature: a person struggling to conquer or to survive a force of nature—a pioneer carving a farm out of the wilderness (conquer), or an explorer lost in the desert (survive)

man vs. animal: taming a wild horse, facing a wild animal on a camping trip, etc.

There are many other external conflicts; the group mentioned above are within the scope of a fourth grade curriculum. Help your class suggest others.

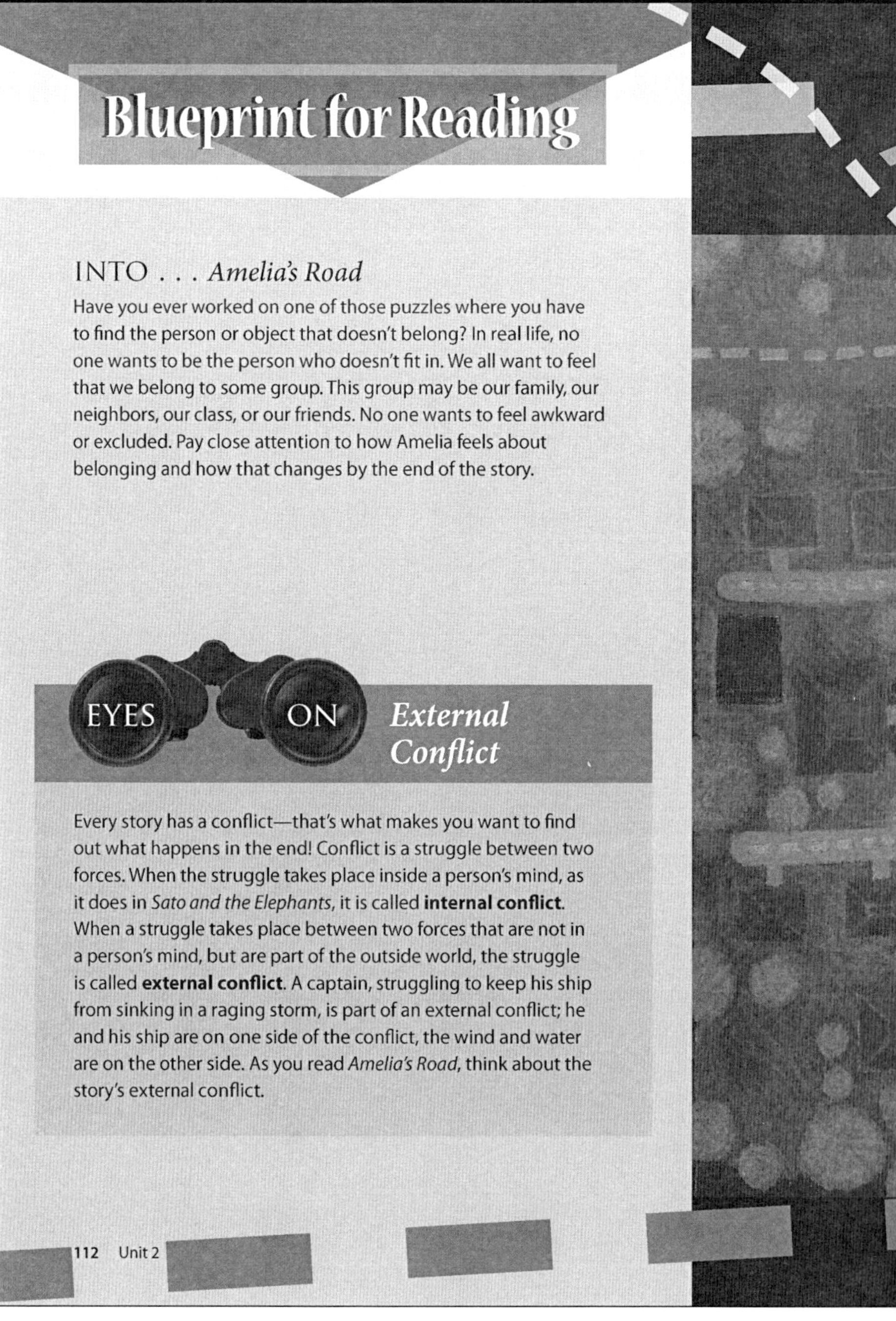
Blueprint for Reading

INTO . . . *Amelia's Road*

Have you ever worked on one of those puzzles where you have to find the person or object that doesn't belong? In real life, no one wants to be the person who doesn't fit in. We all want to feel that we belong to some group. This group may be our family, our neighbors, our class, or our friends. No one wants to feel awkward or excluded. Pay close attention to how Amelia feels about belonging and how that changes by the end of the story.

EYES ON *External Conflict*

Every story has a conflict—that's what makes you want to find out what happens in the end! Conflict is a struggle between two forces. When the struggle takes place inside a person's mind, as it does in *Sato and the Elephants*, it is called **internal conflict.** When a struggle takes place between two forces that are not in a person's mind, but are part of the outside world, the struggle is called **external conflict.** A captain, struggling to keep his ship from sinking in a raging storm, is part of an external conflict; he and his ship are on one side of the conflict, the wind and water are on the other side. As you read *Amelia's Road,* think about the story's external conflict.

112 Unit 2

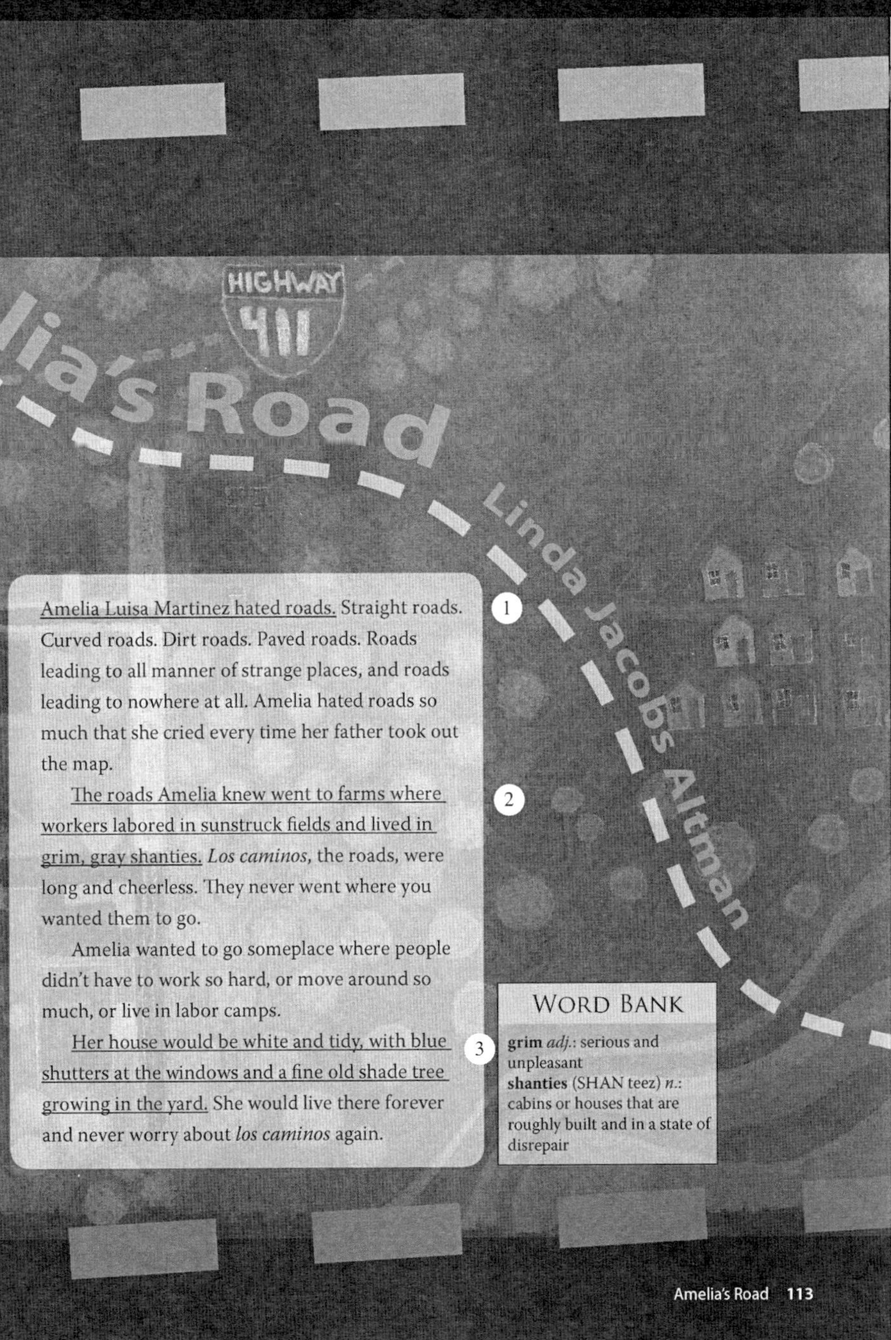

HIGHWAY 411

Amelia's Road

Linda Jacobs Altman

1 Amelia Luisa Martinez hated roads. Straight roads. Curved roads. Dirt roads. Paved roads. Roads leading to all manner of strange places, and roads leading to nowhere at all. Amelia hated roads so much that she cried every time her father took out the map.

2 The roads Amelia knew went to farms where workers labored in sunstruck fields and lived in grim, gray shanties. *Los caminos*, the roads, were long and cheerless. They never went where you wanted them to go.

Amelia wanted to go someplace where people didn't have to work so hard, or move around so much, or live in labor camps.

3 Her house would be white and tidy, with blue shutters at the windows and a fine old shade tree growing in the yard. She would live there forever and never worry about *los caminos* again.

WORD BANK

grim *adj.*: serious and unpleasant

shanties (SHAN teez) *n.*: cabins or houses that are roughly built and in a state of disrepair

Amelia's Road 113

Selection Summary

Amelia is a little girl who hates roads. Roads take her and her migrant farmer parents from farm to farm to do hard work. There is no place called home. More than anything else in the world, Amelia yearns for a place she can call home, a place she can come back to, a place where she belongs.

As the story opens, Amelia's family has arrived at a farm where they will pick apples for several weeks. Amelia is placed in Mrs. Ramos' class at the Fillmore Elementary School. Mrs. Ramos learns Amelia's name and makes sure the entire class does, too. Happy with her new teacher and classmates, Amelia starts for home when she comes across a narrow road. Following it, she discovers a sturdy old tree whose look of permanence fills her with joy. From then on, Amelia visits the tree every day after school.

The cycle of Amelia's life continues, and Amelia knows she will soon have to move on. Before she does, she fills an old metal box with memorabilia and buries it near the tree. Feeling that she has finally found a place where she belongs, she promises herself that she will one day return to the road and to the tree.

Literary Components

1 Exposition: Why would a girl hate roads? The author arouses our curiosity with this odd statement. [Roads are usually representative of freedom, exploration, and advancement; here, they represent almost the opposite.]

2 Setting; Theme: The setting is rural; the feeling is reflected in the words "grim, gray." The story's theme is just beginning to unfold, but is obviously going to be related to the hard life of the migrant worker.

3 Contrast; Characterization: Amelia's dream house is in stark contrast to the "grim, gray shanties" of her real life. We see that Amelia has a dream to work towards.

Guiding the Reading

Literal

Q: What did Amelia hate?

A: Amelia hated roads.

Q: Did it matter what kind of roads they were?

A: No, she hated all roads.

Q: What did Amelia do when her father took out the map?

A: Amelia cried.

Q: What were some of the things that Amelia didn't like about her life?

A: She hated working so hard, living in labor camps, and moving around so much.

Q: How did Amelia imagine her dream house looked?

A: She imagined a place where she could live forever. It would be white and tidy, with blue shutters at the windows and a shade tree in the yard.

Analytical

Q: Why did Amelia cry when her father took out the map?

A: She knew it would only lead to another move and to being uprooted yet again.

Q: What do you think Amelia meant when she said, "They never went where you wanted them to go"?

A: Amelia wished they led to a real home like other children had.

Literary Components

4 Characterization; Theme: In addition to the hard work and poverty, the sense of belonging nowhere accompanies the workers wherever they go.

It was almost dark when their rusty old car pulled to a stop in front of cabin number twelve at the labor camp.

"Is this the same cabin we had last year?" Amelia asked, but nobody remembered. It didn't seem to matter to the rest of the family.

It mattered a lot to Amelia. From one year to the next, there was nothing to show Amelia had lived here, gone to school in this town,
4 and worked in these fields. Amelia wanted to settle down, to belong.

114 Unit 2

Guiding the Reading

Literal

Q: What time of day was it when Amelia's family pulled up to the cabin?

A: It was dusk.

Q: What did Amelia ask that didn't seem to matter to her family?

A: "Is this the same cabin we had last year?"

Q: Why did it matter to Amelia if it was the same cabin as the previous year?

A: She wanted to feel settled down and belong somewhere.

Literary Components

5 Characterization: Unlike Amelia, Mr. Martinez does not have a dream. He has accepted this way of life.

6 Rising Action: Something has changed for Amelia. She has been noticed and made to feel she belongs.

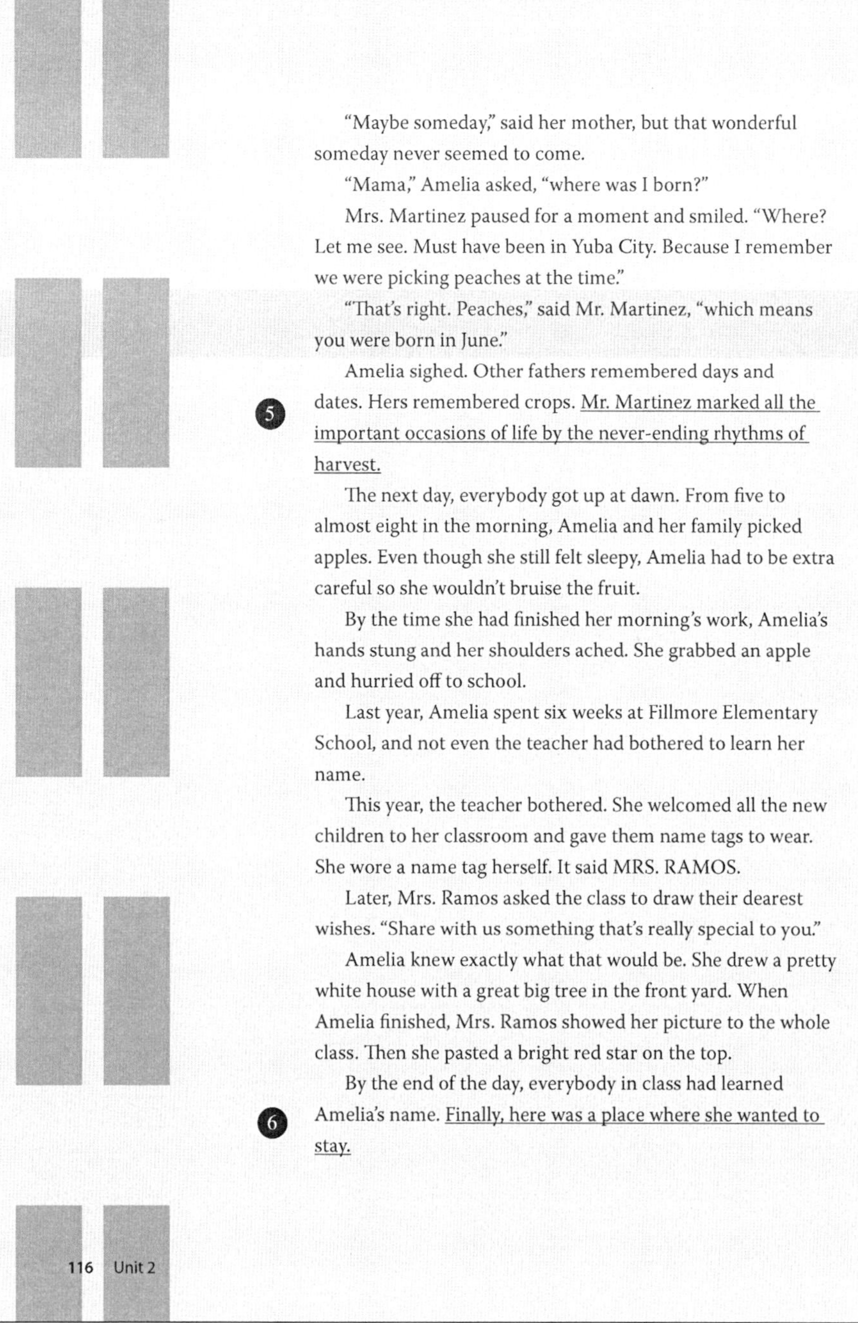

"Maybe someday," said her mother, but that wonderful someday never seemed to come.

"Mama," Amelia asked, "where was I born?"

Mrs. Martinez paused for a moment and smiled. "Where? Let me see. Must have been in Yuba City. Because I remember we were picking peaches at the time."

"That's right. Peaches," said Mr. Martinez, "which means you were born in June."

Amelia sighed. Other fathers remembered days and dates. Hers remembered crops. 5 Mr. Martinez marked all the important occasions of life by the never-ending rhythms of harvest.

The next day, everybody got up at dawn. From five to almost eight in the morning, Amelia and her family picked apples. Even though she still felt sleepy, Amelia had to be extra careful so she wouldn't bruise the fruit.

By the time she had finished her morning's work, Amelia's hands stung and her shoulders ached. She grabbed an apple and hurried off to school.

Last year, Amelia spent six weeks at Fillmore Elementary School, and not even the teacher had bothered to learn her name.

This year, the teacher bothered. She welcomed all the new children to her classroom and gave them name tags to wear. She wore a name tag herself. It said MRS. RAMOS.

Later, Mrs. Ramos asked the class to draw their dearest wishes. "Share with us something that's really special to you."

Amelia knew exactly what that would be. She drew a pretty white house with a great big tree in the front yard. When Amelia finished, Mrs. Ramos showed her picture to the whole class. Then she pasted a bright red star on the top.

By the end of the day, everybody in class had learned 6 Amelia's name. Finally, here was a place where she wanted to stay.

116 Unit 2

Guiding the Reading

Literal

Q: What was Mama referring to when she said, "Maybe someday"?
A: Mama was saying that maybe one day the family could live somewhere permanently.

Q: Where was Amelia born?
A: She was born in Yuba City.

Q: How did her parents remind themselves when and where Amelia was born?
A: They tried to remember what crop they were picking at the time of her birth.

Q: How did Mr. Martinez mark and remember important dates?
A: He connected every important event with the particular crop he was harvesting at the time.

Q: What hours did Amelia's family work?
A: They worked from five (dawn) until eight in the morning.

Q: What were the Martinez family picking at the time of the story?
A: They were picking apples.

Q: Why did Amelia have to be careful even though she was sleepy?
A: She had to be careful not to bruise the fruit.

Q: What school did Amelia attend?
A: She went to Fillmore Elementary School.

Q: What was the new teacher's name?
A: Her name was Mrs. Ramos.

Q: What was different about this new teacher?
A: She made an effort to learn the students' names as well as other things about them.

Q: When Mrs. Ramos asked the children to draw something special, what did Amelia include in her picture?
A: She drew a pretty, white house with a great big tree.

Q: What did Mrs. Ramos do with Amelia's picture?
A: She showed it to the whole class and put a red star at the top.

Analytical

Q: How did Amelia feel about her family using crops as a method of keeping track of dates?
A: She sighed and seemed frustrated. Amelia wished her father would be like other fathers who remembered important dates rather than fruits and vegetables.

Q: Why do you think Amelia was tired?
A: She was up at dawn and worked very hard, especially for a girl her age.

Q: Why did everyone know Amelia's name at the end of the day?
A: Mrs. Ramos had given everyone name tags. In addition, she had shown Amelia's picture to everyone in the class.

Q: Why did Amelia want to stay here?
A: The day in the classroom made her feel comfortable and welcome.

Amelia's Road 117

Literary Components

7 Simile: Amelia feels as bright as the sky.

8 Theme; Visual Image; Symbol: Amelia finds a tree that represents permanence to her—the thing in life she wants most.

9 Theme: The yearning to belong somewhere is a universal one.

10 Conflict: Amelia's desire to belong is thwarted by the family's need to move.

11 Possible Resolution: The reader is told the box is the answer and wonders how a box can solve the problem.

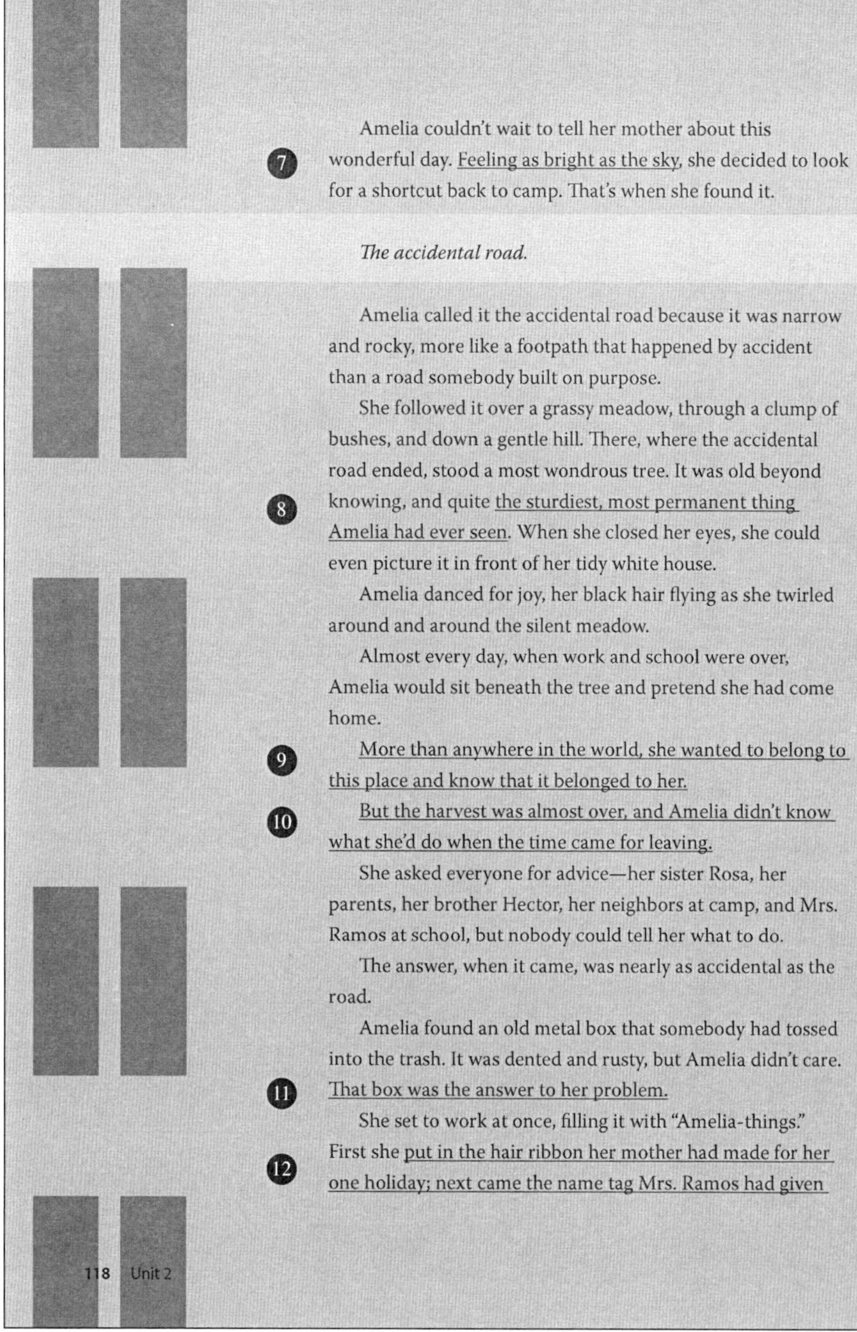

Amelia couldn't wait to tell her mother about this
7 wonderful day. Feeling as bright as the sky, she decided to look
for a shortcut back to camp. That's when she found it.

The accidental road.

Amelia called it the accidental road because it was narrow and rocky, more like a footpath that happened by accident than a road somebody built on purpose.

She followed it over a grassy meadow, through a clump of bushes, and down a gentle hill. There, where the accidental road ended, stood a most wondrous tree. It was old beyond
8 knowing, and quite the sturdiest, most permanent thing
Amelia had ever seen. When she closed her eyes, she could even picture it in front of her tidy white house.

Amelia danced for joy, her black hair flying as she twirled around and around the silent meadow.

Almost every day, when work and school were over, Amelia would sit beneath the tree and pretend she had come home.

9 More than anywhere in the world, she wanted to belong to this place and know that it belonged to her.

10 But the harvest was almost over, and Amelia didn't know what she'd do when the time came for leaving.

She asked everyone for advice—her sister Rosa, her parents, her brother Hector, her neighbors at camp, and Mrs. Ramos at school, but nobody could tell her what to do.

The answer, when it came, was nearly as accidental as the road.

Amelia found an old metal box that somebody had tossed into the trash. It was dented and rusty, but Amelia didn't care.
11 That box was the answer to her problem.

She set to work at once, filling it with "Amelia-things."
12 First she put in the hair ribbon her mother had made for her
one holiday; next came the name tag Mrs. Ramos had given

118 Unit 2

Guiding the Reading

Literal

Q: What did Amelia want to do as soon as she got home?
A: She wanted to tell her mother about her wonderful day.

Q: How did Amelia find the "accidental road"?
A: She decided to take a shortcut.

Q: Why did she call it *accidental*?
A: She called it accidental because it was a narrow and rocky footpath that looked like it had accidentally become a road.

Q: What did Amelia find at the end of the accidental road?
A: She found an old, sturdy, and wonderful tree.

Q: When Amelia closed her eyes, what was she able to imagine?
A: She was able to imagine her dream house, tidy and white.

Q: What did Amelia do almost every day after school and work were over?
A: She would sit under the tree and pretend that she had really come home.

Q: What did Amelia want more than anything in the world?
A: She wanted to belong to this place and know that it belonged to her.

Q: What problem did Amelia face with the thing she wanted most?
A: The harvest was almost over and her family would probably be moving on to another location.

Q: What were the names of Amelia's siblings?
A: Her sister's name was Rosa and her brother's name was Hector.

Q: Whom did Amelia go to for advice?
A: She went to just about everyone!

Q: Did the advice help her?
A: No, nobody was able to tell her what to do.

Q: How were the answer and the road similar?
A: She happened upon both of them accidentally.

Q: What did Amelia find in the garbage?
A: She found an old metal box that was dented and rusty.

Analytical

Q: Why did the tree make such a strong impression on Amelia?
A: It represented something strong and permanent, something she had often dreamed of.

Q: Why did Amelia dance for joy?
A: The strength, the permanence, and the age of the tree were proof to Amelia that what she dreamed of was within her reach. She could see and touch and even, in a way, own something big and strong and permanent.

Q: What made Amelia feel like this was 'her' road?
A: While it appeared that others had made the path in the past, no one seemed to be using it now. It was one of the only places she could call her own.

Amelia's Road 119

Literary Components

⓬ **Theme:** If we cannot say we belong in any one place, we can take *parts* of places or events and make *them* belong to *us*. We can create places in our own hearts, and we are helped by mementos of good times.

⓭ **Resolution:** Amelia feels she belongs to this place and, just as someone will always return home, she feels she will return to her tree.

her; then a photograph of her whole family taken at her last birthday; and after that the picture she'd drawn in class with the bright red star on it.

Finally, she took out a sheet of paper and drew a map of the accidental road, from the highway to the very old tree. In her best lettering, she wrote *Amelia Road* on the path. Then she folded the map and put it into her box.

When all the apples were finally picked, Amelia's family and the other workers had to get ready to move again. Amelia made one more trip down the accidental road, this time with her treasure box.

She dug a hole near the old tree, and gently placed the box inside and covered it over with dirt. Then she set a rock on top, so nobody would notice the freshly turned ground.

When Amelia finished, she took a step back and looked at
⓭ the tree. Finally, here was a place where she belonged, a place where she could come back to.

"I'll be back," she whispered, and then she turned away.

Amelia skipped through the meadow, laughed at the sky, even turned cartwheels right in the middle of the accidental road.

When she got back to the camp, the rest of the family had already started packing the car. Amelia watched them for a moment, then took a deep breath and joined in to help.

For the first time in her life, she didn't cry when her father took out the road map.

ABOUT THE AUTHOR

Linda Jacobs Altman loves to write. A list of her publications is more than five pages long! Ms. Altman has written on a variety of subjects, including the Holocaust, Alzheimer's disease, and the California Gold Rush. She also writes under a variety of names. Linda Jacobs, Linda Jacobs Altman, and Claire Blackburn are all one and the same person! When an author writes under a name that is not his or her real name, the author is using a *pseudonym*, sometimes called "a pen name."

120 Unit 2

Guiding the Reading

Literal

Q: What did Amelia use the metal box for?

A: She filled it with things that were meaningful to her, including: a hair ribbon her mother had made for her, the name tag Mrs. Ramos had given her, a family picture, and the drawing that had received a red star.

Q: What was the last thing that Amelia put in her treasure box?

A: She put in a map of the accidental road with the words "Amelia Road" on it.

Q: When was Amelia's family ready to move again?

A: They were ready when all the apples were picked.

Q: What did Amelia do with the treasure box once she had filled it?

A: She buried it near the old tree and put a rock on top.

Q: Whom was Amelia talking to when she said, "I'll be back"?

A: She was talking to herself and to the place.

Q: What did Amelia do when she saw her family packing up the car?

A: She watched them for a moment, then took a deep breath and joined in to help.

Q: What did Amelia *not* do for the first time in her life?

A: She didn't cry when her father took out the map.

Analytical

Q: Why did Amelia put the rock on top of the dirt?

A: She did it so that people would not notice the fresh dirt and dig up the treasures. She wanted them to stay there until the next time she came back.

Q: Why do you think Amelia buried the box instead of taking it with her?

A: By burying the box she established a connection with the place. It made her feel like she belonged and that she would be back.

Q: Why do you think Amelia was skipping and laughing even though her family was moving?

A: Amelia was still basking in the glow of what she had done; she had established a permanent address. Now, leaving town meant the same thing it meant to ordinary people: a brief—or even lengthy—absence from one's home. She had changed, in her mind, from an itinerant worker with no home, to a person with a home who travels a lot.

Q: Do you think that Amelia's family noticed and wondered about her new attitude towards moving?

A: Answers will vary.

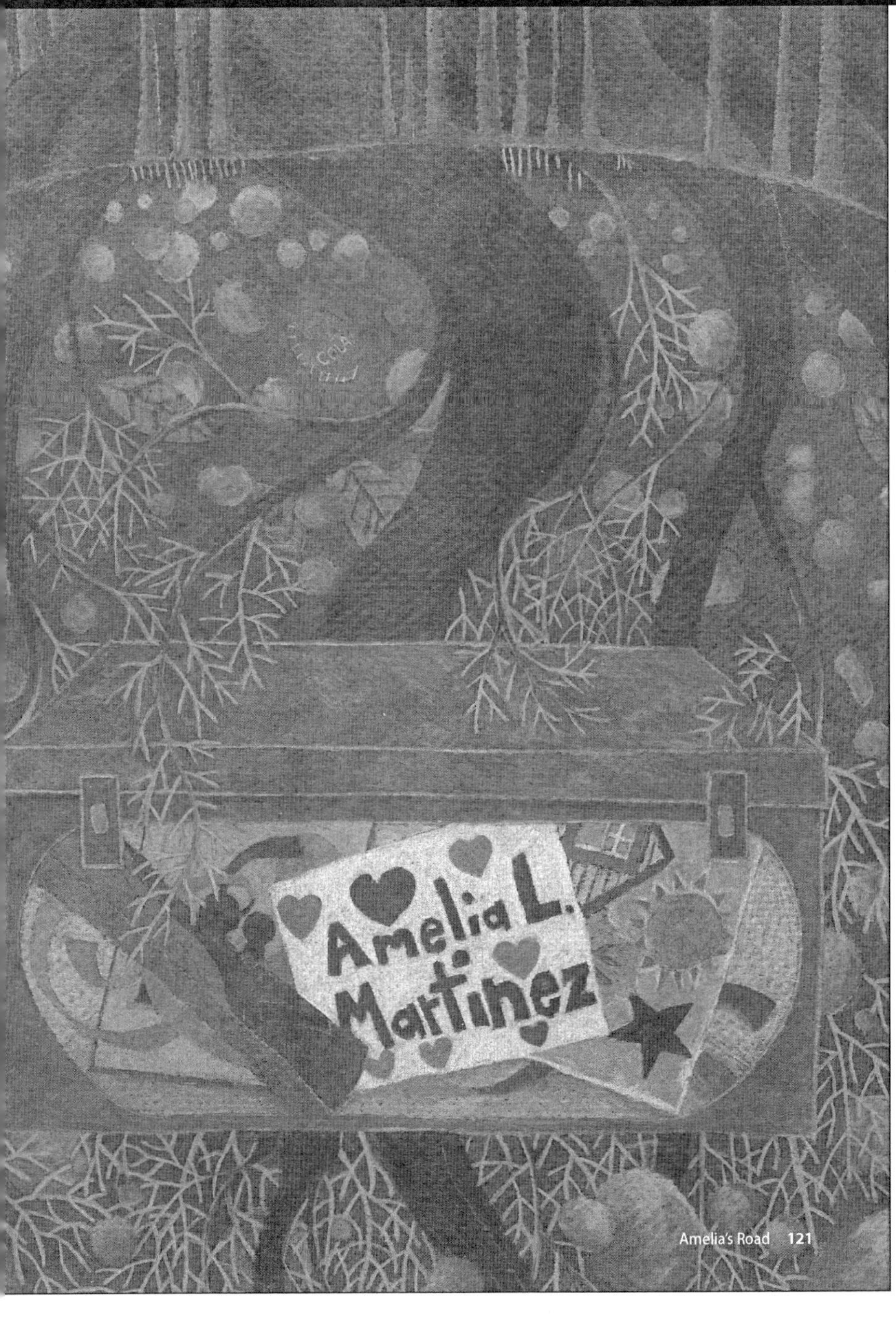
Amelia L. Martinez
Amelia's Road 121

About Since Hanna Moved Away

Poetry Is About Feelings

This poem is a reflection of how we feel when something sad, but not tragic, happens to us. We are a mixture of unhappiness, frustration, anger, and humor. The humor comes when we laugh at ourselves for being so unhappy, frustrated, and angry while still unable to shake those feelings. It is something like the sun coming out before the storm is over.

"Chocolate ice cream tastes like prunes . . ."

"Flowers smell like halibut . . ."

As most people who can joke in the midst of their unhappiness will tell you, their unhappiness is very real; the joking is a way of easing the pain. The language in this poem does a marvelous job of presenting this very human emotional mix. In the story *Amelia's Road,* Amelia deals with her unhappiness—not with humor—but with a constructive plan. The common bond between the story and the poem is the way people can be "in" their feelings and "outside" of them at the same time. Even as we experience pain or suffering, something inside of us is at work, waiting for the chance to jump out and bring us back to a happier state.

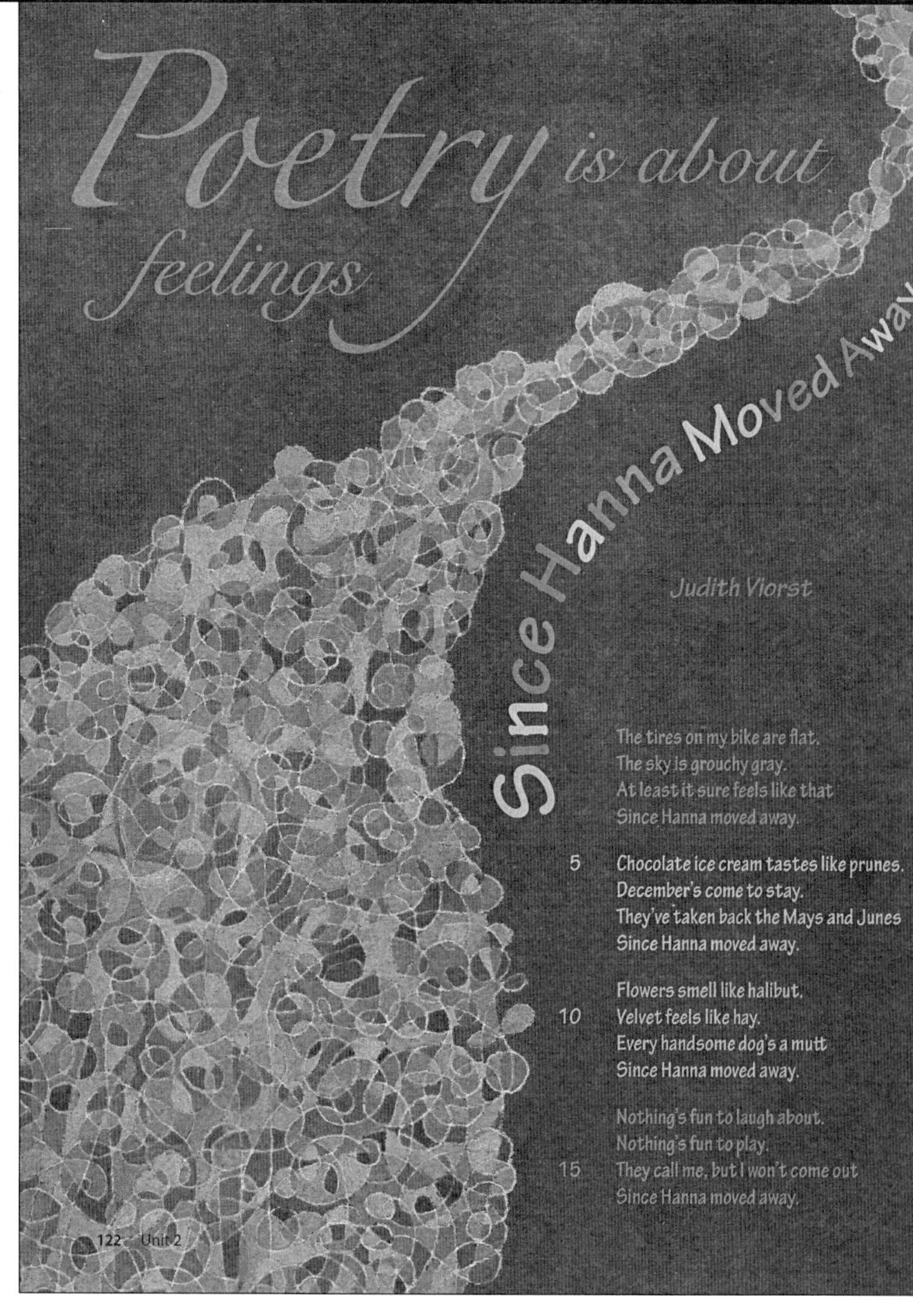

Poetry is about feelings

Since Hanna Moved Away

Judith Viorst

The tires on my bike are flat.
The sky is grouchy gray.
At least it sure feels like that
Since Hanna moved away.

Chocolate ice cream tastes like prunes.
December's come to stay.
They've taken back the Mays and Junes
Since Hanna moved away.

Flowers smell like halibut.
Velvet feels like hay.
Every handsome dog's a mutt
Since Hanna moved away.

Nothing's fun to laugh about.
Nothing's fun to play.
They call me, but I won't come out
Since Hanna moved away.

122 Unit 2

Studying the Selection

FIRST IMPRESSIONS

Do you think Amelia's accidental road and metal box will help her adjust to the next move?

QUICK REVIEW

1. Why did Amelia hate roads and maps?
2. What work did Amelia's family do that required they move from place to place?
3. How did Amelia's family mark and remember important dates?
4. What did Amelia do that made her feel as though she truly belonged in this place?

FOCUS

5. More than anything, Amelia wanted to feel like she belonged. Why is that feeling so important?
6. Amelia feels that Mrs. Ramos is different from other teachers she has had. What might have caused difficulties with other teachers?

CREATING AND WRITING

7. Where do you feel a real sense of belonging? Write a few paragraphs that answer this question.
8. Write about someone who, purely by chance, finds something that changes his or her life. Your story may be either true or fictional.
9. Amelia filled a box with "Amelia-things." Find a container that you like and fill it with items that are meaningful to *you*. You may create replicas of precious objects with craft materials, or make photocopies of documents or drawings instead of using the originals. Add a little note to each item explaining why you chose to include it.

Amelia's Road 123

First Impressions

Answers will vary. Certainly the strong positive memory will be encouraging. Knowing that somewhere a part of her has a real, permanent home will make her feel that she *can* belong. While Mrs. Ramos and all the children may not be the same should she return sometime in the future, the memory of belonging will be comforting and reassuring.

Quick Review

1. Roads and maps represented being uprooted to Amelia. They also represented poverty and hard labor.
2. They were migrant farmworkers, whose job it was to pick whatever fruits and vegetables were ready to be harvested.
3. The family used harvest seasons to gauge time and mark occasions.
4. Amelia filled a box with mementos and buried it at the end of her accidental road.

Focus

5. Every person has the need to feel loved and to have a sense of belonging. While Amelia had a loving family, she still yearned for a permanent residence as well as for friends and neighbors. She didn't want to always be the new one in town. It is comforting to come home to the same place every day and to be greeted along the way by familiar people.
6. Previous teachers might not have understood Amelia and her life experience. Teachers may have been critical of her academic performance or displeased by her lack of energy (the result of her early morning work in the fields). Your students may come up with various suggestions such as: Amelia, looking for guidance, may have asked a classmate for help and been accused of talking out of turn; Amelia's shyness may have looked like snobbishness; her sadness may have appeared to be disdain for the teacher, and so on.

Creating and Writing

7. Answers will vary.
8. Answers will vary.
9. Projects will vary. Encourage your students to really think about what they want to include in their 'things' box. Provide craft materials if needed. Allow students to share the contents of their boxes if they feel comfortable doing so.

Background Bytes

The labor of migrant farmworkers is essential for bringing crops to market in almost every state of the nation. In fact, eighty-five percent of the fruits and vegetables that we eat in the United States are handpicked and/or grown or developed with hand care.

Without farmworkers, the U.S. multi-billion dollar fruit and vegetable industry could not function. It is a fact that agriculture is absolutely reliant upon an "influx of seasonal labor at critical periods in crop development."

Such seasonal labor is provided nearly exclusively by migrant, seasonal farmworker families. Their hand labor is essential for producing blemish-free fruits and vegetables that are found in stores.

The work of dealing with agricultural products is fraught with dangers, not the least of which is the constant exposure to pesticides, herbicides, and fertilizers—all of which are toxic. Laborers work for hours in the sun; working with farm machinery may also be hazardous.

Most of these pickers and plowers and planters earn less than $7,500 a year. The vast majority of migrant farmworkers are American citizens—or are working here with permission to do so from the government. Most have stable and permanent residences in the southern United States, especially California, Texas, and Florida.

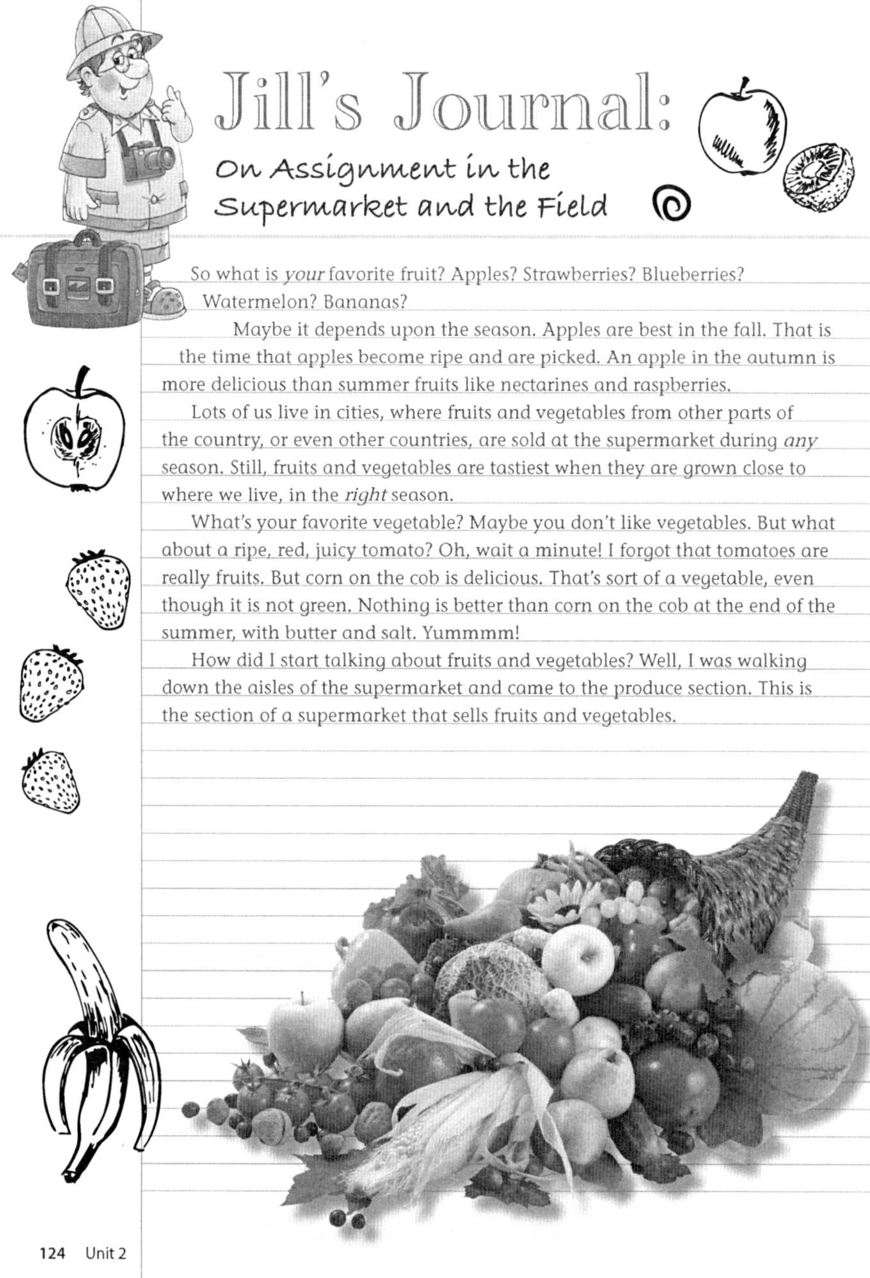

Jill's Journal:

On Assignment in the Supermarket and the Field

So what is *your* favorite fruit? Apples? Strawberries? Blueberries? Watermelon? Bananas?

Maybe it depends upon the season. Apples are best in the fall. That is the time that apples become ripe and are picked. An apple in the autumn is more delicious than summer fruits like nectarines and raspberries.

Lots of us live in cities, where fruits and vegetables from other parts of the country, or even other countries, are sold at the supermarket during *any* season. Still, fruits and vegetables are tastiest when they are grown close to where we live, in the *right* season.

What's your favorite vegetable? Maybe you don't like vegetables. But what about a ripe, red, juicy tomato? Oh, wait a minute! I forgot that tomatoes are really fruits. But corn on the cob is delicious. That's sort of a vegetable, even though it is not green. Nothing is better than corn on the cob at the end of the summer, with butter and salt. Yummmm!

How did I start talking about fruits and vegetables? Well, I was walking down the aisles of the supermarket and came to the produce section. This is the section of a supermarket that sells fruits and vegetables.

124 Unit 2

Okay. Where do these crops come from? We know that farmers and their families are supposed to plant the crops and harvest them. When we are little kids, lots of us see books about farms—at least farms the way they used to be a long time ago.

I decided then and there I wanted to go someplace where crops are being picked. I wanted to see who does it and what it is like.

Well, here I am in California and I am standing right now in a field where everyone is picking, picking, picking. It is only 4:00 A.M. I am yawning. How can anyone work at 4:00 A.M.? But even young people are out here working until they have to go to school.

The people who do it are trying to get ahead in life. So they work hard to save money for a house and maybe, one day, a farm of their own. The crops can't wait for the people. They have to be picked at the right time, no matter what the weather is. That is another reason why the people have to work such long hours. When the kids come home from school, they have to start working all over again. They give almost all the money they earn to their parents.

This is hard work! I have to keep stooping and my back hurts. All around me, people have to climb to get high up, then they climb down, then they climb up. And they carry such heavy loads. A ten-year-old girl named Iselda tells me I must wear gloves. Otherwise I could get sick, because the plants are treated with poisons to kill insects. She says she is allergic to the chemicals that are sprayed on tobacco and strawberries. Touching the leaves gives her a bad reaction.

"Actually," she says, "this is not a bad place. There are clean bathrooms and places to wash our hands. We don't have to go down to a brook to wash and to try to clean our clothes. There is pollution from the plants and soil in the water, and my Mama says we can't go near the water."

"Iselda, is there anything good about being a farmworker who moves from place to place?" Iselda thinks for a moment. "Well, I do like meeting lots of different people. I like seeing different places. And, I know one thing about myself: I can stick to a job and work hard. That makes me pretty grown up, doesn't it?" She leans her head close to me. "I will tell you a secret." She smiles a little smile. "I have always dreamed of becoming a teacher. Do you think I could?"

Power Skill:

What Is Fiction? What Is Nonfiction?

Review the definitions of fiction and nonfiction. Remind students that it is not always immediately clear what is fact and what is fiction. Fiction is made up, but is often based on the author's experiences, and must make sense to readers. Nonfiction is presumably based on the facts, but sometimes we don't really know what happened in a given incident. Also, different individuals interpret events differently. Even with nonfiction, human bias invariably creates some distortion.

Briefly review the selections in Unit One. Which were fiction? Which, nonfiction? How can we tell? What about the semi-autobiographical piece by Laura Ingalls Wilder, *Two Big Bears*? Ask your students why some parts of the story might have been fictionalized. Which parts? What might be left out to make a smoother, more interesting story?

Exercise

Provide students with oak tag and lots of cut-out magazine and newspaper pictures and words from which to choose for their farmworker collages. You will need many pictures of fruits and vegetables, supermarkets, fruit markets, people eating vegetables, and so forth. Include classrooms, books, words, or letters (such as parts of the alphabet), and any other drawings or photos suggestive of school and education. Also include pictures of farm machinery, people picking crops, and whatever else feature elements of the farm labor experience. Maps, cars, road routes, gas stations, and any other components of their lives as travelers will also be useful.

POWER SKILL:

What Is Fiction? What Is Nonfiction?

Fiction and nonfiction are words you will hear a lot in your literature or English classes. Maybe you know what these words mean already. But here goes:

Fiction	Fiction is a story or book in which the plot and the characters are created by the author. Short stories, novels, plays, and even some poetry are fiction. Fiction is not true, but it *seems* true because it makes sense. It may not have *actually* happened, but it *could* have happened.
Nonfiction	Nonfiction is an essay, an article, or a book in which the people and events that are described are actually real. The people are alive or have lived in the past. The events the author writes about have actually occurred. Nonfiction includes biographies, autobiographies, stories about historical events, newspaper articles, science and mathematics literature, and what we just call "true stories."

Amelia's Road is fiction, but migrant farmworkers are real. The story probably makes sense to you, because you are able to understand Amelia's feelings.

Exercise

Create a collage about migrant farmworkers. This must be real. In your collage you will include pictures of the many different crops that the farmworkers pick. Remember, every fruit and vegetable you eat may be picked by farmworkers. Also include pictures that show some of the difficult parts of the lives of farmworkers: They don't have enough money, they live in shacks when they are moving around, they don't get to stay in school long, they are always saying goodbye to friends. Add anything else you can think of.

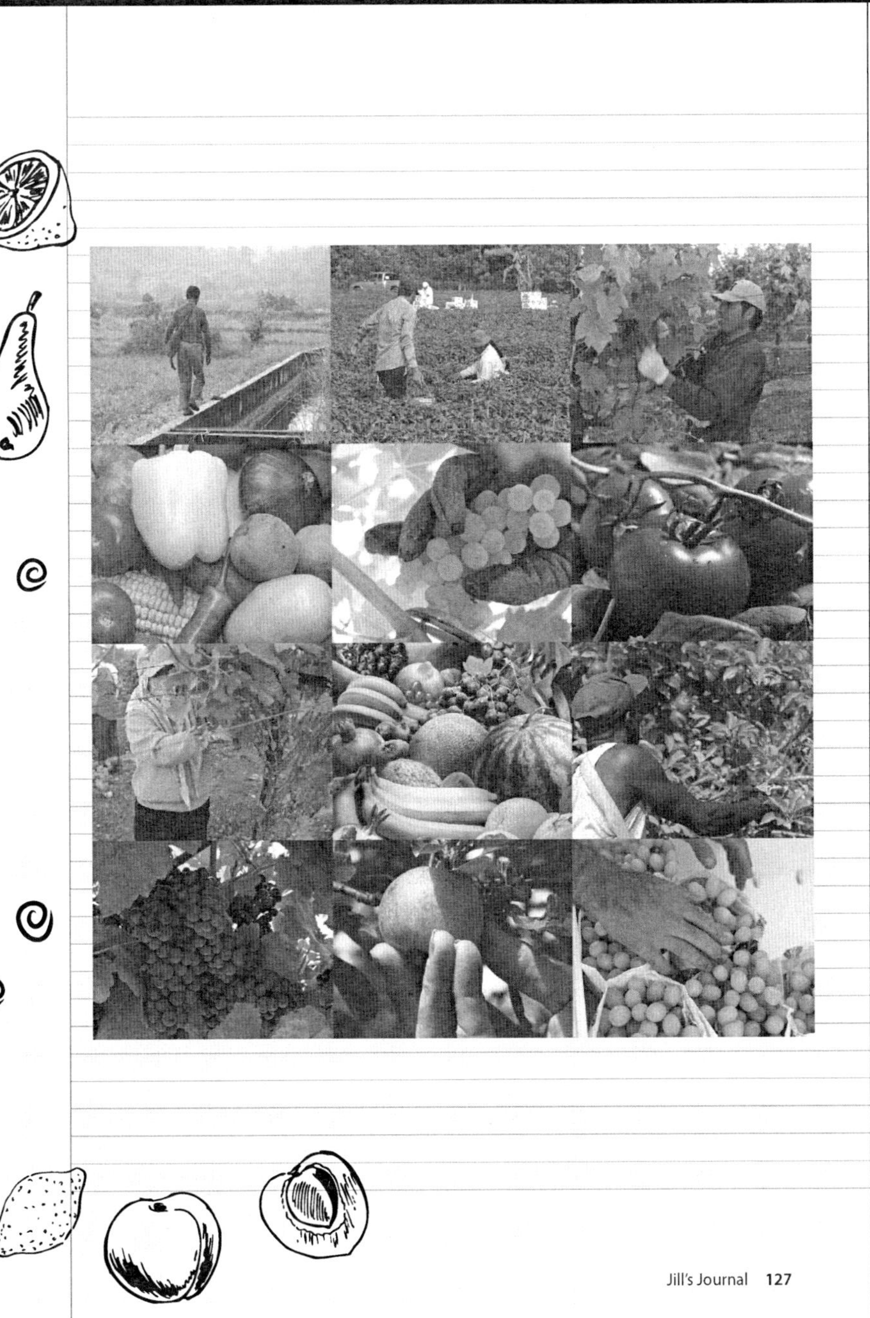

Lesson in Literature

What Is Sequence?

The Tree House

1. Enforcing rules is harder.
2. The rules were made to help each member of the family take responsibility for him- or herself, and to help the family function smoothly and peacefully.
3.
   - Tommy announces there will be rules for his tree house.
   - Tommy thinks of many possible rules for his tree house.
   - Tommy asks his mother how she came up with the family rules.
   - Tommy writes down the house rules.
   - Tommy makes a sign welcoming all to his tree house.

Lesson in Literature . . .
The Tree House

What Is Sequence?

- **Sequence** means order. The numbers 1, 2, 3, 4, 5 are listed here in sequence. The numbers 3, 5, 1, 4, 2 are listed out of sequence.
- When the events of a story are given in sequence, the story is clear and easy to follow.
- When a story is disorganized and events are described out of order, the reader or listener will have difficulty following the story.
- Sequence is especially important in instructions, recipes, and eyewitness reporting.

Think About It!

1. Which is harder: making rules or enforcing them?
2. In your own words, explain what the purpose of most of the rules in Tommy's tree house was.
3. Put the following events in their proper sequence. Rewrite the following five events in their correct order.
   - Tommy asks his mother how she came up with the family rules.
   - Tommy thinks of many possible rules for his tree house.
   - Tommy announces there will be rules for his tree house.
   - Tommy makes a sign welcoming all to his tree house.
   - Tommy writes down the house rules.

128 Unit 2

Vocabulary

quibbled (KWIH buld) *v.*: argued about some small, unimportant detail
delegate (DELL uh gut) *n.*: one person sent by a group of people to represent them at a convention
sympathetic (SIM puh THET ik) *adj.*: understanding and supportive
cobblestone (KOB ul stone) *n.*: a small, naturally rounded stone, used in paving roads
parchment (PARCH ment) *n.*: a stiff, heavy, ivory-colored paper made from the skins of sheep or goats
haughty (HAW tee) *adj.*: snobbish; arrogant
absurd (ub ZURD) *adj.*: ridiculous
magistrate (MADJ iss trayt) *n.*: a government worker who enforces the law
apprentice (uh PREN tiss) *n.*: a person who works for another in order to learn a trade

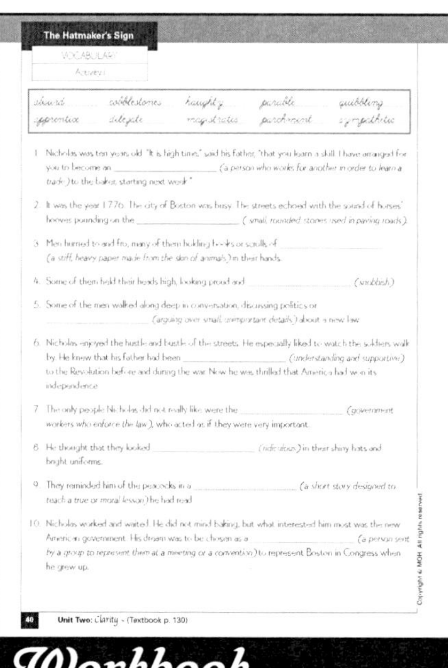
The Hatmaker's Sign
VOCABULARY
Activity I
absurd cobblestones haughty parable quibbling
apprentice delegate magistrates parchment sympathetic
40 Unit Two: Clarity - (Textbook p. 130)

Workbook

The Hatmaker's Sign
VOCABULARY
Activity II
absurd delegate haughty parable quibbling
apprentice cobblestones magistrates parchment sympathetic
Unit Two: Clarity - (Textbook p. 130) 41

Workbook

After his father hammered the last nail into the wood frame of the tree house in the backyard, Tommy announced to his family, "There will be rules in my tree house."

"Rules?" His mother laughed. "What rules?"

"Rules that everyone has to follow," Tommy said proudly.

Tommy's mother smiled at her ten-year-old son. "We have rules in our house, Tommy. The trick is to get people to follow them. How will you do that?"

Tommy knew what his mother was talking about. He followed his parents' rules, most of them, anyway. He cleared the table after dinner. He did his homework at night. He brushed his teeth before bed. He took out the garbage at night. He made his bed—well, sometimes he made his bed and sometimes he didn't.

Sometimes he forgot.

"If someone around this house made his bed every morning...," his mother said.

"He tries," his father added.

"He could try harder," his mother said, "and he could put his clothes away in his drawers or in the hamper."

Suddenly, Tommy had an idea. "I'll write them down!"

"That's a wonderful idea!" his mother said.

That night Tommy wrote and wrote. He made a list of rules, but the list grew and grew. How many rules should he have? He wrote out twenty rules, but some rules sounded like other rules. Then he thought of exceptions to rules. After a while he wasn't sure which rules ought to be rules and which ought to be dropped. Who knew rules for a tree house could be so complicated? Were parents allowed in the tree house? Were friends and neighbors? Were eating and drinking allowed in the tree house? Was homework allowed in the tree house? Was anyone not allowed to enter? Should there be a rule for anyone who entered? A secret handshake? A special knock? What about cleaning up the tree house? What rules should he write down for that?

Finally, he went to his mother. "I'm stuck," he said. "How did you come up with the rules of our house?"

"Well," she said. She sat softly on the sofa and patted a spot beside her for him to sit. "Well," she said again. "We have rules so we can work together and get along as a family, Tommy. We have rules so we all take responsibility by taking care of ourselves and each other." She ran her fingers through his hair and smiled. "So that's why you have to make your bed in the morning."

The next morning Tommy was up early. He made his bed. At breakfast he handed his mother a sheet of paper. It read:

Tree House Rules

All are welcome in this tree house. The only rule of this tree house is to take good care of the tree house and anyone who is in the tree house.

"That's the best set of rules I ever read," Tommy's mother said.

> **Unit Theme:** *Clarity*
>
> **Target Skill:** *Recognizing the elements of sequence in a well-organized story*
>
> **Genre:** *Parable*

Getting Started

This parable is really a story about the writing of the Declaration of Independence. According to the story, when Thomas Jefferson finished writing the Declaration of Independence, he considered it perfect. He was right. It was. Time and history have tested it, and it remains unparalleled in its force and beauty. Ask your class the following questions:

- Can they think of any piece of literature, art, music, or other man-made work that is "perfect"—or as close to perfect as possible? (A few examples might be: Beethoven's Fifth Symphony; the Lincoln Memorial; the game of baseball; their mother's cherry pie.)
- Criticism:Is it helpful or destructive? When a person submits a piece of work for criticism (as Jefferson did), are there any positives to the process? What are they? Are there any negatives? What are they? (Positives would include: the work might be broadened, improved, or clarified by someone else's viewpoint and input. Negatives: the suggestions might diminish, dull, or cheapen the perfect piece of work. The artist might be so sensitive that criticism would stymie his creativity.)
- The Critics: If someone is asked to evaluate a work, should he give his true opinion, or should he conceal what he really thinks to spare the feelings of the creator of the work? Does it depend on the circumstances? If it does, describe the varying circumstances.

Into ...
The Hatmaker's Sign

Unsolicited advice—what do we do with it and how do we react to it? Some important points to make about advice are the following:

- Not all advice is good.
- Not all advice is bad.
- Not all advice should be acted upon.
- Not all advice should be rejected.
- The person giving the advice may not have thought of everything you've thought of.
- You may not have thought of everything the advice giver has thought of.
- Although you don't have to follow anyone's advice, you do have to be respectful of everyone.

In the story, Thomas Jefferson is given advice by his fellow congressmen. The situation in the story, and the one that should be discussed in class, is where one person, who has worked at and thought extensively about a project, is subjected to casual, shallow suggestions and criticism that have little validity. Jefferson's reaction to the suggestions was hurt and anger. Ben Franklin's parable eased his pain and gave him the patience to wait out the storm of criticism. It showed him that if you take the critics too seriously, you will end up with nothing. On the other hand, if you have the patience and good humor to wait them out (and if you really are right), they will come around to your way of thinking in the end.

Eyes On Sequence

A recipe is a good way to help students understand sequence. Ask your students to give you instructions about how to make a peanut butter and jelly sandwich. (If you bring the actual ingredients to class it can be an entertaining experience that they will be unlikely to forget!) If the students tell you to put the peanut butter on the bread, you can challenge them by saying that they have not yet told you to take the lid off the jar or the bread out of the bag. [If you want to be funny, you can literally take the jar of peanut butter and stand it on top of the loaf of bread. As you wait for direction, they will recognize their mistake.]

Another way to illustrate sequence is to write an inaccurate timeline of a typical student's life. Then ask the students to put the events in chronological order. For example, you may want to write something like the following on the board:

- I broke my leg last year at the roller skating party.
- I was born.
- I entered fourth grade.
- We went on a family trip to Florida when I was three years old.
- My older brother was born.

List sequence words on the board, including: *first*, *after*, *then*, and *finally*. This will help the students organize information and recognize sequence.

Introduce the idea of organizing or listing events in an order that is *not* chronological. For example: a sportscaster might tell you what happened in all the baseball games across the country from morning to night, and then go back and tell you about other sporting events that took place throughout the same day. The sportscast is organized by sport, not by which event took place first.

The Hatmaker's Sign is told in chronological order but is interrupted by a "story within a story," the parable that Ben Franklin tells Thomas Jefferson. As you discuss the story with the class, make sure they do not confuse the events in the parable with what actually happens in the story.

Additionally, take this opportunity to explain that a parable is a brief story that illustrates a life lesson. Point out that it is different from a fable, in that fables generally use animals, plants, and forces of nature as characters, but parables generally feature human characters.

Blueprint for Reading

INTO . . . *The Hatmaker's Sign*

It is usually free. People love to give it but don't want to receive it. It can be terribly confusing or very clear. It can be very good or extremely bad. Some people ask for it and then throw it away. What is it? *Advice!*

Have you ever worked long and hard at a job and been very satisfied with the results? Then, just as you were congratulating yourself on a job well done, along came the critics. "It needs a little more color"; "Maybe you should move that to the right"; "It's good, but you made it too small." If you were so polite that you followed every suggestion, what would happen is—well, read *The Hatmaker's Sign*, and you'll find out!

Sequence

"Whip six egg whites. Remove cake from oven. Sift two cups of flour. Allow cake to cool. Add one teaspoon of vanilla. Set oven at 350°. Put the icing on. Mix two cups of sugar with the flour and baking powder." What's wrong with these instructions? It's obvious! *They are not in any order!* Without an order, instructions are impossible to follow.

Just as instructions must be given in order, a story's events must also have some **sequence**, or order. We usually tell a story in the order that the events happened. Sometimes, though, the story is told as a *flashback*, a memory of something that happened in the past. As you read *The Hatmaker's Sign*, notice the sequence of events and how the author organized the story.

130 Unit 2

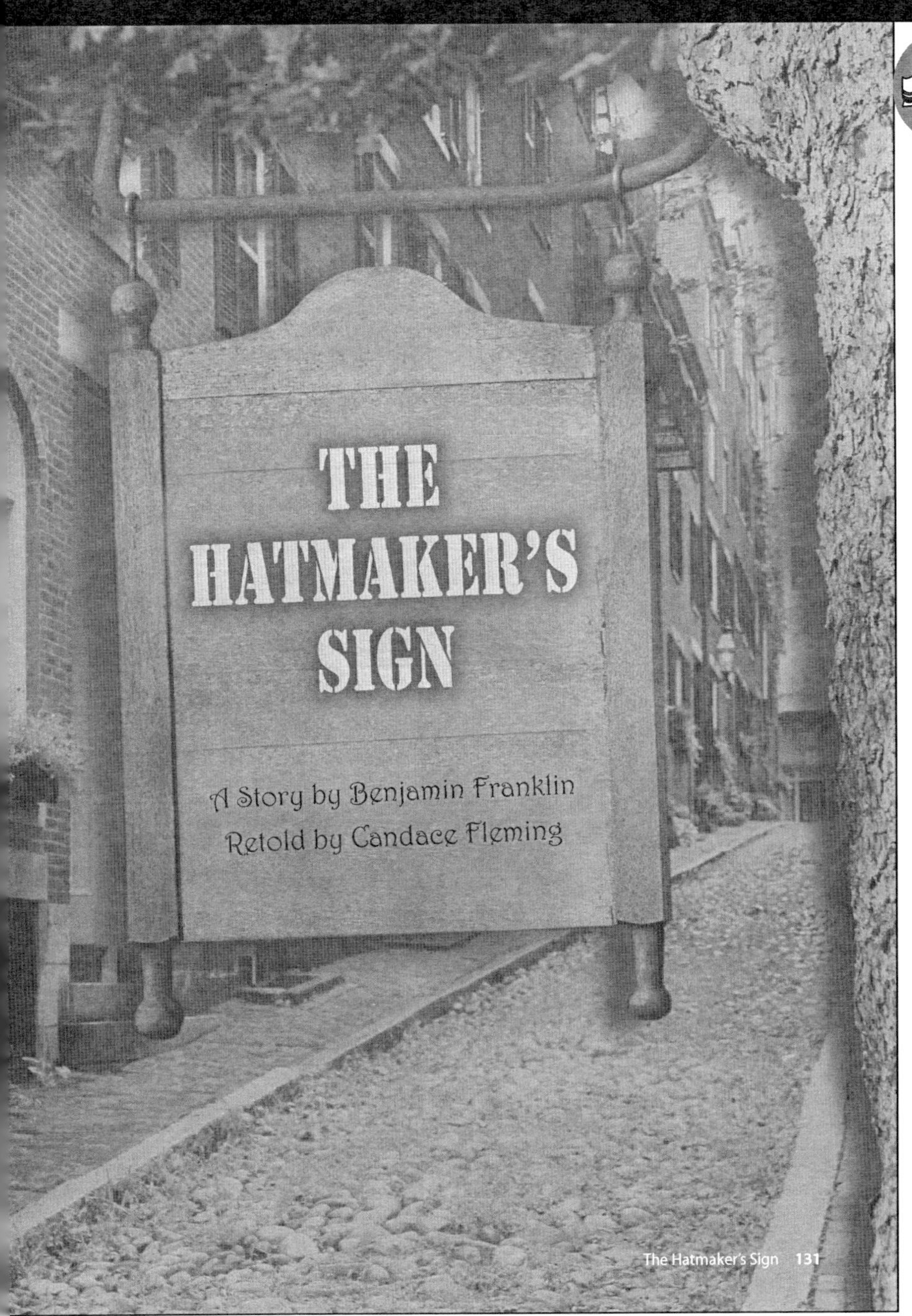

Selection Summary

Thomas Jefferson has just written the Declaration of Independence. He knows it is perfect. But the delegates of the Continental Congress, when shown the perfect piece of work, begin to quibble, criticize, and nitpick. Chagrined, Jefferson slumps in his chair, angry and embarrassed. A wise and kindly Benjamin Franklin tells him the following parable.

A hatmaker once designed a sign for his new hat shop. On the sign was a picture of a hat and the words "John Thompson, Hatmaker. Fashionable hats sold inside for ready money." As he prepared to have the sign made and hung, one person after another quibbled, criticized, and nitpicked every part of it. By the time they were through, all that was left on the sign was a blank space. The sign maker, seeing the blank space, suggested putting onto the sign exactly what the hatmaker had planned to put there in the first place.

Thomas Jefferson hears Benjamin Franklin out and waits to see what will happen. Sure enough, when the smoke clears and the debate is over, Jefferson's work is deemed perfect by one and all.

Literary Components

1 Historical Reference: The author effortlessly places us in Revolutionary War days by mentioning the name Thomas Jefferson. The time and place need very little further elaboration.

2 Repetition; Rhyme; Poetic Tone: The author's use of repetition and rhyme creates the feeling that something of importance and worthy of respect is about to be introduced.

3 Historical Reference: We now know what part of Thomas Jefferson's fascinating life is being referenced.

4 Wording: The author uses a variety of verbs to make the scene more colorful.

5 Rising Tension: The tension (literally) of the plot rises as Jefferson's perfect work is torn to shreds by the critical congressmen.

6 Idiom: Ben Franklin's expression is reflective of the late 1700s in America.

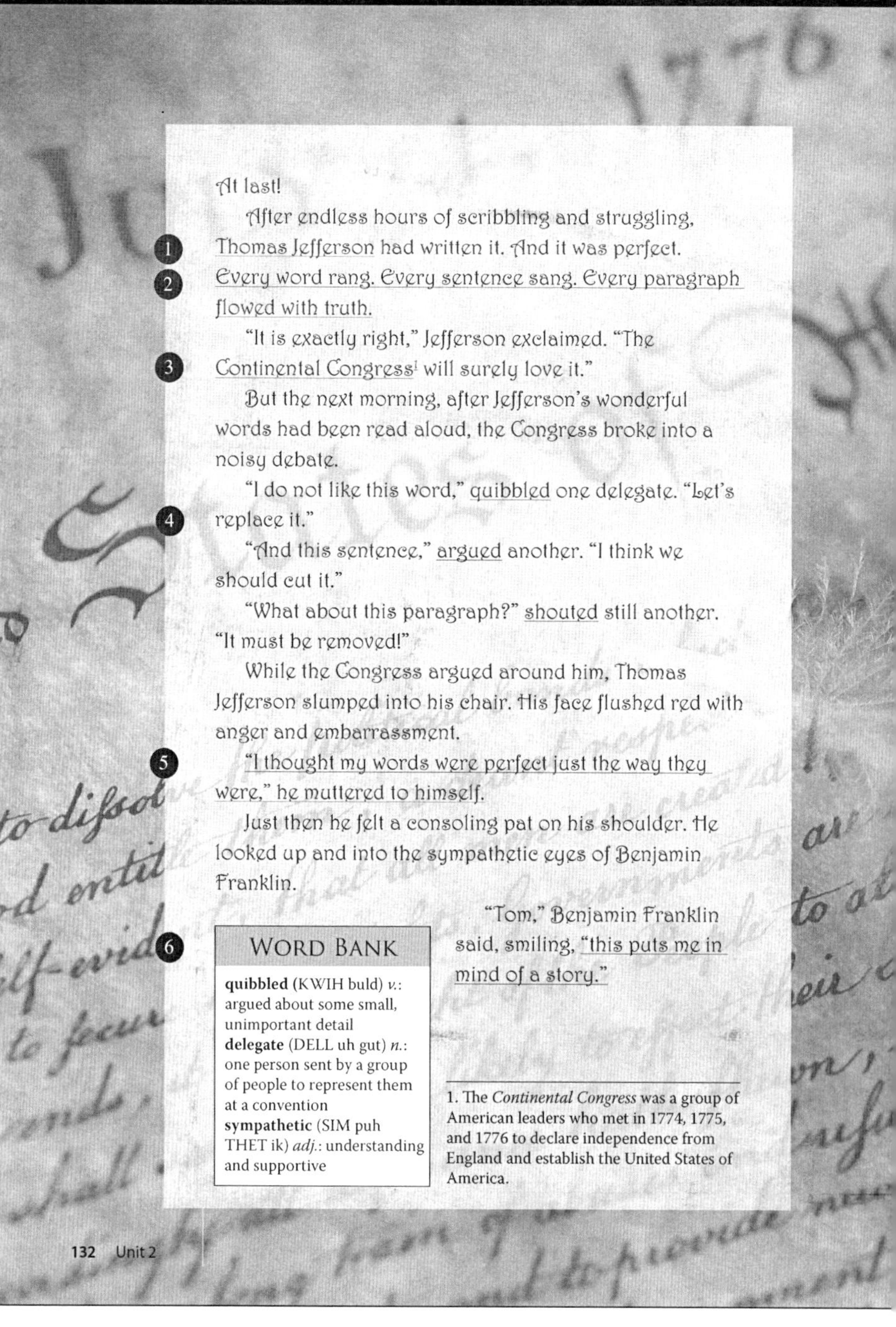

At last!

After endless hours of scribbling and struggling,
1 Thomas Jefferson had written it. And it was perfect.
2 Every word rang. Every sentence sang. Every paragraph flowed with truth.

"It is exactly right," Jefferson exclaimed. "The
3 Continental Congress[1] will surely love it."

But the next morning, after Jefferson's wonderful words had been read aloud, the Congress broke into a noisy debate.

"I do not like this word," quibbled one delegate. "Let's
4 replace it."

"And this sentence," argued another. "I think we should cut it."

"What about this paragraph?" shouted still another. "It must be removed!"

While the Congress argued around him, Thomas Jefferson slumped into his chair. His face flushed red with anger and embarrassment.

5 "I thought my words were perfect just the way they were," he muttered to himself.

Just then he felt a consoling pat on his shoulder. He looked up and into the sympathetic eyes of Benjamin Franklin.

6 "Tom," Benjamin Franklin said, smiling, "this puts me in mind of a story."

WORD BANK

quibbled (KWIH buld) *v.*: argued about some small, unimportant detail
delegate (DELL uh gut) *n.*: one person sent by a group of people to represent them at a convention
sympathetic (SIM puh THET ik) *adj.*: understanding and supportive

1. The *Continental Congress* was a group of American leaders who met in 1774, 1775, and 1776 to declare independence from England and establish the United States of America.

132 Unit 2

Guiding the Reading

Literal

Q: Who wrote something that was perfect?
A: Thomas Jefferson wrote it.

Q: What else do you know about what he wrote other than the fact that it was perfect?
A: He struggled a long time to write it. It flowed with truth.

Q: Did the members of the Continental Congress react in the way in which Thomas Jefferson had anticipated?
A: No, they argued and wanted to make a lot of changes.

Q: What did Thomas Jefferson do when he heard the Congress argue?
A: He slumped into his chair.

Q: Why was Thomas Jefferson angry and embarrassed?
A: He was hurt because he thought his document was perfect and everyone was criticizing his work.

Q: Who approached Thomas Jefferson after he realized that not everyone thought his words were perfect?
A: Benjamin Franklin came over to Mr. Jefferson.

Q: Did Benjamin Franklin also suggest ways for Thomas to improve his writing?
A: No, he was sympathetic and tried to console him.

Q: What was Benjamin Franklin reminded of after going over to Thomas Jefferson?
A: He thought of a story.

Analytical

Q: What were you able to tell from the fact that Thomas Jefferson slumped into his chair?
A: He was hurt and disappointed.

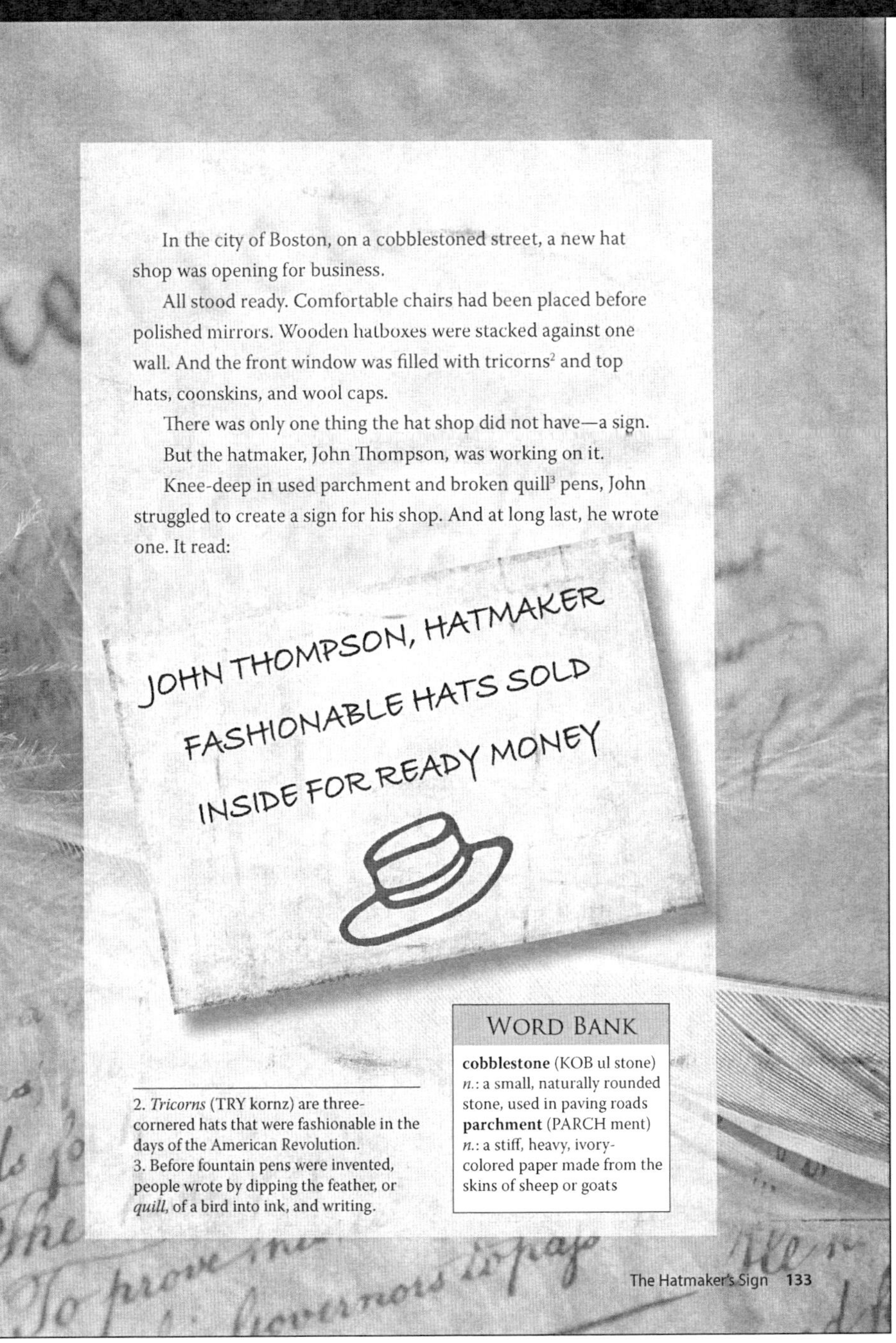

In the city of Boston, on a cobblestoned street, a new hat shop was opening for business.

All stood ready. Comfortable chairs had been placed before polished mirrors. Wooden hatboxes were stacked against one wall. And the front window was filled with tricorns[2] and top hats, coonskins, and wool caps.

There was only one thing the hat shop did not have—a sign.

But the hatmaker, John Thompson, was working on it.

Knee-deep in used parchment and broken quill[3] pens, John struggled to create a sign for his shop. And at long last, he wrote one. It read:

WORD BANK

cobblestone (KOB ul stone) *n.*: a small, naturally rounded stone, used in paving roads

parchment (PARCH ment) *n.*: a stiff, heavy, ivory-colored paper made from the skins of sheep or goats

2. *Tricorns* (TRY kornz) are three-cornered hats that were fashionable in the days of the American Revolution.
3. Before fountain pens were invented, people wrote by dipping the feather, or *quill*, of a bird into ink, and writing.

The Hatmaker's Sign 133

Guiding the Reading

Literal

Q: Where did Benjamin Franklin's story take place?

A: It took place in Boston.

Q: Who was opening a new business?

A: John Thompson was opening a business.

Q: What type of shop was it?

A: It was a hat shop.

Q: What did John prepare for his new business?

A: He prepared comfortable chairs, polished mirrors, wooden hatboxes, and all types of hats.

Q: What was the one thing that was missing?

A: He did not have a sign for his shop.

Q: What did John finally settle on for his sign?

A: He used the words, "JOHN THOMPSON, HATMAKER FASHIONABLE HATS SOLD INSIDE FOR READY MONEY" with a picture of a hat below the text.

Analytical

Q: How can you figure out that "John struggled to create a sign for his shop" without even reading those words?

A: The used parchment on the floor and broken pens indicate failed attempts.

Literary Components

6 Idiom: Ben Franklin's expression is reflective of the late 1700s in America.

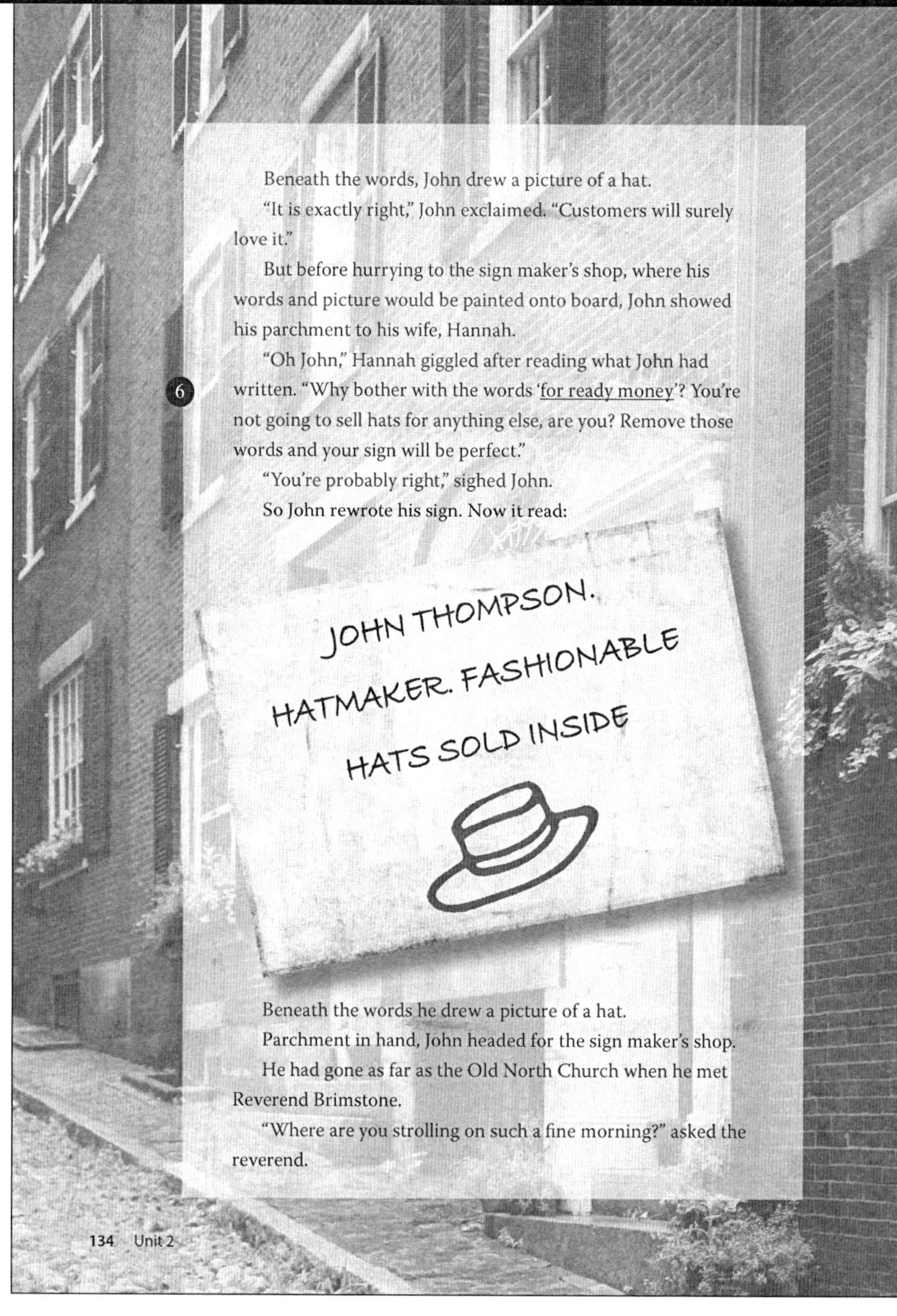

Beneath the words, John drew a picture of a hat.

"It is exactly right," John exclaimed. "Customers will surely love it."

But before hurrying to the sign maker's shop, where his words and picture would be painted onto board, John showed his parchment to his wife, Hannah.

"Oh John," Hannah giggled after reading what John had
6 written. "Why bother with the words 'for ready money'? You're not going to sell hats for anything else, are you? Remove those words and your sign will be perfect."

"You're probably right," sighed John.

So John rewrote his sign. Now it read:

Beneath the words he drew a picture of a hat.

Parchment in hand, John headed for the sign maker's shop.

He had gone as far as the Old North Church when he met Reverend Brimstone.

"Where are you strolling on such a fine morning?" asked the reverend.

134 Unit 2

Guiding the Reading

Literal

Q: How did John feel about the sign he made?

A: He thought that it was perfect and that people would love it.

Q: Whom did John show his sign to before he left the house?

A: He showed it to his wife, Hannah.

Q: What changes did Hannah suggest?

A: She suggested that he remove the words "for ready money."

Q: How did John react to his wife's correction?

A: He sighed, but he thought she was probably right so he rewrote the sign.

"To the sign maker's shop," replied John. He held out his parchment.

Reverend Brimstone read it.

"May I make a suggestion?" he asked. "Why don't you take out the words 'John Thompson, Hatmaker'? After all, customers won't care who made the hats as long as they are good ones."

"You're probably right," sighed John.

And after tipping his tricorn to the reverend, John hurried back to his hat shop and rewrote his sign. Now it read: 7

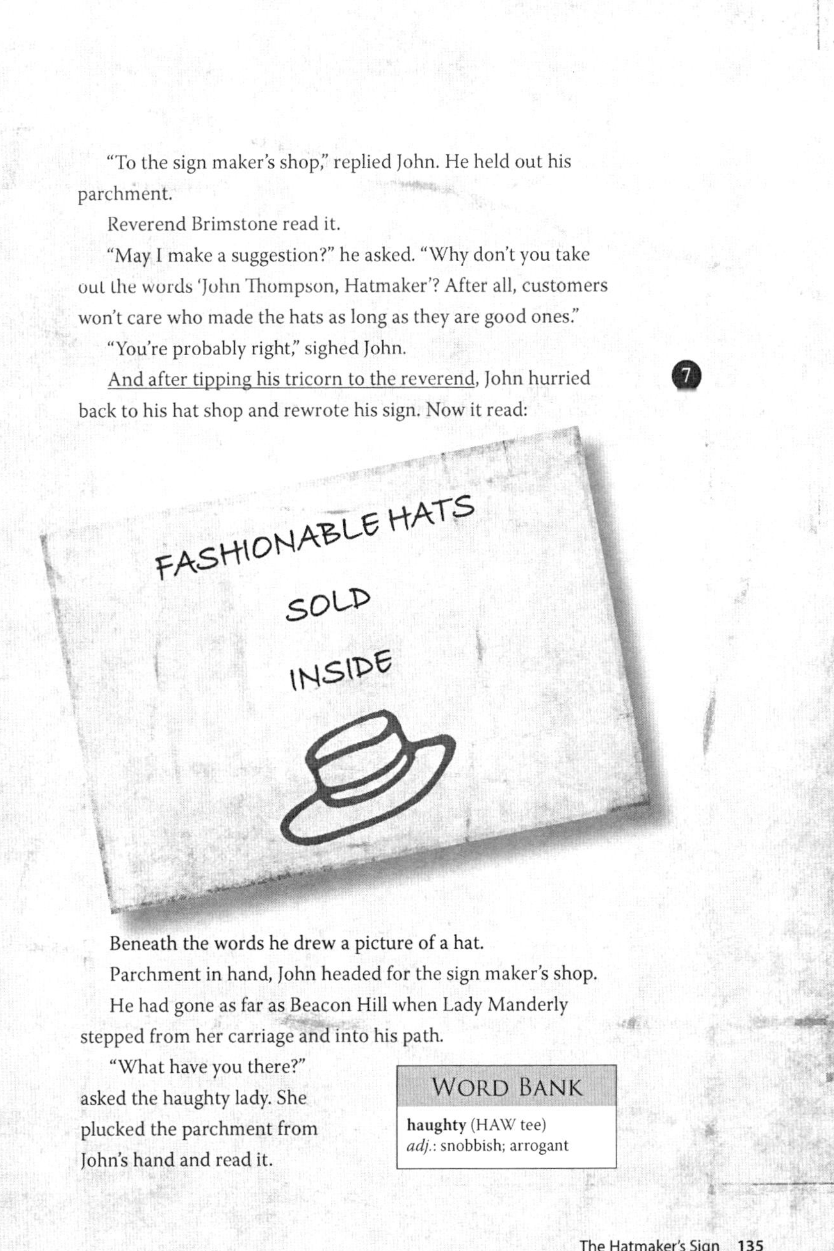

Beneath the words he drew a picture of a hat.

Parchment in hand, John headed for the sign maker's shop.

He had gone as far as Beacon Hill when Lady Manderly stepped from her carriage and into his path.

"What have you there?" asked the haughty lady. She plucked the parchment from John's hand and read it.

> **Word Bank**
> **haughty** (HAW tee) *adj.*: snobbish; arrogant

Guiding the Reading

Literal

Q: Who stopped John on his way to the sign maker's shop?

A: Reverend Brimstone stopped him along the way.

Q: How did the Reverend know about the sign?

A: He asked John where he was headed. He discovered it was to the sign maker's shop and proceeded to read the parchment.

Q: What did the Reverend suggest to John?

A: He told John to take his name off the sign. He felt that customers would want to know that they were getting quality hats, not who was making them.

Q: What did John Thompson do after he finished his conversation with Reverend Brimstone?

A: He went back to rewrite the sign.

Q: Who did John meet at Beacon Hill?

A: He met Lady Manderly.

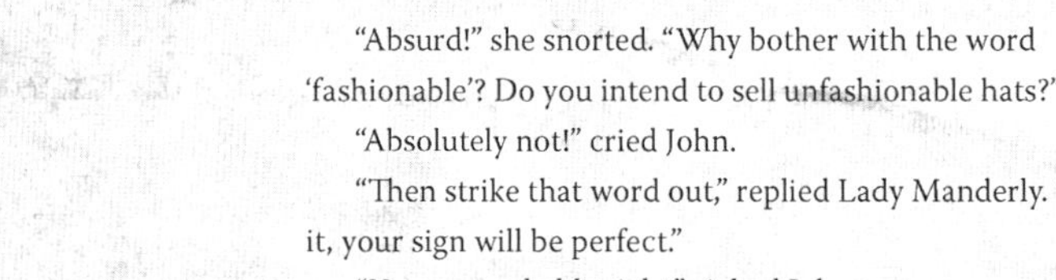

"Absurd!" she snorted. "Why bother with the word 'fashionable'? Do you intend to sell unfashionable hats?"

"Absolutely not!" cried John.

"Then strike that word out," replied Lady Manderly. "Without it, your sign will be perfect."

"You are probably right," sighed John.

And after bidding the lady farewell, John hurried back to his hat shop and rewrote his sign. Now it read:

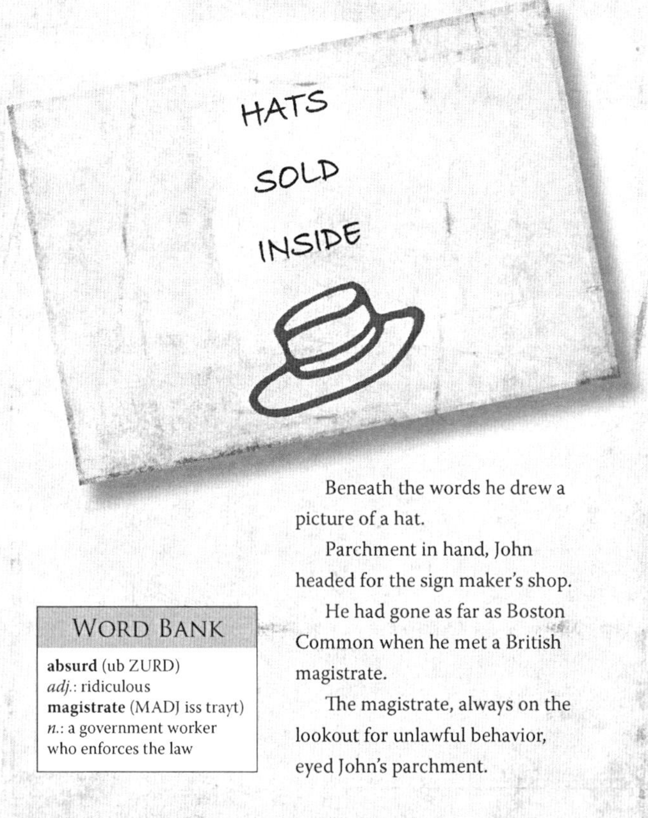

Beneath the words he drew a picture of a hat.

Parchment in hand, John headed for the sign maker's shop.

He had gone as far as Boston Common when he met a British magistrate.

The magistrate, always on the lookout for unlawful behavior, eyed John's parchment.

Word Bank

absurd (ub ZURD)
adj.: ridiculous
magistrate (MADJ iss trayt)
n.: a government worker who enforces the law

Guiding the Reading

Literal

Q: What was the Lady's recommended change to the sign? Why?

A: She told John to take out the word "fashionable" because, after all, who would want to shop in a place that sells unfashionable hats?

Q: What did John do after meeting Lady Manderly?

A: He redid his sign once again.

Q: Whom did John meet at Boston Common?

A: He met the British magistrate.

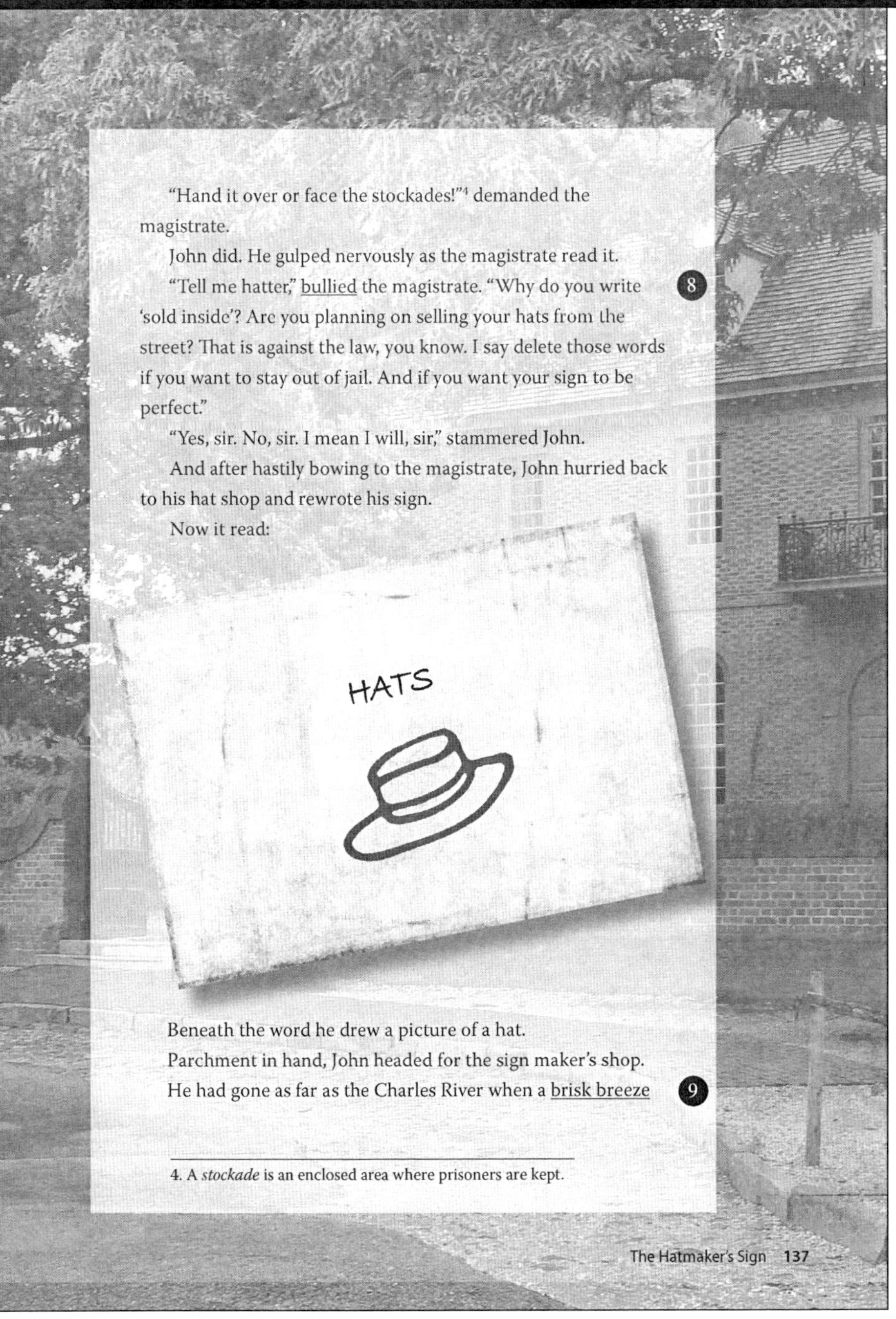

Literary Components

8 Expressive Language: Notice that for every character, the author uses a different verb to indicate speech. Hannah "giggles," the reverend "asks," Lady Manderly "snorts" and "replies," and the magistrate "bullies."

9 Alliteration: "Brisk breeze" has a nice sound to it.

Guiding the Reading

Literal

Q: What type of person was the magistrate?

A: He was tough and threatening. The magistrate bullied John and looked for unlawful behavior.

Q: What did John do before leaving the magistrate?

A: He bowed to him.

Analytical

Q: Why did John gulp nervously and stammer his response?

A: The magistrate sounded rough and threatening and made John feel nervous and uncomfortable. One may suspect, as well, that John was getting increasingly frustrated by everyone's advice.

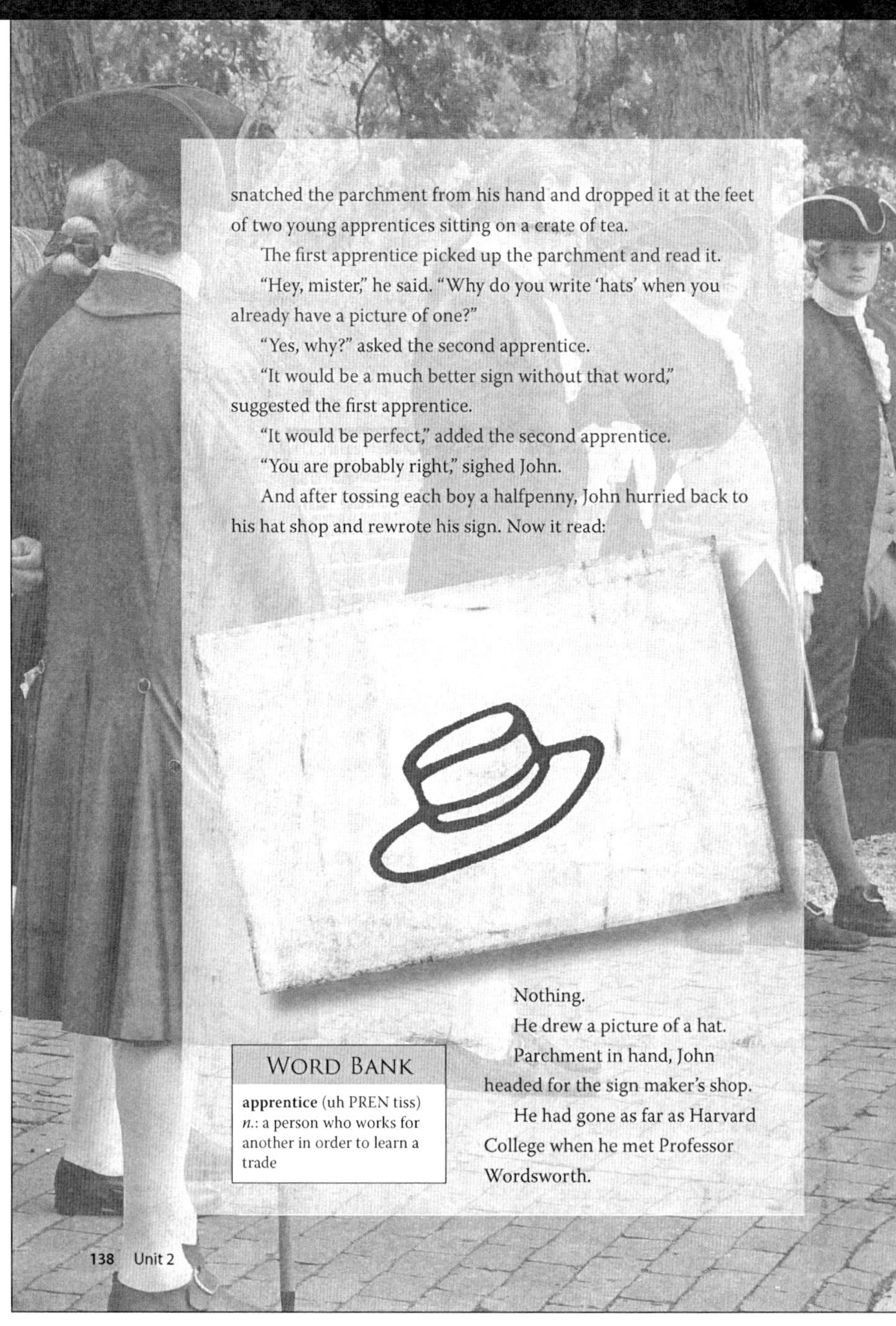

snatched the parchment from his hand and dropped it at the feet of two young apprentices sitting on a crate of tea.

The first apprentice picked up the parchment and read it.

"Hey, mister," he said. "Why do you write 'hats' when you already have a picture of one?"

"Yes, why?" asked the second apprentice.

"It would be a much better sign without that word," suggested the first apprentice.

"It would be perfect," added the second apprentice.

"You are probably right," sighed John.

And after tossing each boy a halfpenny, John hurried back to his hat shop and rewrote his sign. Now it read:

Nothing.

He drew a picture of a hat.

Parchment in hand, John headed for the sign maker's shop.

He had gone as far as Harvard College when he met Professor Wordsworth.

WORD BANK

apprentice (uh PREN tiss) *n.*: a person who works for another in order to learn a trade

138 Unit 2

Guiding the Reading

Literal

Q: How did John happen to talk to the apprentices about his sign?

A: The breeze blew the parchment right to their feet.

Q: What did the apprentices say would make John's sign perfect?

A: Using just the picture without words would make the sign perfect.

Q: What did John give the apprentices?

A: He gave each of them a halfpenny.

Q: Whom did John meet at Harvard College?

A: He met Professor Wordsworth.

John shoved his parchment under the professor's nose. "Please, sir," he said. "Would you tell me what you think of my sign?"

The surprised professor straightened his spectacles and peered at the picture.

"Since you ask my opinion, I shall give it," said Professor Wordsworth. "However, I must ask you a question first. Are you displaying your hats in your shop's front window?"

John nodded.

"Then this picture is useless," declared the professor. "Everyone will know you sell hats simply by looking in your window. Eliminate the picture and your sign will be perfect."

"You are probably right," sighed John.

And after pumping the professor's hand in thanks, John hurried back to his hat shop and rewrote his sign.

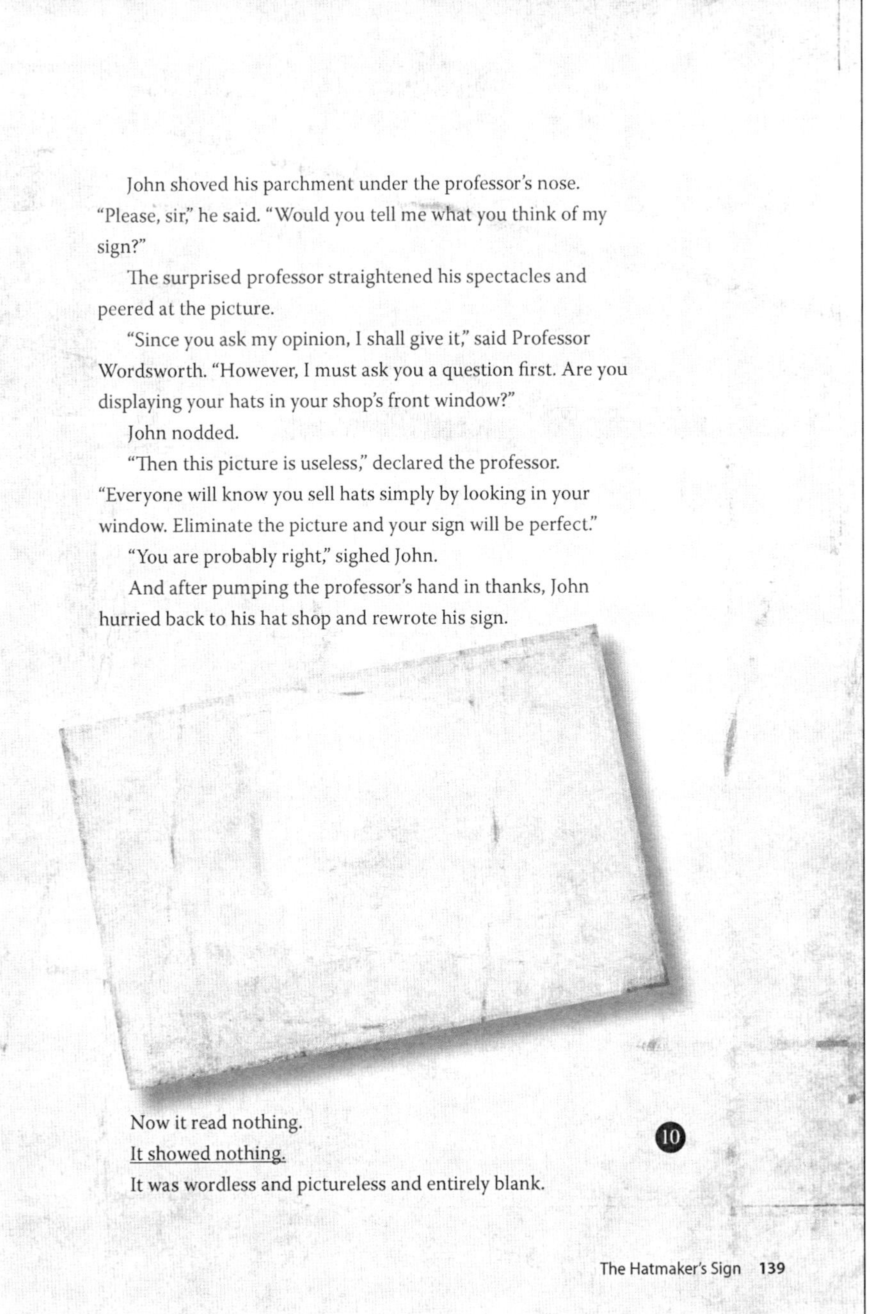

Now it read nothing.
It showed nothing.
It was wordless and pictureless and entirely blank. ⑩

Literary Components

⑩ **Repetition:** In keeping with the story's simple style, the author uses repetition to make his point.

Guiding the Reading

Literal

Q: What was the professor's opinion regarding the sign?

A: He declared that if John planned to display hats in the window, there was no need for the picture.

Q: What was left on John's sign after his conversation with Professor Wordsworth?

A: There was absolutely nothing left on the sign.

Analytical

Q: How was the meeting with the professor different from the other ones?

A: The other people offered their opinions without asking John if he was interested in what they had to say. In this case, John asked Professor Wordsworth for his opinion and the professor said that he would give it because John had asked for it.

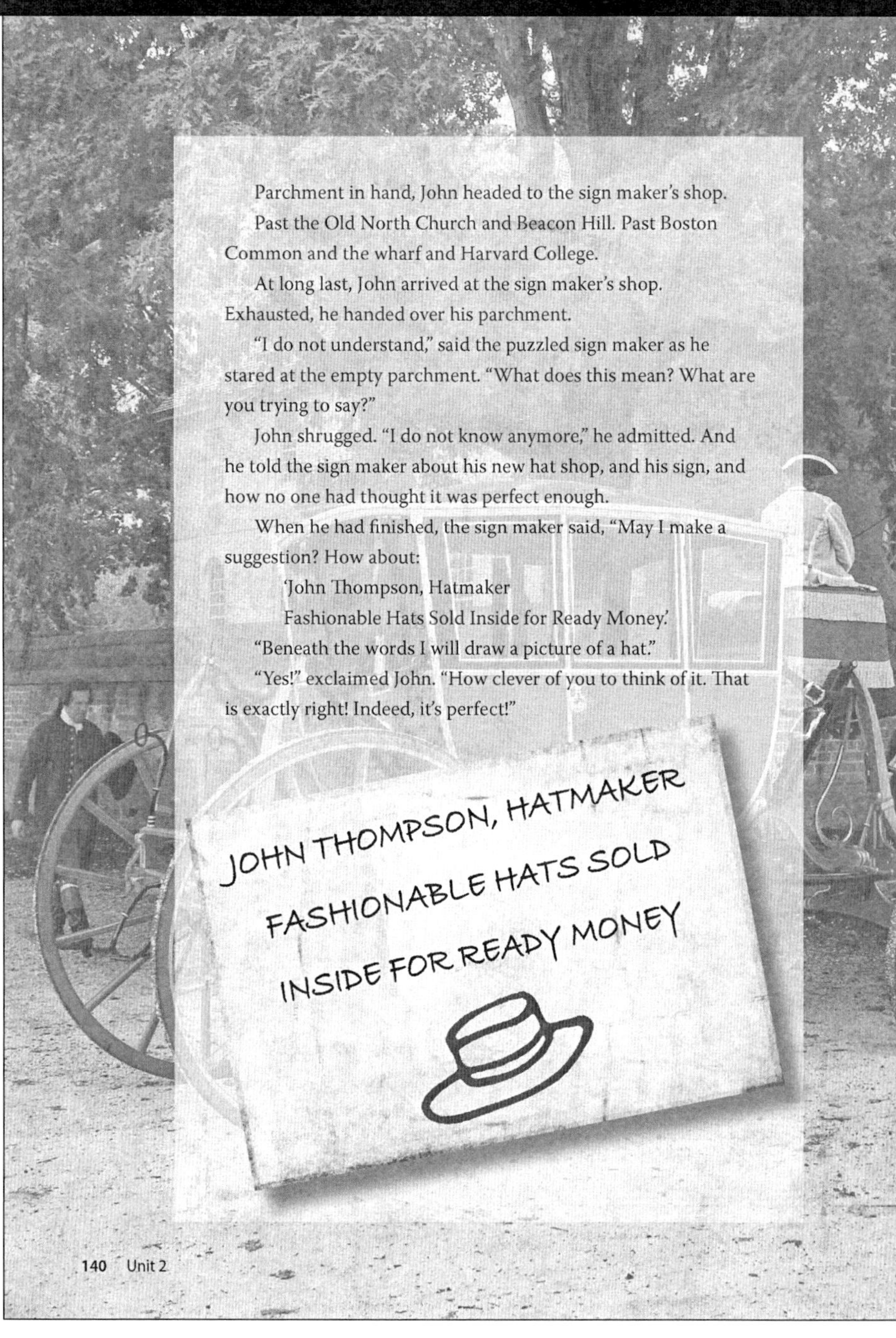

Parchment in hand, John headed to the sign maker's shop.

Past the Old North Church and Beacon Hill. Past Boston Common and the wharf and Harvard College.

At long last, John arrived at the sign maker's shop. Exhausted, he handed over his parchment.

"I do not understand," said the puzzled sign maker as he stared at the empty parchment. "What does this mean? What are you trying to say?"

John shrugged. "I do not know anymore," he admitted. And he told the sign maker about his new hat shop, and his sign, and how no one had thought it was perfect enough.

When he had finished, the sign maker said, "May I make a suggestion? How about:

'John Thompson, Hatmaker
Fashionable Hats Sold Inside for Ready Money.'

"Beneath the words I will draw a picture of a hat."

"Yes!" exclaimed John. "How clever of you to think of it. That is exactly right! Indeed, it's perfect!"

140 Unit 2

Guiding the Reading

Literal

Q: Why was the sign maker puzzled when John handed him the parchment?

A: It was blank.

Q: What was John's response when the sign maker asked, "What are you trying to say?"

A: "I don't know anymore."

Q: What was the sign maker's suggestion?

A: He suggested using the words and picture that John had planned to use in the first place.

Analytical

Q: Why do you think John was exhausted by the time he reached the sign maker's house?

A: First of all, he'd had a long walk. Second of all, the interruptions and criticisms were tiring. Third of all, he had to keep going back home to fix the sign.

Q: How do you think that the sign maker came up with the same exact words that John had thought of?

A: The fact that the sign maker came up with the original sign is the "punch line" of Ben Franklin's tale. It is typical Ben Franklin humor. It is also the entire point of the little story: the hatmaker, knowing his business, had instinctively come up with the best possible sign. Just so, Thomas Jefferson, knowing his business, had come up with the best possible Declaration of Independence. It would just take a little time for people to see that.

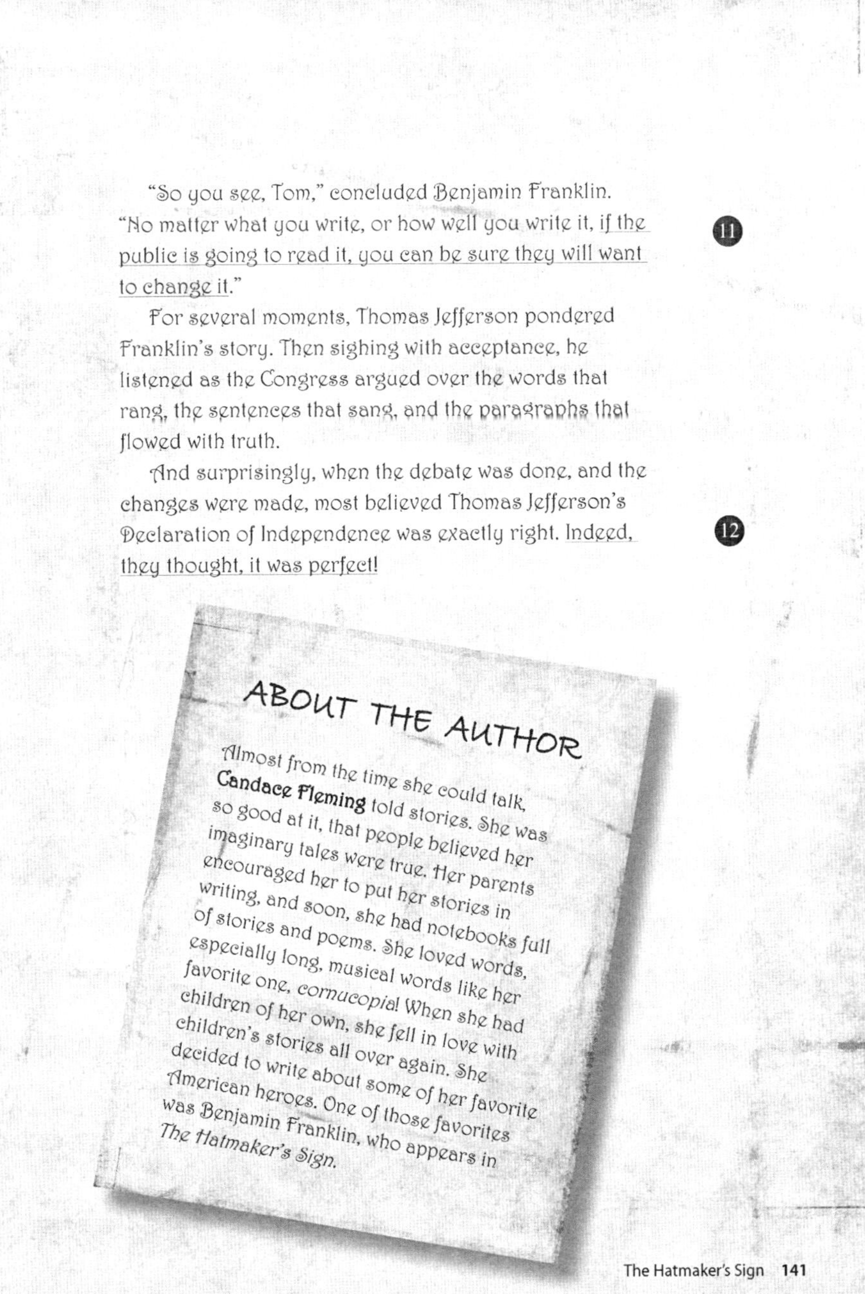

"So you see, Tom," concluded Benjamin Franklin. "No matter what you write, or how well you write it, if the public is going to read it, you can be sure they will want to change it." 11

For several moments, Thomas Jefferson pondered Franklin's story. Then sighing with acceptance, he listened as the Congress argued over the words that rang, the sentences that sang, and the paragraphs that flowed with truth.

And surprisingly, when the debate was done, and the changes were made, most believed Thomas Jefferson's Declaration of Independence was exactly right. Indeed, they thought, it was perfect! 12

ABOUT THE AUTHOR

Almost from the time she could talk, **Candace Fleming** told stories. She was so good at it, that people believed her imaginary tales were true. Her parents encouraged her to put her stories in writing, and soon, she had notebooks full of stories and poems. She loved words, especially long, musical words like her favorite one, *cornucopia*! When she had children of her own, she fell in love with children's stories all over again. She decided to write about some of her favorite American heroes. One of those favorites was Benjamin Franklin, who appears in *The Hatmaker's Sign*.

The Hatmaker's Sign 141

Literary Components

11 Style: The author cleverly has Benjamin Franklin speak in lines that could have been taken from *Poor Richard's Almanac*. Everything he says sounds like an aphorism!

12 Perfect Conclusion: The story comes full circle, as one knew it would.

Guiding the Reading

Literal

Q: How did Thomas, like John, respond to the corrections?

A: He sighed and hesitantly accepted them.

Q: What did Congress do in the end?

A: They continued to argue about the words in Tom's document. After only a few changes, they felt that his work was really perfect!

Q: What was the name of the famous document authored by Thomas Jefferson?

A: The document was known as the Declaration of Independence.

Analytical

Q: Why did Benjamin Franklin tell Thomas this story?

A: He wanted him to understand that his work was outstanding and that it is the nature of people to have something to change or add. He wanted Thomas to deal with the criticism good-humoredly, while not losing sight of the excellence of what he had wrought. Ben gave Thomas a boost in terms of his mood and his confidence.

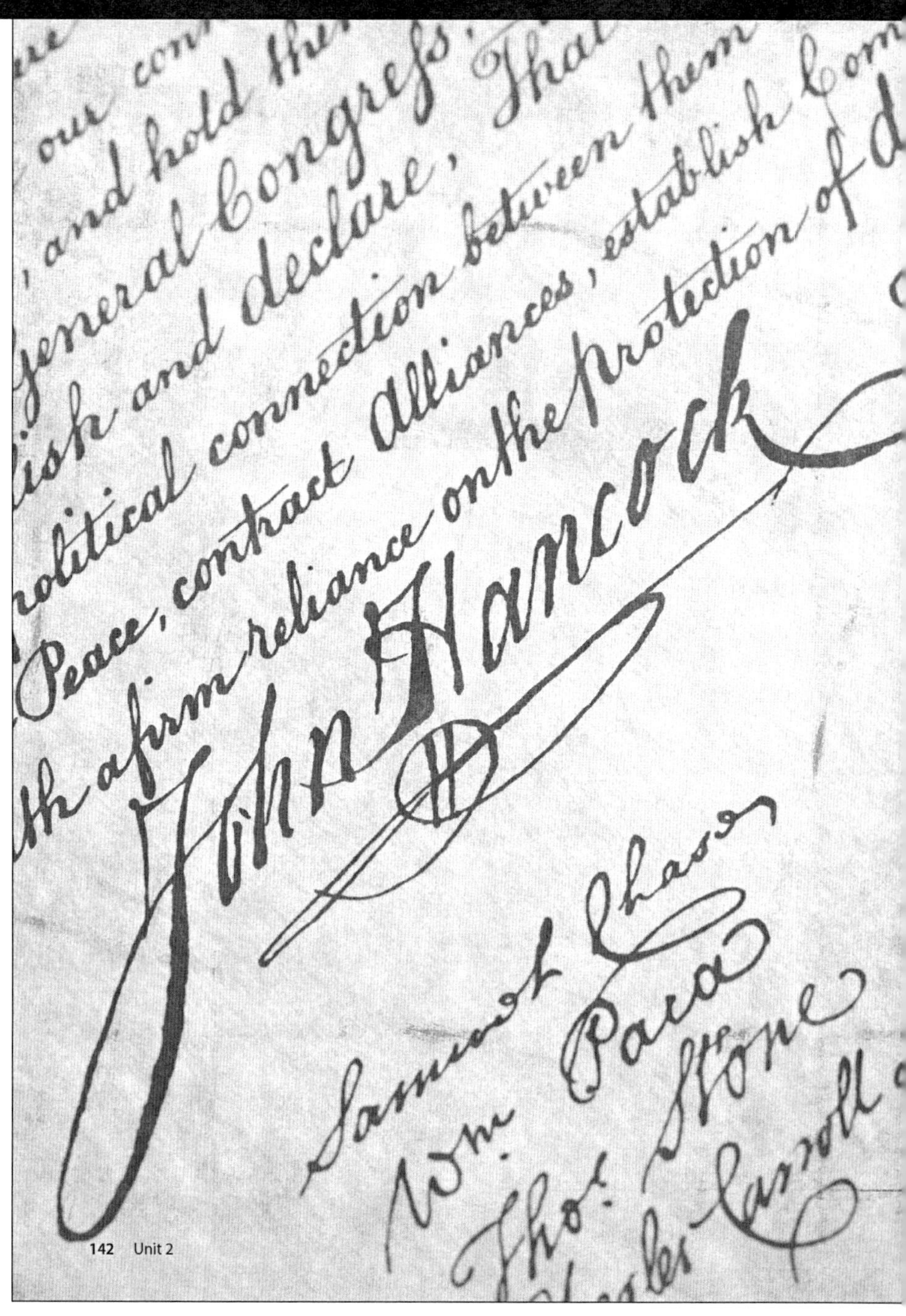
John Hancock
Samuel Chase
Wm. Paca
Thos. Stone
142 Unit 2

Studying the Selection

FIRST IMPRESSIONS

If you were John, how would you have decided what to write on the sign?

QUICK REVIEW

1. As the story opens, what had Thomas Jefferson just completed?
2. In Ben Franklin's story, what had John Thompson prepared for the opening of his new store?
3. What was the only thing left on John's sign after he spoke with the apprentices?
4. Who finally suggested that John use the same words and picture that he had planned to use in the first place?

FOCUS

5. Why was John exhausted by the time he reached the sign maker's shop?
6. Write down one thing you noticed about the sequence of the story that made it organized and easy to read.

CREATING AND WRITING

7. Did John want everyone's advice to help him decide what the sign should say? Write a few sentences describing John's feelings.
8. Write a short fictional story about a child who worked hard on something and was disappointed later on when others did not like it or take it seriously.
9. Make a creative sign for a new store or business that you would like to open.

The Hatmaker's Sign 143

First Impressions

Answers will vary.

Quick Review

1. The document was the Declaration of Independence.
2. He prepared comfortable chairs, polished mirrors, wooden hatboxes, and various hats.
3. A picture was the only thing that remained on the sign.
4. After the sign maker looked at the blank sign and heard the whole story, he suggested the exact same wording that John had written at the start.

Focus

5. He had been stopped so many times. Each time he rewrote the sign and headed out for the sign maker's shop again. John was physically exhausted but also worn out from everyone criticizing the wording on his sign.
6. The most prominent feature of the story is the way the "story within a story" interrupts the action. Another would be the "rhythm" of the parable: John meets a person, the person inquires about the sign, the person offers a ridiculous piece of advice, John acts upon it, then moves on to the next person, and the drama is acted out again. This always happens in the same order. In addition, the order of the changes to the sign adds flair to the story. The author pares down the sign slowly, leaving the picture of the hat until the last.

Creating and Writing

7. It can be inferred from his reactions that John was not particularly pleased with the advice he received. He repeatedly sighs when he heads back to make the changes.
8. Answers will vary. Give your students a few examples. Below are two you may use.

   Ted had a great idea for his solar system project. He would use wire hangers to attach the special balls he made for each planet. If he bent the wire in just the right way, he could make the planets revolve around the sun. After working for weeks, Ted brought the project to school, hoping everyone would be impressed. Instead, his friends made fun of him for using hangers instead of something better. They also thought that his ball for Mars looked lopsided. Ted knew that he had done a good job and had not received any help from adults, but he still felt terribly hurt.

   Ellen wanted to get a wonderful gift for her mother's fortieth birthday. The problem was, she had no money to spend. Finally, she thought of something she could do that her mother would appreciate. She gathered various supplies, went to her room, and began working on a coupon booklet for Mom. The pages included coupons for household chores and errands that Ellen would do for her mother. While Ellen was picturing the smile on her mother's face, her brother looked over her shoulder to see what she was doing. He laughed out loud and said, "Do you really think that is what Mom wants for her birthday?!"
9. Responses will vary.

What Is Foreshadowing?

A Baseball Card

1. The words "he was also a courageous man," hint at the theme: courage.
2. When Michael's father looks at him closely, and Michael thinks his father is angry, we suspect there is something more to the cards than we know about.
3. Answers will vary.

Lesson in Literature . . .

WHAT IS FORESHADOWING?

- **Foreshadowing** is found in many stories. It is a term for the clues the author places in the first part of a story that hint at what will happen later in the story.
- Foreshadowing takes many forms. It can be part of the story's setting—for example, *a dark, rainy day*. It can be a few words spoken by a character. In a play, it can be background music.
- Foreshadowing keeps the reader guessing. Will something happen, or won't it? Were these words a clue, or weren't they?

The day his father told him the story of Jackie Robinson, Michael started his baseball card collection. Before long he had enough cards to fill two shoeboxes he kept beneath his bed. Each night before he fell asleep, he flipped through his cards, studying the players' biographies and statistics and looking into each player's eyes. He asked, "Are you as good as Jackie Robinson was? Are you as courageous as Jackie Robinson was?" He remembered what his father told him: "Jackie Robinson was not only a talented baseball player; he was a courageous man."

When his grandmother visited, Michael told her about Jackie Robinson and his baseball card collection. She smiled and said, "I have a surprise for you." The next weekend when he visited her house, she took an old hat box out of a closet. Inside were baseball cards. "You can have any of them, Michael," she said. That afternoon he studied them one by one. When he came to an old, faded card at the bottom, a wide smile grew across his face. It was the one card he hoped for. It was a Jackie Robinson card.

At home that night he showed the Jackie Robinson card to his father. "Grandma said I could keep it," he said.

"She did?" his father said, and looked at him just as closely as he looked at the worn edges of the old Jackie Robinson card. Because of that look, Michael thought his father was angry.

But it was Michael's mother who knocked on his bedroom door that night. He was under the covers, the hat box of cards opened on his lap. She sat on the edge of his bed. "What did your father tell you about Jackie Robinson?" she asked.

Michael repeated the story of Jackie Robinson, a second baseman for the old Brooklyn Dodgers of the 1940s and 1950s and the first African-American player in major league baseball. Jackie Robinson, Michael told his mother, was a courageous man because he didn't fight back when angry fans taunted him because they wanted only white players in the major leagues. "Mom, I love all my baseball cards," he said. "But I

Unit Theme:	*Clarity*
Target Skill:	*Recognizing hints and clues in a story and predicting outcome*
Genre:	*Autobiographical Fiction*

A BASEBALL CARD

- Foreshadowing can be found not only in mysteries, but also in comedies, sad stories, happy stories, and even poetry.

THINK ABOUT IT!

1. In the first paragraph, Michael remembers his father saying, "Jackie Robinson was not only a talented baseball player; he was a courageous man." Which words in this line hint at the story's theme?
2. What hint does the reader get that the baseball cards have a special meaning to Michael's father?
3. Were you able to predict what Michael would do before you came to the end of the story?

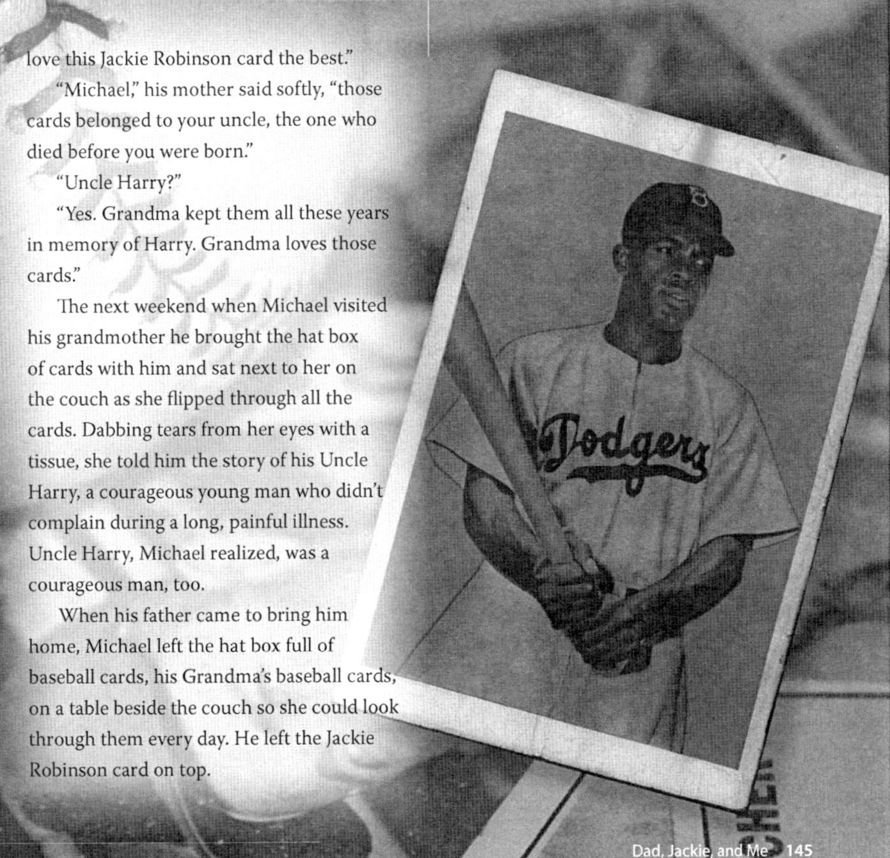

love this Jackie Robinson card the best."

"Michael," his mother said softly, "those cards belonged to your uncle, the one who died before you were born."

"Uncle Harry?"

"Yes. Grandma kept them all these years in memory of Harry. Grandma loves those cards."

The next weekend when Michael visited his grandmother he brought the hat box of cards with him and sat next to her on the couch as she flipped through all the cards. Dabbing tears from her eyes with a tissue, she told him the story of his Uncle Harry, a courageous young man who didn't complain during a long, painful illness. Uncle Harry, Michael realized, was a courageous man, too.

When his father came to bring him home, Michael left the hat box full of baseball cards, his Grandma's baseball cards, on a table beside the couch so she could look through them every day. He left the Jackie Robinson card on top.

Getting Started

Play a baseball game (preferably a real one, otherwise, an imaginary one) with your class and explain the terms used in the story as you go along. Without actually referring to the upcoming story, you may find the opportunity to bring up some of the story's lessons. For example, if someone is not athletic and is being teased or is made to feel unwelcome on the team, you can discuss how that person feels. (This relates to Jackie's teammates harassing him as well as Dad's inability to catch a ball properly.) Or you can give a student (perhaps a volunteer) some odd-looking clothes or hat to wear during the game. See what comments are made. Does it affect the student's ability to play? Aside from the connection to the story, it is a good opportunity to cultivate the kind of team spirit that is sensitive to the feelings of individuals.

Into . . .
Dad, Jackie, and Me

Prejudice in our society has been discussed endlessly. Prejudice with all its political overtones should not be the focus of the classroom discussion of this story. It would be far more useful to discuss prejudice as one more human failing that can and must be rectified. Prejudice has its roots in ignorance and arrogance. It is rooted in ignorance, in that the prejudiced person has all sorts of fictional ideas about the object of his prejudice. It is rooted in arrogance, in that the prejudiced individual does not recognize that, in the blink of an eye, he could suffer the same fate as the person against whom he is prejudiced (in this story it would be prejudice against his race or religion like Jackie suffered, or a physical impairment, like Dad suffered).

To reinforce this idea, you may choose to do the following activity. Divide the class into three groups. Do not choose groups based on race, gender, or academic ability, but, rather, by some arbitrary factor, such as those who are wearing a ponytail, glasses, the color blue, or something of that nature. One group should be excused from homework that night, one should have regular homework, and the last third should be given extra homework. Do not accept any complaints. You may tell the group with extra homework that if they complain they will receive more work to do. Leave room for discussion before the day's end. Explain that this was just a way to demonstrate what prejudice is all about, and you were not actually assigning extra homework. Should glasses really be a deciding factor in who receives homework? Is it fair for a teacher to do that? On the other hand, you can point out that children do need extra work at times, whether supplemental or enrichment, for their own benefit. Ask your students how it felt to belong to each group.

Blueprint for Reading

INTO . . . *Dad, Jackie, and Me*

What would it feel like if people did not want to talk or play with you? What if you were told that you were not smart enough or strong enough to join a group? Have you had an experience where you were not given a fair chance? As we learned in *Supergrandpa,* people make unfair judgments at times. When we develop an unfavorable opinion about someone or something without having a lot of information, it is called *prejudice*. Prejudice comes with a lot of unpleasant "partners," such as meanness, intolerance, and selfishness. As you read *Dad, Jackie, and Me,* identify the characters who suffer from the prejudice of others.

Predicting Outcome

There are people who would love to see into the future. While this is not possible, we often get hints about a future event. The trouble is, we usually don't really notice these hints until after the event takes place! For example, if your friends were planning a surprise party for you, even if they tried their best to keep everything a secret, clues and hints would probably come out. You might notice that something was different, but you wouldn't think about it much. Later on, though, when you were at the surprise party, you would remember the hints and clues and say, "Oh! So that's why you did that..."

In a short story or book, an author will often plant information near the beginning of the story that hints at what is going to happen later on. The hints and clues are called **foreshadowing.** For the reader, deciding which parts of the story are foreshadowing is like working out a puzzle. Using the clues to guess what will happen at the end is like trying to solve a mystery. As you read *Dad, Jackie, and Me,* see if you can identify the foreshadowing and predict what will happen later.

146 Unit 2

Eyes On
Predicting Outcome

A surprise party is an example that your students can relate to. You may discuss the kinds of hints that a child would notice as the planners are trying to keep the secret. For example, a parent might send the birthday child on a useless errand to get her out of the house, or a sibling might give a silly reason for not opening the freezer that holds the ice cream cake. Allow the students to share their own "foreshadowing" experiences with the class.

Point out that there are many ways to weave foreshadowing into a story. A gloomy, eerie setting may indicate a scary or tragic climax. A seemingly extraneous detail should be suspect in the reader's mind as a possible clue. On the other hand, remind them that authors sometimes plant false clues to mislead the reader, so as to have a really good surprise ending.

Predicting outcomes is an important skill. Read the following hints one at a time to your student, then ask the class what they predict will happen:

- Gina and Cindy were best friends. One day, Gina said to Cindy, "Wouldn't it be amazing to be related?! I guess that's too much to ask for."
  They work on a family tree project and find a common relative.
- Wendy is about to go on stage and Dave shouts the well-known phrase, "Break a leg!" Beth tells Dave, "Why did you have to say that?!" "It's just a common saying, Beth. Just relax."
  Wendy breaks her ankle halfway through the performance.
- Neil notices a figure lurking in a corner with a bulky package under his coat.
  Your students can predict a variety of nasty things that might happen next. Then suggest that perhaps the man was hiding a birthday present.

The following are examples of foreshadowing from *Dad, Jackie, and Me.*

- "I dreamed of the day I could see it all for myself."
- "The Dodgers were going to go all the way!"
- "There's no way Dad can meet Jackie Robinson. Besides, Jackie doesn't know sign language. How would they talk to each other?"
- "Jackie never drops the ball," he signed. "He catches it with one hand, not like me."

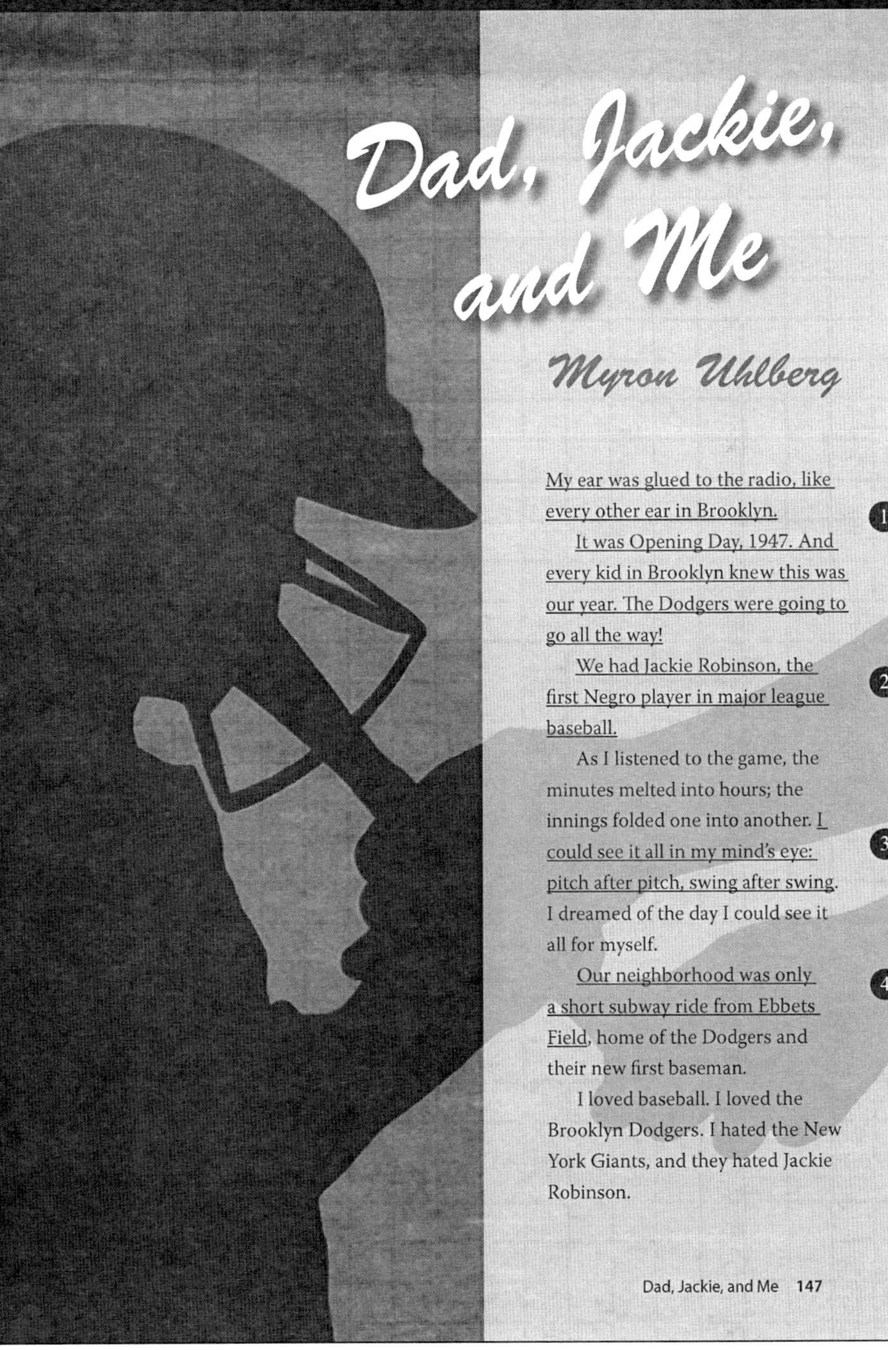

Dad, Jackie, and Me

Myron Uhlberg

My ear was glued to the radio, like every other ear in Brooklyn. 1

It was Opening Day, 1947. And every kid in Brooklyn knew this was our year. The Dodgers were going to go all the way!

We had Jackie Robinson, the first Negro player in major league baseball. 2

As I listened to the game, the minutes melted into hours; the innings folded one into another. I could see it all in my mind's eye: 3 pitch after pitch, swing after swing. I dreamed of the day I could see it all for myself.

Our neighborhood was only 4 a short subway ride from Ebbets Field, home of the Dodgers and their new first baseman.

I loved baseball. I loved the Brooklyn Dodgers. I hated the New York Giants, and they hated Jackie Robinson.

Dad, Jackie, and Me 147

Selection Summary

Like every other kid in Brooklyn in 1947, Myron (the narrator) is a Dodgers' fan. Unlike most kids, he has a father who is deaf. The family lives near Ebbets Field, home of the Dodgers. One day, Dad, who was never very interested in baseball, says he wants to go to a game. Dad wants to meet Jackie Robinson, the first black baseball player in the major leagues. Myron is thrilled, for he has never been to Ebbets Field.

When the game starts and Jackie runs out onto the field, Dad cheers. The fans of the Giants, the opposing team, jeer and hurl epithets at Jackie. This saddens Dad, but it doesn't surprise him. Inspired by Jackie Robinson, Dad begins to take a great interest in baseball. He and Myron practice at home and they begin to attend games together, always cheering loudest for Jackie. When a player from an opposing team spikes Jackie Robinson, Dad leads the crowd in yelling "NO FAIR." Jackie himself seems emotionless. As the summer wears on, Jackie and the Dodgers keep winning. Jackie, the object of slurs and insults, keeps his face blank, never reacting, never complaining.

The Dodgers win the pennant, but they still have one game to play. Dad and Myron go to see their hero, Jackie. As usual, Jackie plays fantastically. In the last inning, Jackie, at first base, catches a line drive, for the last out of the game. He looks at the ball in his glove, then turns and throws the ball right to Dad. Dad reaches up and catches the ball with his bare hand. Perhaps Jackie smiled ... and so ends the 1947 baseball season.

Guiding the Reading

Literal

Q: The Opening Day in 1947 was for what event?

A: It was for major league baseball.

Q: Where did the story take place?

A: It took place in Brooklyn, New York.

Q: What team was the author rooting for?

A: He was a Dodgers' fan.

Q: Which player did the author single out to mention and why?

A: He mentioned Jackie Robinson because he was the first Negro—African American—to play in the major leagues.

Q: Where did the Dodgers play?

A: They played in Ebbets Field.

Q: Who did the Giants hate, according to the author?

A: They hated Jackie Robinson.

Literary Components

1 **Setting; Characterization; Idiom:** In a few short sentences, the author tells us all we need to picture a young Brooklyn Dodgers fan who lives in—where else?—Brooklyn and who talks everyday, ordinary Brooklynese.

2 **Historical Reference:** Jackie Robinson made history as the first black baseball player in the major leagues.

3 **Expressive Language:** The author conveys the power of radio and the outstanding commentators who "delivered" the games to the listeners.

4 **Setting:** A working-class neighborhood is described.

Literary Components

5 Rising Action: We learn two things: that the author's father is deaf and that he is more interested in Jackie Robinson the person than in the Brooklyn Dodgers.

6 Idiom: This slang expression makes the speaker sound very real.

7 Descriptive Language: The speaker uses slang and colloquialism, but is also at home using poetic-sounding metaphors.

One day, my father came home early from work. He walked into my bedroom and announced, "We're going to Ebbets Field."

He didn't say it out loud. My father was deaf, so he signed the words with his hands. I couldn't believe it. Dad had never seemed to care much about baseball.

5 <u>"I want to meet Jackie Robinson," Dad signed.</u>

I was finally going to see a real game. Today the Dodgers
6 were playing the Giants. And <u>we were going to cream 'em</u>.

I got my glove and ball, Dodgers cap, and scorecard. I stuck my lucky pencil behind my ear. As we went down the steps, I tossed the ball to Dad. But he'd never played baseball like me. He dropped it.

I couldn't wait to get to the ballpark. But the whole ride I kept thinking, There's no way Dad can meet Jackie Robinson. Besides, Jackie doesn't know sign language.

How would they talk to each other?

The line to get in to Ebbets Field snaked around Sullivan Place and up to Bedford Avenue. My dad let me hold my ticket. I clutched it for dear life.

Finally, we were through the turnstile. My dad held my hand as we moved with the rest of the crowd through <u>the gloomy</u>
7 <u>underbelly of the stadium</u>, up the dark ramp. Then we tumbled into bright sunlight.

I shut my eyes against the glare. When I opened them again, my breath caught in my throat. I had never seen anything so perfect as the inside of Ebbets Field.

There, laid out at my feet, was the emerald green field, each blade of grass reflecting the light from the afternoon sun.

The angles of the field were sharply marked in two lines of white chalk.

The dirt base paths formed a perfect diamond carpet dotted with fat canvas bags at each base and a black rubber plate at home.

I knew if I lived to be a hundred, I would never again see a sight so beautiful.

148 Unit 2

Guiding the Reading

Literal

Q: What surprise did Dad have for his son?
A: He had tickets to go to a game at Ebbets Field.

Q: Why did this surprise the author?
A: Dad had never seemed to be interested in base-ball.

Q: What was Dad's reason for wanting to go to the game?
A: He said that he wanted to meet Jackie Robinson.

Q: How did Dad tell his son about the exciting news?
A: He was deaf and signed the information to him.

Q: Which teams were going to play the day they went to the game?
A: The Brooklyn Dodgers and the New York Giants were going to play against each other.

Q: How well did Dad play baseball?
A: He did not play well at all. He had never played much and he always dropped the ball.

Q: What was the author thinking during the ride to Ebbets Field?
A: He was thinking that Dad would not be able to meet Jackie Robinson and, even if he could, he would not be able to communicate with him since Jackie did not know sign language.

Q: Why did he have a catch in his throat?
A: He was overwhelmed by what he thought was the most beautiful sight he had ever seen.

Q: How is the field described?
A: "There, laid out at my feet, was the emerald green field, each blade of grass reflecting the light from the afternoon sun. The angles of the field were sharply marked in two lines of white chalk. The dirt base paths formed a perfect diamond carpet dotted with fat canvas bags at each base and a black rubber plate at home."

Q: How does he express his excitement?
A: He says that even if he lives to one hundred he will never see anything quite like this.

Analytical

Q: What did the author mean when he said, "We were going to cream 'em"?
A: He meant that the Dodgers would beat the Giants.

Q: Why might it be difficult to meet Jackie Robinson personally?
A: He was a famous and very busy person.

Q: Can hearing people communicate with deaf people even if they do not know sign language?
A: Yes, many deaf people read lips well or have hearing aids or cochlear implants to help them communicate better. (Cochlear implants had not been invented yet when this story took place.)

Dodgers
42
150 Unit 2

"Hey, peanuts! Hey, hot dogs! Get 'em while they're hot!"

Dad and I sat on the right field line, right behind first base, Jackie's position.

The Dodgers Sym-Phony was marching up and down the aisles playing "The Worms Crawl In, the Worms Crawl Out." The music was earsplitting. Dad couldn't hear it, but he laughed along with everyone else at the sight of the raggedy band's tattered clothes, cowbells, and whistles.

When the game started and Jackie ran out on the field, Dad yelled real loud, "Jackiee, Jackiee, Jackiee!" Only it didn't come out that way. It sounded like, "AH-GHEE, AH-GHEE, AH-GHEE!" Since my dad couldn't hear, he had no way of knowing what the words should sound like.

Everyone looked at my dad. 8

I looked at my shoes.

As Jackie stood at first base, the Giants began hooting and hollering. They called Jackie names. Horrible names. "What are they saying?" Dad asked.

"Bad things," I said.

"Tell me." Some of those words I had to finger spell. I knew no sign for them. Dad listened with a sad little smile on his face.

In the ninth inning, Jackie bunted, and beat the throw to first. Then he stole second.

On the next Dodgers hit, he moved to third. The score was tied at four-all.

The Giants pitcher took a long windup, and Jackie dashed 9
for home. We all jumped to our feet yelling, "Jackiee, Jackiee, Jackiee!"

"AH-GHEE, AH-GHEE, AH-GHEE!" Dad screamed.

This time, nobody seemed to notice.

Forget about the Giants. They were nothing! We had Jackie Robinson.

Every day when Dad came home from work, he started asking me questions. Not about school. About baseball. He wanted to know everything I knew. Especially about Jackie Robinson.

Literary Components

8 Repetition: The repetitive words highlight the author's embarrassment.

9 Dramatic Moment: Any reader who is a baseball fan knows that this is a moment that neither the writer nor his father will ever forget. It may not be the climax of the story, but it is certainly a climactic moment in the life of Myron Uhlberg!

Guiding the Reading

Literal

Q: What were people selling during the game?
A: They were selling peanuts and hot dogs.

Q: Where were Dad and his son sitting?
A: They were sitting on the right field line, right behind first base, which was Jackie's position.

Q: Why was Dad laughing along with everyone if he could not hear the band?
A: He was laughing at the band's clothes, cowbells, and whistles.

Q: What did Dad do when Jackie came out onto the field?
A: He screamed aloud, "Jackiee, Jackiee, Jackiee!"

Q: Why did everyone look at Dad, if he was just yelling, "Jackie!" (a common thing at a game)?
A: Dad could not hear himself and his words did not sound like the word 'Jackie,' but like, "AH-GHEE."

Q: Who called Jackie Robinson terrible names?
A: The Giants called him names.

Q: What did Dad want to know from his son?
A: He wanted to know what was going on and what they were saying about Jackie.

Q: Why didn't the boy know the signs but rather had to finger spell?
A: They were words that were terrible that he did not use and were not in his general vocabulary. (Finger spelling is a method of manually spelling out difficult words or names and other proper nouns.)

Q: When did Jackie really get everyone's attention?
A: It happened during the ninth inning.

Q: Why does the author say that the Giants were nothing?
A: Because he felt having Jackie Robinson was everything.

Q: What did Dad ask each day when his son came home from school?
A: He asked him many questions about baseball.

Analytical

Q: Why did the author look at his shoes?
A: He was embarrassed that everyone was looking at his deaf father and that his behavior stood out.

Q: Why didn't anyone notice Dad's interesting screams this time?
A: They were preoccupied and the noise level was very high.

Literary Components

10 Characterization: Dad's character is beginning to unfold. We learn he is an idealist because he wants to cheer the first black Dodger. Perhaps he identifies with Jackie who, like he, is not in the mainstream of society. Here, we see that Dad doesn't mind a bit of pain if it furthers achievement. He is persistent and not easily discouraged.

11 Characterization: Jackie Robinson doesn't respond to the crowd. Is this because he is shy? Single-minded? Unfeeling? Is this to protect himself from those who would taunt him or worse? We aren't told.

12 High Point: The gradual revealing of Dad's character, the excitement of the game, and the racial prejudice that lurks just under the surface of the story all converge at this semi-climactic moment.

"What's Jackie's batting average?"

".247," I said.

"How's that figured?"

I explained.

"What's an RBI?" he asked.

"Runs batted in."

"Fielding average. What's that mean?"

I told him.

"You teach me baseball," he signed.

"Okay," I said.

One night, Dad came home with a baseball glove.

"Let's have a catch," he signed.

We tossed the ball back and forth until Mom called us for supper. Dad missed the ball every time. The only way he could hold it was by trapping the ball against his chest with
10 both hands. That had to hurt, but Dad just smiled.

"Jackie never drops the ball," he signed. "He catches it with one hand. Not like me."

All that week we practiced. Dad dropped the ball most every time. Even when I threw it underhand.

"Throw it regular," Dad said.

Dad and I kept going to games whenever we could. Every time Jackie came out to his position, Dad chanted right along with the crowd. AH-GHEE, AH-GHEE, AH-GHEE.

11 Jackie never looked over at us. He just stared down the line at the next hitter.

One Sunday, the Dodgers were playing the St. Louis Cardinals. What a game! Our pitcher had a no-hitter going.

And then it happened. On a simple grounder that he knew he couldn't beat, a Cardinal player crossed first base and spiked Jackie—on purpose! Fifty-two thousand eyes popped. Twenty-six thousand jaws dropped. Twenty-six thousand tongues were stilled.

Then, in that awful silence, my father jumped to his feet.

12 "NOOOO!" he screamed. "NOT FAIR! AH-GHEE, AH-GHEE, AH-GHEE!"

152 Unit 2

Guiding the Reading

Literal

Q: What is an RBI?
A: It is a "run batted in."

Q: How well did Dad play baseball even when the author tried to teach him?
A: He did not play very well.

Q: Did practice help him improve?
A: No.

Q: How did Dad catch the ball?
A: He trapped the ball against his chest with both hands.

Q: What did Dad say about Jackie and the ball?
A: Jackie never drops the ball and catches it easily with one hand.

Q: Did Jackie ever notice Dad and son when they were enthusiastically cheering for him?
A: It did not seem as though he did.

Q: Who was playing whom at the game that Sunday?
A: The Dodgers were playing the St. Louis Cardinals.

Q: What did one of the Cardinals do to Jackie on purpose?
A: He crossed first base and spiked Jackie.

Q: What was the reaction of the crowd?
A: "Fifty-two thousand eyes popped. Twenty-six thousand jaws dropped. Twenty-six thousand tongues were stilled." This means the people were quiet from shock and excitement.

Q: Who was the first to respond?
A: Dad started screaming that what was done to Jackie was unfair.

Analytical

Q: Who was the student and who was the teacher when it came to baseball?
A: In this case, the child was his father's teacher.

Q: Why do you think Dad had such an interest in baseball if we knew from the beginning of the story that he was not interested in it and didn't know how to play?
A: Dad is fascinated by Jackie Robinson's acceptance into major league baseball. His strong sense of fairness is thrilled by this move on the part of baseball. At the same time, he identifies with Jackie as an outsider and is eager to cheer him on.

Dad, Jackie, and Me 153

B
Dodgers
154 Unit 2

The Brooklyn crowd went nuts. They leapt to their feet and joined my father. "JACK-IE, JACK-IE, JACK-IE!"

The name bounced off the brick walls, climbed the iron girders, and rattled around under the wooden roof.

But Jackie just stood at first base, his face a blank mask, blood streaming down 13
his leg. It was almost as if he didn't hear the crowd.

All that month, Dad and I followed everything Jackie did. We read and reread every report of every game that was printed in *The New York Daily News*.

Dad started a scrapbook. If there was any mention of Jackie Robinson, he cut out the article and pasted it in his scrapbook.

The scrapbook got thicker.

The Dodgers kept winning.

And the opposing teams kept riding Jackie Robinson.

But Jackie never reacted. He didn't even seem to notice. And he never 14
complained.

The Dodgers clinched the pennant that season when the Cards beat the Cubs. Dad and I went downtown the next day to see the big parade to honor Jackie. And back in the neighborhood, we had a block party to celebrate.

It didn't matter whether the Dodgers won the last game of the season, since we were already over the top. But Dad and I didn't care. We went to Ebbets Field anyway. We went to see Jackie Robinson.

In the third inning, Jackie smacked the ball to deep left field for a double. Then
he flew home like the wind, his feet barely touching the base path. 15

The Brooklyn crowd went crazy. "Go, Go, Go, Jackieeee!"

"GOO, GOO, GOO, AH-GHEEEE!" my dad screamed right along with them.

Finally, late in the day, as deep shadows stretched across the infield, Jackie caught a line drive hit down the first base line. It was the last out of the game.

As the crowd cheered, Jackie stood alone at first base, staring at the ball in his
glove. Then he turned and threw it into the stands—right to my father! 16

That's when my dad did something he had never done before. He reached up and caught the ball in his bare hand!

I'm not sure, but I think I saw Jackie Robinson smile. My dad dropped the ball 17
into my empty glove.

And just like that, the baseball season of 1947 was over.

Literary Components

13 Characterization: Again, we are frustrated and mystified by Jackie's blankness. Is he angry at his enemies? Does he value the support of the crowd? Does he care about anybody one way or the other? Does he care only about winning the game? We are not told. We would like to see him respond to his defenders, but we are not given that satisfaction.

14 Characterization: The author reports things as they appear, not offering any opinion about Jackie's lack of reaction.

15 Simile: The young writer speaks poetically, conveying his feeling (as he did earlier when he described his first glimpse of Ebbets Field) that there is no greater work of art than the game of baseball, its players, and its fields.

16 Climax: Jackie suddenly responds! Dad's unwavering belief in and support of him are rewarded.

17 Conclusion: The moment is fleeting and even Jackie's smile is momentary, but the ball in Dad's glove is real enough, and proof of that great moment in the great summer of 1947.

Guiding the Reading

Literal

Q: What happened after Dad broke the silence?

A: A lot of people joined in.

Q: What did Jackie do?

A: He just stood at first base, his face a blank mask with blood streaming down his leg.

Q: What did Dad do with all the articles he cut out?

A: He put them in a scrapbook.

Q: What happened when the opposing teams kept riding Jackie Robinson?

A: He acted as though he did not notice. He never reacted or complained.

Q: Why did the author go downtown with his Dad?

A: They wanted to see the parade honoring Jackie Robinson.

Q: During which inning did Jackie throw a ball deep into left field?

A: During the third inning.

Q: Who made the last out of the game?

A: Jackie did, by catching a ball at the first base line.

Q: What was Jackie doing while the crowd cheered?

A: He stood alone at first base staring at the ball in his glove.

Q: Whom did Jackie throw the ball to?

A: He threw it to Dad.

Q: What did Dad do when Jackie Robinson threw the ball to him?

A: Amazingly, he caught it with his bare hand.

Analytical

Q: How do you know that a lot of people were screaming loudly?

A: "The name bounced off the brick walls, climbed the iron girders, and rattled around under the wooden roof."

Q: What do you think the other team expected Jackie to do when they mistreated him?

A: Some hoped that he would quit; others hoped he would lose his temper so there could be a good fight; and others were probably so mean and ornery that they just wanted him to be there to be bullied.

Q: What was so surprising about the fact that Dad caught the ball?

A: He had never learned to catch a ball properly.

Author's Note

This story is a work of fiction. Parts of it, however, are based in truth.

My father, who was deaf and spoke only with his hands, worked as a printer for *The New York Daily News*. One night in 1947, he brought home the paper—the ink not quite dry—and excitedly showed me the bold headline: BROOKLYN DODGERS SIGN JACKIE ROBINSON. Beneath it was a photo of two smiling men: the president of the Brooklyn Dodgers, Branch Rickey, and the grandson of a slave, Jackie Robinson.

"Now, at last," my father signed to me, "a Negro will play in the major leagues!"

And from the day he joined the Brooklyn Dodgers until the day he retired, Jackie Robinson was the main topic of conversation in our small Brooklyn apartment during every baseball season.

My father could not throw or catch a baseball, let alone hit one. As a boy in 1910, he attended a deaf residential school, where playing sports was not encouraged. In those days most people considered deaf children severely handicapped and thought teaching them sports a waste of time. What could my deaf father possibly have in common with this Negro baseball player, Jackie Robinson?

During Jackie's first year as a Dodger, my father took me to many games. He told me to watch carefully how the opposing team would single Jackie out for unfair treatment, how they would actively discriminate against him on the field just because his skin was brown. "Just you watch,"

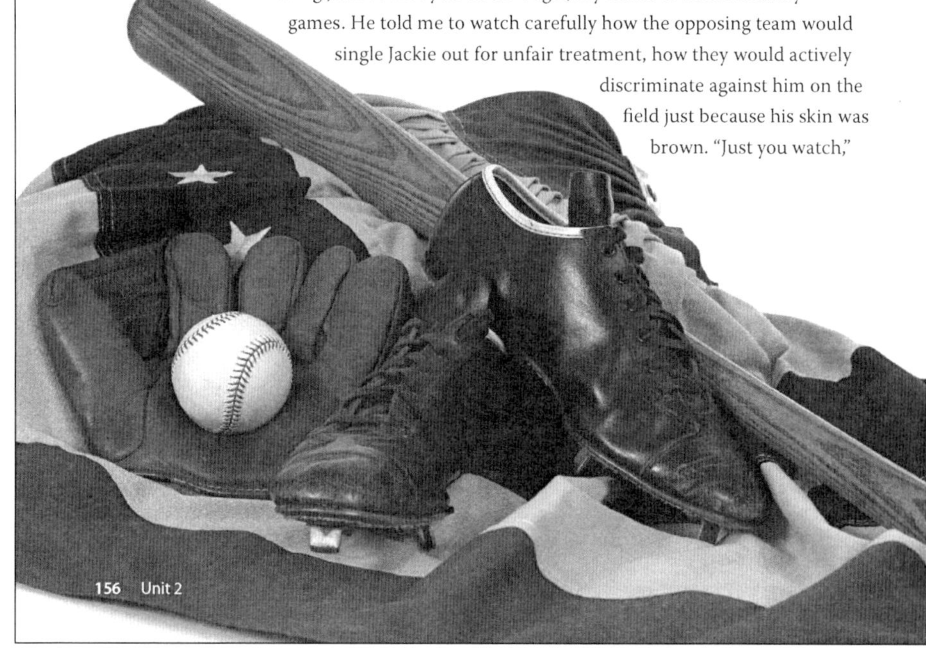

he said. "Jackie will show them that his skin color has nothing to do with how he plays baseball. He will show them all that he is as good as they are."

Throughout his life my father also experienced the cruelty of prejudice. "It's not fair that hearing people discriminate against me just because I am deaf," he told me. "It doesn't matter, though," he always added. "I show them every day I am as good as they are."

One summer day, late in that rookie season of 1947—during which Jackie had quietly endured racial taunts, threats on his life, numerous bean balls, and even deliberate spikings—my father told me about another hero.

"There was a deaf man born in 1862," he signed to me, "who was also a baseball player. His name was William Ellsworth Hoy, but his teammates quickly nicknamed him 'The Amazing Dummy.'

"In those days no one could imagine that a deaf man could play major league baseball. The deaf were thoughtlessly called 'deaf and dumb.' It was common for the hearing to refer to a deaf person as a 'dummy.'

"But Dummy Hoy showed them all," my father continued. "He played fourteen years in the major leagues. He was smart and fast like Jackie, and in his rookie year he stole a record eighty-two bases. One day, he threw three men out at home plate from the outfield, which had never been done before. And, most importantly, he taught umpires to use hand signals to call balls and strikes."

As he told that story, I began to understand the connection between Jackie Robinson and my deaf father. Like Dummy Hoy before them, they were both men who worked to overcome thoughtless prejudice and to prove themselves every day of their lives.

—M.U.

ABOUT THE AUTHOR

Myron Uhlberg was born in 1933 to Lou and Sarah Uhlberg, who "just happened to be deaf." Although he never thought of his parents as handicapped, he observed that some people were prejudiced against them, simply because they were deaf. In his book, *Dad, Jackie, and Me*, he explains how his father, like Jackie Robinson, was sometimes the victim of prejudice. In real life, Jackie was the main topic of conversation at the Uhlberg home. From the day he joined the Dodgers, Jackie Robinson was Lou Uhlberg's hero. For Myron, though, the real hero was his own Dad.

About Analysis of Baseball

Poetry Is About the Things We Cheer

Analysis of Baseball claims to be about baseball—and it is—but it is *really* about the way we talk about baseball.

"Ball hits
bat, or it
hits mitt.
Bat doesn't
hit ball, bat
meets it."

It's also about the way we *experience* baseball.

"That's about
the bases
loaded,
about 40,000
fans exploded."

Baseball is not just played. It is shared. The team and the fans go together like a bat and a ball. Baseball is more than a game. It is more than a lot of rules. It is more than a team. It is more than the fans. It is nearly a culture.

The short, sharp lines of the poem are the language of the sportsman, not the philosopher. They convey what's important to the average fan:

"Ball fits
mitt . . . sometimes
ball gets hit
(pow) . . ."

And, though it's "done for fun," what the true bottom line for every baseball fan is—

"It's about
home, and it's
about run."
—the final score!

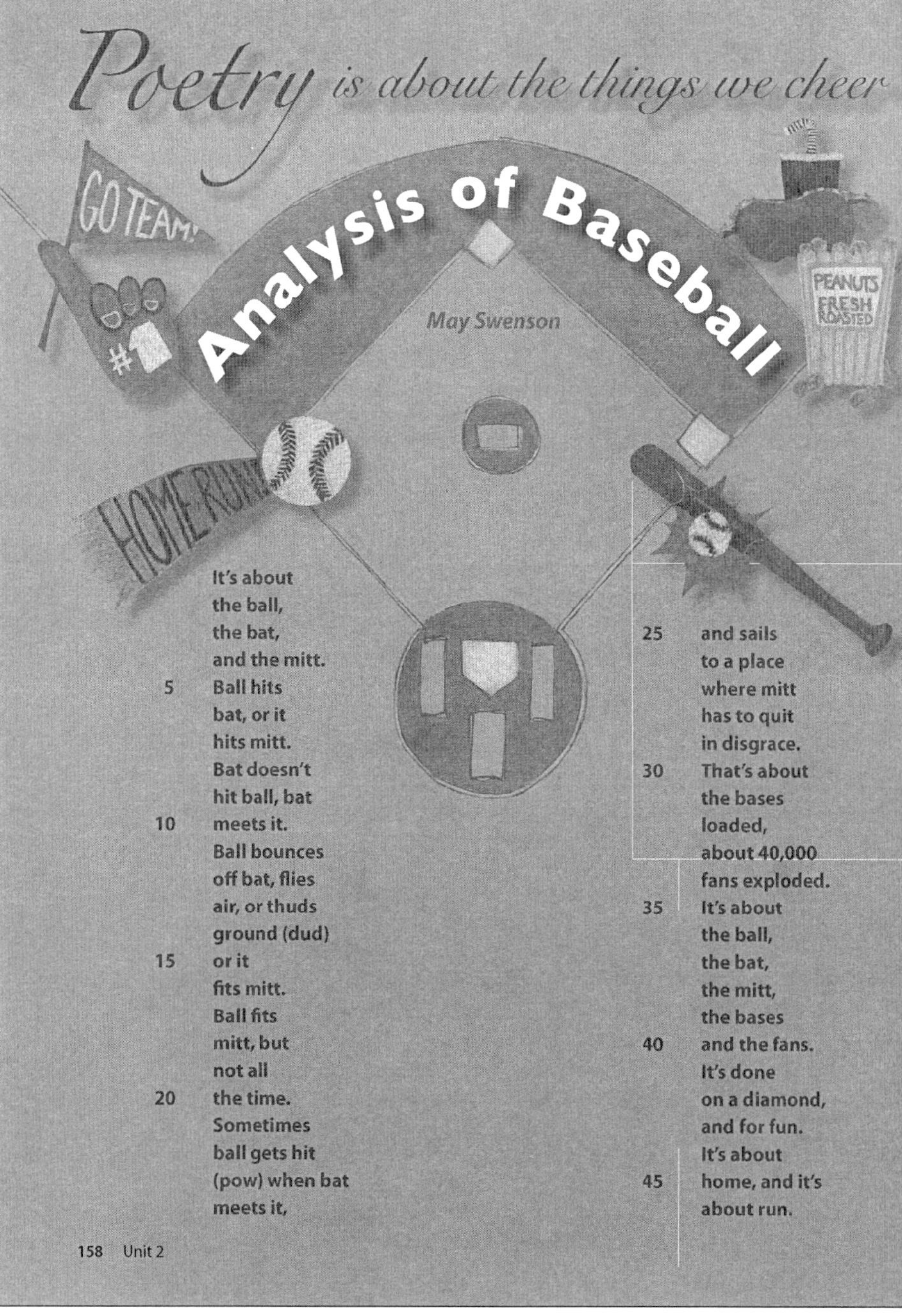

Poetry is about the things we cheer

Analysis of Baseball

May Swenson

It's about
the ball,
the bat,
and the mitt.
Ball hits
bat, or it
hits mitt.
Bat doesn't
hit ball, bat
meets it.
Ball bounces
off bat, flies
air, or thuds
ground (dud)
or it
fits mitt.
Ball fits
mitt, but
not all
the time.
Sometimes
ball gets hit
(pow) when bat
meets it,
and sails
to a place
where mitt
has to quit
in disgrace.
That's about
the bases
loaded,
about 40,000
fans exploded.
It's about
the ball,
the bat,
the mitt,
the bases
and the fans.
It's done
on a diamond,
and for fun.
It's about
home, and it's
about run.

158 Unit 2

Studying the Selection

FIRST IMPRESSIONS

Do you think that anyone on Jackie's own team was prejudiced against him? Why or why not?

QUICK REVIEW

1. What team was the narrator a fan of?
2. Because he was a fan, how did he spend most of his free time?
3. What surprise did Dad have for his son?
4. What important step had the Dodgers taken by asking Jackie Robinson to join the team?

FOCUS

5. What lifelong lessons can the boy learn from his father and Jackie?
6. Did you think Dad would ever meet Jackie Robinson? What are some clues that the author places in the story that allow you to think he will?

CREATING AND WRITING

7. People were prejudiced against Jackie because of his race and against Dad because of his deafness. Sometimes people make prejudiced comments thinking that you agree with them. What would you say to someone who made a prejudiced comment about either Jackie or Dad, thinking that you felt the same way? Write two or three sentences in which you tell the person not to include you in this prejudiced way of thinking.
8. Write a short story about an athlete who joins a team but finds that the team members have made up their minds to dislike the newcomer. Plan the story in your mind so that you know what happens in the end before you start writing. Place clues in the story that help the reader predict the ending.
9. Pretend you are "the voice of the Brooklyn Dodgers" on the radio. It is the last game of the season and Jackie comes to bat. He hits a ball deep into left field and... Write four or five lines that you, the radio announcer, say on the air. You may use lots of capital letters and exclamation points to show the excitement in your voice!

Dad, Jackie, and Me 159

First Impressions

Although the question asks about the Dodgers, many students will respond by saying that the Giants were the ones who hated Jackie. While this is true, you can point out the possibility of prejudice within the team.

One can argue either way. Team spirit would dictate that they not feel prejudice against a fellow teammate, but unfortunately that is not always the case. It is a fact that Jackie Robinson endured constant insults and abuse not only from baseball fans and Giants players, but also from his fellow Dodgers. Some players on the team said they would rather sit out the game than play alongside Jackie. The situation finally eased up when the Dodgers manager threatened to trade players if they did not leave Jackie Robinson alone and just play the game. He emphatically said that he didn't care whether Jackie was black or yellow or had zebra stripes—he was going to play.

Quick Review

1. The author was a fan of the Brooklyn Dodgers.
2. He listened to every game on the radio, dreamed about baseball, and cut out newspaper articles on baseball. When he was at his first game, he said, "I knew if I lived to be a hundred, I would never again see a sight so beautiful."
3. Dad surprised his son with tickets to Ebbets Field to watch a baseball game.
4. They were the first major league team to hire an African American. (There were black-only leagues but this was the first time white and black players played on the same team.)

Focus

5. Dad was confident and proud of who he was despite his deafness. He persevered even when people thought he was unable to do things because of his disability or for some other reason. For example, he kept trying to catch a baseball even though he was not very successful. He was upbeat, devoted, and caring, and had his son's best interests in mind. Dad also taught his son what was fair and just.

   Jackie ignored most of the negative comments shouted at him. He had courage and he also had the wisdom not to respond to the bigots. He was a pioneer in the field of sports.
6. Dad says, "I want to meet Jackie Robinson."

   The narrator says, "There's no way Dad can meet Jackie Robinson. Besides, Jackie doesn't know sign language. How would they talk to each other?"

   Dad is the first and loudest to yell Jackie's name. He becomes so interested in Jackie that he goes to almost every game and practices catching. He is the first to scream in protest when Jackie is spiked.

   All these are clues that *something* will happen. The reader knows a story must lead somewhere, and the fact that the story starts out with a stated goal—Dad meeting Jackie—makes the reader feel something will happen. As in any good story, the reader isn't *sure*, but only feels the two will make some contact.

Creating and Writing

7. Answers will vary. Mention that it sometimes takes courage to shun someone, or a group of people, who want to include you in their feelings of prejudice.
8. Answers will vary.
9. Answers will vary.

Lesson in Literature

What Is a Main Idea?

Turtle, Tortoise, or Terrapin?

1. "What makes a turtle a turtle?"
2. a.
3. Turtles have flippers and can swim in water. The tortoise has legs and moves on land. The terrapin has webbed feet and can swim and move on land.

Lesson in Literature . . . Turtle, Tortoise, or Terrapin?

What Is a Main Idea?

- Every literary form, whether it is a drama, a poem, a novel, a short story, or an essay, must have a **main idea**.
- In an essay, such as the one that follows, each *paragraph* also has a main idea.
- In a well-written paragraph, all the details will be closely connected to its main idea.
- As you read any written work, ask yourself, *What is the main idea here?*

Think About It!

1. Select one sentence from the first paragraph which clearly states the essay's main idea.
2. Which of the following topics is not covered in the second paragraph?
   a. what turtles eat
   b. where turtles live
   c. the size and weight of turtles
3. Read the third paragraph carefully. The main difference between turtles, tortoises, and terrapins is the way they move around and where they live. Describe that difference.

Vocabulary

basking (BASS king) *v.*: lying in something pleasantly warm (like the sun)

predator (PREH duh tor) *n.*: an animal that hunts other animals for food

thrives *v.*: grows and improves

habitat (HAB ih TAT) *n.*: the place where a plant or animal is naturally found

sanctuaries (SANK chew AIR eez) *n.*: a portion of land set aside by the government, where wildlife can live in safety from hunters

expedition (EX puh DISH un) *n.*: a journey or voyage made to a distant place for a certain purpose

commercial (kuh MUR shul) *n.*: made by companies to be sold in stores; not homemade

rehabilitation (REE huh BIH luh TAY shun) *n.*: a returning to good health

ornery (OR nuh ree) *adj.*: mean

transport (trans PORT) *v.*: to move; to carry

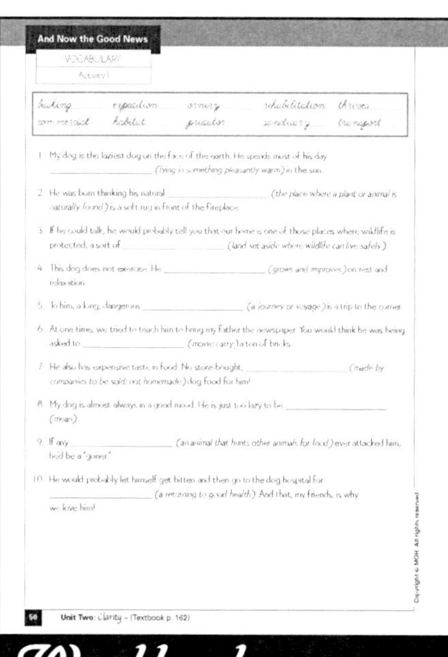

Workbook

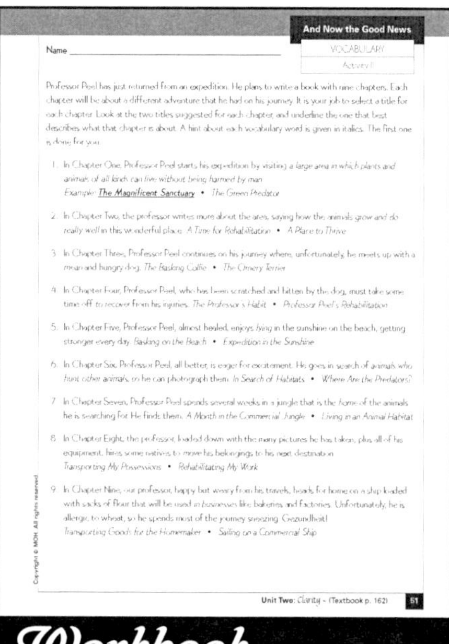

Workbook

Unit Theme:	*Clarity*
Target Skill:	*Recognizing the main idea, and understanding how story details support it*
Genre:	*Nonfiction Essay*

It's easy to recognize a turtle, right? Its hard shell, thumb-like head, and slow walk give it away. What if, though, that turtle inching along in the grass or basking on the log beside the pond is not a turtle but a tortoise or a terrapin? What makes a turtle a turtle?

Everyone believes they know a turtle when they see one, but did you know there are about 300 species of turtles? Some are aquatic, which means they live in water. Others are terrestrial, which means they live on land. Some turtles are amphibious; that is, they live both in water and on land. Some, like the giant tortoise of the Galápagos Islands, can weigh up to seven hundred pounds; others, like the Northern spider tortoise of Madagascar, can weigh less than an ounce and fit in the palm of your hand. Turtles like the red-eared slider are kept as pets in home terrariums, while others like the great leatherback sea turtle are highly endangered.

Turtles are generally divided into these three groups: sea turtles, tortoises, and terrapins. Aquatic turtles, or sea turtles, swim in warm waters throughout the world and migrate to lay their eggs on secluded beaches. A unique feature of the sea turtle is that it has flippers for swimming instead of legs. Sea turtles also have descriptive names like loggerhead, flatback, leatherback, and green and black sea turtles. Many terrestrial, or land-dwelling, turtles are known as tortoises. A very common land turtle is the North American box turtle, which is identifiable by its domed shell and thumb-like head. Its smaller cousin is the American mud turtle. Unlike a sea turtle, a tortoise has legs and is unable to swim or even float. Amphibious turtles, some of which are known as terrapins, are common in North America and have names such as the wood, painted, snapping, and spotted turtles. Unlike a sea turtle or a tortoise, a terrapin, whose habitat is both water and land, has webbed feet for swimming, usually in freshwater ponds, streams, and lakes, and in the case of the diamondback terrapin, in tidal marshes and ponds.

So you see a turtle. What is it? Is it a sea turtle, tortoise, or terrapin? If it looks like a turtle, then most likely it is a turtle. But take a closer look. How big is it? Is its habitat the ocean, the woods, or a freshwater lake? Does it have flippers, short legs, or webbed feet? A problem for turtle lovers is that there are so many species of turtles to recognize, but the joy of turtle lovers is that there are so many species of turtles to enjoy. Is it a sea turtle, tortoise, or terrapin? It doesn't matter. If it's a turtle, it's one of nature's most interesting species.

And Now the Good News 161

Read aloud from the beginning of the selection until the end of the paragraph that begins "Zoos were once prisons." (page 166) Then, read the following questions and answers and ask your students to choose the correct answer.

1. *The Red Data Book* is published every year and lists
   a. the locations in which alligators are most likely to cause problems.
   b. animals which are no longer endangered.
   c. the days that are "doomsdays."
   d. all animals that are in danger of extinction.
2. Why were alligators once in danger of extinction?
   a. Many were killed near golf courses and airport runways.
   b. Other animals were eating them.
   c. People were using alligator skins for shoes and luggage.
   d. The pollution nearby was killing them.
3. When a large predator like the alligator thrives
   a. the crocodiles thrive, too.
   b. dozens of smaller animals thrive with it.
   c. the water holes remain clean.
   d. millions of birds come to live nearby.
4. An ecosystem is
   a. the system by which an animal becomes endangered.
   b. the study of economics.
   c. a community of living things, their environment, and relationships.
   d. a system to help prevent animals from becoming extinct.
5. Where is the Serengeti?
   a. Africa
   b. Eastern Europe
   c. South America
   d. Australia
6. About 90% of the mammals and 75% of the birds in American zoos
   a. are considered endangered.
   b. were born in captivity.
   c. did not make it into the *Red Data Book*.
   d. are not being treated properly.
7. What types of animals are often illegally trapped in nets?
   a. dolphins, seals, and sea turtles
   b. whales and porpoises
   c. salmon, tuna, and swordfish
   d. sharks
8. What is one thing that is being done to prevent these animals from getting caught in nets?
   a. Extra security people are being sent out to watch the fishermen.
   b. They are trying to design safer nets.
   c. Boats are being put on new and limited schedules.
   d. They are trying to lure the animals away from the shore.
9. Zoos used to be compared to
   a. jungles.
   b. invertebrates.
   c. prisons.
   d. pet shops.
10. Ling-Ling is
   a. a type of alligator.
   b. the name of the country with the most endangered animals.
   c. a special ring attached to animals that keeps track of them in the wild.
   d. a panda bear.

Into . . . And Now the Good News

Use examples to help your students understand preservation. To preserve is to protect something of value, to keep it alive and lasting. The thing being preserved can be a material item: keeping it in a glass case preserves a document. It can be a value: soldiers fight to preserve their liberty. It can be something as simple as food being kept from spoiling: to preserve fruit is to make jam (which will not spoil) out of it. In *And Now the Good News*, preservation is a term used in reference to protecting animal habitats.

Explain to your students that this essay was not written solely for those who are animal activists and who will devote themselves to protecting animal habitats. Its purpose is to create awareness in all of us of the need to protect endangered animals. As they read through the selection, ask students to think about why it is important to save these animal habitats. The article clearly wants the reader to recognize that whole ecosystems are affected when animals become endangered or extinct. This, in turn, affects our water and food supplies, as well as the environment as a whole. The author stresses at the end of the article that everyone has the ability to help and make change. You can ask your students for suggestions about how they can help the environment.

Blueprint for Reading

INTO . . . *And Now the Good News*

Have you ever visited an historical village? Have you eaten food from a package or jar that listed "preservative" as one of its ingredients? Is there a photograph or piece of china that has been saved and handed down from generation to generation in your family? In one way or another, each of these has been preserved. *Preservation* is the process of keeping something safe and in good condition. In this story, another type of preservation is discussed—the preservation of endangered animals and their habitats. As you read *And Now the Good News,* think about why this preservation is so important.

EYES ON *Main Ideas and Details*

Have you ever seen a rag doll? It just flops around. Do you know why? It has no backbone! A poorly written story can be like that. If it has no "backbone"—no one idea holding it together—it just flops around. A good story has one **main idea** that holds it together. In a nonfiction piece such as the one you are about to read, the main idea is easy to find. It is usually presented in the title or the first few paragraphs. Once the main idea is presented, the writer must show how each new idea is connected to the main idea.

162 Unit 2

Eyes On Main Ideas and Details

The concept of main idea is not a difficult one. A simple illustration can be found in response to the motherly question, "What did you have for lunch?" Most children know that their mother wants to know, for example, whether tuna or chicken was served. When a child answers, "bread, salt, juice, and ketchup," the parent will invariably persist, "Yes, but what was the *main* course?" When a story is written, the writer must have one or two main ideas. All the details in the story must be clearly connected to the main ideas.

Just as every story or essay must have a main idea, so too, on a smaller scale, every paragraph must have a main idea around which it is built. The main idea is stated in the paragraph's **topic sentence**, which is usually found at or near the beginning of the paragraph.

Tell your students to imagine that they have just returned home from a birthday party. If their mother were to ask about the party, what would be an appropriate response?

a. Bob served a great cake with decorations.

b. It was a lot of fun and I really enjoyed myself.

c. I think Jason's party is next.

After your students offer their opinions, discuss each of the choices: **a.** would be considered a detail; **b.** could serve as a main idea or topic sentence; and **c.** is not relevant at all.

Now read the following paragraph to your students. Ask them to identify the topic sentence and the sentence that does not belong.

Rosalyn is a talented girl, but she is very shy. She spends a lot of free time sketching and painting on her own. When the school play tryouts were announced, Rosalyn wanted to offer her services, but was too shy. Sheila is also very shy. Though Rosalyn thought she would never have a chance to contribute to the play, someone noticed her drawings and asked her to paint scenery. Rosalyn is still soft-spoken, but is able to use her talents for the benefit of others.

The main idea is that Rosalyn, a talented, yet shy, girl, has yet to share her talents with anyone. The first sentence could serve as the topic sentence. "Sheila is also very shy" does not belong in this paragraph.

Have students trace their hand on a piece of colored card stock and cut it out. Either give them a topic or have them choose their own. The main idea should be written in the palm of the hand and the topic sentence on the thumb. Details should be written on each of the remaining fingers.

As you read through *And Now the Good News*, ask your students to find the main ideas and topic sentences of the lengthier paragraphs.

And Now the Good News

from *And Then There Was One*

Margery Facklam

A "doomsday" book lists all the animals in danger of extinction. Its official name is *The Red Data Book*. It's published each year by the International Union for Conservation of Nature and Natural Resources. In a book of so much bad news, can we ever find anything good? ❶ ❷

The good news is that some animals get off the list, when they make a comeback. The American alligator was once in danger of extinction because a lot of people thought that alligator skin looked better on shoes and luggage than on the alligator. Then a law was passed in the 1970s to protect the big reptiles from harm. Now there are so many alligators

And Now the Good News 163

Selection Summary

This nonfiction piece is about the various positive developments in the campaign to conserve wildlife. The first case in point is the alligator, which was once in danger of extinction. There are now so many alligators that they are causing a variety of problems. That is to say, they are causing problems for people; as to their fellow creatures, they are actually helping them to thrive. The author teaches us that when a large predator thrives, dozens of smaller animals thrive with it. Protecting a predator helps save whole ecosystems.

Many laws have been established to protect wildlife. Jungle animals may not be caught and placed in zoos. Dolphins, seals, and sea turtles may not be trapped for marine exhibits. Zoos are more animal-friendly than they used to be, with areas designed specifically to resemble the natural habitat of the animal that occupies it. One problem with animals born in zoos is that it is difficult for them to adapt to the wild, even if freed.

The National Wildlife Refuge System protects a wide variety of birds. Bald eagles and whooping cranes have grown in number, helped along by rangers in the system. The Endangered Species Act protects species such as rhinoceroses and tigers, snow leopards, and pandas. The author concludes by urging all people to protect the environment and all the living things that dwell in it.

Guiding the Reading

Literal

Q: What is the official name of the "doomsday" book?
A: It is called the *Red Data Book*.

Q: What is the purpose of the *Red Data Book*?
A: It lists all the animals in danger of extinction.

Q: How often is it published?
A: It is published once a year.

Q: Who publishes the book?
A: It is published by the International Union for Conservation of Nature and Natural Resources.

Q: What is the good news in this book?
A: Some animals have been taken off of the 'danger of extinction' list.

Q: Which animal is no longer on the list?
A: The American alligator.

Q: What caused alligators to appear on the list at first?
A: People used alligator skin for shoes and luggage.

Q: What stopped people from using so many alligator skins?
A: A law was passed in the 1970s to protect them from harm.

Literary Components

❶ **Opening Sentence:** This nonfiction piece gets right down to business. The first sentence sets the tone: factual rather than emotional, scientific rather than poetic.

❷ **Writing Technique:** The author keeps us interested by varying her prose. After a few rather dry facts, she asks a question of interest to most readers. We read on with interest.

Literary Components

3 Transition: The author moves on to the next topic with a good transition, linking the alligator to a discussion of ecosystems.

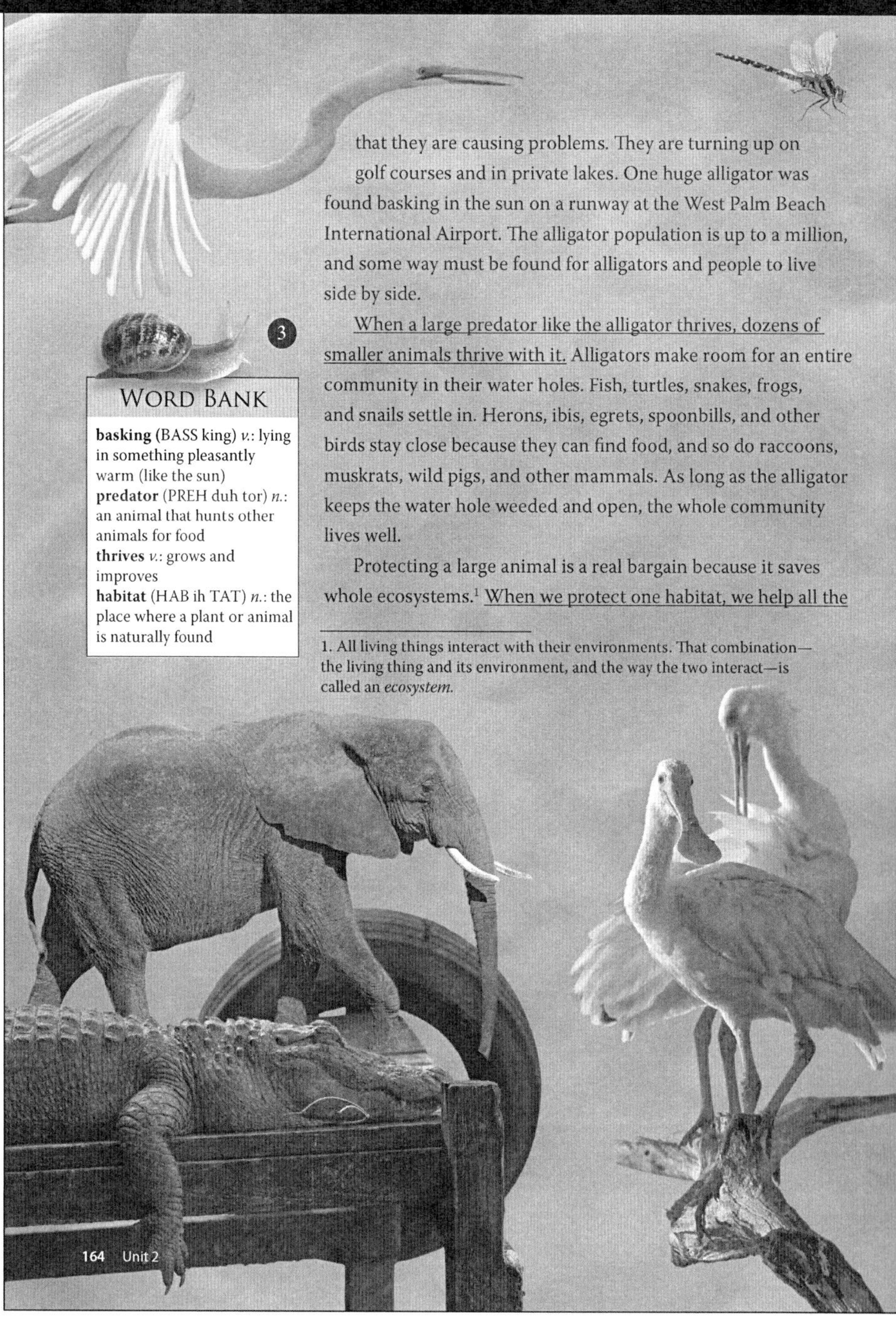

that they are causing problems. They are turning up on golf courses and in private lakes. One huge alligator was found basking in the sun on a runway at the West Palm Beach International Airport. The alligator population is up to a million, and some way must be found for alligators and people to live side by side.

3 When a large predator like the alligator thrives, dozens of smaller animals thrive with it. Alligators make room for an entire community in their water holes. Fish, turtles, snakes, frogs, and snails settle in. Herons, ibis, egrets, spoonbills, and other birds stay close because they can find food, and so do raccoons, muskrats, wild pigs, and other mammals. As long as the alligator keeps the water hole weeded and open, the whole community lives well.

Protecting a large animal is a real bargain because it saves whole ecosystems.[1] When we protect one habitat, we help all the

WORD BANK

basking (BASS king) *v.*: lying in something pleasantly warm (like the sun)
predator (PREH duh tor) *n.*: an animal that hunts other animals for food
thrives *v.*: grows and improves
habitat (HAB ih TAT) *n.*: the place where a plant or animal is naturally found

1. All living things interact with their environments. That combination—the living thing and its environment, and the way the two interact—is called an *ecosystem.*

164 Unit 2

Guiding the Reading

Literal

Q: How are alligators causing problems now?

A: There are so many of them that they are showing up on golf courses and in private lakes. One was even found on an airport runway.

Q: About how many alligators are there now?

A: There are about a million.

Q: Which other animals live near the alligators' water holes?

A: There are fish, turtles, snakes, frogs, and snails. Some birds such as herons, ibis, egrets, and spoonbills stay nearby as well as raccoons, muskrats, wild pigs, and other mammals.

Q: Why is the safety and presence of alligators important to these other animals?

A: They all depend on each other. They are all members of a community called an ecosystem, in which each creature makes its own unique contribution.

Q: Why is it a bargain to protect a large animal?

A: It saves whole ecosystems, not just a single species.

4 animals that live there. In order to help the African elephant, we must
5 help all the animals of the Serengeti.[2] In that 5,000-square-mile area, there are more than 400 species of birds, 50 kinds of mammals, and tens of thousands of insects and other invertebrates.[3]

6 Zoos and wildlife sanctuaries are part of the good news. About 90 percent of the mammals and 75 percent of the birds in American zoos were born in captivity. No longer can an expedition go into the jungle and capture a tiger or monkeys. No one is allowed to catch a dolphin in the open ocean for a marine exhibit or research without permission from the government.

2. The *Serengeti* (SAIR en GET ee) is a plain in Tanzania which has a huge wildlife reserve.
3. *Invertebrates* are animals that do not have a spine.

WORD BANK

sanctuaries (SANK chew AIR eez) *n.*: a portion of land set aside by the government, where wildlife can live in safety from hunters

expedition (EX puh DISH un) *n.*: a journey or voyage made to a distant place for a certain purpose

And Now the Good News 165

Literary Components

4 Key Sentence: After the author talks about alligators and names many small animals that thrive when alligators are protected, she moves from the particular to the general. She talks about how protecting *any* large animal and its habitat benefits all the small animals that live there. This is a good writing technique for a report or nonfiction piece.

5 Key Sentence: The author then reverses the argument and adds that protecting the small animals in a habitat benefits the large animals that live there.

6 Staying on Course: The author reminds us that her topic is "good news about some threatened species." Her repetition of the phrase "good news" reminds us of the topic and ties the paragraphs together.

Guiding the Reading

Literal

Q: Why must we help all of the animals of the Serengeti in order to help the African elephant?

A: There are hundreds of different species of mammals, birds, and insects and they are all interdependent and work with each other. (In some cases, this actually means that they eat each other for food, as in all food chains.)

Q: What is no longer allowed without permission from the government?

A: The capture of wild animals is no longer allowed.

Analytical

Q: Why is it important to know that so many endangered animals in American zoos were born in captivity?

A: Knowing this fact helps us realize that the laws against trapping and capturing these animals in the wild are working.

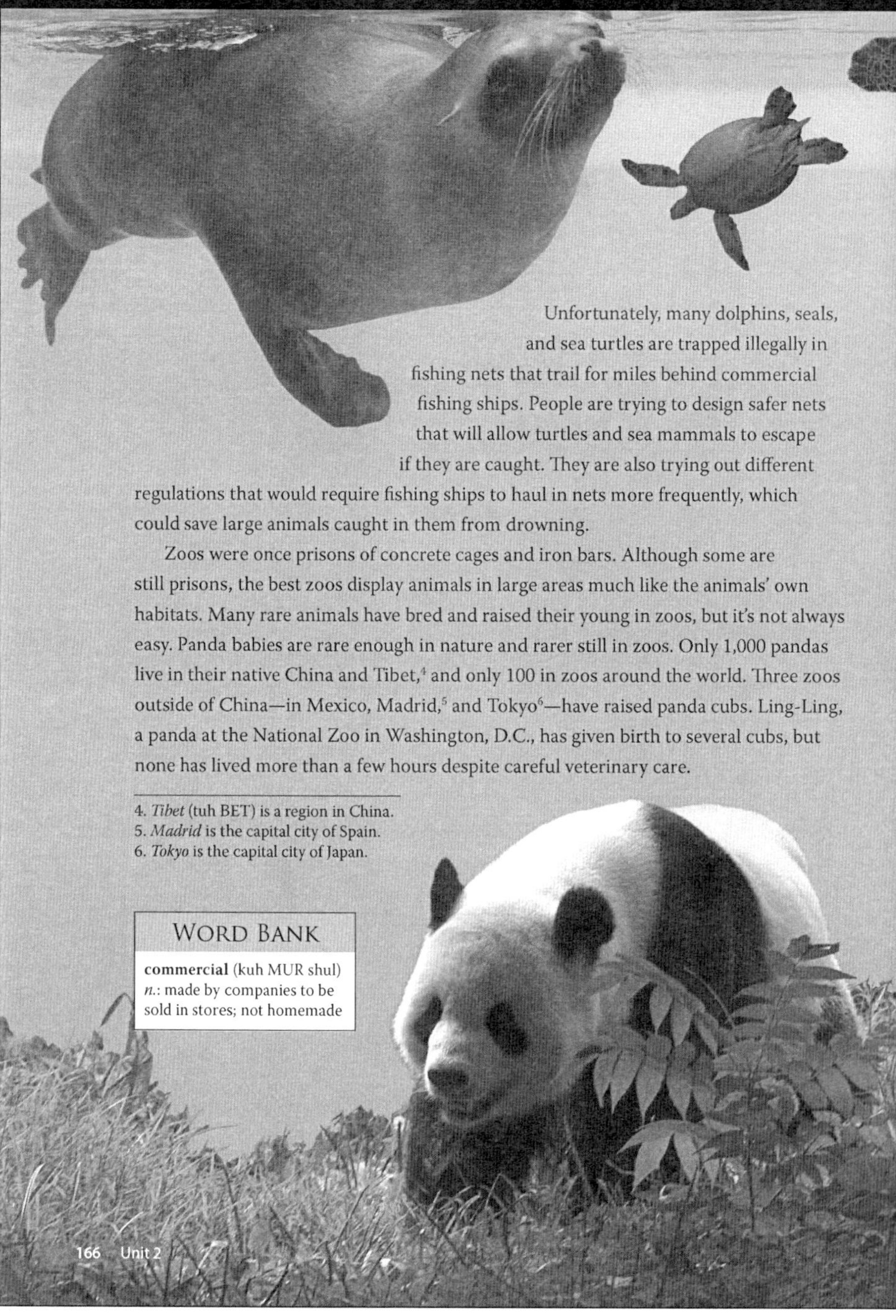

Unfortunately, many dolphins, seals, and sea turtles are trapped illegally in fishing nets that trail for miles behind commercial fishing ships. People are trying to design safer nets that will allow turtles and sea mammals to escape if they are caught. They are also trying out different regulations that would require fishing ships to haul in nets more frequently, which could save large animals caught in them from drowning.

Zoos were once prisons of concrete cages and iron bars. Although some are still prisons, the best zoos display animals in large areas much like the animals' own habitats. Many rare animals have bred and raised their young in zoos, but it's not always easy. Panda babies are rare enough in nature and rarer still in zoos. Only 1,000 pandas live in their native China and Tibet,[4] and only 100 in zoos around the world. Three zoos outside of China—in Mexico, Madrid,[5] and Tokyo[6]—have raised panda cubs. Ling-Ling, a panda at the National Zoo in Washington, D.C., has given birth to several cubs, but none has lived more than a few hours despite careful veterinary care.

4. *Tibet* (tuh BET) is a region in China.
5. *Madrid* is the capital city of Spain.
6. *Tokyo* is the capital city of Japan.

WORD BANK

commercial (kuh MUR shul) *n.*: made by companies to be sold in stores; not homemade

166 Unit 2

Guiding the Reading

Literal

Q: What marine animals are trapped illegally?

A: Dolphins, seals, and sea turtles.

Q: How are they trapped?

A: They are trapped in fishing nets, behind fishing ships.

Q: What do zoos do to make animals' living spaces less like prisons and more comfortable for the animals?

A: They create large areas that are similar to the animal's own habitat.

Q: What rare animal is mentioned here?

A: The panda bear is mentioned.

Q: Where are panda bears from originally?

A: They are from China and Tibet.

Q: How many pandas live in those countries?

A: About 1,000 pandas live in China and Tibet.

Q: How many pandas live in zoos worldwide?

A: About 100 pandas live in zoos.

Q: Which three zoos outside of China have raised panda cubs?

A: The zoos in Mexico, Madrid, and Tokyo have raised panda cubs.

Q: Where does Ling-Ling live?

A: Ling-Ling lived in the National Zoo in Washington, D.C. (Ling-Ling died of unknown causes on December 30, 1992. She was twenty-three years old.)

Q: Why doesn't the National Zoo have more pandas?

A: Ling-Ling gave birth to several cubs but they did not survive more than a few hours.

Analytical

Q: What is the meaning of the phrase "zoos were once like prisons"?

A: Zoos were small and made of concrete and iron bars reminiscent of prisons.

For many wildlife experts, the big goal is to breed animals in captivity and return them to their native homes. But that's not as easy as it sounds. You might think that all you'd have to do is open a cage to let an animal know it's free, but that doesn't always work. In Indonesia, workers at one rehabilitation center try to move once-captive orangutans back into the jungle, but many of the animals won't go. The big red apes like to hang around the feeding station, where bananas and other good food are handed out. When workers take them by the hand and lead them into

8 the forests, some orangutans drag their feet like ornery children. A few may stay alone in the forest overnight, but the next morning they are back in time for breakfast. Part of the problem is too little forest and too many captured orangutans that need homes in it.

The National Wildlife Refuge System cares for 400 habitats from the Florida Keys to Alaska. They protect green sea turtles and monk seals in Hawaii, whooping cranes in Texas, and trumpeter swans in Montana. They provide safe feeding and resting grounds for the annual migrations of thousands of ducks, geese, and other birds.

WORD BANK

rehabilitation (REE huh BIH luh TAY shun) *n.*: a returning to good health

ornery (OR nuh ree) *adj.*: mean

And Now the Good News 167

Literary Components

7 Real-Life Examples to Support General Statement: A good writer of nonfiction will instruct the reader about their topic by making general statements and then back them up with examples from real life that illustrate or support the statements.

8 Simile: There is room for imagery even in nonfiction writing. A good simile such as this one makes us smile while giving us a colorful picture of the subject.

Guiding the Reading

Literal

Q: After keeping the animals in captivity, what is the ultimate goal of some wildlife experts?

A: Their goal is to return the animals to their native homes.

Q: Is it easy to put them back into their habitats?

A: No, many do not want to go back.

Q: How did the orangutans in Indonesia take to being freed?

A: They did not want freedom. The workers lured them into the forest with good food. The animals slept in the forest overnight but were back for breakfast.

Q: What is another problem in trying to return all of the orangutans to the forest?

A: There are too many to fit in the forest. They need more space.

Q: How many habitats does the National Wildlife Refuge System care for?

A: They care for 400 habitats.

Q: What are some examples of these habitats?

A: They protect green sea turtles and monk seals in Hawaii, whooping cranes in Texas, and trumpeter swans in Montana.

Analytical

Q: Why do you think it is difficult for the animals to return to the wild?

A: They become accustomed to life in captivity.

Bald eagles have found help in the refuge system, too. When the eagle was chosen as our national symbol in 1782, there were probably 75,000 of the big birds nesting in the U.S. territory. Today there are fewer than 3,000. It wasn't until 1940, when bald eagles were on the edge of extinction, that Congress passed a law to protect them. But even when they were safe from hunters, eagles' eggs were destroyed by DDT because the adult birds had eaten fish contaminated by the pesticide.

Now the wildlife experts take the first clutch of eggs[7] from an eagle's nest and put them in an incubator until they hatch. With her eggs gone, the eagle will lay a second clutch of eggs, which she will raise. When an eagle is found without eggs, or whose chicks have died, the scientists place three-week-old eaglets from an incubator in its nest. The foster parents usually adopt the chicks and raise them as their own.

7. A *clutch of eggs* is a group of eggs that are all laid at the same time.

Guiding the Reading

Literal

Q: What is the national symbol of the United States?
A: The national symbol is the bald eagle.

Q: How many bald eagles were there in 1782 when the symbol was chosen?
A: There were about 75,000.

Q: What has happened to the eagles since then?
A: The number has decreased to 3,000.

Q: When did Congress pass a law to protect the bald eagle?
A: The law was passed in 1940, when the eagles were on the edge of extinction.

Q: Even after the law was passed, what problem did the eagles have?
A: The adult birds would eat fish that were contaminated by the pesticide DDT.

Q: What do wildlife experts do with eagle eggs they take from the nest?
A: They put them in an incubator and care for them until they find eagles who do not have eggs.

Sometimes they use a process called *hacking*. Rangers build nests on platforms high atop towers in wilderness areas where there are no eagles. They place eight-week-old eaglets in these nests. At first, humans feed the eaglets, although they are careful to stay out of sight. They use a puppet that looks like an eagle, because they don't want the young eagles to *imprint* on humans. The first moving object a newly hatched baby bird sees is "imprinted" on its brain as its mother. Gradually, the eaglets are fed less and less to encourage them to fly off and hunt their own prey. It's a long, slow process, but it works.

Guiding the Reading

Literal

Q: What process is used to help bring these eaglets back into the wild?

A: The process is called hacking.

Q: Why do the human rangers use an eagle puppet?

A: They use a puppet so that the baby eagles will imprint on the image of an eagle rather than on a human.

Q: Is this process quick and easy?

A: No, it is long and slow, but it works.

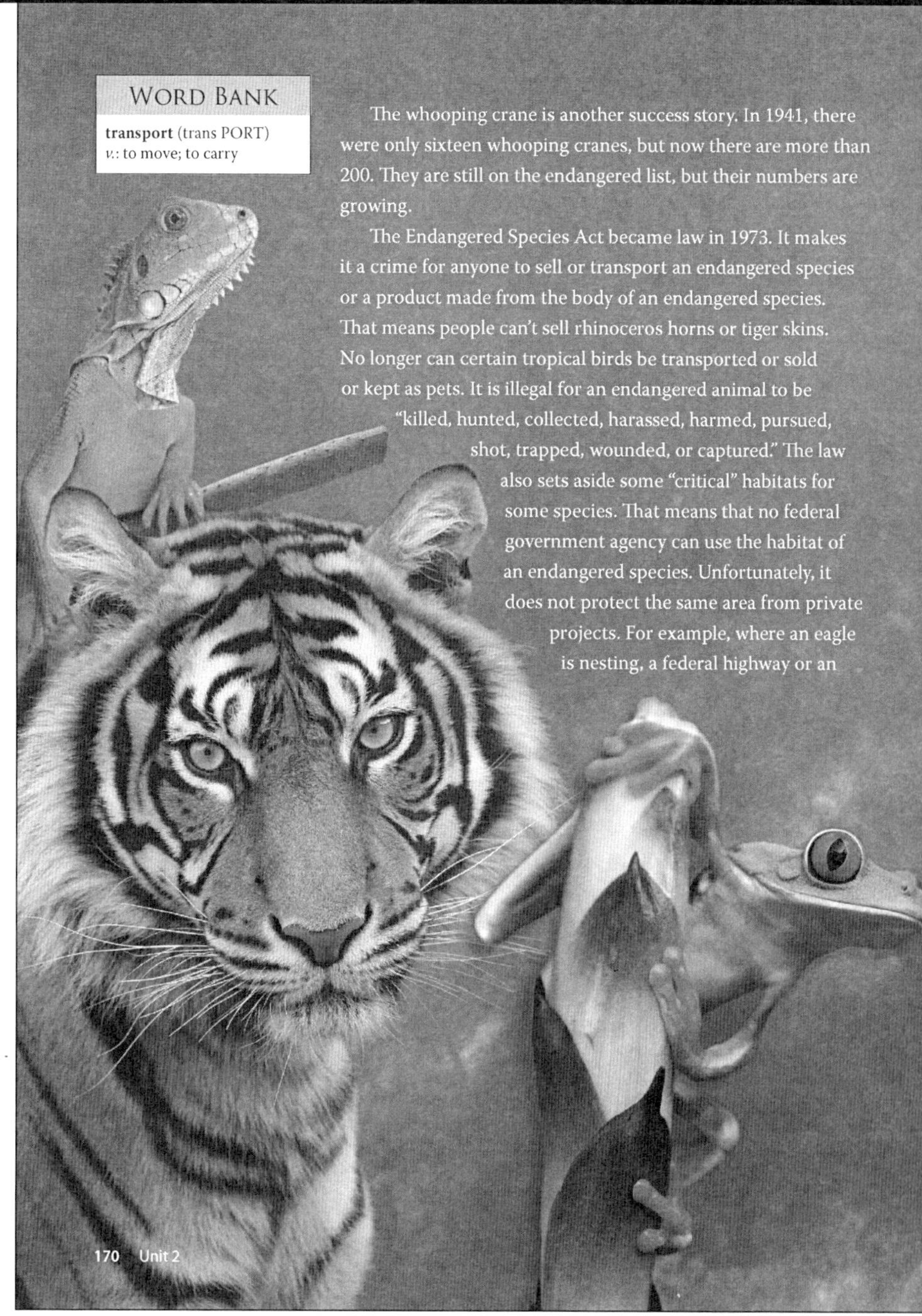

WORD BANK

transport (trans PORT)
v.: to move; to carry

The whooping crane is another success story. In 1941, there were only sixteen whooping cranes, but now there are more than 200. They are still on the endangered list, but their numbers are growing.

The Endangered Species Act became law in 1973. It makes it a crime for anyone to sell or transport an endangered species or a product made from the body of an endangered species. That means people can't sell rhinoceros horns or tiger skins. No longer can certain tropical birds be transported or sold or kept as pets. It is illegal for an endangered animal to be "killed, hunted, collected, harassed, harmed, pursued, shot, trapped, wounded, or captured." The law also sets aside some "critical" habitats for some species. That means that no federal government agency can use the habitat of an endangered species. Unfortunately, it does not protect the same area from private projects. For example, where an eagle is nesting, a federal highway or an

170 Unit 2

Guiding the Reading

Literal

Q: How successful have they been with whooping cranes?
A: They have been very successful. The number of whooping cranes in the world has increased from sixteen to 200.

Q: What law was enacted in 1973?
A: The Endangered Species Act.

Q: What did it do?
A: It officially made it a crime for anyone to sell or transport an endangered species or a product made from the body of an endangered animal.

Q: What are some examples of animal parts that people have used in the past?
A: Rhino horns, tiger skins, and tropical birds have been used illegally.

Q: What are some words used to describe what it is illegal to do to an endangered animal?
A: It is illegal for an animal to be, "killed, hunted, collected, harassed, harmed, pursued, shot, trapped, wounded, or captured."

Q: What else does the law say?
A: The law forbids the use by any government agency of certain habitats that are critical to the survival of some species.

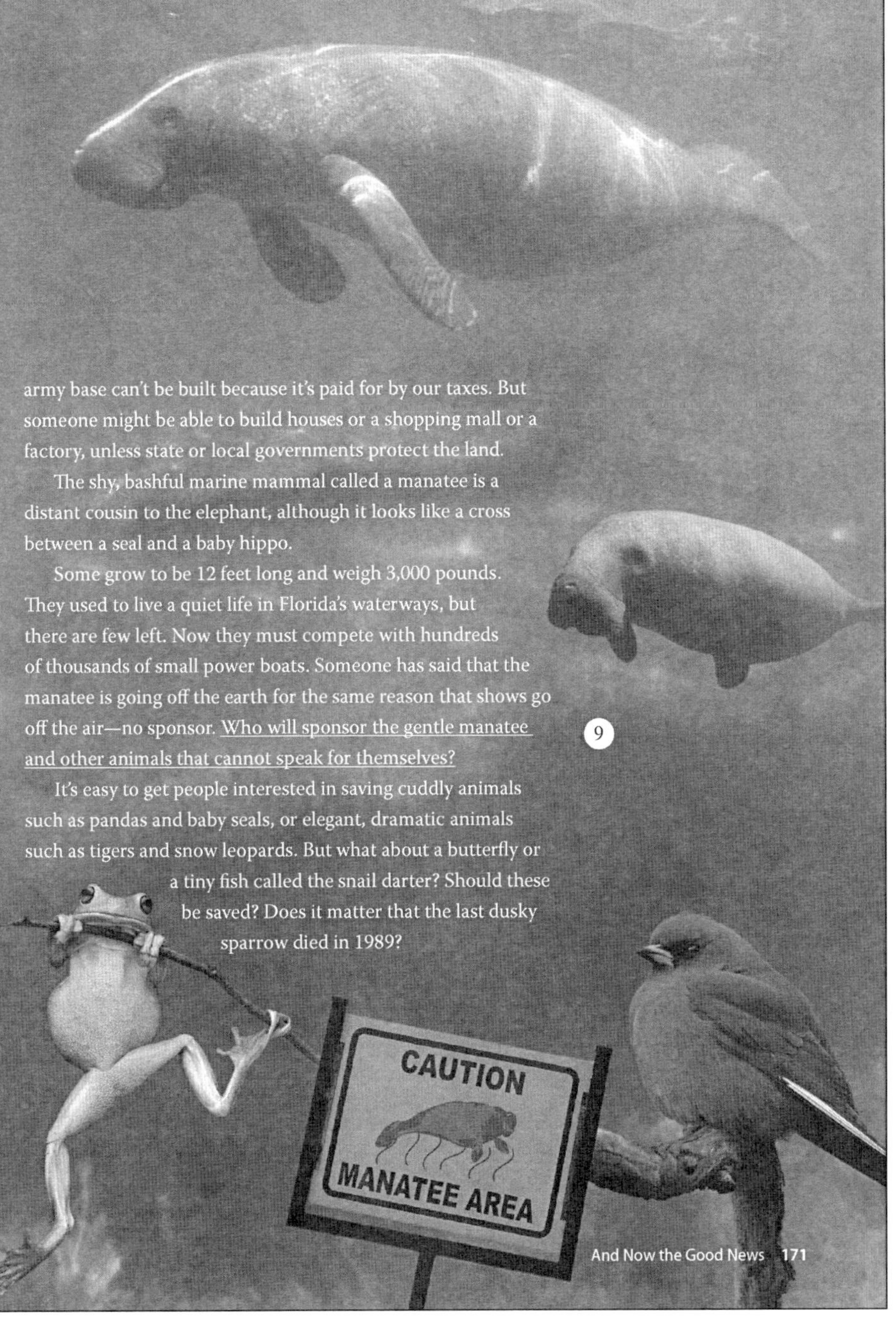

army base can't be built because it's paid for by our taxes. But someone might be able to build houses or a shopping mall or a factory, unless state or local governments protect the land.

The shy, bashful marine mammal called a manatee is a distant cousin to the elephant, although it looks like a cross between a seal and a baby hippo.

Some grow to be 12 feet long and weigh 3,000 pounds. They used to live a quiet life in Florida's waterways, but there are few left. Now they must compete with hundreds of thousands of small power boats. Someone has said that the manatee is going off the earth for the same reason that shows go off the air—no sponsor. Who will sponsor the gentle manatee and other animals that cannot speak for themselves? (9)

It's easy to get people interested in saving cuddly animals such as pandas and baby seals, or elegant, dramatic animals such as tigers and snow leopards. But what about a butterfly or a tiny fish called the snail darter? Should these be saved? Does it matter that the last dusky sparrow died in 1989?

And Now the Good News 171

Literary Components

9 Rhetorical Question: Again, the author uses a question to good effect. This time, the question has no answer and is more a cry of pain than a real question. The author's hope, one presumes, is that the reader will silently answer, "I will!"

Guiding the Reading

Literal

Q: Who can use these habitats?
A: A private person can use them for a project unless the government steps in to protect the land.

Q: What kind of animal is the manatee?
A: It is a shy marine mammal that is a distant cousin to the elephant. The manatee looks like a cross between a seal and a baby hippopotamus.

Q: How large is a manatee?
A: It is about 12 feet long and weighs 3,000 pounds.

Q: Why are there so few manatees left?
A: They have to compete with hundreds of thousands of small power boats along Florida's coast.

Q: Which animals are people naturally interested in?
A: It is easy to get people interested in cuddly animals such as a panda or baby seals, or elegant, dramatic animals such as tigers and snow leopards.

Q: Which animals need to be saved but do not attract as much attention?
A: One example is a small fish called the snail darter.

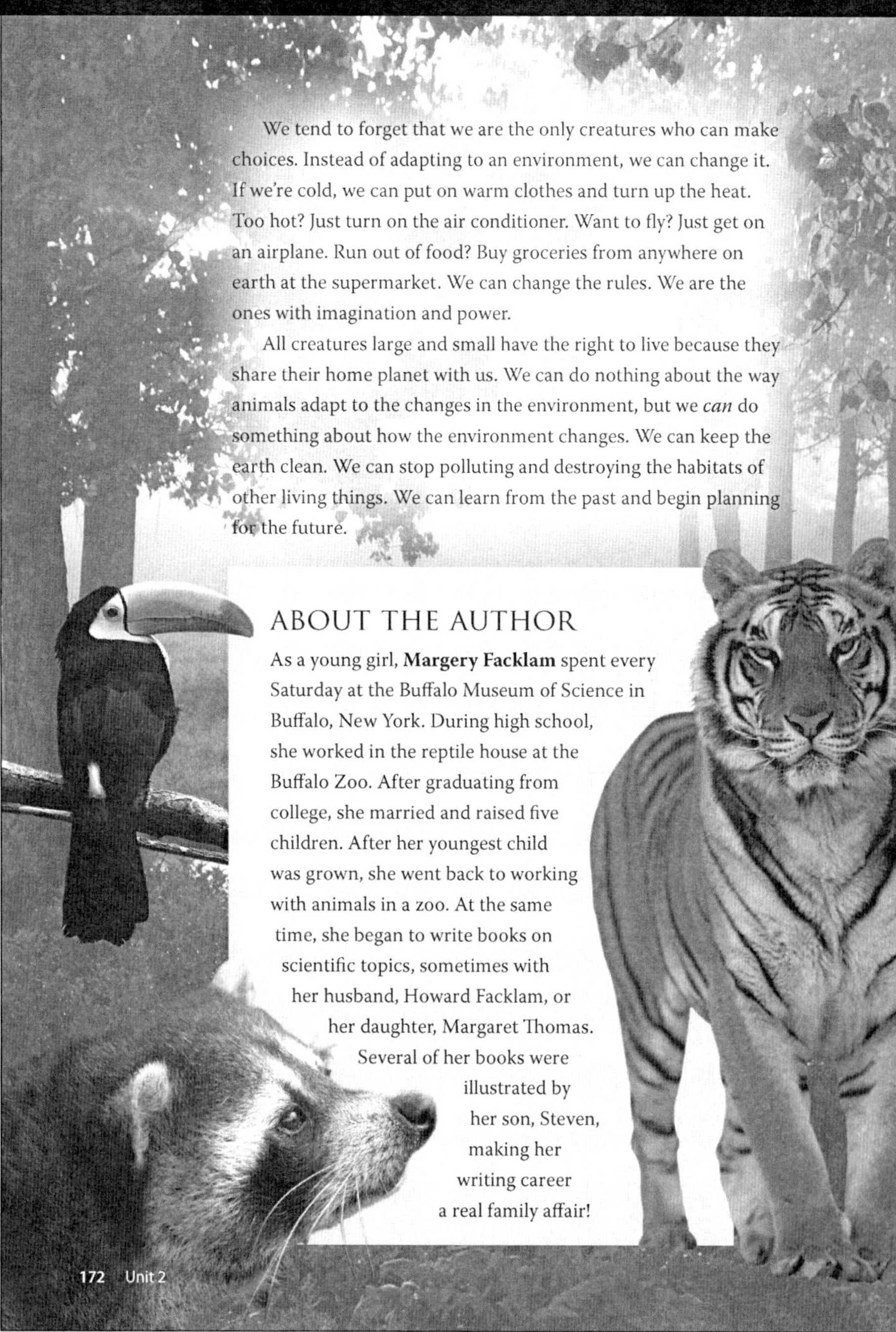

We tend to forget that we are the only creatures who can make choices. Instead of adapting to an environment, we can change it. If we're cold, we can put on warm clothes and turn up the heat. Too hot? Just turn on the air conditioner. Want to fly? Just get on an airplane. Run out of food? Buy groceries from anywhere on earth at the supermarket. We can change the rules. We are the ones with imagination and power.

All creatures large and small have the right to live because they share their home planet with us. We can do nothing about the way animals adapt to the changes in the environment, but we *can* do something about how the environment changes. We can keep the earth clean. We can stop polluting and destroying the habitats of other living things. We can learn from the past and begin planning for the future.

ABOUT THE AUTHOR

As a young girl, **Margery Facklam** spent every Saturday at the Buffalo Museum of Science in Buffalo, New York. During high school, she worked in the reptile house at the Buffalo Zoo. After graduating from college, she married and raised five children. After her youngest child was grown, she went back to working with animals in a zoo. At the same time, she began to write books on scientific topics, sometimes with her husband, Howard Facklam, or her daughter, Margaret Thomas. Several of her books were illustrated by her son, Steven, making her writing career a real family affair!

172 Unit 2

Guiding the Reading

Literal

Q: What is it that we can and cannot do about animals and the environment?

A: We cannot do anything about the ways that animals adapt to the changes in the environment, but we can do something about how the environment changes.

Q: What are some things we can do to help the environment?

A: People can stop polluting, stop destroying the habitats of other living things, and learn from the past and begin planning for the future.

Analytical

Q: What is the purpose of a sponsor for an animal?

A: The purpose is to speak out on its behalf.

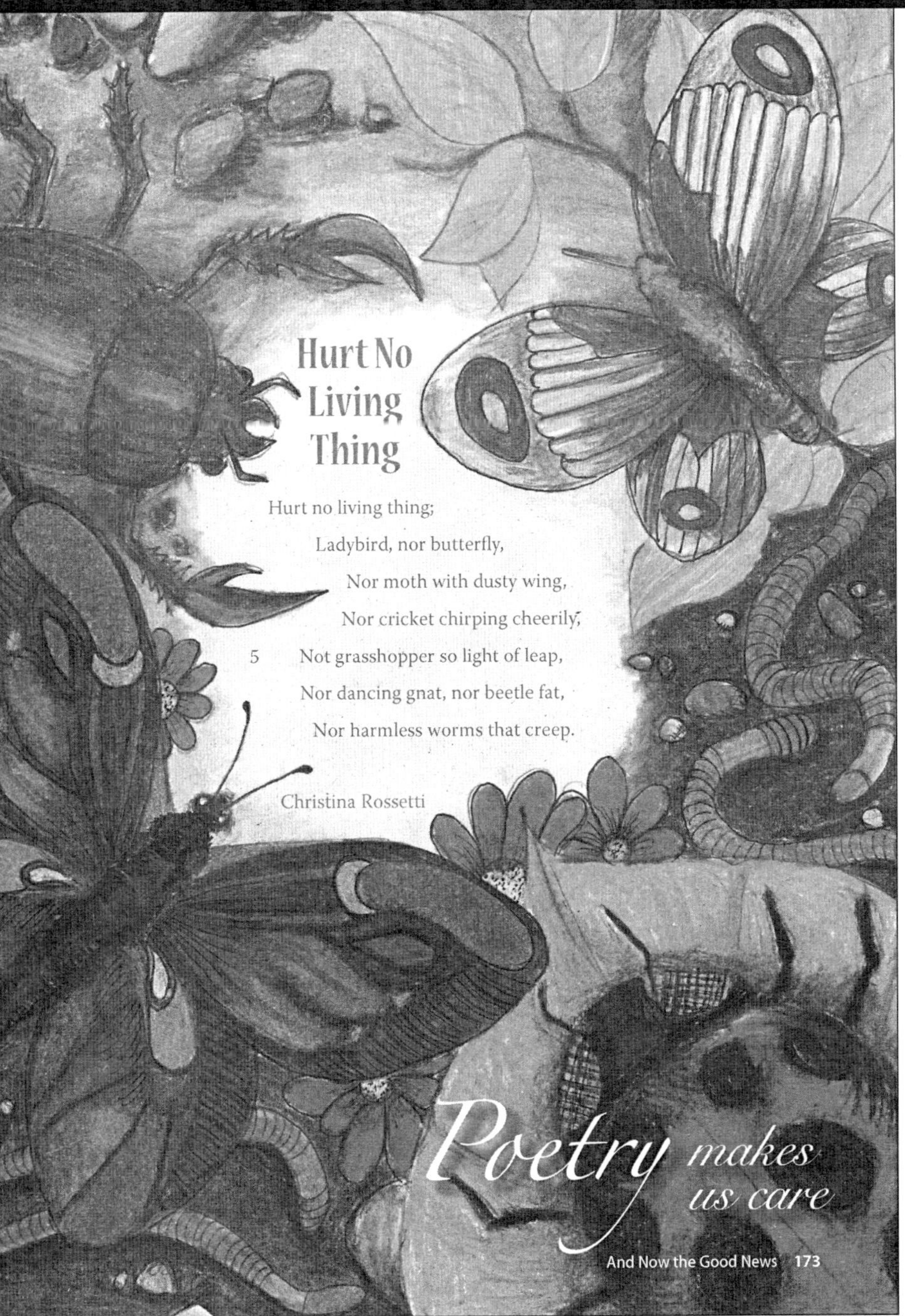

About Hurt No Living Thing

Poetry Makes Us Care

This delicate poem *makes us care* by viewing every living thing as beautiful in its own way. A good poet helps us to see things from a new angle, and Christina Rossetti wishes to teach us to see all of nature, even those creatures whom we consider irritating or ugly, in a new light. The average brown moth, who would turn your good wool sweater into Swiss cheese if it could, has a poetic "dusty wing," while the itch-producing gnat is described as "dancing." The worm is harmless, so let him be, urges the poet, and even the beetle is not obnoxious, just fat. What Rossetti does here briefly is teach us to look at every living thing as an exquisite and unique gift to be appreciated.

First Impressions

By preserving a single animal's habitat, we affect the lives of many other species of mammals, birds, and insects. Because animals depend on each other, if one piece of the ecosystem's puzzle is removed, it can impact hundreds of other creatures and forms of plant life. It is important to recognize that damaging the environment not only affects all of these animals, but also eventually comes to affect our lives. A recent example (2008) is the plight of honeybees that are dying by the thousands. Scientists have not yet determined the cause, but are sure that it must be a result of something we are doing to the environment. One might think that people can manage without honey (which is used in many processed foods), but the lack of bees means less pollination for acres of crops that we depend on for food staples.

Quick Review

1. It lists annually all animals in danger of extinction.
2. Protecting a large animal saves whole ecosystems, not just a single species.
3. Answers will vary.
4. Selling or transporting an endangered species or a product made from one of these animals is illegal. Certain animals cannot be sold as pets. It is illegal for an endangered animal to be "killed, hunted, collected, harassed, harmed, pursued, shot, trapped, wounded, or captured."

Focus

5. Through the efforts of many groups and individuals, some endangered animals have come off the "doomsday" list.
6. **Main Idea:** Animals are now protected by federal laws.

   Topic Sentence: The Endangered Species Act became law in 1973.

   Details: People can't sell rhinoceros horns or tiger skins.

   Tropical birds can't be pets anymore.

   No government agency can use the habitat of an endangered species.

Creating and Writing

7. Responses will vary. Suggest ideas such as family, photos, keepsakes, and so on.
8. Answers will vary.

Studying the Selection

FIRST IMPRESSIONS

Why is it important to preserve animal habitats?

QUICK REVIEW

1. What is the purpose of *The Red Data Book*?
2. Why is it a "bargain" to protect a large animal?
3. List five animals that were mentioned as endangered.
4. What became illegal as a result of the Endangered Species Act of 1973?

FOCUS

5. Why do you think this selection is entitled *And Now the Good News*?
6. Look on page 170 at the paragraph that begins with the words, "The Endangered Species Act." Reread this paragraph. What is the main idea? Write it down. The topic sentence is the first sentence of the paragraph. Write three important details that connect to the topic sentence.

CREATING AND WRITING

7. Write about something other than wildlife that you feel should be preserved and protected. This can be something that is important only to you or that is important to large numbers of people.
8. Write about a group of fourth graders who can communicate with animals. What do they discuss with endangered animals?
9. Choose an endangered animal from your teacher's list. Create an ad campaign that will interest people in helping these animals. Think of a slogan and a logo as well as an ad. Remember that while you need to present true information, you must also try to touch the hearts of people.

174 Unit 2

9. Be sure to explain what logos and slogans are.
   Bring in books from the school or public library on endangered animals for your students to use. There are hundreds of endangered species but the following are a few:

American Bison	Chimpanzee	Night Parrot
Bactrian Camel	Giant Panda	Ostrich
Blue Whale	Gray Wolf	Tasmanian Tiger
Brown Bear	Humpback Whale	Wild Yak
Cheetah	Monito Gecko	

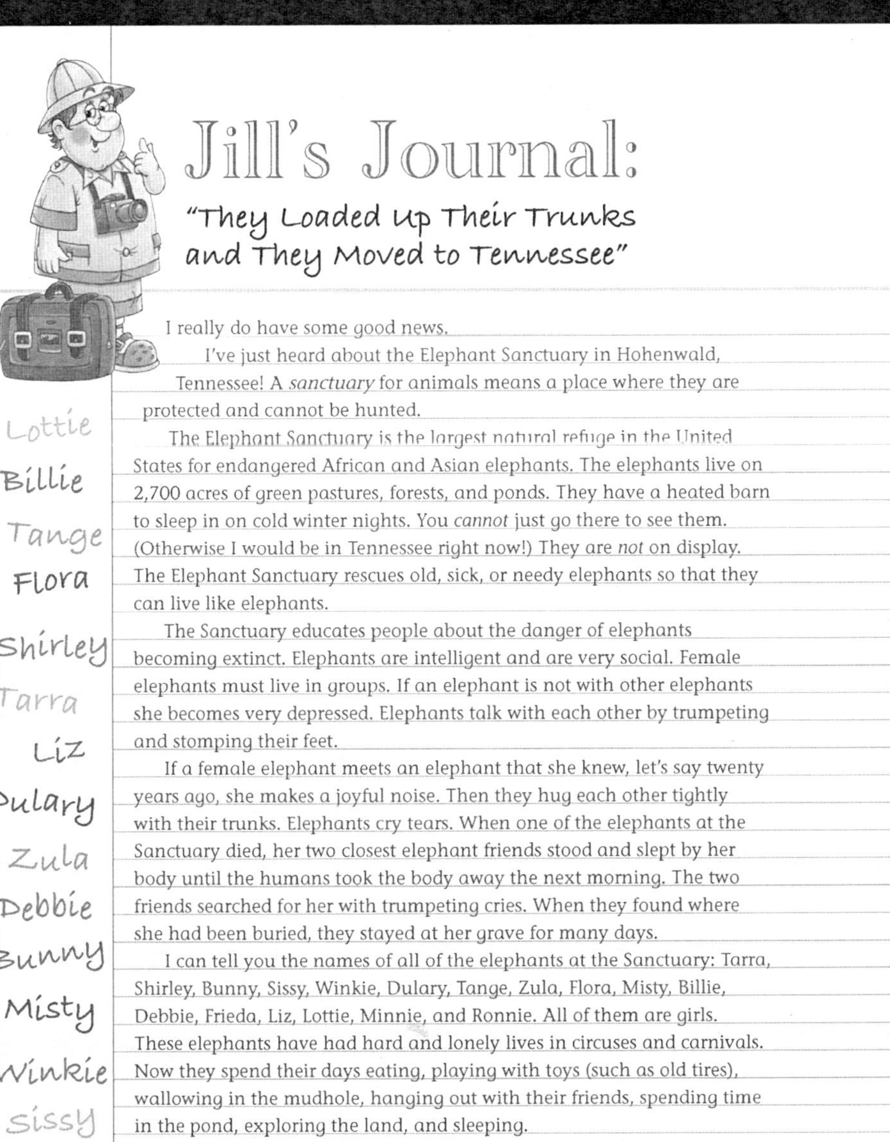

Jill's Journal:

"They Loaded Up Their Trunks and They Moved to Tennessee"

I really do have some good news.

I've just heard about the Elephant Sanctuary in Hohenwald, Tennessee! A *sanctuary* for animals means a place where they are protected and cannot be hunted.

The Elephant Sanctuary is the largest natural refuge in the United States for endangered African and Asian elephants. The elephants live on 2,700 acres of green pastures, forests, and ponds. They have a heated barn to sleep in on cold winter nights. You *cannot* just go there to see them. (Otherwise I would be in Tennessee right now!) They are *not* on display. The Elephant Sanctuary rescues old, sick, or needy elephants so that they can live like elephants.

The Sanctuary educates people about the danger of elephants becoming extinct. Elephants are intelligent and are very social. Female elephants must live in groups. If an elephant is not with other elephants she becomes very depressed. Elephants talk with each other by trumpeting and stomping their feet.

If a female elephant meets an elephant that she knew, let's say twenty years ago, she makes a joyful noise. Then they hug each other tightly with their trunks. Elephants cry tears. When one of the elephants at the Sanctuary died, her two closest elephant friends stood and slept by her body until the humans took the body away the next morning. The two friends searched for her with trumpeting cries. When they found where she had been buried, they stayed at her grave for many days.

I can tell you the names of all of the elephants at the Sanctuary: Tarra, Shirley, Bunny, Sissy, Winkie, Dulary, Tange, Zula, Flora, Misty, Billie, Debbie, Frieda, Liz, Lottie, Minnie, and Ronnie. All of them are girls. These elephants have had hard and lonely lives in circuses and carnivals. Now they spend their days eating, playing with toys (such as old tires), wallowing in the mudhole, hanging out with their friends, spending time in the pond, exploring the land, and sleeping.

Jill's Journal 175

About the Elephant Sanctuary

Founded in 1995, the Elephant Sanctuary, with 2,700 acres, is the largest natural habitat refuge in the United States. The Sanctuary is located in Hohenwald, Tennessee, 85 miles southwest of Nashville, and was established for the rescue of endangered African and Asian elephants.

The mission of the Elephant Sanctuary is two-fold: (1) "To provide a haven for old, sick or needy elephants in a setting of green pastures, old-growth forests, spring-fed ponds and a heated barn for cold winter nights. (2) To provide education about the crisis facing these social, sensitive, passionately intense, playful, complex, exceedingly intelligent and endangered creatures."

The Elephant Sanctuary
P. O. Box 393
Hohenwald, TN 38462
(931) 796-6500

Background Bytes

What is the Endangered Species Act? Here is some information that may be useful as background material for *And Now the Good News.*

The Endangered Species Act (ESA) was passed in 1973 to protect plant and animal species that are at risk of extinction. Species protected by the ESA are classified in two categories: *Endangered* or *Threatened.* A species' classification is determined by how many remain in the wild and the degree to which their survival is jeopardized. Endangered species are likely to become extinct throughout a significant portion of the area where it lives. Threatened species are likely to become Endangered in the near future.

You may recall that, as part of the background for *Sato and the Elephants,* we provided a large amount of information about elephants. To enhance your discussion of Jill's visit to an elephant sanctuary, you may wish to refer to p. 3 of the Teacher Resources Section.

Power Skill:

Making a Table, or in This Case, An Elechart!

Help your students compare the information in the actual *Jill's Journal* article with the data in the chart on pages 178-179. You may want to make copies of part of it for your students. This will show them how much easier it is to look at a table than it is to read prose descriptions. Ask them questions from the data in the table. For example, how many elephants choose bamboo as their favorite food? (Answer: Four.) How many like broccoli best? (Answer: Two.) Which elephants eat foods in addition to the regular categories? Here, the answer can be found by checking the Other column.

Do your students know how to figure averages? If they add up the total number of pounds of hay and vegetation that all of the elephants consume in a day (2,130), and divide by the number of elephants (17), they will have the average per elephant consumption. (2,130/17 = 125.3 almost)

Ask them why they think it is easier to look at the table and absorb information (or not). If they can learn to both read and create tables, they will find that they can store and manipulate data much more easily.

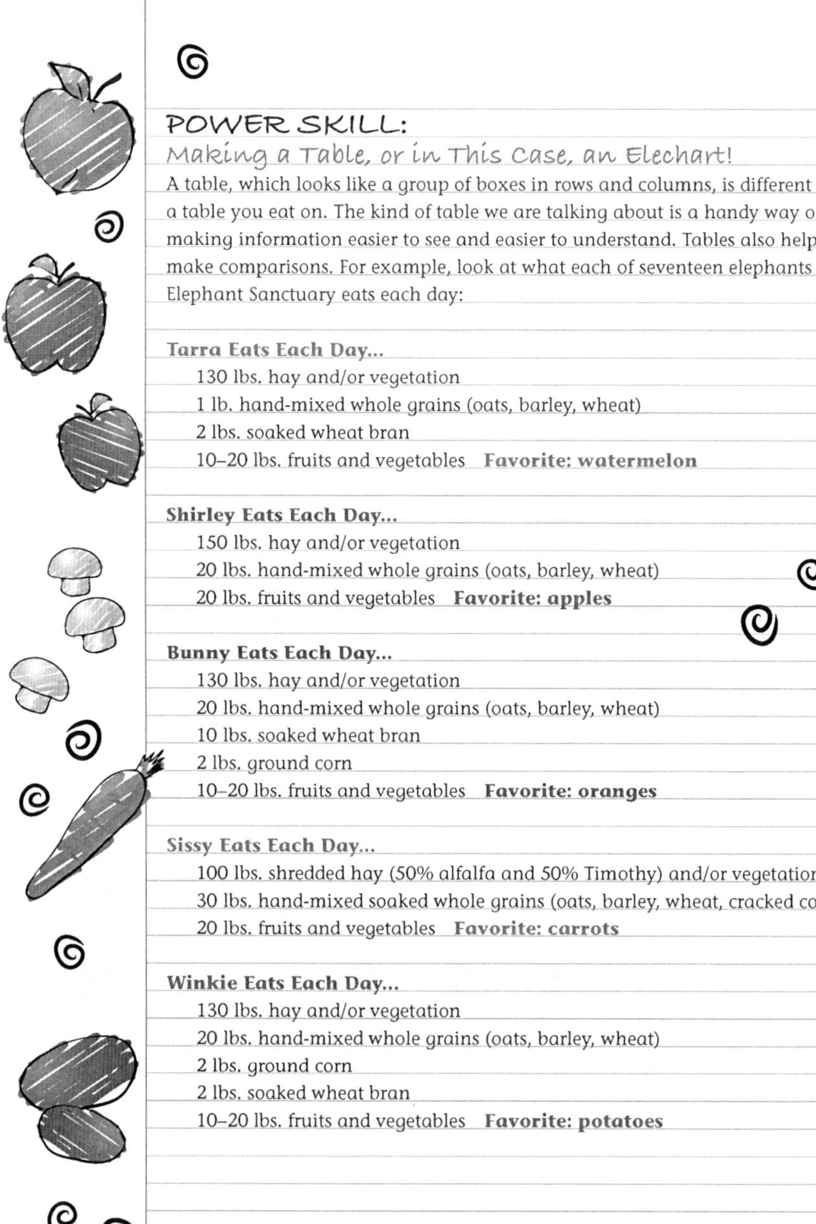

POWER SKILL:

Making a Table, or in This Case, an Elechart!

A table, which looks like a group of boxes in rows and columns, is different from a table you eat on. The kind of table we are talking about is a handy way of making information easier to see and easier to understand. Tables also help us make comparisons. For example, look at what each of seventeen elephants at the Elephant Sanctuary eats each day:

Tarra Eats Each Day...
130 lbs. hay and/or vegetation
1 lb. hand-mixed whole grains (oats, barley, wheat)
2 lbs. soaked wheat bran
10–20 lbs. fruits and vegetables **Favorite: watermelon**

Shirley Eats Each Day...
150 lbs. hay and/or vegetation
20 lbs. hand-mixed whole grains (oats, barley, wheat)
20 lbs. fruits and vegetables **Favorite: apples**

Bunny Eats Each Day...
130 lbs. hay and/or vegetation
20 lbs. hand-mixed whole grains (oats, barley, wheat)
10 lbs. soaked wheat bran
2 lbs. ground corn
10–20 lbs. fruits and vegetables **Favorite: oranges**

Sissy Eats Each Day...
100 lbs. shredded hay (50% alfalfa and 50% Timothy) and/or vegetation
30 lbs. hand-mixed soaked whole grains (oats, barley, wheat, cracked corn)
20 lbs. fruits and vegetables **Favorite: carrots**

Winkie Eats Each Day...
130 lbs. hay and/or vegetation
20 lbs. hand-mixed whole grains (oats, barley, wheat)
2 lbs. ground corn
2 lbs. soaked wheat bran
10–20 lbs. fruits and vegetables **Favorite: potatoes**

176 Unit 2

Dulary Eats Each Day...
120 lbs. hay and/or vegetation
10 lbs. hand-mixed whole grains (oats, barley, wheat bran)
15 lbs. fruits and vegetables
Favorite: sugar cane

Tange Eats Each Day...
130 lbs. hay and/or vegetation
5 lbs. hand-mixed grains (oats, barley)
1 lb. soaked wheat bran with blackstrap molasses
10–20 lbs. fruits and vegetables **Favorite: watermelon**

Zula Eats Each Day...
130 lbs. hay and/or vegetation
7 lbs. hand-mixed grains (oats, barley, wheat bran with blackstrap molasses)
3 lbs. soaked wheat bran with blackstrap molasses
10–20 lbs. fruits and vegetables **Favorite: watermelon**

Flora Eats Each Day...
130 lbs. hay and/or vegetation
7 lbs. hand-mixed grains (oats, barley, rice bran with blackstrap molasses)
10–20 lbs. fruits and vegetables **Favorite: bananas**

Misty Eats Each Day...
120 lbs. hay and/or vegetation
10 lbs. hand-mixed whole grains (oats, barley, wheat)
10 lbs. fruits and vegetables **Favorite: bananas**

Billie Eats Each Day...
120 lbs. hay and/or vegetation
10 lbs. hand-mixed whole grains (oats, barley, wheat bran)
17 lbs. fruits and vegetables **Favorite: hickory tree branches**

Debbie Eats Each Day...
120 lbs. hay and/or vegetation
10 lbs. hand-mixed whole grains (oats, barley, wheat bran)
15 lbs. fruits and vegetables **Favorite: bamboo**

Frieda Eats Each Day...
130 lbs. hay and/or vegetation
20 lbs. hand-mixed whole grains (oats, barley, wheat bran)
30 lbs. fruits and vegetables **Favorite: broccoli**

Liz Eats Each Day...
130 lbs. hay and/or vegetation
20 lbs. hand-mixed whole grains (oats, barley, wheat bran)
30 lbs. fruits and vegetables **Favorite: broccoli**

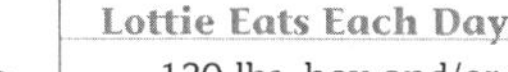

Lottie Eats Each Day...
120 lbs. hay and/or vegetation
12 lbs. hand-mixed whole grains (oats, barley, wheat bran)
15 lbs. fruits and vegetables **Favorite: bamboo**

Minnie Eats Each Day...
120 lbs. hay and/or vegetation
10 lbs. hand-mixed whole grains (oats, barley, wheat bran)
15 lbs. fruits and vegetables **Favorite: bamboo**

Ronnie Eats Each Day...
120 lbs. hay and/or vegetation
10 lbs. hand-mixed whole grains (oats, barley, wheat bran)
15 lbs. fruits and vegetables **Favorite: bamboo**

Is there a better way to list all of this information? Of course there is—in a table! Follow the instructions in the Exercises below.

Exercises

1. A table has rows and columns for its categories. Your table is an Elechart that is going to include ten elephants. So you will need ten rows plus the rows you use for your headings. You pick which ten elephants you want to use, out of the seventeen described above. Don't use the two we have given in the example.

   Your columns will be: Elephant's Name, Hay & Vegetation, Whole Grains (Lbs., Type), Other, Fruits & Vegetables, Favorite. So your table will have seven columns. Notice that Whole Grains is a major category and Lbs. and Type are subcategories. Remember to leave lots of space if you draw your lines before you put in the information.

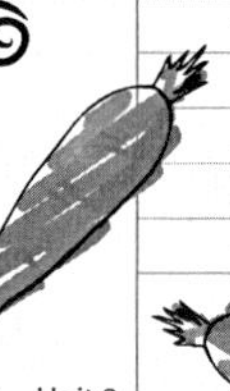

178 Unit 2

Exercises

Exercise 1

My Elechart

1	2	3	4	5	6	7
Elephant's name	**Hay & Vegetation**	**Lbs.**	**Whole Grains Type**	**Others**	**Fruits & Vegetables**	**Favorites**
Zula	130 lbs.	7 lbs.	Oats, barley, wheat bran w/ blackstrap molasses	3 lbs. soaked wheat bran w/ blackstrap molasses	10 -20 lbs.	Watermelon
Flora	130 lbs.	7 lbs.	Oats, barley, rice bran w/ blackstrap molasses		10 - 20 lbs.	Bananas
Tarra	130 lbs.	1 lb.	Oats, barley, wheat	10 lbs. soaked wheat bran	10 - 20 lbs.	Watermelon
Shirley	150 lbs.	20 lbs.	Oats, barley, wheat		20 lbs.	Apples
Bunny	130 lbs.	20 lbs.	Oats, barley, wheat	10 lbs. soaked wheat bran & 2 lbs. ground corn	10-20 lbs.	Oranges
Sissy	100 lbs. 50% alfalfa 50% Timothy	30 lbs.	Soaked oats, barley, wheat, cracked corn		20 lbs.	Carrots
Winkie	130 lbs.	20 lbs.	Oats, barley, wheat	2 lbs. soaked wheat bran & 2 lbs. ground corn	10-20 lbs.	Potatoes
Dulary	120 lbs.	20 lbs.	Oats, barley, wheat bran		15 lbs.	Sugar cane
Tange	130 lbs.	5 lbs.	Oats, barley	1 lb. soaked wheat bran w/ blackstrap molasses	10-20 lbs.	Watermelon

Look at the last row in the model. The word Lbs. appears in columns 2, 3, and 6. You can see that a table makes it possible to add quantities.
To get you started, here is your model table:

My Elechart

Column 1	2	3	4	5	6	7
Elephant's Name	Hay & Vegetation	Whole Grains		Other	Fruits & Vegetables	Favorite
		Lbs.	Type			
Zula	130 lbs.	7 lbs.	Oats, barley, wheat bran with blackstrap molasses	3 lbs. soaked wheat bran with black strap molasses	10-20 lbs.	watermelon
Flora	130 lbs.	7 lbs.	Oats, barley, rice bran with blackstrap molasses		10-20 lbs.	bananas
Total	Lbs.	Lbs.			Lbs.	

2. How many pounds of hay and vegetation do all of your ten elephants eat each day?

3. How many pounds of fruits and vegetables do your ten elephants eat each day?

Exercise 1 Chart, Continued

1	2	3	4	5	6	7
Elephant's name	**Hay & Vegetation**	**Lbs.**	**Whole Grains Type**	**Others**	**Fruits & Vegetables**	**Favorites**
Misty	120 lbs.	10 lbs.	Oats, barley, wheat		10 lbs.	Bananas
Billie	120 lbs.	10 lbs.	Oats, barley, wheat bran		17 lbs.	Hickory tree branches
Debbie	120 lbs.	10 lbs.	Oats, barley, wheat bran		15 lbs.	Bamboo
Frieda	130 lbs.	20 lbs.	Oats, barley, wheat bran		30 lbs.	Broccoli
Liz	130 lbs.	20 lbs.	Oats, barley, wheat bran		30 lbs.	Broccoli
Lottie	120 lbs.	12 lbs.	Oats, barley, wheat bran		15 lbs.	Bamboo
Minnie	120 lbs.	10 lbs.	Oats, barley, wheat bran		15 lbs.	Bamboo
Ronnie	120 lbs.	10 lbs.	Oats, barley, wheat bran		15 lbs.	Bamboo
Total	2, 130 lbs.	232 lbs.			262 lbs. minimum	

2. The figures above are for seventeen elephants.
3. Again, the figures above are for all seventeen elephants.

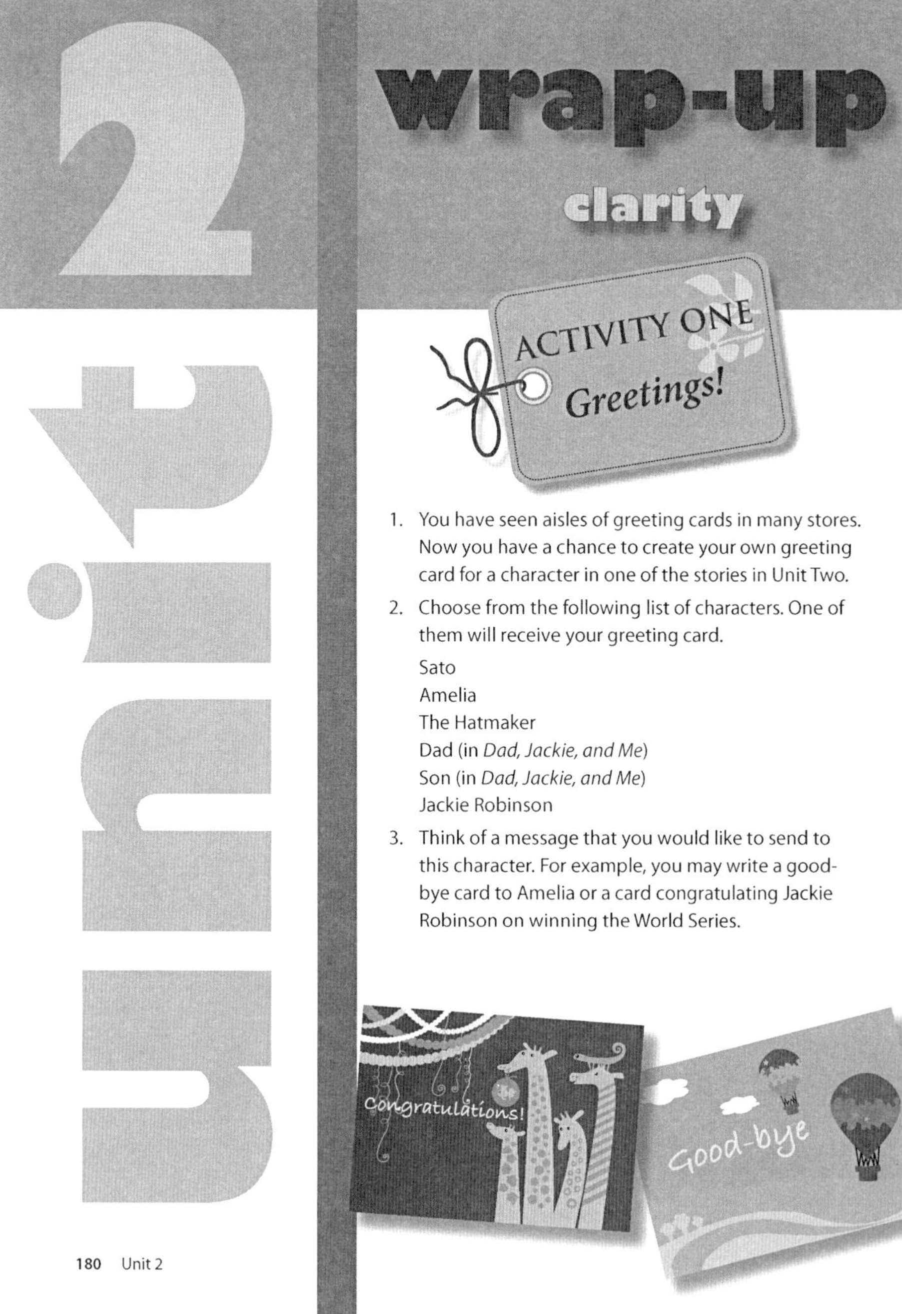

1. You have seen aisles of greeting cards in many stores. Now you have a chance to create your own greeting card for a character in one of the stories in Unit Two.
2. Choose from the following list of characters. One of them will receive your greeting card.

   Sato
   Amelia
   The Hatmaker
   Dad (in *Dad, Jackie, and Me*)
   Son (in *Dad, Jackie, and Me*)
   Jackie Robinson
3. Think of a message that you would like to send to this character. For example, you may write a good-bye card to Amelia or a card congratulating Jackie Robinson on winning the World Series.

Sato and the Elephants

Amelia's Road

The Hatmaker's Sign

Dad, Jackie, and Me

And Now the Good News

4. Using craft materials, make a greeting card and write your message inside. Be creative!
5. Post the cards for all to see.

ACTIVITY TWO

Story Cinquains

1. A **cinquain** (sing KAYN) is a particular type of poem that has five lines.

   Line 1: one word—the topic (noun)

   Line 2: two words that describe the topic (adjectives)

   Line 3: three words that describe what the topic does (verbs)

   Line 4: four words that describe your feelings about the topic (can be a complete sentence)

   Line 5: a synonym for the topic or one word that sums it up
2. Choose one character or theme from Unit Two. Some themes of the stories in this unit are: making mistakes and learning from them, the sense of belonging, accepting criticism, prejudice, and preservation.
3. Write a cinquain about the character or theme you have chosen. Follow the line pattern above. There are very few words in this poem so choose your words carefully. Try to use specific and lively words and to avoid overused words.

unit 2 wrap-up continued

4. Samples:

one word	*Fear*
two words	*Strong emotion*
three words	*Makes one shiver*
four words	*Control, challenge, confront, overcome*
a synonym	*Fright*

Supergrandpa
Energetic senior
Enjoys bicycle riding
Caring, motivated, modest, inspirational
Winner!

5. Share your cinquain aloud with your class. Compare your poem to those that are written on the same topic.

ACTIVITY THREE

Review Board

1. Your teacher will divide your class into groups.
2. Each group represents a committee that writes reviews to be included in a monthly literature magazine. A review is a paragraph telling a bit about the book without revealing the most important parts or the ending. It gives the reader an idea of why they might want to read this book. A review can include positive and negative ideas about the story.
3. Discuss the stories included in Unit Two—*Sato and the Elephants, Amelia's Road, The Hatmaker's Sign, Dad, Jackie, and Me*, and *And Now the Good News*. Choose

three stories for which you would like to write reviews.

4. Together, write three reviews, each one about a different selection. Be sure to edit and proofread your work.
5. When you are done, write the reviews neatly so that they can be included in a class review binder.
6. As the year goes on, students may add reviews of any book they have read, not just stories in this textbook.

ACTIVITY FOUR *Moment of Clarity*

1. Imagine looking outside through a foggy window. You wipe away the moisture and, suddenly, the view is crystal clear. Sometimes our thoughts, like the foggy window, are unclear. An experience, a comment, even some idea that enters our mind, can make things clear. When we come to understand something that we did not really understand before, we have *clarity*.

2. In this unit, many characters achieve clarity towards the end of the story. It is like an 'aha!' moment.

    For example:

    Sato had, until now, carved ivory without thinking too much about where the ivory came from. Sato faces the fact that the beautiful ivory he wishes to carve can be had only if someone kills an elephant. Once he makes this connection, he has clarity. It is clear to him he can no longer use ivory for his carvings.

    The hatmaker (and Thomas Jefferson) realize that, in spite of what all the critics have to say, their work is nearly perfect—just as they thought.

3. Write an essay about a personal situation where you reached a 'moment of clarity.' Perhaps you discovered a new solution to an old problem. You may have learned something new about a person that changed your feeling about that individual. You might have conquered some fear by looking inside yourself and uncovering strength you didn't know you had. Describe the problem you started with and then explain what it took for you to see the situation clearly.

unit 3

head, hands, heart

Characters

Hutchman's Heroes

1. At first, the children's problem is finding a way to keep their teacher from leaving. When that proves unrealistic, their problem is finding a way to show their appreciation for her.
2. The characters are simple, except for Mrs. Hutchman, who is a little more complex.
3. Answers will vary.

Lesson in Literature . . . Hutchman's Heroes

CHARACTERS

- A character can be a person, an animal, or some imaginary creature.
- We watch how each character behaves.
- Some characters are described in a simple way, and we see only one or two personality traits. For example, the girl is mischievous and bright, or the boy is serious and shy.
- Other characters are more complicated. We see many sides of their personality and character.

THINK ABOUT IT!

1. What is the problem that the children face?
2. Why did the children love Mrs. Hutchman?
3. List three of the characters in the story and describe each one with a single adjective. For example: *Mary. Kindhearted.*

186 Unit 3

Vocabulary

composed (kum POZED) *v.*: made up of

executive (egg ZEK yoo tiv) *n.*: a person who has a position of leadership in a business or company

chute (SHOOT) *n.*: a narrow, sloping passageway for delivering items from a higher to a lower level

vertical (VUR tih kul) *adj.*: going up and down, not from side to side

income (INK um) *n.*: the money an individual or business makes during a given time period

Workbook

Workbook

It was the worst thing that could happen to the fourth grade at Sandy Hook Elementary School. When Michael found out, he couldn't believe it and walked off by himself. When Bobby saw his friend alone, he joined him. When Ruth found out, she felt like crying. She ran over to Eileen and told her the bad news. As soon as Eileen heard, tears came to her eyes, and she told Susan. But it was Margaret who finally asked, "What's wrong? Why is everyone so sad?"

The rumor was true. Their teacher, Mrs. Hutchman, was leaving Sandy Hook before the end of the school year. Everyone loved Mrs. Hutchman. In the mornings she smiled when she greeted them, and in the afternoons she smiled when she said good-bye. But during lessons Mrs. Hutchman expected a lot of them. Behind her long dark hair and black-framed glasses, she asked them challenging questions. When they answered, she studied their faces as if her look could draw knowledge out of them.

She called a class meeting. "I have an announcement," she said, looking from child to child, "but many of you know it already."

"Why are you leaving us?" asked Margaret, who was usually very quiet. "Don't you want to teach us anymore?"

Mrs. Hutchman smiled. "Margaret," she said, "I love teaching you, but my husband's job transferred him to Florida. We have to move out of town."

The next day the entire class sat in a circle at recess.

Ruth took charge. "We need a plan."

"Let's convince her to stay," Eileen said optimistically.

"Let's misbehave for the rest of the year," said Bobby who liked to misbehave.

Susan stood up. "Let's buy her a present."

"No," Margaret said, her eyes shining. "Let's *be* her present."

Michael turned to look at Margaret. "How can we be a present?"

"We can make a present of our best work for Mrs. Hutchman and give it to her on her last day," she said proudly.

"I like that idea," Michael said.

He and Ruth divided their classmates into groups. The children who liked writing decided to write a story for Mrs. Hutchman. Those who liked geography planned a map of the route to Florida. The children who liked stories selected one of Mrs. Hutchman's favorite children's books to give to her as a gift. The children who liked science decided to write a report for her on dangerous animals of the Everglades.

On Mrs. Hutchman's last day the class threw her a good-bye party. For gifts, she received wonderful samples of all her students' best work. "You are my heroes," she said. "These gifts will always remind me of you. But tomorrow I expect you to get right down to work for Miss Washington, your new teacher."

That was Mrs. Hutchman. They were going to miss her a lot.

Eddie, Incorporated 187

Unit Theme:	*Head, Hands, Heart*
Target Skill:	*Learning about characters through language, actions, thought, and feelings*
Genre:	*Realistic Fiction*

Getting Started

Begin a discussion with your students about business. Ask if they have ever participated in a business venture, such as a lemonade stand, selling Girl Scout cookies, or candy for a school fundraiser. Ask those who have no "business experience" of their own, if they have a friend who does.

Was running a business harder than expected? Was it simple? Were there any difficulties? Was the business successful?

In addition, ask your students if they have ideas and dreams about opening a particular business of their own.

Into . . .
Eddie, Incorporated

Teamwork is the coordinated effort of a group of individuals for a common cause. Ask your students for examples of "teamwork situations." A few would be:

- cleaning the playroom with siblings
- preparing supper with Mom and two or more siblings
- working on an assembly line, whether in a factory or a project at home
- planning a surprise party for a friend

A popular phrase found on many motivational posters is **T**ogether **E**veryone **A**chieves **M**ore. Ask your students if they were ever assigned to work on a project with a group, yet felt that the members of the group were not team players. Working together does not always come easily, but there are ways to successfully form a team. Ask your students to help you write a list of "tips for teamwork." Some examples are:

Courtesy: Every member of the team should listen courteously to the ideas of the others.

Matching: Try to match the person's talents and interests with the job assigned to that person, if possible.

Flexibility: On the other hand, don't insist on having the job you want, if you are needed in another area.

Focus: Don't be distracted by other people or projects. Work with your team to get the job done.

As you read the story with your class, see if they can identify some of the tips on the list with the behavior of the characters. Here are some examples of the behaviors followed by the tips that may have been on your list:

- When Elizabeth presents her idea for renting a plane to trail a banner about their business, Eddie sees that she is creative. He suggests that she be in charge of advertising.

Tip: *Don't ridicule anyone's ideas.*

Tip: *Recognize which people have which talents.*

Tip: *Try to give people the jobs that they are best at and which they enjoy the most.*

- When Billie Watson suggests they interrupt the meeting to shoot some baskets, Eddie refuses and says, "We've got business."

Tip: *When you're working with the team, don't let outsiders distract you.*

Eyes On Character

Characterization includes both a description of a character's appearance and physical attributes and a portrayal of his or her character traits and personality. In general, the more complex a character, the more believable the character and the story are.

Blueprint for Reading

INTO . . . *Eddie, Incorporated*

Anyone who has been involved in sports knows that no one person can make the team win. There must be a team effort. Imagine a basketball game in which all the players want to shoot baskets. No one is willing to pass the ball. No one is willing to guard. Everyone wants to be a star. The team may win once or twice, but they will never be a championship team. The world of sports is not the only area where people need to be team players. We are often in situations where we must work with others. Starting and running a business is one of those situations. As you read the next story, think about how the friends work together to build *Eddie, Incorporated.*

EYES ON *Character*

Almost everyone is fascinated by other people. Most books, stories, plays, songs, and articles are written about people! There are many ways to find out what a person is really like. Can you think of a few?

When we meet a new person, there is no narrator to say, "Tim is ten years old and was born in Ohio. He is shy but a loyal friend." We learn about people in different ways. When we read about a person, the writer uses many methods to tell us about them. Often, the writer will place clues here and there so that the character's personality slowly unfolds before us. Read the following paragraph:

Pat prepared to study for her American history test with Anna, the new girl in her class. She had already started studying but there was a lot of material to review. Textbook and notes were on her desk and a pencil was in her blonde hair. The red, white, and blue cookies were just the right snack. Even though most people did not want to study with Anna, Pat did not mind. She just wanted to do well on the test.

What do you know about Pat from this paragraph? Look carefully for clues. We can learn about characters from their language, actions, thoughts, and feelings.

188 Unit 3

A character's traits and emotional makeup do not need to be described by the narrator. *Showing* the reader is generally more effective. For example:

- Sarah is a kind soul who is loved for her many acts of kindness.
- On Sundays, Sarah visits both the local nursing home and the food shelter. She volunteers at a home for children twice a week.

It is clear from both sentences that Sarah is a kind person, though in the second sentence it is not stated outright.

In the paragraph provided in the student edition, the following traits are stated or suggested: prepared, organized, studious, kind (helping Anna when others would not), sense of humor (refreshments), and blonde.

If you would like to expand upon the lesson on characterization, ask the students to pick an important adult in their lives whom they like or admire, such as a parent, grandparent, teacher, or older sibling. Have them make a list of this person's traits. Where possible, they should jot down examples that illustrate each attribute. Then have them write a "showing" character sketch (a paragraph is sufficient) of that individual.

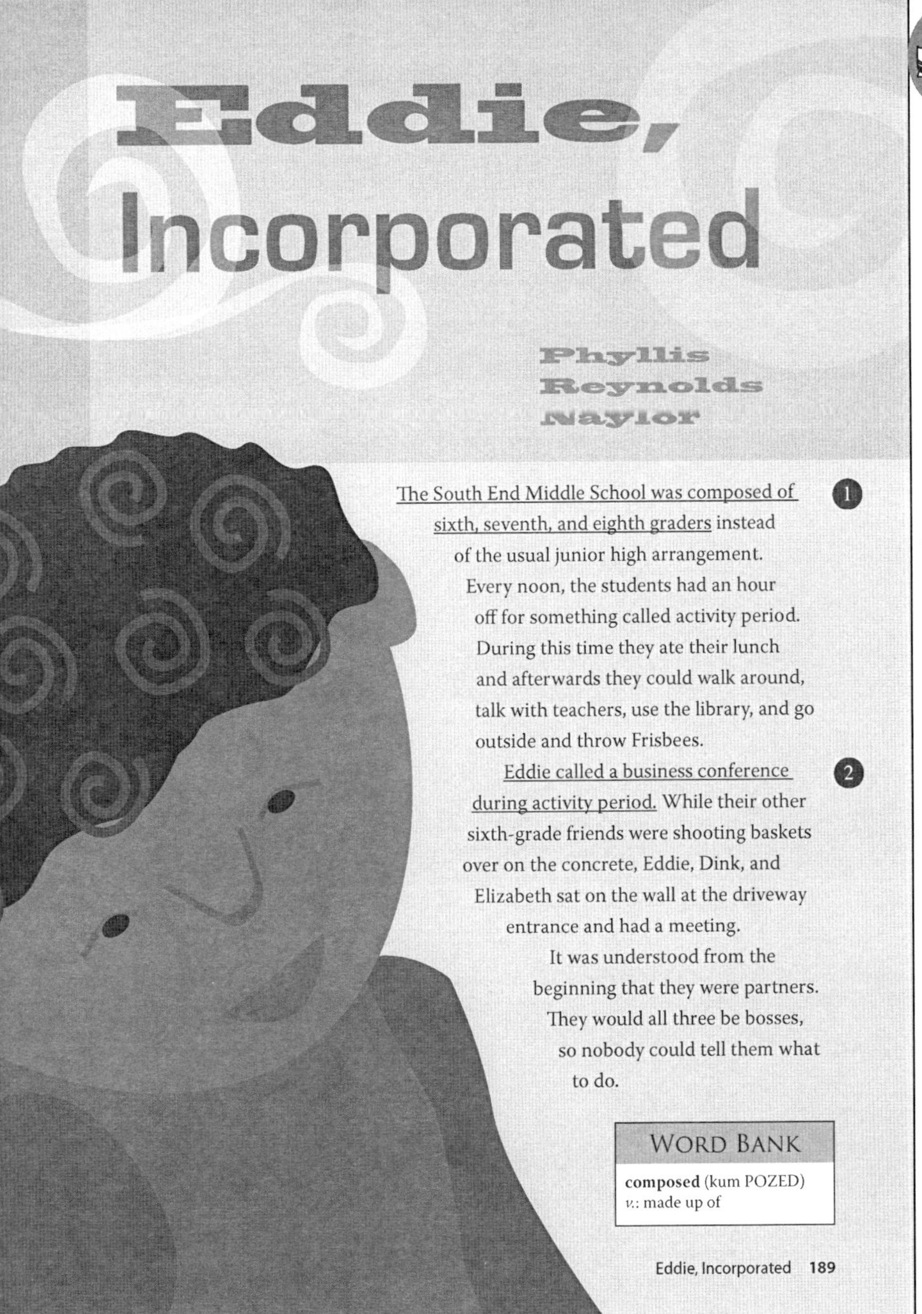

Eddie, Incorporated

Phyllis Reynolds Naylor

The South End Middle School was composed of sixth, seventh, and eighth graders instead of the usual junior high arrangement. Every noon, the students had an hour off for something called activity period. During this time they ate their lunch and afterwards they could walk around, talk with teachers, use the library, and go outside and throw Frisbees. 1

Eddie called a business conference during activity period. While their other sixth-grade friends were shooting baskets over on the concrete, Eddie, Dink, and Elizabeth sat on the wall at the driveway entrance and had a meeting. 2

It was understood from the beginning that they were partners. They would all three be bosses, so nobody could tell them what to do.

WORD BANK

composed (kum POZED) *v.*: made up of

Eddie, Incorporated 189

Selection Summary

Eddie, Dink, and Elizabeth are three sixth graders who decide to open a business. The first decision they make is that all three will be bosses. Once this is established, they proceed to take the steps necessary to make any small business work. They start by assigning the posts of advertising, supply, and operations. We discover that Eddie's, Dink's, and Elizabeth's business is aluminum recycling and the plan is to collect, clean, and sell discarded aluminum cans. Like most youthful entrepreneurs (and many not so youthful ones), they count their eggs way before they are hatched. Plans for how to spend the profits abound.

Eddie's father instructs Eddie—and the young reader—in practical business applications. One thing we learn is the risks and benefits of paying a worker a salary rather than guaranteeing a percent of the profit. We learn about operating expenses. We see how advertising can be ignored or defaced, how a good breakfast starts off the workday right, and, above all, that you can't *do* business if you don't *get* business. In short, this story provides a realistic look at the excitement and struggle involved in setting up a small business.

Literary Components

1 **Setting:** The author sets the scene in a very understated way. From the simple opening statement we learn that the story takes place in a typical American public school, that the characters will be of middle school age, and that the time period is modern.

2 **Exposition:** The story begins to unfold as we hear about a business meeting. Eddie, Dink, and Elizabeth are introduced.

Guiding the Reading

Literal

Q: What school did Eddie attend?

A: He went to South End Middle School.

Q: Which grades were housed in the South End Middle School?

A: Grades six, seven, and eight were there.

Q: When was the students' activity period?

A: The activity period was at noon for one hour.

Q: What did the students generally do during the activity period?

A: The students ate lunch, walked around, talked with teachers, used the library, threw Frisbees, and played basketball.

Q: What did Eddie arrange during activity hour?

A: He arranged a business conference.

Q: Who else joined the meeting?

A: Elizabeth and Dink.

Q: What did they decide right from the start?

A: They decided that they would all be equal partners and bosses.

Analytical

Q: What is meant by "friends shooting baskets over on the concrete"?

A: It means that kids are playing basketball on the playground.

Literary Components

3 Characterization: We learn that Elizabeth is the creative member of the team.

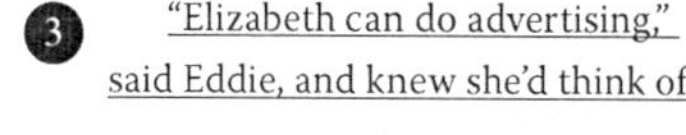

"We've got to have advertising," said Eddie.

Elizabeth lifted her face toward the warm May sun and closed her eyes for a moment. She wore huge, round, blue-tinted glasses, and her hair was pulled up in a large topknot.

"What we need," she said, "is to rent a plane that would fly all over Detroit trailing a banner that said, 'Anselmino's Aluminum Recycling Now Open for Business.' "

She even looked like an executive.

3 "Elizabeth can do advertising," said Eddie, and knew she'd think of

Word Bank

executive (egg ZEK yoo tiv) *n.*: a person who has a position of leadership in a business or company

Guiding the Reading

Literal

Q: What was Eddie's first suggestion?

A: He thought they should do some advertising.

Q: What do you know about the setting so far?

A: The story takes place at South End Middle School during activity period. There is a business meeting near the wall of the driveway entrance. It is a warm, sunny day in May.

Q: What type of business were the kids planning on starting?

A: They were going to start an aluminum recycling business.

Q: What was Elizabeth's suggestion for advertising?

A: She wanted to rent a plane with a banner to fly all over Detroit.

something, even without the plane. "We also need someone in charge of supply—to find out where the cans are and go after them."

"I could use Dad's garbage can carrier and go around collecting," Dink said. He was wearing a tee-shirt with Godzilla[1] on the front. He didn't look like an executive, but he did look as though he could walk over half of Detroit pushing a one-hundred pound load. 4

"You've got it," said Eddie. "Vice-president in charge of supply."

"Hey, Eddie," Billy Watson called. "Let's shoot a few baskets."

"Not now," said Eddie. "We've got business." 5

1. *Godzilla* (gud ZILL uh)

Literary Components

4 Characterization: We learn that Dink is big and strong.

5 Characterization: We learn that Eddie is mature, responsible, and not easily distracted.

Guiding the Reading

Literal

Q: Why did Eddie decide to put Elizabeth in charge of advertising?

A: He knew that she would think of a good advertising idea even without the plane.

Q: What did Dink offer when Eddie said they needed someone in charge of supply?

A: "I could use Dad's garbage can carrier and go around collecting."

Q: What did Eddie turn down in order to work on his business?

A: He turned down a game of basketball with Billy Watson.

Analytical

Q: Did Eddie think the plane idea would work? How do you know this?

A: No. "He knew she'd think of something without the plane." It was not a realistic plan.

Q: Why do you think Eddie agreed to give Dink the position of Vice President in Charge of Supply?

A: He offered, there were only three people to choose from, and his suggestion about using his father's things sounded good. He was also strong and "looked as though he could walk over half of Detroit pushing a one-hundred pound load."

Literary Components

6 Detail; Characterization: From the very detailed description we learn that these young people are organized and realistic. They have thought about what they will need for their business and have taken measures to ensure they are well-prepared.

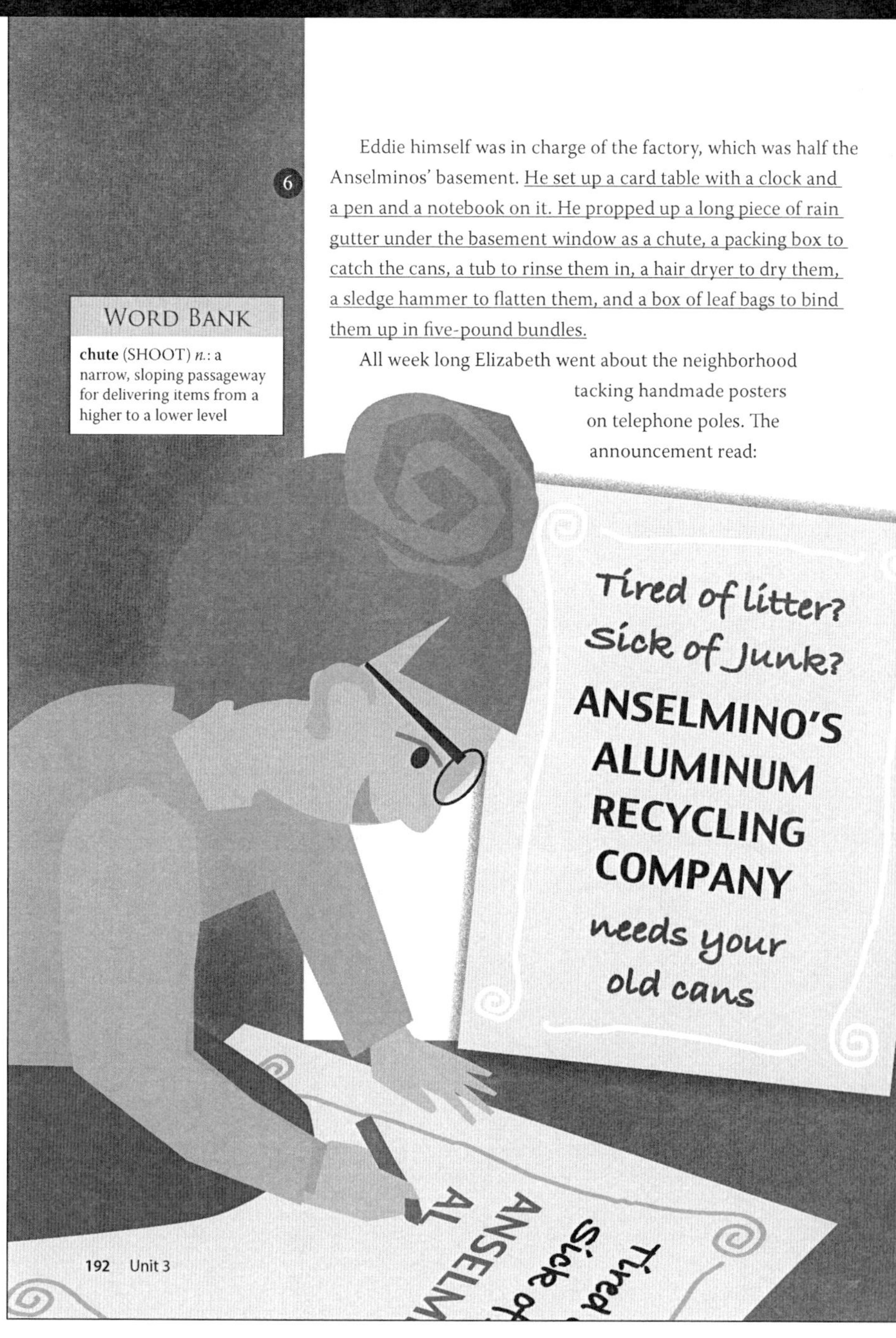

Eddie himself was in charge of the factory, which was half the Anselminos' basement. 6 He set up a card table with a clock and a pen and a notebook on it. He propped up a long piece of rain gutter under the basement window as a chute, a packing box to catch the cans, a tub to rinse them in, a hair dryer to dry them, a sledge hammer to flatten them, and a box of leaf bags to bind them up in five-pound bundles.

All week long Elizabeth went about the neighborhood tacking handmade posters on telephone poles. The announcement read:

WORD BANK

chute (SHOOT) *n.*: a narrow, sloping passageway for delivering items from a higher to a lower level

192 Unit 3

Guiding the Reading

Literal

Q: Where was the new recycling company located?

A: It would be located in the Anselmino's basement.

Q: Elizabeth was in charge of advertising and Dink was in charge of supply. What was Eddie in charge of?

A: Eddie was in charge of the factory.

Q: What were some of the things Eddie prepared in the basement factory?

A: He prepared a card table, a clock, pen, and notebook. He also set up a rain gutter for a chute, a box to catch the cans, a tub, a hairdryer, a sledge hammer, and leaf bags.

Q: How did Elizabeth choose to advertise in the end?

A: She hung handmade posters on telephone poles all around the neighborhood.

And then it listed Eddie's address and phone number.

Dink had painted a big OPEN sign on the back of a dart board to set up outside the house. The Anselmino Aluminum Recycling Company would begin its first day of business on Saturday, May 17, at nine o'clock.

7 "I'll be here at eight-thirty, in case there's a line," Elizabeth said to Eddie on Friday.

8 "And we ought to put in a night deposit box so people will have some place to put their cans after we're closed," Dink suggested. He said he would make one and bring it with him on Saturday.

Even Eddie's brother Joseph was interested in the company.

9 "How much can you get for aluminum cans, Eddie?" he asked at dinner.

"Seventeen cents a pound."

Joseph figured it out on the calculator he had wedged between his leg and the seat of his chair. "Only five hundred and eighty-eight pounds and

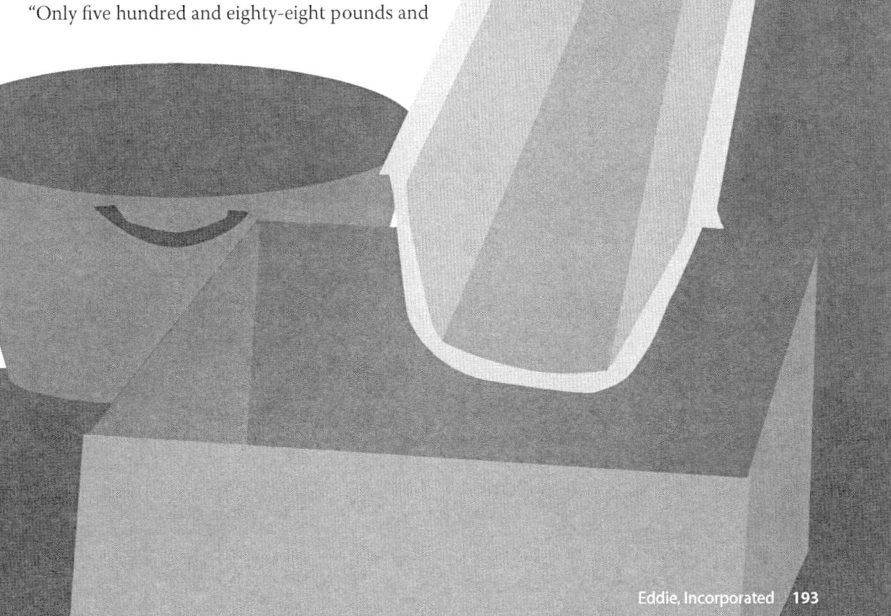

Literary Components

7 Foreshadowing: Elizabeth suggests there will be many people interested in donating old cans. Will there be? The reader can only wonder.

8 Foreshadowing; Characterization: We are given further hints that the business will do well. We also see that both Elizabeth and Dink are willing workers, volunteering to do extra jobs.

9 Rising Action: As talk of profits increases, we wait to see how the business will do.

Guiding the Reading

Literal

Q: Whose address and phone number were on the posters?

A: Eddie's address and phone number were on the posters.

Q: When would the Anselmino Aluminum Recycling Company open?

A: It would open on Saturday, May 17, at nine o'clock.

Q: Why did Elizabeth offer to come at eight-thirty?

A: She offered to help early in case there was a line.

Q: What did Dink suggest they add?

A: He said they should install a night deposit box where people could put cans after they closed.

Q: How much money could they make from collecting aluminum cans?

A: They could earn seventeen cents a pound.

194 Unit 3

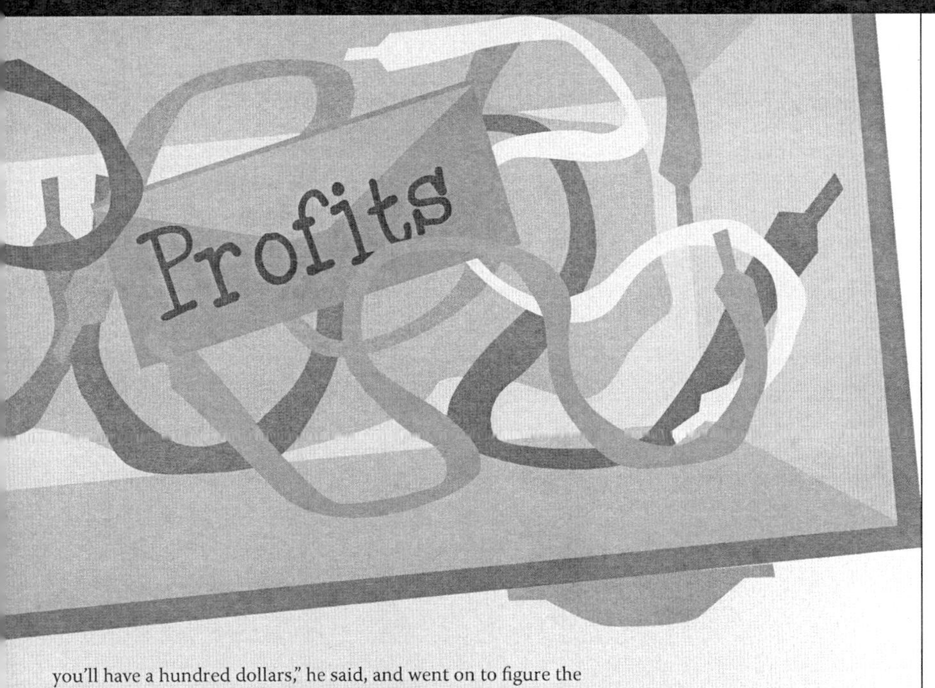

you'll have a hundred dollars," he said, and went on to figure the interest.

"What are you going to do with the profits?" Eddie's other brother, Roger, asked Eddie. "Have you thought of investing it somewhere? The bank gives five and one half percent."

Actually, Eddie had been thinking of putting it in the back of his top dresser drawer under the extra shoelaces, but he said he'd consider investing.

"And what about Dink and Elizabeth?" Mr. Anselmino asked. "Are you putting them on salary, or do they share the profits?"

Eddie wasn't sure.

"If they're on salary," his father said, "that means you pay them a certain amount each week regardless of how much the company takes in. If the company loses money, you'll have to pay them out of your allowance or something. But if the company makes money, they still get only their salary and you get all the rest."

It wasn't difficult to decide that one. Eddie, Dink, and Elizabeth were a team. It would be share and share alike. Even if they made a hundred dollars the first day, they'd split it three ways.  10

Literary Components

10 Theme: Eddie, Dink, and Elizabeth work well together. None of them wants a boss. They all volunteer to do extra work, not relying on someone else to do it. And they want to share the profits equally.

Guiding the Reading

Literal

Q: Who else was interested in the business?

A: Eddie's older brothers Joseph and Roger showed interest.

Q: How many pounds of cans would they need to make $100?

A: They would need 588 pounds!

Q: What did Roger suggest that Eddie do with the profits?

A: He said he should invest them and earn 5½% interest.

Q: Even though Eddie said he would consider investing, what was he really thinking of doing?

A: He was going to put it in the back of his top dresser drawer under the extra shoelaces.

Q: What did Mr. Anselmino ask Eddie about the money they would earn?

A: He asked if Dink and Elizabeth were going to be on salary or if they would share the profits.

Q: What is the difference between a salaried worker and one that shares the profits?

A: A salaried worker makes a specific amount each week/month whether or not there is a profit. If there is a profit, the worker gets a salary and the owner gets the rest of the money earned. If there is a loss, the worker still gets the same salary and the owner loses money.

Q: What did Eddie decide about salary?

A: All three would share the profits evenly.

196 Unit 3

"We're sharing the profits," he said, and realized he was beginning to sound like Roger. It was a good feeling, especially when he understood what he was talking about. 11

"Who's going to pay for the leaf bags you took out of the tool shed?" asked Mrs. Anselmino.

"We'll take it out of our earnings," Eddie told her. They hadn't even opened for business and already they were sixty-three cents in debt. 12

He woke at five the next morning and looked out the window to see if a line was forming yet. The street was still dark and empty. He knew he wouldn't sleep anymore, so he got up, dressed, and went out on the porch to wait.

The paper boy came by, followed by his dog. The mutt was holding something in his mouth that looked familiar. Eddie went down the steps and took it away from him. It was one of the advertisements for the Anselmino Aluminum Recycling Company.

"Hey, where'd he get this?" Eddie called after the boy.

The paper boy shrugged. "I don't know. It was blowing around on the street back there."

Literary Components

11 Theme: Another of the story's themes is "understanding business." The author clearly wants to explain how businesses work to the young reader.

12 External Conflict: Although this business is fortunate in that there is no conflict among the owners, the business as a whole must struggle with expenses.

Guiding the Reading

Literal

Q: What time did Eddie wake up the next morning?

A: He woke up at five in the morning.

Q: What was the paper boy's dog holding in his mouth?

A: The dog was holding a ripped poster advertising Anselmino Aluminum Recycling Company.

Analytical

Q: Which words in the beginning of the story give you a hint about what decision Eddie would make about salary?

A: "It was understood from the beginning that they were partners. They would all three be bosses, so nobody could tell them what to do."

Q: Why did Eddie have a good feeling when he said, "We're sharing the profits"?

A: He felt it sounded knowledgeable and confident.

Q: What was Mrs. Anselmino concerned about?

A: Who was going to pay for the leaf bags and, in general, who was going to take responsibility for every aspect of the business?

Q: How did they manage to be in debt already?

A: They had to pay for the leaf bags.

Q: Why wouldn't Eddie be able to fall asleep again?

A: He was anxious, excited, and curious.

Literary Components

13 **More External Conflict:** Somebody does not want Eddie, Incorporated to succeed.

14 **Characterization; Humor:** Eddie is a normal kid. He is angry at the thoughtless defacing of his ads and thinks dark, humorous thoughts.

15 **Characterization; Setting:** Eddie has a kind-hearted, caring Mom who is supportive of his efforts.

Eddie went down to the corner. The poster had been ripped off the telephone pole. There was still a piece of it left. He walked over to the next street. That poster was there, but someone had drawn two tanks on it, having a war, with smoke and bombs
13 all over the words. At the next telephone pole, someone had crossed out Eddie's telephone number and scribbled in the number for the fire department instead.

He went back home and sat on the steps. This neighborhood didn't have too many old cans; it had too many rotten children. Anselmino's Children Recycling Company, that's what it ought
14 to be. They ought to go around collecting bratty kids in Dink's garbage cart, weigh them in, tie them in sacks, and send them off to Siberia.

Mrs. Anselmino found Eddie still on the porch at seven o'clock and made him come in for breakfast. She put a plate of scrambled eggs before him and a sausage and an English muffin and then, on the spur of the moment, she poured him a half cup of coffee and filled the cup up with cream.

15 "Now," she said, "you're ready for business."

Guiding the Reading

Literal

Q: What had happened to many of their posters?

A: One was ripped, one had drawings all over it, and one had Eddie's telephone number crossed out and the number for the fire department in its place.

Q: What did Eddie think there were a lot of in his neighborhood besides cans?

A: He thought there were many rotten children.

Q: What did he think he should do with them?

A: Collect the bratty kids in Dink's garbage cart, weigh them in, tie them in sacks, and send them off to Siberia.

Q: At what time did Mrs. Anselmino find Eddie on the porch?

A: She saw him at seven o'clock.

Q: What did she serve him for breakfast?

A: She gave him scrambled eggs, sausage, and an English muffin.

Q: What did she add at the last minute that she said made him ready for business?

A: She gave him a half a cup of coffee with a lot of cream.

Analytical

Q: What made Eddie think that there were lots of rotten kids?

A: Many of them ruined Elizabeth's posters for no good reason.

Q: Did Eddie really mean it when he said the children should be sent off to Siberia?

A: No, he was just frustrated.

Q: Why do you think Mrs. Anselmino felt that coffee made Eddie ready for business?

A: It made him look more like a typical businessman, and gave him a grown-up attitude.

Q: What made Eddie feel good again?

A: On one level, it was the food that he needed to give him energy after being up so early. On the other hand, his mother's breakfast and love lifted his spirits a bit.

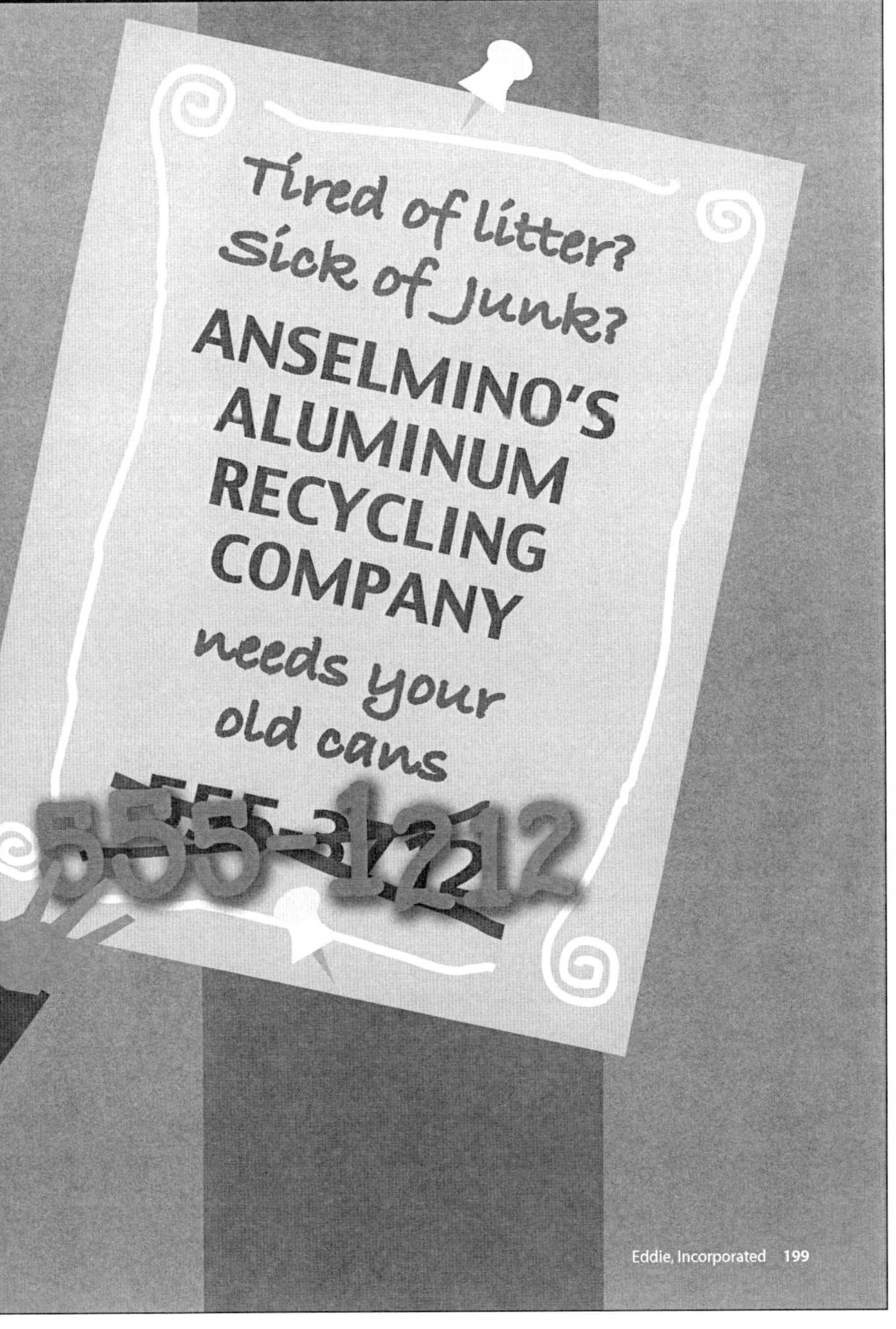
Tired of litter?
Sick of Junk?
ANSELMINO'S
ALUMINUM
RECYCLING
COMPANY
needs your
old cans
555-1212

He was beginning to feel good again.

Dink and Elizabeth arrived at eight-thirty. Dink had brought a night-deposit box made out of an ice cream container. On the curb at the end of the driveway he placed the dart board sign saying, OPEN.

At five minutes till nine, they took their places—Dink outside the basement window, Elizabeth at the bottom of the chute, and Eddie at the card table desk.

On the top of the first page of his notebook, Eddie wrote, "The Anselmino Aluminum Recycling Company" and, as an afterthought, added, "Incorporated," though he wasn't sure what it meant.

Underneath, he made six vertical columns with a ruler. At the top of the first column he wrote, "Date." At the top of the second,

WORD BANK

vertical (VUR tih kul) *adj.*: going up and down, not from side to side

Guiding the Reading

Literal

Q: When did Dink and Elizabeth arrive?

A: They came at eight-thirty.

Q: How did Dink make his night-deposit box?

A: He used an ice cream container.

Q: Where did each of them go at 8:55?

A: Dink stood outside the basement window, Elizabeth was at the bottom of the chute, and Eddie sat at his card table desk.

Analytical

Q: Do you have any idea what 'incorporated' means?

A: Answers will vary. (It means "combined in one body or group to form a legal organization or corporation.")

he wrote "Number of cans." At the top of the third, "Number of pounds." At the fourth, "Income," the fifth, "Expenses," and at the top of the final column he wrote "Profit." Then, after a moment, he added, "...or Loss."

Nine o'clock came, nine-fifteen, and at twenty after, Dink yelled, "Somebody's coming!" 16

There were footsteps on the driveway outside, and the sound of the mailman's voice. He wanted to know where the aluminum deposit was, and Dink directed him to the open window.

The sleeve of a blue uniform came through the window and deposited one empty iced tea can in the rain gutter.

Clunk-ity...Clunk-ity...thunk. 17

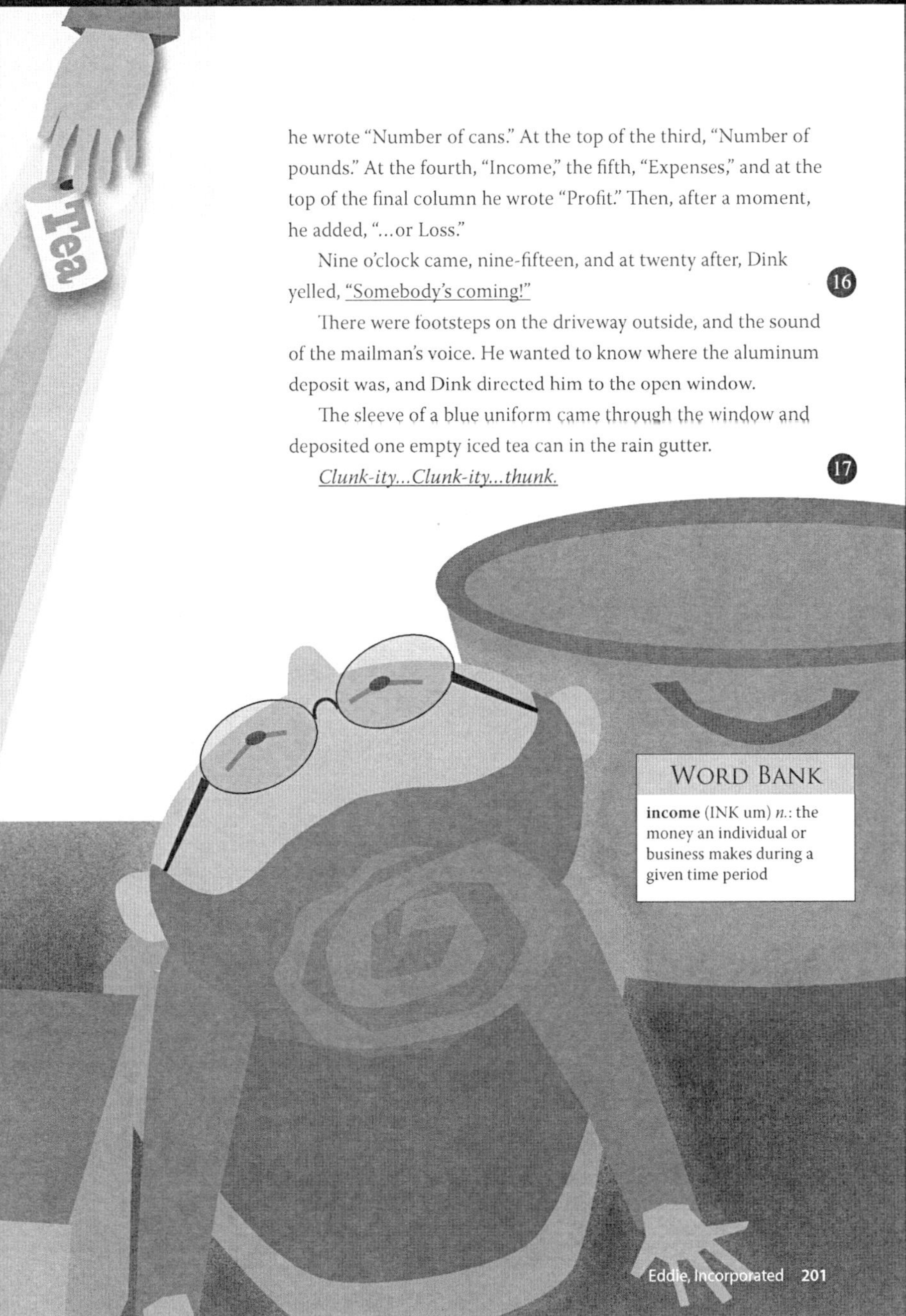

WORD BANK

income (INK um) *n.*: the money an individual or business makes during a given time period

Literary Components

16 Rising Action: Finally, Eddie, Incorporated is open for business.

17 Onomatopoeia; Sound Effects: The author makes us feel as though we are hearing the cans as they come down the chute.

Guiding the Reading

Literal

Q: How did Eddie organize his Recycling Company notebook?

A: He made six vertical columns with a ruler. Each column had a heading: date, number of cans, number of pounds, income, expenses, profit and loss.

Q: How long was it until they received a customer?

A: The first customer arrived at nine-twenty.

Q: Who was the first customer and what did he bring?

A: The mailman brought one empty iced tea can.

Literary Components

18 Idiom: The casual language is part of the realistic tone of the entire story.

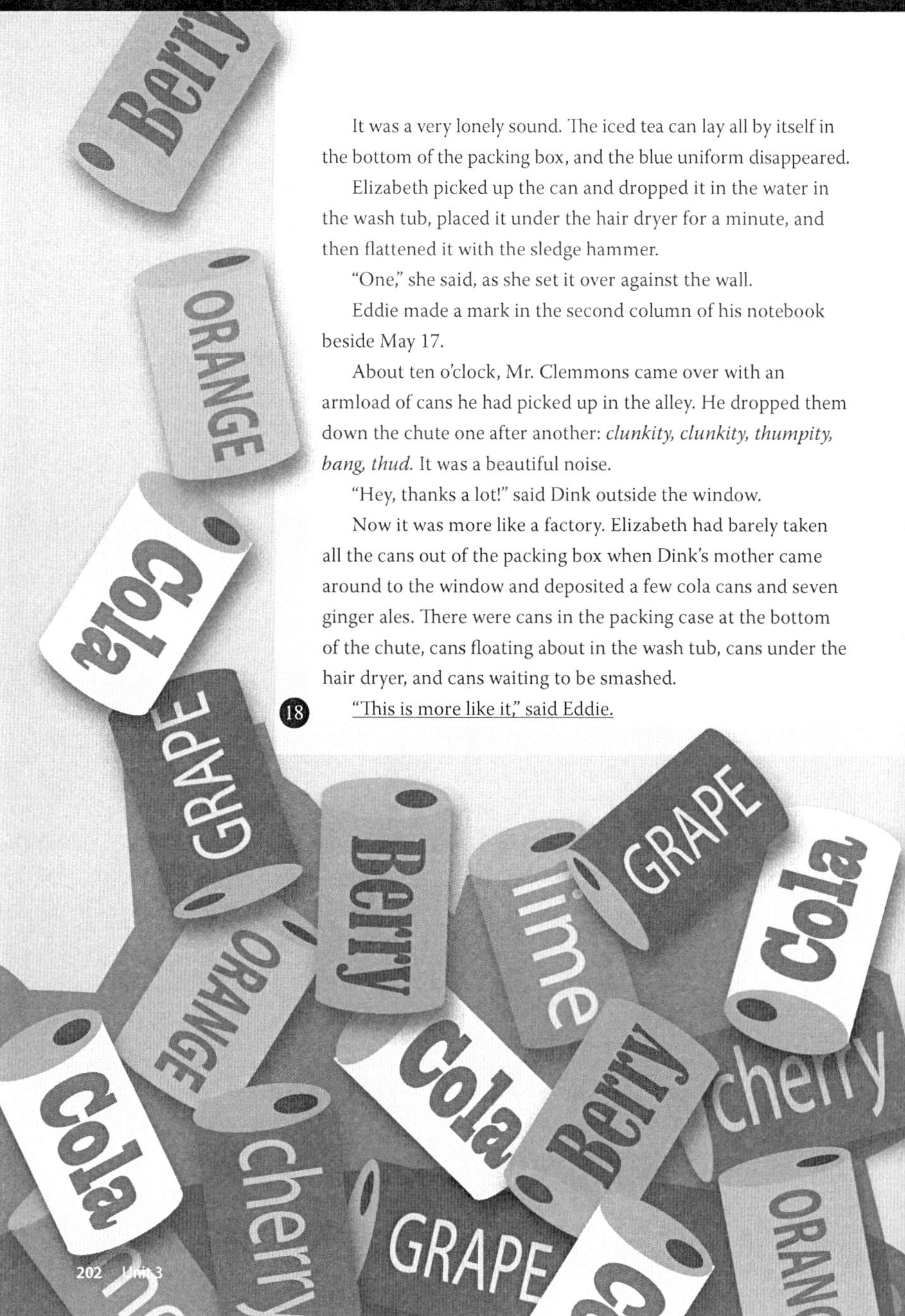

It was a very lonely sound. The iced tea can lay all by itself in the bottom of the packing box, and the blue uniform disappeared.

Elizabeth picked up the can and dropped it in the water in the wash tub, placed it under the hair dryer for a minute, and then flattened it with the sledge hammer.

"One," she said, as she set it over against the wall.

Eddie made a mark in the second column of his notebook beside May 17.

About ten o'clock, Mr. Clemmons came over with an armload of cans he had picked up in the alley. He dropped them down the chute one after another: *clunkity, clunkity, thumpity, bang, thud.* It was a beautiful noise.

"Hey, thanks a lot!" said Dink outside the window.

Now it was more like a factory. Elizabeth had barely taken all the cans out of the packing box when Dink's mother came around to the window and deposited a few cola cans and seven ginger ales. There were cans in the packing case at the bottom of the chute, cans floating about in the wash tub, cans under the hair dryer, and cans waiting to be smashed.

18 "This is more like it," said Eddie.

202 Unit 3

Guiding the Reading

Literal

Q: Who brought cans at ten o'clock?
A: Mr. Clemmons brought an armload of cans he picked up in the alley.

Q: What did Dink's mother bring?
A: She brought a few cola cans and seven ginger ales.

Q: What made it seem more like a factory?
A: There were many cans at each location—the bottom of the chute, floating in the water, under the hair dryer, and waiting to be crushed.

Analytical

Q: The story tells us, "It was a very lonely sound," and then later, "It was a beautiful noise." How do cans sound lonely?
A: They were eagerly anticipating a lot of business but after twenty minutes all they got was one can. The one solitary can seemed lonely compared to what they expected. When the number increased it was beautiful because it made them feel good and accomplished.

Things slowed a little over the lunch hour. Mrs. Anselmino brought down some salami sandwiches, and they took turns eating and standing out on the driveway to direct people to the deposit window.

Billy Watson and some boys from the South End Middle School rode over on their bikes, stuck their heads in the window and yelled crazy things. One of them rolled a rock down the chute. But after they went away, Elizabeth's father arrived with two grocery sacks full of cans.

"Way to go!" whooped Dink from outside as he poured the cans down the rain gutter.

Eddie and Elizabeth were working as fast as they could.

About three o'clock the hair dryer began to smell funny, and Eddie decided that maybe it needed a rest, so they finished drying the cans with a towel.

Guiding the Reading

Literal

Q: What happened over lunch hour?

A: Business slowed while they ate salami sandwiches.

Q: Why did they take turns eating in the driveway?

A: They took turns so that they wouldn't miss customers and would be able to direct them to the deposit window.

Q: What did Billy Watson and his friends do?

A: They yelled insults at Eddie and his friends as they passed by and put a rock down the chute.

Q: Who brought two grocery sacks full of cans?

A: Elizabeth's father brought them.

Q: Why did they finish drying the cans with a towel?

A: They used a towel because the hair dryer started to smell.

Analytical

Q: Why do you think Billy Watson and his friends yelled and threw a rock down the chute?

A: Answers will vary.

Literary Components

19 External Conflict: An unforeseen problem arises. Who would have thought someone could misinterpret the instructions? How will the three kids deal with Mrs. Harris?

20 Characterization: Dink reveals his good heart. Even though Mrs. Harris' cans are a bother, Dink chooses not to hurt her feelings.

At four, old Mrs. Harris came by pulling a little wagon. It was piled high with cans, and she stooped down outside the window and began dropping them one at a time down the chute.

19 Eddie and Elizabeth stared. <u>There were baked beans cans and creamed corn cans and scalloped potato cans and about twenty fruit cocktail.</u> Only one of the cans was aluminum; the rest were tin, and the baked bean can still had a frankfurter in the bottom.

"Why didn't you stop her, Dink?" Elizabeth called up after the woman had left.

20 <u>"I didn't have the heart," he said.</u> "She pulled that wagon four blocks, so I just thanked her, and she said there were more cans where those came from."

At five o'clock, Eddie took the OPEN sign and put it behind the house. He closed the basement window and put the night deposit box in front of it. Then he and Dink and Elizabeth went back to the basement to tally up the day's profits.

Guiding the Reading

Literal

Q: Why did Eddie and Elizabeth stare at Mrs. Harris?

A: There were assorted cans and some were very dirty. Only one of the cans was aluminum while the rest were tin.

Q: Why didn't Dink say anything to Mrs. Harris?

A: He felt bad for her since she had pulled them in a wagon for four blocks.

Q: What did they do at five o'clock?

A: They took down the OPEN sign, closed the basement window and put the night deposit box in front of it. Elizabeth tallied up the day's profits.

Analytical

Q: Why did Elizabeth ask Dink about stopping old Mrs. Harris?

A: Most of her cans were tin and their business was for aluminum cans.

There were one-hundred and thirty-six cans. Eddie brought down the bathroom scale to see how many pounds that would be. They began putting the flattened cans on the scales one at a time.

The marker barely moved. Three cans…four cans…

"Maybe the scale is broken," said Elizabeth.

Around ten cans, they could tell that the marker had moved halfway between zero and one. It took twenty-one cans to make a pound. 21

Carefully they divided the cans into little heaps of twenty-one each. Six piles of cans with ten left over. Six pounds of cans at seventeen cents a pound.

Eddie went to his desk and figured it out. One dollar and two cents. He entered it under "income." Then he remembered the sixty-three cents they owed for the leaf bags and put that in the column marked "expenses." One dollar and two cents

Literary Components

21 Turning Point: The business is now more than just an idea. A day of work has come and gone. Reality sets in. It takes an awful lot of cans to make up a pound. Is it worth all the work?

Guiding the Reading

Literal

Q: How many cans were there in total?

A: There were one hundred and thirty-six.

Q: Why did they think the scale was broken?

A: They kept putting cans on the scale and it did not seem to be registering.

Q: How many cans did it take to make a pound?

A: Twenty-one cans.

Q: What was the total income?

A: The income was $1.02.

Literary Components

22 Turning Point: Reality sets in even more deeply!

23 Falling Action: Eddie is beginning to come to a resolution.

24 Resolution: It seems likely that Eddie, Incorporated will not last too long. But one feels that Eddie, Elizabeth, and Dink now have the experience to start a new venture that *will* be profitable.

 22 minus sixty-three cents left a profit of thirty-nine cents. And thirty-nine cents divided between Eddie, Dink, and Elizabeth was thirteen cents apiece.

"At least you didn't go in the hole," Mr. Anselmino said at dinner that evening.

"And people know where to bring the cans now," said Roger.

"And he paid off his debt to me the very first day," said Mrs. Anselmino.

Joseph had not brought his pocket calculator to the table that evening, but Eddie could tell, by the way he pressed his fingers against the table top one at a time, that he was figuring something out in his head. "Thirteen cents a day, six days a week, fifty-two times a year, at five and a half percent..." he was saying to himself.

But Eddie wasn't interested in what he could make if the Anselmino Aluminum Recycling Company lasted a year.  23 He was wondering if it would last a month.  24 Eight hours a day for only thirteen cents was just a little more than one-and-a-half cents an hour, which meant he'd have to work a day and then some just to afford a stamp to mail his income tax. Bosses had more problems than anybody.

206 Unit 3

Guiding the Reading

Literal

Q: Why did they make only thirteen cents each?

A: They had to pay for the leaf garbage bags and then divide the remaining profits.

Q: Who said that people now know where to bring the cans?

A: Roger said it.

Q: What impressed Mrs. Anselmino?

A: She was pleased that they paid off their debt right away.

Q: What was Joseph calculating at the dinner table?

A: He was trying to figure out how much the Anselmino Aluminum Recycling Company could make in one year.

Q: What was Eddie thinking at the same time?

A: He was thinking about whether the business would last a month. He was wondering if working so many hours for so little pay was worth it.

Analytical

Q: What did Mr. Anselmino mean when he said, "At least you didn't go in the hole"?

A: He meant that at least they did not owe anyone money.

ABOUT THE AUTHOR

Born to write is the only way to describe **Phyllis Reynolds Naylor**! From the time her mother began reading books to her, she has made up her own stories. As a first grader, little Phyllis made up stories about the pictures in her reader and told them to her teacher! In the fifth grade, she would rush home every day to write down her latest story. Soon after she graduated from college, she began to write full-time and has so far published 115 books! Mrs. Naylor lives in Maryland with her husband. They have two grown sons, Jeff and Michael.

First Impressions

Answers will vary. Ask students to support their opinions with examples from the story.

Quick Review

1. They agreed that they would be equal partners and bosses.
2. Elizabeth was in charge of advertising, Dink was in charge of supply, and Eddie took care of the factory.
3. They could earn seventeen cents a pound. In order to earn one hundred dollars, they would need 558 pounds of aluminum cans.
4. The table with the clock and pen on it, the rain gutter chute, the box to catch the cans, the tub to rinse them, the hair dryer, the sledge hammer, and the box of bags all arranged to prepare the cans for recycling gave the basement the look of a factory. However, it *really* looked like a factory when they had a lot of cans coming in and were very busy.

Focus

5. Eddie and his friends obviously felt strongly about their venture. Two points can be made: one, that they wanted to feel mature and start their very own successful business and two, that they strongly believed they were doing something good for the environment.
6. **Eddie:** While Eddie insisted that all three were equal, it was originally his idea and he played a *leadership* role in the business. He was *forward-looking* and liked to plan. He was *organized* in the way he gathered the supplies and set them up and the way he made the chart in his notebook. He displayed *responsibility* by coming on time and reimbursing his mother right away. Eddie was very *motivated.* Invite your students to mention other attributes, as long as they support their ideas with lines from the story. Point out to your students that Eddie is the main character so we know the most about him.

   Elizabeth: Elizabeth was *creative* and did her job *responsibly*.

   Dink: Dink was *kind* (Mrs. Harris) and was quick to offer *help* and ideas, such as the night drop.

   They were all *motivated, hard-working,* and *worked together* as a team. They each *contributed* ideas, *listened* to each other, and did *not complain* about the work involved when something did not go smoothly or if the workload was not divided evenly. Both Elizabeth and Dink showed up early to work the first Saturday.

Studying the Selection

FIRST IMPRESSIONS

Do you think Eddie, Dink, and Elizabeth worked well together as a team?

QUICK REVIEW

1. What did Eddie and his friends agree on first, before they started to discuss the business details?
2. What job was each person given?
3. How much money could the group earn from collecting and recycling cans?
4. What made the basement feel like a factory?

FOCUS

5. Why would Eddie and his friends give up their activity period and the regular games with classmates to work on their business?
6. What character traits helped Eddie, Elizabeth, and Dink start their business?

CREATING AND WRITING

7. Write about a group of children working together on a school project. Include a problem they had and how they solved it.
8. Choose one character from the story. Develop his or her characteristics further. Let the reader get a more detailed peek into his or her life. Include more character traits, interests, talents, physical details, strengths, and weaknesses. Write one paragraph about the character. Then write one more paragraph about this character that includes something that takes place a few weeks after the story, *Eddie, Incorporated.*
9. Your teacher will divide your class into groups of three or four students. Brainstorm with your group about what rules and strategies are most important for teamwork and success. Once you have written down your ideas, find a creative way to share them with your classmates. Make an easy to remember rhyme, a pocket checklist, an attractive poster, or another method. This way, you will all remember to practice these guidelines for future projects.

208 Unit 3

Creating and Writing

7. Answers will vary.
8. Answers will vary. Identifying general character traits and descriptive words during class discussion will make it easier for some students to complete this assignment.
9. Responses will vary. While it is important for the students to think of teamwork strategies on their own, be sure to circulate among the groups and guide the process. You may wish to refer to the list of ideas in the *Into* section.

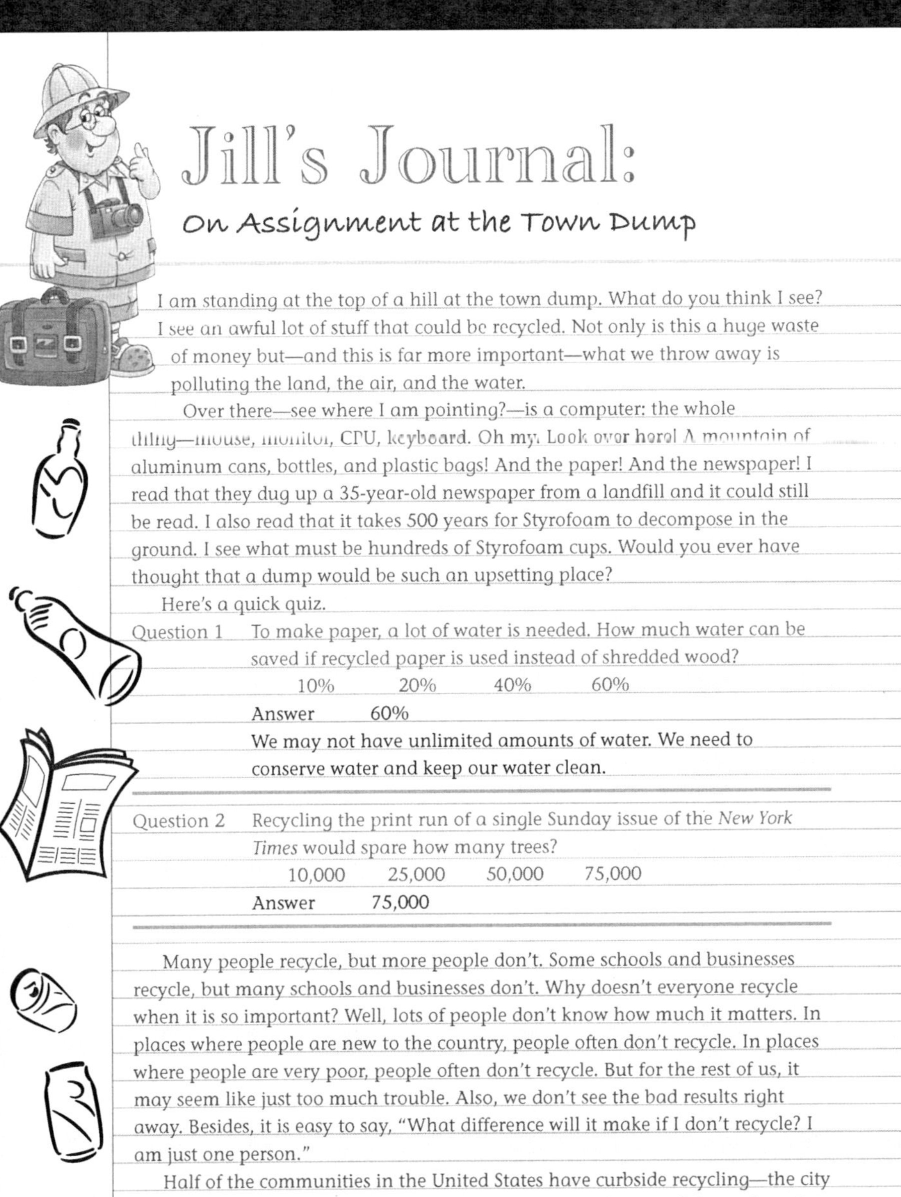

Jill's Journal:

On Assignment at the Town Dump

I am standing at the top of a hill at the town dump. What do you think I see? I see an awful lot of stuff that could be recycled. Not only is this a huge waste of money but—and this is far more important—what we throw away is polluting the land, the air, and the water.

Over there—see where I am pointing?—is a computer: the whole thing—mouse, monitor, CPU, keyboard. Oh my. Look over here! A mountain of aluminum cans, bottles, and plastic bags! And the paper! And the newspaper! I read that they dug up a 35-year-old newspaper from a landfill and it could still be read. I also read that it takes 500 years for Styrofoam to decompose in the ground. I see what must be hundreds of Styrofoam cups. Would you ever have thought that a dump would be such an upsetting place?

Here's a quick quiz.

Question 1 To make paper, a lot of water is needed. How much water can be saved if recycled paper is used instead of shredded wood?

10% 20% 40% 60%

Answer 60%

We may not have unlimited amounts of water. We need to conserve water and keep our water clean.

Question 2 Recycling the print run of a single Sunday issue of the *New York Times* would spare how many trees?

10,000 25,000 50,000 75,000

Answer 75,000

Many people recycle, but more people don't. Some schools and businesses recycle, but many schools and businesses don't. Why doesn't everyone recycle when it is so important? Well, lots of people don't know how much it matters. In places where people are new to the country, people often don't recycle. In places where people are very poor, people often don't recycle. But for the rest of us, it may seem like just too much trouble. Also, we don't see the bad results right away. Besides, it is easy to say, "What difference will it make if I don't recycle? I am just one person."

Half of the communities in the United States have curbside recycling—the city picks up the recycling each week when it comes to get the rest of the trash and the garbage. That means that all that the household must do is have some extra

Jill's Journal 209

Background Bytes

You will want to review the definition of *recycle* with your students:

recycle *v.*: to process old items such as newspapers, glass, plastic, and cans so they can be used to make new products

Some people argue that recycling is not profitable. They are rightfully concerned about the cost of large trucks riding across the city using lots of gas and polluting the air with their exhaust, in order to pick up a few aluminum cans. Perhaps they have images of the soap and hot water going down the drain to wash those cans.

Their concerns are valid. However, when people suggest that recycling is not profitable, and may even be detrimental to the environment, they are not including the costs of *not recycling* in their calculations. They are not thinking of the energy costs over the life of a product, and the new energy costs that accrue if the item has to be completely replaced. Likely, they are not thinking of the air, water, and soil pollution that result from capturing the raw materials, from manufacturing, and, ultimately, from throwing away the product.

Energy costs of manufacture include electricity. Two of the principal causes of acid rain, sulfur and nitrogen compounds, are electricity generation and factories. Coal power plants are the most polluting. Thus, acid rain, which is killing off lakes and river estuaries across the globe, is largely a byproduct of manufacturing. This process is significantly diminished when materials are reused.

Recycling means far less acid rain. The percentage of energy saved by using recycled instead of raw materials to manufacture is 40% for glass, 60% for steel, 95% for aluminum, 40% for newspapers, and 70% for plastics. (*Natural Resource Defense Council*)

The alternatives to recycling are landfills, where trash is buried, and incinerators, where trash is burned. In 2000, Americans were recycling or composting about 30% of their trash. Of the remaining 70%, 55% was land filled and 15% was incinerated. (*Environmental Protection Agency,* 2000) Both of these forms of solid waste disposal have serious hidden costs.

One of the hidden costs of devoting acres of land to landfill is what is called *opportunity cost.* Opportunity cost refers to the loss of the more profitable use to which a landfill site might have been put, were it not being used to hold mountains of garbage and trash.

Other hidden costs of landfill disposal are the contamination of both soil and groundwater, when highly toxic materials leach into the soil from high-technology solid waste. In 2006, Americans threw away 130 million mobile phones—65,000 tons of waste. This waste contained toxic chemicals such as arsenic, beryllium, copper, lead, cadmium, nickel, and zinc. These chemicals have been linked to cancer and neurological disorders. (*University of Colorado Recycling*)

There are four to eight pounds of lead in every computer monitor. There is lead in most of the solder points in electronic product circuit boards. Computers also contain PVCs, retardants, chromium, mercury, beryllium, and cadmium—all carcinogens or neurotoxins. Between 1997 and 2004, 315 million computers became obsolete, along with millions of other electronic products. (*Silicon Valley Toxics Coalition,* 2004) How many individuals and businesses made certain that their computers did not end up in landfills?

In the United States, 86% of the landfills are currently leaking toxic materials into lakes, streams, and aquifers. Once groundwater is contaminated, it is extremely expensive and difficult—if not impossible—to clean it up. (*Environmental Protection Agency,* 2003) In 2002, 45% of the nation's assessed waters were unsafe for fishing, swimming, or supporting aquatic life—up from 40% in 1998. (*Natural Resources Defense Council,* 2002)

The hidden cost of not recycling paper and newspaper is the loss of habitat for animals and plant species, when old growth and rainforests are logged. Loss of habitat is one of the major pressures towards extinction of species.

The push towards recycling will lead to a more beautiful America. This will be an America where the highways and byways are no longer peppered with every manner of litter; recycling will lead to an America in which there are not more roads in the National Forests than in the entire U.S. Interstate Highway system (as is the case today). (*National Forest Protection Alliance*)

Paper Products

Americans throw away one billion trees' worth of paper every year. Each year the average household throws away 13,000 pieces of paper. Fifty million homes could be heated for twenty years on the amount of wood and paper we throw away each year.

One-third of all trees cut down are used for the manufacture of paper.

If you are ever wondering whether it is important to recycle your school or household paper (of all types), consider that the pulp and paper industry is the world's fifth largest industrial consumer of energy. The paper industry uses more water to produce a ton of product than any other industry. Making paper from recycled content rather than from virgin fiber creates 74% less air pollution and 35% less water pollution.

The Environmental Defense Fund estimates that if the entire U.S. catalog industry switched its publications to just ten percent recycled-content paper, the savings in wood alone would be enough to build a nearly six-foot high fence across the length of the United States seven times. (*Worldwatch Institute*, 2004)

One year's worth of America's unrecycled holiday cards would fill a football field ten stories high. (*BRING Recycles*, 2003)

Forty-three percent of land filled or incinerated municipal discards, by weight, is packaging and containers, disposable products such as paper and plastic plates and cups, diapers, junk mail, trash bags, and tissue paper and towels.

Aluminum & Steel

With the energy it takes to make one new aluminum can from bauxite ore, twenty cans can be made from recycled aluminum.

The energy saved each year by steel recycling is equal to the electrical power used annually to power 18 million homes—or enough energy to last Los Angeles residents for eight years. (*Steel Recycling Institute*, 2003)

Four to five tons of bauxite ore are needed for one ton of aluminum ingot.

plastic trash containers and toss their recyclables in the right containers. Sometimes, of course, it also means that a container or a can needs to be washed before it is thrown away—but it doesn't have to be scrubbed!

It is understandable that people don't want extra work. But everything that matters needs care. Our world is precious, and we must take care not to spoil it. We want the water to be clean and pure. We want the air we breathe to be fresh and healthy. We want to make sure the fish can live in the oceans and that no animal is hunted to extinction.

Recycling should not be thought of as a chore. We should look at it as an opportunity to demonstrate how much we value the wonderful world we live in.

POWER SKILL:
Conduct an Experiment; Keep a Log of the Results

Do you know what a logbook is? It's the daily record or journal kept by the captain of a ship on a journey. This is your journey into recycling for two weeks. You are the captain of the ship. You will keep a log of your daily progress with your Recycling-in-Class Experiment.

This activity needs to begin with a solid plan, just as the characters in the story made a solid plan.

1. First, the teacher must appoint a student to lead a class discussion on what steps the class will take to recycle all the trash created by them in school. The project will last two weeks.
2. In your town, what does it take to recycle? Is there curbside pickup, or do you need to take your recyclables to a recycling center? Does the city provide containers, or do you need to provide your own? What types of trash is recyclable where the school is located?
3. Start by calling City or Town Hall to find out what the regulations are. Cities usually require that recyclables be put in three groups, as follows: (1) newspapers; (2) paper and cardboard boxes; (3) aluminum cans, steel cans, glass bottles and jars, plastic bags, and plastic containers. Plastic containers have numbers on the bottom. Turn over a plastic milk bottle and you will see the number 1 inside a triangle. Many towns only pick up #1 and #2 plastic. Other cities take every number plastic container.
4. When you have this information—about curbside pickup vs. recycling center; about whether the city provides containers; about what is recycled and what is not; about whether you need large blue or clear plastic recycling bags from the supermarket—tell your teacher what you have learned.
5. Your class will need to make a decision about whether they can bring in or purchase three extra plastic waste bins or whether to use doubled paper supermarket bags. You will also need to determine where these extra bins or bags will stand.

210 Unit 3

Bottles & Containers

Americans throw out more than 270 million beer and soda drink bottles every day. (*Container Recycling Institute*, 2001)

Forty states do not require deposits on soda bottles. In those forty states, 29% of the bottles are recycled. Ten states require a nickel deposit. In those ten states, the container-recycling rate is 72%. One state, Michigan, requires a dime deposit. In Michigan, the redemption rate is 95%. When environmental groups fought for deposits on bottles, the soda and bottle industry spent billions of dollars to defeat the proposed legislation.

Recycling glass instead of making it from silica sand reduces mining waste by 75% and energy use by 40%. The process of making new glass from old causes 20% less air pollution than making new glass. (*Lehigh County Solid Waste Management*, 2003)

Glass will take more than one million years to decompose in our landfills.

Appliances

Only 52% of all major appliances are recycled in the United States. (*Environmental Protection Agency*, 1999)

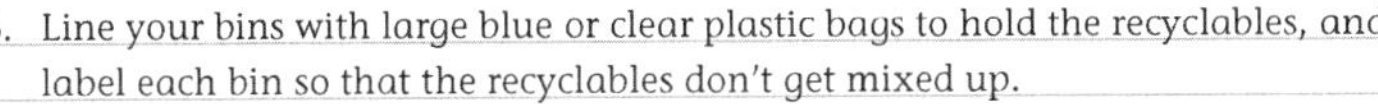

6. Line your bins with large blue or clear plastic bags to hold the recyclables, and label each bin so that the recyclables don't get mixed up.
7. Finally, the class needs a notebook in which to make daily entries. The first entry should briefly describe the first class meeting about setting up the recycling project. Each day write down the events connected with your project. How do people in your class feel about doing this? How many of each type of container is recycled each day? Enter your information clearly, so that you will be able to make a table of the daily recycling at the end of the week. The rows will be the days. The columns will be for aluminum cans, glass bottles or jars, plastic containers, paper and magazines, and newspapers.

Exercises

Your exercises will include the following:

1. Your recycling project, to be conducted for two weeks.
2. Your logbook, in which you will keep a daily record.
3. Your table, Our Two-Week Recycling-in-Class Experiment, which will look like this:

Our Two-Week Recycling-in-Class Experiment

Day	Aluminum Cans	Glass Bottles and Jars	Plastic Bottles, Containers, and Disposable Cups	Paper and Magazines	Newspapers
[starting day]					

All of your aluminum cans, other cans, glass bottles, and plastic are kept in the same container—if that is how your city collects or divides it. It is important to have a separate count of what is being thrown out.

Jill's Journal 211

Power Skill:

Conduct an Experiment; Keep a Log of the Results

As you talk with your students about the Power Skill, make certain you tell them that you will be conducting your own Two-Week Recycling Experiment at your own home and that you will be recycling along with them.

At the beginning of the project, show them your own spiral notebook and your own entries. It may be helpful to even express your impatience or exasperation with the project, and how you grow beyond that initial reaction.

We suggest that you, yourself, contact City or Town Hall, so that you are familiar with, and can convey to your class, information regarding whether or not there is curbside pickup, and if not, the location of reclamation or recycling centers. You can also post a list in class—and include this list in your notice to parents—of what exactly can be recycled at the curbside and at the recycling center.

Exercises

1. Help the students get organized.
2. Show students how you have set up your own logbook.
3. Your table, My Two-Week Recycling-in-Class Experiment, which will look like the chart below.

Our Two-Week Recycling-in-Class Experiment

Day	Aluminum Cans	Glass Bottles and Jars	Plastic Bottles, Containers, and Disposable Cups	Paper and Magazines	Newspapers
[starting day]					

Major and Minor Characters

Snowstorm!

1. The snowstorm has stranded them in their house. At the end of the story we see that the main problem is that the heroine cannot get to her school play.
2. The narrator is the major character. We are not given her name. Mom, Meg, Fred, Dad, and Sam are all minor characters.
3. Answers will vary, but we would suggest persistence and creativity.

Lesson in Literature . . .

MAJOR AND MINOR CHARACTERS

- A **major** character is one of the **main** characters in a story. The action, dialogue, and narration are centered on these characters.
- The author will give the reader a lot of information about the main character.
- A **minor** character is one who does not play an important role in the story.
- The author may use minor characters to make the story more realistic, to represent one idea, or to add to the plot.

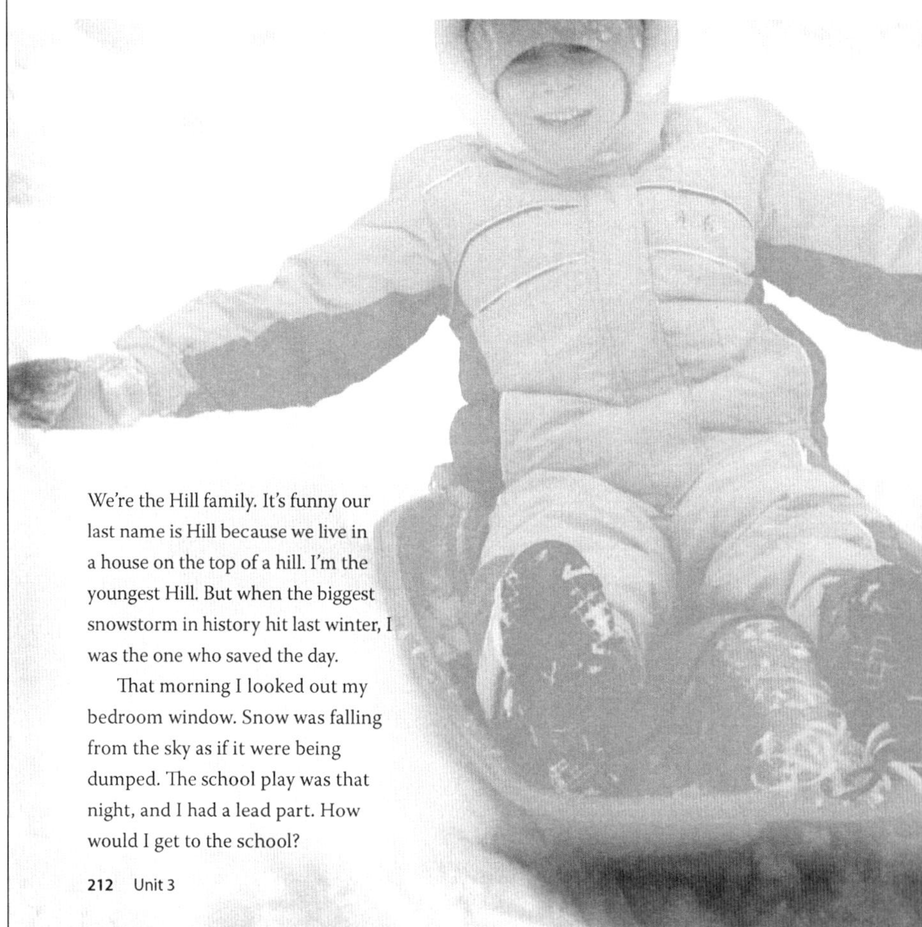

We're the Hill family. It's funny our last name is Hill because we live in a house on the top of a hill. I'm the youngest Hill. But when the biggest snowstorm in history hit last winter, I was the one who saved the day.

That morning I looked out my bedroom window. Snow was falling from the sky as if it were being dumped. The school play was that night, and I had a lead part. How would I get to the school?

212 Unit 3

Vocabulary

horizon (huh RY zun) *n.*: the place in the distance where the earth and sky seem to meet

plucked (PLUKD) *v.*: pulled out, like feathers from a bird

commotion (kuh MO shun) *n.*: noise and disturbance

herded (HURD id) *v.*: drove or led (cows)

churned *v.*: shook and beat milk to turn it into butter

whiff *n.*: a slight smell

singe (SINJ) *v.*: to burn slightly

trough (TROFF) *n.*: a long, boxlike container used to hold food or water for animals

affected (uh FEK tid) *v.*: influenced

miscalculated (mis KAL kyuh LAY tid) *v.*: judged incorrectly

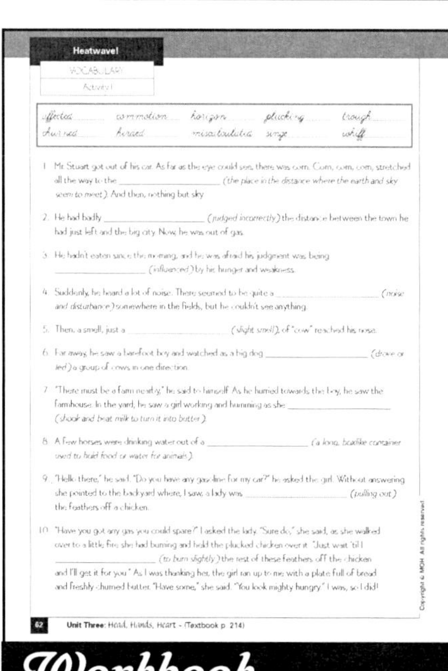

Heatwave!

VOCABULARY

Activity I

affected commotion horizon plucking trough
churned herded miscalculated singe whiff

Unit Three: Head, Hands, Heart • (Textbook p. 214)

Workbook

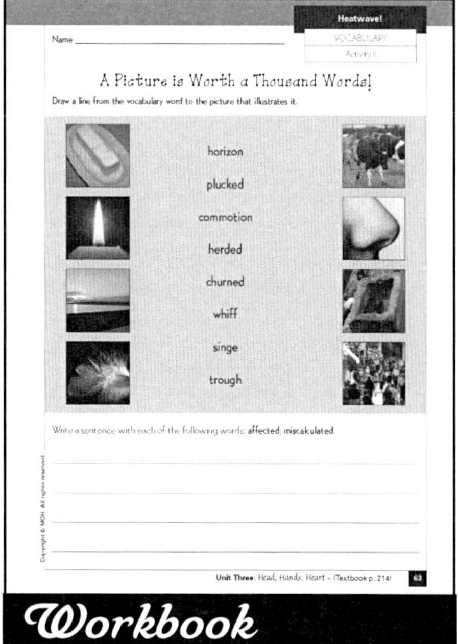

Heatwave!

VOCABULARY

Activity II

Name ____________

A Picture is Worth a Thousand Words!

Draw a line from the vocabulary word to the picture that illustrates it.

horizon
plucked
commotion
herded
churned
whiff
singe
trough

Write a sentence with each of the following words: affected, miscalculated

Unit Three: Head, Hands, Heart • (Textbook p. 214) 63

Workbook

Snowstorm!

THINK ABOUT IT!

1. What is the problem that must be solved by the characters in the story?
2. Who is the major character in the story? Name two minor characters.
3. In your opinion, what are the two most important personality traits of the major character in this story?

I ran downstairs.

My sister Meg and my brother Fred were pulling on coats, hats, boots, and gloves.

"Can I help?" I asked.

"No," they said together. "You're too young."

Mom stood in the kitchen, shouting into the phone, "The car is stuck! What do we do?"

"Can I help?" I asked her.

"No, honey," Mom said, "stay inside."

At the front door Dad and my oldest brother Sam took turns shoveling out a short path from our front door.

"Need any help?" I asked.

"No," my father said. "You're not big enough."

Snow fell and fell. That afternoon I pulled on snow boots, a heavy coat, and a hat and gloves. I was determined to help. So I climbed out of my bedroom window and stood on top of a mountain of snow almost as high as the second floor. The snow was so high I walked onto the roof of the garage!

"Be careful!" my father shouted from below.

I looked down. Dad and Sam shoveled. Meg and Fred shoveled. Mom stood in the doorway.

Seeing them, I knew it was up to me not to work but to think. How would I get down the hill and to the school play?

"Everybody!" I said loudly. "I have an idea!"

Meg and Fred stared up at me.

"I'll use the sled," I shouted.

Meg looked at Fred. Fred looked at Sam. Sam looked at Mom. Mom looked at Dad.

"You'll use the sled!" Dad repeated, shouting up to me. "I'll get Uncle Bill to meet you at the bottom of the hill and drive you to the school. Pack your things!"

"She'll use the sled!" everyone in the family said together.

Before I knew it, I was sledding down the hill. Beside me, my precious cargo was in a small basket strapped to the sled. In it was my costume for the school play. I was going to make it to opening night after all. Thanks to my family and, of course, my sled, I saved the day and the play.

Unit Theme: *Head, Hands, Heart*

Target Skill: *Recognizing the difference between major and minor characters*

Genre: *Fantasy Fiction*

Getting Started

Heatwave! is a humorous tale that has a creative blend of fantasy and reality. It invites the reader to go along with its ridiculous claims and laugh at the outlandish events. The freewheeling stream of consciousness coupled with the lightning fast dialogue and description create the fun. Like its cousin, the tall tale, the story works because the audience is in on the joke and is mentally "egging on" the storyteller to greater and greater feats of imagination.

Point out to your students that *they* often use exaggerated language. Children are in the habit of using superlatives such as "I'm starving!" "It's freezing in here!" or "I told you a million times!" Make a list on the board of examples of common exaggerations. As a challenge, ask your students to avoid using such phrases for a week.

Begin a simple, realistic narrative and then ask one student to add a sentence or two. Continue around the room allowing each student to add another few sentences. Remind them to keep it somewhat realistic but to have some fun adding some elements of the fantastical!

Into . . . Heatwave!

Ingenuity is the quality of being clever, inventive, and resourceful. It involves skill and imagination. We use ingenuity all the time. A simple example would be how we substitute one ingredient for another when cooking and baking, if we don't have the called for ingredient on hand.

Inventions are often the result of creative problem solving and ingenuity. The invention of the sandwich is a good example. Legend has it that the year 1762 was a busy one for the fourth Earl of Sandwich, John Montagu. To save time when eating, he asked his cook to place his meat in between two slices of bread. Voila! A sandwich! Today we call ingenuity "thinking outside the box." This means that, when confronted with a problem, we try to look at it from a new angle to find a way to solve it. We all use our ingenuity to a degree. Girls who get to school and find that the hem of their skirt has come out will use a staple, scotch tape, or even a paper clip to hold it up! A boy who finds himself stuck in the rain may grab a plastic bag or newspaper to keep his hat or clothing from getting soaked. Invite your students to share some ingenious solutions they have come up with for everyday problems.

One more thing to share with your class is the oft quoted adage, "Necessity is the mother of invention." Ask your students to think of a few illustrations of this saying.

Eyes On Major and Minor Characters

Choose any story with which your students are familiar to illustrate the terms *major* and *minor* characters. Have the students identify the major and minor characters of the story.

Use the students' own lives to further differentiate between major and minor characters. First, using yourself as an example, go to the board and write the names of some key individuals in your life. Then write the names of some people you frequently encounter but who do not make a significant difference in your daily life. Instruct your students to take out a piece of paper and divide it in half. Have them list their lives' "major characters" on one half, and their lives' "minor" ones on the other. For most of your students, the major characters will include family members, teachers, close friends, and neighbors. "Minor characters" will be people like the mailman, the grocer, or the neighbor that we wave to from time to time.

In a story, major characters are usually mentioned throughout. There may be multiple main characters. Generally, main characters develop and change over the course of the story.

Blueprint for Reading

INTO . . . *Heatwave!*

In 1904 a World's Fair was held in St. Louis. One of the most popular treats for sale was ice cream. Arnold Fornachou, an ice cream vendor, was selling bowl after bowl of it to eager customers when, suddenly, he noticed he was out of bowls! What could he do? If the ice cream melted it would be worthless. Another vendor, Ernst Hamwi, was selling *zalabia*, a crisp waffle. Seeing Arnold's panic, he grabbed a *zalabia*, rolled it into a cone shaped holder, and rushed over to the ice cream stand to show Arnold how the waffle could be used to hold ice cream. Americans have not stopped enjoying ice cream cones since that day!

When Ernst Hamwi grabbed the waffle, he was using his *ingenuity*. That means he was using his ability to think of new, creative solutions to a problem. When you use your ingenuity, you refuse to let a problem stop you; you explore every possible solution from every possible angle. As you read *Heatwave!*, notice how the main character uses ingenuity to help her family.

Major and Minor Characters

As we have seen, a story has both **main**, or **major**, characters and **minor** characters. Imagine telling the story of *Goldilocks and the Three Bears* to a group of young children. Would you need to give a lengthy description of Goldilocks' parents? No, and there is a good reason for that. Goldilocks' parents are only minor characters in the tale and do not help move the story along. The main, or most important, characters are Goldilocks and the three bears. Anyone they happened to meet on their walk in the woods would be minor.

In the following story, see if you can determine which characters play a key role and are **major characters**, and which play only a small part and are **minor characters**.

214 Unit 3

Minor characters play various roles. Some are small but useful parts of the background or plot. Others play a more significant role but contribute only to one section of the story or in one particular way. Minor characters often remain static as opposed to major characters who change throughout the narrative.

In *Heatwave!*, the author is a major character as is the heat wave itself, which takes on a persona of its own as the antagonist. Pa, Ma, and Hank play minor roles, and are not key to the main story line.

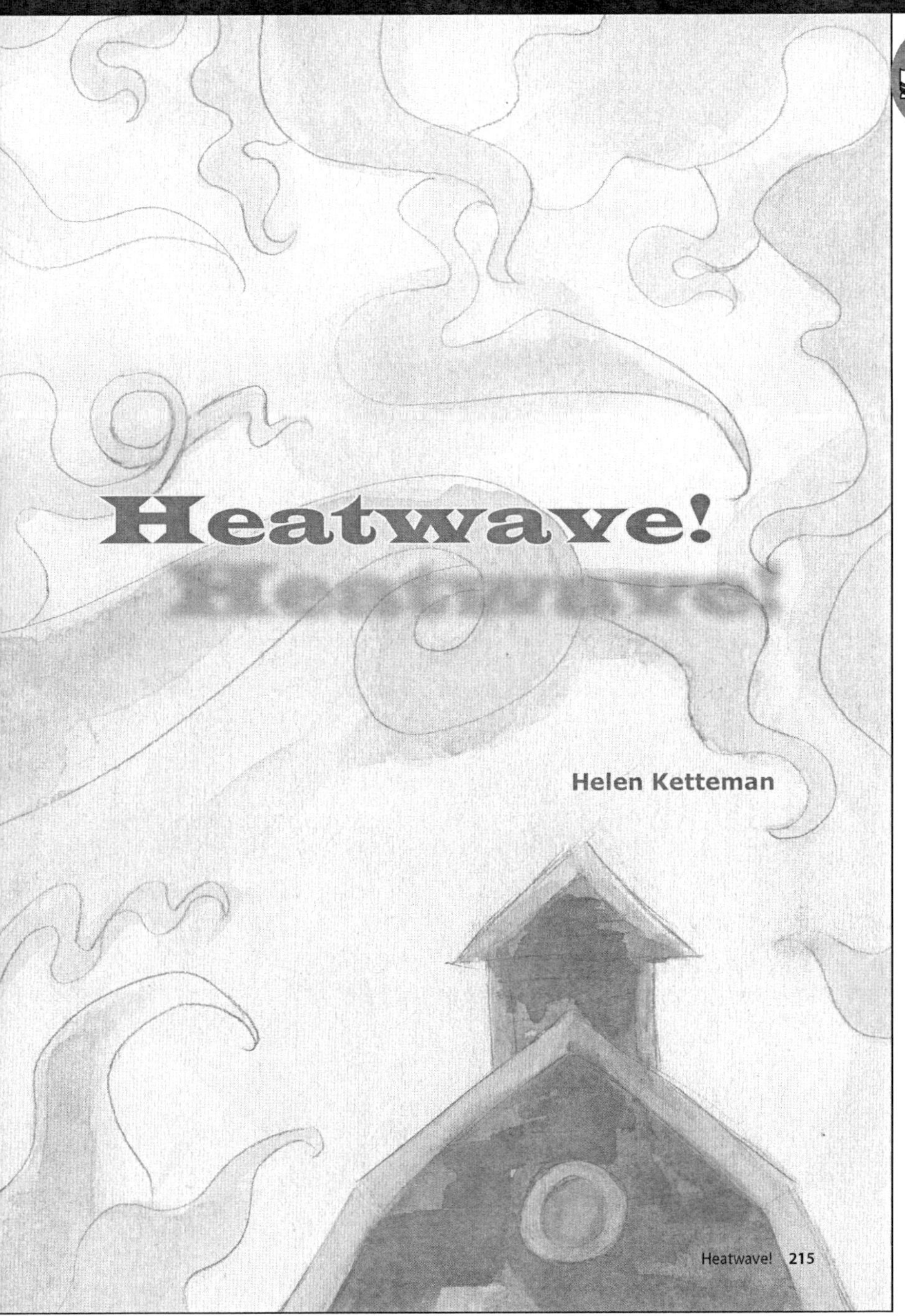

Selection Summary

No message. No moral. No history. No fatal flaw or wounded ego. Just fun! When a story opens by telling you of a flock of geese who fly into a clump of "crinkled, yellow air" and emerge "plucked, stuffed, and roasted," you know you can sit back and relax.

Heatwave! is very visual, very tangible. A lot of the humor comes from the manic pace, the stream of consciousness, the plays on words, the concretizing of the abstract. If you are the analytical type, you can take the funny images and analyze why they are funny, using some of the explanations above. Otherwise, you can just let your class enjoy this silly, funny piece.

My big brother, Hank, used to tease me that girls couldn't be farmers. But he sure changed his tune the day the Heat Wave hit.

I was feeding the chickens when I heard a loud roar. I looked out across the horizon and saw a big old clump of crinkled, yellow air rolling across the sky. A flock of geese flew in one side and came out the other side plucked, stuffed, and roasted.

I hollered for Ma and Pa and Hank, but before they got outside, the Heat Wave hit. The mercury blasted out of the porch thermometer like a rocket. Ma's flowers pulled themselves up by their roots and crawled under the porch looking for shade.

WORD BANK

horizon (huh RY zun) *n.*: the place in the distance where the earth and sky seem to meet
plucked (PLUKD) *v.*: pulled out, like feathers from a bird

Guiding the Reading

Literal

Q: What did Hank always tease about?
A: He said that girls could not be farmers.

Q: What changed Hank's opinion?
A: The Heat Wave changed the way he thought about girls.

Q: What was the author doing when she heard a loud roar?
A: She was feeding the chickens.

Q: How did she describe what she saw on the horizon?
A: She saw a "big old clump of crinkled, yellow air rolling across the sky."

Q: What happened before Ma, Pa, and Hank came outside?
A: The Heat Wave hit.

Q: What did Ma's flowers do?
A: They pulled themselves up by their roots and crawled under the porch looking for shade.

Analytical

Q: What did she mean when she said, "A flock of geese flew in one side and came out the other side plucked, stuffed and roasted"?
A: Answers will vary. The heat was so great that it prepared and cooked the geese. As with many lines in this story, it is hyperbole.

Q: Do you think the mercury really shot out like a rocket?
A: Answers will vary. Again, this is comic hyperbole. (Hyperbole differs from exaggeration. Exaggeration is a stretch of the truth; hyperbole doesn't even pose as truth, it is unabashedly unbelievable.)

Heatwave! 217

218 Unit 3

By the time everybody ran outside, the Heat Wave had gotten snagged on the barn's weather vane. It was near harvest time, so we raced to the cornfield to save what we could. But by the time we got there, it was already too late. The corn had started popping. It looked like a blizzard had hit. One of our old hound dogs turned blue and froze when he saw it. I wrapped him in a blanket, and he thawed out okay.

Guiding the Reading

Literal

Q: It was near what time of year for farmers?

A: It was near harvest time.

Q: Where did the family race to first?

A: They went to the cornfield to save what they could.

Q: What did they see when they arrived?

A: The corn had started to pop.

Q: What did it look like from all of the popping corn?

A: It looked like a blizzard had hit.

Analytical

Q: Why did the hound dog turn blue and freeze when he saw the popcorn?

A: He reacted that way because he thought the popcorn was really snow.

Then we heard a commotion in the pasture. We raced over. The cows were hopping around like rabbits. The ground had gotten too hot, so we herded them inside the barn. They still looked miserable, though. Pa figured their milk had gotten too hot, so we set to milking. As it turned out, the cows had jumped so much, they'd churned their milk to butter. It came out melted. We'd milked the last of the butter when I had an idea.

We scrubbed a couple of shovels and the beds of the pickup trucks, then I sent Pa and Hank to the field to fill the pickups with popcorn.

When they were done, they brought the trucks around, and we all pitched in and poured the butter over the popcorn. Then Hank and Ma drove the truck to the drive-in down the road. In no time at all, they sold every last bit of that popcorn, then hurried home.

We still had plenty of worries. We hurried to the field where we had oats planted. Sure enough, they had dried out. I tried wetting them down, but that didn't turn out to be such a good idea.

Soon I felt something slimy and thick rising up around my ankles. In another minute, it was waist high, and I could barely move. Turned out I'd created a whole field of oatmeal. It was lumpy, just like Ma's, and I about drowned in the stuff.

WORD BANK

commotion (kuh MO shun) *n.*: noise and disturbance
herded (HURD id) *v.*: drove or led (cows)
churned *v.*: shook and beat milk to turn it into butter

Guiding the Reading

Literal

Q: Why did everyone race to the pasture?
A: They ran to find out what the commotion was all about.

Q: What were the cows doing when they got to the pasture?
A: They were hopping around like rabbits.

Q: Why were they hopping around?
A: They were hopping because the ground had gotten too hot.

Q: Where did they put the cows?
A: The cows were put in the barn.

Q: Why did they start milking the cows?
A: Pa figured their milk had gotten too hot.

Q: What came out instead of milk?
A: Melted butter came out.

Q: Why did melted butter come out?
A: The cows' jumping churned the milk into butter.

Q: What was the author's idea when she saw all that butter?
A: She thought it would be a good idea to pour it over all of the popcorn in the field.

Q: What did Hank and Mom do with all that delicious popcorn?
A: They sold it at the drive-in theater down the road.

Q: Where did the family go next?
A: They went to the field where the oats were planted.

Q: Why did the author decide to water the oats?
A: They had dried out from the Heat Wave.

Q: Why wasn't it a good idea?
A: It turned into lumpy oatmeal.

Q: How much oatmeal was there?
A: There was enough to go up to the author's waist.

Heatwave! 221

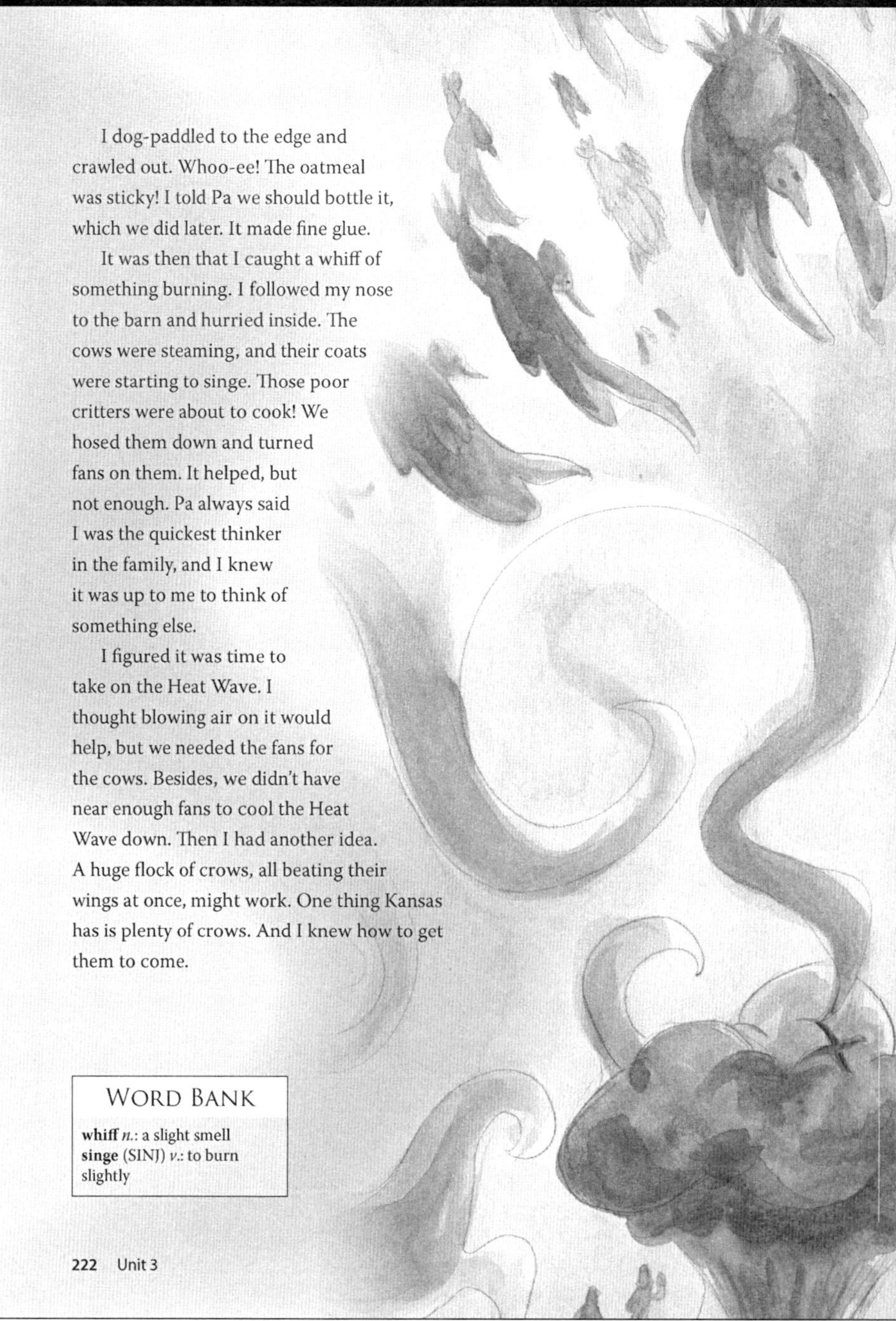

Guiding the Reading

Literal

Q: What did they do with all that oatmeal?
A: It was bottled to use as glue.

Q: What did she smell burning?
A: The cows were so hot that their coats were starting to burn.

Q: What did they do to cool them down?
A: They hosed them down and turned on fans.

Q: How did the author know it was up to her to come up with another good cooling idea?
A: Pa always said that she was the quickest thinker in the family.

Q: What was her first idea to cool the air?
A: She was going to blow air from fans.

Q: Why wouldn't it work?
A: They needed the fans for the cows and there were not enough.

Q: What was the second idea?
A: The idea was to get a huge flock of crows to beat their wings at once.

Q: Where does the story take place?
A: It takes place in Kansas.

Q: What did they have plenty of in Kansas?
A: They had many crows.

Analytical

Q: Do you think fans would have been enough to fight the Heat Wave even if they had not been needed for the cows?
A: Answers will vary. They would not do the job in reality, but in a story like this, who knows?

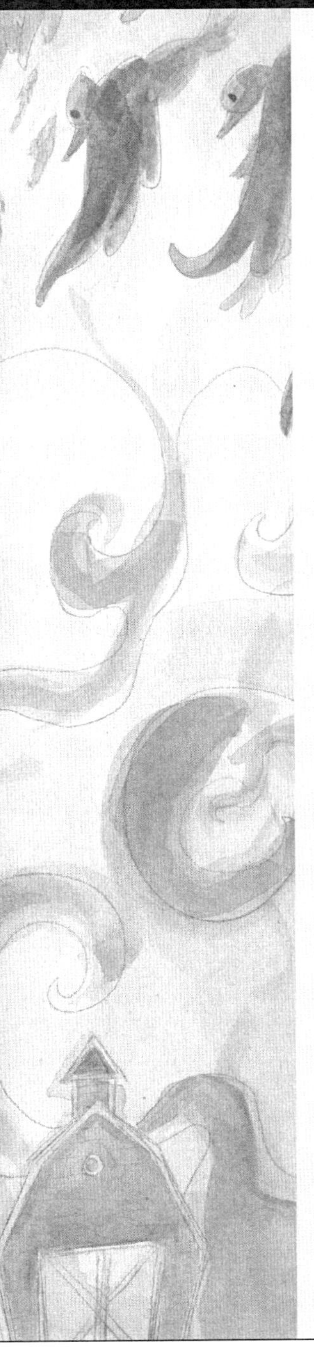

We dumped several fifty-pound bags of flour and a bunch of yeast in the trough by the barn, then stirred in water with shovels. That dough rose so fast we had to run for our lives. It rolled over several chickens, then picked up the tractor and Sally the mule. Ended up big as the barn.

A few minutes later, the dough started baking in the heat. Smelled awful good, and that's what I was counting on. Crows can't resist the smell of baking bread, and soon every crow in Kansas came flocking to the farm. Their wings made so much wind, we had to tie ourselves around a giant tree trunk to keep from being blown away. It felt cooler already.

The trouble was, those crows didn't keep flying. They lit on the bread and started eating. The temperature shot right back up, and I figured we might be licked.

The crows pecked at the bread until they freed Sally and the chickens. None of them were a bit worse for wear. In fact, they were right frisky. I figured all that yeast had caused their spirits to rise.

WORD BANK

trough (TROFF) *n.*: a long, boxlike container used to hold food or water for animals

Guiding the Reading

Literal

Q: How did the author attract many crows to come?
A: She made dough by dumping the ingredients in the barn.

Q: Why did they have to "run for their lives"?
A: The dough rose so fast, it was filling up the barn and pushing its way out.

Q: What did the dough do as it grew?
A: It rolled over several chickens, and then picked up the tractor and Sally the mule.

Q: What helped the dough to rise and bake so fast?
A: The extreme heat helped it rise quickly.

Q: What was it that attracted the crows?
A: The delicious aroma of baking bread.

Q: How many crows came to the farm?
A: Every crow in Kansas came.

Q: Did it work? Did the crows cool things off?
A: Yes, they made a lot of wind and cooled things off.

Q: What did the author and her family do when the crows came?
A: They tied themselves to a tree trunk to keep from blowing away.

Q: What happened when the crows started to eat the bread?
A: The temperature went up again and it was very hot.

Q: What happened to the chickens and the mule?
A: As the crows ate, the animals were freed.

Q: Did the dough seem to bother them?
A: No, the author thought it did not affect them—if anything, it made them friskier.

Analytical

Q: How do you think they knew they had to attach themselves to the tree?
A: Answers will vary. Either they anticipated the strength of the birds, or they realized what was about to happen as the wind began to get stronger. Students may suggest that stories like this need no commentary!

Q: What did she mean when she said, "all that yeast had caused their spirits to rise"?
A: She was trying to be funny. Figuratively, this means that its spirits, its mood, will get better. Literally, it means that the dough grew.

224 Unit 3

Seeing Sally gave me one more idea. I told Pa to hitch her to the plow, and she plowed up a section of land in record time. While Pa was plowing, I found what I needed. I gave everyone lettuce seeds, and we started planting. Those seeds sprouted as soon as they hit the dirt.

The bigger the lettuce grew, the cooler the air got. That Heat Wave put up a fight, all right. It rippled and twisted and squirmed like a bucking bronco. But as the lettuce cooled the air more, the Heat Wave started shrinking, until it finally disappeared altogether.

The weather vane and the barn cooled down, and the cows stopped steaming, too. They didn't seem much affected, except the fuzz on their hides never grew back. Ma had to knit them all sweaters for the winter.

WORD BANK

affected (uh FEK tid) *v.*: influenced

Guiding the Reading

Literal

Q: What gave the author the next idea?

A: Seeing Sally gave her the next idea.

Q: What did Pa do?

A: He hitched Sally to the plow and plowed up a section of land.

Q: What did the author do?

A: She found lettuce seeds, distributed them to Ma, Pa, and Hank and they all planted them.

Q: How long did it take for the seeds to sprout?

A: They sprouted immediately, as soon as they hit the dirt.

Q: Did planting the lettuce help?

A: Yes, it gradually cooled the air and made the Heat Wave disappear.

Q: What changes were there after the Heat Wave left?

A: Everything cooled down and went pretty much back to normal except for the fuzz on the animals' hides that never grew back.

Analytical

Q: How do you think that lettuce can cool the air?

A: Answers will vary. Students will suggest various ideas, such as: the leaves will grow fast and their flapping will cause cool winds.

Q: Why do you think that "Heat Wave" is capitalized?

A: Answers will vary. One possibility is that it was so big that she felt it deserved extra emphasis. Another is that it changed her life.

So that's how I saved the farm, by planting lettuce. In case you're wondering how lettuce could cool the air, it wasn't just any kind of lettuce, you see. It was iceberg lettuce. I did make one mistake, though. I miscalculated the amount of lettuce I needed and planted too much.

Kansas had an awful early snowfall that year, but none of us ever let on why.

WORD BANK

miscalculated (mis KAL kyuh LAY tid) *v.*: judged incorrectly

About the Author

About the Author

Helen Ketteman grew up in a quiet town in Georgia, turning to books for the excitement and adventure she craved. When she married, she and her husband moved to Chicago, where their two sons were born. The family then moved to Seattle, Washington, and Helen started to write picture books for children ranging in age from preschool to fifth graders. Mrs. Ketteman has published sixteen picture books so far. She travels all over the country speaking and meeting with teachers and librarians. Who knows? She may come to *your* city one day!

Guiding the Reading

Literal

Q: What explanation does the author give for her lettuce idea working?

A: It was called *iceberg* lettuce.

Q: What was one mistake that she made?

A: She miscalculated and planted too much lettuce.

Q: What was the result of the excess lettuce?

A: There was an early snow.

Q: What secret did the author and her family have?

A: They knew why Kansas had an early snowfall that year.

Analytical

Q: What difference does it make whether it was iceberg lettuce or another kind of lettuce?

A: The "ice" in iceberg is used figuratively. "Ice" is a word that brings to mind a cooling image.

Heatwave! 227

About Be Glad Your Nose Is on Your Face

Poetry Is Silly

How far is silly from creative? Not far. First of all, you have to be creative to juxtapose all sorts of odd things. It is the juxtaposition of odd things that makes silliness funny. When children think of putting a nose between their toes or on top of their heads, they laugh. Then, you have to creatively link these two odd things in a humorous way,

> "For you'd be forced to smell your feet."
>
> "Your brain would rattle from the breeze."

So, not that we want to detract from the pure enjoyment of silliness for its own sake, we want to point out to the educator that silliness is not at all a waste of time. It trains the mind to look at things from a new angle and to make connections and associations between two things or ideas that one would not normally make. This is the stuff of which inventions are thought of and discoveries are made.

Be Glad Your Nose Is On Your Face

Be glad your nose is on your face,
not pasted on some other place,
for if it were where it is not,
you might dislike your nose a lot.

Imagine if your precious nose
were sandwiched in between your toes,
that clearly would not be a treat,
for you'd be forced to smell your feet.

Your nose would be a source of dread
were it attached atop your head,
it soon would drive you to despair,
forever tickled by your hair.

Within your ear, your nose would be
an absolute catastrophe,
for when you were obliged to sneeze,
your brain would rattle from the breeze.

Your nose, instead, through thick and thin,
remains between your eyes and chin,
not pasted on some other place—
be glad your nose is on your face!

Jack Prelutsky

Studying the Selection

FIRST IMPRESSIONS

At what point in the story did you realize that the author's ingenious tale was not realistic?

QUICK REVIEW

1. In what way did Hank tease his sister?
2. What happened to the cornfield when the Heat Wave hit?
3. Was watering the oats a good idea? Why or why not?
4. What did the author use to attract the crows?

FOCUS

5. Which silly parts of the story made you laugh the most? Why is it good to read some stories that are not realistic and serious?
6. What important role did Pa and Hank play even though they were minor characters?

CREATING AND WRITING

7. The story does not mention how the family protected themselves from the heat throughout the Heat Wave. Write a paragraph about how the family protected themselves. Your ideas should be creative and funny.
8. Write a short and original fantasy involving the weather.
9. Choose three items from home or school and think of a new and unusual use for each. For example, a bottle cap could be used as a cookie cutter and an iron could be used to warm up food. Then, share your ideas with the class.

First Impressions

Answers will vary.

Quick Review

1. He said that girls could not be farmers.
2. The heat turned it into popcorn.
3. Watering the oats was not a good idea, because it turned them into lots of lumpy oatmeal.
4. She made dough and knew the smell of baking bread would attract them.

Focus

5. Answers will vary. It is enjoyable and healthy to laugh. Exercising our imagination and creative side are important not only in writing, but for sharpening our problem solving skills.
6. Aside from their general help, they made some important comments. Pa's confidence in the author's quick thinking encouraged her to think up a solution. Hank's comments also pushed her to prove herself and her abilities.

Creating and Writing

7. Answers will vary.
8. Answers will vary.
9. Answers will vary. Provide time for the students to present their ideas to the class.

What Is Dialogue?

How Can a Horse Run so Fast?

1. Horses.
2. Julie learns that her mother knows a lot about horses.
3. Answers will vary. Some examples follow. From the narrative: Julie knew that as a girl her mother loved horses; Julie didn't realize her mother still loved horses; the setting is a grassy hill. From the dialogue: Horses can run at forty miles an hour; horses' legs are different than ours; Eileen was afraid of horses at first.

Lesson in Literature . . .

WHAT IS DIALOGUE?

- **Dialogue** is the conversation that takes place between the characters in a story or play.
- Quotation marks are placed around lines of dialogue.
- Dialogue tells us what the characters are thinking and doing. It may also *foreshadow* future events.
- Sometimes the conversation between two characters tells the story for the author.

THINK ABOUT IT!

1. In one word, what is the subject of the dialogue between Julie and her mother?
2. What does Julie learn about her mother as the dialogue continues?
3. What is one thing you learned about Julie from the dialogue?

How Can a Horse Run so Fast?

"How can a horse run so fast?" Julie asked her mother. Julie Walker and her mother Eileen sat together on a grassy hill overlooking a pasture. Below them two foals (young horses) galloped awkwardly around in circles.

"They're amazing, aren't they?" Eileen said to Julie with a hint of awe in her voice.

Julie looked at her mother. "They look clumsy to me," she said.

"They're clumsy now," Eileen said, smiling, "but I guess you can say that horses are built for speed. Thoroughbreds, the racing horses, have been clocked at over forty miles per hour. That's with a saddle and a rider!"

While mother and daughter had eaten a picnic lunch, they had enjoyed watching the two foals run around. Julie had named them Midnight and Sparky.

"They have funny-looking legs," Julie said.

"Their legs are just different than ours," Eileen replied. "Their legs don't have knees and ankles or muscles like ours, Julie. Their legs are only skin and hair, bone, tendons, ligaments, cartilage, and hooves."

Julie's eyes widened as she listened to her mother talk about horses. "How do you know so much about horses?"

Eileen smiled, remembering her love of horses from her childhood. "When I was your age, I loved horses. I loved to watch them run in races and jump in competitions. All I wanted to do was to learn to ride."

"Weren't you afraid?" Julie asked.

"At first I was afraid," Eileen said.

"Isn't it dangerous to ride?"

"No," Eileen said cautiously. "Horses are strong animals, Julie, but with proper riding lessons anyone can enjoy riding a horse." Eileen paused briefly to look closely at her daughter. "I know I enjoyed riding," she said.

Julie knew that as a girl her mother loved horses, but she didn't realize until just then that her mother still loved everything about horses. "Did you ever ride in competitions?" she asked her mother.

"Yes, I was an equestrian," Eileen said with a laugh. "I rode in a few show jumping competitions, but I liked all kinds of riding, because some horses walk, others trot, some lope, some jump, and others gallop. It all depends on the horse and the rider." Eileen felt like a teacher giving a lesson.

"I think I'd like to learn to ride," Julie said softly. "But not one of these foals. They're too clumsy for me."

Mother and daughter laughed together. "Of course not, Julie. Not yet. These foals are too young for riding, but just wait. In a couple of years you may be taking a riding lesson and the horse you're on will be Midnight or Sparky."

"I think I'll recognize them," Julie said.

"I bet you will," Eileen said. "I know I remember every horse I ever rode."

Julie looked at her mother's face. Now she knew why her mother loved everything about horses.

The Wright Brothers 231

Getting Started

Read aloud through page 235 until the paragraph that ends with the words, "the wind didn't seem nearly as strong."

1. What were the The Wright Brothers' names?
   a. Wilbur and Oliver
   b. William and Otis
   c. Wilbur and Orville
   d. Willis and Orville
2. What did people say about Mrs. Wright?
   a. She spent too much time with birds and fish.
   b. She spoiled her children.
   c. She was too old to be going on picnics.
   d. Her apple pies were the best in town.
3. Where did the Wright family live?
   a. Detroit
   b. Howell
   c. Buffalo Grove
   d. Dayton

Unit Theme: *Head, Hands, Heart*

Target Skill: *Learning about a character's attributes through what they say*

Genre: *Fictionalized Biography*

4. What did Mrs. Wright tell her children about birds?
   a. the name and song of each bird
   b. where each type of bird went during winter
   c. which bird was their state bird
   d. what kinds of worms and other food they ate
5. What did Mrs. Wright tell Wilbur about the flight of birds?
   a. Their lightweight bones make it easier to fly.
   b. Flapping their wings makes them go faster.
   c. Their beaks help them to change direction.
   d. When the feathers ruffle it helps their flight.
6. After Will's question, what did Mrs. Wright tell him about the wind?
   a. The wind blows up and down and helps birds go up.
   b. Birds can sense which direction the currents are blowing.
   c. Birds don't fly as much in windy conditions.
   d. Wind blows only towards or away from you.
7. What was Mrs. Wright's reaction when her boys said they could make wings for people?
   a. She laughed and thought it was a silly idea.
   b. She suggested they go to work on the project when they get home.
   c. She told them that people had tried it before unsuccessfully, so they should forget about it.
   d. She advised them to try when they got older.
8. According to the story, why did Wilbur and Orville keep asking their mother questions?
   a. They liked to pester her.
   b. Their father was not home very often so they asked their mother instead.
   c. She listened and gave them sensible answers.
   d. They had a report to do for school.
9. What problem did Wilbur have during the snowstorm?
   a. He had a hard time walking to the barn.
   b. As he shoveled, more snow continued to fall.
   c. He was very bored staying in the house all day.
   d. He felt cold even with two sweaters.
10. How did Wilbur solve his snowstorm problem?
   a. He found a good idea in a book at home.
   b. His mother gave him a good idea.
   c. He remembered what a teacher had taught him.
   d. As he was falling asleep, he thought of a solution.

Into . . . The Wright Brothers

Children often confuse confidence with arrogance. Explain to them that the two are very different. Arrogance is the feeling that one is better than others. Confidence really is not focused on other people at all. It is a sense that one can do what needs to be done, a feeling that one is competent to cope with whatever comes his way, and a feeling that one's own opinion and performance is satisfactory and worthwhile. Confident people are willing to take risks and are not haunted by fear of failure. They are willing to offer friendship and approval and are not hampered by fear of rejection. Self-confidence is a crucial building block for a child's future. Confident people have lots of room in their world for other people; they are not threatened by another's success or good fortune, because they are happy with their own abilities and accomplishments. Self-confident people believe that they have to move forward and see what new goal they can set, what new contribution they can make. Any adult who has contact with children should make a conscious effort to instill confidence in them. It is what makes them healthy and successful adults.

In *The Wright Brothers*, Mrs. Wright made her children feel that their ideas and aspirations were of value. She did not mock them in any way, but encouraged them to be creative and gave them the confidence to believe in themselves.

Eyes On Dialogue

Students tend to overuse dialogue in their own writing. They like to write pages of dialogue that are often simple conversations that include: hi, how are you, okay, so what's new, etc. It is important for students to recognize that dialogue should serve a purpose. It should provide us with a better understanding of a character.

The following are a few examples.

- *"Well, when you're a little older maybe you can try," their mother said.*
  This is typical of Mrs. Wright, who balances a sense of realism with a desire to encourage creativity in her children.
- *"It looks like it would fall apart if you sat on it," Al Johnston said, and he laughed too.*
  This gives us a good indication of how the boys mocked Will and Orv.
- *"We'll draw one, you and I," Wilbur said. "We can't run to Mother every time we want to make something."*
  This illustrates another lesson learned by Wilbur and Orville: self-reliance.

Blueprint for Reading

INTO . . . from *The Wright Brothers: Pioneers of American Aviation*

Do you remember learning to ride a bike? When you first started, you probably didn't think you could do it and you wobbled back and forth. Then came that wonderful moment when you just *knew* you could! That *knowing*, that confidence, kept the bike straight as you pedaled. A big step toward succeeding at something is having the confidence that you can succeed. Do you think you can get a part in the school play? Do you believe that you can get a better grade next time? Would you be willing to approach an older, popular student? Do you think that you can make a difference?

As you will see, the Wright brothers could not have accomplished what they did without self-confidence. *Self-confidence* means being positive and believing in yourself and your abilities. As you read the story, think about what contributed to the boys' self-confidence.

Dialogue

Dialogue helps us understand characters and makes them more believable. Read the following dialogue.

"I am going to organize the lists and call Mrs. Tanner. Tammy, you get some extra drinks and napkins. Ben, you can get some extra paper. In order for this project to work, be prepared to follow my instructions very carefully."

What do you know about the person speaking? Even though you don't know the person's name or too many details about the speaker, you have learned something about the speaker's personality. The speaker is an organized, take-charge person. As you read the following story, notice how much the dialogue reveals about the characters.

232 Unit 3

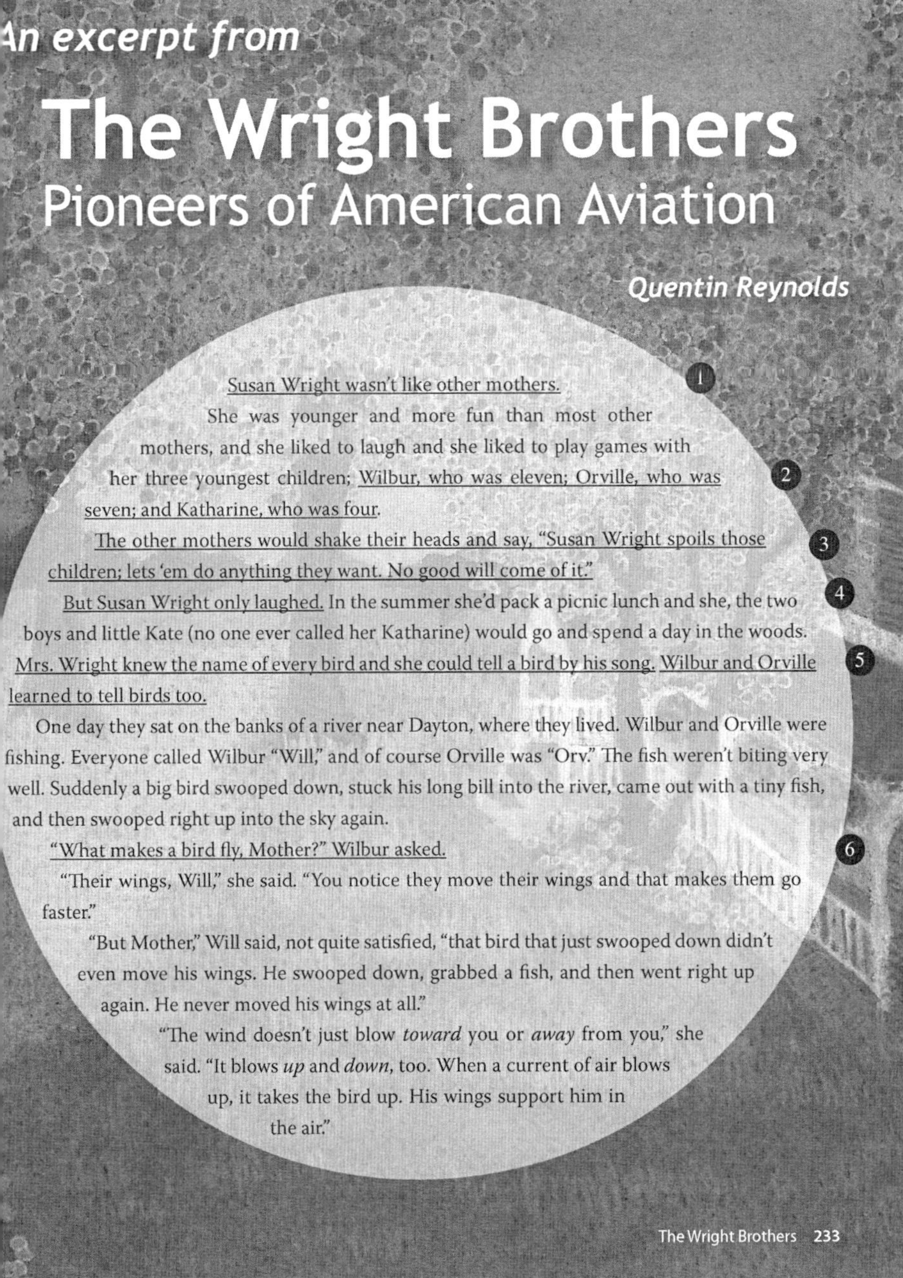

An excerpt from

The Wright Brothers
Pioneers of American Aviation

Quentin Reynolds

Susan Wright wasn't like other mothers. ❶ She was younger and more fun than most other mothers, and she liked to laugh and she liked to play games with her three youngest children; Wilbur, who was eleven; Orville, who was seven; and Katharine, who was four. ❷

The other mothers would shake their heads and say, "Susan Wright spoils those children; lets 'em do anything they want. No good will come of it." ❸

But Susan Wright only laughed. ❹ In the summer she'd pack a picnic lunch and she, the two boys and little Kate (no one ever called her Katharine) would go and spend a day in the woods. Mrs. Wright knew the name of every bird and she could tell a bird by his song. ❺ Wilbur and Orville learned to tell birds too.

One day they sat on the banks of a river near Dayton, where they lived. Wilbur and Orville were fishing. Everyone called Wilbur "Will," and of course Orville was "Orv." The fish weren't biting very well. Suddenly a big bird swooped down, stuck his long bill into the river, came out with a tiny fish, and then swooped right up into the sky again.

"What makes a bird fly, Mother?" Wilbur asked. ❻

"Their wings, Will," she said. "You notice they move their wings and that makes them go faster."

"But Mother," Will said, not quite satisfied, "that bird that just swooped down didn't even move his wings. He swooped down, grabbed a fish, and then went right up again. He never moved his wings at all."

"The wind doesn't just blow *toward* you or *away* from you," she said. "It blows *up* and *down*, too. When a current of air blows up, it takes the bird up. His wings support him in the air."

The Wright Brothers 233

Selection Summary

Young Wilbur and Orville Wright are lucky. Their mother, Susan, has a curiosity about the world that she imparts to her sons. She has a scientific bent of mind and easily applies scientific principles to daily living. When, during a fierce storm, Wilbur tells his mother how hard it was to walk from the barn to the house, she teaches him about wind resistance. "The thing to do is to lean forward into the wind," she says, planting the seed of an idea in his mind.

It is not long before Wilbur finds a good way to use this new information. With Susan's help, the boys design a sled unlike any that their friends have. This sled is longer and lower than any other one in town. It is built on the principle that the less wind resistance, the faster the sled will move. Susan teaches the boys another important lesson: the finished product will be only as good as the design and pattern drawn before it is built. Susan teaches the boys to be perfectionists about their measurements for both the pattern and the actual sled. Susan's knowledge of mathematics is a great asset to the boys' efforts.

The great day comes and the boys line up their sled at the top of the hill next to the other boys' sleds. The other boys tease them about their odd-looking sled and the fact that their mother helped design it. But the teasing stops as Orville and Wilbur, lying on the sled—to reduce wind resistance, of course—fly down the slope. And when they reach the bottom, the sled continues to fly… until it comes to a slow, smooth landing.

Guiding the Reading

Literal

Q: In what ways was Susan Wright unlike other mothers?
A: She was younger, more fun, and played with her children. People said she let her children do whatever they wanted.

Q: Did it bother Susan Wright when people said that she spoiled her children?
A: No, she laughed.

Q: What was Katharine's nickname?
A: Her nickname was Kate.

Q: What did Mrs. Wright teach her kids about birds?
A: She told them the name of every type of bird and its song.

Q: Where did the Wrights live?
A: They lived in Dayton (Ohio).

Q: What were the boys' nicknames?
A: They were Will and Orv.

Q: What did Will ask his mother about birds?
A: "What makes a bird fly, Mother?"

Q: What was his mother's answer?
A: The faster they flap their wings, the faster they go.

Q: What problem did Wilbur have with his mother's answer?
A: The bird he saw swoop down for fish didn't seem to be flapping its wings at all—so how could his mother be right?

Q: What did Will learn about the way the wind blows?
A: The wind currents do not just blow towards you or away from you, but up and down too. When air blows up, it takes the bird up and supports him.

Literary Components

❶ **Characterization; Exposition:** The reader is immediately drawn into the story. We learn something of one of the main characters: that she is not like other mothers, and we want to know how she is different.

❷ **Characterization:** We are introduced to the other main characters.

❸ **Voice:** A good device used here is having the neighbors describe Susan, rather than the narrator do so.

❹ **Characterization:** Susan is independent, undeterred by what anyone thinks. We will find this quality central to the plot.

❺ **Characterization; Foreshadowing:** Mrs. Wright knows lots of things about the natural world. An interest in birds foreshadows what comes next.

❻ **Thematic Thread:** A fascination with swift movement and, of course, flight, starts to reveal itself here.

"If we had wings, then we could fly too, couldn't we, Mother?" Wilbur asked.

"But G-d didn't give us wings." She laughed.

"Maybe we could make wings," Wilbur insisted. 7

"Maybe," his mother said thoughtfully. "But I don't know. No one ever did make wings that would allow a boy to fly."

"I will some day," Wilbur said, and Orville nodded and said, "I will, too." 8

"Well, when you're a little older maybe you can try," their mother said.

That was another thing about Susan Wright. Most other mothers would have said, "Oh, don't be silly, who ever heard of such nonsense!" But not Susan Wright. She knew that even an eleven-year-old boy can have ideas of his own, and just because they happened to come from an eleven-year-old head—well, that didn't make them foolish. She never treated her children as if they were babies, and perhaps that's why they liked to go fishing with her or on picnics with her. And that's why they kept asking her 9
questions. She always gave them sensible answers.

They asked their father questions too, but he traveled for his work and was away a lot.

"It's getting chilly," Mrs. Wright said suddenly. "Look at those gray clouds, Will."

Wilbur looked up. "It's going to snow, I bet," he said happily. 10

"No more picnics until next Spring," his mother said. "Yes, it looks like snow. We'd better be getting home."

As they reached home, the first big white snowflakes started to fall. They kept falling all that night and all the next day. It was the first real snowstorm of the year.

In the morning the wind was blowing so fiercely that Wilbur found it hard to walk to the barn where the wood was stored. The wind was so strong it almost knocked him down. He burst through the kitchen door with an armful of wood for the stove, and he told his mother about the wind.

"The thing to do is to lean forward into the wind," she said. "Bend over, and that way 11
you get closer to the ground and you get under the wind."

That night, when Wilbur had to make the trip for more wood, he tried his mother's idea. To his surprise it worked! When he was bent over, the wind didn't seem nearly so strong.

After a few days the wind stopped, and now the whole countryside was covered with snow. Wilbur and Orville, with little Kate trailing behind, hurried to the Big Hill not far from the house.

Orville's schoolmates were all there with their sleds. It was a good hill to coast down because no roads came anywhere near it, and even if they had, it wouldn't have

Literary Components

7 Characterization; Theme: Wilbur, like his mother and brother, think in terms of the possible. The theme of flight continues.

8 Foreshadowing: Some very obvious foreshadowing is present here, as anyone familiar with the story of the Wright brothers knows. The invention of the airplane, which this line foreshadows, is not described in this story. It appears later on in the book from which this story is excerpted.

9 Characterization; Theme: The boys are characterized as having much curiosity about the world around them. The theme of learning by asking questions, and the point that no question is a silly one, is advanced here.

10 Transition: The author here uses the snow to move smoothly into the next topic, which is how the Wright brothers learn about wind resistance.

11 Theme: This lesson will be a very strong theme not only in this story but, one can guess, throughout the book, as the Wright brothers apply this knowledge to their airplane.

Guiding the Reading

Literal

Q: After he heard how wind blows, what did Will wonder about?
A: He wondered whether people would be able to fly if they had wings.

Q: What was his mother's response?
A: G-d did not make us that way and no one ever made wings for people.

Q: Will sounded determined to do what about wings?
A: One day he would make wings that would allow humans to fly.

Q: Who agreed with him?
A: Orville agreed that he would make wings with Will.

Q: Did his mother laugh at Will and his ideas?
A: No, she understood that eleven-year-olds can have good ideas too. She never treated the boys like babies or made them feel silly.

Q: Why did the boys always ask their mother questions?
A: She took an interest in them and gave sensible answers.

Q: What prediction did Will have about the weather?
A: He looked at the gray clouds and predicted snow.

Q: Was Will's weather report accurate?
A: Yes, the first real snowstorm of the year started that day.

Q: Why did Wilbur have such a hard time getting wood from the barn?
A: The wind was so fierce that it almost knocked him down.

Q: What did Mrs. Wright suggest to Wilbur regarding the wind?
A: She told him to lean forward toward the ground in order to get under the wind.

Q: What happened when Will tried his mother's idea?
A: It actually worked!

Q: Where did the Wright children go after the snow stopped?
A: They went to the Big Hill.

Q: Who else was at the Big Hill aside from the Wright children?
A: Orville's schoolmates were there.

Analytical

Q: How did Mrs. Wright's behavior help develop her sons' potential?
A: Her interest in and respect for the boys' thoughts and ideas encouraged them to probe and learn and never to be afraid to ask questions.

Literary Components

12 Setting: The author gracefully slips the year into the narration.

13 Rising Action: Now that we know the characters fairly well, and have been introduced to the theme, the core plot of the story begins.

12 mattered. This was 1878 and there were no automobiles. Horse-drawn sleighs traveled the roads in winter. The horses had bells fastened to their collars, and as they jogged along the bells rang and you could hear them a mile away.

Most of the boys had their own sleds; not the flexible fliers boys have now, but old-fashioned sleds with two wooden runners. No one ever thought of owning a "bought" sled. In those days a boy's father made a sled for him.

The boys who had sleds of their own let Wilbur and Orville ride down the hill with them. Ed Sines and Chauncey Smith and Johnny Morrow and Al Johnston all owned sleds, but they liked to race one another down the long hill. When this happened Wilbur and Orville just had to stand there and watch. Late that afternoon the boys came home, with little Kate trailing behind, and their mother noticed that they were very quiet. She was wise as well as fun, and she soon found out why they were unhappy.

"Why doesn't Father build us a sled?" Wilbur blurted out.

"But Father is away, Will," his mother said gently. "And you know how busy he is when he is at home. He has to write stories for the paper and he has to write speeches.
13 Now suppose we build a sled together."

Wilbur laughed. "Whoever heard of anyone's mother building a sled?"

"You just wait," his mother said. "We'll build a better sled than Ed Sines has. Now get me a pencil and a piece of paper."

"You goin' to build a sled out of paper?" Orville asked in amazement.

"Just wait," she repeated.

Will and Orv brought their mother a pencil and paper, and she went to her husband's desk and found a ruler. Then she sat down at the kitchen table. "First we'll draw a picture of the sled," she said.

"What good is a picture of a sled?" Orville asked.

"Now Orville, watch Mother." She picked up the ruler in one hand and the pencil in the other.

"We want one like Ed Sines has," Orville said.

"When you go coasting, how many boys will Ed Sines's sled hold?" she asked.

"Two," Wilbur said.

"We'll make this one big enough to hold three," she said. "Maybe you can take Kate along sometimes." The outline of a sled began to appear on the paper. As she drew it she talked. "You see, Ed's sled is about four feet long. I've seen it often enough. We'll make this one five feet long. Now, Ed's sled is about a foot off the ground, isn't it?"

Orville nodded, his eyes never leaving the drawing that was taking shape. It was beginning to look like a sled now, but not like the sleds the other boys had.

"You've made it too low," Will said.

Guiding the Reading

Literal

Q: Why was the Big Hill a good place to sled?
A: No roads came anywhere near it and there were only horse-drawn sleighs that had warning bells.

Q: What kind of sleds did most boys have?
A: They had old-fashioned, homemade sleds with two wooden runners.

Q: Who made the boys' sleds?
A: Usually their fathers made them.

Q: When would the Wrights just stand and watch?
A: They would have to watch when the other boys raced one another down the hill.

Q: What did Mrs. Wright notice about her children when they arrived home that afternoon?
A: They were very quiet.

Q: Why were the boys unhappy?
A: Their father had not built a sled for them.

Q: What did their mother tell them?
A: She reminded them that their father was away often and was very busy when he was home. Then she suggested that they build a sled together.

Q: Why did Wilbur laugh?
A: It was funny to think that his mother would make a sled. He had never heard of a mother doing that before.

Q: Did the laughter bother Mrs. Wright?
A: Not at all. She went ahead with the plans for the sled.

Q: Why were the boys confused when their mother asked for pen and paper?
A: They could not understand how you could build a sled from paper.

Q: What kind of sled did the boys want?
A: They wanted a sled like the one their friend, Ed Sines, had.

Q: What change to Ed Sines' model did Mother make in her drawing?
A: She made the sled a three-seater instead of a two-seater.

Q: Who would sit in the third seat?
A: Kate would sit there.

Analytical

Q: Did the Wright boys have their own sleds?
A: No, some boys let them use theirs or they just watched.

“You want a sled that’s faster than Ed’s sled, don’t you?” His mother smiled. “Well, Ed’s sled is at least a foot high. Our sled will be lower—closer to the ground. It won’t meet so much wind resistance.” 14

“Wind resistance?” It was the first time Wilbur had ever heard the expression. He looked blankly at his mother.

“Remember the blizzard last week?” she asked. “Remember when you went out to the woodshed and the wind was so strong you could hardly walk to the shed? I told you to lean over, and on the next trip to the woodshed you did. When you came back with an armful of wood you laughed and said, ‘Mother, I leaned ’way forward and got under the wind.’ You were closer to the ground and you were able to lessen the wind resistance. Now, the closer to the ground our sled is the less wind resistance there will be, and the faster it will go.”

“Wind resistance...wind resistance,” Wilbur repeated, and maybe the airplane was born in that moment. Certainly neither Will nor Orville Wright ever forgot that first lesson in speed. 

Literary Components

14 Theme: The reader begins to understand why the earlier story about Wilbur coming from the barn was inserted.

15 Foreshadowing: The author assumes that the reader knows who the Wright brothers are.

Guiding the Reading

Literal

Q: What other changes did Mrs. Wright make in her sketched plans?
A: The sled would be a foot longer and closer to the ground.

Q: Why did Mrs. Wright make it closer to the ground?
A: Less wind resistance would allow it to go faster.

Q: What example did Mrs. Wright use?
A: She reminded Wilbur how he had bent over during the blizzard.

Analytical

Q: What is wind resistance?
A: Wind pushes at an object as the object pushes against it. The less surface there is on the object pushing against the wind, the less the wind will push against the object.

Q: Why was this first lesson in speed so important to Wilbur?
A: It would influence his designing of an airplane later on.

Literary Components

16 Theme: Along with the theme of the importance of wind resistance, the theme of getting it right on paper will be carried out throughout the story and the book.

17 Rising Action: For the young reader, the action has finally begun.

"How do you know about these things, Mother?" Wilbur asked.

"You'd be surprised how much mothers know, Will." She laughed. She didn't tell the boys that when she was a little girl at school her best subject had been arithmetic. It just came naturally to her. It was the same when she went to high school. And when she went to college, algebra and geometry were her best subjects. That was why she knew all about things like "wind resistance."

Finally she finished the drawing. The boys leaned over the table to look at it. This sled was going to be longer than Ed's sled and much narrower. Ed's sled was about three feet wide. This one looked as if it would be only half that wide.

"You made it narrow," Wilbur said shrewdly, "to make it faster. The narrower it is, the less wind resistance."

"That's right." His mother nodded. "Now let's put down the exact length of the runners and the exact width of the sled."

"But that's only a paper sled," Orville protested.

16 "If you get it right on paper," she said calmly, "it'll be right when you build it. Always remember that."

" 'If you get it right on paper, it'll be right when you build it,' " Wilbur repeated, and his mother looked at him sharply. Sometimes Will seemed older than his eleven years. Little Orville was quick to give you an answer to anything, but as often as not he'd forget the answer right away. When Will learned something he never forgot it.

"Mother, you make all your clothes," Wilbur said thoughtfully. "You always make a drawing first."

"We call that the pattern," his mother said. "I draw and then cut out a pattern that's exactly the size of the dress I am going to make. And..."

"If the pattern is right, it'll be right when you make the dress," he finished. She nodded.

17 "Now you two boys get started on your sled." She smiled. "There are plenty of planks out in the barn. Find the very lightest ones. Don't use planks with knots in them. You saw the planks to the right size, Will—don't let Orville touch the saw."

"May we use Father's tools?" Wilbur asked breathlessly.

His mother nodded. "I don't think your father will mind. I know you'll be careful with them. Just follow the drawing exactly," she warned once more.

The two boys, followed by little Kate, hurried out to the barn. Both realized that this was an important occasion. Wilbur always chopped the wood for the stove when his father was away, but he had never been allowed to use the gleaming tools that lay in his father's tool chest.

Three days later their sled was finished. They pulled it out of the barn and asked their mother to inspect it. She had her tape measure with her and she measured it.

Guiding the Reading

Literal

Q: What did Mother answer when asked how she knew all these things?

A: "You'd be surprised how much mothers know."

Q: What was one of the reasons Mother knew about wind resistance?

A: She was an excellent math student.

Q: What did Wilbur figure out on his own after looking at the picture?

A: He realized that making the sled narrower would reduce wind resistance.

Q: What important lesson did Mrs. Wright teach Orville when he said that it was only a paper sled?

A: "If you get it right on paper, it'll be right when you build it."

Q: What did Will realize about his mother's dresses?

A: The pattern she drew before making a dress was just like the sketch they had prepared for the sled.

Q: Where did the boys get the wood to build their sled?

A: The wood was from the barn.

Q: Who was allowed to use the saw?

A: Only Will was allowed to use the saw.

Q: What did Mother say about Father's tools?

A: Father would not mind if they used the tools; she knew they would be careful.

Q: How long did it take for Will and Orv to complete the sled?

A: They finished it in three days.

Analytical

Q: Mrs. Wright says to the boys, "You want a sled that's faster than Ed's sled, don't you?" She is obviously encouraging them to compete with their friends. Do you think this is good?

A: Your students may argue that one should not try to outshine one's friends. This is a very complex and important topic. In this case, everything turned out fine. The boys wound up with a better sled, which they happily shared with their friends. They didn't ridicule their friends or keep the sled all to themselves. One can imagine they would happily share the "wind resistance" secret with anyone who wanted to learn about it. Trying to outdo what already exists is the fuel on which progress runs.

Q: Why do you think Mrs. Wright let the boys build the sled all by themselves?

A: It was a learning experience. It built up their skill, creativity, and belief in themselves.

The Wright Brothers 239

240 Unit 3

The runners were exactly the length she had put down in her drawing. In fact, the boys had followed every direction she had given them. The runners gleamed. Orville had polished them with sandpaper until they were as smooth as silk. 18

"We thought of one other thing, Mother," Will said. "We found some old candles in the woodshed. We rubbed the runners with the candles. See how smooth they are?"

Mrs. Wright nodded. She had forgotten to tell the boys that, but they'd thought it out for themselves. "Now try your sled," she told them.

Followed by Kate, the boys dragged their new sled to the hill only a half a mile away, where their pals were coasting. They looked at the new sled in amazement. It was long and very narrow. It looked as though it wouldn't hold anyone. The runners were thin compared to those on their own sleds.

"Who made that for you?" Ed Sines asked.

"Mother showed us how," Wilbur said proudly. Some of the boys laughed. Whoever heard of a boy's mother knowing how to make a sled?

"It looks as if it would fall apart if you sat on it," Al Johnston said, and he laughed too.

"Come on, we'll race you down the hill," another cried out.

"All right, two on each sled," Wilbur said. He wasn't a bit afraid. He was sure the drawing had been right, and because he and Orv had followed the drawing, he knew that the sled was right.

They lined the four sleds up. Will and Orv sat on their sled, but it didn't "fall apart." Suddenly Wilbur got an idea.

"Get up, Orv," he said. "Now lie down on the sled…that's it…spread your legs a bit." Will then flopped down on top of his brother. "Less wind resistance this way," he whispered.

"Give us all a push," Ed Sines yelled.

And then they were off. It was an even start. The four sleds gathered speed, for at the top the slope was steep. Will looked to the right. Then to the left. He brushed the stinging snow out of his eyes but he couldn't see the other sleds. He looked behind. They were straggling along, twenty and now thirty feet in back of him. The new sled skimmed along, the runners singing happily. Both Will and Orv felt a strange thrill of excitement. They approached the bottom of the long hill. The other sleds were far, far behind now. 19

Usually when the sleds reached the bottom of the hill they slowed down abruptly and stopped. But not this sled. It kept on; its momentum carried it on and on a hundred yards farther than any of the other sleds had ever reached. Finally it stopped.

Shaking with excitement, Will and Orv stood up.

"We flew down the hill, Orv," Will said breathlessly. 

Literary Components

18 Characterization: We see the preciseness of these brothers which will ultimately enable them to become great inventors. We also see the respect they give their mother.

19 Climax: We're pretty sure they'll win, but not positive.

20 Moment of Realization; Foreshadowing; Theme: Wilbur and Orville have tasted "flight." They won't give up until they actually fly in the air.

Guiding the Reading

Literal

Q: What did Mrs. Wright think about the final product?

A: After measuring and inspecting it, she saw that they had followed all the directions and it was beautiful.

Q: How did the boys make the runners smooth?

A: First they used sandpaper, and then they rubbed them with wax candles.

Q: What was the reaction of all the other boys when they got to the hill?

A: They looked at the new sled in amazement and wondered how it would hold anyone.

Q: What did their friends say when they heard that their mother helped them make the sled?

A: They laughed and thought it would fall apart. Then they challenged the Wrights to race down the hill.

Q: Why wasn't Will nervous?

A: He felt confident because they'd followed the drawing exactly.

Q: What new idea did Will have about wind resistance right before they went down the hill?

A: His idea was to lie down on the sled.

Q: At first, did it look like anyone in particular was going to win?

A: No, it was an even start.

Q: Why wasn't Will able to see the other boys even when he pushed the snow out of his eyes?

A: They were all far behind him.

Q: How did Orv and Will feel about their new sled?

A: They had a strange thrill of excitement.

Q: What was different about the Wright brothers' sled when it reached the bottom of the hill?

A: The momentum kept it going for a hundred yards after it reached the bottom of the hill. The other sleds slowed down and stopped when they reached the bottom.

Analytical

Q: What does the fact that they thought of the candles on their own show?

A: It shows that they have begun to think creatively and independently. This is just what Mrs. Wright wanted from her children, and bore fruit in their many inventions.

"We flew," Orv repeated.

Now Ed and Al and Johnnie ran up, excited at what had happened. No sled had gone so far or so fast as the one Will and Orv had built.

"You *flew* down the hill," Ed Sines gasped. "Let me try it?"

Wilbur looked at Orv, and some secret message seemed to pass between them. They had built this sled together, and it was the best sled there was. They'd always work together building things.

"Orv," Will said, "I've got an idea. This sled can do everything but steer. Maybe we can make a rudder for it. Then we can make it go to the right or to the left."

"We'll get Mother to draw one," Orv said.

"We'll draw one, you and I," Wilbur said. "We can't run to Mother every time we want to make something."

By now little Kate had come running down the hill.

"You promised," she panted. "You said you'd take me for a ride."

"Come on, Kate." Will laughed. "The three of us will coast down once. And then you can try it, Ed."

They trudged up the hill, pulling the sled. Two words kept singing in Wilbur's ears. "We flew...we flew...we flew..."

Orville and Wilbur Wright continued to plan and work together. They used the Wright Cycle Shop for many projects. They made over and improved bicycles, they built a printing press on which they printed a newspaper, and together they planned and built a glider. This was the very plane they flew at Kitty Hawk, North Carolina. They improved it and added an engine, and for the first time, on December 17, 1903, a glider flew under its own power. The glider, which Wilbur and Orville had built, was the first airplane to fly with a man on board. This invention made the Wright brothers famous all over the world.

The brothers always remembered the lesson they had learned from their mother. They always worked by a plan. "Get it right on paper, and it'll be right when you build it," Susan Wright had said. That is exactly what they did.

Guiding the Reading

Literal

Q: Was Ed Sines still making fun of the Wright boys after their sled went down the hill?

A: No. He was impressed and said, "You flew down the hill," and wanted a chance to try the new sled.

Q: What secret message seemed to pass between Will and Orv?

A: They had successfully built something together; they felt good about it and would do it again in the future.

Q: What new idea did Will have for the sled?

A: He thought to make a rudder to help it steer.

Q: What was Will's reaction when Orv said they should ask Mother to draw a rudder?

A: He said that the boys should do it themselves and not run to their mother for everything.

Q: Who had a ride before Ed?

A: Kate got a ride before Ed.

Q: What two businesses were the Wright brothers involved in before they started working on flying machines?

A: They owned a bicycle shop and published a newspaper.

Q: Where did they fly their first glider?

A: In Kitty Hawk, North Carolina.

Q: How did they fly their first glider?

A: They added an engine.

Q: What happened on December 17, 1908?

A: The Wright brothers' glider flew under its own power. It was the first airplane to fly with a man on board.

Q: Which lesson (among others) did they apply that stuck with them throughout?

A: "Get it right on paper, and it will be right when you build it."

Analytical

Q: The fact that the boys discussed a new rudder idea on their own showed what?

A: It showed that they had applied the lessons their mother had been teaching them.

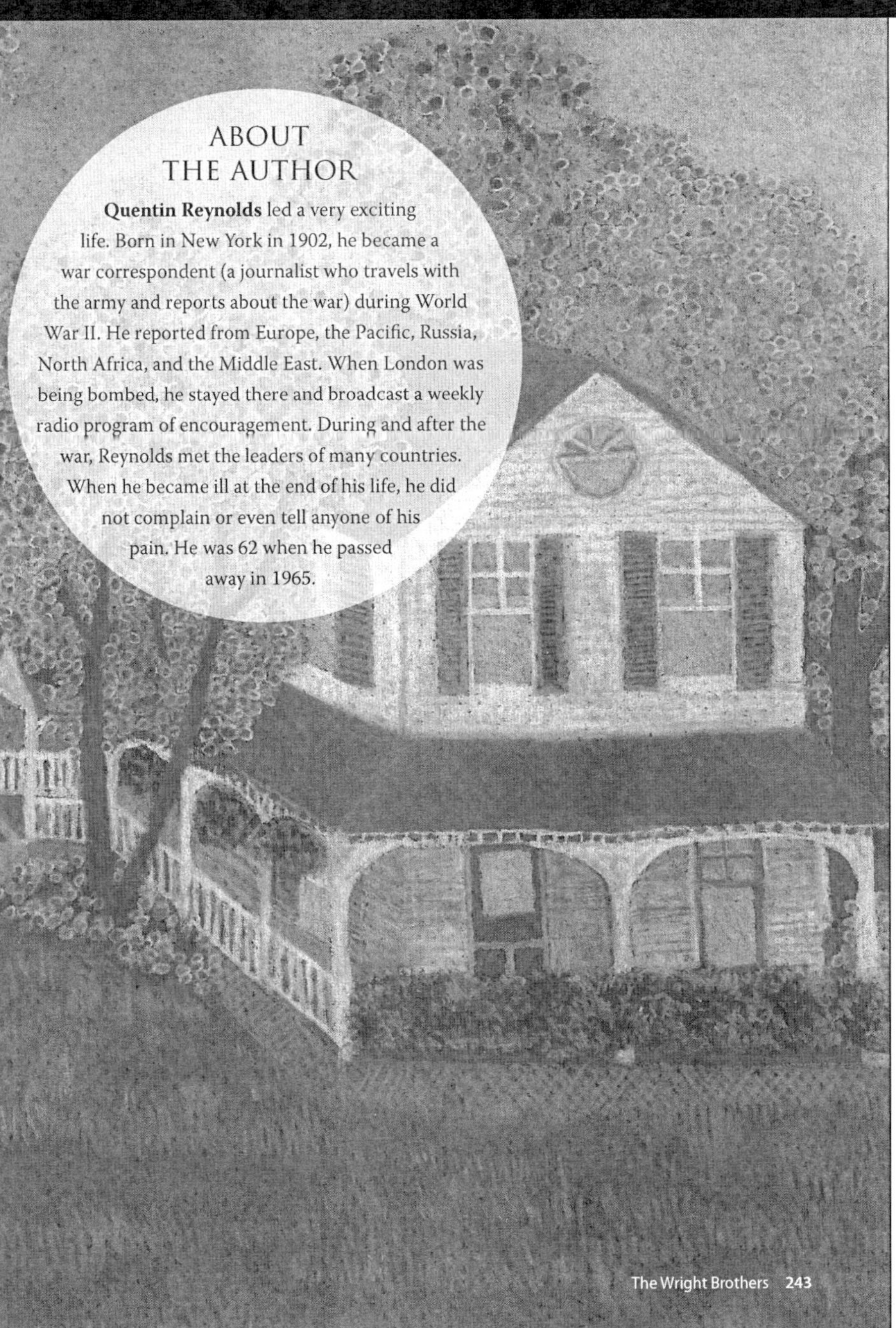

ABOUT THE AUTHOR

Quentin Reynolds led a very exciting life. Born in New York in 1902, he became a war correspondent (a journalist who travels with the army and reports about the war) during World War II. He reported from Europe, the Pacific, Russia, North Africa, and the Middle East. When London was being bombed, he stayed there and broadcast a weekly radio program of encouragement. During and after the war, Reynolds met the leaders of many countries. When he became ill at the end of his life, he did not complain or even tell anyone of his pain. He was 62 when he passed away in 1965.

About The Inventor Thinks Up Helicopters

Poetry Teaches Us to Ask Questions

The Inventor Thinks Up Helicopters is actually one long question. It is the same question that haunts every inventor before the inventor's idea becomes a reality: why is [such and such] not possible? The more detailed the question, the more likely the idea will materialize. As the inventor envisions the invention, he or she becomes more and more confident that the answer to the question is, *it is possible*!

The Inventor Thinks Up Helicopters is loaded with poetic devices.

It has assonance …

"a
v**er**tical
wh**ir**ling …
sw**er**ves"

"st**ee**ring
v**eering**"

"fl**ee**t as a b**ee**tle"

"j**ou**nce
b**ou**nce"

"d**o**t
n**o**t"

It has consonance …

"**Testing** his **st**eeri**ng**
Twi**st**i**ng** and veeri**ng**"

It has alliteration …

"whirling
winding
testing …
twisting"

It has similes …

"Hops like a cricket
Swerves like a dragonfly
Fleet as a beetle"

… and metaphors …

"Why not
a …
bug
a pasture the size of a dot"

It ends with a question to which we already know the answer.

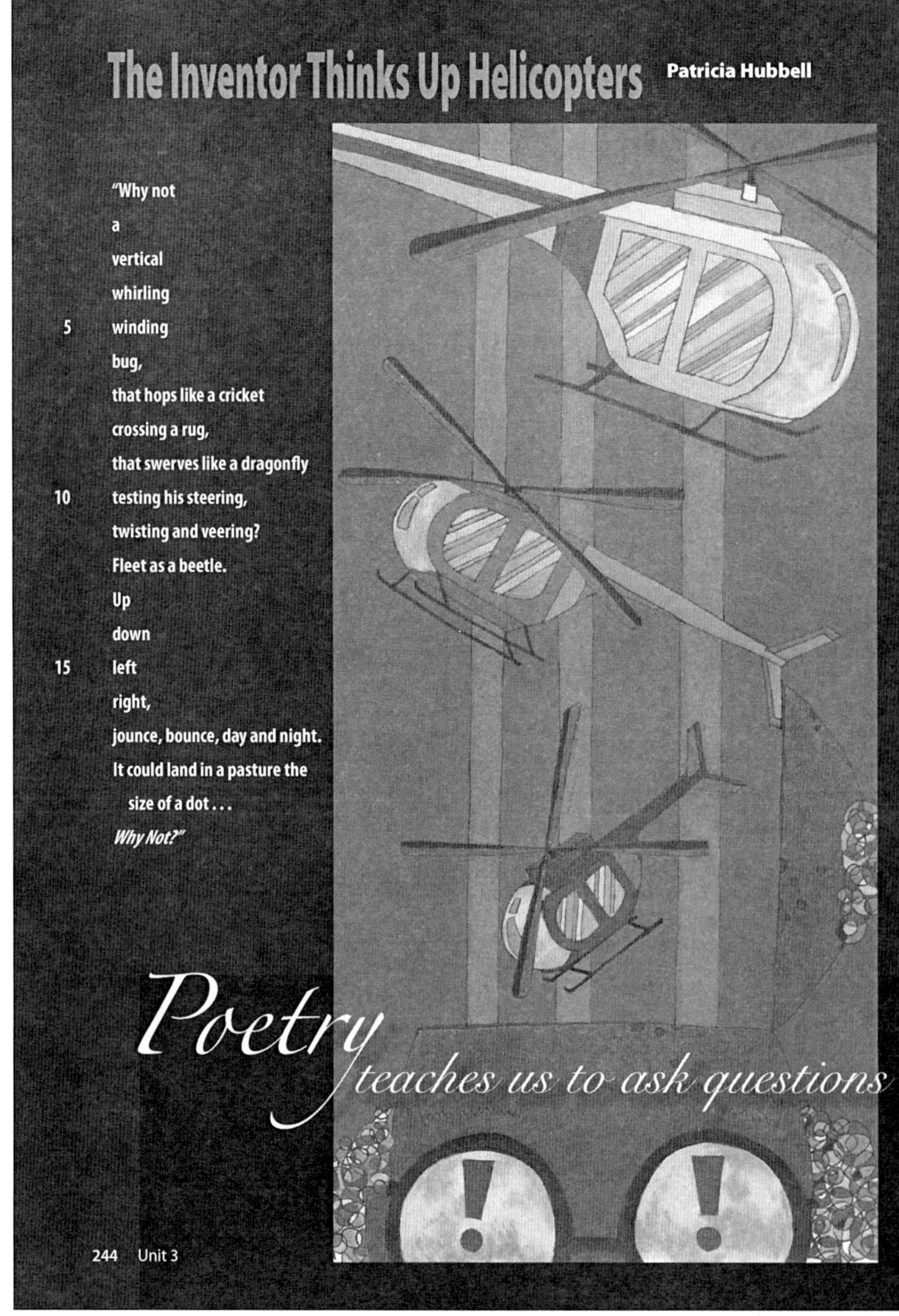

The Inventor Thinks Up Helicopters

Patricia Hubbell

"Why not
a
vertical
whirling
winding
bug,
that hops like a cricket
crossing a rug,
that swerves like a dragonfly
testing his steering,
twisting and veering?
Fleet as a beetle.
Up
down
left
right,
jounce, bounce, day and night.
It could land in a pasture the
size of a dot . . .
Why Not?"

Poetry teaches us to ask questions

244 Unit 3

Studying the Selection

FIRST IMPRESSIONS

Why do you think the Wright brothers were such confident young men?

QUICK REVIEW

1. What lesson did Wilbur learn during the snowstorm?
2. What did all the neighborhood children like to do for fun during the winter?
3. Who actually built the new sled and how long did it take?
4. What two ideas did Will and Orv come up with all on their own?

FOCUS

5. What are three lessons you can learn from this selection?
6. Choose three lines of dialogue from different parts of the story that reveal something important about a character.

CREATING AND WRITING

7. Write about something that you have always wanted to do but are afraid you will fail at. What makes you feel you will not succeed? Next to your reasons for thinking you *cannot* reach this goal, write down some plan to help you reach it.
8. Write a realistic but fictional story about how the Wright brothers—or fictional characters— try to help humans fly. The story may be serious, humorous, or a mixture of the two. Remember: It should be realistic, not a fantasy.
9. Draw a sketch of something you would like to build. Use a ruler or other drawing tools and try to be as accurate as possible.

The Wright Brothers 245

First Impressions

Thanks to their mother's patience, encouragement of their questioning, and respect for their ideas, the Wright boys grew into confident young men.

Quick Review

1. He learned to lean forward to create less wind resistance.
2. They liked to ride sleds down the hill.
3. Wilbur and Orville made the new sled themselves over the course of three days.
4. They came up with the idea of rubbing candle wax on the runners and the idea of building a rudder to steer the sled.

Focus

5. Answers will vary, but some include:
   - You never know what you can do until you try.
   - Mother knows best.
   - Planning makes perfect.
   - Do not be embarrassed to ask questions.
   - Peer pressure should not prevent you from doing something.

   Working together on a project is more fun and has a better chance at succeeding.
6. Answers will vary. Some possibilities include:
   - "If we had wings, then we could fly too, couldn't we, Mother?" Wilbur asked.
   - "Well, when you're a little older maybe you can try," their mother said.
   - "Bend over, and that way you get closer to the ground and you get under the wind."
   - "Now suppose we build a sled together."
   - "If you get it right on paper," she said calmly, "it'll be right when you build it."
   - "It looks like it would fall apart if you sat on it," Al Johnston said, and he laughed too.
   - "You flew down the hill," Ed Sines gasped. "Let me try it?"
   - "We'll draw one, you and I," Wilbur said. "We can't run to Mother every time we want to make something."

Creating and Writing

7. Answers will vary. The feared objective may be something as simple as approaching a potential friend. It may be asking for tutoring to achieve academic success, or learning to play a musical instrument. Many factors can discourage a person from trying. Fear of embarrassment, rejection, or ridicule may play a big role. Other considerations may be financial, inconvenience, lack of confidence in one's skill or intelligence, or simply fear of the unknown.
8. Answers will vary.
9. Answers will vary. Provide different rulers and tracing shapes to help your students.

Background Bytes

Biographers of the Wright brothers invariably look for clues to the boys' genius and their dedication to their projects. (Their work in the early 1900s on flyers shows that they were relentless in their experimentation. Even serious accidents—in some of which fatalities occurred—did not deter them.)

Neither boy received formal credit for finishing high school. (Wilbur completed the work, but the family left town before graduation.) Neither went to college. (There had been plans for Wilbur to go to Yale; a serious hockey accident and his mother's illness seem to have precluded that.) Nor did they have the financial wealth that would have made it possible for them to work on the flyers without concern for supporting themselves. So what was the source of their vision, their brilliance, and their commitment?

Why did Wilbur believe that he could build a printing press (and then succeed at it)? Why did they believe that they could design and build bicycles (and, again, succeed)? Why take on the age-old dream of humankind to fly like a bird? In this last, they created one of the greatest technological marvels of all time, and changed the future of the world.

In *The Wright Brothers: A Centennial Tribute*, Bob Gardner writes of Susan Wright:

> *Inventiveness and mechanical ability were often a presence in the Wright household. Older brother Lorin improved a hay baling machine and Wilbur built a device for folding papers while he was responsible for folding a ... publication. The strongest mechanical aptitude, however, was demonstrated by the mother, Susan Wright.*
>
> *She was resourceful in adapting household tools or utensils to unexpected uses. She designed clothes, built a sled for her children, and her family said that she 'could mend anything.'*

Dr. Subodh Mahanti writes "with her mechanical skill, she could build simple household appliances and toys for children." He is convinced that the boys inherited their mechanical genius from their mother.

Apparently, the Wrights, both teachers, were credited by their children as having provided an environment in which curiosity was never stifled and intellectual growth was fostered. From all accounts, the children were encouraged to read widely and the family libraries were large. Their mother had an innate mathematical sense and ventured into engineering activities unusual for a woman at that time. Finally, their father was also editor of a newspaper and dedicated in his work.

In 1889, when Wilbur was 22 and Orville was 17, Susan Wright died. She had been ill with tuberculosis. Their sister Katharine, who was 15 at the time, assumed the responsibility of running the household. She and her father wholeheartedly supported the near total immersion of the two brothers in their experimentation. The Wright Flyer was really a family project: their father gave them $1000 to fund their work. Their sister also assisted financially after she had graduated from Oberlin College.

Wilbur wrote at one point, "For some years I have been afflicted with the belief that flight is possible to man. My disease has increased in severity and I feel that it will soon cost me an increased amount of money if not my life. I have been trying to arrange my affairs in such a way that I can devote my entire time for a few months to experiment in this field."

But when the Wright brothers were unable to make much headway after intensive application to the problem of flight, they were very much disappointed. Wilbur wrote: "When we left Kitty Hawk at the end of 1901, we doubted that we would ever resume our experiments. Although we had broken the record for distance in gliding, and although Mr. Chanute, who was present at that time, assured us that our results were better than had ever before been attained, yet when we looked at the time and money which we had expended, and considered the progress made and the distance yet to go, we considered our experiments a failure. At this time I made the prediction that men would sometime fly, but that it would not be within our lifetime."

Jill's Journal:

On Assignment in Dayton, Ohio

It is May 1877. I have been invited by Mrs. Susan Wright to take tea this afternoon at 3:00. I am so pleased. Her handwritten invitation was delivered early this morning to the boardinghouse where I am staying.

My hostess, Mrs. Granville Dooley, has said that the gardener will take me over in the buggy. How very considerate people are in these times!

The Wright family has lived in Dayton, Ohio at 7 Hawthorn Street for a little longer than six years. (I have been told that their youngest son, Orville, was born there.) The house, which is quite stately, was newly built for them when they moved here in 1871. It must be quite a change for Milton Wright, Mrs. Wright's husband. Why, he was born in a log cabin!

Well, we have arrived. I have checked my pocket watch and it is just 3:00 on the nose. The buggy ride was surprisingly smooth. No bumps. (Can you imagine? There are less than twelve miles of paved roads in Dayton until 1900!)

The Wrights have been married since 1859. I am looking forward to meeting their five children. Let me see now, there's Reuchlin, who is 16 already. Lorin—he's 13 or 14. Wilbur is 10. Orville is five and little Katharine is two.

Mrs. Wright greets me at the door. How exciting to meet a person from history! Have you ever wondered what people actually looked like long ago or what fashions were like? Did you ever wish you could go back in time?

Well, I am here to say that her clothing is very fine. She is wearing a black dress that looks like it is made of taffeta or silk—it has a grainy, shiny texture. Of course, it is long—it goes down to her laced up shoes. At the neck it has a scalloped white lace collar that closes with a white bow. The dress has those wonderful puffy sleeves, snugly fitting cuffs and shoulders, and a narrow waist. I do wish we could wear such styles today. Mrs. Wright's hair is dark brown, parted in the middle and tucked into a bun at the back.

"How kind of you to come," she says. "My husband is away on one of his journeys, but all of the children are here for you to meet." She gestures with her right hand to the house. "Please come in. We are so glad you could join us for tea."

We enter a room where the walls are lined with books. "This is the downstairs library. My husband's books are kept in the upstairs library." She

246 Unit 3

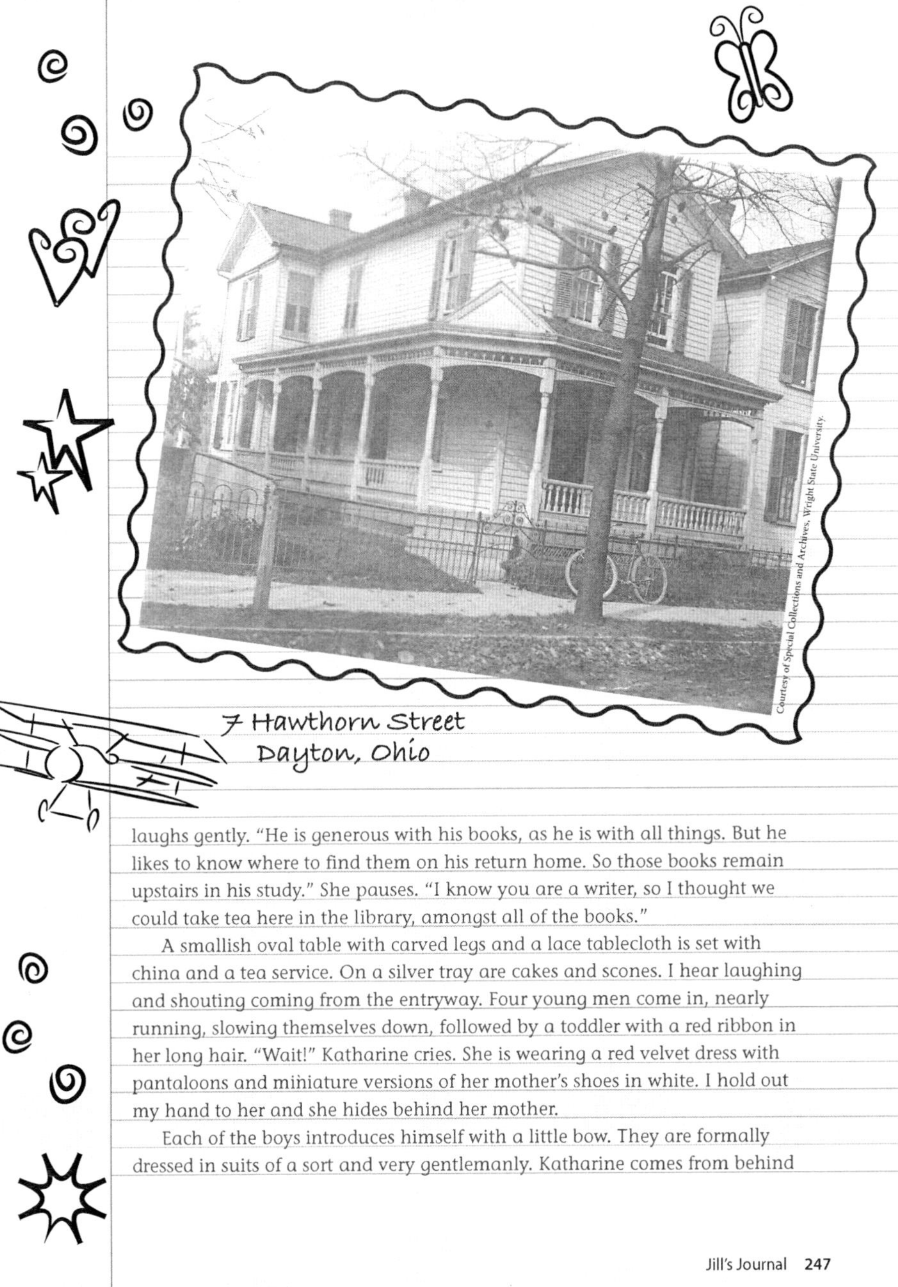

laughs gently. "He is generous with his books, as he is with all things. But he likes to know where to find them on his return home. So those books remain upstairs in his study." She pauses. "I know you are a writer, so I thought we could take tea here in the library, amongst all of the books."

A smallish oval table with carved legs and a lace tablecloth is set with china and a tea service. On a silver tray are cakes and scones. I hear laughing and shouting coming from the entryway. Four young men come in, nearly running, slowing themselves down, followed by a toddler with a red ribbon in her long hair. "Wait!" Katharine cries. She is wearing a red velvet dress with pantaloons and miniature versions of her mother's shoes in white. I hold out my hand to her and she hides behind her mother.

Each of the boys introduces himself with a little bow. They are formally dressed in suits of a sort and very gentlemanly. Katharine comes from behind

Jill's Journal 247

Chronology	
1889	The boys start a printing business. Their mother, Susan, dies on July 4. Orville decides to quit school.
1892	The Wright Cycle Company is formed.
1896	Orville survives six weeks with typhoid. Wilbur reads about the death of a famous glider pilot and becomes interested in flying.
1899	Wilbur writes to the Smithsonian for information about aeronautics on May 30.
1900	The brothers test their first glider at Kitty Hawk, North Carolina, in September and October.
1901	They test the 1901 glider in July and August. The brothers build a wind tunnel to test the drag and lift of various wing shapes.
1902	They test their third glider in September and October.
1903	Orville makes the historic first flight on December 17 at Kitty Hawk, North Carolina.
1904	Wilbur and Orville move their testing to Huffman Prairie, a pasture east of Dayton.
1905	They perfect their airplane and begin looking for buyers of their invention.
1908	Wilbur does demonstration flights in Europe. Orville flies for the U.S. Army in Fort Myer, Virginia, and is severely injured in a crash; his passenger is killed.
1909	Wilbur and Orville are welcomed home to Dayton in a two-day gala celebration at which they receive a Congressional gold medal.
1912	Wilbur dies of typhoid May 30, aged 45.
1917	Milton Wright dies on April 3, aged 88.
1932	A national monument to the Wright brothers is dedicated at Kitty Hawk on March 3.
1948	Orville dies on January 30, aged 77.

Their ability to persist nonetheless was really remarkable. "They built their own wind tunnels to test systematically wings of different shapes for the pressures and forces acting on them. After making careful analysis of their data they could find out where the earlier experimenters went wrong. By using their own aerodynamic data, the Wright brothers built new gliders."

As a consequence, in 1902, they succeeded in breaking all the previous records on gliding. Their 1902 glider was the very first aircraft in which the fundamental problems of flight—lift and three-axis control—were finally solved. All that remained was the need for refinements.

Roddam Narasimha writes, "Indeed one can say that the Wright brothers set the style and method of aircraft design that is followed to this day; only the tools are now vastly more powerful."

her mother to curtsy. "I am delighted to meet each of you," I say, smiling.

We are about to sit in the circle of chairs that has been set out, when Reuchlin blurts out, "Mother, I think I have fixed your sewing machine!" Mrs. Wright says, "Why Reuch, that's my boy!" She pronounces his name *Roosh*. Reuch says, "Well, Mother, I just did as you suggested." Wilbur turns to me and says proudly, "My Mother can fix or make anything." Mrs. Wright lowers her head modestly.

The children munch their cakes quietly as we talk. Mrs. Wright reminds me that the Civil War was not so long ago. "So many fine young men died. But my husband and I were very much opposed to the evils and suffering of slavery. Of course, he is still very much concerned with the problems of our countrymen."

I wish I could tell her how her sons will change the world. I wish I could tell her what a fine person Katharine will be, how she will care for and help Orville and Wilbur, and how Lorin will assist his brothers.

I remind myself that in my mind I must stay here in 1877. I should enjoy and be grateful for the opportunity to sit with this wonderful woman and her young family.

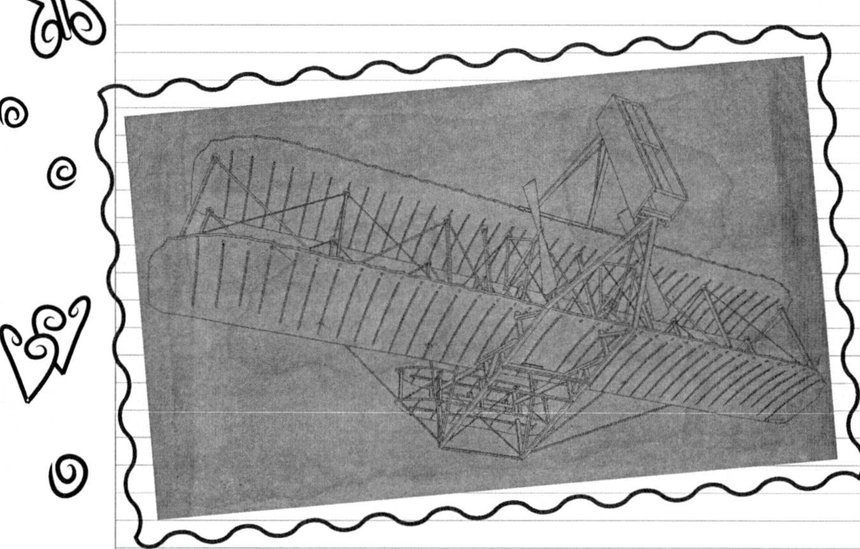

POWER SKILL:

How Does an Author Successfully Transport Us to Another Time and Place?

When a story is set in a certain time period, the author includes many details that help the reader feel right at home in that era. As you read Jill's Journal, you may not have even noticed how many small bits of the 1870s you took in as you focused on the plot and characters. However, if you had to write a piece of fiction set in a different time period, you would have to do quite a bit of research to find out what clothing your characters should wear, what their houses should look like, what kind of manners they should have, and even how their spoken English should differ from our modern English. The following exercise will help you organize what you know about life in the 1870s. Draw a simple cluster. In the center circle write "The 1870s." Into each one of the cluster circles, write one detail of setting, costume, language, manners, or anything else that helped create the 1870 atmosphere in the story.

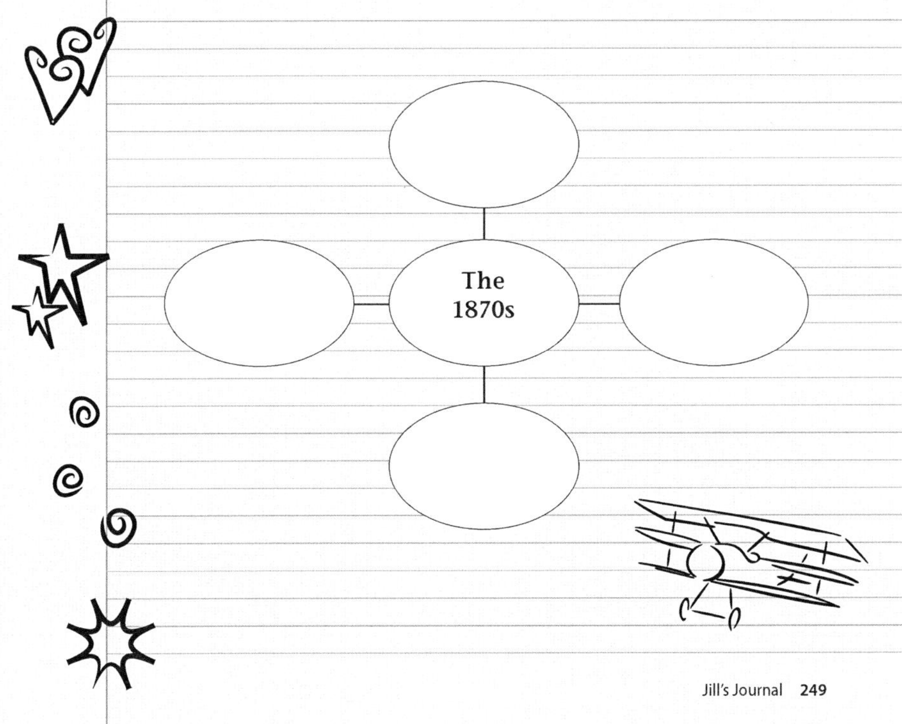

Power Skill:

How Does an Author Successfully Transport Us to Another Time and Place?

A simple cluster looks like a ferris wheel. Put the words "the 1870s" at the center of the wheel. In the "cars" or circles around the hub, the students can have some or all of the following details:

- taking tea
- a handwritten invitation
- a boardinghouse
- the buggy
- someone (Milton Wright) who had been born in a log cabin
- a pocket watch
- fewer than twelve miles of paved road in the city
- a black taffeta dress worn to tea
- laced up shoes
- scalloped white lace collar, puffy sleeves, etc.
- a bun
- silver tray, cakes, and scones, etc.
- boys formally dressed in suits
- the Civil War was not long ago

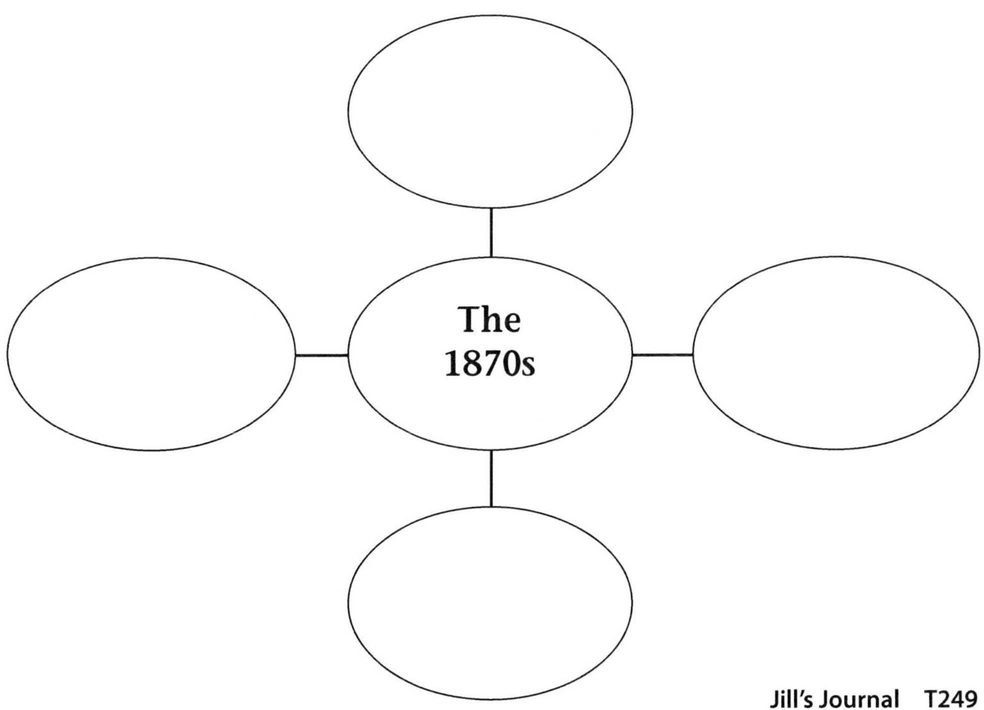

What Is Internal Dialogue?

Bicycle

1. Bobby: "Today is not a good day for a bicycle lesson."
   Tom: "Why not? It's not raining or cold."
   Bobby: "What's the big deal about learning to ride a bike, anyway?"
   [The question doesn't ask for a third line, but some students may wish to add this.]
2. Mr. Keller is smiling and happy. Bobby looks worried and strained.
3. Answers will vary.

Lesson in Literature . . .

WHAT IS INTERNAL DIALOGUE?

- *Internal* means inside. *Dialogue* is conversation. **Internal dialogue** is a conversation that takes place inside the mind of a character.
- Internal dialogue reveals what the character is thinking, feeling, or planning to do.
- Everyone experiences internal dialogue. We call it *thinking*.
- In a story, internal dialogue is different from ordinary dialogue. It is not usually written as a conversation between two speakers. It is written as part of the narration.

THINK ABOUT IT!

1. The first paragraph describes Bobby's thoughts. These thoughts could have been divided between two different people. Imagine that, instead of *thinking* these lines, Bobby was *talking* to his friend Tom. Write a dialogue between Bobby and Tom, using quotation marks. It should start like this:

   Bobby: "
   Tom: "
2. Sometimes, we can tell what people are thinking by the looks on their faces. When Mr. Keller arrives, what is the look on his face? What is the look on Bobby's face? Make sure you base your answer on the words in the story that describe the feelings of both characters.
3. Copy one line of dialogue out of the story. Make sure you include the quotation marks. Then copy out one line of narrative that describes an internal dialogue. That line will not have quotation marks.

BICYCLE

Today was not a good day for a bicycle lesson, Bobby thought. It wasn't raining or cold, but he was sure he didn't want to learn to ride today. What's the big deal about learning to ride a bike, anyway?

He was at the park, waiting for his neighbor Mr. Keller who had volunteered to give him a few lessons. "You'll be a bicycle rider in no time!" Mr. Keller had told him.

Bobby wondered if Mr. Keller was right.

He looked across the grass and down the street. Mr. Keller must have forgotten about the lesson. He decided he'd waited long enough, but he hadn't taken ten steps for home when his stomach sank. There was Mr. Keller on a bike riding across the empty parking lot. He circled around him, whistling and smiling. "This will be you in a few minutes!"

Bobby felt panicky.

It wasn't that he didn't like bikes. He did. He loved watching bicyclists ride past his house on sleek, shiny racing bikes. He liked the excitement on the faces of boys and girls his age when they rode their bikes to school or to the park. Bobby even liked when he saw a father on a bike with a child in a seat behind him or a mother and a daughter pedaling happily on a tandem bike.

He just wasn't sure if he could do it! He couldn't imagine staying up on a bike by balancing on two wheels and knew he'd never figure out the steering or the brakes.

"Let's get started," Mr. Keller said.

Mr. Keller instructed him on climbing onto the bike, and he explained balancing, steering, and braking. "But you just have to try it, Bobby. Don't worry if you fall. It's trial and error. Everybody falls at first."

Those last words caught Bobby's attention. "Everybody falls?" he asked.

"Everybody," Mr. Keller said. "You learn by falling. Each fall brings you closer to riding."

After hearing that, Bobby inched his leg over the bar. So what if I fall a couple of times? Everybody falls. I'll be closer to riding!

Mr. Keller pushed the bike as Bobby pedaled hard. "I'm here," Mr. Keller said, running along beside him. "Hold the handle bar straight! Pedal, Bobby!" It was a few seconds before Bobby realized that Mr. Keller had stopped running. He was riding on his own! "Remember the brakes!" he heard Mr. Keller call from far behind.

He was a bicycle rider!

Later, he fell once and fell again. Of course, it took time to learn the steering and the braking. But Mr. Keller was right. Each fall brought him closer to riding. In no time he learned to ride a bicycle. It was a lesson he would never forget.

The Imperfect/Perfect Book Report 251

- **Unit Theme:** *Head, Hands, Heart*
- **Target Skill:** *Internal dialogue tells us what the characters are thinking.*
- **Genre:** *Realistic Fiction*

Getting Started

Ask students to write a paragraph (or more) about one of their favorite books. They must include reasons for why they liked the book. They should write a very brief plot outline without revealing too much information. Share the paragraphs with the class. Consider writing a book review of your own.

Into . . . The Imperfect/ Perfect Book Report

Competition is a fact of life. It exists not only in the classroom, but in many other areas as well. It begins with 'my Daddy is stronger than yours' and reaches to the highest offices of government. Competition is as old as mankind, and no amount of talk can eradicate it. We must therefore harness it. To do so, we must ask ourselves the following questions:

- *Why are we competing?*
- *What are we competing against?*
- *What are we competing to achieve?*
- *How are we competing?*

Are we competing because we want to improve, advance, learn something new, or improve a skill? These are positives. Are we competing to shore up a bad self-image? To put down somebody else? To live up to someone else's demands or expectations? These are negatives.

What are we competing against?

Are we competing against our own former achievement? Are we competing against a challenge? The status quo? These are positives. Are we competing against one particular individual whom we wish to outdo? Are we competing against a well-meaning or idealistic group? These are negatives.

What are we competing to achieve?

Do we want to become better informed, more able to contribute to the world, climb the unconquered heights and plumb the undiscovered depths? Is competition the spark that lights a fire in us? These are positives. Do we wish to take every prize, to grab more than our share of honor, power, or money? Do we wish to show the world that, try as they may, they will never surpass us? These are negatives.

How are we competing?

Do we encourage others to join the race? Are we happy with someone else's success? Do we share our winnings? Do we remain humble? Do we compete with enthusiasm and generosity and above all, fairness? These are positives. Will we do whatever it takes to win? Are we bad losers? Are we arrogant when we win? Do we desperately need to win all the time? Do we play the game unfairly? These are negatives.

Competition can be healthy, but it can also destroy an individual's quality of life and self-worth. When people are driven to compete, they are motivated to perform at higher levels and achieve what they did not know was possible. However, the same competitive spirit can lead a person to blindly hurt others or themselves on their way to reaching their goal. In sports, competition can be fun. In many other situations, competition is not enjoyable.

Blueprint for Reading

INTO . . . *The Imperfect/Perfect Book Report*

People are cheering! The scoreboard is flashing! Teammates are urging each other to play their best! It is a lively baseball game and only one team can win. Playing against each other with lots of energy and the belief that the best team will win is called *competition*. People are constantly competing against one another, but is it always a good thing? Read the following story and see what you think about the competition that exists between the main character and her classmates.

Internal Dialogue

Do you ever wish that you had special powers and could hear what your parents or friends were thinking? While that is not likely to happen, we are given the opportunity to find out what characters in stories are thinking. **Internal dialogue** tells us about the characters' inner thoughts. *Internal* means inside, and *dialogue* is conversation. When we "overhear" internal dialogue, it is as if we are hearing the characters talking to themselves. As you read, notice how internal dialogue adds to this story.

252 Unit 3

It is very important to tell your students that above all else, people must aim to do their own personal best. Compete with yourself! Julio is a wonderful example of this.

Suggestion: To illustrate healthy competitiveness, draw on the story of how the Wright brothers built a better sled. Unhealthy competitiveness is, of course, the subject of this story.

Eyes On Internal Dialogue

Internal dialogue should serve a purpose. While its substance may range from the mundane to the revelatory, a character's internal dialogue should provide insight into the story line or character. Internal dialogue may be used to provide a different perspective from that of the narrator. This will be discussed in a later section when point of view is addressed.

There are two types of internal dialogue. In one type, the narrator tells us what a character is thinking. In the other more formal and dramatic type, the character's thoughts are quoted as though they were being spoken aloud.

There was no doubt about it. Zoe Mitchell was just as smart as Cricket Kaufman. Everyone who had known Cricket since she had been the star of the morning kindergarten class, back when she was five years old, agreed. Finally, she had met her match. ❶ ❷

In some ways, it made Cricket feel strange not to be the best student in the class. But at the same time, she worked harder than ever and found that she liked school better and better. ❸ She was learning so many new things. It was hard to decide if it was because now she was in fourth grade or because she was working not to let Zoe get ahead of her. Lucas Cott was smart too, but it wasn't the same thing. Maybe it was because he was the smartest boy in the class and she had been the smartest girl. Now, whenever test papers were handed back, Cricket craned

Selection Summary

Cricket Kaufman is the unrivaled star of her class—that is, until Zoe Mitchell joins the fourth grade class at her school. Cricket has met her match. Neck and neck in the race for excellence, Zoe and Cricket rack up the A's and 100's. They are friends and rivals. Mrs. Schraalenburgh, the teacher, remains above the fray. She is interested in drawing the best out of each student and praises effort more than results.

When Mrs. Schraalenburgh assigns a book report, Cricket decides this is a good opportunity to reassert herself as the top student in the class. She chooses to write her report on a book that she has recently given to Zoe. From memory, she writes a long, detailed report on the book. She puts time and effort into making sure the writing is neat, then additional time and effort into constructing a beautiful cover for the report.

Surprised to find that Zoe has done her report on the same book, Cricket waits for the reports to be graded, confident that her outstanding work will be praised. Imagine her surprise and chagrin when, with a pat on the back, her teacher hands her the report saying, "I'm sure you'll do better next time ..." Chagrin turns to dismay when Cricket sees the "B-" on her report, while one of the poorest students gets an "A" on his report, not to mention the "A" earned by her arch rival, Zoe.

The story ends when a chastened Cricket, helped along by a kindhearted and generous Zoe, resolves to be less competitive in the future.

Guiding the Reading

Literal

Q: Which two girls were considered the smartest in the class?

A: Zoe Mitchell and Cricket Kaufman were considered the smartest.

Q: How long had Cricket been known as a star student?

A: It had been since kindergarten.

Q: Why didn't Lucas Cott seem to affect Cricket as much as Zoe did?

A: He was the smartest boy, not the smartest girl.

Analytical

Q: What is meant by the words, "Finally, she had met her match"?

A: There was someone who was on the same level as Cricket and might challenge her.

Literary Components

❶ **Exposition; Characterization; Setting; External Conflict:** In a few short lines we learn the following: the story takes place in modern times in a public school setting. The leading characters are two smart, probably competitive girls. The struggle between the two seems to be what the story will be about (a bit of **foreshadowing**, too).

❷ **Colloquialism:** This is a nicely turned phrase.

❸ **Characterization:** Cricket has earned her position as smartest girl. She is a hard worker and truly loves to learn. The competition with Zoe has actually served to sharpen her skills as a student, not to distract her from learning.

Literary Components

❹ **Thematic Thread:** The writing in this paragraph is very good and tight. Although the author adds some new information, it only serves to strengthen the main point, which is repeated at the end of the paragraph: that the two girls are equally smart.

❺ **Theme; Point/Counterpoint:** The counterpoint to the theme of competitiveness and excelling is the philosophy of Mrs. Schraalenburgh, who stresses effort as equally important as results.

❻ **Theme:** Again, a good point for debate. What is meant by the phrase "everyone was treated equally"? Were those who didn't even try given as much respect as those who did? Were those who excelled because they worked hard given the same reward as those who did not try as hard, or who did try but did not succeed?

❼ **Theme; Characterization; External Conflict; Internal Dialogue:** The theme of competitiveness is carried out in the character of Cricket. Competition between two of anything (here, it is two girls) is a form of external conflict. Cricket's thoughts about how to gain recognition and reassert herself as best student form her internal dialogue.

4 her head to see what mark Zoe had gotten. Almost always, the two girls had performed equally well.

Mrs. Schraalenburgh beamed proudly at them both when they each got 100 percent on the fractions test in arithmetic. But she also congratulated Julio for improving his score. When Cricket walked to the back of the room to use the pencil sharpener, she was able to see that Julio had almost as many problems wrong as he had gotten right. Mrs. Schraalenburgh was a funny teacher. She always said she was proud of all her students and to prove it she never singled one person out above the others. 5 Maybe that was why it wasn't quite so bad that Zoe Mitchell was such a good student. If Cricket wasn't the teacher's pet this year, neither was Zoe. No one was. With a different "personality of the day" selected each morning, and students like Julio being congratulated even when they could only answer half the questions, everyone was treated equally. 6

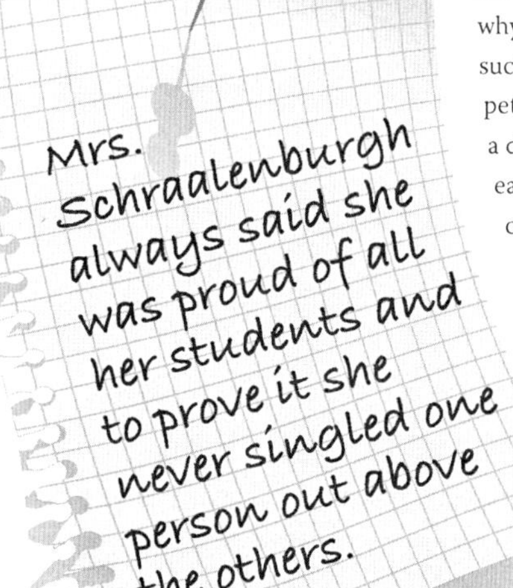

Still, when Mrs. Schraalenburgh said that once a month everyone had to write a book report, Cricket was delighted. She loved reading and a book report would be fun for her to write. She would do one that was so much better than everyone else's that Mrs. Schraalenburgh would have to admit that she was the very best student in the class. 7 Although Cricket was pleased with the new assignment, there were loud groans from the back of the room.

"Quiet!" Mrs. Schraalenburgh scolded. "If you have something to say, raise your hands and I will call on you." She looked at Lucas, who had made the loudest groan.

"Don't you like to read, Lucas?" asked the teacher.

Guiding the Reading

Literal

Q: What didn't Mrs. Schraalenburgh ever do?
A: She never singled out one person above the others.

Q: How did Cricket know the truth about Julio's test?
A: She peeked at his paper when she went to use the sharpener in the back of the room.

Q: Do you think it was right for Cricket to glance at Julio's paper?
A: No, she had no right to look at someone else's paper.

Q: Who was the teacher's pet?
A: Mrs. Schraalenburgh did not have a teacher's pet.

Q: What were the students required to do once a month?
A: They had to write a book report.

Q: Why was Cricket pleased about the book report assignment?
A: She liked to read and write and thought that it would be an opportunity to prove that she was better than everyone else.

Q: Was everyone in the class as glad about the book report as Cricket was?
A: No, there were many loud groans.

Q: Who groaned the loudest?
A: Lucas.

Q: What rule did Mrs. Schraalenburgh remind her class about?
A: She reminded them to raise their hands before speaking.

Analytical

Q: Why did Mrs. Schraalenburgh praise Julio even though he got so many wrong?
A: Since Julio's score has improved, we can assume he has been trying hard. She is praising his effort and his progress.

8 "Sure," said Lucas. "But I don't like writing book reports."

"A book report is a way of sharing something that you have enjoyed with the rest of the class," said Mrs. Schraalenburgh. "It should tell your classmates whether or not they too should read that book."

Lucas did not look convinced. Cricket knew he read a lot of books. She saw him checking them out of the school library when the class had library time. But she also knew he was lazy about doing homework. She, on the other hand, couldn't wait to begin. 9 She would make the best book report that anyone ever did. Then, perhaps finally, Mrs. Schraalenburgh would know what a great student she was.

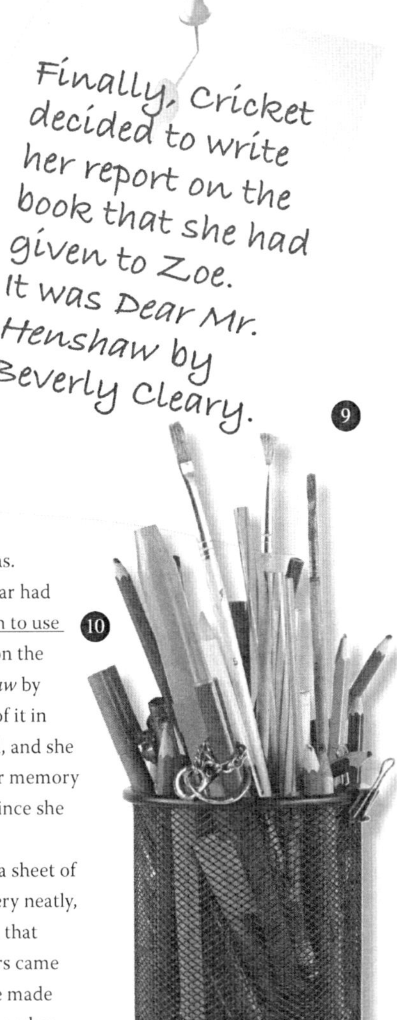

Cricket had read so many books since the school year had begun that at first she couldn't make up her mind which to use for her report. 10 Finally, she decided to write her report on the book that she had given to Zoe. It was *Dear Mr. Henshaw* by Beverly Cleary. It was too bad she couldn't find a copy of it in the library. But Cricket remembered the story very well, and she thought she could write a report from her memory. Her memory was very good and it had been only a couple of weeks since she had read the book.

Cricket sat down and wrote, covering both sides of a sheet of loose-leaf paper as she told all about the book. Then, very neatly, she copied it over. She used a razor-edged marking pen that she had bought with her allowance last week. The letters came out clear and neat, but near the bottom of the page, she made a mistake. Cricket didn't want to have any crossing-out on her report. So she took a fresh piece of paper and copied her report over again, very slowly this time so that she wouldn't make

Literary Components

8 Dialogue: You may contrast regular "dialogue" with internal dialogue.

9 Theme; Characterization; Internal Dialogue: As in #7, the author continues to build on her theme, revealing Cricket's thoughts in which she calculates her ability to outshine everyone else.

10 Internal Conflict: This is a very mild example of internal conflict.

Guiding the Reading

Literal

Q: How did the teacher explain the purpose of a book report?
A: She said that writing and presenting a report is a way of sharing something that you have enjoyed with the rest of the class. "It should tell your classmates whether or not they too should read that book."

Q: What did Cricket know about Lucas's schoolwork?
A: He was lazy about doing homework.

Q: Why did Cricket have trouble deciding what book to use?
A: She had read so many books since the start of the year.

Q: Which book did Cricket choose to use for the book report?
A: She chose *Dear Mr. Henshaw* by Beverly Cleary.

Q: Why didn't she have a copy of the book?
A: She could not find one in the library.

Q: How did Cricket plan to write her book report without the book?
A: Her memory was very good and she thought she remembered the book very well.

Q: Where did Cricket get her new pen?
A: She bought it with her allowance.

Q: What did the first copy of Cricket's book report look like?
A: It was very neat until she made a mistake at the bottom.

Q: Why did Cricket start a new copy of her book report?
A: She did not want to have any crossing-outs.

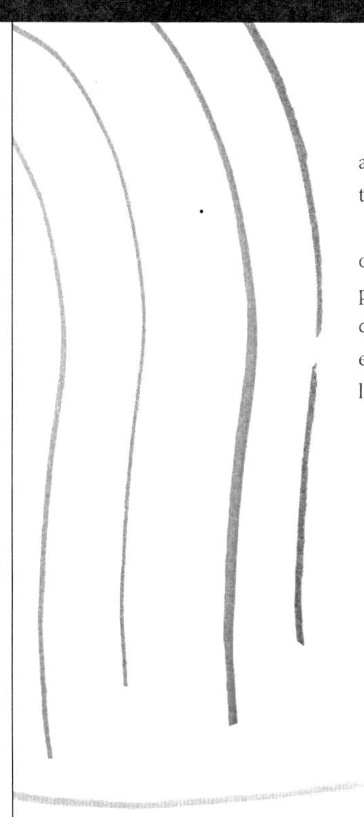

another error. When she was finished, it looked beautiful. It was the neatest piece of homework that she had ever done.

Then, to enhance the report, she decided to make a special cover for it. She took two sheets of red-colored paper. With her pencil and a ruler, she drew lines across the top of the page. She did it very, very lightly so that afterward she would be able to erase the lines. Then, using the block letters that they had been learning to do in art class, she wrote the title and the author.

Dear Mr. Henshaw
By Beverly Clearly

Book Report By
Cricket Kaufman

Underneath, she drew a picture of a boy sitting at a desk and writing. People who hadn't read the book might think it was supposed to be a picture of Cricket writing her book report, but if you read the book or at least read Cricket's report about it, you would know that it was supposed to be Leigh Botts, the main character in the story. He was always writing letters to his favorite author, who was named Mr. Henshaw. Cricket colored in the picture with her markers, and she erased the lines from the top of the paper.

Cricket had her own stapler. She used it to staple the top cover and the back cover to the page with her report. When she was finally finished, it was time for bed. She had missed her

Guiding the Reading

Literal

Q: What special addition did she make to the book report this time?

A: She made a nice red cover with block lettering.

Q: What was on the cover?

A: Cricket wrote the title, author, and her own name on the cover. She also drew a picture on the cover.

Q: Why did Cricket think people might make a mistake about her illustration?

A: She was afraid people would think it was a picture of herself working on her book report. But if they read the book, or at least her report, they would understand that it was a picture of Leigh Botts, the main character in the story.

Q: What do you know so far about the characters in *Dear Mr. Henshaw* from this story?

A: Leigh Botts is the main character and he was always writing letters to Mr. Henshaw.

Analytical

Q: Do you think that Cricket would have made another copy if it weren't for her competition with Zoe?

A: Answers will vary. It seems that she would have. She appears to be a true perfectionist.

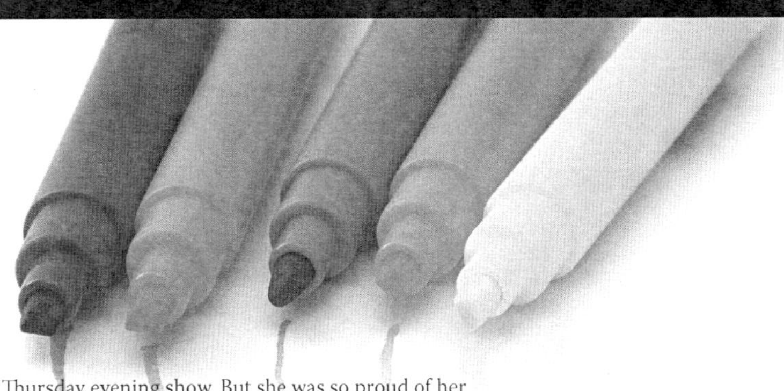

favorite Thursday evening show. But she was so proud of her completed book report that she didn't even mind. Wait until Mrs. Schraalenburgh sees my wonderful report, she thought. She knew that the teacher would have to be very impressed with her careful work. 11

The next morning Cricket proudly handed in her report.

"You didn't tell us we had to make covers," said Connie Alf when she saw Cricket's masterpiece.

"We didn't have to make covers," said Julio. Cricket looked at the paper he was putting on the teacher's desk. Wait until Mrs. Schraalenburgh saw that he had written a report about *Mr. Popper's Penguins*, which she had read to them at the beginning of September. It was cheating to write a report about a book that you hadn't even read. Listening didn't count. And besides, everyone in the class already knew about the story. Julio will be in big trouble, Cricket decided. 12

"I wrote about the book that you gave me," Zoe whispered to Cricket as she put hers in the pile. 13 "It was a great book and it was fun to write about it." She smiled at Cricket. But Cricket did not smile back. 14 It hadn't occurred to her that Zoe would use the same book that she did for her report.

"How long was your report?" Cricket asked her.

"It was all one side and a little bit of the other side of the paper," said Zoe.

Cricket began to feel better. Her report was longer and her report had a fancy cover. 15 Her report had to be a lot better than Zoe's. In fact, having another report on the same book to compare with hers would make Mrs. Schraalenburgh realize all the more how much effort Cricket had put into the assignment.

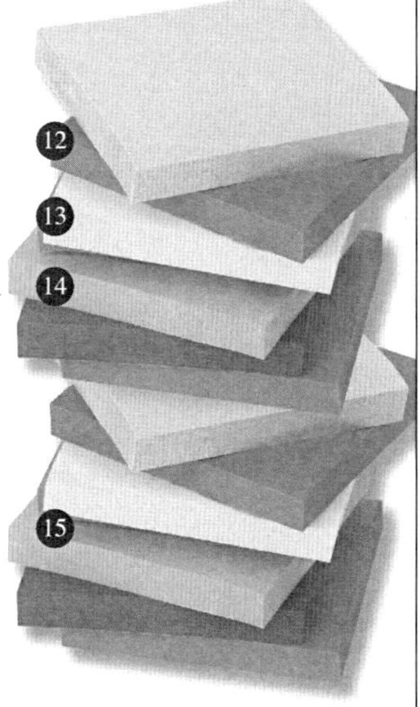

Literary Components

11 Characterization; Internal Dialogue: Cricket is a hardworking perfectionist. She knows her work is good and hopes her teacher will praise her for it.

12 Internal Dialogue: Again, Cricket's thoughts are competitive and not sympathetic to the poorer students in the class.

13 Apparent Turning Point: Suddenly, everything changes. The "easy win" that Cricket had anticipated in the race to be best turns into a face-off with her only real competitor, Zoe.

14 Characterization: The character of Zoe offers the reader a second way to excel. Although she is just as smart as Cricket, she wears her excellence with grace. She is not threatened by competition and is actually happy to have a peer.

15 Internal Dialogue: The author tells us what Cricket is thinking. Although the thoughts are given in the form of a narration, not in dialogue form, we still call this "internal dialogue."

Guiding the Reading

Literal

Q: What was Cricket thinking at the end of the evening?

A: She did not mind spending all that time on the book report. She was sure that Mrs. Schraalenburgh would be very impressed with her work.

Q: What worried Connie Alf when she saw Cricket's book report?

A: She did not know that they were required to make covers.

Q: Who told Connie that they did not need to make covers?

A: Julio told her.

Q: What book did Julio use for his book report?

A: He used *Mr. Popper's Penguins.*

Q: Why did Cricket think that Julio would be in trouble when Mrs. Schraalenburgh saw his report?

A: He had not actually read the book. Mrs. Schraalenburgh had read it aloud to the class at the beginning of the year.

Q: What did Zoe whisper to Cricket as she handed in her report?

A: Zoe told Cricket that she had used the book Cricket had given her for her book report.

Q: What was Cricket's reaction?

A: She was surprised and concerned.

Q: What made Cricket feel a little better?

A: Zoe told her that her paper was a little shorter than Cricket's and did not have a fancy cover.

Q: At the end of class, what was Cricket's feeling about the book reports?

A: She thought it might be good to have two reports on the same book. This way, her teacher would compare the two and surely think that hers was better.

Analytical

Q: Do you think that it is a good idea to compare the work of two students?

A: Answers will vary. Always ask students to support their answers. Additionally, you can ask whether they think there is an absolute answer.

Literary Components

16 Poor English: Mrs. Schraalenburgh should know better. The word "share" encompasses the word "together." Using both is redundant.

17 Rising Action: The reader waits to see what will happen.

18 Rising Action; Tension: Anyone who has been a student knows how hard it is to wait for papers to be handed back!

19 Characterization: Cricket loves the approval she works very hard to get.

20 Climax: Suddenly, all the tension, waiting, and build-up of the story come crashing down. In that one, sympathetic pat on the back, Cricket's world is—for the moment—shattered.

She smiled at Zoe. It was a good thing that they had both written about the same book, after all.

Mrs. Schraalenburgh took all the reports and put them inside her canvas tote bag. "I'll take these home to read over the weekend," she promised. "On Monday, I'll give them
16 back and we'll share them together."

17 All weekend Cricket glowed inside as she thought about her wonderful book report. She just knew that her teacher was going to love it. She couldn't wait until they were returned on Monday. Mrs. Schraalenburgh would probably write on the report how fabulous it was.

The reports were not returned to the students until after 18
lunch on Monday. Cricket could hardly sit still as the teacher walked about the room handing them back. She decided she would try and keep a straight face. It would be hard not to grin from ear to ear 19
when she was reading the teacher's comments. But on the other hand, it would look as if she were showing off when other students such as Julio got bad marks on their reports. She held her breath as Mrs. Schraalenburgh stood at her desk and sorted through the remaining papers in her hand.

"Here's yours, Cricket," said the teacher. She patted Cricket on the back. "I'm sure you'll do better next 20
time, so don't worry too much about your grade."

Cricket couldn't imagine what the teacher was referring to. There was nothing written on the red cover of her report, but when she opened it up, she saw a B– written on the top of the page. Cricket couldn't believe it. How could she possibly have gotten such a low mark? This was an A+ report. It didn't make sense. Then Cricket noticed that on the inside of the back cover, Mrs. Schraalenburgh had written a message.

258 Unit 3

Guiding the Reading

Literal

Q: What did Mrs. Schraalenburgh tell the class before she left?
A: She would read the reports at home over the weekend and return them on Monday. The students would share them with the class on Monday as well.

Q: What was Cricket thinking about all weekend?
A: She was in a good mood. She thought that her teacher would surely love her report and write a comment about how fabulous it was.

Q: When were the reports returned?
A: They got them back after lunch on Monday.

Q: What was going through Cricket's mind while waiting for Mrs. Schraalenburgh to return her report?
A: Cricket was trying to control herself. She had trouble sitting still. She did not want to give too big a grin because it might make others feel bad or look like she was showing off.

Q: What did the teacher tell Cricket when she handed her the report?
A: "I'm sure you'll do better next time, so don't worry too much about your grade."

Q: What was Cricket's reaction to Mrs. Schraalenburgh's comment?
A: She did not know what her teacher meant.

Q: What grade did Cricket get on her book report?
A: Her grade was a B minus.

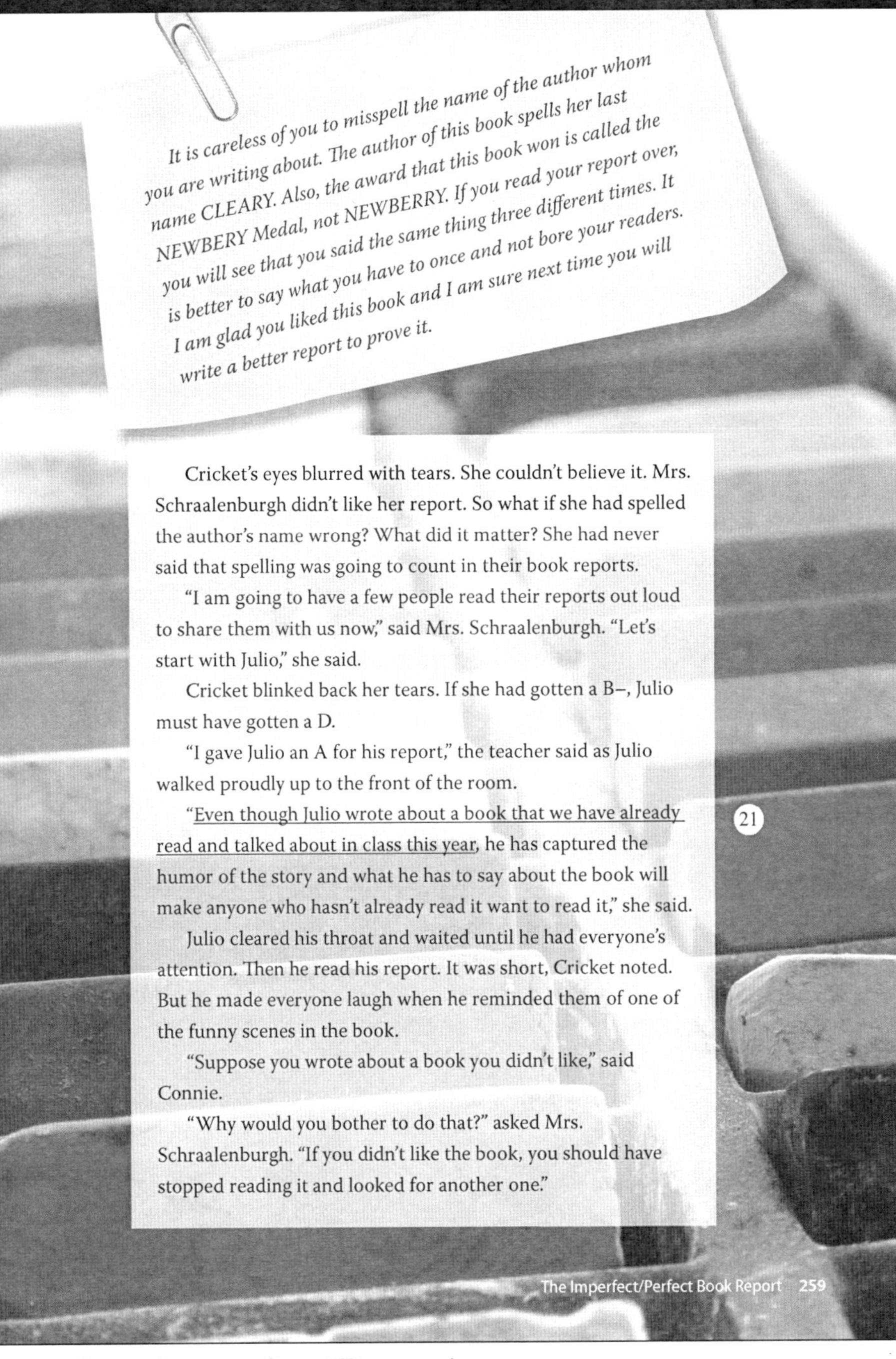

It is careless of you to misspell the name of the author whom you are writing about. The author of this book spells her last name CLEARY. Also, the award that this book won is called the NEWBERY Medal, not NEWBERRY. If you read your report over, you will see that you said the same thing three different times. It is better to say what you have to once and not bore your readers. I am glad you liked this book and I am sure next time you will write a better report to prove it.

Cricket's eyes blurred with tears. She couldn't believe it. Mrs. Schraalenburgh didn't like her report. So what if she had spelled the author's name wrong? What did it matter? She had never said that spelling was going to count in their book reports.

"I am going to have a few people read their reports out loud to share them with us now," said Mrs. Schraalenburgh. "Let's start with Julio," she said.

Cricket blinked back her tears. If she had gotten a B–, Julio must have gotten a D.

"I gave Julio an A for his report," the teacher said as Julio walked proudly up to the front of the room.

"Even though Julio wrote about a book that we have already read and talked about in class this year, he has captured the humor of the story and what he has to say about the book will make anyone who hasn't already read it want to read it," she said. 21

Julio cleared his throat and waited until he had everyone's attention. Then he read his report. It was short, Cricket noted. But he made everyone laugh when he reminded them of one of the funny scenes in the book.

"Suppose you wrote about a book you didn't like," said Connie.

"Why would you bother to do that?" asked Mrs. Schraalenburgh. "If you didn't like the book, you should have stopped reading it and looked for another one."

The Imperfect/Perfect Book Report 259

Literary Components

21 Characterization; Good Conversation

Topic: Mrs. Schraalenburgh's character is one that should be discussed. She is very intent on treating everyone equally. A boy who has written a report about a book he never read is given an A. Why? A girl who unknowingly misspelled the author's name is criticized. Is this equal treatment?

Guiding the Reading

Literal

Q: What were some of the reasons that Mrs. Schraalenburgh gave Cricket the B minus?

A: She misspelled important words, like the author's last name and the award the book received. She repeated ideas a few times.

Q: Did her teacher write anything positive in her comment?

A: Yes. "I am glad you liked this book and I am sure next time you will write a better report to prove it."

Q: What was Cricket's reaction after she read the comment?

A: Her eyes blurred with tears.

Q: What did Cricket think about spelling?

A: She did not think that it was so important and never heard her teacher say that spelling would be counted on the report.

Q: What assumption did Cricket make about Julio's report?

A: She was sure that if she'd gotten a B minus, he must have gotten a D.

Q: What grade did Julio actually receive?

A: His grade was an A.

Q: Even though Julio wrote about a book that the class had read in class, what good things did Mrs. Schraalenburgh say about his report?

A: "He has captured the humor of the story and what he has to say about the book will make anyone who hasn't already read it want to read it."

Q: How did the class react to Julio's report?

A: They laughed and enjoyed it.

Q: What did Connie ask?

A: "Suppose you wrote about a book you didn't like."

Q: What did Mrs. Schraalenburgh say that surprised the students?

A: "If you didn't like the book, you should have stopped reading."

Analytical

Q: Why did Cricket make these simple mistakes?

A: She did not have the book in front of her when she wrote the report.

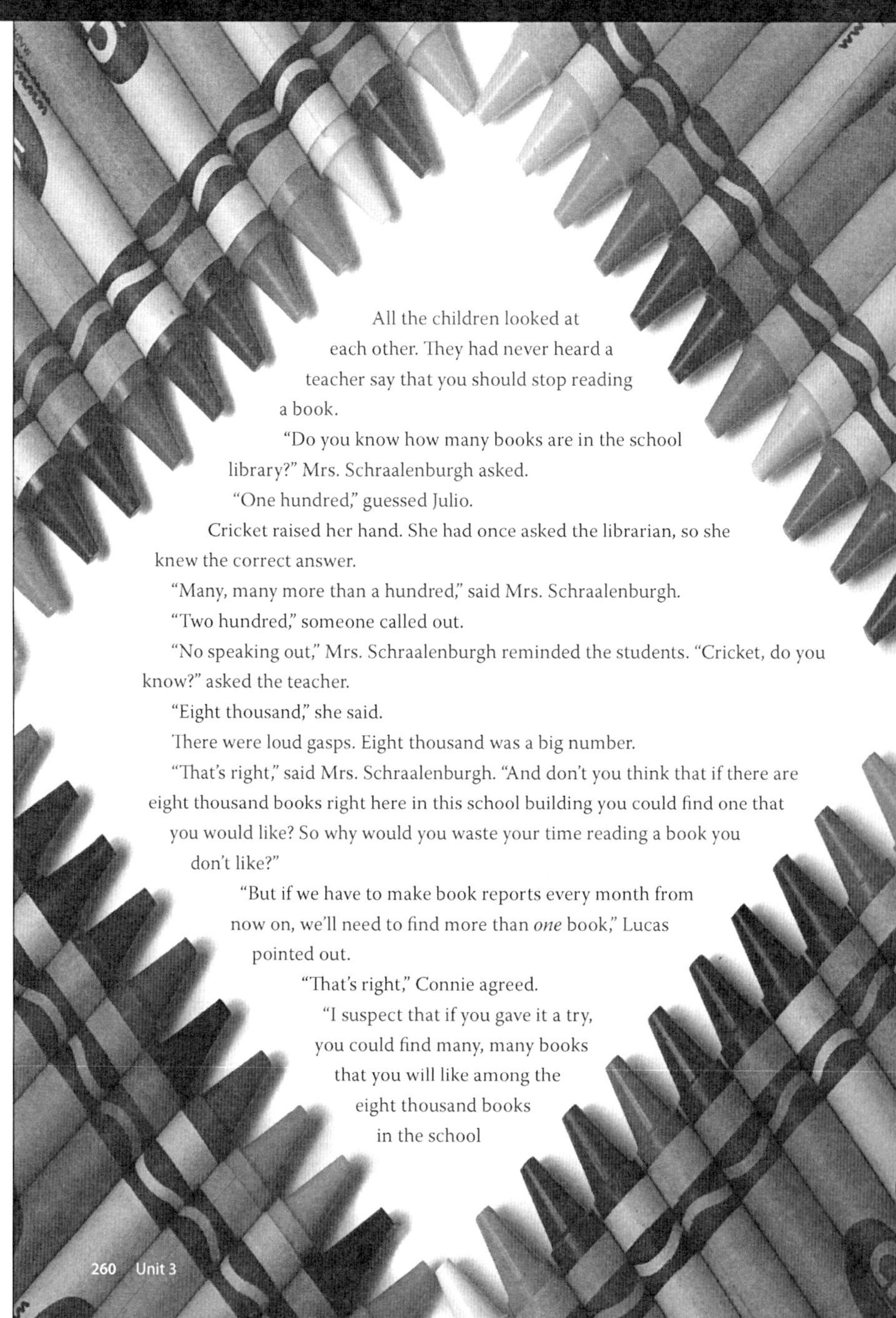

Guiding the Reading

Literal

Q: How many books were in the school library?

A: There were eight thousand books.

Q: How did Cricket know how many there were when her classmates guessed much lower numbers?

A: She had once asked the librarian.

Q: Why did Mrs. Schraalenburgh ask the class about the library books?

A: She wanted to show them how many choices there are in books and to assure them that they could find one that they liked!

Q: What complaint did Lucas have?

A: They did not have to find only one book that they liked, but one book a month for their book reports.

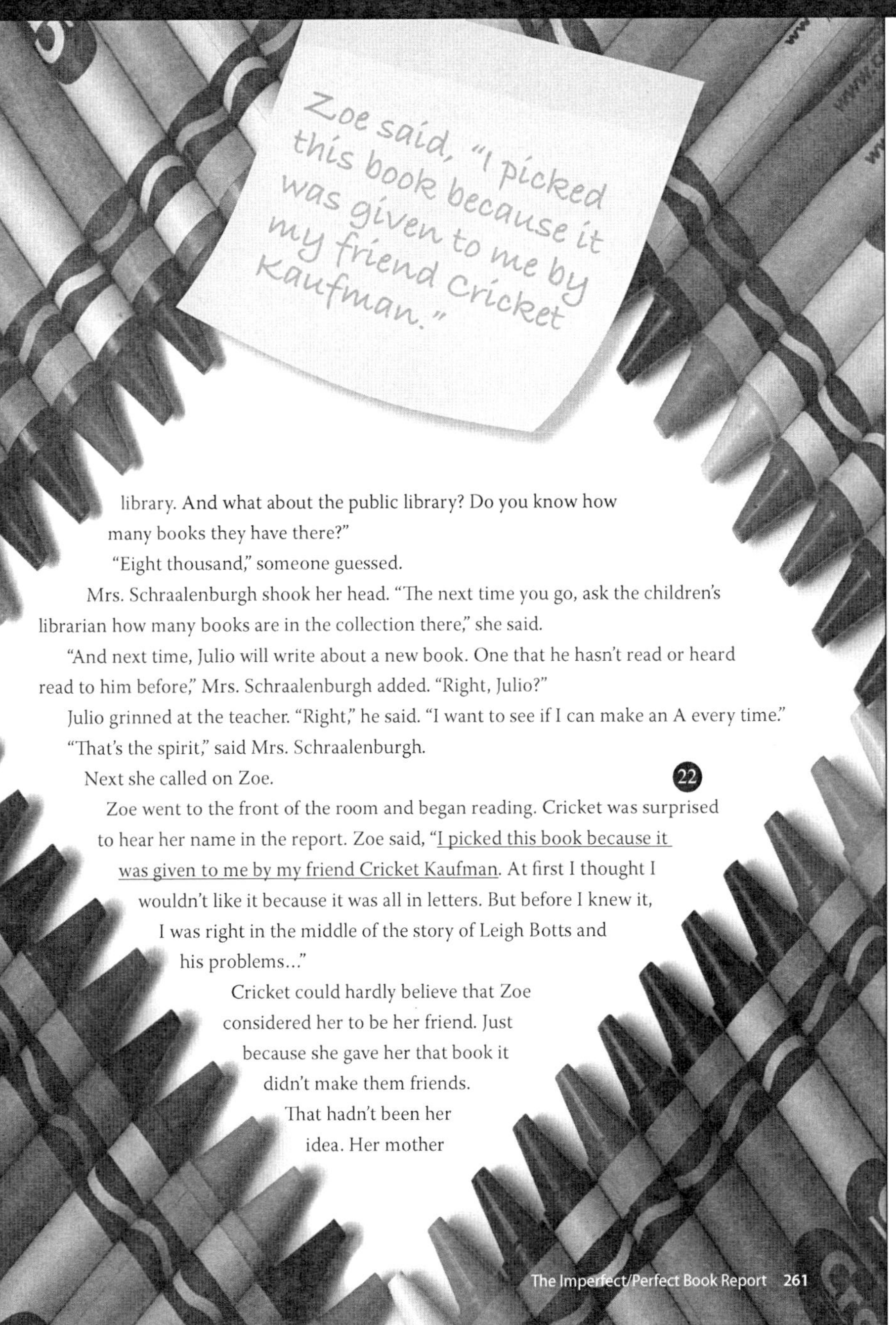

library. And what about the public library? Do you know how many books they have there?"

"Eight thousand," someone guessed.

Mrs. Schraalenburgh shook her head. "The next time you go, ask the children's librarian how many books are in the collection there," she said.

"And next time, Julio will write about a new book. One that he hasn't read or heard read to him before," Mrs. Schraalenburgh added. "Right, Julio?"

Julio grinned at the teacher. "Right," he said. "I want to see if I can make an A every time."

"That's the spirit," said Mrs. Schraalenburgh.

Next she called on Zoe. (22)

Zoe went to the front of the room and began reading. Cricket was surprised to hear her name in the report. Zoe said, "I picked this book because it was given to me by my friend Cricket Kaufman. At first I thought I wouldn't like it because it was all in letters. But before I knew it, I was right in the middle of the story of Leigh Botts and his problems..."

Cricket could hardly believe that Zoe considered her to be her friend. Just because she gave her that book it didn't make them friends. That hadn't been her idea. Her mother

The Imperfect/Perfect Book Report 261

Literary Components

(22) **Characterization:** Again, Zoe is pictured as an easygoing, generous spirit who has no calculating side to her.

Guiding the Reading

Literal

Q: Did anyone know how many books there were in the public library?

A: No. Mrs. Schraalenburgh said that they should ask the librarian next time they go to the library.

Q: What did Julio plan to do for his next book report?

A: He planned to write about a new book and try to get an A.

Q: Who was the next person to read a book report aloud?

A: Zoe was next.

Q: Why was Cricket's name mentioned in Zoe's report?

A: Zoe told the class that Cricket had given her the book she was going to talk about.

Q: Why did Zoe think she would not like the book at first?

A: It was all in letter form.

Q: What did Zoe say that surprised Cricket?

A: She could not believe that Zoe called her a friend in public. It was her mother's idea to give the book to Zoe and that did not mean that she was Zoe's friend.

Literary Components

23 **Characterization:** Cricket's first priority is not the truth.

24 **Theme:** The author wants to make a point here about "overachievers." Again, this point can certainly be discussed. Aren't most great accomplishments done by people who "go the extra mile," who work to make their job stand out even if no "extra credit" is guaranteed?

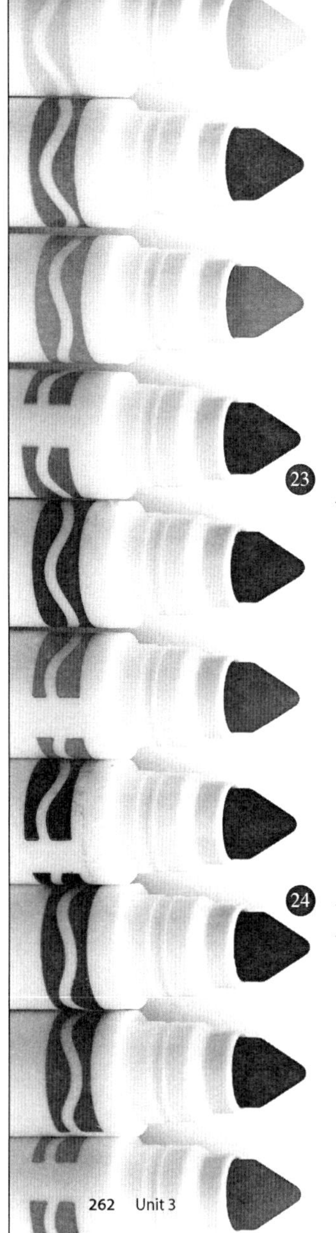

had insisted that she bring a gift when she went to Zoe's party. And now Zoe had gotten an A writing about it when Cricket had only got a B–. It just didn't seem fair.

Zoe finished reading her report. "How many people want to read that book, now that they have heard about it?" asked Mrs. Schraalenburgh.

Every hand in the class except Cricket's went up.

"Now you know why Zoe got an A on her report. She has done an excellent job of sharing her pleasure with all of us. I notice that Cricket didn't raise her hand. But she doesn't have to read the book. She already did," said the teacher, smiling at Cricket. "And when she gave a copy of it to Zoe as a present, she was sharing her pleasure of the book in still another way."

23 Cricket could have said that when she bought the book for Zoe, she hadn't even read it yet. But she didn't. She liked what Mrs. Schraalenburgh said about her sharing the pleasure of the book by giving it as a present. It almost made up for the bad mark she got.

Mrs. Schraalenburgh wrote Beverly Cleary's name on the chalkboard so that everyone could copy it and said, "Now when you go to the library, you'll know who the author is." Cricket blushed to see the correct spelling on the board. It had really been foolish on her part to write a book report when she didn't have the book right in front of her to copy the author's name. She wouldn't make that mistake again.

A few other students read their book reports too. Cricket noticed that none of them had made covers for their reports. 24 It had been silly of her to waste her time making a fancy cover if Mrs. Schraalenburgh didn't give her extra credit for it.

"There isn't time to read any more reports," said Mrs. Schraalenburgh after a while. "This was just to get us started. Next month, we will have oral book reports and everyone will have a turn. So start looking for a good book to read. Don't wait until the last minute."

The bell rang for dismissal. Zoe edged over to Cricket. "Thanks again for the book," she said.

262 Unit 3

Guiding the Reading

Literal

Q: What seemed unfair to Cricket?
A: It seemed unfair that Zoe and Cricket used the same book but received different grades.

Q: How many people wanted to read *Dear Mr. Henshaw* after hearing Zoe's report?
A: Everyone raised their hand indicating that they wanted to read it, except for Cricket.

Q: Why was Mrs. Schraalenburgh smiling when Cricket did not raise her hand?
A: Mrs. Schraalenburgh assumed that Cricket did not raise her hand because she had already read it. Her teacher knew this because she had graded Cricket's report.

Q: Why didn't Cricket tell her teacher the truth about why she'd given Zoe the book?
A: She liked what Mrs. Schraalenburgh said about sharing her enjoyment of the book by giving it as a present.

Q: What was Cricket feeling when Mrs. Schraalenburgh wrote Beverly Cleary's name on the board?
A: She felt embarrassed and foolish that she had not spelled the author's name correctly on the cover of her report.

Q: Why did Cricket change her opinion about her creative cover?
A: She realized that no one else had made one and Mrs. Schraalenburgh did not give her extra credit for it. She was silly to have wasted her time because she still got the B minus.

Q: Why did the class stop reading book reports after Zoe finished hers?
A: Mrs. Schraalenburgh told the class that next month they would have an oral book report where everyone would have to read aloud. This month's reading was just to get everyone started.

Q: What suggestion did Mrs. Schraalenburgh have for the upcoming book report?
A: She suggested that they not wait until the last minute to choose a good book.

Q: What did Zoe say to Cricket at the end of class?
A: She thanked her for the book again.

Analytical

Q: Which students would probably listen closely to Mrs. Schraalenburgh's advice?
A: Julio and Cricket would prepare differently for their next book report.

Cricket nodded her head. She was relieved that Zoe didn't ask her what grade she had gotten on her report. If the situation had been reversed and Cricket had received an A and Zoe had not read her report aloud, Cricket knew she would have been dying to ask. 25

"I'll bet we have the same taste in books," said Zoe. "Maybe we could go to the library together after school sometime. You could show me the books you've read and I could show you the ones I've read."

Cricket found herself smiling at Zoe. It sounded as if it might be fun. There had never been another girl in school who liked to read as much as she did. Maybe Zoe was right. Maybe she would be a friend to her. 26

"Okay," she agreed. And suddenly, it didn't matter so much what grade she had gotten on her report. Next time she would get an A. And if Zoe got one too, it wouldn't be so terrible. After all, they were the two smartest girls in Mrs. Schraalenburgh's class. 27

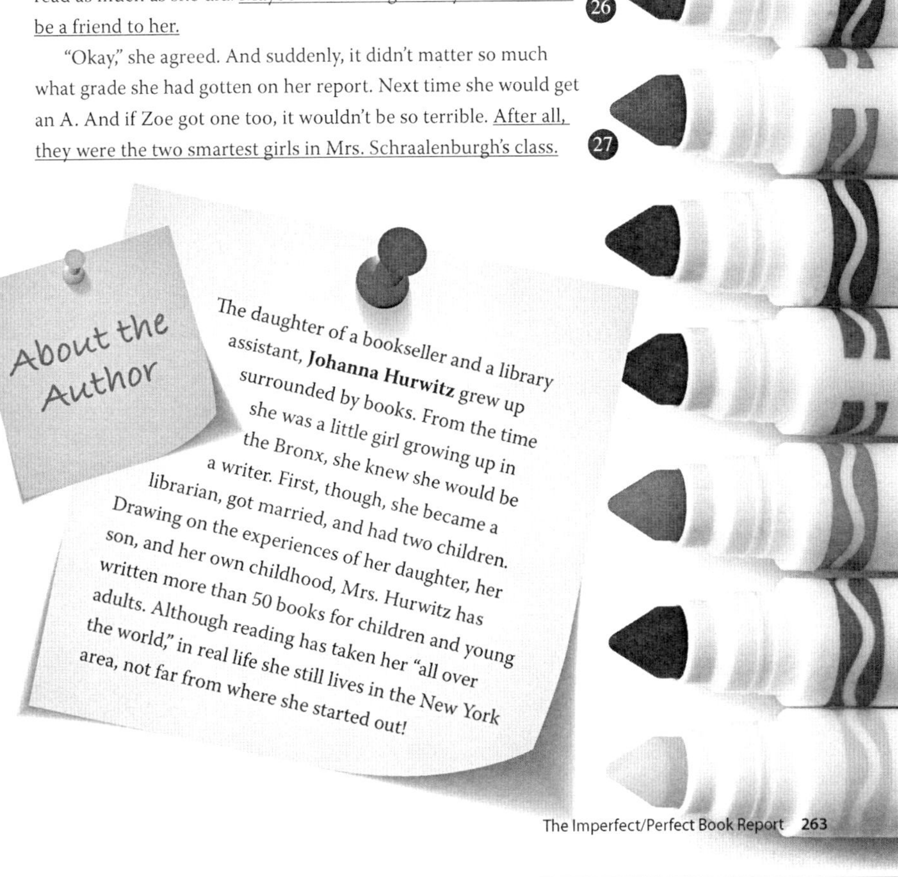

About the Author

The daughter of a bookseller and a library assistant, **Johanna Hurwitz** grew up surrounded by books. From the time she was a little girl growing up in the Bronx, she knew she would be a writer. First, though, she became a librarian, got married, and had two children. Drawing on the experiences of her daughter, her son, and her own childhood, Mrs. Hurwitz has written more than 50 books for children and young adults. Although reading has taken her "all over the world," in real life she still lives in the New York area, not far from where she started out!

Literary Components

25 Internal Dialogue; Dawning Self-Awareness: The author tells us what Cricket is thinking and that she realizes that Zoe is a whole lot nicer than she is!

26 Resolution: The story comes to a close as Cricket realizes that being at the top can be lonely, and having some company there can be rewarding.

27 Theme: Has Cricket learned her lesson or not? She is still highly competitive. She is just willing, now, to share the top spot with one other person. Will she continue to hope everyone else does poorly? Will she influence Zoe?

Guiding the Reading

Literal

Q: Why was Cricket relieved?

A: She was glad that Zoe did not ask her what grade she'd gotten on the book report.

Q: What did Zoe think she had in common with Cricket?

A: She thought that both girls had the same taste in books.

Q: What suggestion did Zoe have?

A: The girls should go to the library together and show each other good books that they had read.

Q: What sounded like fun to Cricket?

A: She liked the thought of becoming friends with someone who liked to read as much as she did.

Q: What would happen next time if both Cricket and Zoe received an A on their book report?

A: It would not be so terrible since they were both the smartest girls in the class.

Analytical

Q: Why does the author use the words, "Cricket found herself smiling at Zoe"?

A: Cricket did not expect that she would react with pleasure to any of Zoe's comments. She had been upset with her. She just found herself smiling.

Q: Why didn't it matter what grade she had received on the book report?

A: She liked the idea of being Zoe's friend. She knew she would get an A the next time, and she knew she would remain at the top of the class. She was willing to share the top spot with Zoe because she realized that having someone who is your equal can be enjoyable, and lead to many shared good times.

About You and I

Poetry Is About You and Me

An infant knows only his own needs. As the infant grows into a toddler, he becomes aware of others as distinct entities. As the toddler develops, he has a growing awareness that others have needs. We could almost define maturity as the extent to which a person recognizes that

"... every you is an I to itself"

This poem's message can be looked at as a psychological truth,

"Every you everywhere in the world is an I;

Every I in the world is a you!"

but it also has ethical significance. One who truly recognizes that *you are an I*, will "love his fellow man as himself," and see all men as his brothers:

"It makes us both the same somehow"

Trying to imagine what it is like to be someone else is a fascinating exercise. Writers in particular must do this to create characters with depth. But it is also an exercise we should all do for the many benefits it brings. It helps us to understand others, to sympathize with them, to avoid judging them, to rejoice with them, and to grieve with them. It helps us to be as one with them without losing an iota of our own uniqueness.

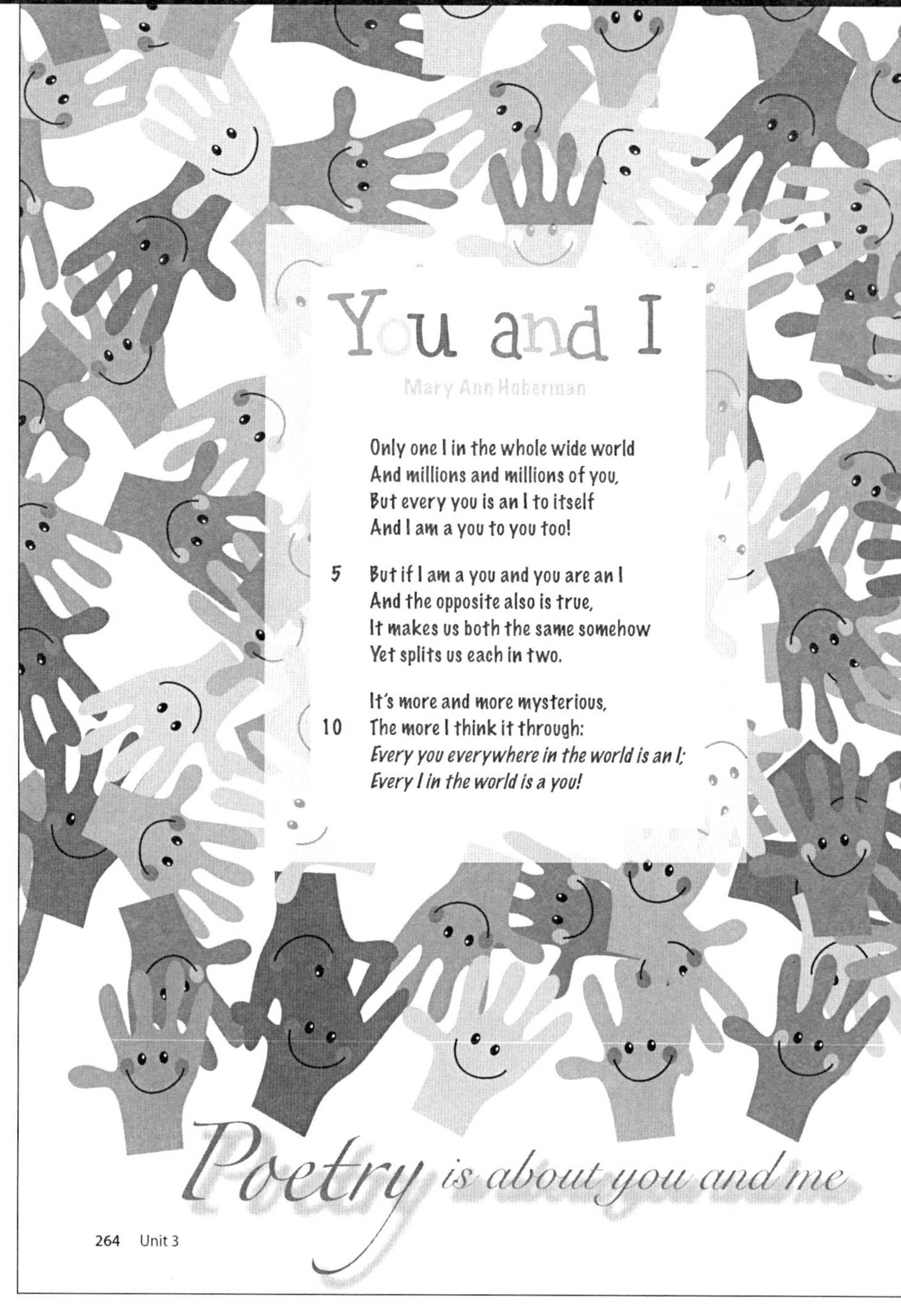

You and I

Mary Ann Hoberman

Only one I in the whole wide world
And millions and millions of you,
But every you is an I to itself
And I am a you to you too!

But if I am a you and you are an I
And the opposite also is true,
It makes us both the same somehow
Yet splits us each in two.

It's more and more mysterious,
The more I think it through:
Every you everywhere in the world is an I;
Every I in the world is a you!

Poetry is about you and me

264 Unit 3

Studying the Selection

FIRST IMPRESSIONS

Do you think Cricket was the only one competing, or were other students, such as Zoe or Julio, also in competition with each other?

QUICK REVIEW

1. Which two girls were the smartest in Mrs. Schraalenburgh's class?
2. How did things change for Cricket when Zoe joined her class?
3. What book did both girls use for their book report?
4. Why did Cricket receive a much lower grade than she expected?

FOCUS

5. Why, at the end of the story, did Cricket feel it didn't matter so much what grade she had gotten on her report?
6. "Wait until Mrs. Schraalenburgh sees my wonderful report, she thought." What does this line of internal dialogue tell us about Cricket? Why is it important to the story?

CREATING AND WRITING

7. Write about a time that you had a positive or negative experience competing with a classmate or a sibling.
8. Write about a child your age who moves to a new town. The child will be the main character in your story. Your main character meets a new neighbor of the same age, and immediately thinks that they cannot be friends. Later on this changes. Your story should include answers for some of the following questions:
   - Why did the main character move to a new town?
   - What was it that made the main character think that the neighbor could not be their friend?
   - What was it that made the neighbor seem unfriendly?
   - What did the neighbor think about the main character?
   - Do some of the feelings change? How and why?

   Try to use internal dialogue in your story to help answer these questions.
9. Your teacher will give you a piece of cardboard that looks like a book cover. Write the title and author of a book you would like to recommend to your classmates on your cover. Add an illustration and one or two sentences telling why you think that your classmates would like this book. Put the finished book cover on the bulletin board for everyone to enjoy.

First Impressions

The story doesn't give us too many clues, however, it is likely that everyone was competing at some level, because that is the nature of most groups. Because grades are given in school, competition is almost inevitable in the classroom.

Quick Review

1. Cricket and Zoe were the smartest girls in the class.
2. Cricket was used to being the smartest from the time she was in kindergarten. She was not accustomed to sharing the spotlight or having any competitors.
3. They both used *Dear Mr. Henshaw* for their book reports.
4. She did not spell the author's name correctly and was repetitious in her writing. The fact that she did not use the actual book prevented her from doing a better job.

Focus

5. Cricket had recognized that while grades were important, there were other things of value. She recognized the importance of Julio's efforts, the need to be responsible and accurate, Mrs. Schraalenburgh's understanding, and friendship. She anticipated a new friendship with a friend who also enjoyed reading—a friend who was her equal. She also realized that competition, to the degree in which she displayed it, was not beneficial.
6. This line of internal dialogue is important because it reveals Cricket's competitive and egotistical nature. It also provides a hint (foreshadowing) that something is going to happen to deflate Cricket.

Creating and Writing

7. Answers will vary.
8. Answers will vary. Encourage your students to use the technique of internal dialogue to tell their story and reveal their characters' thoughts.
9. Provide your students with book-shaped cutouts or have the students make their own from colorful poster board. Each student should write the title and author of a book they would like to recommend on their 'book' (spelled correctly, of course). They should include an illustration and one or two sentences that summarize why they would highly recommend this book to others. You may choose to ask each student to create more than one 'book.' Another option would be to keep the bulletin board up and continue to add to it throughout the year.

Point of View

Beyond the Mountains

1. The story is told through a narrator.
2. Answers will vary.
3. Anthony and the narrator may be the same person. If they are not, Anthony has shared his thoughts with the narrator and it is clear that the narrator's point of view is the same as Anthony's.

Lesson in Literature . . .

BEYOND THE MOUNTAINS

POINT OF VIEW

- A story's point of view depends on who is telling the story.
- Sometimes a story is told from the narrator's point of view.
- Most nonfiction works are written from the narrator's point of view.
- In works of fiction, a story may be told from a character's point of view.

THINK ABOUT IT!

1. Is this story told only through a narrator, or is dialogue used to reveal some of the plot?
2. In the second paragraph, we learn how Anthony felt about his host family. Write two sentences to describe Anthony's visit from the point of view of the host family.
3. In your opinion, do the narrator and Anthony have the same point of view? Explain your answer.

Vocabulary

battered (BAT erd) *adj.*: damaged by rough and careless treatment

passion (PASH un) *n.*: an enthusiasm for something

realign (REE uh LYN) *v.*: to return to their proper position

tooling (TOOL ing) *v.*: driving or riding in a vehicle

semicircular (SEM ee SUR kyuh lur) *adj.*: shaped like half of a circle

pirouettes (PEER oo ETS) *n.*: a dance step in which the dancer whirls about on one foot

interchangeable (IN tur CHAYNGE uh bul) *adj.*: two things that can be used in place of one another

proposal (pruh PO zul) *n.*: a suggested plan

gingerly (JIN jur lee) *adv.*: with great care

inspired (in SPY ehrd) *v.*: filled with a sense of purpose

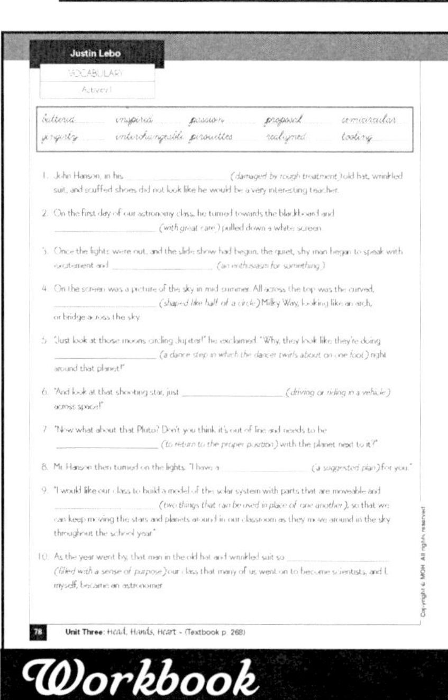

Justin Lebo

VOCABULARY

Activity I

battered	inspired	passion	proposal	semicircular
gingerly	interchangeable	pirouettes	realigned	tooling

1. John Hanson, in his ________________ (*damaged by rough treatment*) old hat, wrinkled suit, and scuffed shoes did not look like he would be a very interesting teacher.
2. On the first day of our astronomy class, he turned towards the blackboard and ________________ (*with great care*) pulled down a white screen.
3. Once the lights were out, and the slide show had begun, the quiet, shy man began to speak with excitement and ________________ (*an enthusiasm for something*).
4. On the screen was a picture of the sky in mid summer. All across the top was the curved, ________________ (*shaped like half of a circle*) Milky Way, looking like an arch, or bridge across the sky.
5. "Just look at those moons circling Jupiter!" he exclaimed. "Why, they look like they're doing ________________ (*a dance step in which the dancer twirls about on one foot*) right around that planet!"
6. "And look at that shooting star, just ________________ (*driving or riding in a vehicle*) across space!"
7. "Now what about that Pluto? Don't you think it's out of line and needs to be ________________ (*to return to the proper position*) with the planet next to it?"
8. Mr. Hanson then turned on the lights. "I have a ________________ (*a suggested plan*) for you."
9. "I would like our class to build a model of the solar system with parts that are moveable and ________________ (*two things that can be used in place of one another*), so that we can keep moving the stars and planets around in our classroom as they move around in the sky throughout the school year."
10. As the year went by, that man in the old hat and wrinkled suit so ________________ (*filled with a sense of purpose*) our class that many of us went on to become scientists, and I, myself, became an astronomer.

78 Unit Three: Head, Hands, Heart ~ (Textbook p. 268)

Workbook

Justin Lebo

VOCABULARY

Activity II

Name ________________________________

Who? What? Where? When? Why? And How?

1. *Where* would you wear your **battered** hat?
   a. to a family picnic and baseball game
   b. to an elegant wedding reception
2. *What* are you more likely to have a **passion** for?
   a. calcium with vitamin D in pill form
   b. chocolate ice cream with whipped cream
3. *What*, on your family's car, might need to be **realigned**?
   a. the paint job
   b. the wheels
4. *Who* might you see **tooling** around?
   a. a little boy on a bike
   b. a handyman repairing your roof
5. *Why* would one want a **semicircular** driveway?
   a. so that a driver does not need to back out
   b. so that the surface will never need fixing
6. *Who* can be seen doing **pirouettes**?
   a. a musician
   b. a dancer
7. *How* can you tell if two parts are **interchangeable**?
   a. if the instructions tell you they are
   b. if the instructions warn you not to use one part in place of another
8. *Where* would one hear a **proposal**?
   a. on a radio station that plays old favorites
   b. in a meeting of people looking for a new idea for their business
9. *What* would you handle **gingerly**?
   a. a football
   b. a rattlesnake
10. *Why* might you feel **inspired**?
    a. because you just heard a good speech
    b. because you just caught the flu

Unit Three: Head, Hands, Heart ~ (Textbook p. 268) 79

Workbook

Anthony didn't know what to expect when his airplane landed in Managua, Nicaragua. He had lived his whole life in the United States, and this trip was the first time he had ever set foot in a foreign country. He was nervous. All he knew about Nicaragua was that it was a Central American country between Honduras and Costa Rica and the Pacific Ocean and the Caribbean Sea. Would he understand the people? Would the people understand him? How could he possibly understand anything about a poor country in Central America?

The first thing Anthony observed was the beauty of Nicaragua. As his group of college students traveled in the capital city of Managua, he noticed the magnificent mountains surrounding the city. In the city he saw big houses where wealthy people lived, but he also saw many shacks on the outskirts of the city where poor people lived. He saw something else, too. The Nicaraguan people, rich and poor, were just like the people he knew at home in the United States. The family that hosted him for two nights during his stay in Managua seemed a lot like his own family back home.

When Anthony and his group traveled into the country, a poor farming family hosted them for two nights. In the country Anthony met families that lived together in very small houses. He met hardworking parents, mostly mothers, who cooked, worked in the fields, and took care of their children. He met children who worked alongside their mothers and who loved to play games with visitors. Despite their circumstances, Anthony understood that these poor people were like anybody he might meet in his hometown in the United States. Although they spoke Spanish and didn't own as many possessions as most Americans, the people he met were full of love and life. He began to feel a strong attachment to the people of Nicaragua.

Anthony, though, was most impressed by something else he saw in Nicaragua. When his group visited an orphanage for handicapped children, he was surprised by the large number of children who lived there. When he realized that they had no homes and no families, he was even more surprised by their friendliness, joy, and excitement when visitors arrived. Anthony didn't think he would ever forget the little girl who took him by the hand to show him around the orphanage.

On his way to the airport, just before he left Nicaragua, Anthony caught another glimpse of the mountains. At the beginning of his trip, he thought his lasting memory of Nicaragua would be the beauty of those mountains, but at the end of his trip he knew differently. His lasting memory of Nicaragua would be the beauty of its people. He would never forget their kindness, friendliness, and hospitality. *Someday,* he thought, *I'll come back to Nicaragua. Someday, I'll come back.*

Justin Lebo 267

Unit Theme: *Head, Hands, Heart*

Target Skill: *Recognize and identify point of view. Who is telling the story?*

Genre: *Nonfiction Article*

Getting Started

Read aloud through page 272 until the words, "Maybe he could do more..."

1. How old was Justin Lebo?
   a. seventeen
   b. ten
   c. fourteen
   d. twelve and a half
2. What was Justin's hobby?
   a. ice hockey
   b. stamp collecting
   c. photography
   d. bike racing
3. Where did Justin buy his old bikes?
   a. at garage sales
   b. through advertisements
   c. at city hall auctions for lost and abandoned bikes
   d. at major bike shop sales
4. Which sentence best describes the Lebo garage?
   a. It looked like a dinosaur's home.
   b. There were tools of almost every kind.
   c. It looked like a bike shop.
   d. The old rocking chair and scrap of carpet made it cozy.
5. What did Justin do when he got really stuck on repairs?
   a. He went to Mel at the bike shop.
   b. He asked his older brother for help.
   c. He put the bicycle aside and went to work on the next one.
   d. He looked for a solution in his many books about bikes.
6. What did Justin call the old bikes that he bought at garage sales?
   a. oldies
   b. stale wheels
   c. race gems
   d. junkers
7. What was the name of the place that Justin called about donating bikes?
   a. Home Away from Home
   b. Kilbarchan Home for Boys
   c. Boys' Town of America
   d. Annie Oakley Home for Boys
8. How did Justin know about this place?
   a. A classmate lived at the home.
   b. He once saw it advertised on the bus.
   c. He used to live near the home.
   d. He just picked it out of the phone book.
9. What happened when Justin and his mother went back to the car after delivering the first two bikes?
   a. They realized that they were low on gas.
   b. The boys tried to return the bikes.
   c. They decided to go for pizza after all that hard work.
   d. They watched the boys carry the bikes into the building.
10. How did Justin feel after he gave away the bicycles?
    a. happy and satisfied
    b. tired and proud
    c. angry and frustrated
    d. responsible and smart

Into . . . Justin Lebo

People tend to believe that material possessions will bring them happiness. Although this is true up to a point, it is a truism that as wealth increases the "happiness returns" diminish. John B. Rockefeller (1839-1937), a well-known millionaire, once said, "I have made many millions but they have brought me little happiness." Multi-millionaire Andrew Carnegie is quoted as saying, "Millionaires rarely smile." Whether wealth brings happiness and, if it does, how much, is a popular subject of discussion, especially among the less-than-wealthy.

What almost everyone *will* agree on is that giving of oneself will ultimately bring the giver a deep-felt satisfaction. Everyone has the ability to give something to someone somewhere at some time. Having successfully made some contribution, people tend to cultivate the giving habit, a testimony to the pleasure that comes with giving. Performing a selfless act does not require risking one's life. It is simply doing something kind without thought to personal gain. Having extra money is not a prerequisite to helping people. There are many opportunities to help others with one's talents, abilities, and resources. (See *Studying the Selection*, #7.) Ask your students to think of opportunities for helping in various ways. Use Justin Lebo as a starting point. Children can do wonders by singing to the elderly or helping a small child on the school bus. Those who are studious and organized can provide a reminder board or tutoring for upcoming tests. Students who have a good sense of humor can help cheer up those who are ill. Anyone with artistic skills can send get-well cards to others, and so on. Some students may suggest major projects, but that is not the goal of this discussion. Explain that taking a few extra minutes to say "Good morning" to a homebound neighbor or "hello" to a new student—especially a lonely or less popular one—is the kind of daily giving we are aiming for.

Eyes On Point of View

Point of view is fun to explain. Make up two or three situations, humorous or serious, and encourage your students to describe them from various points of view. A simple example: a snowstorm. Ask one student to be a mail carrier; one to be a ten-year-old; one to be a bride whose wedding is scheduled for the day of the snowstorm; one to be a principal; and one to be the owner of a snowplow. Tell each to describe the snowstorm from his or her point of view. As you can see, the possibilities are endless!

Tell your students that most stories are told by a narrator with an apparently objective or neutral point of view. But that is not always the case; a narrator can be biased. Again, you can play a game with them having various narrators telling the same story from varying points of view. Finally, explain that in some stories the words, thoughts, or actions of characters help tell the story. Those words, thoughts, or actions give the reader a second point of view.

Blueprint for Reading

INTO . . . *Justin Lebo*

What does it mean to be *selfless*? The suffix *-less* means "without," or "not having." Care*less* means without care. Hope*less* means without hope. Self*less* means without self, without thinking of *yourself*. When you are selfless, you put someone or something before yourself. The *someone* may be a friend, a parent, or anyone who needs your help. The *something* may be an organization that needs your support. But being selfless does not mean that you give everything and get nothing. As you read, see if you can understand what Justin gained from being selfless and giving.

EYES ON *Point of View*

A birthday party was held at the home of four-year-old Brian Melton. When his father came home, Brian ran to the door and said, "Daddy! You missed all the fun! A bottle of red soda exploded when we opened it and got all over everything! The kids said it was the best party ever!" When Mr. Melton walked into the kitchen, Mrs. Melton said, "Jim, this was the worst birthday party I have ever given! A bottle of red soda exploded and ruined my carpet." As Mrs. Melton was sighing, Brian's older sister, Joannie, walked in looking bored. "Mom, I don't know how you put up with those little kids. All they do is eat and run around." Mr. Melton wrinkled his brow. He couldn't figure it out. It sounded as though there had been three different parties in his house: an exciting one, a terrible one, and a boring one! Which one was it?

The answer is, of course, that the party was all three—exciting, terrible, and boring—depending on your **point of view**. Your *point of view* is the way you look at a situation. As you read *Justin Lebo*, see if you can identify the point of view from which the story is being told.

WORD BANK

battered (BAT erd) *adj.*: damaged by rough and careless treatment

passion (PASH un) *n.*: an enthusiasm for something

268 Unit 3

Something about the battered old bicycle at the garage sale caught ten-year-old Justin Lebo's eye. What a wreck! It was like looking at a few big bones in the dust and trying to figure out what kind of dinosaur they had once belonged to. 1 2

It was a BMX bike with a twenty-inch frame. Its original color was buried beneath five or six coats of gunky paint. Now it showed up as sort of a rusted red. Everything—the grips, the pedals, the brakes, the seat, the spokes—were bent or broken, twisted and rusted. Justin stood back as if he were inspecting a painting for sale at an auction. Then he made his final judgment: perfect. 3

Justin talked the owner down to $6.50 and asked his mother, Diane, to help him load the bike into the back of their car.

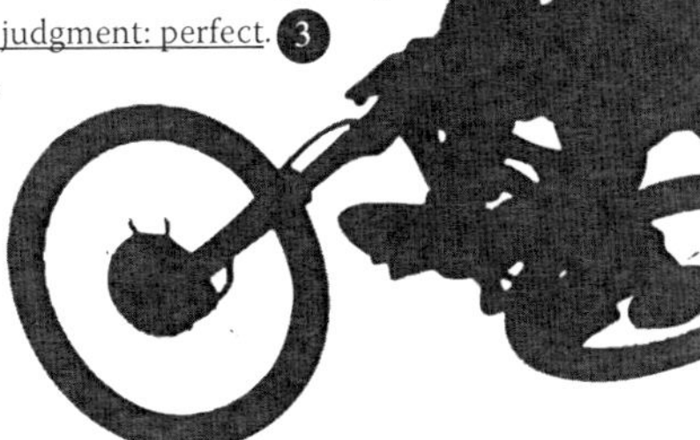

When he got it home he wheeled the junker into
4 the garage and showed it proudly to his father. "Will you help me fix it up?" he asked. Justin's hobby was bike racing, a passion the two of them shared. Their

Justin Lebo 269

Selection Summary

Justin Lebo is a ten-year-old boy who lives in Patterson, New Jersey. As the story opens, Justin is at a garage sale, trying to talk the owner of a battered, bent, and broken bike into selling it to him for $6.50. What will Justin do with it? He and his father will spend many happy hours restoring the bike. After they restore two such bikes, they decide to donate them to the children of Kilbarchan Home for Boys. The bikes are vastly appreciated by the boys—and a hobby is born. Justin resolves to restore a used bike for every boy in the home before the year is out. He has six months to make nineteen bikes.

Justin becomes a one-boy foundation. He asks his parents to provide matching funds for his own donations. He drafts his mother to drive him to garage sales and thrift shops. He works for hours taking apart old bikes and putting the useable parts together to make new bikes. Time is running out and he has completed only ten bikes. Justin gets a break when a neighbor writes a letter to a local newspaper describing Justin's project. The paper does a story on Justin and "overnight," everything changes. Bikes and money begin to flow in. Bike-building help materializes in the form of Mel, the bike shop owner. Justin beats his deadline, bringing joy to the boys in the home and inspiration to all who hear of his project.

Justin does not stop when his project is complete. He takes on new challenges, volunteering to make bikes for a series of groups and causes. Making other people happy makes him happy. And, in his words, "that's why I do it."

Guiding the Reading

Literal

Q: How old was Justin Lebo?
A: He was ten years old.

Q: What caught Justin's eye at the garage sale?
A: He saw a battered old bicycle.

Q: What kind of bike was it?
A: It was a BMX with a twenty-inch frame. Buried beneath several layers of paint, the original color was red. Almost every part of the bike was bent or broken.

Q: What did Justin ask his father when he arrived home with the old bike?
A: He asked his father to help him fix it.

Q: What hobby did Justin and his Dad share?
A: They had a passion for bike racing.

Analytical

Q: What is a *junker*?
A: It is something that is essentially junk, ready to be thrown out, but can be used for parts or perhaps even rebuilt.

Q: Was $6.50 the original price at the garage sale?
A: No. Justin "talked the owner down," which means he convinced him to lower the price.

Literary Components

1 **Setting; Characterization:** From the opening line, we learn that the setting is somewhere in the United States in modern times. Justin Lebo appears to be an ordinary ten-year-old who likes old bikes.

2 **Simile:** This is a wonderful example of a simile. Point out the phrase "it was like," as the indicator for a simile.

3 **Rising Action; Narrative Voice:** The reader becomes curious about why Justin finds battered bikes "perfect," and wants to read on. An unseen narrator will tell the story.

4 **Characterization:** Justin's parents seem to be good people and we see how well he gets along with both of them.

Literary Components

5 Narrative Voice; Background: The narrator interrupts the action to catch us up on the background to the story.

6 Characterization: Justin is someone who continuously strives to outdo himself. He is independent and likes to handle problems himself, if possible.

7 Minor Theme: Justin's excellent relationship with his parents is a backdrop to the action.

5 garage barely had room for the car anymore. It was more like a bike shop. Tires and frames hung from hooks on the ceiling, and bike wrenches dangled from the walls.

After every race, Justin and his father would adjust the brakes and realign the wheels of his two racing bikes. This was a lot of work, 6 since Justin raced flat out, challenging every gear and part to perform to its fullest. He had learned to handle almost every repair his father could and maybe even a few things he couldn't. When Justin got really stuck, he went to see Mel, the owner of the best bike shop in town. Mel let him hang out and watch, and he even grunted a few syllables of advice from between the spokes of a wheel now and then.

WORD BANK

realign (REE uh LYN) *v.*: to return to their proper position

7 Now Justin and his father cleared out a work space in the garage and put the old junker up on a rack. They poured alcohol on the frame and rubbed until the old paint began to yield, layer by layer. They replaced the broken pedal, tightened down a new seat, and restored the grips. In about a week, it looked brand new.

Justin wheeled it out of the garage, leapt aboard, and started off around the block. He stood up and mashed down on the pedals, straining for speed. It was a good, steady ride, but not much of a thrill compared to his racers.

270 Unit 3

Guiding the Reading

Literal

Q: Why didn't the garage have room for the car?

A: There were bikes, bike parts, and tools all over the place.

Q: What would they do after each race?

A: They would adjust the brakes and realign the wheels of their two racing bikes.

Q: What did Justin know about fixing bikes?

A: He had learned just about everything his father knew and maybe even a few things that he did not.

Q: Who was Mel?

A: He was the owner of the best bike shop in town who let Justin hang around and watch him work. Mel helped Justin when he was not able to fix something himself and would sometimes give Justin advice.

Q: What did Justin and his father use to strip away some of the paint layers?

A: They rubbed the bike with alcohol.

Q: What else did they fix on the bike?

A: They replaced the broken pedal, put on a new seat, and restored the grips.

Q: How long did it take to repair the old junker?

A: It took about a week.

Soon he forgot about the bike. But the very next week, he bought another junker at a yard sale and fixed it up, too. After a while it bothered him that he wasn't really using either bike. Then he realized that what he loved about the old bikes wasn't riding them: it was the challenge of making something new and useful out of something old and broken. 8

Justin wondered what he should do with them. They were just taking up space in the garage. He remembered that when he was younger, he used to live near a large brick building called the Kilbarchan Home for Boys. It was a place for boys whose parents couldn't care for them for one reason or another.

He found "Kilbarchan" in the phone book and called the director, who said the boys would be thrilled to get two bicycles. The next day when Justin and his mother unloaded the bikes at the home, two boys raced out to greet them. They leapt aboard the bikes and started tooling around the semicircular driveway, doing wheelies and pirouettes, laughing and shouting.

WORD BANK

tooling (TOOL ing) *v.*: driving or riding in a vehicle
semicircular (SEM ee SUR kyuh lur) *adj.*: shaped like half of a circle
pirouettes (PEER oo ETS) *n.*: a dance step in which the dancer whirls about on one foot

Literary Components

8 **Theme:** Although a more "spiritual" theme will emerge, the theme of fixing what is broken, making the useless into something useful, starts in a very tangible, material way. Choosing to rejuvenate old bikes, rather than viewing them as junk to be thrown out, is one of Justin's characteristics.

Guiding the Reading

Literal

Q: What did Justin do with the bike when he was done with the repairs?
A: He took one ride and then forgot about it.

Q: What did he do the following week?
A: He bought another junker bike at a yard sale.

Q: What started to bother Justin?
A: He was not using the bikes that he bought at sales.

Q: What challenge did he enjoy?
A: He liked making something new out of something old and broken.

Q: What was Kilbarchan?
A: It was a home for boys whose parents could not care for them for one reason or another.

Q: Why did Justin call the director of the home?
A: He offered them two refurbished bicycles.

Q: What happened when Justin and his mother arrived at Kilbarchan?
A: Two boys raced out to greet them. They started riding the bikes and having fun right away.

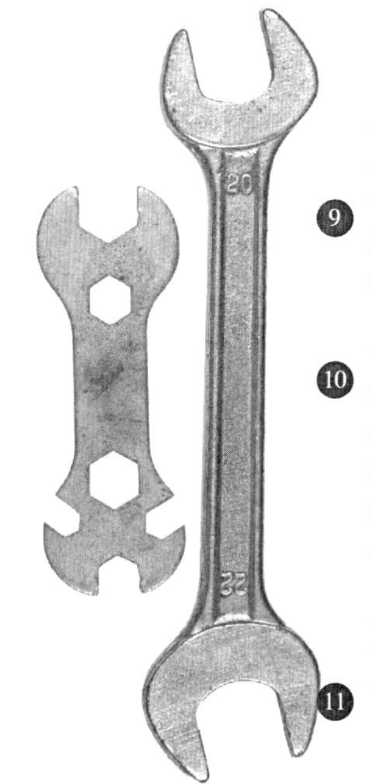

The Lebos watched them for a while, then started to climb into their car to go home. The boys cried after them, "Wait a minute! You forgot your bikes!" Justin explained that the bikes

9 were for them to keep. "They were so happy," Justin remembers. "It was like they couldn't believe it. It made me feel good just to see them happy."

On the way home, Justin was silent. His mother assumed he was lost in a feeling of satisfaction. But he was thinking about

10 what would happen once those bikes got wheeled inside and everyone saw them. How would all those kids decide who got the bikes? Two bikes could cause more trouble than they would solve. Actually, they hadn't been that hard to build. It was fun. Maybe he could do more…

"Mom," Justin said as they turned onto their street, "I've got an idea. I'm going to make a bike for every boy at Kilbarchan for the holidays." Diane Lebo looked at Justin out of the corner of

11 her eye. She had rarely seen him so determined.

When they got home, Justin called Kilbarchan to find out how many boys lived there. There were twenty-one. It was

12 already June. He had six months to make nineteen bikes. That was almost a bike a week. Justin called the home back to tell them of his plan. "I could tell they didn't think I could do it," Justin remembers. "I knew I could."

Justin knew his best chance was to build bikes almost the way GM or Ford builds cars: in an assembly line.[1] He would start with frames from three-speed, twenty-four-inch BMX bicycles. They were common bikes, and all the parts were interchangeable. If he could find enough decent frames, he could take parts off broken bikes and fasten them onto the good frames. He figured it would take three or four junkers to produce enough parts to make one good bike. That meant sixty to eighty bikes. Where would he get them?

WORD BANK

interchangeable (IN tur CHAYNGE uh bul) *adj.*: two things that can be used in place of one another
proposal (pruh PO zul) *n.*: a suggested plan
gingerly (JIN jur lee) *adv.*: with great care

1. In an *assembly line*, a product is manufactured piece by piece. As each part of the product is made, it is passed to the next worker, who adds the next piece to it, and so on, until the entire product is completed.

272 Unit 3

Literary Components

9 Voice: In the middle of the narrative, the narrator inserts lines spoken by Justin. The lines are in quotation marks, so the reader recognizes that these words were actually spoken by Justin. This is a nonfiction piece, so the lines are "real."

10 Internal Dialogue: The narrator now shifts to internal dialogue, telling us what Justin is thinking.

11 Characterization: This author views determination and exceptional behavior as a virtue. Justin is trying to excel at helping others. Point out that in *The Perfect/Imperfect Book Report*, Cricket was trying to excel for purely selfish reasons.

12 External Conflict: The struggle here will be against time. Justin will race to finish the bikes while the weeks fly by.

Guiding the Reading

Literal

Q: What happened when the Lebos got back in the car to go home?
A: The boys told them that they'd forgotten their bikes.

Q: How did Justin feel after he gave away the bikes?
A: It made him feel good to see others so happy.

Q: What did Mrs. Lebo think when Justin was quiet on the way home?
A: She assumed that he was thinking about the satisfying feeling that comes along with helping someone.

Q: What was Justin really thinking?
A: He was wondering what would happen once the rest of the boys saw the bikes. He was afraid the bikes would cause more problems than they solved. Then he began to think of what else he could do to help.

Q: What idea did Justin share with his mother?
A: He wanted to fix up enough bikes for every boy in Kilbarchan.

Q: What was Mrs. Lebo's response to Justin's idea?
A: She did not say anything, she only looked at him. She noticed that he was extremely determined.

Q: How many boys in total were at Kilbarchan?
A: There were twenty-one.

Q: How many more bikes did Justin need to repair?
A: He would need to repair nineteen more.

Q: How long would it take him to fix the nineteen bikes?
A: It was June and he set a goal of six months for himself—he wanted each boy to have a bike by the end of the year. He would have to produce about one bike a week.

Q: What did he tell the adults at Kilbarchan?
A: He told them of the plan that he had.

Q: What lesson did Justin learn from car companies like GM and Ford?
A: He learned to work on his project using an assembly line.

Q: What bike did he want to use for each one?
A: He would use three-speed, twenty-four inch BMX bicycles.

Q: Why did Justin use this bike in particular?
A: They were common and the parts were easily interchangeable.

Q: How many bikes did Justin think he would need to have one useable bike?
A: He would need three or four junkers.

Q: About how many bikes would he need in total?
A: He would need between sixty and eighty bikes.

Garage sales seemed to be the only hope. It was June, and there would be garage sales all summer long. But even if he could find that many bikes, how could he ever pay for them? That was hundreds of dollars.

He went to his parents with a proposal. "When Justin was younger, say five or six," says his mother, "he used to give some of
13 his allowance away to help others in need. His father and I would donate a dollar for every dollar Justin donated. So he asked us if it could be like the old days, if we'd match every dollar he put into buying old bikes. We said yes."

Justin and his mother spent most of June and July hunting for cheap bikes at garage sales and thrift shops. They would haul the bikes home, and Justin would start stripping them down in the yard.

But by the beginning of August, he had managed to make only ten bikes. Summer vacation was almost over, and school and homework would soon cut into his time. Garage sales would dry up when it got colder, and Justin was out of money. Still, he was determined to find a way.

14 At the end of August, Justin got a break. A neighbor wrote a letter to the local newspaper describing Justin's project, and an editor thought it would make a good story. One day a reporter entered the Lebo garage. Stepping gingerly through the tires and frames that covered the floor, she found a boy with cut fingers and dirty nails,

Literary Components

13 Theme: Helping those less fortunate than you is one of the story's themes. Justin will work hard, sacrifice time, effort, and money to help others. He will have strong support from his parents, friends, and the community at large. *Shared values* are another theme. Justin, his parents, and all those who help him have shared values. When many share the same values, much can be achieved.

14 Turning Point: We will see that one external conflict—Justin's determination versus the lack of money to pay for the bikes—is won by Justin.

Guiding the Reading

Literal

Q: What was Justin's greatest concern?

A: Even if he managed to find enough bikes at garage sales over the summer, how would he pay for all of them?

Q: What did Justin's parents agree to do in order to help?

A: They would contribute a dollar for every dollar he spent.

Q: Where did he get that idea?

A: When he was as young as five or six, he often gave away part of his allowance. At that time, his parents donated a dollar for every dollar that Justin donated.

Q: What did Justin and his mother do for most of June and July?

A: They went to many garage sales and thrift shops to find cheap bikes.

Q: How many bikes had Justin repaired by the beginning of August?

A: He'd managed to finish ten bicycles.

Q: What problems did Justin face in August?

A: Since summer vacation would be over soon, school and homework would not leave much time to work on bikes. Also, there would not be many garage sales with the approach of fall. Most of all, Justin did not have any more money to spend for bike purchases.

Q: Was Justin going to give up because of the many obstacles that stood in his way?

A: No, he was determined to find a way to make things work.

Q: How did the reporter find out about Justin and his project?

A: A neighbor wrote a letter to a local newspaper and one of the editors thought it would make a good story.

Literary Components

 **Voice; Characterization:** Again, the author inserts real quotes into the narrative. We see that what we had guessed about Justin is true: he hates the limelight and self-aggrandizement. He is the ideal person who helps for the sake of helping and seeks neither credit nor praise.

banging a seat onto a frame. His clothes were covered with grease. In her admiring article about a boy who was devoting his summer to help kids he didn't even know, she said Justin needed bikes and money, and she printed his home phone number.

Overnight, everything changed. "There must have been a hundred calls," Justin says. "People would call me up and ask me to come over and pick up their old bike. Or I'd be working in the garage, and a station wagon would pull up. The driver would leave a couple of bikes by the curb. It just snowballed."

By the start of school, the garage was overflowing with BMX frames. Pyramids of pedals and seats rose in the corners. Soon bike parts filled a toolshed in the backyard and then spilled out into the small yard itself, wearing away the lawn.

More and more writers and radio reporters called for interviews. Each time he told his story, Justin asked for bikes and money. "The first few interviews were fun," Justin says, "but it reached a point where I really didn't like doing them. The

274 Unit 3

Guiding the Reading

Literal

Q: How does the author describe the reporter's first look at Justin Lebo?

A: He was a boy with cut fingers and dirty nails. His clothes were covered in grease.

Q: What information did she include in her article?

A: Justin was a boy who devoted his summer to helping kids he did not know. He was in need of bikes and funds. She printed the phone number where people could reach him.

Q: How did the newspaper article affect Justin's project?

A: He received about one hundred calls and people were constantly donating old bicycles for him to use.

Q: By the time school started, what did the Lebo garage look like?

A: It was overflowing with bikes and their parts.

Q: Was the first reporter the only one who took interest in Justin's project?

A: No, he received many interview requests from writers and radio reporters.

Q: What did Justin ask for each time he shared his story with a reporter?

A: He asked for more bikes and money to continue his project.

Q: Did Justin enjoy giving interviews?

A: No, he did not.

Analytical

Q: What did Justin mean when he said, "It just snowballed"?

A: Just as a snowball grows bigger as it rolls down a hill, so too, his bike business grew and gained momentum.

publicity was necessary, though. I had to keep doing interviews to get the donations I needed."

By the time school opened, he was working on ten bikes at a time. There were so many calls now that he was beginning to refuse offers that weren't the exact bikes he needed.

As checks came pouring in, Justin's money problems disappeared. He set up a bank account and began to make bulk orders of common parts from Mel's bike shop. Mel seemed delighted to see him. Sometimes, if Justin brought a bike by the shop, Mel would help him fix it. When Justin tried to talk him into a lower price for big orders, Mel smiled and gave in. He respected another good businessman. They became friends.

The week before the holidays Justin delivered the last of the twenty-one bikes to Kilbarchan. Once again, the boys poured out of the home and leapt aboard the bikes, tearing around the snow.

And once again, their joy inspired Justin. They reminded him how important bikes were to him. Wheels meant freedom. He (16)

WORD BANK

inspired (in SPY ehrd) *v.*: filled with a sense of purpose

Justin Lebo 275

Literary Components

(16) **Theme:** The only thanks Justin wants is to see the joy of the Kilbarchan boys when they get the bikes.

Guiding the Reading

Literal

Q: If he did not like the interviews, why did he agree to them?
A: He needed the publicity in order to get the necessary materials and funding.

Q: At what point did Justin refuse the offers?
A: By the time school started, he was busy working on ten bikes at a time. If a caller did not have the exact bike or parts that he needed, he declined the offer.

Q: What did Justin do once he received a large amount of money?
A: He set up a bank account.

Q: How did the relationship between Justin and Mel change throughout this project?
A: They became friends.

Q: Did Justin reach his goal of delivering a bike for every boy in Kilbarchan before the end of the year?
A: Yes.

Analytical

Q: How do you know that Justin was a good businessman?
A: He was responsible about the money, he made wise decisions such as ordering in bulk, and he negotiated prices with Mel. He also seemed to have a good work ethic.

Literary Components

17 Theme: Helping others brings great happiness to the helper.

18 Voice; Theme: In Justin's own voice we see a small part of another theme that is not fully developed in the story. It is the theme of independence, which a bike—and a book—represent to Justin.

thought how much more the freedom to ride must mean to boys like these who had so little freedom in their lives. He decided to keep on building.

"First I made eleven bikes for the children in a foster home my mother told me about. Then I made bikes for all the women in a homeless shelter. Then I made ten little bikes and tricycles for the kids in a home for sick children. Then I made twenty-three bikes for the Paterson Housing Coalition."

In the four years since he started, Justin Lebo has made between 150 and 200 bikes and given them all away. He has been careful to leave time for his homework, his friends, his coin collection, his new interest in marine biology, and of course his own bikes.

Reporters and interviewers have asked Justin Lebo the same question over and over: "Why do you do it?" The question seems to make him uncomfortable. It's as if they want him to say what a great person he is. Their stories always make him seem perfect, which he knows he isn't. "Sure it's nice of me to make the bikes," he says, "because I don't have to. But I want to. In part, I do it for myself. I
17 don't think you can ever really do anything to help anybody else if it doesn't make you happy.

"Once I overheard a kid who got one of my bikes say, 'A bike is
18 like a book; it opens up a whole new world.' That's how I feel, too. It made me happy to know that kid felt that way. That's why I do it."

ABOUT THE AUTHOR

Phillip Hoose writes books, essays, stories, and articles. He has written on a wide variety of subjects, including stories about endangered species, a perfect World Series game, and a championship basketball team. He wrote one of his most popular books, *Hey, Little Ant,* with his daughter Hannah, who was only nine years old at the time. Mr. Hoose works for an organization dedicated to protecting the habitats of endangered species. He lives in Portland, Maine where, in addition to writing books, he writes and performs his own songs.

276 Unit 3

Guiding the Reading

Literal

Q: What was Justin feeling and thinking after he gave away all the bicycles he had worked so hard to repair?

A: The joy felt by the boys inspired Justin. He thought about how much the freedom to ride meant to boys who had so little freedom in their lives.

Q: What did Justin Lebo do after his project for the Kilbarchan Home was complete?

A: He decided to continue building new bikes to give to others.

Q: Name some of the organizations that benefited from Justin's kindness.

A: He made bikes for children in a foster home, women in a shelter, seriously ill children, and for the Paterson Housing Coalition.

Q: How many bicycles did Justin make and give away during the four years since he started?

A: He gave away between 150 and 200 bikes.

Q: What were some of Justin's other interests?

A: Justin had a coin collection and a new interest in marine biology.

Q: What question was Justin asked most by reporters?

A: "Why do you do it?"

Q: What answer did Justin usually give?

A: "I don't think you can ever really do anything to help anybody else if it doesn't make you happy."

Q: How did one of the boys who got a bike describe the feeling of owning a bike?

A: "A bike is like a book; it opens up a whole new world."

Analytical

Q: In brief, what is the answer to the question, "Why do you do it?"

A: It makes others happy and that makes Justin happy.

Q: Why did it make Justin Lebo feel uncomfortable when people asked him why he put so much effort into his bike project?

A: He was sincere about helping others and making them happy. He did not wish to be in the spotlight or appear to be someone great. He agreed that it was a nice thing for him to do but he does it partially to make himself happy.

About Holding Up the Sky

Poetry Shares Big Ideas

This poem is thought-provoking. It tells the fable of a hummingbird who lies on his back with his feet in the air to keep the sky from falling. When an elephant taunts him for thinking one tiny hummingbird can hold up the sky, the hummingbird answers:

> "Not alone. But each must do what he can.
> And this is what I can do."

Your more literal-minded students may find the fable's message a bit hard to digest. Why should the hummingbird be admired for believing something ridiculous, or for wasting his energy on an impossible job? He might be better off burrowing into the earth to find a secure hiding place. As for the elephant's question,

> "Do you really think …
> that those tiny feet could help hold up the sky?"

The comedians in your class may provide the hummingbird with the obvious repartee,

> "Well it hasn't fallen yet, has it?"

However, once we accept the fable's premise (that the sky is going to fall in, or that it is all right for the hummingbird to think it will), the message is clear. The hummingbird is heroic because he is willing to give heart and soul to save the world. The same idea was taken very seriously, indeed, when phrased by Tennyson,

> "Ours is not to reason why,
> Ours is but to do and die"

The theme of the poem is that every creature has something to contribute, and that even if the contribution seems miniscule, the spirit driving the contribution is gigantic. The power of the spirit combined with the many and varied efforts of all creatures to "save the world" will bring success.

HOLDING UP THE SKY

A TALE FROM CHINA

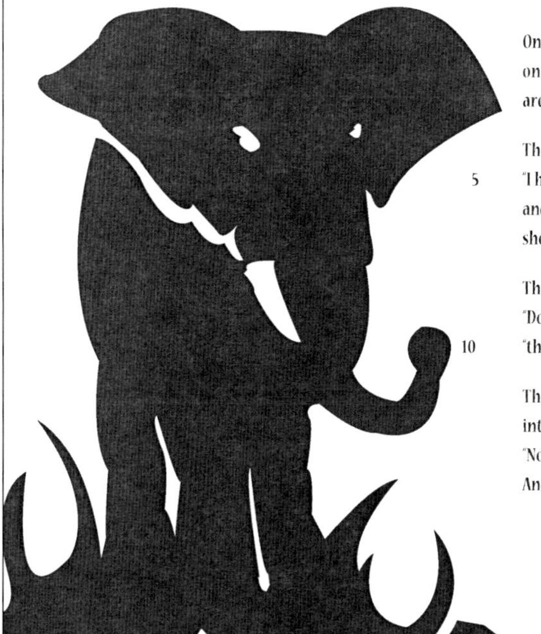

One day an elephant saw a hummingbird lying
on its back with its tiny feet up in the air. "What
are you doing?" asked the elephant.

The hummingbird replied,
"I heard that the sky might fall today,
and so I am ready to help hold it up,
should it fall."

The elephant laughed cruelly.
"Do you really think," he said,
"that those tiny feet could help hold up the sky?"

The hummingbird kept his feet up in the air,
intent on his purpose, as he replied,
"Not alone. But each must do what he can.
And this is what I can do."

Poetry shares big ideas

278 Unit 3

Studying the Selection

FIRST IMPRESSIONS

Who gained more from the bicycle project—Justin or the boys?

QUICK REVIEW

1. What did Justin look for at garage sales?
2. What did Justin do with the junkers he brought home?
3. How did Justin collect enough bicycles and money for this project?
4. To whom did Justin donate twenty-one bikes?

FOCUS

5. Why was freedom an important concept in this story?
6. Write at least two sentences describing some event in the story from the point of view of one of the following individuals: Mel, Mom, or the director of the Kilbarchan Home for Boys.

CREATING AND WRITING

7. Everyone has their own unique combination of talents. Write about how you can contribute to individuals and groups in your community. You may write about your past involvement in a project or an idea you have for the future.
8. Write about a group of students who raise money to help needy children attend summer camp. Include details about the campaign. Describe the feelings about the project from the point of view of the students and of the needy children.
9. Think of a creative way to make a model bicycle. You can use any material such as pipe cleaners or aluminum foil. Speak to your teacher about which materials you would like to use. When your model is complete, write a meaningful slogan on it, such as, "Giving is a cycle."

Justin Lebo 279

First Impressions

Answers will vary. The likely answer will be that they both benefited.

Quick Review

1. Justin looked for old bikes, especially BMXs.
2. He fixed them and sometimes asked his father or Mel, the owner of the bike shop, for assistance with the repairs.
3. At first, he was having difficulty getting the help he needed. His parents contributed money on top of what Justin himself had given to the project. Once the reporters publicized what Justin was doing, the contributions were overwhelming.
4. Justin gave the bikes to the children in the Kilbarchan Home for Boys.

Focus

5. Justin understood that the bikes allowed the boys at Kilbarchan to have a sense of freedom and independence. This was especially important, since they had very little freedom in other aspects of their lives. Justin's own freedom allowed him to make decisions and to spend his time and money helping others.
6. Answers will vary.

Creating and Writing

7. Answers will vary. If the students have difficulty getting started, provide a few examples, such as playing an instrument for patients in the hospital or lending something that you already have.
8. Answers will vary.
9. Responses will vary. Bring in a variety of materials for your students. You may plan a day for planning and then bring the materials to class or allow your students to work on the project at home. The sayings will vary. Accept any slogan that demonstrates an understanding of the assignment.

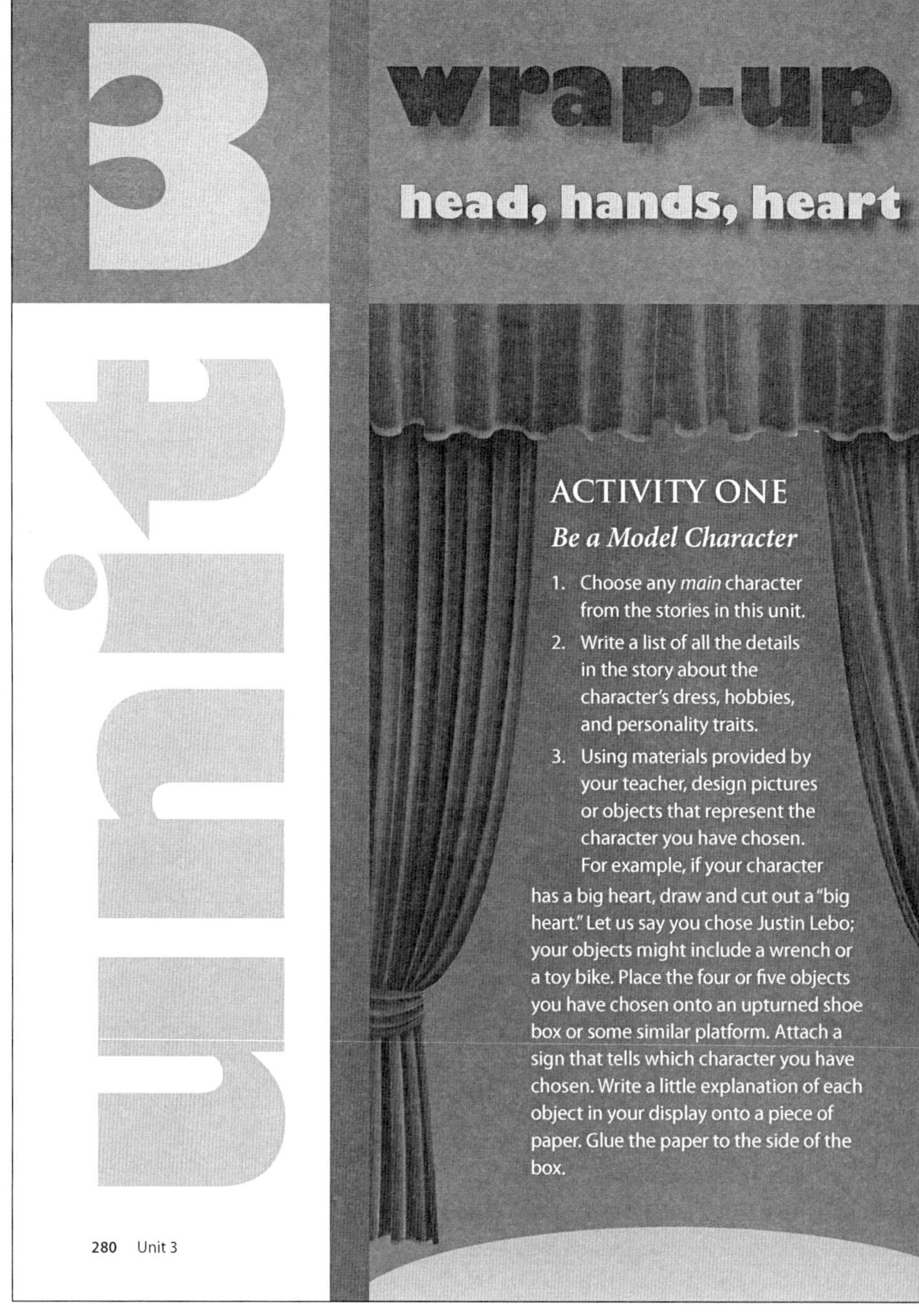

ACTIVITY ONE

Be a Model Character

1. Choose any *main* character from the stories in this unit.
2. Write a list of all the details in the story about the character's dress, hobbies, and personality traits.
3. Using materials provided by your teacher, design pictures or objects that represent the character you have chosen.

For example, if your character has a big heart, draw and cut out a "big heart." Let us say you chose Justin Lebo; your objects might include a wrench or a toy bike. Place the four or five objects you have chosen onto an upturned shoe box or some similar platform. Attach a sign that tells which character you have chosen. Write a little explanation of each object in your display onto a piece of paper. Glue the paper to the side of the box.

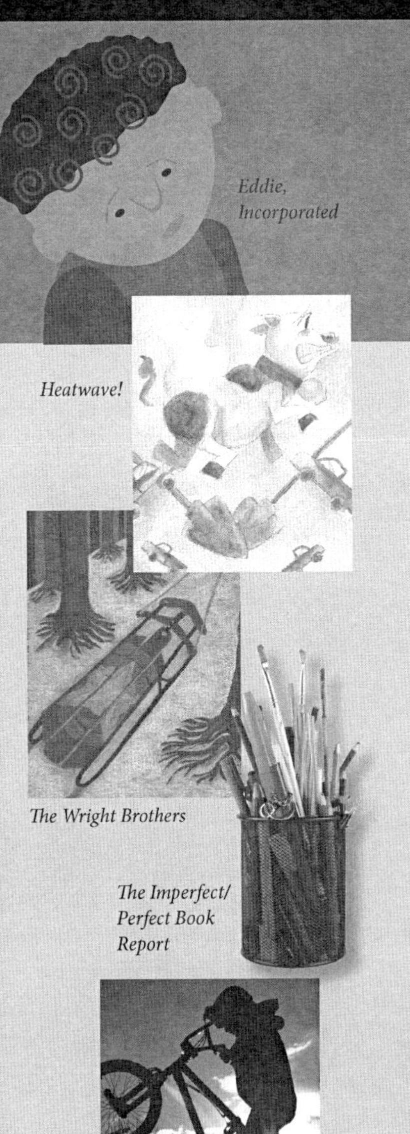

ACTIVITY TWO

The Same Game

1. For this activity, you may choose any major or minor character from the stories in this unit.
2. Choose a character that you are the most like.
3. List the ways that you are like the character. Include things like the way you look, your personality, and your favorite hobbies and sports activities. Compare the way you feel about school and the subjects you like most and least.
4. You may also list some differences.
5. Tell the class in an interesting and clear speaking voice how you are most like the character you have chosen.

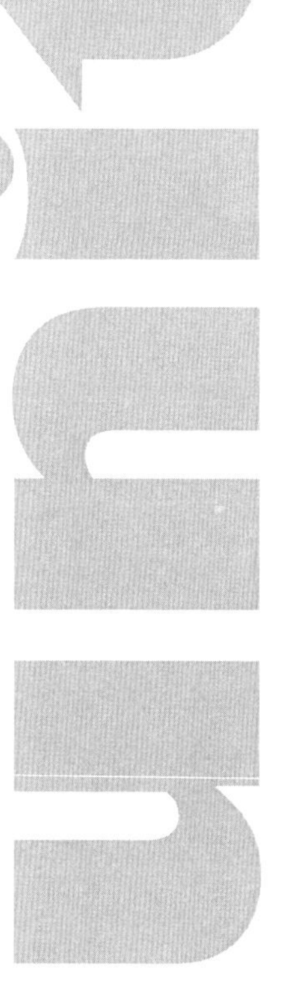

wrap-up continued

Activity Three

1. For this activity, you will work in groups of two or three.
2. Your job is to take one character from Unit Three and place him or her in a different story in Unit Three. How will the character react? How will the others feel? Will this character help solve a problem or will the character cause new problems? Does your character become friendly with the other characters in the story? What information or insight can this character share with the others in the story?

ACTIVITY FOUR

Characters change and learn over the course of a story. Choose a character from one of the stories in this unit and write a paragraph about how the character changed from the beginning to the end of the story. What caused the character to change?

- Was it some event?
- The influence of another character?
- A sudden understanding?
- Growing older?
- A combination of these or other things?
- Did the character change for the better or the worse?

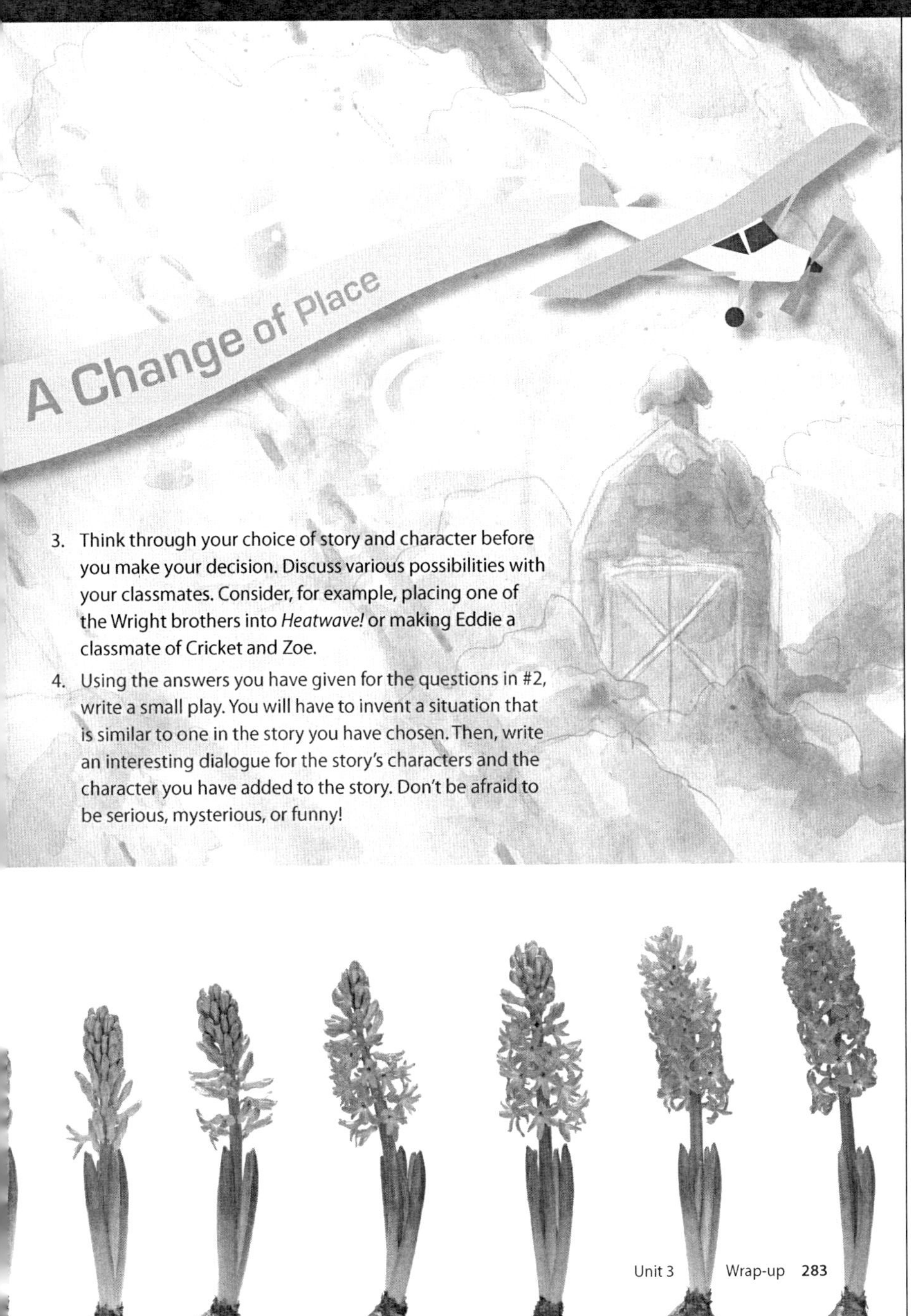

A Change of Place

3. Think through your choice of story and character before you make your decision. Discuss various possibilities with your classmates. Consider, for example, placing one of the Wright brothers into *Heatwave!* or making Eddie a classmate of Cricket and Zoe.
4. Using the answers you have given for the questions in #2, write a small play. You will have to invent a situation that is similar to one in the story you have chosen. Then, write an interesting dialogue for the story's characters and the character you have added to the story. Don't be afraid to be serious, mysterious, or funny!

Poetry

Poetry Is . . .

Sound and Rhythm
Sound, Rhythm, and Rhyme
Saying a Lot in a Few Words
A Picture
Rhyme
Fun to Write
Free

Contents

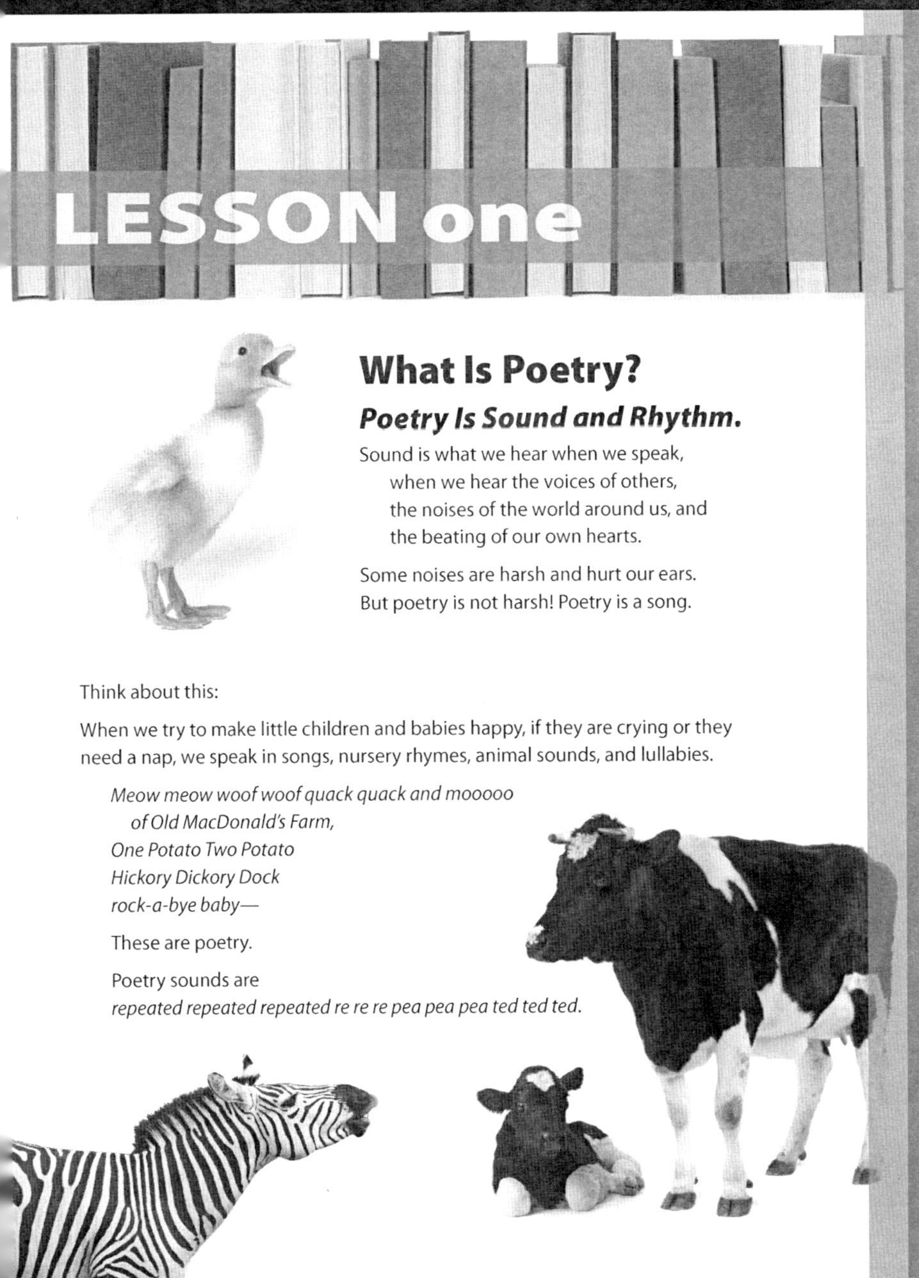

LESSON one

What Is Poetry?

Poetry Is Sound and Rhythm.

Sound is what we hear when we speak,
when we hear the voices of others,
the noises of the world around us, and
the beating of our own hearts.

Some noises are harsh and hurt our ears.
But poetry is not harsh! Poetry is a song.

Think about this:

When we try to make little children and babies happy, if they are crying or they need a nap, we speak in songs, nursery rhymes, animal sounds, and lullabies.

Meow meow woof woof quack quack and mooooo
of Old MacDonald's Farm,
One Potato Two Potato
Hickory Dickory Dock
rock-a-bye baby—

These are poetry.

Poetry sounds are
repeated repeated repeated re re re pea pea pea ted ted ted.

Poetry 287

Lesson One
What Is Poetry?

What is the key to poetry? Poetry uses the pleasure we take in sound and the repetition of sound. Poetry is also often about rhythm: a beat that is inherent in the syllables of each line of verse. Both the patterns of sound and rhythm are the primary building blocks of most poetry.

Poetry is not taught. It is shown. It is revealed. We show children a celebration of sounds. Read each of the poems in the Poetry Unit first to yourself and then to your class, or before the students themselves begin reading an assigned poem. Show that you enjoy the poem as you read aloud. Remember: Keep time where there is a beat, use dramatic expression where you are able, speak loudly, and pace yourself. Make certain your students know the meaning of all the words the poet uses.

Lesson One has four poems:

Birds' Square Dance by Beverly McLoughland

Thistles by Karla Kuskin

Whirligig Beetles by Paul Fleischman

This Is the Key by Anonymous

You can best prepare yourself to share these poems with your students, if you:

- read the poem silently several times
- speak the poem out loud softly
- speak the poem out loud loudly
- beat out the rhythm of the poem with your hand or foot, if the poem has a regular (or irregular) pattern of rhythm

When you are finished reading one poem, think about these questions:

How did the words feel in your mouth?

What sounds did you hear?

Which sounds did you hear repeated?

How did the poem leave you feeling?

Poets repeat sounds just as composers repeat notes. Repetition enchants us and enables us to remember oral histories, poetry, and songs. Repetition calms and reassures us. This is why poetry is an ancient tradition in nearly all cultures.

Poetry, then, is closest to our favorite literary forms and to comforting and entertaining experiences of sound: songs, lullabies, nursery rhymes, tongue twisters, and all forms of wordplay. One of the ways we talk to very little children is through the use of nursery rhymes and funny songs with funny sounds and animal noises. Poetry should be second nature to us.

When it comes to your students, remember that poetry not only *must* be read out loud, at some point in the semester it needs to be memorized and performed. As children, we like to speak dramatically and make dramatic gestures. Now your students can relearn these behaviors!

Birds' Square Dance

New Words

cassowary: large birds of New Guinea, Australia, the Aru Islands, and Ceram, closely related to the emu

chachalaca: tropical birds that live in trees and resemble wild turkeys but are longer legged and have a well-developed feathered crest, that are native to Central America and Mexico

kittiwake: a type of gull

noddy tern: any of several stout-bodied terns, chiefly of tropical and subtropical seas

do-si-do (doe see doe)**:** Two dancers begin by facing each other, then move clockwise so as to first pass right shoulders ("pass by the right"), then back-to-back, then left shoulders, ending where they began.

Cockatoo, bluefoot booby, marabou, cassowary, toucan, noddy, oriole, chachalaca, bobolink, kittiwake, loon, puffin, parakeet, curlew, crow, pipit, and *tern* are the names of seventeen different kinds of birds.

About the Poem

This exuberant Beverly McLoughland poem is meant to be danced and shouted, and uses a traditional square dance beat. Each line has four beats, with the stress on beats one and three. In Lines 2 and 4 of all five stanzas, the fourth beat is implied.

The listing of birds, here, is a kind of repetition, a kind of counting out (as in *One Potato, Two Potato*). The poem opens and closes with traditional square dance words: *Swing your partner* and *Do-si-do. Swing your partner* sets the tone of the poem and *Do-si-do* concludes the story.

Birds' Square Dance has no theme. It is a celebration of sound, beat, and movement. In addition to the repetition of birds' names, the author repeats the vowel sound *ooo*: *Cockat**oo**, Bl**ue**foot, b**oo**by, Marab**ou**, T**ou**can, L**oo**n, Curl**ew**.*

When this sort of vowel repetition occurs within words it is called **assonance**. The author also rhymes the final words of Lines 2 and 4 of each stanza:

Cockatoo ... Marabou
toe ... Oriole (an almost rhyme called a *slant rhyme*)
right ... tight
feet ... Parakeet
crow ... Do-si-do

What other forms of repetition does the author use?

Syllable sound:

*M**ara**bou ... C**asso**wary ... n**oddy***
Chacha**la**ca
***Bobo**link*

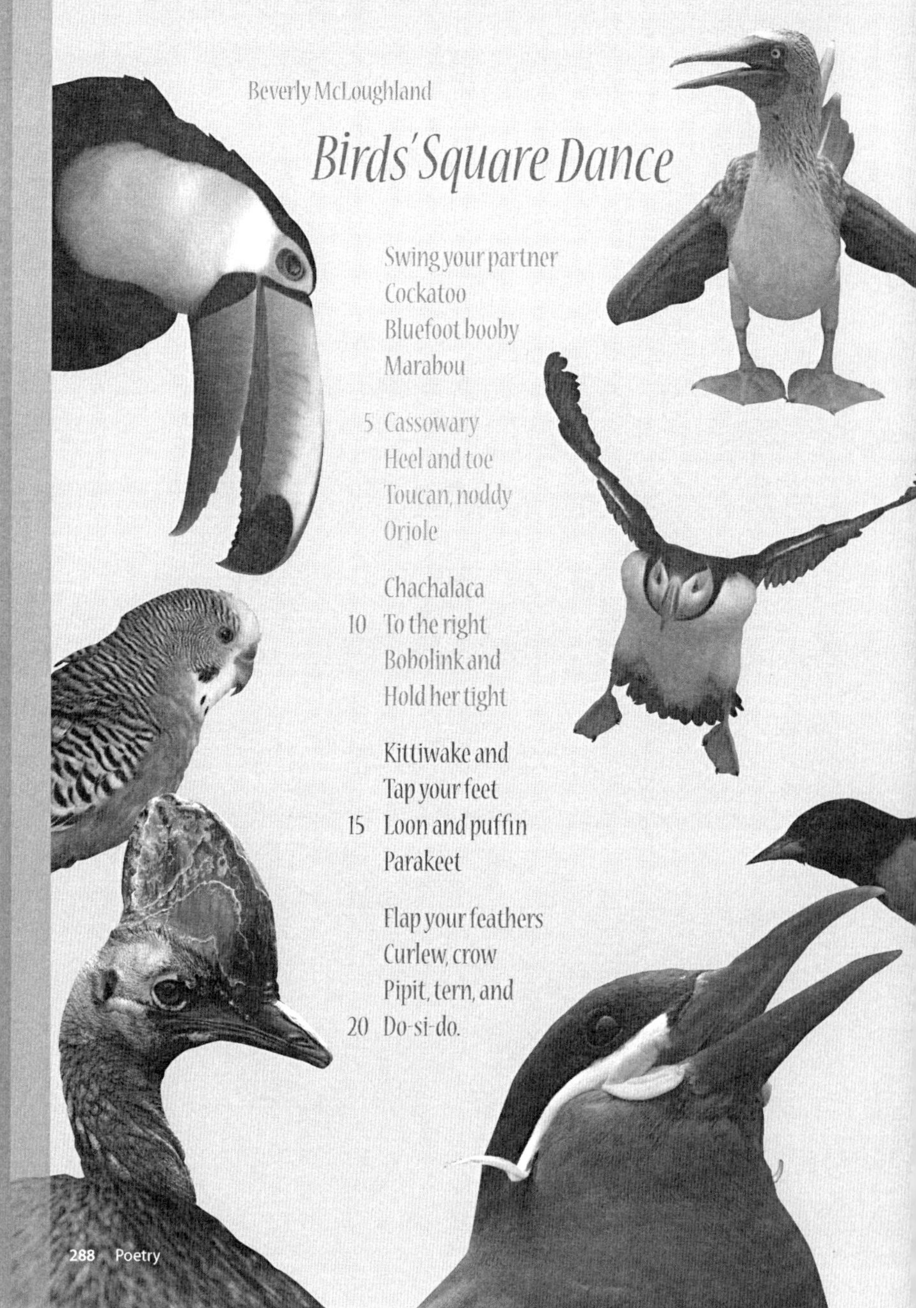

Beverly McLoughland

Birds' Square Dance

Swing your partner
Cockatoo
Bluefoot booby
Marabou

Cassowary
Heel and toe
Toucan, noddy
Oriole

Chachalaca
To the right
Bobolink and
Hold her tight

Kittiwake and
Tap your feet
Loon and puffin
Parakeet

Flap your feathers
Curlew, crow
Pipit, tern, and
Do-si-do.

288 Poetry

Initial and Internal Consonant:
Words with a ***k*** sound:

***C**o**ck**atoo, **C**assowary, Tou**c**an, Chachala**c**a, Bobolin**k**, **K**ittiwa**k**e, Para**k**eet, **C**urlew, **C**row*

The repetition of initial consonants is called **alliteration**. The repetition of internal consonants is called **consonance**. The author also repeats other consonants:

b ***B**luefoot **b**oo**b**y, **B**o**b**olink*
t *Cocka**t**oo, **t**oe, **T**oucan, **t**igh**t**, **t**ap, **t**ern*
f ***f**eet, **F**lap, **f**eathers*
p ***p**uffin, **P**arakeet, **P**i**p**it*

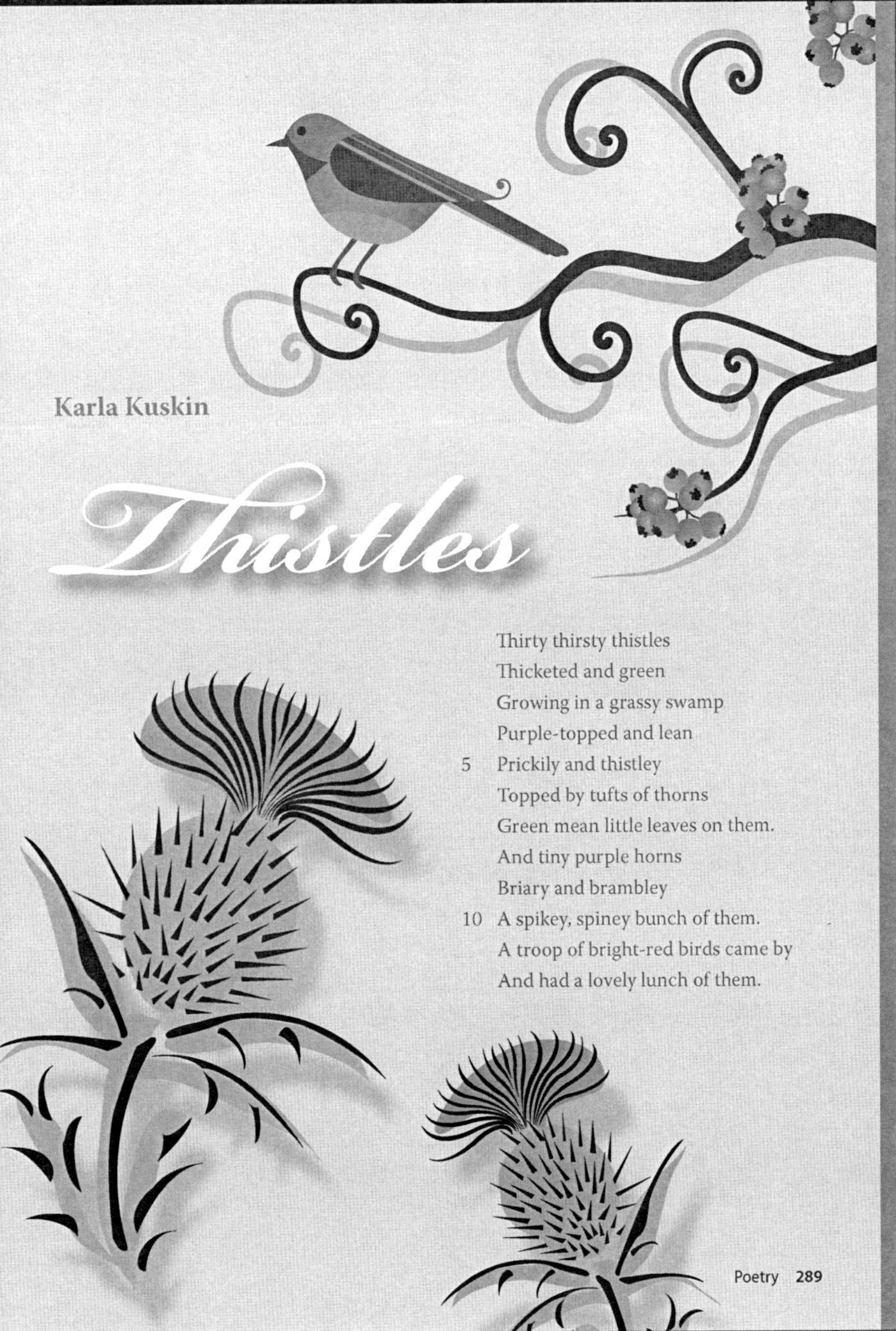

Karla Kuskin

Thistles

Thirty thirsty thistles
Thicketed and green
Growing in a grassy swamp
Purple-topped and lean
Prickily and thistley
Topped by tufts of thorns
Green mean little leaves on them.
And tiny purple horns
Briary and brambley
A spikey, spiney bunch of them.
A troop of bright-red birds came by
And had a lovely lunch of them.

Poetry 289

Thistles

About the Poem

Clearly, this poem is a tongue twister, with lots of alliteration and consonance thrown at us every which way (which is how tongue twisters twist our tongues). *Thistles* is a lesson in the repetition of consonants. The author also threads this one-stanza poem with vowel repetition (another way to trip a tongue, in combination with the tricky consonant combinations).

Does the poem have a theme? Perhaps. We learn a lot about those thistles in ten lines. And then they are eaten and gone in one fell swoop (just two lines!) by a troop of bright-red birds who come to dine. In nature, that which seems solid and stable can disappear in an instant!

Alternating lines rhyme (2 with 4, 6 with 8, and 10 with 12). The last rhyme is sweet: *bunch of them … lunch of them.*

Rhythmically, the poem is as follows:

Thirty thirsty thistles
    6 beats (stress on syllables 1, 3, 5)
Thicketed and green
    5 beats (stress on syllables 1, 3, 5)
Growing in a grassy swamp
    7 beats (stress on syllables 1, 3, 5, 7)
Purple-topped and lean
    5 beats (stress on syllables 1, 3, 5)
Prickily and thistley
    6 beats (stress on syllables 1, 3, 5)
Topped by tufts of thorns
    5 beats (stress on syllables 1, 3, 5)
Green mean little leaves on them.
    7 beats (stress on syllables 1, 3, 5, 7)
And tiny purple horns
    6 beats (stress on syllables 2, 4, 6)
Briary and brambley
    6 beats (stress on syllables 1, 3, 5)
A spikey, spiney bunch of them.
    8 beats (stress on syllables 2, 4, 6, 8)
A troop of bright-red birds came by
    8 beats (stress on syllables 2, 4, 6, 8)
And had a lovely lunch of them.
    8 beats (stress on syllables 2, 4, 6, 8)

The effect of the poet's altering the stress pattern of the poem is not a fourth grade discussion, but you certainly will want to point out to your students that this occurs, in order to help them keep time.

Ask your students to find the repetition of these letters: *th, ir, istle, ick, gr, p, t, sp,* and *br.* Are there any other repeated initial consonants they see?

The poet also uses internal rhyme (words within lines rhyming): *green mean* and then the matching assonance of *leaves.*

You may want to point out that the color *red* in the next to the last line comes as a shock, after all of that green and purple, just as we are surprised that along come some birds who make quick work of the well-armored thistles.

Whirligig Beetles

Do you students know that *whirl* means to turn in a circle?

The word *whirligig*, which is a noun, is something that continuously whirls, moves, or changes.

Whirligig beetles are a family of water beetles that have a firm oval, usually dark, body with a bronzy luster. Most of the time, they live on the surface of water where they move swiftly about in curves. They swim rapidly in circles when alarmed. They are also distinguished by their divided eyes, which can see both above and below water.

Their grouping behavior helps them avoid being hunted and is a survival mechanism. They have a bubble of air trapped underneath their abdomens which allows them to dive and swim under the water for a long time.

About the Poem

This poem for two voices (or two groups of voices) captures the seemingly ecstatic, compulsive whirling of whirligig beetles. The poem, incredibly, conveys the *feeling* of whirling. One is almost whirling as one reads it and is dizzy by its end.

The poem is to be read by two groups in a fashion similar to a round. Group I starts the poem and has five stanzas or separate sections of the poem. For Group I, stanza 1 has three lines. Stanza 2, six lines. Stanza 3, six lines. Stanza 4, only one line! Stanza 5 has nine lines.

Group II starts one line later than Group I. For Group II, the poem has only three stanzas. Stanza 1 has six lines. Stanza 2 has six lines. Stanza 3 has sixteen lines!

Your students will need to be very clear about the rhythm. Each line consists of two slow beats on the stressed syllables or six fast beats matching each syllable. For most of the poem—up to Line 22—the stressed syllables are syllables 2 and 5.

Make sure your students are also clear about how many lines they are silent (while the other group speaks). They should continue beating out the rhythm when it is their turn to be silent. Then they will be able to come in on cue. See the chart on the far side of the following page (p. T291). All the lines in the poem are counted as long as one group is speaking. The poem has 33 lines.

The poem does not rhyme. Repetition comes from the counterpoint of the two voices, which weave in and out of the poem, very nearly saying all of the same words and echoing each other, and from all of the *ing* endings.

Since the author uses lots of alliteration (repetition of initial consonants), you may want to ask your students to identify the repeated letters. Make sure they know what a consonant is.

The poem shows what can be done poetically with a lot of synonyms. If you or your students want to mimic this piece at some point, a thesaurus will be invaluable.

Does the poem have a theme? If one knows that these beetles whirl in order to avoid being eaten by predators, then the variety of movements they can make to survive stands in sharp contrast to the vulnerability of the thistles.

Make sure your students know what *serpentine* (like a serpent or snake; winding or turning one way and another) and *tortuous* (marked by repeated twists, bends, or turns; winding) mean.

In the chart the stressed syllables are in bold.

Whirligig Beetles

Paul Fleischman

We're whirligig beetles
we're swimming in circles,
black backs by the hundred.

We're spinning and swerving
as if we were on a
mad merry-go-round.
We never get dizzy
from whirling and weaving
and wheeling and swirling.

The same goes for turning,
revolving and curving,
gyrating and twirling.
The crows fly directly,
but we prefer spirals,
arcs, ovals, and loops.

"As the whirligig swims"

circular
roundabout
backtracking
indirect
serpentine
tortuous
twisty,
best possible
route.

We're whirligig beetles
we're swimming in circles,
black backs by the hundred.
We're spinning and swerving
as if we were on a
mad merry-go-round.

We never get dizzy
from whirling and weaving
and wheeling and swirling.
The same goes for turning,
revolving and curving,
gyrating and twirling.

The crows fly directly,
but we prefer spirals,
arcs, ovals, and loops.
We're fond of the phrase
"As the whirligig swims"
meaning traveling by
the most circular
roundabout
backtracking
indirect
serpentine
tortuous
twisty and
turny,
best possible
route.

290 Poetry

This Is the Key

This is the key of the kingdom:
In that kingdom there is a city.
In that city there is a town.
In that town there is a street.
In that street there is a lane.
In that lane there is a yard.
In that yard there is a house.
In that house there is a room.
In that room there is a bed.
On that bed there is a basket.
In that basket there are some flowers.
Flowers in a basket.
Basket on the bed.
Bed in the room.
Room in the house.
House in the yard.
Yard in the lane.
Lane in the street.
Street in the town.
Town in the city.
City in the kingdom.
Of the kingdom this is the key.

Anonymous

Poetry 291

Group I	Group II	Line
We're **whirl**igig **bee**tles	1-**2**-3 4-**5**-6	1
we're **swim**ming in **cir**cles,	We're **whirl**igig **bee**tles	2
black **backs** by the **hun**dred.	we're **swim**ming in **cir**cles,	3
1-**2**-3 4-**5**-6	black **backs** by the **hun**dred.	4
1-**2**-3 4-**5**-6	We're **swim**ming and **swerv**ing	5
We're **swim**ming and **swerv**ing	as **if** we were **on** a	6
as **if** we were **on** a **(6 beats)**	mad **mer**ry-go-**round.** **(5 beats)**	7
mad **mer**ry-go-**round.** **(5 beats)**	1-**2**-3 4-**5**-6	8
We **nev**er get **diz**zy	1-**2**-3 4-**5**-6	9
from **whirl**ing and **weav**ing	We **nev**er get **diz**zy	10
and **wheel**ing and **swirl**ing.	from **whirl**ing and **weav**ing	11
1-**2**-3 4-**5**-6	and **wheel**ing and **swirl**ing.	12
1-**2**-3 4-**5**-6	The **same** goes for **turn**ing,	13
The **same** goes for **turn**ing,	re**volv**ing and **curv**ing,	14
re**volv**ing and **curv**ing,	gy**rat**ing and **twirl**ing.	15
gy**rat**ing and **twirl**ing.	1-**2**-3 4-**5**-6	16
The **crows** fly di**rect**ly,	1-**2**-3 4-**5**-6	17
but **we** prefer **spi**rals,	The **crows** fly di**rect**ly,	18
arcs, **o**vals, and **loops.** **(5 beats)**	but **we** prefer **spi**rals,	19
1-**2**-3 4-**5**-6	arcs, **o**vals, and **loops.** **(5 beats)**	20
1-**2**-3 4-**5**-6	We're **fond** of the **phrase** **(5 beats)**	21
"As the **whirl**igig **swims**"	"As the **whirl**igig **swims**"	22
1-2-**3** 4-5-**6**	meaning **trav**eling **by**	23
1-2-**3** 4-5	the most **cir**cular **(5 beats)**	24
circular **(3 beats)**	**round**about **(3 beats)**	25
roundabout	**back**tracking	26
backtracking	**in**direct	27
indirect	**ser**pentine	28
serpentine	**tor**tuous	29
tortuous	**twis**ty and	30
twisty **(2 beats)**	**tur**ny **(2 beats)**	31
best **pos**sible **(4 beats)**	best **pos**sible **(4 beats)**	32
route. **(1 beat)**	**route.** **(1 beat)**	33

This Is the Key

About the Poem

This Is the Key is a mysterious and probably very old nursery rhyme. We are led into a town, down a street, a lane, into a yard, into a house to find a basket of flowers. There are no verbs other than *is*, and yet one has the sense of motion, of moving through all of these places.

Apparently, the basket of flowers is the key to the kingdom. Why would a basket of flowers be the key? Could natural beauty and the blossoming of life be an answer to some of the puzzles of life? Discuss this with your students. Whatever you come up with—*that* is the theme.

Talk with your students about the meaning of the word *key*. Of course, most of us know that a key is a metal object used to lock or unlock something. But *key* is also used in the abstract as something that reveals the solution to a problem or mystery.

The poem has twenty-two lines: Lines 11 and 12 form its center, both in terms of the structure of the poem and thematically. Here lies the basket of flowers that are the key to the kingdom and the key to the poem.

Think About It

1. After you have read the poem to your class (beating time with your hand or foot), have your students practice the poem. You may want to give them time in class to rehearse individually and in small groups.
2. In *Birds' Square Dance*, the poet uses the sound *ooo* in *Cockat**oo**, Bl**ue**foot, b**oo**by, Marab**ou**, T**ou**-can, L**oo**n*, and *Curl**ew***.
3. Here are twenty-four tongue twisters, so that each student will have a different one to recite.
   - Sure the ship's shipshape, sir.
   - If Stu chews shoes, should Stu choose the shoes he chews?
   - What a shame such a shapely sash should such shabby stitches show.
   - A big black bug bit a big black bear, made the big black bear bleed blood.
   - Toy boat. Toy boat. Toy boat.
   - Which wristwatches are Swiss wristwatches?
   - A skunk sat on a stump and thunk the stump stunk, but the stump thunk the skunk stunk.
   - The boot black bought the black boot back.
   - Six sick slick slim sycamore saplings.
   - Knapsack straps.
   - Unique New York.
   - Cheap ship trip.
   - The sixth sick sheik's sixth sheep's sick.
   - Shy Shelly says she shall sew sheets.
   - Lesser leather never weathered wetter weather better.
   - Moose noshing much mush.
   - Many an anemone sees an enemy anemone.
   - Thieves seize skis.
   - Chop shops stock chops.
   - Preshrunk silk shirts.
   - A bloke's back bike brake block broke.
   - Lily ladles little Letty's lentil soup.
   - Six slippery snails, slid slowly seaward.
   - Three twigs twined tightly.
4. a. The six words in *Thistles* that begin with *th* are ***th**irty, **th**irsty, **th**istles, **th**icketed, **th**orns*, and ***th**istley*.

   b. The three words that begin *gr* are ***gr**een, **gr**owing*, and ***gr**assy*.

   c. Three words begin with *br*: ***br**iary, **br**ambley*, and ***br**ight-red*. Two words begin *sp*: ***sp**ikey* and ***sp**iney*.
5. a. *Whirligig Beetles* takes a lot of practice. The easiest way for your students to practice is for them to clap their hands and beat their feet in time to the words. Have them practice one stanza at a time.

THINK about it

1. Read *Birds' Square Dance* to yourself, silently. Then read *Birds' Square Dance* out loud. Now read *Birds' Square Dance* tapping your foot and clapping your hands to the beat. Which sounds did you hear repeated? Write them down.
2. In *Birds' Square Dance*, the poet uses the sound *ooo* (as in *boo hoo*) seven times. Write down the seven words that have the sound *ooo*.
3. *Thistles* is a tongue twister. Your teacher will give you a tongue twister to practice and say before your class. Which consonants are repeated in *your* tongue twister? Write them down.
4. a. Write down the six words in *Thistles* that begin with *th*. (Do not include the word *them*, because it is a different *th* sound.)

   b. Write down the three words (one of these is used twice) that begin *gr*.

   c. Now, write down the words that begin *br* and those that begin *sp*.
5. a. This exercise must be led by your teacher. *Whirligig Beetles* is meant to be read in two groups. During part of the reading, one group is quiet while the other recites. The easiest way to recite in the correct rhythm is to clap your hands and tap your foot as you say the words out loud. In order to keep the rhythm you have to keep clapping and tapping even when it is not your group's turn to read.

   b. Your teacher will assign you to Group One or Two. Remember: When your group is not reciting, keep beating time.
6. *This Is the Key* goes forward and back. Which line is at the exact center of the poem? Write down your answer.
7. You are going to write a poem just like *This Is the Key*. Your poem will have only ten lines. Five will go forward and five will go back. Here are some beginning lines to choose from:

   This is the door to the house...
   These are the steps to the library...
   This is the gate to the path...

   You may choose to think of one of your own.

292 Poetry

   b. Divide the class into two groups called Group I and Group II. Group I will start the poem and will recite five stanzas or separate sections of the poem. For Group I, stanza 1 has three lines. Stanza 2, six lines. Stanza 3, six lines. Stanza 4 only one line! Stanza 5 has nine lines.

   Group II starts one line later than Group I. For Group II, the poem has only three stanzas. Stanza 1 has six lines. Stanza 2 has six lines. Stanza 3 has sixteen lines.
6. The line at the exact center of the poem is:
   "In that basket there are some flowers."
7. Your students are going to write a poem just like *This Is the Key*. Here is an additional list of opening lines:
   This is the cover that opens the book
   This is the road to the city
   This is the forest
   This is the nation
   This is the school
   This is the flag
   This is the room

Poetry Is Sound, Rhythm, and RHYME!

Poetry Is Nonsense

Have you ever heard the expression "it tickles my funny bone"? Even if you haven't, you will surely agree that that is what a limerick does! Limericks are not written to teach a lesson or to describe a beautiful scene. They are there just to make you laugh! Part of what makes them so much fun to read and write is that they are all written in the same form. Limericks all have five lines. What else do they all have? (Hint: The answer includes the words rhythm and rhyme.)

Limericks are most enjoyable when read aloud. Reading the limerick correctly is part of the fun. In the examples that follow, the syllables that should be stressed when being recited are italicized.

An *old* man was *seen* in the *park*.
He *raked* leaves from *dawn* until *dark*.
"I *can't* stand the *noise*,
Of *dogs*, girls, and *boys*,
But it's *worse* when the *dogs* start to *bark*."

A lot of limericks have the name of a place as the last word in the first line:

A *kid* in my *class* at my *school*,
Could *add* and sub*tract* on a *stool*.
Where he *stood* on his *head*,
Till his *face* turned quite *red*,
We *all* thought it *real*ly quite *cool*.

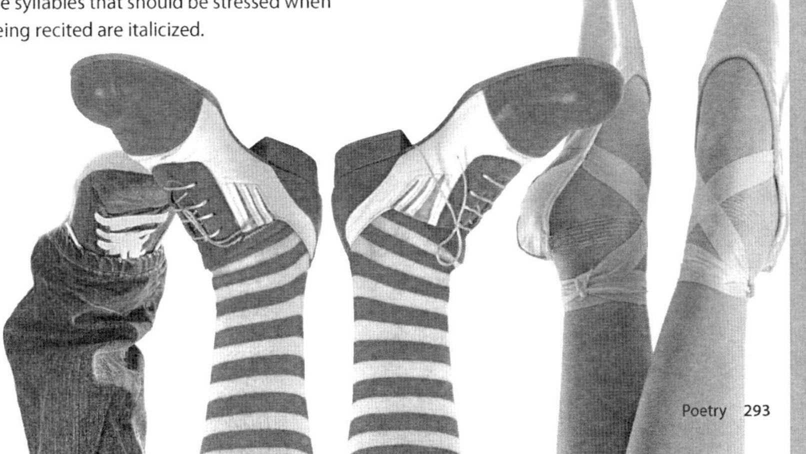

Lesson Two

Poetry Is Sound, Rhythm, and Rhyme!

A **limerick** is a five-line poem that is usually funny. Often, limericks are about human eccentricities or foibles. These little nonsense poems have the rhyme scheme *aabba*: The final words of the first two lines and the last rhyme, as do the final words of the second and third.

Traditionally, the 1st, 2nd, and 5th lines have eight beats, with the stress on the 2nd, 5th, and final beats. The 3rd and 4th lines have five (or six) beats, with the stress again on the 2nd and final beats.

As with all the categories, there are many exceptions to these rules. The rules are just a guide.

Note: Some of the words or concepts in the limericks presented in the textbook may not be well understood by your students. Make sure they know the definitions of all the words so that they can appreciate the humor of the limericks. The following is a small guide to words that your students may not know:

Ogden Nash

- **ingenious:** clever; creative
- **frugal:** the opposite of extravagant; saving money wherever possible
- **keys:** these keys refer to musical keys as in "c major" or "a minor"

Anonymous

- **gap:** a wide space
- **span:** bridge

Graham Lester

- **gullible:** easily fooled or tricked
- **phony:** fake

Anonymous

- **pickled:** preserved by salting
- **internal workings:** his digestive organs (stomach, etc.)

Limericks

The supreme master of the limerick was Edward Lear, an Englishman who lived from 1812 to 1888. He was the twentieth child in his family—raised by his oldest sister—and he was brilliant. He had epilepsy, asthma, and acute bouts of depression; nonetheless, he was a prolific writer and a gifted artist. He produced both serious and comic works. One of his fans was Queen Victoria to whom he gave drawing lessons. In spite of his poor health, he traveled widely. His work has been enjoyed for more than 150 years.

In *The Complete Book of Nonsense*, Lear published more than two hundred limericks, each of which was paired with an original drawing. This is a book you may want to look for at the library and share with your students. Below are some examples.

There was an Old Man with a nose,
Who said, "If you choose to suppose,
That my nose is too long,
You are certainly wrong!"
That remarkable Man with a nose.

There was an Old Lady of Chertsey,
Who made a remarkable curtsey;
She twirled round and round,
Till she sunk underground,
Which distressed all the people of Chertsey.

There was an Old Person of Buda,
Whose conduct grew ruder and ruder;
Till at last, with a hammer,
They silenced his clamour,
By smashing that Person of Buda.

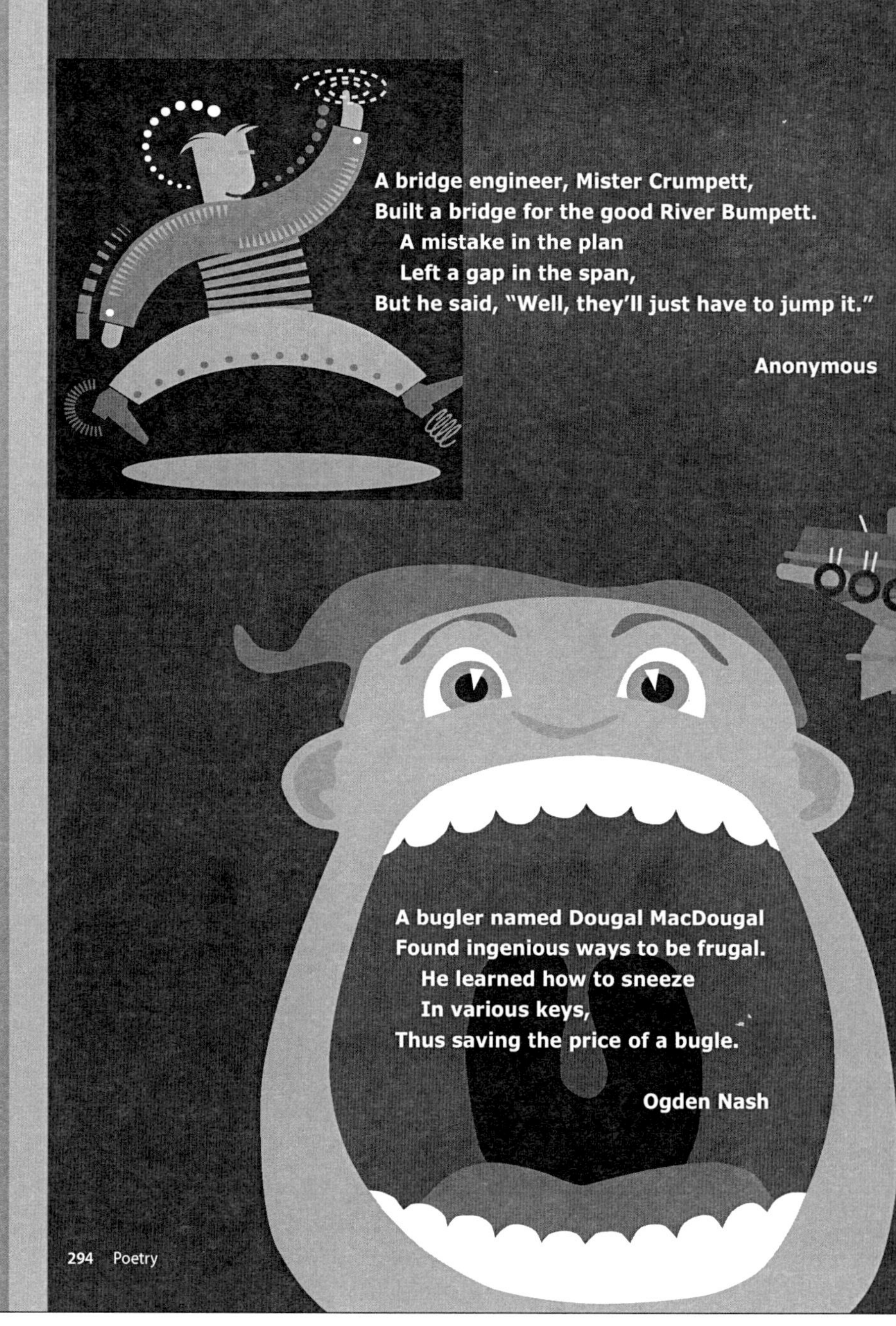

There was an Old Man of Nepaul,
From his horse had a terrible fall;
But, though split quite in two,
By some very strong glue,
They mended that Man of Nepaul.

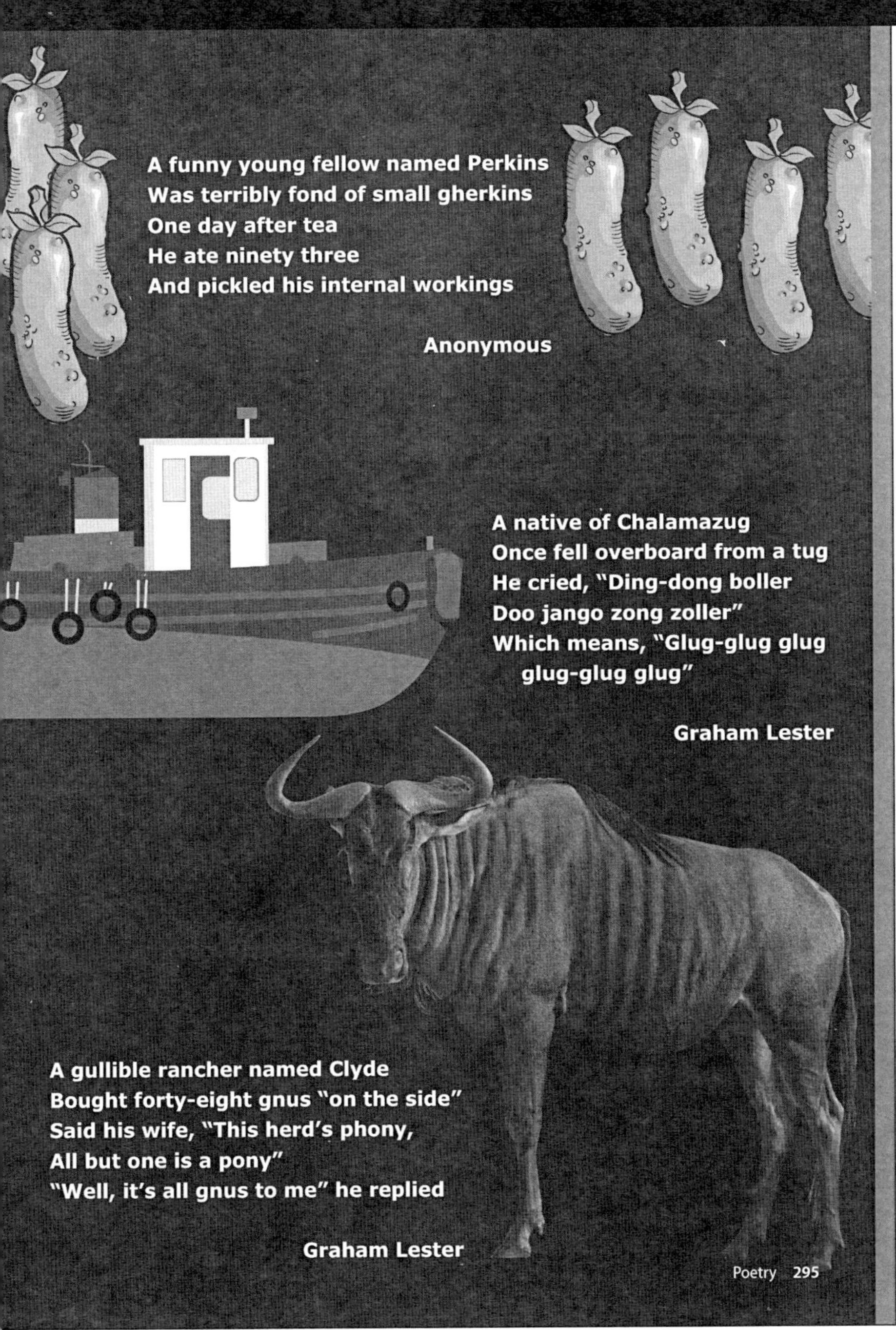

A List of Rhymes

Here are some rhymes to share with your students. Some limericks use personal names as the opening rhyme. For example:

There once was a toddler named Jane,
Who never had been on a train,
She walked everywhere
With her stuffed teddy bear
'Til she flew to LA in a plane.

You may want to help your students create a list of such rhymes as a resource for their own limerick writing. Ask them to help you generate a list of rhymes for Al, Ann, Bob, Dave, Flo, Jim, Jill, Kate, Lynn, Pat, Sam, etc. Make certain that they know to go through the alphabet sequentially when they are trying to think up rhymes. For example:

ate, bait, date, fate, freight, gate, hate, late, Kate, mate, Nate, plate, equate, rate, sate, slate, skate, state, trait, wait, weight

To help get you started, here are some others. We have not included words that may not be familiar to fourth graders. Ask the students to help you build such lists.

all, ball, brawl, call, crawl, fall, gall, hall, mall, Paul, Saul, shawl, small, squall, stall, tall, wall

bill, chill, dill, drill, fill, frill, gill, grill, hill, ill, Jill, kill, mill, nil, pill, Phil, quill, sill, skill, spill, still, till, trill, will

beat, cheat, eat, feat, feet, greet, heat, meet, neat, Pete, pleat, seat, sheet, sleet, sweet, treat, tweet, wheat

ail, bale, Braille, dale, fail, flail, Gail, gale, hale, hail, jail, kale, mail, nail, pail, pale, quail, rail, sail, scale, snail, stale, tale, tail, trail, vale, veil, whale

boo, coo, chew, clue, cue, do, due, few, flu, flue, goo, glue, grew, hue, knew, Lou, mew, moo, new, rue, sue, screw, skew, slew, spew, stew, strew, to, too, two, true, view, woo, who, you, zoo

best, blessed, confessed, chest, dressed, guest, guessed, jest, lest, messed, nest, pest, pressed, quest, rest, test, vest, west, zest

These lists are just to get you started. Clearly, there are a lot more easily rhymed words out there!

The Rhyming Contest

After you and your class have created these lists, divide the class into groups of three to four students. Each group will have one student assigned to be the recorder for the group. You will call out a word and then give the groups several minutes (perhaps you can use an egg timer) to write down as many rhymes as they can come up with for that word. Then you go on to the next word. This is a fun activity and good practice for limerick writing.

Think About It

1. A *sol*dier who *came* here from *France,*
   Had *stripes* down the *legs* of his *pants,*
   His *jack*et was *small,*
   Cause *he* was so tall,
   Instead of a *gun,* he'd a *lance.*
   Now *he'll* never *learn* how to *dance.*
   How *far* could he *get* from the *ants!*
   Now *his* horse is *learning* to *prance.*
2. Jane Smith came from Kalamazoo,
   Her *pet* was her *dear* cockatoo.
   Mar*ie* was all *white,*
   She *rarely* took *flight,*
   A *finger* she'd *bite,*
   She *never* would *fight,*
   Of *very* great *height,*
   She *slept* well at *night,*
   She *was* quite a *sight,*
   And *never* took *fright,*
   But her *squawk* made Jane *cry,* "Boo *hoo!*"
3. A young man from Philly, PA,
   (pronounced "pea *ay*")
   Said, "*This* is a *beautiful* day.
   He *took* off his *coat,*
   Then *he* cleared his *throat,*
   And *said,* "What more *is* there to *say*?"
   Said, "*My* horse could *do* with some *hay.*"
   And *said,* "Soon he is *going* to *neigh.*"
   Was *happy* and *cheerful* and *gay.*
   And said, *Everything's going* my *way.*
   Said, "*Dancing* is *always okay.*"
   And *that's* when he *started* to *sway.*
4. A *child* went to *play* at the *shore,*
   And *found* it was *really* a *bore.*
   The *sun* was too *hot,*
   A *sunburn* he *got,*
   Now *he* never *swims* any *more.*
   The *sand* scratched his *feet,*
   Now *that* was no *treat!*
   There was *sand* in the *food,*
   Now *that* was no *good,*
   He *started* to *frown,*
   When he *thought* he would *drown*…

Here are four limericks
for you to complete!

1. A *sol*dier who *came* here from *France,*
   Had *stripes* down the *legs* of his *pants,*
   His *jack*et was *small,*
   Cause *he* was so tall,
   ______________________.
2. Jane Smith came from *Kalamazoo,*
   Her *pet* was her *dear* cockatoo.
   Mar*ie* was all *white,*
   ______________________.
   But her *squawk* made Jane *cry,* "Boo *hoo!*"
3. A young man from Philly, PA,
   (pronounced "pea *ay*")
   ______________________.
   He *took* off his *coat,*
   Then *he* cleared his *throat,*
   And *said,* "______________________."
4. A *child* went to *play* at the *shore,*
   And *found* it was *really* a *bore.*
   ____
   ____
   Now *he* never *swims* anymore.

5. It is time to write your own limerick. Think of your three rhyming words in the 1st, 2nd, and 5th lines before you begin.
   Hint: When you are trying to find rhymes, start with one sound, and then go through the alphabet with it.
   For example: ***and, band, canned, fanned, grand, hand, land, manned, planned, sand, stand.***

6. Your teacher will pair you with another student. Rehearse one of the five limericks in your book or your *own* limericks, so that the two of you can recite a limerick or two for the class.

296 Poetry

5. Review the first drafts of your students' limericks. Suggest improvements, where necessary, and give them the opportunity to rewrite. Then help students choose partners for their limerick recitations. Give them some time to rehearse. Encourage them to have fun with this.

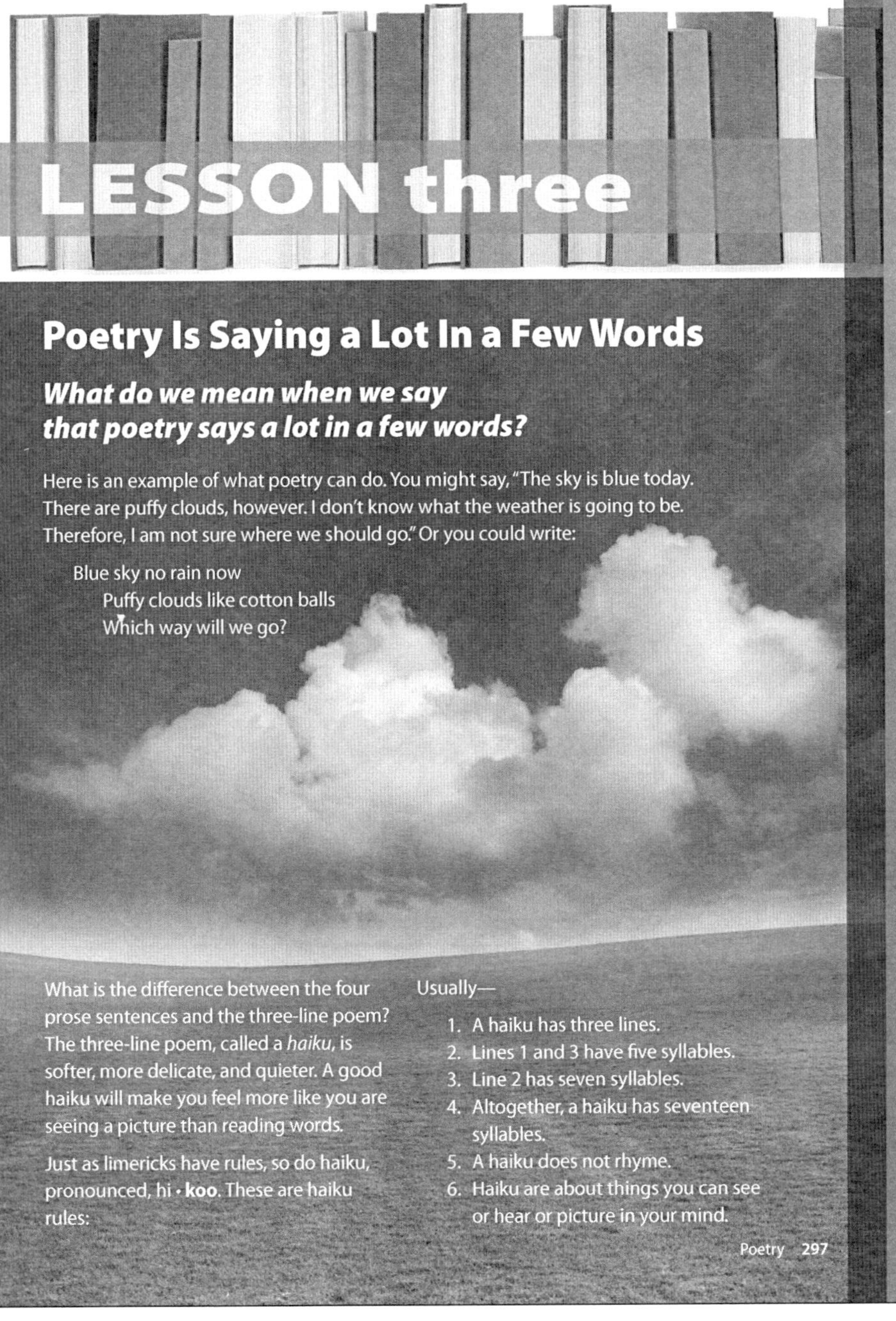

LESSON three

Poetry Is Saying a Lot In a Few Words

What do we mean when we say that poetry says a lot in a few words?

Here is an example of what poetry can do. You might say, "The sky is blue today. There are puffy clouds, however. I don't know what the weather is going to be. Therefore, I am not sure where we should go." Or you could write:

Blue sky no rain now
Puffy clouds like cotton balls
Which way will we go?

What is the difference between the four prose sentences and the three-line poem? The three-line poem, called a *haiku,* is softer, more delicate, and quieter. A good haiku will make you feel more like you are seeing a picture than reading words.

Just as limericks have rules, so do haiku, pronounced, hi • **koo**. These are haiku rules:

Usually—

1. A haiku has three lines.
2. Lines 1 and 3 have five syllables.
3. Line 2 has seven syllables.
4. Altogether, a haiku has seventeen syllables.
5. A haiku does not rhyme.
6. Haiku are about things you can see or hear or picture in your mind.

Poetry 297

Lesson Three

Poetry Is Saying a Lot In a Few Words

As we indicate in the textbook, these are the traditional haiku rules:

1. A haiku has three lines.
2. Lines 1 and 3 have five syllables.
3. Line 2 has seven syllables.
4. Altogether, then, a haiku has seventeen syllables.
5. A haiku does not rhyme.
6. Haiku are usually based on images (the pictures in your mind) and observations (what you can see or hear).
7. Haiku should give the reader a feeling.

Discuss the rules for haiku with your class. Then talk about the subtle, soft quality of the three three-line poems in the textbook. What does the poet see? What feelings emerge from reading these little, spare poems?

Syllabification

Do all of your students know what a syllable is?

Review the list of syllabified words on page 300 in the student textbook. Have the class look up some of the words in the dictionary, to show that the syllables have been separated correctly. Often, it is not clear with which syllable a consonant should go.

On the board, make columns, as we have done in the textbook, headed: **One Syllable**, **Two Syllables**, **Three Syllables**, **Four Syllables**. Call on members of the class to give you words from a particular category, one category to a line. Sometimes it is difficult to find four-syllable words that continue the theme, and you may need the help of a thesaurus.

Is your class familiar with a thesaurus? If you or they are looking for words within a particular category or synonyms that have the "right" number of syllables, a good thesaurus can be extremely helpful. Students may want to have access to a thesaurus when they are writing their own haiku.

After your discussion of syllabification, pass out a list of words (or write them on the board), and have students indicate the number of syllables next to each word. This is simply a check to determine whether some students need further preparation.

Haiku

Haiku is an old Japanese form of verse. Properly written haiku has extraordinary compression and is subtly suggestive. These terms or specifics are not necessarily the goal for fourth grade, but children surprise us with their intuitive sense of what the form calls for.

A great haiku uses imagery that comes from intense or careful observation or listening. Haiku were first seen in the 16th century. The medium was developed by the poet Basho (1644-1694), under whose pen the form became increasingly refined. Ideally, a haiku presents a pair of contrasting images, one suggestive of time and place, the other a vivid but fleeting observation. Working together, they evoke mood and emotion. The poet does not comment on the connection but leaves the synthesis of the two images for the reader to perceive.

In this short, fourth grade lesson on haiku you may not be able to reach so high, but a sense of the goal will help you guide your students.

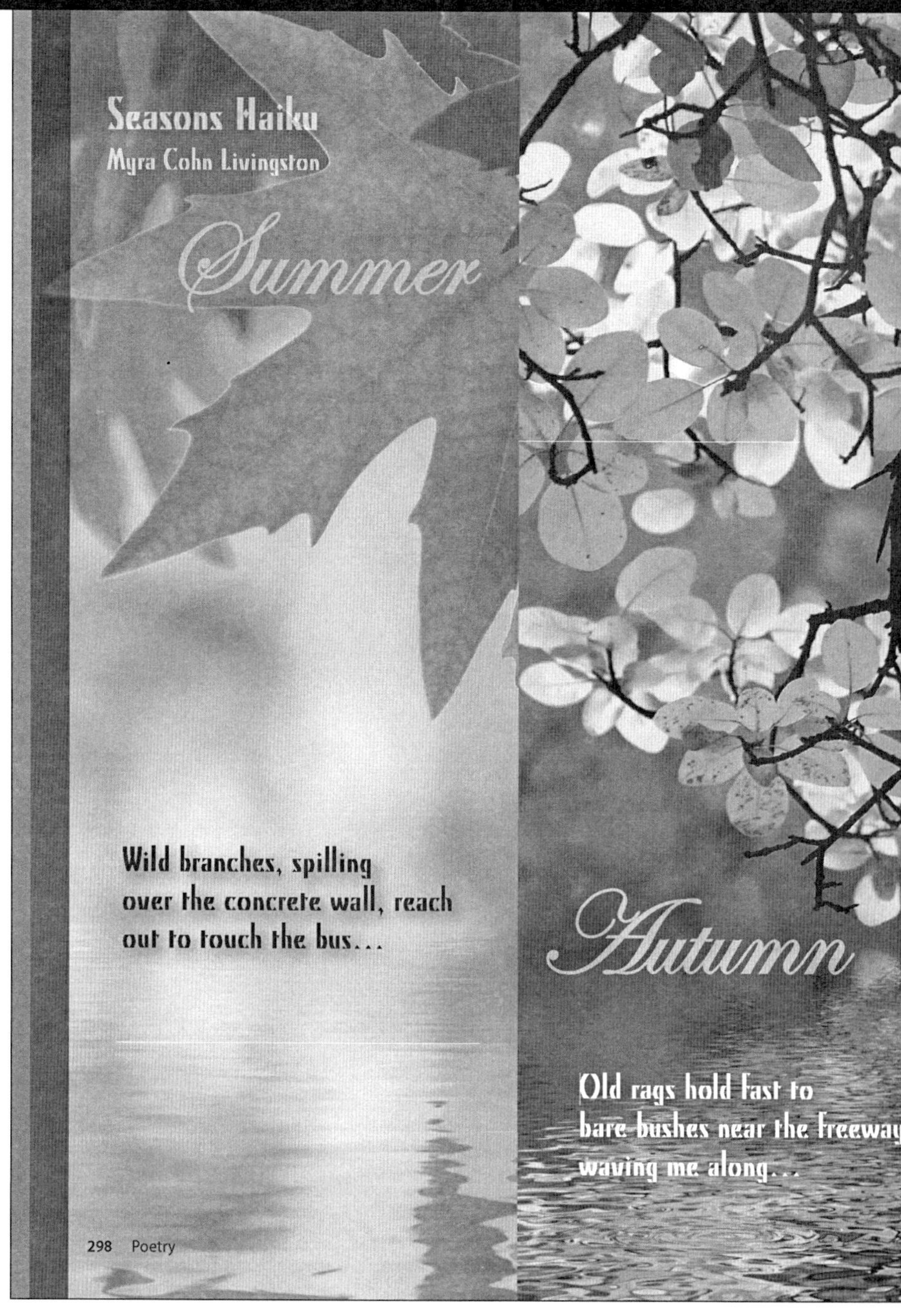
Seasons Haiku

Myra Cohn Livingston

Summer

Wild branches, spilling
over the concrete wall, reach
out to touch the bus...

Autumn

Old rags hold fast to
bare bushes near the freeway
waving me along...

298 Poetry

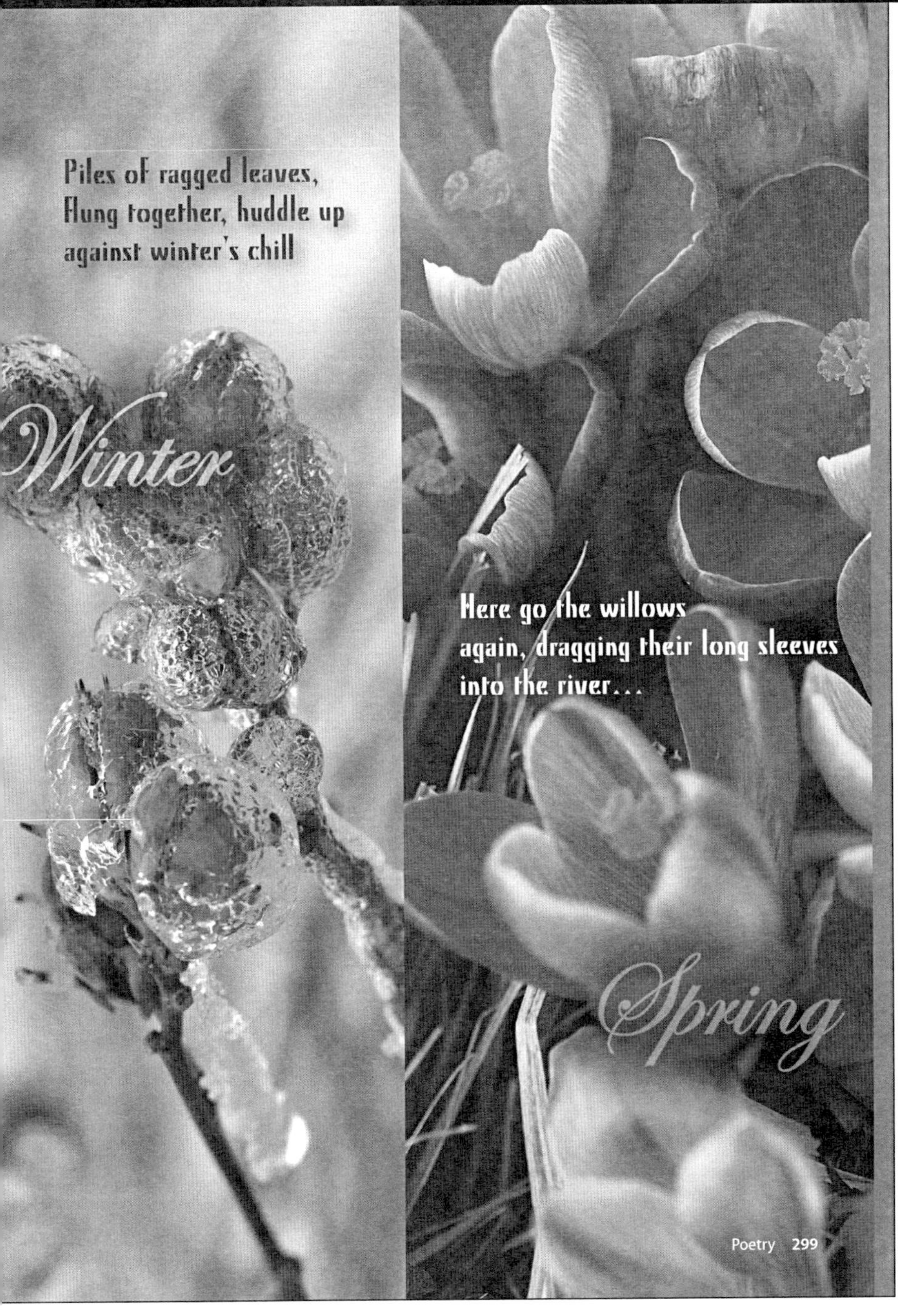
Piles of ragged leaves,
flung together, huddle up
against winter's chill
Winter
Here go the willows
again, dragging their long sleeves
into the river...
Spring
Poetry 299

Think About It

1. There are 5 syllables in the first line, 7 syllables in the second line, and 5 syllables in the third line. Each haiku has a total of 17 syllables.
2. You may wish to draw the suggested chart and make copies of it for your students to fill in. The following words should be in each column:
   Column 1: wild; reach; touch; bus; hold; fast; bare; near; piles; leaves; flung; chill; here; their; long
   Column 2: branches; spilling; over; concrete; brushes; freeway; waving; along; ragged; huddle; against; winter's; willows; again; dragging; into; river
   Column 3: together
3. Talk with the class about the categories suggested in the textbook: the seasons, animals, colors. Ask them for more suggestions. Other ideas: parts of a car, foods, ingredients for a cake, the weather, physical environments (for example, desert, mountains, lake, ocean, city). Stress the importance of sensory images and observations and the emergence of a feeling.

1. Go back and reread the four haiku. Count the syllables in each one, line by line. How many syllables are there in each line? How many syllables are in each haiku? Write down your answer.

Examples of Words Divided into Syllables

Now let's make sure you know what a syllable is. It is easy to explain by giving examples. Look at the examples line by line.

One Syllable	Two Syllables	Three Syllables	Four Syllables
car	au•to	Toy•o•ta	au•to•mo•bile
sport	base•ball	bas•ket•ball	to•bog•gan•ing
pleased	con•tent	sat•is•fied	com•fort•a•ble
pain	dis•tress	suf•fer•ing	mel•an•chol•y
flute	cel•lo	pi•an•o	har•mon•i•ca
ape	mon•key	go•ril•la	o•rang•u•tan
red	pur•ple	ma•gen•ta	aq•ua•ma•rine

2. On a piece of paper, draw a chart like the one shown. Your chart should have three columns. Number the columns one through three. Using words of four letters or more, write a list of one-syllable words into the column labeled "1." Write a list of two-syllable words under the column labeled "2." Write one three-syllable word in the third column. The words should be taken from the haiku poems on the previous pages.

3. Write four haiku. First, pick a topic that will provide you with four different pictures. Here are some examples: the seasons, animals, and colors—or think of a category of your own. Remember, your haiku will have three lines with syllables of 5/7/5. Haiku are supposed to be "word pictures." They describe something you can see or hear in your imagination.

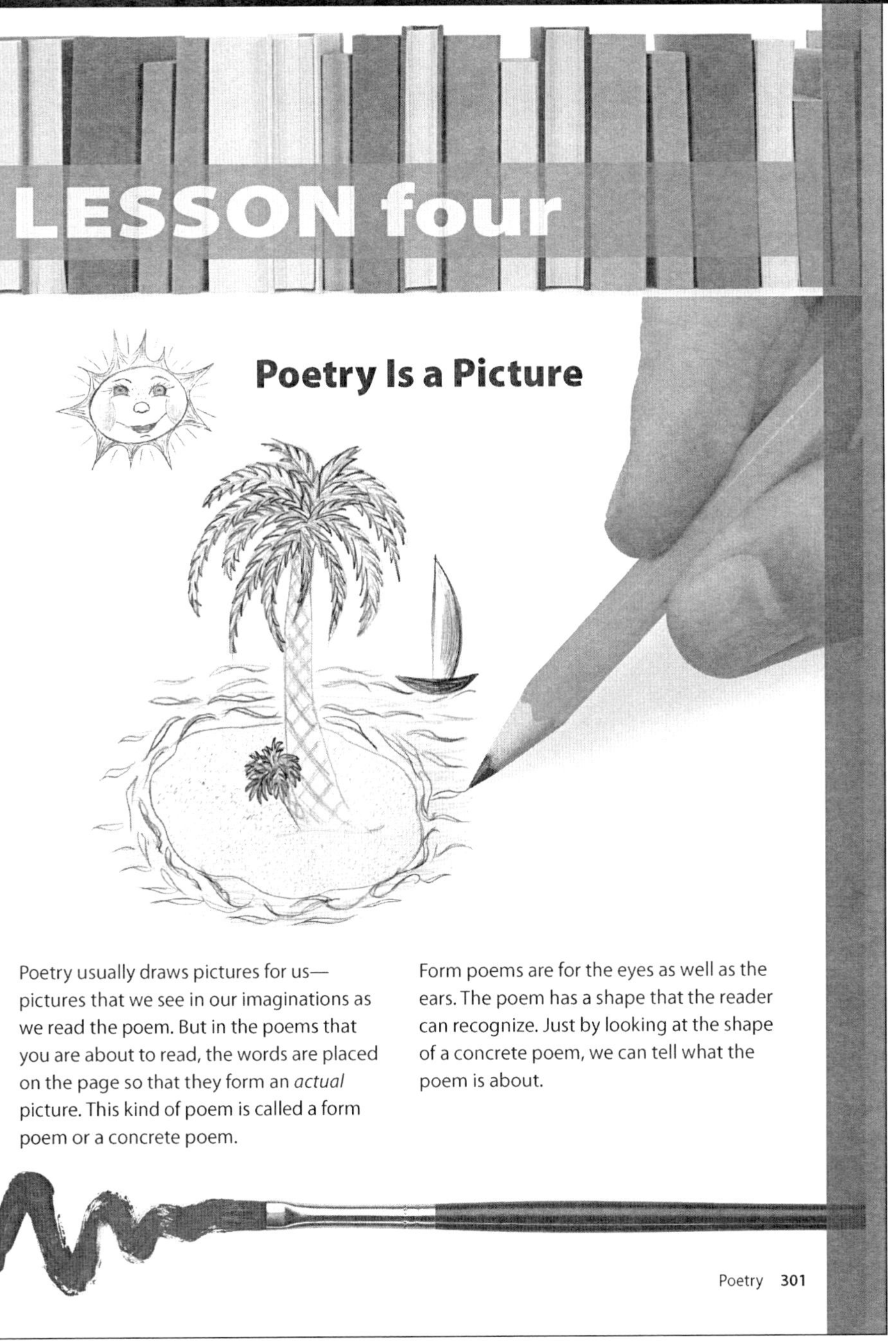

LESSON four

Poetry Is a Picture

Poetry usually draws pictures for us—pictures that we see in our imaginations as we read the poem. But in the poems that you are about to read, the words are placed on the page so that they form an *actual* picture. This kind of poem is called a form poem or a concrete poem.

Form poems are for the eyes as well as the ears. The poem has a shape that the reader can recognize. Just by looking at the shape of a concrete poem, we can tell what the poem is about.

Poetry 301

Lesson Four

Poetry Is a Picture

Form poetry is not only fun for students; its creation involves more than one physical sense (hearing and seeing) and more than one skill (writing and creating pictures).

Many people, both children and adults, have difficulty writing, and would be hard put to write a good poem. People become self-conscious trying to write. But watch ordinary folks in a hands-on pottery studio. Adults who never allow themselves to make art are suddenly taking their work very seriously. They are too involved in the process to think about themselves.

Form poetry works similarly for students. The making of the picture distracts them from their self-consciousness. Making art loosens the bonds and enables us to skirt some of the usual obstacles to creativity.

Talk with the class about shapes for poems. Together, generate a list of ideas for shapes on the board. In addition to the suggestions in the textbook, other possibilities include:

a spiral
a tent
a kite
a vase of flowers
a maze
a clock
a cube
a balloon

In fact, shapes that require dimension (such as a cube or a ball) are especially intriguing.

Caution your students that after they have chosen a shape, they should first work on and write out their poem in ordinary fashion. It is hard to see what you are doing when the words are going every which way.

You may want to give students time in class, as well as help with collage and poster board supplies, for their form poem projects.

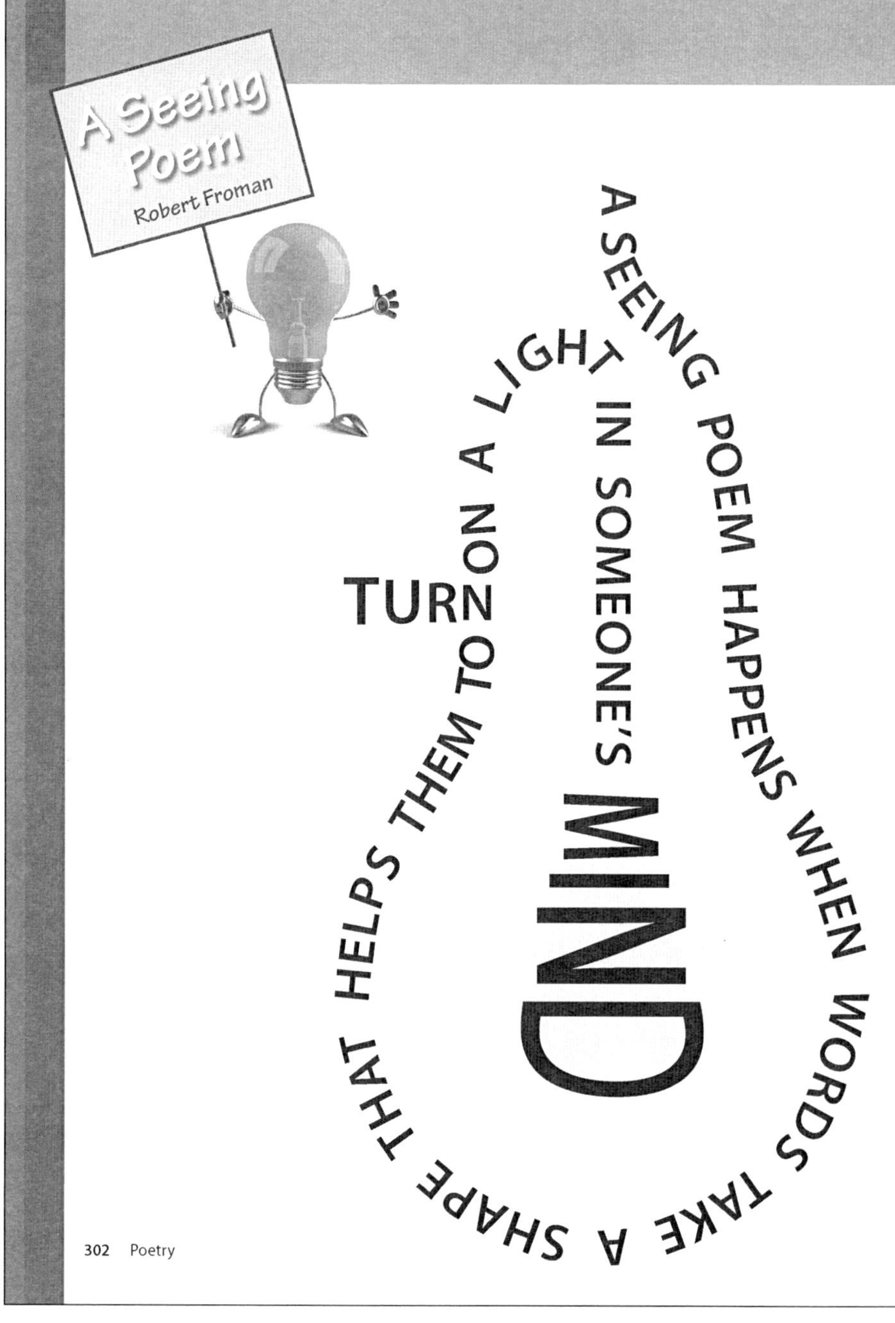
A Seeing Poem
Robert Froman
A SEEING POEM HAPPENS WHEN WORDS TAKE A SHAPE THAT HELPS THEM TO TURN ON A LIGHT IN SOMEONE'S MIND

POPSICLE

Joan Bransfield

popsicle
popsicle
tickle
tongue fun
licksicle
sticksicle
please
don't run
dripsicle
slipsicle
melt, melt
tricky
stopsicle
plopsicle
hand all
s
t
i
c
k
y

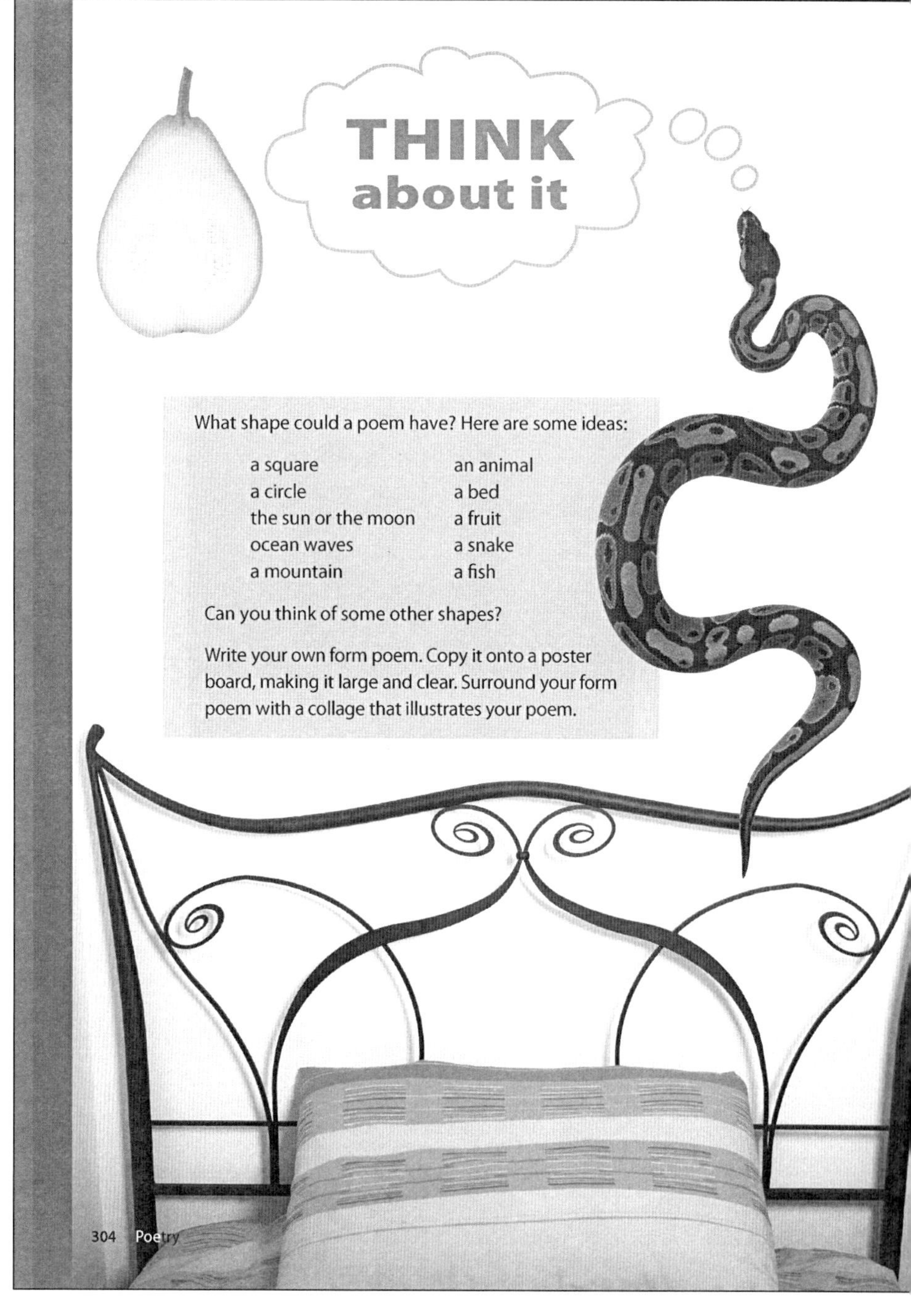

THINK about it

What shape could a poem have? Here are some ideas:

a square	an animal
a circle	a bed
the sun or the moon	a fruit
ocean waves	a snake
a mountain	a fish

Can you think of some other shapes?

Write your own form poem. Copy it onto a poster board, making it large and clear. Surround your form poem with a collage that illustrates your poem.

304 Poetry

LESSON five

Poetry Is Rhyme

You did lots of rhyming with limericks, so you really know what a rhyme is. But what is the definition of the word *rhyme*? When the end sounds of two words are the same, they rhyme. *Good* and *should* rhyme because *-ood* and *-ould* sound the same.

Rhyming poems are written in a variety of ways. Sometimes every two lines rhyme. For example:

> Rain, rain go ***away***
> Come again some other ***day***.

Sometimes, the second and fourth lines rhyme. For example:

> *Let me root, root, root for the home team*
> *If they don't win it's a* ***shame***
> *For it's one, two, three strikes you're out*
> *At the old ball* ***game***

The pattern in which the lines of a poem rhyme is called a **rhyme scheme**. A rhyme scheme shows which lines rhyme with which. Sometimes a rhyme scheme can be tricky. Look at the well-known nursery rhyme *Jack and Jill*.

> Jack and Jill
> Went up the hill,
> To fetch a pail of water.
>
> Jack fell down,
> And broke his crown,
> And Jill came tumbling after.

In this poem there are three lines in each verse. The first two lines of each verse rhyme:

> *Jill* and *hill*
> *down* and *crown*

The surprise comes in the third line. When we read the first verse, we think the third line is just "lonely," and rhymes with nothing. But we find its match when we read the second verse—it is the third line of the second verse!

> *water* and *after*

Lesson Five

Poetry Is Rhyme

Rhyme scheme is one of those topics that are far easier to teach by illustration than by definition. Every child knows that some poems rhyme in an *aabb* pattern, while others rhyme in an *abab* pattern. They just don't know how to verbalize this fact. It will be much easier to let them teach themselves about the different types of rhyme schemes than for you to attempt to describe them in a theoretical way. All you really need to do is give them one tool: the use of the label *a*, *b*, *c*, etc. Once they can do that, they can recognize and write down the rhyme scheme of any poem.

Compare and Contrast

Exercise #1 on page 308 calls upon students to make a table that helps them compare and contrast *Dust of Snow* and *The Shark*.

Compare is used to mean, "to examine the character or qualities of, in order to discover the *similarities*."

Contrast is used to mean "to examine the character or qualities of similar or comparable objects, in order to discover their *differences*."

Before students do the exercises, you will want to make sure you include a comparison of the two poems in your class discussion.

The Shark

About the Poem

The Shark is a wonderful performance piece because of its sly, dark, amused tone. Practice reading it aloud, so that you can give your class an imaginative dramatic reading.

The poem is seventeen lines and thirteen sentences long. The poem is written in couplets of rhymed pairs—except for the final three lines, which comprise a rhyming unit of three. The rhyme scheme is *aa bb cc dd ee ff gg eee.*

The Shark concerns itself with the desire to consume that drives the shark and has some very clever touches:

It opens and closes with the words, *My sweet,* which imply a ludicrous familiarity with the reader.

At the center of the poem, the central premise,

With those two bright eyes and that one dark thought.
He has only one, but he thinks it a lot.
And the thought he thinks but can never complete
Is his long dark thought of something to eat.

Reiterated at the end as,

That one dark thought he can never complete
Of something—anything—somehow to eat.

The poet repeats the word *swim(s)* in three consecutive lines—which really gives the sense that something's swimming around. *Dark* is repeated four times and his bright eyes are mentioned twice. There is superb consonance that is really a mouthful in Line 13 (*gulper, ripper, snatcher, grabber*), which has more beats than any other line in the poem (13).

The poem closes with a cautionary threat that makes for high drama.

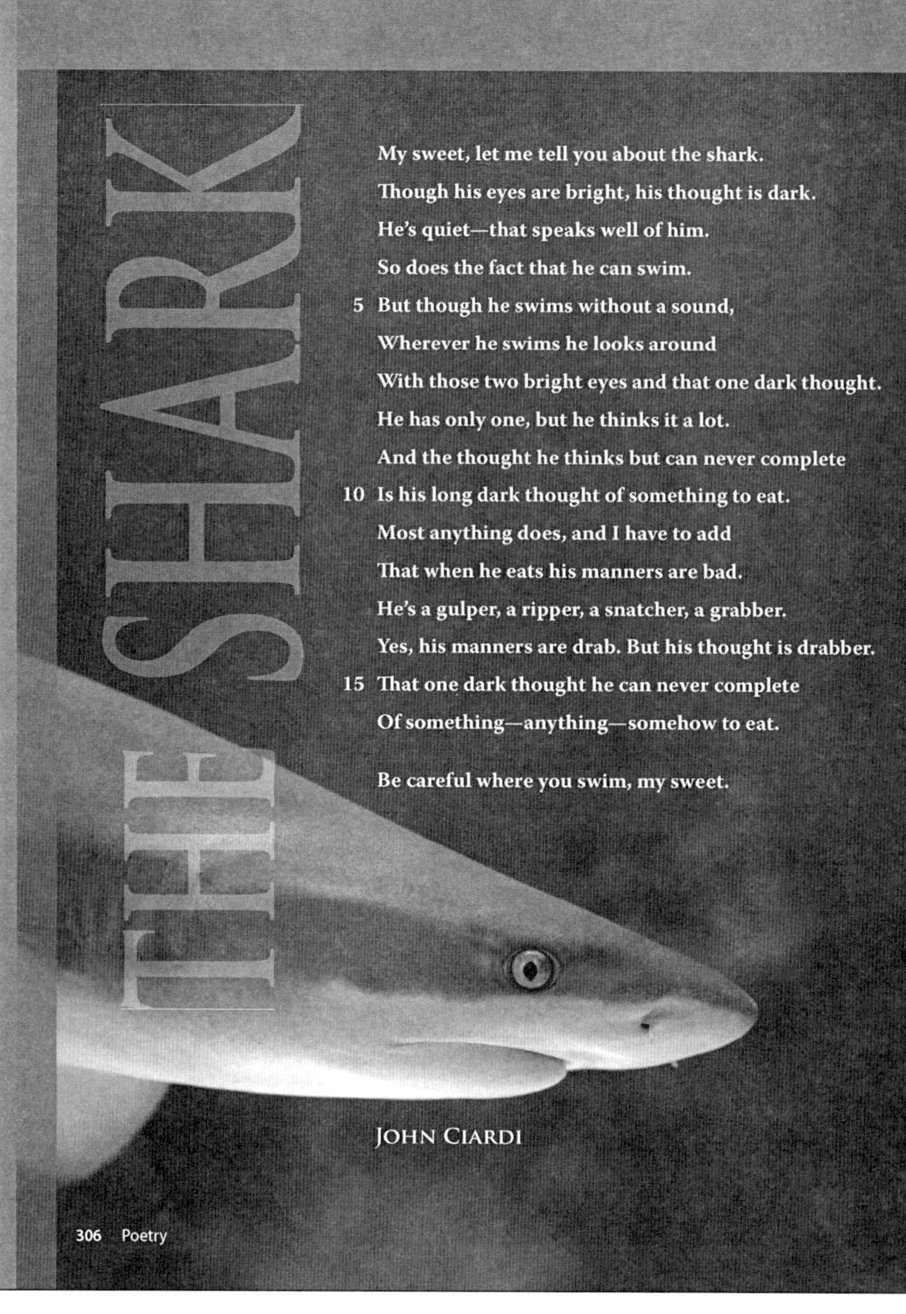

THE SHARK

My sweet, let me tell you about the shark.
Though his eyes are bright, his thought is dark.
He's quiet—that speaks well of him.
So does the fact that he can swim.
But though he swims without a sound,
Wherever he swims he looks around
With those two bright eyes and that one dark thought.
He has only one, but he thinks it a lot.
And the thought he thinks but can never complete
Is his long dark thought of something to eat.
Most anything does, and I have to add
That when he eats his manners are bad.
He's a gulper, a ripper, a snatcher, a grabber.
Yes, his manners are drab. But his thought is drabber.
That one dark thought he can never complete
Of something—anything—somehow to eat.

Be careful where you swim, my sweet.

JOHN CIARDI

306 Poetry

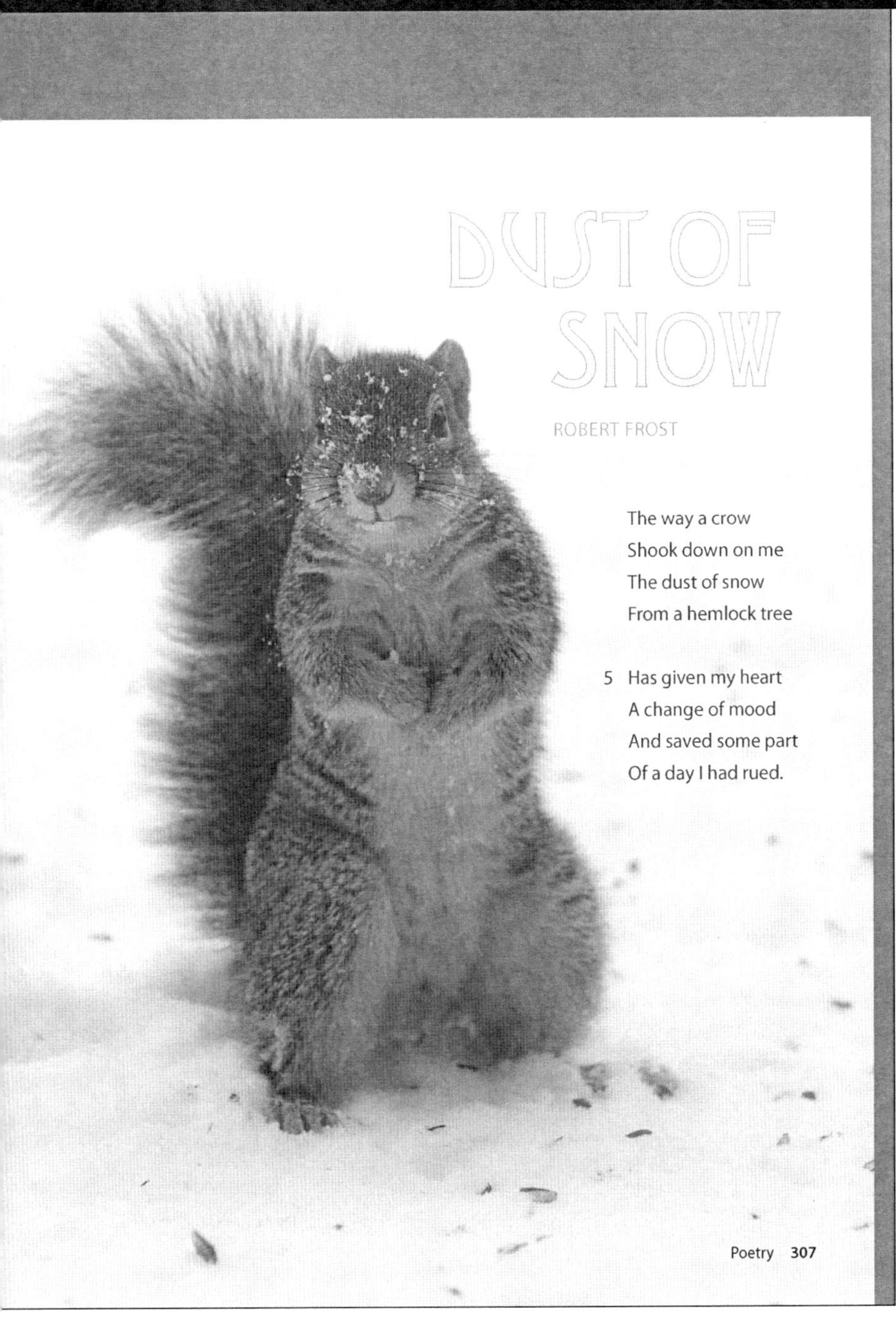

DUST OF SNOW

ROBERT FROST

The way a crow
Shook down on me
The dust of snow
From a hemlock tree

Has given my heart
A change of mood
And saved some part
Of a day I had rued.

Poetry 307

Dust of Snow

About the Poem

At first glance, *Dust of Snow* seems a simple eight-line poem of two stanzas, with a rhyme scheme of *abab cdcd.* All but two of the words have only one syllable. The beats per line are 4-4-4-5 (first stanza) and 5-4-4-6 (second stanza).

The vocabulary is easy, except for the final word, *rued,* which means, "felt penitence, remorse, or regret for." Certainly, this was not a day to which the speaker of the poem was looking forward!

We learn that poets create pictures with similes or metaphors. But *Dust of Snow* has no similes or metaphors. In fact, the poem does not even have a single adjective. What about the repetition we've heard so much about? There appears to be none in this poem, except the rhyming sounds and the rhythmic consistency.

Dust of Snow, then, can be taught as a nice little poem for the fourth grade, a poem about a person who didn't feel very cheerful on a particular day, but whose mood was lightened by a crow's shaking snow down onto him from a pine tree.

But Robert Frost is a very careful poet of exquisite sensibility. His use of particular words to convey theme is often so quiet, so subtle as to escape notice—unless we set about trying to figure out just what he is doing. Often, one needs to look up words he uses, to check whether they have a second meaning, to check whether his words cast a shadow we don't readily perceive.

Some of what Frost has done here may be a little sophisticated for the understanding of fourth graders. You will have to decide what you can take from the discussion that follows, either for yourself or for your students.

For this poem, we need to think about symbols. What is a symbol? A **symbol** is a visible thing that stands for or suggests something invisible or intangible. You can give your students examples of symbols, and they will likely be able to understand this. A lion is a symbol of courage. A key may represent freedom. The American flag may represent liberty. In general, all flags are visual symbols of the nations they represent. A skull and crossbones is a symbol of poison. A heart is a symbol of love. The shining sun may be a symbol of warmth and happiness. Think about this. Do other symbols come to mind? Now ask yourself (and perhaps the class) what a crow is symbolic of. What about hemlock? And where do we often hear the word "dust"?

Crows and ravens (which belong to the same family of birds) often feature in European legends as signs of doom or death. Presumably, this is because of their startling glossy black plumage, their shrill cries, and their tendency to eat carrion. It has been claimed that they circle above scenes of death, such as battles.

Hemlock is defined as "any of several poisonous herbs" and as "a drug or lethal drink prepared from the poison hemlock." Even though Frost refers to the hemlock tree, not hemlock the herb, this dark echo remains.

Dust, of course, is evocative of every man's ultimate return to "dust" in death.

Crow, hemlock, and *dust* all carry strong connotations of death and set the tone of the first stanza. This is the darkness that is lifted for the second stanza and for the conclusion of the poem by the actions of the crow.

Hemlock is also "any of a genus of evergreen coniferous trees of the pine family." It is significant that the tree beneath which the speaker of the poem stands remains green even in winter. Even in winter, when plants appear to be dead, most trees are leafless, and the earth seems to have died, some trees remain green—a harbinger of spring, of life and cheer to come.

Think About It

1.

	Dust of Snow	*The Shark*
Rhyme Scheme (Which lines rhyme?)	*abab cdcd*	*aabbccddeeffggeee*
Number of Lines (Don't count the indented lines!)	Eight	Seventeen
Number of Sentences	One	Thirteen
Mood of the Poem (Serious? Funny?)	Serious	Darkly funny
What Is the Poem About?	A person's dark mood is lifted by a crow's shaking snow down upon him.	A shark is driven by one desire: the desire to eat.
Author	Robert Frost	John Ciardi

2. a. He means a day about which he felt remorse and sorrow. If he had rued the day, he was dissatisfied, and felt regret about events that had happened.

   b. He might be more cheerful. He might be looking forward to the day. Or, he might just be going through the day without any particular feeling one way or the other.

1. Robert Frost's *Dust of Snow* and John Ciardi's *The Shark* are very different from each other—except that both poems have rhymes. Create a table like the one below. (You will need extra space for Rhyme Scheme and What Is the Poem About?.) Fill in the table. When you have finished, you will have *compared* and *contrasted* the two poems.

	Dust of Snow	The Shark
Rhyme Scheme (Which lines rhyme?)		
Number of Lines (Don't count the indented lines!)		
Number of Sentences		
Mood of the Poem (Serious? Funny?)		
What Is the Poem About?		
Author		

2. a. The word *rued* means regretted—to be very sorry about something. What does Robert Frost mean when he says, "a day I had rued"? How did the poet feel about the day, if he rued it?

   b. The crow changed the poet's mood. How did he feel after the crow shook snow on him?

Poetry Is Fun to Write

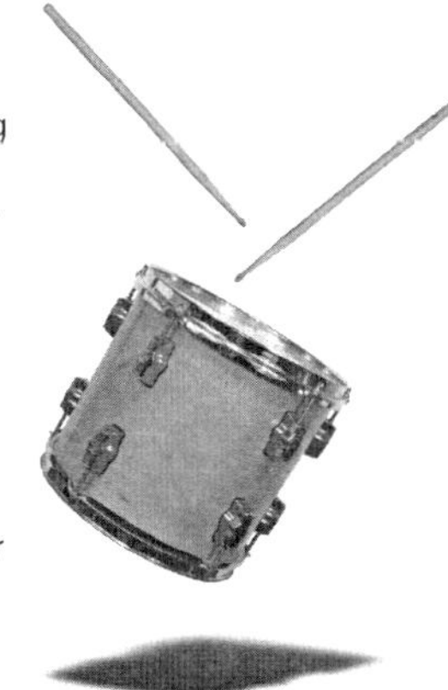

Have you ever thought that you could write a poem by making a list? Have you ever thought that you could take a list and make it into a poem? You can! Each of the poems you will now read uses a list. *Some Opposites* is a list of opposites. *Tortillas Like Africa* begins and ends with a story about "Isaac and me" making tortillas, but the middle six lines are a list of countries.

The use of lists is a way that these two poems are alike. How are these two *different*?

Some Opposites has a regular rhythm of eight or nine beats per line. Also, every two lines of *Some Opposites* rhyme.

Count the beats in each line of *Tortillas Like Africa*. Do the lines all have the same beat? Now look at the last words of the lines. Do the lines rhyme?

Poems that don't have a regular beat and don't rhyme have a special name: FREE VERSE! *Tortillas Like Africa* is free verse.

What, then, makes free verse poetry? Free verse often has a lot of repetition. Lines may be repeated. Phrases may be repeated. Words may be repeated. Sounds may be repeated.

Free verse poems, like other poetry, may have odd punctuation: no periods, commas where there should be periods, and commas where there should be no punctuation.

Free verse poems may have capital letters in the middle of sentences. It may have very long sentences or no sentences. A line may leave you hanging, on the edge of a cliff, waiting for the next line to complete the idea. You will see how this works in the poetry lesson that follows.

REPEAT

Lesson Six
Poetry Is Fun to Write

Both of the poems in this unit incorporate lists. *Some Opposites* is a list of opposites. You may want to review this list with your students. The phenomena for which opposites are named are listed in this chart:

Phenomenon	Its Opposite
standing still	*walking up or down a hill* *Running backwards, creeping, crawling* *leaping off a cliff and falling* *turning somersaults* *any other mode of travel*
a doughnut	*a cookie with a hole around it*
two	*a lonely me* *a lonely you*
a cloud	*a white reflection in the sea* *a huge blueness in the air*
opposite	?

Tortillas Like Africa begins and ends with a story about the speaker and Isaac (his brother?) making tortillas in the first and last stanzas, but the two middle stanzas are a list of countries that their tortillas resemble. Of the eight countries mentioned, five are described.

Africa	
Colombia	
Greenland	
Italy	the boot country
Mexico	[their] homeland to the south
Chile	thin as a tie
France	square as a hat
Australia	with patches of jumping kangaroos

To prepare your students for writing their own list poems, ask them to describe other countries on the classroom map. You can also throw out the names of zoo animals and ask for "poetic" descriptions. For example, a zebra is not just white and black stripes, but may look like a thunderbolt or venetian blinds. An elephant has what? Why, ears like triangles, a nose like a hose, and skin gray as gravel. A camel has one or two mountains and the line of the horizon on its back. A cat is a purr and a hiss, a dog a woof woof, and so forth. You want to guide your students into thinking in terms of the shapes or activities phenomena suggest—*not* their precise description. The same idea can be applied to friends, clothes in the closet, or items in a drawing.

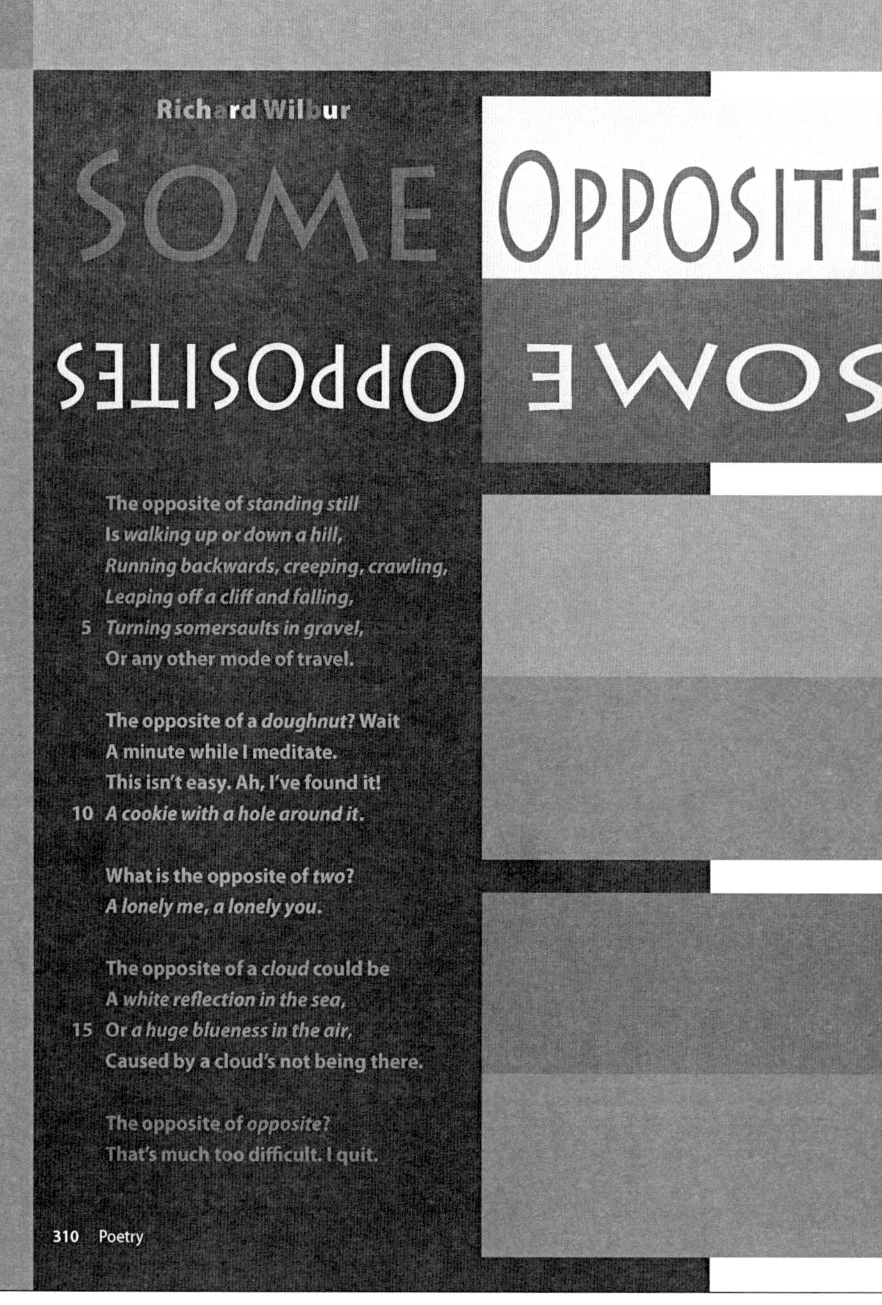

Richard Wilbur

SOME OPPOSITES

The opposite of *standing still*
Is *walking up or down a hill,*
Running backwards, creeping, crawling,
Leaping off a cliff and falling,
Turning somersaults in gravel,
Or any other mode of travel.

The opposite of a *doughnut?* Wait
A minute while I meditate.
This isn't easy. Ah, I've found it!
A cookie with a hole around it.

What is the opposite of *two?*
A lonely me, a lonely you.

The opposite of a *cloud* could be
A white reflection in the sea,
Or *a huge blueness in the air,*
Caused by a cloud's not being there.

The opposite of *opposite?*
That's much too difficult. I quit.

310 Poetry

Discuss what characterizes these two poems in order to identify their major differences.

Some Opposites has a regular rhythm of eight or nine beats per line. Every couplet (each pair of lines) rhymes. Your students can count the beats in each line, and you write the numbers down on the board. Your students can also identify the rhymes.

Now, have your students count the beats in each line of *Tortillas Like Africa.* Write *these* numbers on the board. Go over the last word of each line. Clearly there is no rhyming here.

You can now review **free verse** with your class. Free verse poems don't have a regular (consistent from line to line) beat and don't rhyme. Therefore, *Tortillas Like Africa* is free verse.

Talk with students about what it is about *Tortillas Like Africa* that makes it poetry. (You and the class will have more practice with this in Lesson Seven with *Good Hotdogs* and *Jackrabbit.*) Free verse often has a lot of repetition. Lines may be repeated. Phrases may be repeated. Words may be repeated. Sounds may be repeated.

Which lines are repeated in *Tortillas Like Africa?* No full lines are repeated.

Which phrases?

When we
Here was

Which words?

tortillas
When
dough
board
roll(ing)(ed)
round

Which sounds?

Check out the ***d*** in ***d****ough*, ***d****ust*, *boar****d***

the ***o*** sound in *d****o****ugh*, *b****o****wl*, *g****o****es*, *r****o****ll(ing)(ed)*

the ***oo*** sound in *kangar****oo****s* and *m****oo****n*

the consonants ***s*** and ***t*** in *twist* and *stretch*

You and your class can surely find other repetitions of sound.

What odd punctuation is there in this poem? Count the number of words in the first stanza. Would this be written as only one sentence in prose? What about the *absence* of a comma at the end of the first line of the last stanza? *Tortillas Like Africa* clearly has a large number of capital letters in the middle of its few sentences in the first and last stanzas. Moreover, notice the funny line break at the end of Line 4. *Here goes* what?

Typical of what we think of as *poetic,* the poem has lots of nice images that create pictures in the mind's eye: *the shapes of faraway lands, thin as a tie, square as a hat, with patches of jumping kangaroos,* and *a pocked moon.* The poet uses strong, precise verbs that we can hear or imagine: *squeezed, spanked, palmed, giggled,* and *threw.* But the finest and oddest image, with its nouns derived from verbs, is the final one. These tortillas look like *the twist and stretch of the earth taking shape.* It is hard to figure out just what that means, but its power is nonetheless undiminished.

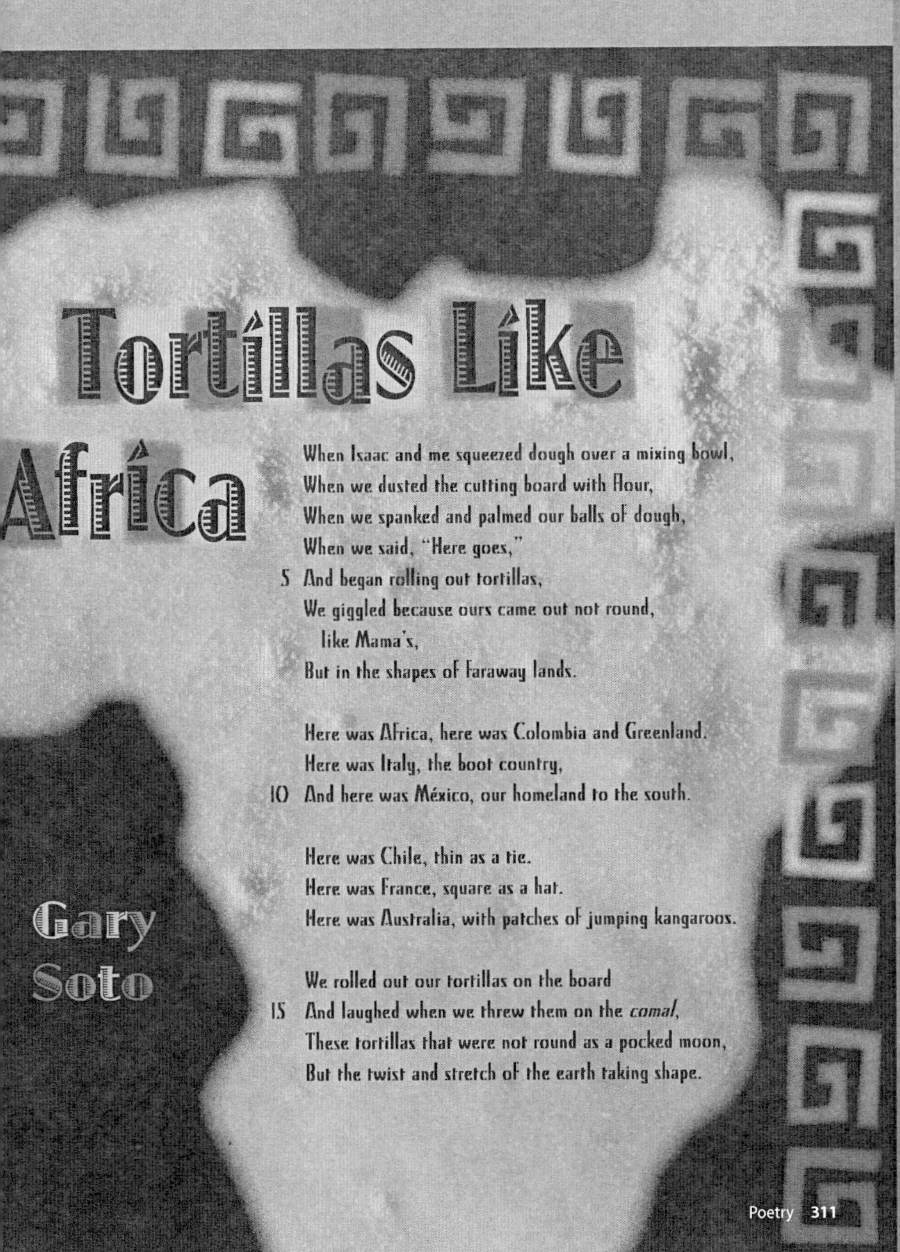

Tortillas Like Africa

Gary Soto

When Isaac and me squeezed dough over a mixing bowl,
When we dusted the cutting board with flour,
When we spanked and palmed our balls of dough,
When we said, "Here goes,"
And began rolling out tortillas,
We giggled because ours came out not round,
like Mama's,
But in the shapes of faraway lands.

Here was Africa, here was Colombia and Greenland.
Here was Italy, the boot country,
And here was México, our homeland to the south.

Here was Chile, thin as a tie.
Here was France, square as a hat.
Here was Australia, with patches of jumping kangaroos.

We rolled out our tortillas on the board
And laughed when we threw them on the *comal*,
These tortillas that were not round as a pocked moon,
But the twist and stretch of the earth taking shape.

Think About It

1. Students may use our topics (or their own), and if it helps, they can begin with one of the couplets given. Look at your students' first drafts, and offer suggestions regarding including more details and some images.
2. See chart on page T309 for answers.
3. A similar phenomenon or the phenomenon itself.
4. See list on page T309 for answers.
5. Answers will vary.

THINK about it

Here's what you have to do...

Take a look in your refrigerator.
What do you see?

A brown apple with a bite
Guess it didn't taste quite right.

Take a look at your dresser drawer.

Two pens, some stamps, and, look! six keys!
Some dust that always makes me sneeze.

Now look in your closet?

A white blouse ironed, wrinkle-free,
It has a pocket for my key.

How about a list of your friends?

Benjamin, sometimes angry but wise
A better friend than three other guys.

How about a list of the animals at the zoo?

A zebra like a thunderbolt,
A momma horse with her new colt.

You have been given these two-line openers so that you can do the following:

1. Write your own list poem of eight or more lines. You can use one of the suggested topics or one you think up yourself. Make this a rhyming poem. Rhyme every two lines or every other line. Remember that this is more than a list. You should include some detailed descriptions, as well as thoughts and feelings.
2. Richard Wilbur's list includes *standing still, a doughnut, two,* and *a cloud.* Write down his list, and next to each item write its opposite (or opposites, where he gives more than one).
3. What do you think is the opposite of *opposite?*
4. Make a list of the countries in Gary Soto's poem. Write each country on a separate line. Three of the countries have no description. But next to each country that *does,* write the words he uses to describe it.
5. Now is your chance to write a free-verse list poem. You may use the same topic you used for your rhyming poem, one of the other topics that was suggested, or something you have thought of yourself.

Poetry Is Free

What does that *mean—that poetry is free?*

When you write a poem, you let a part of yourself go free. You share some of your thoughts or memories with other people. You let a part of yourself out into the world. Some of your feelings and ideas can go for a long, long walk!

Poetry is also freer. That is, poetry is freer than prose. When you write free verse poetry, you can write in any shape or form. You can let one line hang out like the ledge of a cliff. The next line can be just one word. *You* decide what you want to do with your poem.

You don't have to use punctuation, or you can use punctuation in odd places. You don't have to use capital letters, or you can use MANY capital letters. If you are writing free verse, poetry has very few rules.

Lesson Seven

Poetry Is Free

Ask students if they have ever noticed how writing in a journal (or a diary) or writing a letter can provide a private, satisfying release for their ideas and images—a way of letting feelings go, setting feelings down, or communicating with another person. This can be similar to the way it feels to draw or paint a picture. Since Lesson Seven is the conclusion of the Poetry Unit, now is a good time to begin poetry journals.

For this project, students keep a notebook, or a section of their notebook, in which they write a free verse poem each day. You should set aside regular class time—the same time each day, if possible—for this activity. At the scheduled time, students close their eyes and rest their heads on their arms for three minutes. At the end of the three minutes, students take five minutes to write in verse what they have just seen in their mind's eye.

Every two weeks or so, students can volunteer to write one of their poems on the board. This will be an opportunity for you to talk about how a poem may be made stronger or how its meaning may change if the line breaks, or the punctuation or capitalization are altered.

Read *Good Hotdogs* aloud to your class several times. Discuss the sounds they hear repeated—both vowel and consonant sounds. Then have them complete Exercises 1–4 in the *Think About It* section on p. 320. *Jackrabbit* is a dramatic performance piece. Make several groups of four to six students from the class. Have the groups, themselves, determine how to divide up the poem for performance. Allow class time for rehearsal. It should be interesting to see how the varying divisions create different renditions of the poem.

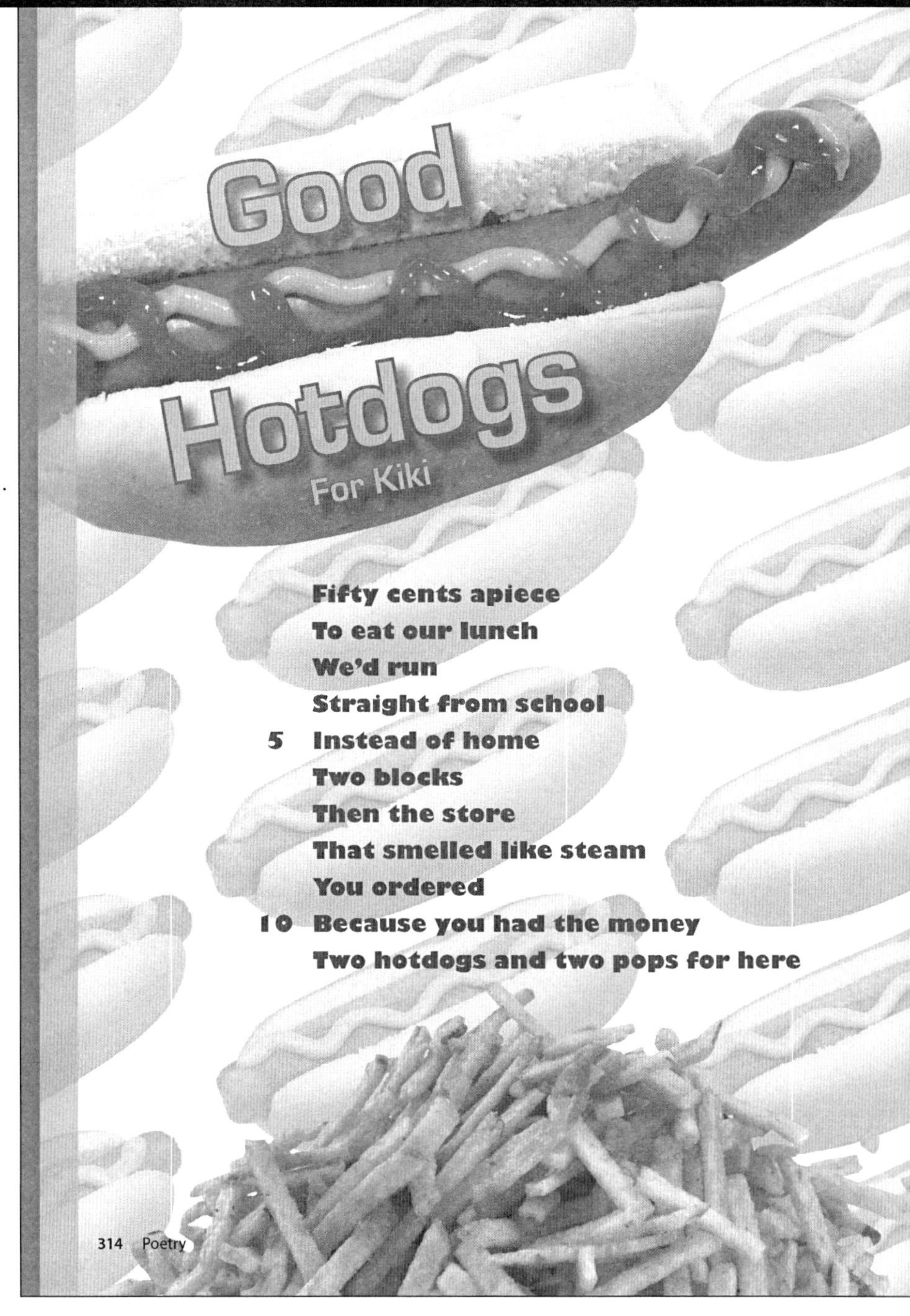

Good Hotdogs

For Kiki

Fifty cents apiece
To eat our lunch
We'd run
Straight from school
Instead of home
Two blocks
Then the store
That smelled like steam
You ordered
Because you had the money
Two hotdogs and two pops for here

Everything on the hotdogs
Except pickle lily
Dash those hotdogs
Into buns and splash on
All that good stuff
Yellow mustard and onions
And french fries piled on top all
Rolled up in a piece of wax
Paper for us to hold hot
In our hands
Quarters on the counter
Sit down
Good hotdogs
We'd eat
Fast till there was nothing left
But salt and poppy seeds even
The little burnt tips
Of french fries
We'd eat
you humming
And me swinging my legs

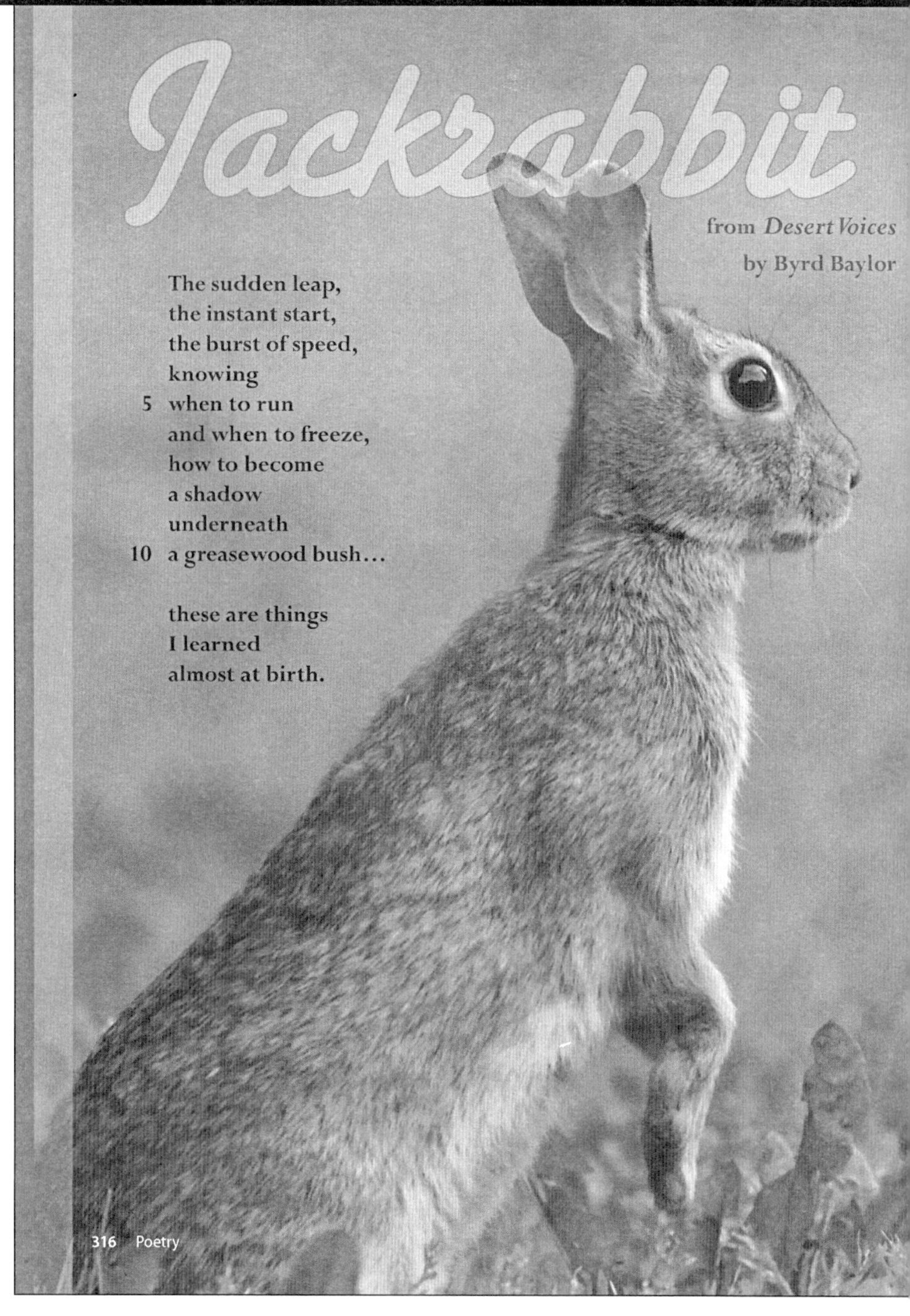

Jackrabbit

from *Desert Voices*

by Byrd Baylor

The sudden leap,
the instant start,
the burst of speed,
knowing
when to run
and when to freeze,
how to become
a shadow
underneath
a greasewood bush...

these are things
I learned
almost at birth.

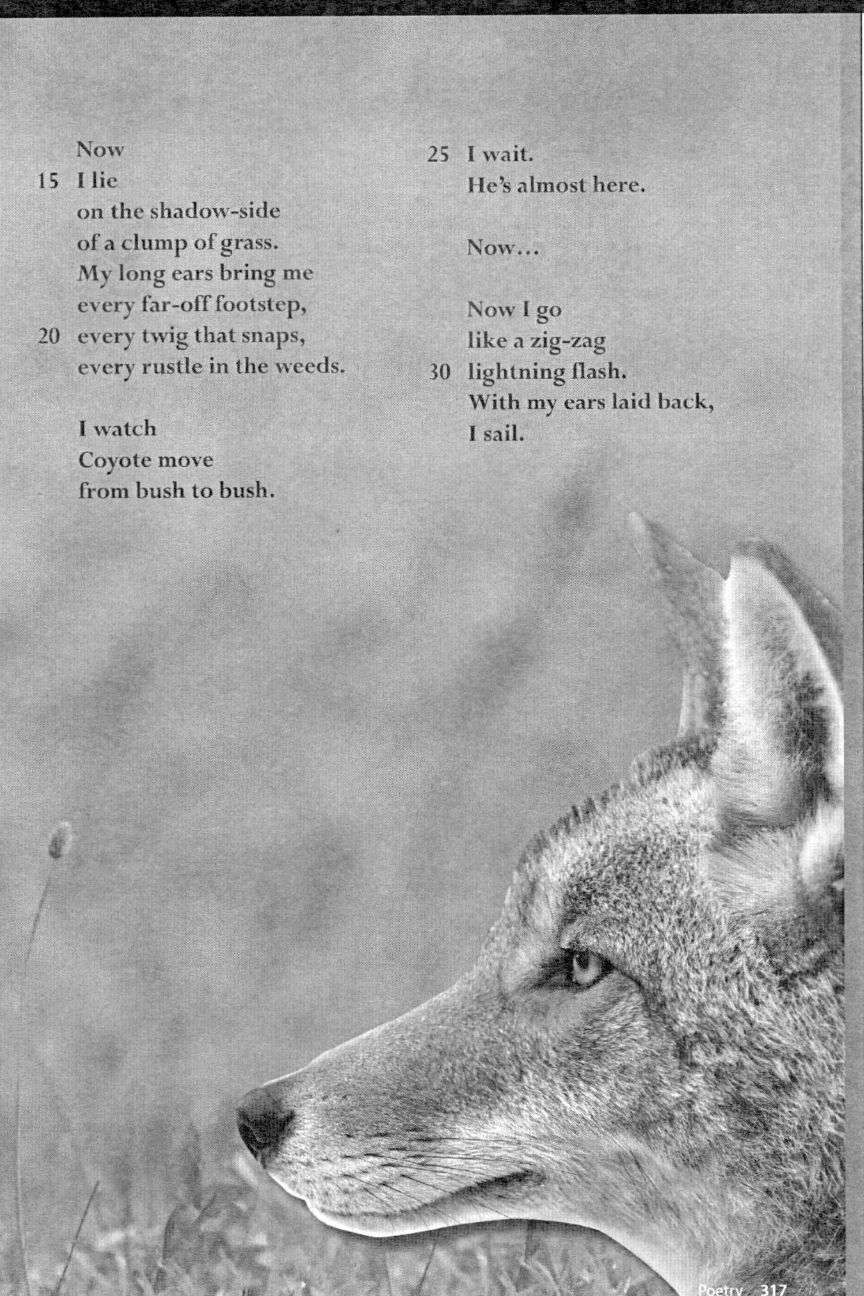

Now
I lie
on the shadow-side
of a clump of grass.
My long ears bring me
every far-off footstep,
every twig that snaps,
every rustle in the weeds.

I watch
Coyote move
from bush to bush.

I wait.
He's almost here.

Now...

Now I go
like a zig-zag
lightning flash.
With my ears laid back,
I sail.

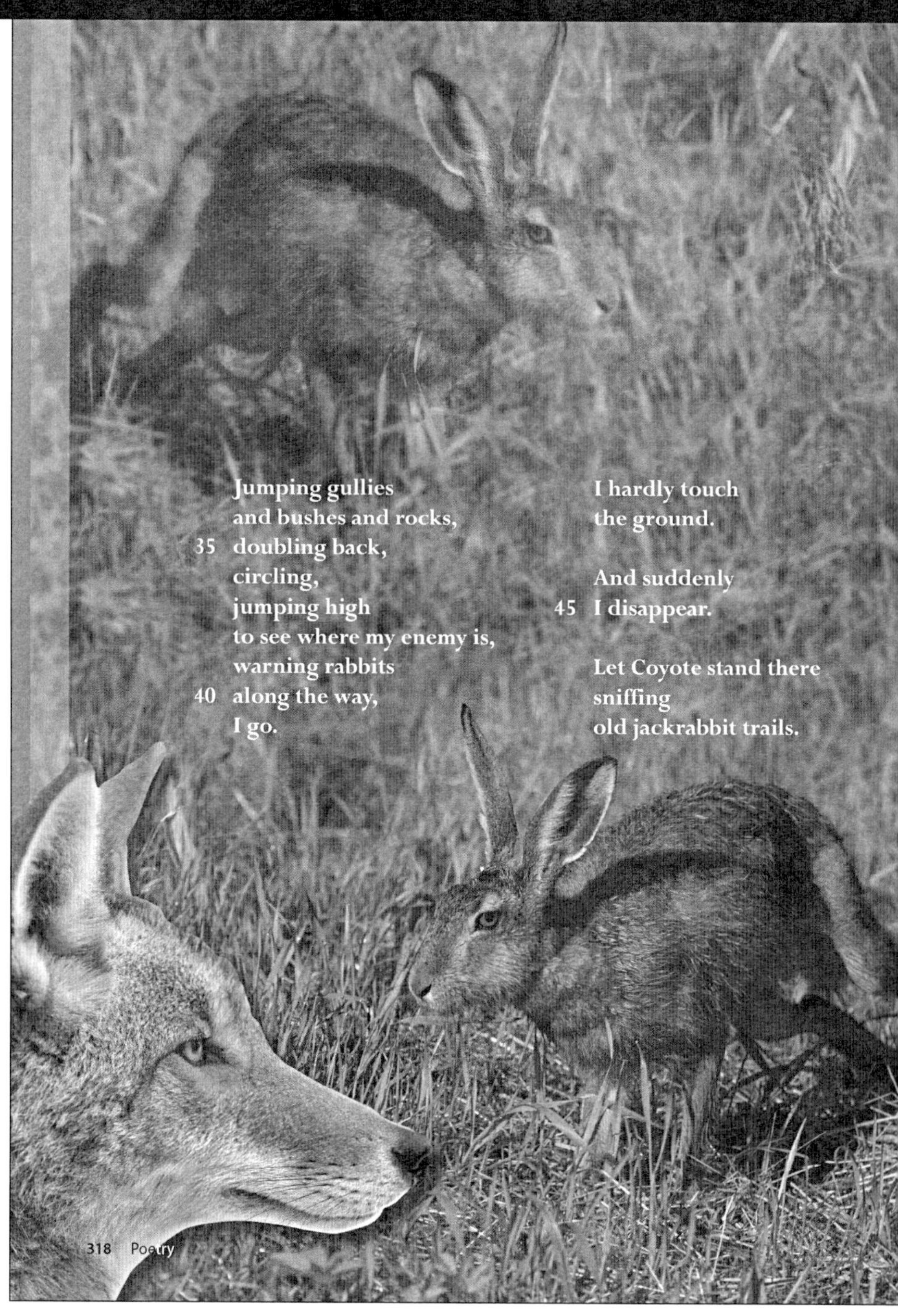

Jumping gullies
and bushes and rocks,
doubling back,
circling,
jumping high
to see where my enemy is,
warning rabbits
along the way,
I go.

I hardly touch
the ground.

And suddenly
I disappear.

Let Coyote stand there
sniffing
old jackrabbit trails.

318 Poetry

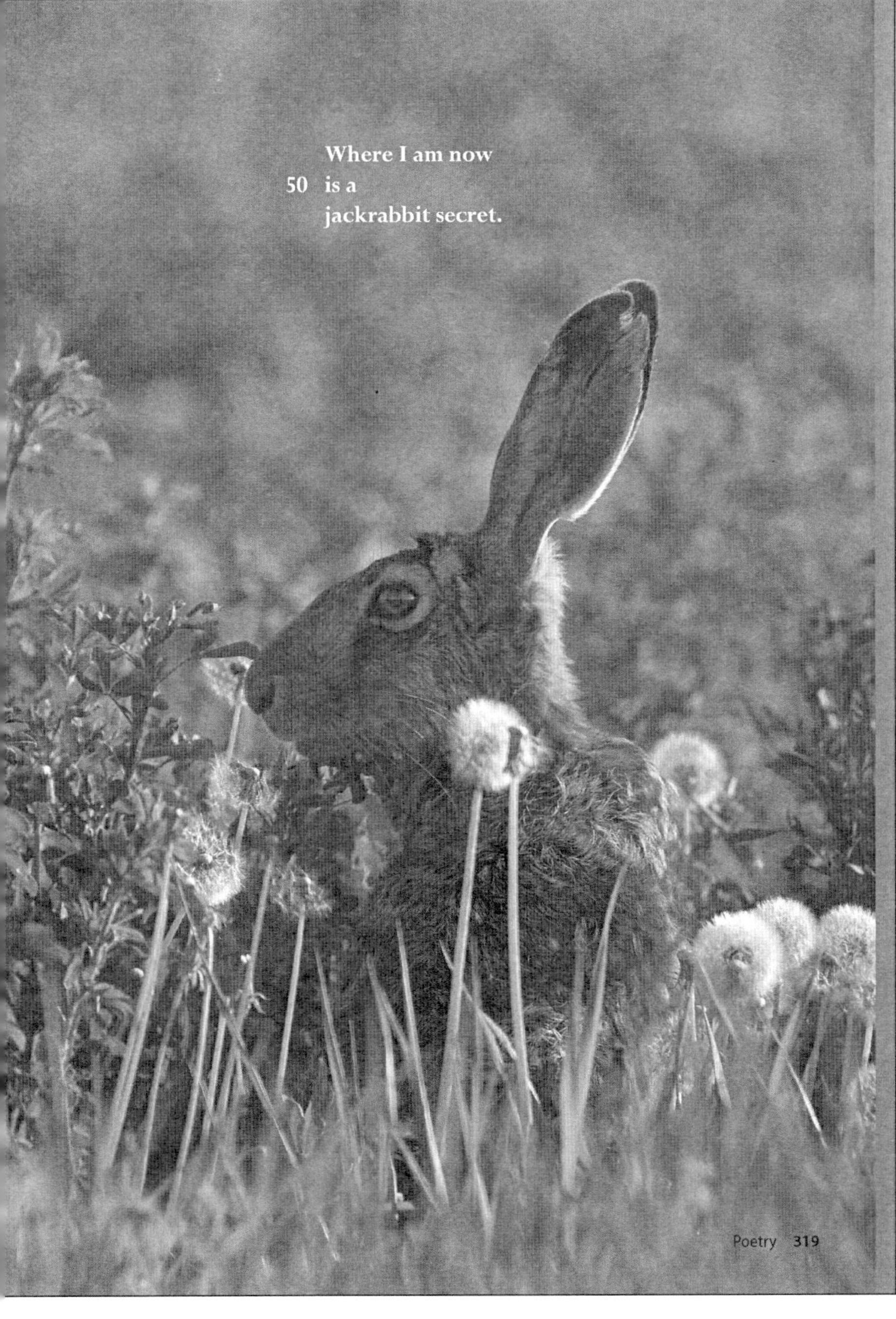

Where I am now
is a
jackrabbit secret.

Poetry 319

Think About It

1. *eat* (3x), *We'd* (3x), *two* (3x), *hotdogs* (4x), *French fries* (2x)
2. This is really a subjective impression. Your reading will help students develop their ideas about this. Of course, you want to make certain they know what *emphasis* means.
3. If you are able, read through students' prose paragraphs before they write their poems.
4. Answers will vary.
5. You may decide that their performance of the poem can substitute for this exercise.

THINK about it

In *Good Hotdogs*, Sandra Cisneros has written a poem for Kiki about a time when they would eat hotdogs together for lunch.

1. Reread the poem and make a list of the words and phrases that are repeated.
2. What two places in the poem are given special importance by the way the lines end?
3. Write one or two paragraphs about a special time you spent with someone. Your memories may be happy or sad.
4. Now, remove the punctuation and change your prose piece into a free verse poem. Give your poem a title and name the person for whom you are writing the poem.

In *Jackrabbit*, Byrd Baylor uses two columns (in some places) and a zigzag form to make her poem look like the track of the jackrabbit as it runs from the coyote.

5. Write about a bird fleeing a cat, a dog chasing another dog, a deer being followed by hunters—or any other story of one creature trying to escape another. Make your poem look a little like the chase. Your poem can be shorter than *Jackrabbit*.

320 Poetry

Poetry 321

- GLOSSARY
- ACKNOWLEDGMENTS
- INDEX OF AUTHORS AND TITLES

glossary

A

abreast (uh BREST) *adv., adj.*: side by side

abrupt (uh BRUPT) *adj.*: sudden

absurd (ub ZURD) *adj.*: ridiculous

abundantly (uh BUN dunt lee) *adv.*: very much

affected (uh FEK tid) *v.*: influenced

agonized (AG uh NYZD) *v.*: worried unhappily

allotment (uh LOT ment) *n.*: the portion of something that is assigned to someone

amateurs (AM uh churz) *n.*: beginners lacking in skill and experience; not experts

anticipation (an TISS ih PAY shun) *n.*: happily looking forward to something

appointment *n.*: position; job

apprentice (uh PREN tiss) *n.*: a person who works for another in order to learn a trade

B

balmy (BAH mee) *adj.*: mild and refreshing weather

basking (BASS king) *v.*: lying in something pleasantly warm (like the sun)

battered (BAT erd) *adj.*: damaged by rough and careless treatment

beacon (BEE kun) *n.*: a light used as a warning signal

bolt *v.*: suddenly run away

brandishing (BRAN dish ing) *v.*: waving and displaying

budge (BUHJ) *v.*: move even slightly

bustling (BUSS ling) *v.*: full of activity

C

calico (KAL ih ko) *n.*: a plain cotton fabric printed on one side

cataloging (CAT uh LOG ing) *v.*: organizing a list of items into groups

celebrities (suh LEB rih teez) *n.*: well-known or famous people

chiseled (TCHIH zuld) *v.*: carved with a *chisel*, a tool with a cutting edge designed to carve a hard material

chores (TSHORZ) *n.*: the everyday work around a house or farm; a small job that must be done regularly

churned *v.*: shook and beat milk to turn it into butter

chute (SHOOT) *n.*: a narrow, sloping passageway for delivering items from a higher to a lower level

clenched (KLENSHT) *v.*: held closed tightly

club (KLUB) *n.*: a heavy stick

clutched (KLUCHD) *v.*: held onto tightly

cobblestone (KOB ul stone) *n.*: a small, naturally rounded stone, used in paving roads

commercial (kuh MUR shul) *n.*: made by companies to be sold in stores; not homemade

commotion (kuh MO shun) *n.*: noise and disturbance

composed (kum POZED) *v.*: made up of

confined (kun FYND) *v.*: restricted; kept from leaving a place

console (kun SOLE) *v.*: comfort

consternation (KAHN stur NAY shun) *n.*: a sudden alarming amazement or dread

consulting (kun SULT ing) *v.*: asking advice of

corroded (kuh RODE id) *adj.*: worn away

crammed (KRAMD) *v.*: crowded; stuffed

craned (KRAYND) *v.*: stretched out their necks (to see)

crest *n.*: the highest part of a hill

crude *adj.*: rough; not well-designed

cultivate (KUL tih vayt) *v.*: to help the plants grow by tending to the soil around them

D

debris (duh BREE) *n.*: the remains of anything destroyed

decreed (dih KREED) *v.*: ordered; commanded

delegate (DELL uh gut) *n.*: one person sent by a group of people to represent them at a convention

dense (DENSS) *adj.*: thick and tightly packed together

desolately (DESS uh lit lee) *adv.*: very sadly

devastation (DEH vis TAY shun) *n.*: destruction and ruin

devour (dih VOW ehr) *v.*: to swallow hungrily

distinctive (dis TINK tiv) *adj.*: unusual; having a special style

distinguished (dis TEENG wishd) *v.*: important and respected

domain (doe MAYN) *n.*: a region inhabited by a certain type of wildlife

donned (DAHND) *v.*: put on

doused (DOWST) *v.*: threw water on

dwarfed (DWORFD) *v.*: appeared small by comparison

E

eaves (EEVZ) *n.*: the overhanging lower edges of a roof

eerie (IH ree) *adj.*: strange and somewhat frightening

effortlessly (EFF urt less lee) *adv.*: easily

embedded (em BED ed) *v.*: set deeply into

engrossed (en GROSED) *v.*: occupied; completely involved in

enraged (en RAYJD) *adj.*: extremely angry

evaporating (ee VAP uh RAY ting) *v.*: disappearing

executive (egg ZEK yoo tiv) *n.*: a person who has a position of leadership in a business or company

expedition (EX puh DISH un) *n.*: a journey or voyage made to a distant place for a certain purpose

F

famine (FAM in) *n.*: a hunger; a major food shortage

flaw *n.*: a defect; an imperfection

flint stones *n.*: hard stones used to produce a spark

G

gingerly (JIN jur lee) *adv.*: with great care

glistened (GLISS und) *v.*: shone

gorge (GORJ) *n.*: a small canyon through which a stream runs

grim *adj.*: serious and unpleasant

grippe (GRIP) *n.*: influenza

gullies (GULL eez) *n.*: small valleys or ravines made by running water

H

habitat (HAB ih TAT) *n.*: the place where a plant or animal is naturally found

haltingly (HALT ing lee) *adv.*: slowly, with hesitation

haughty (HAW tee) *adj.*: snobbish; arrogant

hearth (HARTH) *n.*: the floor of a fireplace

herded (HURD id) *v.*: drove or led (cows)

hoisted (HOYS tid) *v.*: raised

horizon (huh RY zun) *n.*: the place in the distance where the earth and sky seem to meet

hovered (HUV urd) *v.*: waited nearby

huddled (HUH dld) *v.*: gathered closely together

I

impact (IM pakt) *n.*: the force with which one thing hits another

implored (im PLORD) *v.*: begged

income (INK um) *n.*: the money an individual or business makes during a given time period

indebted (in DET ed) *adj.*: owing; obligated to repay something

inspired (in SPY ehrd) *v.*: filled with a sense of purpose

instinctively (in STINK tiv lee) *adv.*: without thinking; from an inborn knowledge, not as a result of having been taught

interchangeable (IN tur CHAYNGE uh bul) *adj.*: two things that can be used in place of one another

inundated (IN un DAY tud) *v.*: flooded

J

jagged (JAG ud) *adj.*: rough, sharp, and uneven

jarring (JAR ing) *v.*: shaking

jauntily (JAWNT ih lee) *adv.*: in a lively, carefree, and slightly proud way

jubilant (JOO bih lunt) *adj.*: full of joy

K

kindling (KIHND ling) *n.*: material that ignites easily, used to start a fire

L

linger (LEENG er) *v.*: to stay somewhere longer than necessary because one does not want to leave

lull *n.*: a temporary calm

lulling (LULL ing) *v.*: putting to sleep by quiet, soothing means

luminous (LOO mih nuss) *adj.*: reflecting light

M

magistrate (MADJ iss trayt) *n.*: a government worker who enforces the law

maneuvered (muh NOO vurd) *v.*: moved about and changed direction as required

manipulate (muh NIP yoo layt) *v.*: handle with skill

matted (MAT ed) *adj.*: thick and tangled

meandered (mee AN derd) *v.*: wound around gently from one place to another

menacing (MEN uh sing) *adj.*: threatening

miscalculated (mis KAL kyuh LAY tid) *v.*: judged incorrectly

misleading (miss LEED ing) *adj.*: words or actions that lead people to believe something that is not true

mock *adj.*: pretend; make-believe

monologue (MAH nuh log) *n.*: a long speech made by one person, with no answer or interruption from the listener

monument (MAHN yoo munt) *n.*: a building, statue, or the like, built in memory of a person or event

mural (MYOOR ul) *n.*: a large picture painted directly on a wall or ceiling

mustering (MUST uh ring) *v.*: gathering; calling upon

N

needlessly (NEED luss lee) *adv.*: unnecessarily

O

ominous (AH mih nuss) *adj.*: threatening; hinting that something bad is about to happen

ornery (OR nuh ree) *adj.*: mean

P

parchment (PARCH ment) *n.*: a stiff, heavy, ivory-colored paper made from the skins of sheep or goats

pare (PAIR) *v.*: to cut off the outer layer

passion (PASH un) *n.*: an enthusiasm for something

peer *n.*: one who is the equal of another

pelts *n.*: animal skins that have not been prepared for use in clothing or other items

persimmon (pur SIH mun) *n.*: a large, plumlike orange fruit that is sweet when very ripe

picturesque (PIK chur ESK) *adj.*: pleasing, interesting, and noticeable

pirouettes (PEER oo ETS) *n.*: a dance step in which the dancer whirls about on one foot

pitch *n.*: a black, sticky tar

pitches *v.*: falls sharply

plain *n.*: a large flat area of land

plucked (PLUKD) *v.*: pulled out, like feathers from a bird

plunges (PLUNJ iz) *v.*: falls down suddenly

poacher (POE chur) *n.*: a person who hunts or fishes in an area where it is illegal for him or her to do so

podium (PO dee um) *n.*: a small platform for a speaker, orchestra conductor, or the like

portfolio (port FO lee oh) *n.*: a flat, portable case for carrying loose papers, drawings, and the like

poultice (POLE tiss) *n.*: a small moist bandage of cloth or herbs

precision (prih SIZH un) *n.*: being exact about every detail

predator (PREH duh tor) *n.*: an animal that hunts other animals for food

principal (PRIN sih pul) *adj.*: first in importance

propelled (pruh PELD) *v.*: moved; driven

proposal (pruh PO zul) *n.*: a suggested plan

pungent (PUN junt) *adj.*: sharp and strong (used only to describe a taste or smell)

Q

quibbled (KWIH buld) *v.*: argued about some small, unimportant detail

quivered (KWIV erd) *v.*: shook slightly

quivery (KWIH vuh ree) *adj.*: shaky

R

raja (RAH zha) *n.*: the title of a chieftain or prince in India and areas of southeast Asia

realign (REE uh LYN) *v.*: to return to their proper position

reef *n.*: a ridge of rocks or sand near the surface of the water

rehabilitation (REE huh BIH luh TAY shun) *n.*: a returning to good health

relinquish (rih LINK wish) *v.*: let go of

resentment (ree ZENT ment) *n.*: a feeling of displeasure with someone who, one believes, has caused injury or unhappiness

retreated (rih TREE ted) *v.*: moved back toward the place it had come from

S

sanctuaries (SANK chew AIR eez) *n.*: a portion of land set aside by the government, where wildlife can live in safety from hunters

sapling (SAP ling) *n.*: young tree

scavenging (SKAH vun jing) *v.*: taking or gathering something useable from among unwanted things

scoffed (SKOFT) *v.*: mocked; ridiculed

semicircular (SEM ee SUR kyuh lur) *adj.*: shaped like half of a circle

shaft *n.*: the long, straight stem of something

shanties (SHAN teez) *n.*: cabins or houses that are roughly built and in a state of disrepair

siege (SEEJ) *n.*: a serious attack, as in illness

singe (SINJ) *v.*: to burn slightly

snare *n.*: a trap

soar (SORE) *v.*: fly high into the air

sow (rhymes with now) *n.*: an adult, female pig

sprinted (SPRINT ed) *v.*: raced at full speed for a short distance

stealthily (STELL thih lee) *adv.*: softly and secretly

stifling (STYF ling) *adj.*: so hot and still as to make it difficult to breathe

stunned (STUND) *v.*: shocked

susceptible (suh SEP tih buhl) *adj.*: more likely to be affected by something

suspended (sus SPEND ed) *v.*: temporarily stopped

swig *n.*: a mouthful of liquid

sympathetic (SIM puh THET ik) *adj.*: understanding and supportive

T

technique (tek NEEK) *n.*: method

tenement (TEH nuh munt) *n.*: a run-down and often overcrowded apartment house

tepid (TEP id) *adj.*: lukewarm

thatched *adj.*: having a roof made of straw

thaw *v.*: melt

thicket (THIK it) *n.*: many bushes growing close together

thrashes *v.*: beats against

thrives *v.*: grows and improves

timid (TIH mid) *adj.*: shy and easily frightened

tooling (TOOL ing) *v.*: driving or riding in a vehicle

transport (trans PORT) *v.*: to move; to carry

treacherous (TRECH uh russ) *adj.*: very dangerous

trembling (TREMB ling) *v.*: shaking slightly from fear, cold, or excitement

trough (TROFF) *n.*: a long, boxlike container used to hold food or water for animals

trudged (TRUJD) *v.*: walked slowly and heavily

U

undulating (UN dyuh LAY ting) *v.*: moving with a wavelike motion

upheaval (up HEE vul) *n.*: a great disturbance

V

venture (VEN chur) *v.*: to go carefully into an unknown or dangerous place

vertical (VUR tih kul) *adj.*: going up and down, not from side to side

vicious (VISH uss) *adj.*: harsh and cruel

W

wallowed (WAH lode) *v.*: rolled about in a clumsy way

wan (WAHN) *adj.*: pale and weak

wedged (WEJD) *v.*: packed in tightly

whiff *n.*: a slight smell

acknowledgments

Illustrators

Lauren Chaikin: Heatwave!; Dancing Bees

Aviva Goldfarb: Leah's Pony; The Gift

Aviva Gross: Sato and the Elephants; The Garden of Happiness; The Bridge Dancers

Eva Martin: The Way; Purple Snake; Hurt No Living Thing; Today the Dolphins Came to Play

Lydia Martin: Amelia's Road; The Wright Brothers; Earthquake Terror; Toto; Underwater Rescue; Maria's House; Analysis of Baseball; If You Think You Are Beaten; Here She Is; Since Hanna Moved Away; Analysis of Baseball; Be Glad Your Nose Is On Your Face; The Inventor Thinks Up Helicopters; Michael Is Afraid of the Storm; In This Jungle; City I Love

---

Amelia's Road
Amelia's Road Text Copyright © 1993 by Linda Jacobs Altman. Permission arranged with LEE & LOW BOOKS, INC., New York, NY 10016.

Analysis of Baseball
Reprinted with permission of The Literary Estate of May Swenson

And Now the Good News
From AND THEN THERE WAS ONE: THE MYSTERIES OF EXTINCTION by Margery Facklam. Copyright © 1990 by Margery Facklam (text); Copyright © 1990 by Pamela Johnson (illustrations). By permission of LITTLE BROWN & COMPANY.

A Bugler Named Dougal MacDougal
Copyright © 1935 by Ogden Nash. Reprinted by permission of Curtis Brown, Ltd.

Be Glad Your Nose Is On Your Face
From THE NEW KID ON THE BLOCK. TEXT COPYRIGHT © 1984 BY JACK PRELUTSKY. Used by permission of HarperCollins Publishers.

Birds' Square Dance
"Birds' Square Dance" first appeared in RANGER RICK, November, 1988. Reprinted by permission of the author.

The Bridge Dancers
The Bridge Dancers, by Carol Saller, text © copyright 1991 by the author. Reprinted by permission of the author.

City I Love
From HOME TO ME: POEMS ACROSS AMERICA by Lee Bennett Hopkins. Copyright © 2002 by Lee Bennett Hopkins. Reprinted by permission of Orchard Books, an imprint of Scholastic Inc.

Dad, Jackie, and Me
From *Dad, Jackie, and Me*, text © 2005 Myron Uhlberg. Permission to reprint granted by Peachtree Publishers

Dust of Snow
"Dust of Snow," from THE POETRY OF ROBERT FROST edited by Edward Connery Lathem. Copyright 1923, 1969 by Henry Holt and Company. Copyright 1951 by Robert Frost. Reprinted by arrangement with Henry Holt and Company, LLC

Earthquake Terror
From EARTHQUAKE TERROR by Peg Kehret, copyright © 1996 by Peg Kehret. Used by permission of Cobblehill Books, an affiliate of Dutton Children's Books, A Division of Penguin Young Readers Group, A Member of Penguin Group (USA) Inc., 345 Hudson Street, New York, NY 10014. All rights reserved.

Eddie, Incorporated
Reprinted with the permission of Atheneum Books for Young Readers, an imprint of Simon & Schuster Children's Publishing Division from EDDIE, INCORPORATED by Phyllis Reynolds Naylor. Text copyright © 1980 Phyllis Reynolds Naylor.

For You
"For You" from VALENTINE POEMS, edited by Myra Cohn Livingston © 1987 by Karla Kuskin. Used by permission of S©ott Treimel NY.

The Garden of Happiness
THE GARDEN OF HAPPINESS, copyright © 1996 by Erika Tamar, reproduced by permission of Harcourt, Inc.

The Gift
From THE GIFT by Helent Coutant illustrations by Vo-Dinh Mai, copyright © 1983 by Helen Coutant Illustrations copyright © 1983 by Vo Dinh Mai. Used by permission of Alfred A. Knopf, an imprint of Random House Children's Books, a division of Random House, Inc.

Good Hotdogs
From MY WICKED WICKED WAYS. Copyright © 1987 by Sandra Cisneros in English, published by Third Woman Press and in hardcover by Alfred A. Knopf. By permission of Susan Bergholz Literary Services, New York, NY and Lamy, NM. All rights reserved.

A Gullible Rancher Named Clyde
"A Gullible Rancher Named Clyde" by Graham Lester; reprinted by permission of the author.

The Hatmaker's Sign
The Hatmaker's Sign © 1998 by Candace Fleming. Text used with permission of the Author and BookStop Literary Agency. All rights reserved.

Heatwave!
Reprinted by permission of Walker & Company.

Homeward the Arrow's Flight
An excerpt from *Homeward the Arrow's Flight* by Marion Marsh Brown, copyright © 1980, 1995, by Marion Marsh Brown, reprinted by permission of Field Mouse Productions.

The Imperfect/Perfect Book Report
"The Imperfect/Perfect Book Report" from *Teacher's Pet* by Johanna Hurwitz. Text © 1988 by Johanna Hurwitz. Reprinted by permission of the author.

In This Jungle
From A CRAZY FLIGHT AND OTHER POEMS by Myra Cohn Livingston. Copyright © 1969 Myra Cohn Livingston. By permission of Marian Reiner.

The Inventor Thinks Up Helicopters
From THE TIGERS BROUGHT PINK LEMONADE by Patricia Hubbell. Copyright © 1988 by Patricia Hubbell. By permission of Marian Reiner for the author.

Jackrabbit
Reprinted with the permission of Atheneum Books for Young Readers, an imprint of Simon & Schuster Children's Publishing Division from DESERT VOICES by Byrd Baylor. Text copyright © 1981 Byrd Baylor.

Johnny Appleseed
"Johnny Appleseed" by Stephen Vincent Benét. From A BOOK OF AMERICANS by Rosemary and Stephen Vincent Benét. Copyright © 1933 by Rosemary and Stephen Vincent. Copyright renewed © 1961 by Rosemary Carr Benét. Reprinted by permission of Brandt & Hochman Literary Agents, Inc.

Justin Lebo
"Justin Lebo" from IT'S OUR WORLD, TOO! by Phillip Hoose. Copyright ©1993, 2002 by Phillip Hoose. Reprinted by permission of Farrar, Straus and Giroux, LLC.

acknowledgments

Leah's Pony
Leah's Pony by Elizabeth Friedrich. (Caroline House, an imprint of Boyds Mills Press, Inc., 1996) Reprinted with the permission of Boyds Mills Press, Inc. Text copyright © 1996 by Elizabeth Friedrich.

March Bear
"March Bear" from *Turtle in July* by Marilyn Singer. Text copyright © 1989 by Marilyn Singer. Reprinted by permission of the author.

Michael Is Afraid of the Storm
Reprinted By Consent of Brooks Permissions.

Mom's Best Friend
Mom's Best Friend © 1992 by Sally Alexander. Text used with permission of the Author and BookStop Literary Agency. All rights reserved.

Name This American
"Name This American" by Hannah Reinmuth is reprinted with the permission of the publisher, PLAYS, The Drama Magazine for Young People/Sterling Partners, Inc. © 1995. This play is for reading purposes only; for permission to produce and/or perform, write to PLAYS, PO Box 600160, Newton, MA 02460.

A Native of Chalamazug
"A Native of Chalamazug" by Graham Lester; reprinted by permission of the author.

One Grain of Rice
From ONE GRAIN OF RICE by Demi. Scholastic Inc./Scholastic Press. Copyright © 1997 by Demi. Reprinted by permission.

Owl Moon
From OWL MOON by Jane Yolen, copyright © 1987 by Jane Yolen, text. Used by permission of Philomel Books, A Division of Penguin Young Readers Group, A Member of Penguin Group (USA) Inc., 345 Hudson Street, New York, NY 10014. All rights reserved.

Popsicle
"Popsicle," from SPLISH SPLASH by Joan Bransfield Graham. Text copyright © 1994 by Joan Bransfield Graham. Illustration copyright © 1994 by Steven Scott. Reprinted by permission of Houghton Mifflin Company. All rights reserved.

Purple Snake
The poem "Purple Snake" from *Confetti: Poems for Children* Text copyright ©1996 by Pat Mora. Permission arranged with LEE & LOW BOOKS Inc., New York, NY 10016.

Sato and the Elephants
Sato and the Elephants by Juanita Havill. Text copyright © 1993 by Juanita Havill. Reprinted by permission of the author.

Seasons Haiku
From CRICKET NEVER DIES A Collection of Haiku and Tanka by Myra Cohn Livingston. Copyright © 1997 Myra Cohn Livingston. Used by permission of Marian Reiner.

The Seven Children
"The First Day" ("The Seven Children"), from IT'S KWANZAA TIME! by Clay and Linda Goss, copyright © 1994, 1995 by Clay and Linda Goss. Used by permission of Philomel Books, A Division of Penguin Young Readers Group, A Member of Penguin Group (USA) Inc., 345 Hudson Street, New York, NY 10014. All rights reserved.

The Shark
"The Shark" from FAST AND SLOW by John Ciardi. Copyright © 1975 by John Ciardi. Reprinted by permission of Houghton Mifflin Company. All rights reserved.

Since Hanna Moved Away
Reprinted with the permission of Atheneum Books for Young Readers, an imprint of Simon & Schuster Children's Publishing Division from IF I WERE IN CHARGE OF THE WORLD AND OTHER WORRIES by Judith Viorst. Text copyright © 1981 Judith Viorst.

Some Opposites
"Some Opposites" from OPPOSITES: POEMS AND DRAWINGS, copyright © 1973 by Richard Wilbur, reprinted by permission of Houghton Mifflin Harcourt Publishing Company.

Stone Fox
TEXT COPYRIGHT © 1980 BY JOHN REYNOLDS GARDINER. Used by permission of HarperCollins Publishers.

Supergrandpa
Super Grandpa, book with audio CD, written and narrated by David M. Schwartz; illustrated by Bert Dodson. © Tortuga Press, 2005.

The Way
"The Way," from *Music of Their Hooves: Poems About Horses* by Nancy Springer. (Wordsong, an imprint of Boyds Mills Press, Inc., 1994) Reprinted with the permission of Boyds Mills Press, Inc. Text copyright © 1994 by Nancy Springer.

Thistles
"Thistles" from THE ROSE ON MY CAKE. Copyright © 1964, renewed 1992 by Karla Kuskin. Used by permission of S©ott Treimel NY.

The Tiger, the Persimmon and the Rabbit's Tail
"The Tiger, the Persimmon and the Rabbit's Tail" from *Korean Folk & Fairy Tales* retold by Suzanne Crowder Han. Copyright © 1991, 2006 by Suzanne Crowder Han. Reprinted by permission of Hollym Corp., Publishers.

Tortillas Like Africa
"Tortillas Like Africa" from CANTO FAMILIAR, copyright © 1995 by Gary Soto, reprinted by permission of Houghton Mifflin Harcourt Publishing Company.

Toto
Copyright © 1971 by Marietta Moskin published by the Coward, McCann, and Geoghegan. Reprinted with permission of the Carol Mann Agency.

Two Big Bears
"Two Big Bears," from pp. 101-116 of *Little House in the Big Woods* by Laura Ingalls Wilder. TEXT COPYRIGHT 1932, 1960 Little House Heritage Trust. Used by permission of HarperCollins Publishers.

Underwater Rescue
TEXT COPYRIGHT © 1990 BY WAYNE GROVER. Used by permission of HarperCollins Publishers.

Whirligig Beetles
TEXT COPYRIGHT © 1988 BY PAUL FLEISCHMAN. Used by permission of HarperCollins Publishers.

The Wright Brothers
From THE WRIGHT BROTHERS by Quentin Reynolds, copyright 1950 by Random House, Inc. Text copyright renewed 1978 by James R. Reynolds and Frederick H. Rohlfs, Esq. Illustrations copyright renewed 1978 by Random House, Inc. Used by permission of Random House Children's Books, a division of Random House, Inc.

You and I
From MY SONG IS BEAUTIFUL by MARY ANN HOBERMAN. Copyright © 1994 by Mary Ann Hoberman. By permission of LITTLE BROWN & COMPANY.

Note: We have expended much effort to contact all copyright holders to receive permission for their works. We will correct any omissions brought to our attention in future editions.

index of authors and titles

Teacher Resources Section

- SUPERGRANDPA
- MOM'S BEST FRIEND
- SATO AND THE ELEPHANTS
- EARTHQUAKE TERROR
- OWL MOON
- MARIA'S HOUSE
- DANCING BEES
- STONE FOX
- FROM JILL'S JOURNAL...
  THE DRAMA OF THE PEOPLE AND THE MOON BEARS

Teacher Resources

Supergrandpa

The story, *Supergrandpa*, reads like a folktale: the characters are presented almost as caricatures of themselves. In fact, Gustaf Håkansson was an actual person, sometimes referred to during his life as the "crazy Swedish cycling legend."

The real Nils Gustaf Håkansson was born in October 1885 in Helsingborg, Sweden. Mr. Håkansson and his wife, Maria Håkansson, lived in a district of Helsingborg called Gantofta. He was a bus driver, and she owned a café.

Mr. Håkansson was always an avid bicyclist. It is said that in 1926, when he was 42, he "conquered" the Swedish mountains by bicycle. This must have made him strong and resilient, and was certainly superb training for what was to come. Bicycle racing is one of the most physically demanding activities—more so than many other sports.

As the story also tells us, in 1951, the man who was to become a legendary veteran cyclist heard of the plan to hold the first *Sverige-Loppet*, or Tour of Sweden race. This was to be the longest stage race ever held in Sweden. (A stage race is made up of several races—or stages—ridden in sequence. The participant with the lowest cumulative time overall is the winner.) The *Sverige-Loppet* was to run nearly the entire length of Sweden, spanning a distance of 1,761 kilometers, or 1,094 miles.

Mr. Håkansson was determined to complete the Tour of Sweden ride from Haparanda to Ystad. Again, as we learn in the story, he was denied a chance to participate officially because the organizers had set the maximum age for all competitors at 40 years. (It may well be that in 1951, 66 was regarded as a more senior age than it is now.) Also, he wasn't one of the top 50 Swedish bicycle racers selected through the Swedish racing organization's "legally sanctioned" preliminary races. Therefore, the officials sent him away.

Because the Tour was run in stages, while the contestants slept, Håkansson was able (remarkably) to continue pedaling. "Official" sources mention that he was able to bicycle up to three days at a stretch! As the public (and then the media) became aware of his participation in the contest, he earned the name *Stålfarfar*, which means "steel Grandpa."

Apparently, when he stopped for a break in Söderhamn, the police requested that he be examined by a doctor. Whatever it was the medical exam involved, it showed Håkansson to be in good health.

It took Gustaf Håkansson 6 days, 14 hours, and 20 minutes to reach Ystad. Contrary to the story, our sources write that he arrived 24 hours before the other contestants. We should remember that he made this rigorous trip with his single-speed Opabike while carrying his own luggage.

"There was a parade with a marching band, fire brigades and Håkansson sat in a cage on a golden seat." Indeed, the king, Gustaf VI Adolf of Sweden, gave him an audience the next day.

Håkansson was subsequently very much in demand. He was paid to appear in advertisements, and he seems to have toured the country as a singer of songs. He made a record at Liseberg, and was deemed "the world's oldest recording artist."

The Tour of Sweden was not the last of Håkansson's bicycling adventures. In 1959, he rode his bicycle to Jerusalem to visit the holy sites. Amazingly—but perhaps not surprisingly, given his record for endurance—his last bicycling adventures were completed *after* his 100th birthday. Nils Gustaf Håkansson died on June 9, 1987 in Ekerö, Stockholm, Sweden. He was nearly 102 years old. His wife, Maria, predeceased him by a year at the age of 104.

Mom's Best Friend

What is a *service animal*? Service animals are animals that are trained individually, over time, to help people with disabilities and to do tasks for them that they are unable to do themselves.

What are *disabilities*? Disabilities are physical or mental limitations that substantially curtail normal activity and functioning. Common disabilities include the inability to see (blindness), the inability to hear (deafness), and the inability to walk or to use one's arms and hands. An individual who has one of these conditions may be unable to carry out tasks or human functions in the usual way.

Thankfully, service animals fill the gap. Service animals may guide people who are blind, alert people who are deaf, pull wheelchairs, protect a person who is having a seizure, or carry out other needed tasks. As *Mom's Best Friend* makes clear, a service animal may also be like a pet when home with the family, but service animals are working animals, and should never be treated by strangers as pets when they are outside of the home. If people stop to pet them or make distracting sounds or talk with them, it may make it harder for the service animal to do its job—and that can jeopardize the welfare of the person the animal is assisting!

According to the Official Website of the City of San Antonio Planning, more than 12,000 people there with disabilities use the assistance of service animals. The San Antonio Planners write that although we are most familiar with guide dogs who aid those who are blind, "many disabling conditions are invisible. Therefore, every person who is accompanied by a service animal may or may not 'look' disabled." Disabled people are certainly not required to carry proof of their disabilities, and service animals are not required to have any special certification.

Between 1970 and 1990, several crucial federal laws were passed to ensure the civil rights of disabled persons using service animals. This legislation includes:

Americans with Disabilities Act, ADA (1990)

Air Carrier Access Act (1986)

Fair Housing Amendments Act (1988)

Rehabilitation Act (1973)

Each of these laws (and the ADA, most importantly) has contributed to allowing persons with disabilities to lead more normal lives. Each allows for the person assisted by a service animal to have increased participation in our society. The disabled person, however, is not the only one to reap benefits: all of the rest of us gain from that person's increased productivity.

The Americans with Disabilities Act (ADA) ensures that businesses and organizations that serve the public *must allow people with disabilities to bring their service animals into all areas of the facility where customers are normally allowed to go.* This federal law covers all businesses open to the public, including restaurants, hotels, taxis and shuttles, grocery and department stores, hospitals and medical offices, theaters, health clubs, parks, and zoos.

Businesses that sell or prepare food must allow service animals in public areas even if state or local health codes prohibit animals on the premises. None of these businesses are permitted to charge those with service animals extra fees. Nor are they allowed to isolate them from—or treat them less nicely than—other patrons.

Fear of animals or allergies is not considered adequate reason to deny access or refuse service to those with service animals. Businesses that violate the Americans with Disabilities Act can be required to pay damages and suffer penalties.

Service Dog Etiquette to Remember:

Do not touch a service animal, or the person whom the animal is assisting, without that person's permission.

Do not feed a service animal. It is doing a job and its owner undoubtedly has the animal on a schedule.

Do not talk to or make noises at a service animal, as you do not want to distract the animal from its job.

Do not expect a disabled person to want to discuss his or her disability nor the guidance his or her service animal provides. No one wants to be treated as though she or he is a special case.

If you have additional questions concerning the ADA and service animals, please call the Department's ADA Information Line at (800) 514-0301 (voice) or (800) 514-0383 (TTY).

Sato and the Elephants

The following will provide you with information on elephants. You may wish to use part of the material later on when discussing the last selection in Unit Two—*Jill's Journal* for *And Now the Good News.* Bear in mind that *And Now the Good News* is a nonfiction piece about endangered species. Facts that would be more relevant to a general discussion about conservation, protection of endangered species, and animal sanctuaries may be saved to be used later on.

About Elephants

Elephants are the Earth's largest land-dwelling mammals. Their bodies are covered with long, coarse hairs and their thick skin helps them to remain cool. An elephant trunk is actually a joined nose and upper lip. The trunk of an elephant is like a fifth limb that the elephant manipulates to gather food and water. The trunk has more than 40,000 muscles.

The two species of elephants each have subspecies. African elephants may be savannah or forest. Asian elephants, with four subspecies, may be Sri Lankan, Indian, Sumatran, or Borneo. The elephants of Asia have long been used for transportation and the movement of heavy objects. In fact, they have been central to Asian culture for thousands of years.

Male elephants average 10' 5" at the shoulder. Female elephants of both species are smaller. From trunk to tail, elephants are up to 30 feet long. Males weigh from 6,000 to 15,000 pounds. In the wild, elephants live up to 70 years.

Elephants eat bark, roots, grasses, leaves, and bamboo. These are the staples of their diet. They also eat crops grown by farmers (probably much to their displeasure), such as sugarcane and bananas. According to one source, adult elephants can eat 300 to 400 pounds of food a day. Perhaps this number is for males, since the figures for the females at the Elephant Sanctuary (refer to *Jill's Journal* for *And Now the Good News* on p. 175) are much lower.

At the beginning of the 20th century, African elephants numbered in the several millions. The population of Asian elephants is estimated to have been around 100,000. The African elephant population today is estimated as being 450,000 to 700,000. There are about 35,000 wild Asian elephants.

Elephants live in closely knit matriarchal family groups of related females. Each group, or herd, is led by the oldest—and frequently largest—female in the herd. Within the herd, elephants form deep family bonds. Adult female elephants and their daughters will spend their entire lives together. Herds may be as small as eight individuals or as large as 100. Calves are raised and sheltered by the entire herd. Young bull elephants are forced out of the herd when they are twelve to fifteen years of age. Males lead solitary lives or live temporarily with other males. It is not clear from the literature whether the matriarchy is as true of African elephants as it is of Asian elephants.

Elephants are extremely intelligent animals and indeed have long memories both for other elephants and for terrain. Their fine memories are essential to the herd leaders during dry seasons when they may need to walk hundred of miles to find watering holes recalled from years past. Through many years of working with and observing elephants, researchers have established that elephants clearly display signs of grief, joy, and anger.

Elephants require the society of other elephants. Recent research has demonstrated that elephants "communicate over long distances by producing a sub-sonic rumble that can travel over the ground faster than sound through air. Other elephants receive the messages through the sensitive skin on their feet and trunks." In this way, the social groups of elephants "talk" with each other.

As human populations require more and more land, elephants are losing critical habitat. Poaching for ivory, which has been on the increase since 1989, also places the future of these majestic creatures at grave risk. According to the Center for Conservation Biology, forest elephants are currently being slaughtered across central Africa, because logging, road building, and the bush meat trade have recently made this elephant population more vulnerable to poaching. Much of the demand for ivory is being driven by the growing economy in China, and the high status the Chinese attach to owning ivory.

Earthquake Terror

Earthquake Facts

The largest recorded earthquake in the United States was a magnitude 9.2 that struck Prince William Sound, Alaska on Friday, March 28, 1964.

The largest recorded earthquake in the world was a magnitude 9.5 in Chile on May 22, 1960.

The **hypocenter** of an earthquake is the location beneath the earth's surface where the rupture of the fault begins. The **epicenter** of an earthquake is the location directly above the hypocenter on the surface of the earth.

It is estimated that there are 500,000 detectable earthquakes in the world each year. 100,000 of those can be felt, and 100 of them cause damage.

Each year the southern California area has about 10,000 earthquakes. Most of them are so small that they are not felt. Only several hundred are greater than magnitude 3.0, and only about 15-20 are greater than magnitude 4.0. If there is a large earthquake, however, the aftershock sequence will produce many more earthquakes of all magnitudes for many months.

The magnitude of an earthquake is a measured value of the earthquake size. The magnitude is the same no matter where you are, or how strong or weak the shaking was in various locations. The intensity of an earthquake is a measure of the shaking created by the earthquake, and this value does vary with location.

There is no such thing as earthquake weather. Statistically, there is an equal distribution of earthquakes in cold weather, hot weather, rainy weather, etc. Furthermore, there is no physical way that the weather could affect the forces several miles beneath the surface of the earth. The changes in barometric pressure in the atmosphere are very small compared to the forces in the crust, and the effect of the barometric pressure does not reach beneath the soil.

Most earthquakes occur at depths of less than 80 km (50 miles) from the Earth's surface.

The world's deadliest recorded earthquake occurred in 1556 in central China. It struck a region where most people lived in caves carved from soft rock. These dwellings collapsed during the earthquake, killing an estimated 830,000 people. In 1976 another deadly earthquake struck in Tangshan, China, where more than 250,000 people were killed.

Florida and North Dakota have the smallest number of earthquakes in the United States.

Alaska is the most earthquake-prone state and one of the most seismically active regions in the world. Alaska experiences a magnitude 7 earthquake almost every year, and a magnitude 8 or greater earthquake on average every 14 years.

Familiarize yourself with these terms to help identify an earthquake hazard:

Aftershock: An earthquake of similar or lesser intensity that follows the main earthquake.

Earthquake: A sudden slipping or movement of a portion of the earth's crust, accompanied and followed by a series of vibrations.

Epicenter: The place on the earth's surface directly above the point on the fault where the earthquake rupture began. Once fault slippage begins, it expands along the fault during the earthquake and can extend hundreds of miles before stopping.

Fault: The fracture across which displacement has occurred during an earthquake. The slippage may range from less than an inch to more than 10 yards in a severe earthquake.

Magnitude: The amount of energy released during an earthquake, which is computed from the amplitude of the seismic waves. A magnitude of 7.0 on the Richter Scale indicates an extremely strong earthquake. Each whole number on the scale represents an increase of about 30 times more energy released than the previous whole number represents. Therefore, an earthquake measuring 6.0 is about 30 times more powerful than one measuring 5.0.

Richter Scale: A measurement of an earthquake's intensity. Each one-point increase on the scale indicates ten times the amount of shaking and 33 times the amount of energy. The energy released by a large earthquake may be equal to 10,000 times the energy of the first atomic bomb.

Seismic Waves: Vibrations that travel outward from the earthquake fault at speeds of several miles per second. Although fault slippage directly under a structure can cause considerable damage, the vibrations of seismic waves cause most of the destruction during earthquakes.

Owl Moon

In this wonderful poem, the speaker uses the word *owling*. What does the phrase, *to owl*, mean? Merriam-Webster says that *owl* is an intransitive verb that is *chiefly dialect*, and means to hoot or stare like an owl. People owl "with hoots that echo eerily down the valley."

There are many different kinds of owls with terrific descriptive names.

North American Owls include:

- Barn Owl
- Barred Owl
- Boreal Owl
- Burrowing Owl
- Eastern Screech-Owl
- Elf Owl
- Ferruginous Pygmy-Owl
- Flammulated Owl
- Great Gray Owl
- Great Horned Owl
- Long-Eared Owl
- Mountain Pygmy-Owl
- Northern Hawk Owl
- Northern Pygmy-Owl
- Northern Saw-Whet Owl
- Short-Eared Owl
- Snowy Owl
- Spotted Owl
- Western Screech-Owl
- Whiskered Screech-Owl

Central American Owls include:

- Balsas Screech-Owl
- Bare-Shanked Screech-Owl
- Barn Owl
- Barred Owl
- Bearded Screech-Owl

- Black-and-White Owl
- Burrowing Owl
- Cape Pygmy-Owl
- Colima Pygmy-Owl
- Costa Rican Pygmy-Owl
- Crested Owl
- Eastern Screech-Owl
- Elf Owl
- Ferruginous Pygmy-Owl
- Flammulated Owl
- Fulvous Owl
- Great Horned Owl
- Guatemalan Screech-Owl
- Mottled Owl
- Mountain Pygmy-Owl
- Northern Saw-Whet Owl
- Pacific Screech-Owl
- Short-Eared Owl
- Spectacled Owl
- Spotted Owl
- Striped Owl
- Stygian Owl
- Tropical Screech-Owl
- Vermiculated Screech-Owl
- Western Screech-Owl
- Whiskered Screech-Owl

There are so many good words here for your students to learn. What is *Colima*? Where is *Costa Rica*? Do your students know what *crested, mottled,* and *spectacled* mean? How about the more exotic words, such as *fulvous, stygian,* and *vermiculated*?

Colima is the name of a city and state in Mexico. Colima is also the name of a volcano and of a kind of spider.

Crested means having a crest, or an ornamental tuft, on the head of a bird or animal—like a wave or a little mountain.

Mottled means marked with spots of different colors.

Spectacles are eyeglasses. *Spectacled* means having color markings or patches of naked skin suggesting a pair of spectacles!

Fulvous is a color: dull brownish yellow, tawny.

Owls are often nocturnal, meaning they are active at night and sleep during the day. As a consequence, even many bird watchers are unaware of the owls that may be living nearby. Owls are very beautiful birds, with a variety of fascinating calls. Although owls are usually solitary, there is a term for a group of owls: a *parliament of owls*. Globally, there are more than 200 species of owls. Owls are carnivores and hunt small mammals, other birds, and some insects. There are a few species of owls whose prey is almost exclusively fish.

Those who participate in the challenge of locating owls consider *owling* an art. Certainly, in order to be an owler, you must know the calls of the owls that interest you. Then, you must learn to imitate the calls very well.

Another tricky part of owling is being able to determine the location of an owl call—when you are lucky enough to hear one—and then, to quietly get nearer to the owl's position. According to owling experts, this is a process that requires a great deal of practice and skill: owl sounds may be very soft, owlers are usually searching in the dark, and even in daylight owls are extremely well-camouflaged.

Owlers sometimes cup their hands behind their ears to better listen. They also may use small flashlights and look for reflection in the owl's eyes. This reflection is called *eye shine*. Owlers often move around in a triangle to get a better sense of where the owl is calling from. Apparently, that is exactly what owls do, as well. Of course, if you are going to try this, keep in mind that owls have better night vision than humans. You are advised to stay in the shadows and under the trees. Their sense of hearing, too, is so refined that owls sometimes track small animals from sound alone. So be quiet! Remember: Owls are as territorial as humans and they don't care for intruders. So, take care!

Maria's House

In *Maria's House*, Maria worries, "There was no way of making a rundown tenement building look beautiful, if you drew it the way it was." Do your students know what a tenement is?

A *tenement* is an apartment building where people live and pay rent. But *tenement* is one of those words that have two different kinds of meanings: (1) a denotative definition, which is a dictionary definition; and (2) a connotative definition, which is a meaning that comes from a feeling or an attitude. In the United States, a tenement is an apartment building; but it also always refers to a crowded, dirty apartment building in very poor condition.

Many tenements are called *walk-ups*, because they have no elevators. In some tenements, people in separate apartments have to share one bathroom. The bathrooms are out in the hallway, rather than in people's apartments.

Tenements are usually located in the older parts of large cities. These old parts of cities are often slums. *Slums* are very crowded areas of the city that have dirty buildings in poor condition. The people who live in slums are very poor.

There was a time when people who were financially comfortable were totally oblivious to how the poor lived in the big cities. The well-off knew nothing about life in the tenements. But in 1890, a man named Jacob Riis, who had emigrated to the U.S. from Denmark in 1870, published a pioneering work of photojournalism.

His book, *How the Other Half Lives*, exposed the plight of the poor on the Lower East Side of Manhattan. Because of technological advances in photography, he was able to shoot pictures of the wretched conditions in the tenements of New York City. He was also able to shoot photos in the dark—which was necessary, because the tenements were dark inside. Riis's work was also innovative, because he mostly attributed the plight of the poor to their terrible environments.

He wrote of the Tenth Ward, which was where many of the poor Jewish immigrants lived. City health officers called the Tenth "the typhus ward." (Typhus is a deadly disease that flourishes where there is poor hygiene, crowding, and lice.) Jacob Riis was advanced in his thinking, when he said that penury and poverty were wedded everywhere to dirt and disease. He also made it clear that the people who lived in the tenements could not be blamed for the conditions of their lives.

He deplored the solid city blocks of tenements that had been built on the Lower East Side. He wrote:

> The average five-story tenement adds a story or two to its stature in Ludlow Street and an extra building on the rear lot, and yet the sign "To Let" is the rarest of all there. Here is one seven stories high. The sanitary policeman whose beat this is will tell

you that it contains thirty-six families ... In this house, where a case of smallpox was reported, there were fifty-eight babies and thirty-eight children that were over five years of age.

He was shocked to observe that even the densest crowding in London never was as dense as it was on the Lower East Side. "The packing of the population has run up the record here to the rate of three hundred and thirty thousand per square mile." Given that there were no skyscrapers, this was an extraordinary number of people on a small piece of land.

For the record, it needs to be said that his work had some major flaws. He was often biased against Italians, Jews, and the Irish. Nonetheless, he wrote in many passages with great feeling for these very people. In fact, he was inspired to write and photograph as he did out of sympathy for his subjects; he was horrified at the way they were forced to live. (Jacob Riis himself had been forced to live in the dreadful police-run poorhouses of New York, during his first months in America.)

Ultimately, his work—which was considered powerful, muckraking journalism—educated wealthy New Yorkers and many politicians "who had no idea such a world existed within a few miles of their own opulent neighborhoods." They were able to see first-hand, through Riis's photographs, what thousands of new Americans had to endure. *How the Other Half Lives* persuaded Theodore Roosevelt—who at that time was the New York City Commissioner of Police—to shut down the police-run poorhouses. After Roosevelt read Riis' book, he called Riis "the best American I ever knew."

Dancing Bees

Many farmers depend upon traveling beekeepers. Why? The wild pollinators—which include wasps, bats, beetles, and bumblebees—are unable to carry large enough quantities of pollen from tree to tree. Therefore, hundreds of beekeepers travel across the country in trailers and big trucks to help out farmers with *billions* of migrant bees. (Really, it's the beekeeper who is the chief migrant. The bees travel in their hives inside huge semi-trucks or trailers. Just think. After the bees are released into their new surroundings, have gathered their nectar, and, just incidentally carried pollen from flower to flower, they return to their very own hives!)

Typically, beekeepers spend their winters in the warm, growing places, such as California or the southern states. In the summer, they travel north to pollinate other crops. In the Dakotas, for example, the traveling bees serve the farmers who grow vast fields of alfalfa and clover. Alfalfa and clover produce some of the finest honey.

John Miller is a traveling beekeeper. In February 2005, he had driven to California where the almond trees had flowered—on more than 580,000 acres. The almond trees were ready for the annual arrival of the beekeepers. John's hives ordinarily would have been hubs of hardworking, fat, brown honeybees. Every previous February, John's bees worked tirelessly, carrying pollen from blossom to blossom. Not so, in 2005! As John describes it, his bees "were wandering in drunken circles at the base of the hive doors—wingless, desiccated, sluggish, and blasé." Within several weeks, nearly half of John Miller's 13,000 hives were empty. He figures at least 300 million of his bees died.

Of course, John was not the only beekeeper to whom this happened: a devastating problem that came to be called "Colony Collapse Disorder" was occurring in the hives of beekeepers across the nation. Why was this such a disaster?

Well, it used to be that the chief work of a beekeeper was to keep bees so that they would make honey. The beekeeper would sell the honey, usually locally. Not so, today. Today, the chief work of a bee is to pollinate the flowers of those foods we love to eat.

How do you feel about blueberries, cherries, and apples? Do people you know like broccoli or onion rings? Lots of people want cucumbers in their salads! What do you think of carrots and beautiful, big, orange pumpkins in the fall? How about zucchini, summer squash, or winter squash? These crops cannot grow without honeybees.

In fact, the work of contemporary beekeepers is one of the lynchpins of modern agriculture. Almond ranchers, for example, cannot produce their crops in quantity without the traveling bees. An almond rancher with hardworking bees can generate 2,400 pounds of almonds per acre. An almond rancher without the bees' pollination services will harvest only 40 pounds per acre. Did you know that almonds are California's chief export?

If our bees are dying, just think of this: "the annual bee migration ... is the glue that holds much of modern agriculture together." Besides the foods mentioned above, honeybees are also crucial for the pollination of lettuce, cranberries, oranges, canola, and a hundred other crops. These foods cannot be grown in the quantities to which we are accustomed and which feed the nation (and the world) without the pollination services of bees. Imagine how prices would rise without the bees!

What is responsible for "the silence of the bees"? Why are the bees dying or simply vanishing? Scientists think that a small, but powerful, group of elements are the cause:

(a) pesticides
(b) invasive parasitic mites
(c) an insufficient supply of food
(d) a new virus that attacks the immune systems of bees

Beginning in 2007, the U.S. Congress granted emergency funds of $20 million annually to the U.S. Department of Agriculture to study the disappearance of honeybees. How else can we help honeybees? Here is a list of things to do.

1. **Build a Beehive for Non-Stinging Bees!** Does your family own a drill? Do you have a backyard, a balcony (or fire escape), or nearby park? If so, this can be fun and not hard. Get a block of wood that isn't pressure-treated. A block that is 2 to 3 feet long, 1 foot high, and 1 foot deep will be perfect. Then with your parents' help, drill holes in it that are 3/32 inch to 5/16 inch in diameter. (If your drill has bits of different sizes, it will be easy to determine the diameter of the hole you are drilling.) The hole should be about 5 inches deep. If the thought of bees makes people in your house or apartment nervous, place your wood block (with the holes exposed) further from the house. If you live in an apartment, you can try placing your wood block at the park (if there is one!). Then wait for the bees to arrive.
2. **Work on growing a garden with members of your family. Or simply make your yard prettier. Make it colorful! Grow several different kinds of flowers, and perhaps some vegetables if you are able.** Even apartment dwellers with a porch, balcony, or fire escape may be able to take a couple of large flower pots—or large empty cans with some holes poked in the bottom so the water can drain—and grow flowers and tomatoes. If you are going to

grow from seed, it will be wise to check out just how to do this successfully, either at the public library or at a nearby store that sells garden supplies.

The National Resource Defense Council (NRDC) advises us to grow local and native plants, because these are the plants the will be just right for local bees. If you grow several different types of plants, you will attract a diversity of bees.

- **Look for flowers of different shapes and colors.** Did you know that bees have good vision? It is interesting that both color and shape matter to the bees!
- **Plant flowers that grow at different times.** The clerk at the place where you buy your flowers will be able to advise you on growing months.

Stone Fox

The word *Indian* was first used by Christopher Columbus (or his contemporaries), who didn't know there was a continent to the west between Spain and the Indies (the Malay Archipelago). When he got to the Caribbean islands, he thought he had arrived in the Indies and the inhabitants were dubbed "Indians."

When we think of the indigenous people of North America, we tend to consider them as a homogeneous group—one people with one culture, having similar practices and languages across the tribes and nations that inhabited the present-day United States of America and Canada. But this was not the case.

How large was this population of indigenous people before 1500? Contemporary estimates by scholars run from a low of 2 million to a high of 18 million. A figure of 9 million probably is a reasonable, conservative guess. In any case, so many people, living in many separate groups in distinct regions across the land, would have to represent many different cultures. Their languages were at least as different from each other as are German, French, Spanish, English, Dutch, and Italian, for example.

Below we have included several word sets (Abenaki-Penobscot, Cherokee, and Choctaw) that may interest your students.

Abenaki-Penobscot Word Set

English	Abenaki-Penobscot
One	Bazegw
Two	Niz
Three	Nas
Four	Yaw
Five	Nôlan
Man	Zanôba *or* Gizôba
Woman	Behanem
Dog	Alemos *or* Adia
Sun	Gizos
Moon	Gizos
Water	Nebi
White	Wôbi
Yellow	Wizôw
Red	Mekwi
Black	Mkazawi
Eat	Micimek
See	Namito
Hear	Nodam
Sing	Linto

Cherokee Word Set

English	Cherokee
One	Sagwu
Two	Ta'li
Three	Tso'i
Four	Nvgi
Five	Hisgi
Man	Asgaya
Woman	Agehya
Dog	Gihli
Sun	Nvda
Moon	Nvda
Water	Ama
White	Unega
Yellow	Dalonige
Red	Gigage
Black	Gvhnige
Eat	Agi'a
See	Agowatiha
Hear	Atvgi'a
Sing	Dekanogi'a

Choctaw Word Set

English	Choctaw
One	Achaffa
Two	Tuklo
Three	Tuchena
Four	Ushta
Five	Talhapi
Man	Hattak
Woman	Ohoyo
Dog	Ofi
Sun	Hvshi
Moon	Hvshi
Water	Oka
White	Hanta *or* Tohbi
Yellow	Lvkna
Red	Humma
Black	Lusa
Eat	Vpa
See	Pi̱sa
Hear	Ha̱klo
Sing	Taloa

The Drama of the People and the Moon Bears

(Based on a Very Similar AAF Play)

Characters:

Moon Bear #1

Moon Bear #2

The Poacher (a poacher is someone who hunts animals that are illegal to hunt)

The Husband of the Poacher

Wildlife Official #1

Wildlife Official #2

Wildlife Official #3

Wildlife Official #4

Wildlife Official #5

Wildlife Official #6

A Vile Bear Bile Farmer

The Vile Bear Bile Farmer's Wife

Store Owner

Store Owner's Husband

Customer #1

Customer #2

Customer #3

Customer #4

Moon Bears #1 and #2 are walking through the woods.

Moon Bear #1: We are wise and peaceful animals. We love to eat berries, nuts, and HONEY! I am 3 years old. I just moved away from my mother.

Moon Bear #2: I am also 3 years old. I also just moved away from my mother. We want to live on our own. Of course, we will be near our mothers.

Moon Bear #1: If no hunter kills us, and if we stay strong, we will live to be 30 years old.

Moon Bear #2: We are walking through the forest now to search for food and to have fun. It is pretty here.

Moon Bear #1: OW! I stepped in a leghold trap!

Moon Bear #2: Me, too! OW! This hurts so much!

Moon Bear #1: I am so afraid.

Moon Bear #2: My leg hurts.

The poacher and her poacher husband now walk into the woods.

The Poacher: Aha! We have caught a Moon Bear!

The Poacher Husband: We have caught two Moon Bears!

The Poacher: Now we can sell these bears to the bile farmers!

The Poacher Husband: The bile farmers will give us money so we can feed our children.

Six Wildlife Officials now enter.

Wildlife Official #1: Aha! We have got two poachers! Poachers. Why are you hunting Moon Bears?

Wildlife Official #2: Moon Bears are endangered. It is against the law to hunt them or to trap them.

The Poacher: We are very poor. We trapped these baby bears because we need money to buy food and clothing for our children.

The Poacher Husband: We can sell these bears to a bile farmer. We will get enough money to buy food for many months.

Wildlife Official #3: Hmmm, we must all go and find the bile farmer.

Everyone exits.

The Six Wildlife Officials enter a bear bile farm.

Wildlife Official #4: I can see many cages with bears in them.

Wildlife Official #5: The bears seem so sad.

Wildlife Official #6: Some of the bears are even hitting their heads against the bars of their cages. They used to be wild and free.

Wildlife Official #1: We must find the Bear Farmer and find out why this is happening.

All of the Wildlife Officials: *(They turn and speak to the audience.)* Please remember what you see here at this bear farm. We will ask for your help later!

The Bear Bile Farmer enters.

Wildlife Official #2: Now, Bear Bile Farmers—both of you!—we have a question. Why do you pay the Poacher and her Poacher Husband to trap the bears so you can keep them in this horrible farm?!

The Bear Bile Farmer: We pay the Poacher and her Poacher Husband because we are very poor. We need the money.

The Bear Bile Farmer's Wife: We need the money to buy food and clothing for our children. If we sell the bears' bile to a store in town, we make enough money to buy food for many months.

Wildlife Official #3: Hmmm, we must go to the town store.

The Store Owner and the Store Owner's Husband enter.

Wildlife Official #3: Now, Store Owner and Store Owner's Husband. We have a question for you.

Wildlife Official #4: This is the question. Why do you pay the Bear Bile Farmer and the Bear Bile Farmer's Wife, who pay the Poacher and the Husband of the Poacher, who trap the Moon Bears, who then have to live in fear in a horrible bear bile farm prison?

The Store Owner: We pay the Bear Bile Farmer and the Bear Bile Farmer's Wife, who pay the Poacher and the Husband of the Poacher, who trap the Moon Bears, because we have many customers who buy bear bile goods.

The Store Owner's Husband: Yes. Indeed. We know we can make lots of money from them. We sell shampoo with bear bile, wine with bear bile, and also medicines with bear bile.

Wildlife Official #3: Hmmm, we must go find the customers.

Four Customers enter the store.

Wildlife Official #5: Now Customers, we have a question for you. Why do you pay the Store Owner and the Store Owner's Husband who pays the Bear Bile Farmer and the Bear Bile Farmer's Wife, who pays the Poacher and the Husband of the Poacher, who trap the sweet Moon Bear babies, who then have to live in fear in a horrible bear bile farm prison?

Customer #1: I pay the Store Owner and the Store Owner's Husband who pays the Bear Bile Farmer and the Bear Bile Farmer's Wife, who pays the Poacher and the Husband of the Poacher, who trap the sweet Moon Bear babies, because I think this shampoo that is made with bear bile makes my hair extra soft and smooth.

Customer #2: I pay the Store Owner and the Store Owner's Husband who pays the Bear Bile Farmer and the Bear Bile Farmer's Wife, who pays the Poacher and the Husband of the Poacher, who trap the sweet Moon Bear babies, because I think that this medicine made with bear bile makes my fever go away.

Wildlife Official #6: Do you know what happens to the bears so that you can have these products?

Customers # 1 and #2: No, we don't know what happens to the bears.

Wildlife Official #6: (*Addresses the audience*) Please tell these customers and the Store Owner and the Store Owner's Husband what is done to the moon bears at the bear farm and what the bear farm is like.

Audience: *Willing audience members should stand up and describe how the bears are kept in cages and are not free to live in the wild.*

The Store Owner and the Store Owner's Husband: But isn't bear bile necessary for making medicine?

All the Wildlife Officials: No! There are 54 other kinds of Chinese medicines that are just as good or even better. And those medicines don't hurt the bears!

Customer #3: Now that I know how awful bear bile farming is, I will never again buy shampoo with bear bile in it. I will not pay money to the Store Owner and the Store Owner's Husband who pay the Bear Bile Farmer and the Bear Bile Farmer's Wife, who pay the Poacher and the Husband of the Poacher, who trap the sweet Moon Bear babies, so the Moon Bears can stay wild and free!

Customer #4: And now that I know how awful bear bile farming is, I will never again buy wine with bear bile in it. I will not pay money to the Store Owner and the Store Owner's Husband who pay the Bear Bile Farmer and the Bear Bile Farmer's Wife, who pay the Poacher and the Husband of the Poacher, who trap the sweet Moon Bear babies, so the Moon Bears can stay wild and free!

The Store Owner: Well, since our customers are not going to buy bear bile goods anymore and will probably tell others to stop buying and to help the Moon Bears ...

The Store Owner's Husband: ... then we must order new products without bear bile! I will not pay money to the Bear Bile Farmer and the Bear Bile Farmer's Wife, who pay the Poacher and the Husband of the Poacher, so that the Poachers will stop trapping the baby bears, and so ...

Everyone, Including Audience: ... so the moon bears can stay wild and free!

WORKBOOK ANSWER GUIDE

Table of Contents

UNIT ONE

THE THINGS THAT MATTER

UNIT TWO

CLARITY

UNIT THREE

HEAD, HANDS, HEART

UNIT FOUR

CARING

UNIT FIVE

DETERMINATION

UNIT SIX

THE GRAND FINALÉ

To the Teacher:

Here are some suggestions regarding how to help your students best use the Activity Workbook.

Vocabulary Activity One

1. Before assigning Activity One, review the vocabulary words with your students. Each student should be clear about the pronunciation and the meaning of every word. Remind your students, also, that sometimes the vocabulary exercises call for the plural form of a vocabulary word given in the singular or vice versa (if the vocabulary word is a noun) or for a different tense of the vocabulary word (if the word is a verb).
2. Some Activity One exercises may use words that are new to the student that are *not* listed in the Word Banks of the textbook. These words are related to the selection thematically and are defined in the Workbook Glossary, not in the textbook Glossary. Familiarize your students with the location of the Workbook Glossary.
3. Many vocabulary words may not be words your students use in ordinary discourse. Vocabulary lists derived from literature tend to be more advanced than the working vocabulary of the average American student. Please give your students practice using the selection vocabulary.

   The fine nuances of the new words they learn will help students think and express themselves with greater specificity. Moreover, if a student is often stumbling over selection words, reading will not be the pleasurable and informative experience it ought to be.
4. We all know that some words have several different meanings. We understand the meaning of such a word based upon the context within which the word is used. Vocabulary words that may have more than one meaning are used in the Activity One exercises *according to the definition given in the textbook Word Bank.* For the most part, the definition prompts given with each Activity One sentence use the very same words as the definition given in the textbook.

Vocabulary Activity Two

Vocabulary Activity Two offers students the opportunity to think creatively and logically about the selection vocabulary. Students are called upon to categorize words, compare meanings, and manipulate the words in ways that develop both inferential reasoning skills and the ability to think deductively. Activity Two requires a solid understanding of the meanings of the words. It should *always follow* Activity One. Again, we suggest your reviewing all the vocabulary pronunciations and definitions before students proceed with Activity Two.

The Six Comprehension Questions

1. The six comprehension questions in the workbook require "higher level" thinking. In other words, for these questions students need to figure things out. Students may be asked to
   - give examples of incidents in the selection that support or express its theme;
   - compare and contrast characters or events in the story;
   - make predictions;
   - draw conclusions based upon information implied or stated in the story;
   - express an opinion and support it with specific details from the selection.
2. You may need to review and discuss the six comprehension questions with your class and with individual students. Depending upon their academic level and maturity, you may find that all or some of the class simply is unable to answer these questions independently. If you can give them sufficient support at the outset, they may develop these skills over the school year.

3. You will help your students by giving them the vocabulary with which to answer the comprehension questions you are asking. Below are terms that it will be helpful to define for them. The first column has sets of terms that are opposites. The second sets of words are more subtly related. As you teach the students these terms, be sure to give examples from one of the selections.

compare : contrast	describe, explain
differences : similarities	features, characteristics, qualities
fact : opinion	narrator, narration
quote : paraphrase	sequence

4. *One Step Further* is just that—an activity that engages students in the highest level of critical thinking. *One Step Further* takes students one step further in using skills of evaluation. Students are asked to express and support opinions and to do original writing as they analyze the selection's theme.
   One Step Further often presents students with a famous quotation that is, through its meaning, connected with the theme of the selection. Students are asked to write a short paragraph about whether and why they agree or disagree with the ideas expressed in the quotation.
   This is an activity in which you must be actively involved. The ideas expressed in the quotations will be easily understood if they are supported by teacher explanation. Be sure to define any difficult words in the quotation.

Graphic Organizer

Graphic organizers help your students visually process information. Help students understand that a graphic organizer is a visual representation of the knowledge they have already acquired from working on questions and activities related to the selection. The graphic organizers are independent activities. Often the directions for a particular graphic organizer is multifaceted; make certain that students understand all of the steps in these directions.

Leah's Pony (Textbook p. 4)

Vocabulary—Activity I (p. 2)

1. clutched
2. debt
3. auctioneer
4. agriculture
5. cultivate
6. sow
7. collateral
8. drought
9. withered
10. gullies

Vocabulary—Activity II (p. 3)

In top drawer:	*In bottom drawer:*	*On top of chest:*
agriculture	auctioneer	clutched
drought	collateral	
gullies	debt	
sow		
wither		
cultivate		

Comprehension Questions—In-Depth Thinking (p. 4)

1. ***Remained the same:***
   - They were living on the same farm.
   - The family remains close-knit throughout.
   - They had chores to do all along, but the nature of the chores changed.
   - Papa was always teaching Leah. An example from the beginning would be how he showed her the way to attach and adjust the saddle. Later on he taught her to be brave both by telling her to be brave and by example.

   Things that changed:
   - The crops grew beautifully at the beginning, but later on they hardly grew at all.
   - Leah and her family seemed much happier and more carefree beforehand.
   - Before the drought that created the Dust Bowl, there were regular farm chores. Afterwards, the family members were busy cleaning the dust and protecting themselves from the wind.
   - After times became difficult, the family could no longer afford what they could in the past. Mama became resourceful and reused things to save money.
   - Leah has grown in many ways by the end of the story.
2. ***Leah and her family:***
   - Papa bought his Leah a special gift, a pony.
   - Papa patiently taught her how to take care of the pony.
   - They all worked together to take care of the farm and keep each other's spirits up.
   - Mama baked fresh hot coffee cake for Leah every Saturday despite the circumstances.
   - Leah was willing to give up something important for her family.

   Leah and her pony:
   - Leah was busy riding the pony the whole summer.
   - Leah took good care of the pony.
   - Leah had a special spot under her pony's mane that she loved to scratch.
   - Leah loved to hear Mr. B. say, "That's the finest pony in the whole county."
   - Leah was concerned that it was hard to keep her pony's coat shiny during the windstorms.
   - It was hard for Leah to make the decision and part with her pony.
   - Leah was sad when the farm was quiet, without the pony's whinny.
   - Leah was thrilled to see her pony back.

   Mr. B. and Leah:
   - Leah loved to go to Mr. B.'s grocery store to hear him shout, "That's the finest pony in the whole county." He probably enjoyed saying it as much as she liked to hear it.
   - Mr. B. sounded concerned when he heard that Leah was willing to sell her pony.
   - From the fact that Leah did not tell Mr. B. the true reason, it seems likely that she felt he cared so much that he wouldn't allow her to sell her pony.
   - Mr. B. returned Leah's pony right after the auction was over.
   - Mr. B. wrote Leah an encouraging note.

   All of the farmers:
   - The neighbors who left stopped to say good-bye.
   - The farmers united behind Leah's family at the auction.
3. Answers will vary.

Comprehension Questions—Drawing Conclusions (pp. 4-5)

4. Answers may vary. Here is one possible answer: At first, Leah's parents did not want to alarm her or worry her unnecessarily. When they realized there would be a public auction, however, they had to tell her.
5. Answers will vary.
6. Answers will vary.

Comprehension Questions—One Step Further (p. 5)

Answers will vary. Be sure that students include responses to all of the questions.

Graphic Organizer (p. 6)

1. Farmer One could have kept the flock of chickens he had bought at the bargain price of ten cents. Instead, he gave the chickens to Mama.
2. Farmer Two could have kept the pickup truck he bought at the ridiculous price of twenty-five cents. Instead, he gave it back to Papa.
3. (*The Neighbors* is filled in.)
4. Mr. B. could have kept Leah's pony, which he had bought for a small sum. Instead, he returned it to her.
5. Leah could have watched as her father lost the farm. She could have said, "What can a little girl do?" Instead, she sold her pony to get the cash she would use at the auction. Her actions saved the farm.

Graphic Organizer (p. 7)

1. It glistened like satin.
2. It was no taller than a man's thumb.
3. The wind blew so hard it turned the sky black with dust.
4. Grasshoppers turned the day to night.
5. She galloped past a house with rags stuffed in broken windowpanes.

Supergrandpa (Textbook p. 24)

Vocabulary—Activity I (p. 8)

1. spy
2. contestants
3. rivalry
4. surpass
5. sprinted
6. craned
7. vigorous
8. scoffed
9. orb
10. triumph

Vocabulary—Activity II (p. 9)

1. mock, ridicule
2. race at full speed for a short distance
3. stretch out one's neck to see
4. a round object
5. an older energetic person
6. a person who takes part in a competition
7. outdo
8. a victory
9. competition
10. strong and active

Comprehension Questions—In-Depth Thinking (p. 10)

1. At first, Gustaf said, "This Tour of Sweden is for me!" He was a frequent bicycle rider and thought he would enjoy the race. After he was challenged by almost everyone, he chose to ride the length of the race to prove that he could do it, to himself and to those around him. When he was recognized as "Supergrandpa" and developed a fan club, he realized he could win, and wanted to, too.
2. Any answer that includes one of the following traits or a variation of it: confidence, creativity, determination, motivation, persistence, drive, receptiveness to encouragement, positive attitude, sense of humor, stamina.
3. (1) Gustaf finds out about the race.
   (2) He is denied permission to participate in the race.
   (3) Gustaf remains determined to bicycle the length of the race.
   (4) Gustaf Håkansson becomes Supergrandpa, known to all of Sweden.
   (5) Gustaf 'wins' the race.

Comprehension Question—Drawing Conclusions (pp. 10-11)

4. Answers will vary.
5. Answers will vary. Some reasonable possibilities would be when:
   - The reader saw his persistence at the very start.
   - Gustaf displayed incredible strength and determination just to pedal all those miles to reach the starting line.
   - Everyone in the crowd rooted for him.
   - The story states, "And suddenly, he wanted to win too!"
6. Answers will vary. It seems that the public was inspired by the fact that an older man would—and could—put forth the effort to finish the race. Perhaps some were prompted to support Gustaf because of the injustice they felt was being done to him. Others simply wanted to be kind and encouraging, once the young child pointed out Gustaf in the crowd. The newspaper article made it sound interesting and inviting to get involved.

Comprehension Questions—One Step Further (p. 11)

Answers will vary. Assist students who have difficulty understanding the meaning of "Don't judge a book by its cover." Then let them respond independently.

Graphic Organizer (pp. 12-13)

[First sign:] What people said to discourage Gustaf.

What did his wife say? But you're too old for a bicycle race.

What did his son say? You'll keel over.

What did his grandchildren say? You can't ride your bike a thousand miles, Grandpa.

What did the first judge say? But this race is for young people.

What did the second judge say? You would never make it to the finish.

What did the third judge say? We can only admit racers who are strong and fit.

[Second sign:] What Gustaf did.

What did Gustaf do the morning after the judges rejected him? He cycled far out of town.

What did Gustaf do to reach Haparanda? He cycled six hundred miles.

What did Gustaf do because he didn't have a number? He cut out a big red zero and pinned it to his shirt.

How did Gustaf get ahead of the other riders? He cycled all night.

What didn't Gustaf do? He hardly slept.

[Third sign:] What people said or did to encourage Supergrandpa.

How did the newspaper make him famous? They put his picture in the paper.

How did people help him when he was hungry? They gave him food and drink.

How did he become known to radio-audiences? Radio interviewers broadcast what he said.

What did they tell him near the end of the race? They told him he could win.

What did they do when he won? They cheered and lifted him onto their shoulders.

Two Big Bears (Textbook p. 40)

Vocabulary—Activity I (p. 14)

1. trembling
2. thaw
3. chores
4. leaves
5. budge
6. club
7. quiver
8. pitch
9. calico
10. hearth

Vocabulary—Activity II (p. 15)

1. b.
2. c.
3. b.
4. a.
5. b.
6. a.
7. c.
8. c.
9. b.
10. c.

Comprehension Questions—In-Depth Thinking (p. 16)

1. **Main/Important:** Pa, Ma, Laura, and the bears

   Minor/Less Important: Mary, Sukey, shopkeeper, and men in shop
2. **Similarities:** Both Sukey and the Bear were large, dark, furry animals. Both were heavy and about the same size. Both animals had large heads.

   Differences:

Sukey	*Bear*
brown	black
short fur	shaggy fur
large gentle eyes	small glittering eyes
3. Answers will vary. Some possibilities include:
   - Ma finished sewing the new clothing from the calico that Pa brought home.
   - All of the snow and icicles completely melted.
   - Pa set up some traps or extra protection from bears.
   - Pa told some more stories.
   - The family started to do some spring-cleaning.

Comprehension Questions—Drawing Conclusions (pp. 16-17)

4. Answers will vary. They might estimate that she is about their own age. Some indications would be: she is new at holding a lantern, she sits on her father's knee, and so on. Discuss with your students the fact that some behaviors of nine-year-olds have remained the same over the generations, while others have changed. They may enjoy giving examples of each category.
5. Ma wanted to be strong and show the girls that she was confident that everything would be all right. She may have been anxious, wondering what caused Pa's delay, but she didn't want Laura and Mary to be burdened with that worry.
6. Answers will vary.

Comprehension Questions—One Step Further (p. 17)

Answers will vary.

Graphic Organizer (pp. 18-19)

1. Papa walks through the woods at night. / *Mama goes to the barn at night.*
2. *Papa thinks he sees a bear.* / Mama thinks she sees a cow.
3. Papa hits the bear with a club. / *Mama hits the "cow."*
4. *After Papa hits the "bear," he finds it is a tree.* / After Mama hits the "cow," she realizes it is a bear.
5. Papa is very courageous. / *Mama is very courageous.*

Mom's Best Friend (Textbook p. 58)

Comprehension Questions—In-Depth Thinking (p. 20)

1. Freedom from the responsibilities of cooking, errands, and general housekeeping, was certainly a vacation for Mom. More than that though, Mom was enthusiastic about getting a new dog guide. Going back to The Seeing Eye brought back a lot of memories for her. In addition, she enjoyed spending time with other blind people. The rest of the family missed Mom and had extra chores to do, which certainly didn't make for a great vacation.
2. Answers will vary. Getting on a crowded bus; going to a zoo where the smells of other animals might be confusing; being near children who are too young to know not to distract a dog guide, are some examples.
3. - Mom needs to exhibit patience on a daily basis. Her inability to see makes each day challenging, but she has learned to handle her disability with grace. She often injects humor into a difficult situation; for example, her description of garbage day is funny rather than resentful or angry.
   - Dog guide training requires a lot of patience. Even after Ursula goes through all the training, she makes mistakes, which can sometimes be painful (bumping into trees), embarrassing, or dangerous (crossing the street).
   - Leslie, her father, and brother must also exercise a lot of patience. They need to be patient with each other, understand that jobs may be done differently from the way Mom does them, and wait for Mom to come home from Morristown. Patience is required again when they must wait for Ursula to get used to the new environment and receive permission to play with her.

Comprehension Questions—Drawing Conclusions (pp. 20-21)

4. Answers will vary.
5. Answers will vary. At first, Leslie, thought mostly about herself—she was concerned about her relationship with Marit and Ursula, instead of about Mom's needs. She was also judgmental when it came to Mom's letters. Perhaps she was even jealous at one point that Mom was having such a good time and spoke so highly of the people and dogs at The Seeing Eye. These emo-

tions are understandable, and Leslie did recognize that her Mom loved her and that this was the best thing for everyone. She also realized that she could develop a new relationship with Ursula. Your students may feel that Leslie's actions were acceptable, or they may say that they would have behaved differently and more maturely. However, it is important to point out that people never really know how they would react in a situation until they are in the other person's position.

6. Answers will vary. If students are not sure what to write about, present a few examples: the digestive system, the ability to bend at all joints, the sense of taste, the fact that we have built-in protection like tears and eyelashes for our eyes, and so on.

Comprehension Questions—One Step Further (p. 21)

Some students will wholeheartedly agree with this statement and say that dogs and other pets are companions that are warm, cuddly, and nonjudgmental. Other students will disagree, saying that pets and people are not in the same category. While some animals may make good pets, they cannot replace a close relationship with a human being. Regardless of their opinions, students will likely look at the situation differently when it involves someone like Mom, who truly depends on her dog companion.

Graphic Organizer (pp. 22-23)

There are obviously no right or wrong answers. Some of your students may mention that many elevators have Braille floor numbers, that ovens probably can be fitted with Braille on/off and degree buttons, that Mom jogs with Dad, and so on. Hopefully, some of your inventive and thoughtful students will come up with new ways to help vision impaired—or otherwise impaired—people to function normally. Don't forget about the case for removing existing impediments or obstacles.

The Tiger, the Persimmon and the Rabbit's Tail (Textbook p. 72)

Comprehension Questions—In-Depth Thinking (p. 24)

1. By the end of the story the tiger is portrayed as fearful. He admits fear to the rabbit and advises the rabbit not to go back to the tree for fear that the 'dried persimmon will get him.' It is likely, though, that after this episode is forgotten, the tiger will assume the superior attitude he is described as having at the beginning of the story.
2. He keeps repeating, "Oh, I can't believe I'm alive," and similar phrases.
3. The tiger tends to jump to conclusions. Not knowing what a persimmon is, he jumps to the conclusion that it is a frightening animal. When he feels the thief on his back, he jumps to the conclusion that he is a persimmon. A "good thinker" investigates and tries to learn the facts before coming to a conclusion.

Comprehension Questions—Drawing Conclusions (pp. 24-25)

4. The rabbit was much more relaxed about the whole situation. His is a less excitable nature, and also a more skeptical one. For all the tiger's boastfulness, the rabbit is actually the more confident of the two. When the tiger warns him about the persimmon, the rabbit says he is the fastest runner in the forest, so can escape if necessary. Throughout the story, the tiger wants to run, whereas the rabbit wants to deal with the problem head-on.
5. Answers will vary. Some will say the thief will not steal again after such a traumatic experience, others may say a thief is a thief.
6. There is something compelling about a baby's cry. The noise can be irritating and it is frustrating to hear a baby cry without knowing the source of its problem. The noise was also unfamiliar to the tiger.

Comprehension Questions—One Step Further (p. 25)

Answers will vary. Encourage humorous dialogues where the animals ridicule the tiger, where the town gossips exaggerate or change the story, or where a slow-witted animal gets it all wrong. Or, your students may be of a more serious bent and have their animals moralize about fear, courage, etc. Some may be politically savvy and have their animals unionize against the tiger, now that he has been shown to be a coward.

Graphic Organizer (pp. 26-27)

- **2nd Row, 2nd Column:** The tiger thought the baby wasn't afraid of him.
- **2nd Row, 3rd Column:** The tiger crept closer.
- **3rd Row, 1st Column:** The mother gave the baby a persimmon and the baby stopped crying.
- **3rd Row, 3rd Column:** The tiger decided to go eat an ox.
- **4th Row, 2nd Column:** The tiger thought it was the persimmon.
- **4th Row, 3rd Column:** The tiger allowed the thief to put a rope around his neck.
- **5th Row, 2nd Column:** He thinks the tiger is a calf.
- **5th Row, 3rd Column:** He jumps on the tiger's back.
- **6th Row, 2nd Column:** He thinks it's the dried persimmon.
- **7th Row, 1st Column:** The thief grabs hold of a branch and climbs through a hole in the tree trunk.
- **7th Row, 3rd Column:** He rolls over and over on the ground in happiness.
- **8th Row, 1st Column:** The tiger tells the rabbit about the dried persimmon.
- **9th Row, 1st Column:** The rabbit sees a frightened man.
- **9th Row, 3rd Column:** He puts his rump in the tree.
- **10th Row, 1st Column:** The thief pulls hard on the rabbit's tail.
- **10th Row, 2nd Column:** The tiger thinks it's the persimmon.

Sato and the Elephants (Textbook p. 94)

Vocabulary—Activity I (p. 28)

1. corroded
2. beacon
3. precision
4. flaw
5. dense
6. eerie
7. pare
8. chiseled
9. tepid
10. trudged

Vocabulary—Activity II (p. 29)

1. to cut off the outer layer of something
2. lukewarm
3. defects, faults
4. strange and frightening
5. walk slowly and heavily
6. thick and tightly packed
7. being exact
8. a light used as a warning signal
9. carved with a special carving tool
10. worn away

Comprehension Questions—In-Depth Thinking (p. 30)

1. Sato knew what he would *not* do. He could not make this piece into a netsuke because it was too large. He also wanted to be sure not to waste any of it. He watched and waited until the ivory 'spoke' to him, until he had a vision of what he should do with it. He was excited with the magical feeling that seemed to instruct him to carve.
2. Sato watched his father work when he was younger. He often told his father, "Someday I will be a great ivory carver like you." Sato looked up to his father and treasured the carving his father had given him.
3. The bullet obviously came from a hunter's gun. A different bullet probably killed the elephant.

Comprehension Questions—Drawing Conclusions (pp. 30-31)

4. Sato felt guilty because he realized that all along he had been encouraging poachers and causing harm to the elephants by demanding ivory for carving. His guilt caused him to resolve not to use ivory at all, but to carve out of stone instead.
5. Sato was happy at the end of the story, but in a different way. Students may answer at different levels, but they should indicate that he was happy to have recognized his mistake and was rectifying it by working with stone instead of ivory. Some may suggest that he was happy and sad at the same time. He'd always wanted to become a master ivory carver. The elephant incident altered his goal. He may not have been as happy on one level, but at a deeper level, he had the satisfaction of knowing he was doing the right thing. This is called peace of mind. Some mature students may be able to recognize that the happiness at the beginning was blissful and innocent. At the story's close, the happiness came from a deeper source.
6. Answers will vary.

Comprehension Questions—One Step Further (p. 31)

Answers will vary. Most people do not like to be reminded of their mistakes. Even if they choose to revisit them, they do not appreciate being reminded of their mistakes by other people. Remembering our mistakes indicates that we have shortcomings and that knowledge is not always pleasant. However, if we understand that every human being errs, and that we can learn tremendous lessons from our blunders, our perspective can change dramatically. This view will not necessarily heal any hurt feelings or reduce any negative repercussions, but it can, at least, turn the mistake into an opportunity for growth.

Graphic Organizer (pp. 32-35)

1. He was famous for the beauty and precision of his ivory figures.
2. He hoped to be an ivory carver like his father.
3. When Akira tells him there aren't as many elephants now, he thinks about where ivory comes from.
4. The vision of a magnificent elephant appears to him.
5. It is a bullet.
6. He understands that an elephant was killed to obtain this ivory.
7. He weeps.
8. He leaves the bullet in the elephant's forehead.
9. He thinks they will kill him.
10. He gives up his dream of becoming a master carver of ivory and resolves to carve stone, instead. He keeps the figure of the elephant with the bullet in its forehead to strengthen his resolve.

Amelia's Road (Textbook p. 112)

Comprehension Questions—In-Depth Thinking (p. 36)

1. Before, Amelia was negative about a number of things. She resented the fact that her family moved around so much and did things differently, like remembering important events by the crops that were being harvested at the time. Amelia desperately wanted to settle down in one place and make friends.

   After, Amelia learned that even with frequent moving, one could make important connections with people and places. She bonded with the students in the class. Mrs. Ramos created an atmosphere where the students were all recognized as individuals, something Amelia craved. When her good work was acknowledged, she felt appreciated. Finally, her road and tree were private and personal, yet represented the wonderful time she had had in school.
2. Amelia was very happy and proud that Mrs. Ramos singled out her work to show to the class. (You may want to use this opportunity to discuss this topic further.)
3. Taking the box with her would have defeated its purpose. She did not want to take these mementos on the road with her. She wanted just the opposite—to put a part of herself into a permanent place.

Comprehension Questions—Drawing Conclusions (pp. 36-37)

1. Answers will vary.
2. Knowing that she had belonged to a group once before would give her confidence that she could fit into a new group. Perhaps she would establish friendships more quickly and even be able to help others in the same position as she. Despite the knowledge that she would have to leave once again, she might try harder this time to make the best of the situation.
3. Answers will vary.

Comprehension Questions—One Step Further (p. 37)

Answers will vary.

Graphic Organizer (pp. 38-39)

Four reasons Amelia felt she did not belong: no house; no school; the teachers didn't know her name; she was always moving. Some other reasons: no neighbors; no friends; no store she regularly shops in; no meeting place (like a pizza shop, etc.); no extracurricular activity or group she can belong to, etc.

Four wonderful things that helped Amelia feel she belonged: Mrs. Ramos welcomed the new children; Mrs. Ramos asked everyone what their name was; Mrs. Ramos showed Amelia's picture to the class; Mrs. Ramos put a star on Amelia's paper; all the children learned Amelia's name. (Note: An extra event is listed.)

The items Amelia put into her box and why: a hair ribbon her mother gave her: it makes her know she belongs to her mother and to her family; the name tag Mrs. Ramos gave her: it makes her feel like a real person with her own name, not just a nameless child nobody knows; a picture of her family: again, she belongs to this family, the family is the one constant in her life; the picture with the star: this makes her feel like an individual who has her own unique talents and abilities, a valuable person who people will want to know; the map of the accidental road: this is a place she belongs, she has made it her own.

The Hatmaker's Sign (Textbook p. 130)

Vocabulary—Activity I (p. 40)

1. apprentice
2. cobblestones
3. parchment
4. haughty
5. quibbling
6. sympathetic
7. magistrates
8. absurd
9. parable
10. delegate

Vocabulary—Activity II (p. 41)

1. arrogant
2. apprentice
3. quibbles
4. delegate
5. parable
6. magistrate
7. parchment
8. sympathetic
9. absurd
10. cobblestones

Comprehension Questions—In-Depth Thinking (p. 42)

1. ***Similarities***
   - Both put forth a lot of effort.
   - Both were asked to make changes.
   - Both were frustrated with the advice.
   - Benjamin Franklin helped Thomas and the sign maker helped John recognize the right thing to do.

   Differences
   - John was working for his own business, while Thomas was working on behalf of the entire country.
   - John took away everything he had done upon the suggestion of others, while Thomas accepted some changes.
   - John accepted the suggestions right away even though he was reluctant, while Tom did not want to accept any changes to his perfect document at all.
2. Reverend Brimstone's comment was polite. He said, "May I make a suggestion?" Lady Manderly's was rude. She snorted while she said, "Absurd!" The magistrate threatened and bullied John; his comment was offensive.
3. Ben Franklin's story helped Thomas Jefferson to wait out the storm of criticism without getting too insulted or angry. Franklin's good-humored way of looking at human nature helped Jefferson to adopt a more patient and positive attitude to the process of having his masterpiece analyzed and critiqued.

Comprehension Questions—Drawing Conclusions (pp. 42-43)

4. Answers will vary.
5. In short, yes. Ben Franklin appears to agree with Jefferson that Jefferson's work is as near perfect as possible. This is why Franklin, in his story, has the sign maker put John's original words and picture back on the sign at the end of the story. The words John has written for the sign symbolize the words Tom has written for the Declaration of Independence.
6. Answers will vary.

Comprehension Questions—One Step Further (p. 43)

Answers will vary.

Graphic Organizer (pp. 44-45)

There is no specific answer guide for this exercise.

Dad, Jackie, and Me (Textbook p. 146)

Comprehension Questions—In-Depth Thinking (p. 46)

1. At first, the narrator is embarrassed of his father in public. On the bus, he thinks about Dad's limitations and how he would not be able to communicate with Jackie. The boy also looks at his shoes when Dad draws the attention of other fans.

   Later on, the son has grown accustomed to attending games with his father and feels more comfortable. Since Jackie is so successful and there is so much cheering, no one seems to notice Dad's screaming and unclear language.

   One could also infer that, since Dad has gotten so involved in baseball, they now share this interest and it creates a bond between father and son.
2. Dad's speech was unclear due to his hearing impairment. Some attendees may have gotten used to having Dad at the games or they were simply absorbed in their own shouting and cheering. (You can take this opportunity to elaborate further. When one does not hear one's own voice, it is difficult to produce clear speech. Point out that there have been many advances in medicine and technology since this story took place. For example, cochlear implants and better hearing aids have drastically changed the lives of the deaf.)

3. Both Jackie and Dad persevere even though they face great obstacles. They ignore a lot of the stares or jeers of others. They are both pursuing something that they love. For Jackie it is baseball, but for Dad it is his son's happiness—which leads him to baseball.

Comprehension Questions—Drawing Conclusions (pp. 46-47)

4. Dad was a devoted father who truly wanted to be part of his son's life and make him happy. Try as he might, he could not improve his baseball skills. He continued because it was so important to the boy and, also, because he was not the type to run from a challenge. Also, it may be that once Dad got involved, he felt connected to Jackie. He was able to relate to him in ways that others could not.
5. Answers will vary. Perhaps he was in shock that his team actually won the final game. Maybe he felt upset that he was not recognized for what he did for the team. Another possibility would be that he was bracing himself for negative comments; not all of his teammates were happy to be playing with Jackie because he was black—and Jackie felt it.
6. Answers will vary.

Comprehension Questions—One Step Further (p. 47)

Answers will vary. The new player may voice anger, optimism, or indifference. The advice may be to fight back, have patience, keep your thoughts to yourself, have faith in the better people, and so on.

Graphic Organizer (pp. 48-49)

The Brooklyn Dodgers' Diamond:

First Base: Thanks to Jackie's tie-breaking hit, they win the first game Dad and the narrator attend.

Second Base: The Dodgers keep winning.

Third Base: The Dodgers win the last game of the season even though it doesn't count.

Home Plate: The Dodgers win the pennant.

Jackie Robinson's Diamond:

First Base: Jackie steals home in one of the games described and the crowd goes wild.

Second Base: Jackie ignores being spiked and the Brooklyn fans yell in his defense.

Third Base: Jackie caught the last ball of the last game of the season. The fans love him.

Home Plate: There is a big parade to honor Jackie.

Dad's Diamond:

First Base: Dad cheers Jackie right along with the crowd.

Second Base: Dad learns everything he can about baseball.

Third Base: Jackie throws a ball right to Dad.

Home Plate: Dad catches Jackie's ball barehanded.

And Now the Good News (Textbook p. 162)

Vocabulary—Activity I (p. 50)

1. basking
2. habitat
3. sanctuary
4. thrives
5. expedition
6. transport
7. commercial
8. ornery
9. predator
10. rehabilitation

Vocabulary—Activity II (p. 51)

1. The Magnificent Sanctuary
2. A Place to Thrive
3. The Ornery Terrier
4. Professor Peel's Rehabilitation
5. Basking on the Beach
6. Where Are the Predators?
7. Living in an Animal Habitat

9. Transporting My Possessions
10. Sailing on a Commercial Ship

Comprehension Questions—In-Depth Thinking (p. 52)

1. Zoos are more animal-friendly. They try to replicate the natural habitat of each animal rather than keep it imprisoned in a cage.
2. They were in danger of extinction, but now the number of alligators has increased to the point that they are causing problems in some areas. Also, it is illegal to hunt alligators for their skins.
3. Rhinoceroses are captured for their horns, tigers for their skins, and tropical birds to be used as fine pets.

Comprehension Questions—Drawing Conclusions (p. 53)

4. Animals raised in captivity do not know how to take care of themselves. They are used to being fed by humans. They are not used to threats like bad weather, lack of food and water, or predators.
5. Protecting animal habitats affects our water and food supply, our air quality, and our general quality of life.
6. People can stop polluting and stop destroying the habitats of other living things. We can be careful not to waste food or water, conserve fuel, and be respectful of all living things.

Comprehension Questions—One Step Further (p. 53)

Answers will vary.

Graphic Organizer (pp. 54-55)

Alligator: fish; turtles; snakes; frogs; snails

African Elephant: birds; mammals; insects; invertebrates

National Wildlife Refuge System: green sea turtles; monk seals; whooping cranes; trumpeter swans; bald eagles

Eddie, Incorporated (Textbook p. 188)

Vocabulary—Activity I (p. 56)

1. composed
2. executive
3. financial
4. income
5. efficiently
6. vertical
7. transactions
8. contracts
9. competently
10. chute

Vocabulary—Activity II (p. 57)

1. c.
2. e.
3. a.
4. h.
5. d.
6. f.
7. b.
8. i.
9. g.
10. j.

Comprehension Questions—In-Depth Thinking (p. 58)

1. At the beginning of the story, Eddie was entirely devoted to starting his business. He was busy with every aspect of it and thought of it as a long-term project. He was sure it would make a big profit. At the end of the story, while the first day had been somewhat successful, he was unsure about whether it would be worthwhile to continue running the company altogether.
2. A worker who earns a salary is paid a certain amount of money every week (or two weeks, or month, etc.) regardless of how much or little the business took in during that time period. (You may wish to explain that if the business loses too much money, the worker will likely be laid off. If the business is very profitable, the salary may go up. But on a normal basis, the salary is the same every pay period.) A worker who earns a share of the profits gets an agreed upon percentage of the profits each pay period.
3. ***Mom:*** gave him food and encouragement; lent him garbage bags; showed how impressed she was with the fact that he paid back his debt so quickly

   Dad: asked if Dink and Elizabeth would share the profits or would be on a salary; was encouraging by telling Eddie that he didn't 'go in the hole'

   Roger: asked what Eddie was going to do with the profits; showed interest in his success at the end

   Joseph: made calculations for Eddie projecting how much money he could take in, plus interest; showed interest in his success at the end

Comprehension Questions—Drawing Conclusions (pp. 58-59)

4. They had everything prepared in advance. Eddie got up very early and could not fall back asleep. Elizabeth and Dink both showed up ready for work a full half hour early.
5. Unfortunately, there are bullies who do cruel things. Sometimes they are under the influence of a bad group of friends. They were probably thoughtless kids who were jealous of Eddie's business idea.
6. Answers will vary. Be sure your students support their answers.

Comprehension Questions—One Step Further (p. 59)

Answers will vary. You may wish to refer back to some of the material in the *Into* section.

Graphic Organizer (pp. 60-61)

- **painted a big OPEN sign:** Dink
- **kept a notebook listing expenses:** Eddie
- **closed the basement window and removed the OPEN sign:** Eddie
- **got there at 8:30 in case there was a line:** Elizabeth
- **collected cans in his father's garbage carrier:** Dink
- **put advertisement posters on poles:** Elizabeth
- **washed and dried the cans:** Elizabeth
- **made a night deposit box:** Dink
- **weighed the cans:** Eddie

Heatwave! (Textbook p. 214)

Vocabulary—Activity I (p. 62)

1. horizon
2. miscalculated
3. affected
4. commotion
5. whiff
6. herded
7. churned
8. trough
9. plucking
10. singe

Vocabulary—Activity II (p. 63)

1. **horizon:** picture of sky and land meeting
2. **plucked:** a picture of a chicken being plucked, or a chicken with a feather floating nearby
3. **commotion:** a picture of a group of people shouting
4. **herded:** a group of cows
5. **churned:** a churn or a stick of butter
6. **whiff:** a nose
7. **singe:** a flame
9. **trough:** a trough

Comprehension Questions—In-Depth Thinking (p. 64)

1. Since the popcorn *looked* like a blizzard, the dog reacted accordingly.
2. There are a few possible answers. The most likely reason would be that it was such a major heat wave, the likes of which people had not seen before, that she capitalized the words to distinguish it from your "garden variety" heat wave. Another would be that it is central to the story.
3. At the beginning of the story, the author says that Hank 'changed his tune' when the Heat Wave came. We can assume that after her display of ingenuity, his opinion changed.

Comprehension Questions—Drawing Conclusions (pp. 64-65)

4. ***External:***

   Hank vs. sister (author)

   Heat Wave vs. family

   Internal: (though not mentioned explicitly)

   Ways to approach the Heat Wave: (a) Go to the cornfield or go to the barn? (b) Use the fan idea or use the lettuce idea?
5. She is observant and creative. She seems confident despite the jibes of her brother, and brave as well. While some of her ideas do not work (the oatmeal), and others don't even get off the ground (she could not use fans because they were needed by the cows), she is not discouraged, but thinks creatively. She has a sense of humor and she is able to delegate jobs to others.
6. Answers will vary.

Comprehension Questions—One Step Further (p. 65)

Answers will vary.

Graphic Organizer (pp. 66-67)

There is no specific answer guide for this exercise.

The Wright Brothers (Textbook p. 232)

Comprehension Questions—In-Depth Thinking (p. 68)

1. Mrs. Wright took a genuine interest in her children. She did not allow them to do just anything they pleased, contrary to what her neighbors thought. (See #4 in *Drawing Conclusions.*) She inspired them to think for themselves and be individuals. She taught them life skills and confidence. While she never ridiculed their ideas with laughter or sarcastic remarks, she also did not give them false hopes. Susan Wright spent time with her children and taught them by being a positive role model. This selection indicates that Mrs. Wright was different than other mothers at the time. This does not mean that parents at the time did not care deeply for children, but during that period, conduct was stricter and people believed that 'children should be seen and not heard.'
2. The Wrights' sled held three people instead of two, it was one foot longer, lower to the ground, and narrower.
3. Not only was the concept of wind resistance important in building an efficient sled, it was one that the Wright brothers would apply in the future to the design of their flying machines.

Comprehension Questions—Drawing Conclusions (pp. 68-69)

4. Susan Wright wanted to provide her children with the freedom to experiment and learn. She wanted them to learn to do things independently and to be unafraid of trying and asking. Above all, she wanted them to believe in themselves.
5. It sets the stage for what is to come. Fascination with the flight of birds inspired the boys to think of ways to enable people to fly. You can mention foreshadowing, though the brothers' airplane building days do not appear in this selection.
6. Susan Wright was a warm mother who enjoyed spending time with her children. It is clear that there was mutual respect. Although their father was often away, it seems that they had tremendous respect for him and his work. The family had picnics, went sledding, and engaged in many other activities. They helped each other out and worked together on projects. Will and Orv got along well and their partnership would last a lifetime. While Kate was sometimes a tag-along, the boys did not seem to mind and took care of their little sister.

Comprehension Questions—One Step Further (p. 69)

"Riches" refers to a person's positive qualities and intangible assets. There are times that people do not recognize their own potential. When someone reminds them how truly rich they are, it encourages them to strive for greater things and to accomplish more.

Graphic Organizer (pp. 70-71)

Low to the ground

1. "… the closer to the ground our sled is the less wind resistance there will be, and the faster it will go."

Thin runners

7. Less resistance from the snow on the ground.

Boys will ride it lying down on their stomachs

6. "… lie down on the sled … Less wind resistance this way…"

Sled is narrow

3. "The narrower it is, the less wind resistance."

Runners are smooth

5. "We rubbed the runners with candles."

Built according to the pattern we drew first

4. "If you get it right on paper, it'll be right when you build it."

Mother showed us how

2. "You'd be surprised how much mothers know…"

The Imperfect/Perfect Book Report (Textbook p. 250)

Comprehension Questions—In-Depth Thinking (p. 72)

1. At the beginning, Cricket viewed Zoe as a threat to her position as the smartest girl in the class. Cricket was busy checking what grades Zoe received. By the end of the story, Cricket had not only come to terms with the fact that Zoe was just as smart as she was, but she appreciated it. Zoe became a potential friend with similar interests.
2. The internal dialogue that the author includes provides us with a very good idea of what Cricket is thinking throughout the story. We do not learn as much about Zoe. However, based on her general behavior, her public pronouncement about Cricket giving her the book, and the way Zoe behaved at the end of the story, it does not appear that she had any inkling about Cricket's negative feelings.
3. Zoe will probably make the same effort and do well. Cricket will be more accurate, and not spend more time on extra credit and less time on the assignment. Julio will choose a book that he has not read before. He will also be more confident as he works, thanks to his A. Hopefully, most of the students will listen to the

teacher's advice to plan and not leave the assignment for the last minute. Some students might select a book that they think they'll enjoy after the discussion on choosing books and the sheer number of books in the library.

Comprehension Questions—Drawing Conclusions (pp. 72-73)

4. Opinions on Mrs. Schraalenburgh will vary. The author clearly thinks she is portraying a good teacher by giving her the following virtues:
   - She always expressed how proud she was of her students.
   - She treated them with respect and as individuals.
   - She did not have teacher's pets.
   - She seemed very kind, but also knew how to discipline the students. (She scolded the students about not speaking until called upon.)
   - She was a good teacher and explained things well.
   - She took advantage of 'teachable moments' as seen from the discussion on the number of library books.
   - She graded the reports right away over the weekend.
   - She combined a positive comment with criticism, as in the case of Cricket's book report.
5. She was careful about certain things, like neatness and the appearance of the cover. She wished to impress the teacher and outshine Zoe in her own personal scholastic competition. She was careless about spelling and the actual content of the report. Because she was so bright, she assumed that it would be just fine.
6. Julio's case is not a one-sided affair. On the one hand, we see that he does try, in that he has improved his arithmetic score and prepared an entertaining book report. On the other hand, he did not follow the rules: he reviewed a book that was read to the class by the teacher. He is never reprimanded nor does his grade suffer in any way. Some students might feel that while Julio should have been encouraged and rewarded for his effort, there should have been some distinction made between a student who actually did the assignment correctly and one who did not. If Julio normally failed, it would seem that a grade of B or even A- would still be very encouraging and rewarding while taking note of the fact that he did not do perfect work. Some students may point out that Julio got a huge boost from getting an A and that it should not bother anyone else whether he had read the book or not.

Comprehension Questions—One Step Further (p. 73)

Answers will vary.

Graphic Organizer (pp. 74-77)

The student's page will look like this:

The Imperfect/Perfect Book Report

By Johanna Hurwitz

The main character of the story is Cricket Kaufman, a fourth grader who is an outstanding student. Zoe Mitchell is in the fourth grade, too, and is just as smart as Cricket. Mrs. Schraalenburgh is the teacher. She is unusual because she never plays favorites. She treats all the students equally and never singles out anyone for being better or worse than the others. [Here the student should say whether this is a good thing or a bad thing.] Mrs. Schraalenburgh assigns a book report. Cricket works very hard at writing the report, even making a cover with an illustration for it. [Here the student offers an explanation for Cricket's willingness to do extra work:] *I think Cricket feels she has to show she is better than everyone else.* She is willing to work for the best grade in the class, and she is sure she will get it. Surprisingly, a boy who did not even do the assignment correctly gets a very good grade. [The student expresses an opinion about awarding a good grade to this boy:] *I'm glad that boy got a chance to get an A. Maybe it will encourage him to work harder in the future.* But Cricket, who always gets A's, got a B-. The teacher told her that she had misspelled the author's name and repeated herself. This makes Cricket feel very bad.

By the end of the story, Cricket tries to change her personality. She tries to enjoy working with a friend instead of always trying to be the best. [Student's opinion of the story:] *I enjoyed reading about this type of girl, because some of the kids in my class are like her. I think we can all learn a lesson from her about working with a friend instead of competing against a friend.*

Teacher: Notice that the report is a mixture of summary and opinion. The combination makes the review both informative and interesting. It also requires that the student think critically.

Justin Lebo (Textbook p. 268)

Vocabulary—Activity I (p. 78)

1. battered
2. gingerly
3. passion
4. semicircular
5. pirouettes
6. tooling
7. realigned
8. proposal
9. interchangeable
10. inspired

Vocabulary—Activity II (p. 79)

1. a.
2. b.
3. b.
4. a.
5. a.
6. b.
7. a.
8. b.
9. b.
10. a.

Comprehension Questions—In-Depth Thinking (p. 80)

1. Dad helped Justin repair the bikes. His parents agreed to match every dollar that Justin put into buying old bikes. His mother drove him to garage sales and thrift shops. His parents allowed him to fill the garage and backyard with bikes and parts.
2. He was responsible about the money, he made wise decisions such as ordering in bulk, and he negotiated prices with Mel. He also seemed to have a good work ethic.
3. Mel was always helpful when a repair was too complicated for Justin. However, it seemed that Justin did not go there all that often and when he did, Mel simply grunted to him. Over time, the two became friends. Perhaps Justin's sincerity and generosity made an impression on Mel. He saw that Justin was not just interested in bike racing, but in helping others. The fact that they

had a joint goal in helping the children created a stronger bond. Justin's selflessness inspired Mel to give more than he might have.

Comprehension Questions—Drawing Conclusions (pp. 80-81)

4. Justin's hobby was fixing old bikes he'd bought at garage sales. There was, however, a limit to how many bikes he could use. At one point, he realized that what he truly enjoyed was making something new and useful out of something old and broken. It was then that he decided to give the refurbished bikes away to those in need.
5. Justin acted very mature and selfless. He handled the reporters well and was confident enough to contact people like Mel and the director of the Home. His perseverance and devotion were admirable. His actions and behavior were not necessarily typical of a ten year old, but this true story does prove that boys his age have the potential to do a great deal.
6. It made people think and inspired them to help others.

Comprehension Questions—One Step Further (p. 81)

Answers will vary. The answer should touch on the fact that giving to others brings happiness, satisfaction, and fulfillment. Of course, giving to others should be done in a way that is selfless, not selfish.

Graphic Organizer (pp. 82-83)

Mr. Lebo helped Justin repair old bikes and taught Justin how to repair them himself. He agreed to match dollar for dollar the money Justin raised.

Mrs. Lebo drove Justin and the first two bikes to Kilbarchan. She supported his idea of remaking bikes for all the children of Kilbarchan. She agreed to match dollar for dollar the money Justin raised.

A neighbor wrote a letter to the local newspaper describing Justin's project.

A reporter wrote an admiring article about Justin's project.

Readers of the article donated many used bikes.

Mel helped Justin fix some of the bikes and gave him a good price on spare parts.

"The kid" who expressed his gratitude made it all worthwhile for Justin.

Earthquake Terror (Textbook p. 326)

Vocabulary—Activity I, Lesson 1 (p. 84)

1. engrossed
2. cataloging
3. stifling
4. jarring
5. relinquish
6. impact
7. bolted
8. evaporated
9. susceptible
10. meandered

Vocabulary—Activity I, Lesson 2 (p. 85)

1. devastation
2. retreated
3. debris
4. suspended
5. ominous
6. dwarfed
7. pungent
8. wedged
9. upheaval
10. undulating

Vocabulary—Activity II, Lesson 1 (p. 86)

1. b.
2. a.
3. b.
4. b.
5. a.
6. b.
7. a.
8. a.
9. a.
10. b.

Vocabulary—Activity II, Lesson 2 (p. 87)

1. ominous
2. suspended
3. wedged
4. undulating
5. pungent
6. dwarfed
7. devastation
8. upheaval
9. debris

Comprehension Questions—In-Depth Thinking (p. 88)

1. Moose's behavior worried Jonathan, though he couldn't tell what the problem was. The eerie silence and stifling air followed by thunder on a clear day all signaled trouble.
2. Jonathan had chosen Moose even thought his parents wanted a different dog. After Abby's accident, Moose provided Jonathan with comfort and companionship. Moose also was smart and sensed the earthquake before Jonathan did and comforted him throughout.
3. ***Different:*** Jonathan takes responsibility for himself, and he also feels responsible for his sister. He is older, so he is much better informed about earthquakes. He seems closer to Moose than his sister. He controls his fear. He is forgiving of Abby's crankiness. Abby is young and looks to her brother for help. She does not try to control her fear. She accuses her brother, who is very tolerant of her, of being rough and hurting her.

   Same: Both children love their parents. Both get along well with Moose.

Comprehension Questions—Drawing Conclusions (pp. 88-89)

4. Jonathan used the information he had learned from his teacher at the earthquake drills. The story about Grandma (earthquakes can be limited to a small area) and Mom's example (of how to deal with Abby's bruises) both provided him with information as well.
5. He compares standing on the earth to riding a surfboard; he compares the way his stomach lurched to the way he felt in an elevator; he compares standing on the ground to riding a roller coaster; he compares being surrounded by the noise of the earthquake to being at the center of an orchestra.

6. Jonathan was a good brother. Even before the earthquake, it was clear that he cared for his sister. He insisted that she walk in front of him so that he could keep an eye on her. During the earthquake, he protected Abby even though he fell and hurt himself repeatedly. He also showed concern and compassion when he explained that it was an earthquake and when he dealt with her bruised knee.

Comprehension Questions—One Step Further (p. 89)

Answers will vary.

One additional quote you may want to mention:

"Courage is not the absence of fear, but rather the judgment that something else is more important than fear."

Graphic Organizer (pp. 90-91)

The sentences should be in this order:

1. "Moose suddenly stood still, his legs stiff and his tail up."
2. "No magpies cawed, no leaves rustled overhead."
3. "Moose barked ... his warning bark, the one he used when a stranger knocked on the door."
4. "He heard a deep rumbling sound in the distance."
5. "Another loud noise exploded as Jonathan lurched sideways."

The Gift (Textbook p. 350)

Vocabulary—Activity I (p. 92)

1. balmy
2. haltingly
3. propelled
4. wan
5. console
6. monologue
7. scavenging
8. glistened
9. luminous
10. linger

Vocabulary—Activity II (p. 93)

balmy = mild weather *that is warm and refreshing*

glistened = shone *and sparkled in the light*

haltingly = slowly *with small stops along the way*

linger = to remain in one place *longer than is necessary*

luminous = reflecting light *in a soft, moonlike glow*

monologue = a speech by one person *when the listener or listeners do not interrupt*

propelled = was moved *by some other force*

scavenging = looking for something of worth *among mostly useless items*

wan = pale *and sickly looking*

Comprehension Questions—In-Depth Thinking (p. 94)

1. Both Anna and Nana Marie needed companionship and developed a close bond very early on. Although they were different in age, they were very similar in nature. Both were sensitive, thoughtful people. Both saw beauty in nature and in memories. Each one appreciated the other.
2. Rita treated Anna like a child and did not really pay attention to her thoughts and opinions. Nana Marie spoke to Anna as an equal. She really listened to Anna and appreciated her company.
3. Answers will vary. For example: *the clump of moss.* "As I sat on the damp ground, I put my hand down and felt something velvety. I looked down and saw emerald color moss growing in the shade of the rock. It was cool and warm at once, just like the evening breeze."

Comprehension Questions—Drawing Conclusions (pp. 94-95)

4. The other gifts were nice and the givers were well-intentioned. However, Anna put much thought into hers and came up with an idea that was unique to Nana Marie's needs—one she knew would be appreciated.
5. Answers may vary. Those who have a close relationship with a grandparent or elderly neighbor may be able to relate better to such a relationship. Other students may find it rather unusual. Some may mention the distinction between a connection with an older person and a real friendship.
6. Answers may vary. What Anna did for Nana Marie was very meaningful. The gift meant a lot to her not only on that day, but would cheer her and warm her heart for a long time to come. It was significant because it opened the door to dealing with her loss of sight and gave her some hope of still experiencing the world.

Comprehension Questions—One Step Further (p. 95)

Answers will vary. A relationship is not always fifty-fifty and each person contributes something different. However, it does not last if it is completely one-sided. A deeper friendship develops when there is give and take on both ends.

Graphic Organizer (pp. 96-97)

1. small; deep; in the woods
2. bottomless; nothing but darkness
3. reflecting the bark of silver beeches; shining like armor
4. wet; soft; thawing
5. wan; February; swallowed by a thick mist; thick
6. damp; had an edge of warmth

Answers will vary for the "gift boxes."

Toto (Textbook p. 368)

Vocabulary—Activity I (p. 98)

1. timid
2. thatched
3. jauntily
4. crude
5. poachers
6. snare
7. menacing
8. mock
9. doused
10. plains

Vocabulary—Activity II (p. 99)

1. b.
2. b.
3. a.
4. a.
5. b.
6. b.
7. b.
8. a.
9. b.
10. a.

Comprehension Questions—In-Depth Thinking (p. 100)

1. Suku had never joined the others in the bush as lion hunters. He was shy and afraid. Toto had never gone beyond the immediate company of his herd.
2. He disliked it, but his fears bothered him more than the taunts.
3. **Suku:** "He approached the trapped elephant carefully. His father had taught him to be aware of wounded animals who could be far more dangerous in fear and pain."

   Toto: "Elephants have no enemies—Mother said so," he told himself bravely.

   A lion is the only animal who might stalk an unprotected elephant child.

   "Young as he was, Toto recognized the smells and sounds of danger."

   "Toto had raised his trunk and spread his ears the way big elephants did when they were ready to attack."

Comprehension Questions—Drawing Conclusions (pp. 100-101)

4. Suku empathized with the injured elephant.

   "But the little elephant seemed to **sense** that Suku **wanted to help** him ..."

   "But Toto, who had spent the night by himself, would not leave that strange two-legged creature with the oddly dangerous smell but the **warm, comforting** sounds."

   "Please, **little one, please** hurry home," Suku pleaded.
5. Opinions will vary. Suku was brave because he did what he believed was right despite his fears. Suku did not really think about being brave until the warden said he was. He knew what he was doing but still felt scared inside.
6. Both Suku and Toto took risks and went out on their own. Suku learned not to be afraid of the valley and began to gain confidence about his own ability to deal with animals. Toto learned to avoid leaving the sanctuary, because the dangers outside were not ones he could deal with.

Comprehension Questions—One Step Further (p. 101)

The quotes might be a little challenging for students to interpret on their own. Discuss the meaning of them briefly and then allow your students to form their own opinions and answer the questions.

Graphic Organizer (pp. 102-103)

Suku

2. Suku lived in the hills.
5. Suku learned to carry water, help make a fire, and pen the cattle.
6. Suku's mother wanted him to go out of the village.
7. Suku was afraid to go too far away.
8. Suku was fearful.

Both

1. Toto and Suku lived in Africa.
3. Both could see the blue and purple mountains from their homes.
4. Both were young.
9. Both Toto and Suku were angry at the poachers.
10. Both Toto and Suku stood where they were when they saw the lion.
11. Both Toto and Suku changed from the beginning of the story.
12. Both Toto and Suku had someone older who came to their rescue.

Toto

2. Toto lived in the valley.
5. Toto learned what food was safe to eat and how to recognize danger.
6. Toto's mother did not want him to stray.
7. Toto was curious and wanted to go far away.
8. Toto was not fearful.

Owl Moon (Textbook p. 386)

Comprehension Questions—In-depth Thinking (p. 104)

1. She is afraid of the extreme cold and the dark shadows. The woods at night scare her. In addition, one might say she is afraid of disappointing her father by talking or doing the wrong thing.
2. The dark, the cold, the woods, the expectation of seeing a huge owl fly in front of the moon, the time alone with Pa, and the anticipation of telling about her bravery to her brothers all contribute to her excitement.
3. "the trees stood still

   as giant statues.

   "... and the snow below it was whiter than the milk in a cereal bowl."

Comprehension Questions—Drawing Conclusions (pp. 104-105)

4. People can communicate with each other through facial expressions and body language. They can also use sign language—either American Sign Language or other accepted gestures or motions.
5. Answers will vary. Here are some: You don't need words because you understand each other perfectly. You don't need warm because you have decided to ignore the cold, as part of the

adventure. You need hope as you wait expectantly for the huge black shadow to cross over the moon.

6. Answers will vary.

Comprehension Questions—One Step Further (p. 105)

Nature is a home, because it is the backdrop of our lives. Aside from actually being the 'home' we live in, we draw upon its resources for everything in our lives. Nature is a teacher in countless ways; we leave it to you to list some of them. For many people, nature is the companion of choice: silent, soothing, reliable, accepting.

Graphic Organizer (pp. 106-107)

There is no specific answer guide for this exercise.

Homeward the Arrow's Flight (Textbook p. 400)

Vocabulary—Activity I, Lesson 1 (p. 108)

1. confined
2. agonized
3. consternation
4. ventured
5. hoist
6. manipulate
7. don
8. wallow
9. maneuvered
10. desolately

Vocabulary—Activity I, Lesson 2 (p. 109)

1. allotment
2. grippe
3. inundated
4. siege
5. appointment
6. resentment
7. vicious
8. ominous
9. lull
10. consult

Vocabulary—Activity II, Lesson 1 (p. 110)

There are obviously no right or wrong answers. Here are a few sample answers:

1. President Lincoln agonized over the idea of going to war.
2. I was confined to my bed for three weeks.
3. He actually put on a suit and donned a hat; after all, it was his own wedding!

Vocabulary—Activity II, Lesson 2 (p. 111)

1. a **point** ment
2. inun **date** d
3. lull (aby)
4. vicious
5. **a llot** ment (a lot)
6. **g** r **ip** pe (pig)
7. **om** in**o** us (moo)
8. **co** ns **u** l **t** i **n** g (count)
9. res **ent** men **t** (tent)
10. siege-I+e=geese

Comprehension Questions—In-Depth Thinking (p. 112)

1. Tom's windows were not sealed properly, allowing cold drafts to come into the house. This likely caused more illness to the members of his family. The Whitefeathers' house was clean and neat and Susan saw that they had good hygiene habits.
2. Susan's own health was often neglected as a result of her work. She managed on very little sleep or on some nights, none at all. She felt that her work came first and if she did not treat her patients, no one else would.
3. Iron Eye was a nickname for her father who, though deceased, was well remembered by the residents of the reservation. He was known for his influence on the people and his iron will. This, and other things she remembered, gave Susan the encouragement she needed to push onward.

Comprehension Questions—Drawing Conclusions (pp. 112-113)

4. Many family members are mentioned, including Susan's father, Iron Eye, and her mother (known as One Woman). Her sisters Rosalie and Marguerite are mentioned, though there were others. They are a close-knit family and have fond memories of the early years. Susan's siblings are somewhat involved with her work as a doctor and they support each other in a number of ways. Warmth comes across, as well as respect for their parents and one another.
5. Susan was not afraid of change in terms of having goals that no one before her had reached, such as being the first Native American woman to become a doctor. She taught others to change the way they took care of their health and hygiene. When circumstances changed such as weather conditions, she did not let that deter her. Finally, when they sat around the kitchen table at the end of the story, they embraced the changes that had taken place even though the memories of their youth still lingered.
6. Susan was involved in making the decision to let the children go home, but the incident with Jimmy was not entirely her fault. It had been a tough decision to make. If they'd waited, they would have lost the window of opportunity to get the children home safely to their parents. Susan felt a great responsibility as the reservation doctor, especially since the people all relied on her judgment.

Comprehension Questions—One Step Further (p. 113)

Be sure to define the word *submission* and make sure your students understand *devotion* and *dedication*, which were also mentioned in the *Into* section.

Answers will vary somewhat, but there should be an understanding that giving of yourself to an important cause is meaningful and displays true strength of character.

Graphic Organizer (pp. 114-115)

The answers are in italics.

- (sample) Susan La Flesche / *the first female native-American doctor in the U.S.*
- *Rosalie* / Susan's sister who lives on the reservation
- Iron Eye / *Susan's father who never gave up trying to help the Omaha people*

- *The Omahas* / the Native Americans who lived on the reservation
- Pie / *Susan's loyal horse whose actions saved the lives of Susan and Jimmy*
- Marguerite / *Susan's sister; a teacher who is married to the very ill Charlie*
- *Charlie* / He is married to Susan's sister Marguerite. He is very sick and doesn't make it through the winter.
- Joe / *A Native American whose wife is about to have a baby. He begs Susan to come through the storm to help his wife.*
- *Minnie Whitefeather* / Joe's wife. Susan comes through the storm to help her give birth.
- Jimmy / *He is a little boy who is found nearly dead in the snow.*
- *Henry* / Charlie's brother who comes for the funeral.

Underwater Rescue (Textbook p. 428)

Vocabulary—Activity I (p. 116)

1. domain	6. hovered
2. reef	7. instinctively
3. embedded	8. needlessly
4. enraged	9. abundantly
5. shaft	10. peer

Vocabulary—Activity II (p. 117)

1. a.	6. b.
2. b.	7. b.
3. a.	8. b.
4. a.	9. b.
5. a.	10. a.

Comprehension Questions—In-Depth Thinking (p. 118)

1. He wanted to help because he saw that the baby was injured badly and without his assistance would die from its wounds or be eaten by sharks. He hesitated because he was unarmed and it was unusual for wild dolphins to approach people.
2. Amazingly, they were able to communicate through motions, sounds, and expressions that led them to trust one another.
3. Answers may vary. Although he thought highly of dolphins and was kind to animals from the very beginning of the story, Wayne's understanding of dolphins and his affection for them increased by the end of the selection. He felt he could connect with them in a way he had not known he could.

Comprehension Questions—Drawing Conclusions (pp. 118-119)

4. One might think that Wayne would be afraid, but he wasn't. He had experience dealing with sea animals and knew that dolphins seldom approached humans.
5. He tells us about the feeling he had that something unusual was about to happen.
6. It is unlikely that such a scenario would occur again. All of the circumstances were extraordinary. The fact that Wayne was alone and unarmed, that the dolphins approached him at all, and that Wayne even knew what to do, were unusual.

Comprehension Questions—One Step Further (p. 119)

People use words to convey thoughts and feelings. But words are often insufficient to express what we feel. Sometimes, we ourselves are not aware of what we really feel or think. At other times, we simply don't have the verbal skills to say what is on our mind. In spite of the limitations of the spoken word, those who understand us are able to "read" us. They interpret our expressions, our tone of voice, the way we are standing or sitting, and a host of other nonverbal signals. Sometimes it takes a friend or parent to tell *us* how we are feeling! When we read about people who communicate with animals and vice versa, we become aware of how rich nonverbal communication can be.

Graphic Organizer (pp. 120-123)

You may want to share the following suggested dialogue with your students before they begin this exercise.

"Now we were face-to-face. This dolphin family had an injured baby. Could they have come to me for help?"

- Diver: I see you need help. Please let me see if I can help you.
- *Dolphin: Our baby is injured. Can you help? Can we trust you?*

"The father dolphin, hovering just inches from me, placed his nose under my arm and pushed up ... The impatient father dolphin wanted me to 'get to work.' "

- Diver: should I begin? Do you trust me? Don't hurt me.
- *Dolphin: Yes, please begin. Our baby is bleeding. We'll protect you.*

"I gently touched the hook shaft, and the baby made a high-pitched cry."

- Diver: Poor baby! I know this hurts but soon it will be better. Hold on, your Mommy is right here.
- *Dolphin: Oww! It hurts so much! Mommy!*

"Suddenly all three dolphins swam away, climbing toward the surface above. I had forgotten they had to breathe every few minutes."

- *Dolphins: Excuse us for a moment. We have to go out for some air. Don't go away.*

"The baby cried out in pain, and the big dolphin clicked several times. It seemed as though the parent dolphins were working with me, encouraging their baby to cooperate."

- Diver: Mom! Dad! Hold onto your baby and comfort him so I can do my work.
- *Dolphins: OK, baby. We're right here. Soon it will be over, then we'll get you a seaweed popsicle.*

"The father dolphin swam right up to me and looked into my eyes behind the diving mask. He nodded his head up and down in a rapid motion and then gently pushed me with his nose."

- Diver: We're all done. I think your baby will be fine. Thank you for letting me help you.
- *Dolphins: How can we ever thank you enough? We see that we can trust some humans!*

"Then I saw a small dolphin. It was in the midst of six other dolphins with a scar clearly visible on its back ... It swam close to the boat ... jumping high out of the water."

- *Dolphin: Hi, Doc! Come on in for a swim!*
- Diver: You look great! Keep in touch!

"I look forward to swimming with the dolphins again. It could happen anytime now."

- Diver: It's been so long since I last saw you!
- *Dolphins: Yes it has, we have always been on the lookout for you.*

The Seven Children (Textbook p. 448)

Comprehension Questions—In-Depth Thinking (p. 124)

1. The youngest might not have been able to read and would require help from the others.
2. They were genuinely concerned about their children's welfare. They probably talked and worried about the possible outcomes of their little experiment. It seemed that when the children arrived the farmer and his wife had been waiting for them.
3. Answers will vary. The parents certainly seemed to have the best interest of their children in mind. They provided for their children and were kind and understanding. They believed in their children and had creative solutions to their children's problems.

Comprehension Questions—Drawing Conclusions (pp. 124-125)

4. It shows that they trusted their father.
5. Answers will vary, but it would probably have taken longer than it did. It is likely that by nightfall they would have felt that they needed each other for basic food and shelter, and moral support.
6. You and your students can have a little fun with this one. Here are a few possible debacles: that night there was a thunderstorm, blizzard, earthquake, tidal wave, etc. That night, they were all struck with poison ivy, stomach flu, hay fever, etc. That night, several escaped convicts were known to have fled to the woods. The possibilities are limitless!

Comprehension Questions—One Step Further (p. 125)

It is doubtful anyone will argue with this statement. You may wish to take out a nickel, dime, or quarter and show the class the inscription *E Pluribus Unum*—In Unity There is Strength—on it. You may ask them why a country like the U.S.A. would choose to put these words on its coins. The very name of the country, The *United* States, indicates how very important unity is, and how very beneficial it is to those who have it.

Graphic Organizer (pp. 126-127)

Under each of the children:

1. I will decide because I am the oldest.
2. But I am the smartest. I should decide what we should do.
3. I'm hungry.
4. I'm thirsty.
5. I'm scared.
6. My legs hurt.
7. I want to go home.

Into the bundles:

1. two flint stones
2. kindling
3. a net of tiny strings
4. a large quilted blanket
5. a canteen of water
6. a loaf of banana bread
7. a piece of cloth

Into the box: They were to make a fire with flint stones and kindling, then set up a tent out of the netting. They were to drink from the canteen of water and eat the banana bread. The cloth was a map showing them how to get home.

The Garden of Happiness (Textbook p. 462)

Comprehension Questions—In-Depth Thinking (p. 128)

1. Plants in general bring joy to people. Aside from that, the sense of everyone working in harmony, at something that gave satisfaction to all, made the garden a very happy place to be.
2. Although the students may want to bemoan the fate of the poor immigrants, they themselves seem to be optimistic about their future. They work at improving their present surroundings while feeling comfortably nostalgic about their various birthplaces. They are cheerful and friendly. One imagines that their children will be highly successful "second-generation" Americans.
3. Answers will vary. Students may say that she would have been sad for a while. Some might add that, after a while, she would find a different hobby or perhaps plant something in her house, waiting for spring to come.

Comprehension Questions—Drawing Conclusions (pp. 128-129)

4. The names of the characters and the vegetables they plant tell us about their nationalities and tastes. This, in turn, tells us about the diverse population and the harmonious way the people worked together on the garden.
5. Marisol was friendly and determined. Students may offer other suggestions as well.
6. Change is a part of life. We have to learn to adapt to change and stride towards the future. A somewhat different lesson is that those who have lived long enough know that many things in life are cyclical. If you wait long enough, you will see what has been 'lost,' return.

Comprehension Questions—One Step Further (p. 129)

Answers will vary.

Graphic Organizer (pp. 130-131)

Character Sunflower

1. Marisol
2. Mr. Ortiz (Puerto Rico)
3. Mrs. Washington (U.S.A.)
4. Mr. Singh (Bangladesh)
5. Mr. Castro (Cuba?)
6. Mrs. Rodriguez
7. Mrs. Garcia (Mexico)
9. Mrs. Anderson (U.S.A.)
10. Mrs. Majewska (Poland)

Foreign Word Sunflower

1. *qué pasa* (what's happening)
2. *valore* (a type of bean)
3. *niña* (girl)
4. *mira* (look)
5. *habichuelas* (kidney beans)
6. *muy grande* (very big)
7. *sloneczniki* (sunflowers)
8. *los girasols* (the sunflowers)
9. *mi cariño* (my darling)
10. *apúrate* (hurry up)
11. *bodega* (store)

Plants Sunflower

1. tomatoes
2. black-eyed peas
3. greens
4. sweet potatoes
5. *valore* (beans)

One Grain of Rice (Textbook p. 482)

Comprehension Questions—In-Depth Thinking (p. 132)

1. The raja was an absolute monarch. That means he had all the power in the land and everyone was afraid to criticize him. A person like this can do what he wants and think he is good because everyone is afraid to tell him about his shortcomings. The one thing that can be said in his favor is that he at least *wanted* to be fair and wise.
2. At the opening of the story, the raja is an absolute monarch who takes most of what the people produce. Although he has a logical reason for what he does, by our standards he is cruel and greedy. Why should the hardworking people be deprived of the rice they have grown? If something had to be stored for the future, it could have been a much smaller percentage of their crops. He does not care about the deprivation his people suffer, nor does he have any sense that the rice belongs to them. By the end of the story, the raja has stopped behaving like a tyrant. Although he is the raja, he keeps his promise to Rani, and allows her to keep all the rice she has amassed. He then makes a second promise to take only as much rice as he needs. He allows her to criticize and correct him. He allows the people to have as much rice as they need. He promises to be humble and obey his own law.
3. It was insensitive for the raja to celebrate while his people were starving. It was bad enough that he was not giving them the rice that they themselves had grown, but to squander it on himself and his courtiers was appalling.

Comprehension Questions—Drawing Conclusions (pp. 132-133)

4. a. The raja was, if nothing else, a poor math student.

   b. The people seem to have been accepting of the raja up to the beginning of the famine. Perhaps they were kept on such a short string of hard work with little to show for it that they could not revolt.

   c. As to whether the raja was cruel: yes he was, although he was more greedy and thoughtless than he was cruel. Perhaps if he had spent the day with a peasant, he would have changed his ways. In his favor we can say that he does not want anyone to suffer, he just wants everything for himself. He is not terribly stubborn, and at the end of the story he changes his ways.
5. Rani's understanding of mathematics and her ability to trick the raja indicate how very smart she was. The fact that she used her brains to help others shows us how caring she was.
6. The people would have starved. Perhaps, they would have stormed the palace and taken the rice by force.

Comprehension Questions—One Step Further (p. 133)

A few examples of "two plus two equal four; four plus four equal eight," and so on would be: one person sneezes. Two catch colds. Those two sneeze and four catch colds, etc. Or, one person sends a picture postcard to two friends. Those two send postcards to two friends each. Those four, etc. Encourage your students to come up with some novel "compounding."

Graphic Organizer (pp. 134-135)

1. ... had no intention of sharing it with the people. He viewed it as all his.
2. ... the raja's servants took most of it, so people went hungry.
3. ... he refused, even though he had promised to give it to them in times of famine.
4. ... he and his servants feasted on the rice.
5. ... she planned to return it to the king so that she could get into the palace to talk to him.
6. ... she knew it was a huge reward.
7. ... it would amount to all the rice in the kingdom.
8. ... gave it all to the poor people.

Maria's House (Textbook p. 500)

Comprehension Questions—In-Depth Thinking (p. 136)

1. Maria hopefully learned a lot from Mama's behavior. Mama was proud of her daughter and her accomplishments, as a mother should be. Mama put others' needs before her own. She worked hard and probably deprived herself of some things in order to pay for Maria's lessons, smocks, and portfolio. Mama always complimented Maria on how pretty she looked, freely giving love, approval, and support to her daughter. Yet, when Maria needed to hear some stern words, Mama cared enough to tell her the truth, unafraid of Maria's dissatisfaction. Mama possessed confidence and character. She wanted her daughter to have these, too, and did what she could to teach Maria to be honest in all aspects of her life.
2. Maria knew her mother well enough to know that she would encourage her to draw her own building—something she did not want to do. In addition, she knew that by admitting she was ashamed of her building, she was saying that her parents had somehow failed her. This was something else she did not want to do.
3. On the way to class that Saturday, Maria was apprehensive. While she felt a bit more confident on the walk to the bus stop, once on the bus, she began to anticipate the problems that would arise in class. She wished that she could have stayed home just this once. Maria dreaded walking into class and putting up her drawing, and hoped that no one would laugh at her. On the way home, Maria probably felt relieved and just a little proud of herself. She perhaps even looked forward to giving her mother the full report of what had happened.

Comprehension Questions—Drawing Conclusions (pp. 136-137)

4. She may have thrown the picture in the garbage simply out of frustration—either at the situation or that she could not actually live in such a house. More likely, she wanted to get rid of it because she did not trust herself. By throwing it out, she was acknowledging that the picture gave a false impression and that the truth lay in her tenement drawing.
5. Answers will vary.
6. Miss Lindstrom probably felt very embarrassed at that moment. First, she had to absorb the surprise of having made a false assumption. Second, she had to cover up her surprise and look nonchalant. Third, she had to decide whether or not to apologize for her wrong assumption. Fourth, she had to admire this young girl for her confidence and honesty. Fifth, she had to resolve never again to make assumptions.

Comprehension Questions—One Step Further (p. 137)

Answers will vary. Here are a few points you might like to share with your students. It is certainly possible to be too little or too much concerned about the opinions of others. Being oblivious to what everyone thinks may be damaging. Being overly concerned about what others think is a losing battle; you can never satisfy all of the people all of the time. A middle road that is a combination of confidence and sensitivity, strong character and awareness of others, independence and intuition is probably ideal for most.

Graphic Organizer (pp. 138-139)

Answers will vary.

The Bridge Dancers (Textbook p. 528)

Vocabulary—Activity I (p. 140)

1. gorge
2. soaring
3. plunged
4. pitching
5. quivery
6. lulled
7. perilous
8. thrashing
9. poultice
10. jubilant

Vocabulary—Activity II (p. 141)

There is no specific answer guide for this exercise.

Comprehension Questions—In-Depth Thinking (p. 142)

1. Callie is energetic and carefree. She is determined, adventurous, and doesn't mind taking risks. She has all kinds of ideas and even her hair seems to resist being bound by any rules.

   Maisie is a serious person and is more cautious and responsible. Maisie foresees consequences better than Callie does. She often looks after Callie and is there when she needs help.
2. Callie begs Maisie with her eyes to overcome her fear and get Mama.
3. She knows that it is not necessary because the girls had suffered the consequences of their actions, which said more than any lecture could.

Comprehension Questions—Drawing Conclusions (pp. 142-143)

4. There are many possibilities. The following are just a few examples.

   "The dirt path is steep from our house down the twisty old hill." (p. 529)

   "Our bridge is just a shaky old skeleton, a tangle of ropes and boards that ripples and wings in the breeze." (p. 529)

   "The next nearest is the Ketchums' place, another mile up the mountain." (p. 529)
5. The bridge is a central part of the story; it links the house, Mama's job, Callie's carefree outings, and Maisie's fears. Each character 'dances across the bridge' in her own way. Mama's 'dance' is the most literal. Callie actually dances near the bridge, though it's possible that she crosses her own 'bridge' when she has her accident and realizes that she may have to curb some of her wild spirit. Maisie has the most abstract 'crossing of the bridge,' when she takes charge of saving Callie.
6. Answers may vary. There were risks involved in not getting Mama and treating Callie on her own. However, she had learned a great deal from her mother and rose to the occasion. She confidently took charge and did whatever Mama would have done to care for her sister's wound. There were also risks in crossing the bridge during a storm. She could have been hurt even worse than her sister was; she could have fallen into the ravine and been killed;

she could have crossed the bridge and not located her mother; her sister could have bled profusely while she was getting her mother.

Comprehension Questions—One Step Further (p. 143)

Ford meant that our confidence and self-image shape our destiny. Confidence in one's abilities magnifies those abilities. Lack of confidence robs us of ability. Talent, skill, smartness, strength, and so on, are not static; they expand and contract in consonance with our sense of who we are. Although, clearly, a tone-deaf person cannot "believe" himself into being a second Mozart, one's mental attitude has a powerful effect on one's capabilities.

Graphic Organizer (pp. 144-145)

10. Maisie's heart jumps when Callie pretends to slip on the bridge.
9. Maisie is afraid for her mother to cross the bridge.
2. Maisie objects to Callie's using the ax, but doesn't really try to stop her.
7. Maisie is too frightened to go get Mama so she starts to doctor Callie herself.
8. Maisie is so afraid to cross the bridge in the storm that the fear stings her eyes.
3. Maisie steps onto the bridge with both feet.
5. Maisie crawls back to the edge of the gorge knowing she cannot cross the bridge.
1. Maisie goes back to Callie and prepares a poultice and some feverfew tea.
6. Maisie stays up all night caring for Callie until Mama arrives.
4. Mama lets Maisie help her with her doctoring.

Dancing Bees (Textbook p. 544)

Comprehension Questions—In-Depth Thinking (p. 146)

1. The bees are able to feel the vibrations of the dance movements.
2. With their tiny brains, the bees are able to create a waggle dance with movements so exact so that all the bees can find the source of food no matter where it is. The bees not only find the nectar, but also can always find the way back to their own hive.
3. The scientists discovered that bees must have a combination of the waggle dance, the whirring wings, and a taste of the food in order to successfully deliver their message.

Comprehension Questions—Drawing Conclusions (pp. 146-147)

4. They probably studied the behavior of the worker honeybees well and then constructed the robot bee. They analyzed what was important and what wasn't. For example, they included a way to dispense a sample of the sugar-water, but knew that the appearance of the robot would not make much of a difference because the hive was dark.
5. We see that scientists the world over (or, at least, in the free world) share information and frequently work together on projects. As the computer makes communication easier, more and more information is shared.
6. Answers will vary.

Comprehension Questions—One Step Further (p. 147)

Answers will vary. Help your students understand this quote. Define any difficult vocabulary.

Graphic Organizer (pp. 148-149)

1. "When a honeybee discovers a rich supply of nectar, it flies back to the hive to tell the other bees exactly where the food is."
2. "If the bee is dancing outside the hive on a flat surface, she lines up with the sun, then turns to point toward the food."
3. "The pattern of a bee's dance is a figure eight."
4. "She repeats the dance over and over again as her sister bees watch."
5. "The most important part of the dance is the straight run through the middle of the figure eight."
6. "In a few minutes, the first bees to figure out where the food is fly away."

Name This American (Textbook p. 552)

Vocabulary—Activity I (p. 150)

1. distinguished
2. celebrities
3. indebted
4. monuments
5. misleading
6. podium
7. observant
8. doubt
9. inquisitive
10. principal

Comprehension Questions—In-Depth Thinking (p. 152)

1. Answers will vary.
2. Answers will vary.
3. Aside from actual knowledge of history, careful listening to the other questions and skillful use of the process of elimination would be helpful tools.

Comprehension Questions—Drawing Conclusions (pp. 152-153)

4. Answers will vary.
5. The humorous naming of the hosts Lady Liberty and Uncle Sam delivers a serious message. Thanks to the freedom that exists in America, people from all walks of life are free to make tremendous contributions to every aspect of life.
6. Answers will vary.

Comprehension Questions—One Step Further (p. 147)

Answers will vary. If your students are not familiar with the term "person of influence," please clarify. Bring examples of politicians, business magnates, media personalities, etc. In contrast, "influential people" usually include mothers, fathers, teachers, and so forth.

Graphic Organizer (pp. 154-157)

Walter Hunt

Eliminate:

famous
made a discovery
did not invent anything
invented an electrical item
invented something bigger than a bread box
invented the comb
invented the pen

Circle:

not well-known
invented something
invented a household item
invented something smaller than a bread box
invented something you could put in your pocket
invented the safety pin

Gutzon Borglum

Eliminate:

famous
a scientist
a painter
a musician
an entertainer

Circle:

name is not well-known
not a scientist
an artist
not a musician
a sculptor
his work is on Mt. Rushmore

Maria Mitchell

Eliminate:

in politics
science does not interest her
is in medicine
not an astronomer
grew up in New York

Circle:

politics do not interest her
a scientist
not in medicine
an astronomer
grew up in Massachusetts
discovered a new comet

Dolley Madison

Eliminate:

living now
not alive during the Revolutionary War
a seamstress who worked on the flag
Martha Washington
Abigail Adams
Mrs. Jefferson
Mrs. Monroe

Circle:

lived 200 years ago
alive during the Revolutionary War
was married to one of the first four presidents
the wife of James Madison

Boss of the Plains (Textbook p. 570)

Vocabulary—Activity I (p.158)

1. distinctive
2. picturesque
3. technique
4. saplings
5. swig
6. bustling
7. crammed
8. huddled
9. pelts
10. matted

Vocabulary—Activity II (p. 159)

- **bustling:** slow-paced
- **crammed:** empty
- **distinctive:** ordinary
- **huddled:** spaced far apart
- **matted:** combed
- **picturesque:** ugly
- **sapling:** old tree

Comprehension Questions—In-Depth Thinking (p. 160)

1. His dream of going west was fulfilled, but his dream of discovering gold was not. On the other hand, since the point of finding gold was to get rich, one can say that that part of the dream came true, too, even if the wealth came from selling hats rather than discovering gold.
2. John's trade and talent served him well. By abandoning his dream of finding gold in the hills and falling back on working at his trade, he reached his goal of growing rich and successful.
3. The Stetson was a quality piece of work. It was well-made, long-lasting, and designed specifically for life on the plains. (By producing this hat, rather than digging for gold, John succeeded at becoming rich while providing a valuable service to people.) It seems from the story that it had little or no competition.

Comprehension Questions—Drawing Conclusions (pp. 160-161)

4. Answers will vary. We are not told much about John's family beyond the basic facts outlined in the beginning of the story. It is possible that Mr. Stetson was disappointed when his son, John, left the family business to follow a dream. Surely, he must have

been proud of him for creating a successful hat business in Philadelphia and following the family tradition.

5. The most important business idea John had was making a product that was really needed. Because he had lived on the plains himself, he knew exactly what kind of a hat would be useful and long-lasting. The second business idea he had was sending sample hats and order forms to every store in the West. This is a combination of calculated risk and good advertising. The third important business idea was rushing to fill the orders once he got them. Finally, giving a catchy name to the new product added style and desirability to the hat.
6. When John was offered five dollars for his hat, it made him realize that his hat was a marketable item. It also made him realize that people would be willing to pay a large sum of money for a hat like it. It didn't take long for John to make his plans to produce more of what he now realized was something he could readily sell.

Comprehension Questions—One Step Further (p. 161)

One famous example is the first ice cream cone, which, legend has it, was actually a waffle used by an ice cream vendor who had run out of bowls. Ask the class if their families have some privately used "invention" that fills a need.

Graphic Organizer (pp. 162-163)

Correct answers are in italics.

First, take a *blanket*. In the middle of it, pile *rabbit's fur*. Next, make an *Indian's bow* and flick it over the fur. Take a swig of *water* and *spray* it over the fur. Take the matted fur and dip it in *boiling water.*

Stetsons are good for the following: It could wave cows into a corral, fan the flames of a newly lit campfire, carry oats to feed a horse, scoop up a refreshing drink of water, come in handy in picking huckleberries, it is a perfect decoy when a cowboy is in trouble, and makes a soft cushion for a cowboy's head.

Stone Fox (Textbook p. 586)

Vocabulary—Activity I (p. 164)

1. amateur	6. abruptly
2. treacherous	7. stunned
3. frigid	8. effortlessly
4. abreast	9. clenched
5. overtake	10. jagged

Vocabulary—Activity II (p. 165)

There is no specific answer guide for this exercise.

Comprehension Questions—In-Depth Thinking (p. 166)

1. ***Similarities:***

   They both deeply cared for those who were close to them.

   They were both determined to win the race. Willy displayed determination in other areas, such as in his dealings with the man at the bank and in the way he related to Stone Fox. Stone Fox showed determination in his campaign to reinstate his people on their native land, in his behavior towards white people, and even in ensuring that Willy be declared the winner.

   Differences:

   Stone Fox was a tough adult with a lot of racing experience. Willy was a young, inexperienced boy.

   Willy was very friendly and outgoing while Stone Fox was stonily silent.

   Willy was reasonable, respectful, and gentle. Stone Fox was at times irrational, angry, and rough.

   Their general backgrounds were extremely different.
2. Willy prepared a lot with Searchlight and started by taking the lead. Stone Fox did not practice. He waited until late in the race to overtake the others and take the lead.
3. Grandfather was immensely proud of his grandson and infused with hope that Willy would win. That gave him a boost of energy. His illness was in part due to the anxiety he had about the farm and the tax collectors.

Comprehension Questions—Drawing Conclusions (pp. 166-167)

4. Some were frightened of Stone Fox. Others did not know what to do. Some individuals probably thought of helping but did not react before Stone Fox took action.
5. Answers will vary, but should be supported, as opposed to a simple 'yes' or 'no' answer.
6. Answers will vary.

Comprehension Questions—One Step Further (p. 167)

While it is true that people have limitations, there are many things that can be accomplished with will and determination. Often, until we push ourselves to the limit, we do not actually know what our potential is.

Graphic Organizer (pp. 168-169)

1. i. The night before the race, little Willy goes to the doctor to get medicine for his grandfather.
2. f. Doc Smith gives Willy a prescription and a piece of cake.
3. c. Willy goes to Lester the pharmacist and gets the medicine.
4. k. On his way home he passes an old barn.
5. g. Inside he finds the five Samoyeds.
6. j. Stone Fox comes up and slaps him.
7. a. His eye is swollen and sore.
8. e. The gun goes off and the race begins.
9. l. Willy and Searchlight take the lead.
10. d. After a while, Stone Fox catches up and takes the lead.
11. h. Searchlight collapses just as they approach the finish. Willy carries him over the finish line.
12. b. Willy and Searchlight are declared the winners.